CONTENTS

CONTENTS

The **Architects'** Handbook

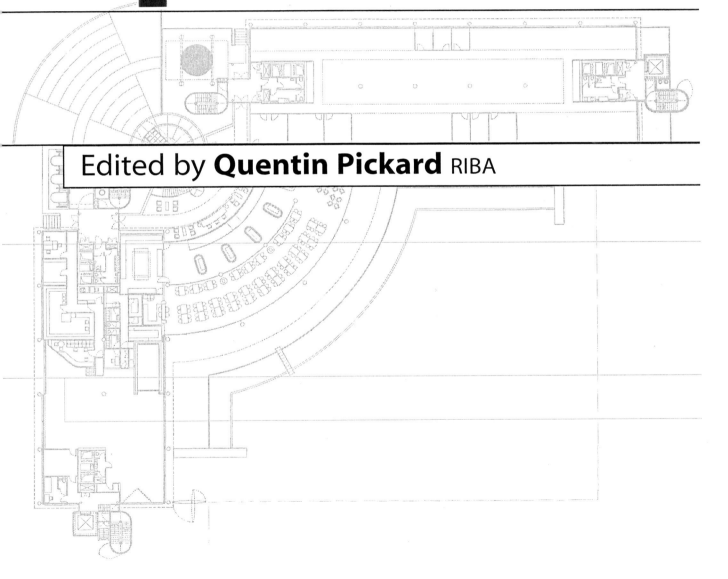

Edited by **Quentin Pickard** RIBA

Blackwell
Publishing

© 2002, 2005 by Blackwell Publishing company

Editorial offices:
Blackwell Publishing Ltd, 9600 Garsington Road, Oxford OX4 2DQ, UK
    Tel: +44 (0) 1865 776868
Blackwell Publishing Inc., 350 Main Street, Malden, MA 02148-5020, USA
    Tel: +1 781 388 8250
Blackwell Publishing Asia Pty Ltd, 550 Swanston Street, Carlton, Victoria 3053, Australia
    Tel: +61 (0)3 8359 1011

First published 2002 by Blackwell Science Ltd, a Blackwell Publishing company
Reprinted 2003
Reissued in paperback 2005 by Blackwell Publishing Ltd
4   2008

ISBN 978-1-4051-3505-4

Library of Congress Cataloging-in-Publication Data (from the hardback edition)
The architects' handbook / edited by Quentin Pickard.
    p. cm.
    Includes bibliographical references and index.
    ISBN 978-1-4051-3505-4 (pbk.)
    1. Architecture—Handbooks, manuals, etc.   2. Architectural drawing—Handbooks, manuals, etc.
1. Pickard, Quentin

NA2520 A67 2002
721–dc21

                                                                           2002025435

A catalogue record for this title is available from the British Library

Set in Classical Garamond
By Vector CSI, Stamford, Lincolnshire, Great Britain
Printed and bound in India by Replika Press Pvt. Ltd

For further information on Blackwell Publishing, visit our website:
www.blackwellpublishing.com/construction

PREFACE

The Architects' Handbook provides visual and technical information for most building types likely to be encountered by architects, designers and building surveyors. For each section, we have tried to ensure a representative sample of recent buildings to reflect the diversity of approach so essential in a well-designed environment. Numerous plans, many sections and elevations, and some three-dimensional views have been included, to give the essential character of a particular building. The distinctive contribution of this book is that it concentrates more on the overall character of buildings, and not on excessive detail or too much technical information. Although we have deliberately avoided comment on the design qualities of buildings, the fact that a building is included indicates that we consider it makes a positive design contribution.

One aspect that became increasingly evident as the book progressed was just how flexible a building designation needs to be: 'business parks', for instance, do not want to be included in 'industrial buildings'; an 'arts centre' should be considered with theatres, and certainly not with 'art galleries'; and is an arts centre really just a superior type of community centre? Many buildings designed to produce physical components, which we used to call 'industrial buildings', are now more akin to offices than industry. There are many similarities between an out-of-town hypermarket shed and a warehouse, yet one is commonly called a 'shop' and the other an 'industrial building'.

The question of how much reference should be made to technical standards and other legislation is never easy to answer. Wherever possible, therefore, such references have been kept to a minimum, and grouped at the end of the book. It should also be remembered that accessibility facilities have been discussed in several sections, and generally it has been assumed that, for instance, a disabled WC must be provided in every building to which the public has access, and it seemed superfluous to mention this in every instance.

The one thing of which we can be certain is that technical requirements will continue to be amended,

and no doubt expanded. Architects and other designers have to keep abreast of seemingly constant changes and will appreciate that it is essential to check that all technical information is up to date.

One sad but inevitable development is the increasing rarity of drawings of good visual appeal. The growth of computer-aided design is resulting in the near-disappearance of visually satisfying drawings. CAD drawings are often unsuitable for book reproduction – there is little distinction in line thickness, much irrelevant detail is included (grid lines, minor dimensions etc.), while other important information often seems impossible to obtain (for instance, scales and north points). To try to ensure that the art of good draughting is not entirely forgotten, a section on drawing practice has therefore been included – a subject that otherwise might not seem to be particularly appropriate for this book.

This work has drawn upon many sources, and considerable efforts have been made to ensure that all copyright material has been properly credited. If by mischance anything has been overlooked, it will be noted in the next edition. Many specialists have been consulted about technical details, and their contributions are gratefully acknowledged; they are listed in the following pages.

Inevitably in a work as extensive as this, some errors are bound to occur, and readers' comments and suggestions (which should be sent to the publishers) will all be noted.

I am very grateful to all the architects, other individuals and organisations who have supplied information, many having gone to considerable lengths to provide the correct drawings or technical details.

Sincere thanks are due to all the contributors for their hard work, and also to Antonia Powell, who undertook a great deal of research. I would also like to thank my publisher, Julia Burden, who offered constant encouragement and suggestions, and Paul Stringer and Mark Straker, who have managed to turn a mass of text and drawings into an excellent final layout. Thanks also to Geoff Lee for his many first-rate drawings.

Quentin Pickard
www.qpickard.co.uk

ACKNOWLEDGEMENTS

BUSINESS PARKS

2: Illustration from English Estates (and others) *Industrial and Commercial Estates, Planning and Site Development*, published by Thomas Telford, London.

7: The September 1997 masterplan of Kings Hill Business Park designed by Wordsearch Communications is reproduced by kind permission of Rouse Kent Ltd.

EDUCATION: UNIVERSITIES AND COLLEGES

1, 2, 4, 7: Illustrations from Department for Education, Architects & Building Branch, Design Note 50, *Accommodation for Changes in Further Education*. Crown copyright is reproduced with the permission of the Controller of Her Majesty's Stationery Office.

FARMS

4, 5, 6, 10, 11, 12, 13, 14, 15, 16, 18, 24, 25: Illustrations reproduced, with permission, from N. H. Noton's *Farm Buildings* (College of Estate Management, Reading, 1982).

7, 8: Reproduced, with permission, from Southorn, N. (1996) Farm *Buildings – Planning and Construction*, Melbourne: Inkata (a division of Butterworth Heinemann).

9, 17, 19, 20, 21: Illustrations reproduced by permission of I. J. Loynes, of ADAS at that time. (ADAS are specialists in agricultural and rural building design.)

26: Reproduced from **Farm Building Progress**, 110, October 1992, p. 5.

HOUSING AND RESIDENTIAL ACCOMMODATION

5, 51: Illustrations from Goodchild, B. (1997) *Housing and the Urban Environment*, Blackwell Science, Oxford.

56, 57: From *Housing Quality Indicators: Research Report and Indicators*, Department of the Environment, Transport and the Regions and the Housing Corporation: Crown copyright 1999. Reproduced with the permission of the Controller of Her Majesty's Stationery Office.

121: From *NHBC Standards* (National House-Building Council, Amersham). Used with permission.

INDUSTRIAL BUILDINGS

29: Diagrams from *Principles of Warehouse Design*, courtesy of the Institute of Logistics and Transport.

LABORATORIES

3, 6, 7, 8, 9, 10: Illustrations reproduced, with permission, from *Laboratories: A Briefing and Design Guide*, by Walter Hain, published by E & FN Spon (an imprint of Taylor & Francis), 1995, pages 14, 15, 17, 24, 26 and 36.

LIBRARIES AND LEARNING RESOURCE CENTRES

1: Illustration © British Museum Central Archives.

3, 4: Illustrations reproduced from information provided by NPS Architectural Services and Library and Information Service, Norfolk County Council.

MUSEUMS AND ART GALLERIES

12, 15: Illustrations from Hall, M. (1987) *On Display: A Design Grammar*, Lund Humphries Publishers Ltd, London.

OFFICES

4–31: Illustrations adapted from the following and used with permission:

British Council for Offices (2000) *BCO Guide 2000: Best practice in the specification of offices*, BCO

Marmot A. and Eley J. (1995) *Understanding Offices*, Penguin Books, Harmondsworth

Raymond S. and Cunliffe R. (1997) *Tomorrow's Office: creating effective and humane interiors*, E & FN Spon, London

Raymond S. and Cunliffe R. (1997) *Corporate reception areas: a design guide*, Eclipse, London

Van Meel J. (2000) *The European Office: office design in the national context*, 010 Publishers, Rotterdam

RELIGIOUS BUILDINGS

12, 13: Illustrations from Bradbeer, F.H. 'Church Design: Principles of Organ Design', Architects' Journal, vol. 146, pp 927–36.

20: From de Breffny B. (1978) *The Synagogue*, Weidenfeld & Nicolson Ltd, London.

21, 24: From Krinsky C.H. (1985) *Synagogues of Europe*, Architectural History Foundation/ Massachusetts Institute of Technology Press, Cambridge, Massachusetts.

SPORTS

85, 86, 87, 88: Illustrations from *Swimming Pools and Ice Rinks*, edited by Geraint John and K Campbell, published by Butterworth Architecture, and reproduced by permission of Butterworth Heinemann, a division of Reed Educational & Professional Publishing Ltd.

ZOOS AND AQUARIUMS

2: Illustration of the elephant and rhinoceros house at London Zoo is used with permission from Casson Condor Partnership.

5, 6, 7: Illustrations reproduced, with permission, from Mallinson, J.J.C. and Carroll, J.B. (1995) 'Integrating Needs in Great Ape Accommodation: Sumatran Orang-Utan *Pongo pygmaeus abelli* "Home Habitat" of JWPT', in: *Proceedings of the International Orangutan Conference: The Neglected Ape*, Nadler R.D., Galdikas B., Sheeran L., and Rosen N. (eds), Plenum Press, New York.

CONTRIBUTORS

EDITOR

Quentin Pickard, BA, RIBA, MiMgt
Since 1978 Quentin Pickard has been a partner in private practice, specialising in conservation and ecclesiastical projects. He studied at Newcastle University and Thames Polytechnic, and has taught part-time at several London universities and at the Architectural Association. As a member of the Aqua Group he is co-author of three books on contract practice and administration. He is currently the RIBA Conservation Advisor and has been instrumental in establishing the Register of Architects Accredited in Building Conservation.

RESEARCH ASSISTANT

Antonia Powell, BSc (Hons)
Antonia Powell studied at South Bank University, and is a senior conservation officer with a local authority in London.

CONTRIBUTORS

Peter Beacock, BA, BArch, MSc, RIBA
(*Community Centres*)
Peter Beacock runs the Architectural Design and Management programme at the University of Northumbria, and has an interest in sustainable design. In addition, he has worked with Wilkinson Hindle Halsall Lloyd Partnership (WHHLP) on a number of recent projects.

Patricia Beecham, BA (Hons), BArch (Hons), RIBA
(*Farms; Museums; Law Courts; Zoos and Aquariums*)
After studying at Newcastle University, Patricia Beecham spent 20 years as a registered architect on a wide variety of projects in private practice in Liverpool, London and Newcastle. During two years in Warsaw she developed a series of guided architectural walks. She is now practising independently.

Fiona Brettwood, BA, Dip Arch, RIBA
(*Community Centres*)
Fiona Brettwood is a partner in Wilkinson Hindle Halsall Lloyd Partnership (WHHLP), which has over 25 years' experience of community architecture, community consultation and design participation. Her recent and current projects are with community projects in the North-East, helping in the development of appropriate facilities for the 21st century.

John Cavilla, BSc (Hons), MCIOB, MAPM, MiMgt
(*Drawing Practice and Presentation*)
After graduating in Building Technology at the University of Manchester Institute of Science and Technology, John Cavilla gained some 22 years' experience in contracting, project management and architecture before becoming a senior lecturer in construction at South Bank University in 1985. Having lectured in a wide range of construction-related subjects at both undergraduate and post-graduate levels, in 2000 he returned to private practice and is a visiting fellow at South Bank University. His areas of specialism include buildability and the role of design within the private finance initiative.

Helen Dallas, MA (EdMan), Dip Arch, RIBA
(*Cinemas, Landscape Works, Vehicle Facilities*)
Following her studies at Newcastle University and North London Polytechnic, Helen Dallas qualified in 1985 and subsequently worked in private practice on residential, commercial and ecclesiastical buildings. A former member of the Aqua Group, she is currently Development Manager for a leading disability charity.

DfES (Department for Education and Skills), Schools Building and Design Unit
(*Education: Schools*)
With special thanks to: **Tamasin Dale, Robin Bishop, Chris Bissell, Sandra Legg, Andy Thompson, Alison Wadsworth, Beech Williamson.**

Previously known as the Architects and Building Branch of the DfEE, the Unit continues to offer design advice and guidance to schools, building professionals and the British Government through its Building Bulletins, seminars and involvement in live case-study projects.

Roger Dixon, Dip Arch, MaPS
(*Health Service Buildings*)
Roger Dixon is an architect and health facility planner with parallel careers in the Health Ministry and in his own practice since 1965. He has worked internationally on project briefing, development control planning and design as well as on research and evaluation.

Brian Edwards, Dip Arch, MSc, PhD, RIBA, RIAS, MRTPI
(*Airports*)
A Professor of Architecture at Edinburgh College of Art/Heriot Watt University in Edinburgh, Brian Edwards has a particular interest in transport architecture and was a member of the design team for Edinburgh Airport. He has authored many journal articles and 15 books, including *The Modern Terminal: new approaches to airport architecture*, published by Spon in 1998.

Howard Goodman
(*Health Service Buildings*)
The late Howard Goodman of MPA and former Health Ministry Chief Architect, 1971–88, initiated this chapter. It was completed by his Ministry and MPA colleagues, Roger Dixon and Tony Noakes. The more than 120 years of leading-edge experience they have brought to the subject includes research, briefing, special development projects, master planning, design guidance and design-in-use evaluation.

Walter Hain, BArch, RIBA
(*Laboratories*)
Walter Hain has been extensively involved in laboratory work on new-build and refurbishment projects in both the public and private sectors.

Sean Jones, BA, BArch, RIBA, Associate Principal, HOK Sport
(*Sports*)
After qualifying at Manchester University, Sean Jones joined HOK Sport (formally Lobb Sports Architecture) in 1985. During his time with the company he has gained experience on a wide variety of projects in the commercial, sports and leisure sectors across the globe, taking major stadiums, sports grandstands and racecourse facilities through from detailed design to project completion. He managed the Cardiff project office which completed the Millennium Stadium at Cardiff Arms Park in time for the Rugby World Cup in 1999, and now manages the team responsible for the new stadium for Arsenal Football Club. He is also heading up the design team for the Faro and Benfica Stadiums which will play key roles in the Euro 2004 football championships.

Grace Kenny, BA (PPE), LèsL (Ling Lit Hist), MA (Fr), PhD (Arch), Dip Trans MIL
(*Education: Universities and Colleges*)
After research at University College London (economics and architecture) Grace Kenny ran the R&D programme at the Architects and Building Branch of the DfES. She now advises higher and further education institutes on space.

Fred Lawson, PhD, MSc, EurIng, CEng
(*Hotels; Restaurants and Catering Facilities*)
Qualified in four chartered institutions, Professor Lawson has undertaken major hotel and tourism projects in over 30 countries, including assignments for the World Bank, United Nations Development Programme, EU and World Tourism Organisation. He has authored ten books on planning and design and, as a leading academic, he has pioneered these subjects in a number of universities.

Di McPhee, BSc (Hons)
(*Crematoria*)

Tony Noakes
(*Health Service Buildings*)
Tony Noakes is an architect specialising in the theory and practice of health building planning and design. In the 1960s he joined the UK Health Ministry team that, for over 30 years, spearheaded the development of health building design in the UK.

Kate Pickard, BA (Hons)
(*Theatres and Arts Centres*)
Born in Australia and raised in Africa and Scotland, Kate Pickard obtained her honours degree in Fine Art and Theatre at De Montfort University, Leicester. She studied Theatre Design in North Carolina while working on local theatre and film sets.

Santa Raymond, Dip Arch, RIBA
(*Offices*)
An architect and interior designer, Santa Raymond is principal of SRC workplace design specialists, and co-author of *Tomorrow's Office: creating effective and humane interiors*. She is also responsible for devising lean office conferences.

Stephen J. Thorpe, BA (Hons) Arch, RIBA, NRAC, MEWI, Threshold Architects
(*Design for Accessibility*)
Having qualified in 1961, Stephen Thorpe has since 1970 been working in the field of designing for accessibility. He contributes as designer, access consultant, expert witness, author and illustrator.

PROFESSIONAL AND SPECIALIST ASSISTANCE ALSO PROVIDED BY
Community Centres: David Cummings
Farms: I.J. Loynes, BSc, MIagrE, Head of Engineering, Harper Adams University College
Fire Stations: Peter J. Smith, Dip Arch, Buildings Officer, London Fire and Civil Defence Authority
Health Service Buildings: Dr Ronnie Pollock, consultant in healthcare planning; Glynis M. Meredith-Windle, Meredith-Windle Associates
Housing: Rex Hawkesworth, ARIBA
Law Courts: Mike Sandquest, Christopher Rainford, Paul Monaghan
Libraries: John Creber, BA, ALA
Theatres: P. Connolly, Theatres Trust Administrator
Youth Hostels: John Bothamley
Zoos: Jeremy J.C. Mallinson, Director, Jersey Wildlife Preservation Trust; Gordon McGregor Reid, Director, North of England Zoological Society; Brian Seward, Assistant Director, Bristol Zoo; Roger J. Wheater, Director, The Royal Zoological Society of Scotland

AIRPORTS

Brian Edwards

INTRODUCTION

Airports are one of the few uniquely 20th-century building types and the terminals their defining piece of architecture. Early airports date from the 1930s but the bulk have their origins in the post-war period. The tailor-made modern terminal began its life in the 1950s, with notable prototypes such as the TWA Terminal at Kennedy Airport, New York (1956) by Eero Saarinen, Turnhouse Airport Edinburgh (1956) by Robert Matthew and O'Hare, Chicago (1955) by C. F. Murphy. These effectively established the typology of the terminal as a split-level container handling arriving and departing passengers on different levels.

Today the airport has matured into a second generation and largely hybrid building type. Modern terminals are no longer simple structures for the processing on to the plane of a few hundred passengers per day. They are multi-level megastructures (four main levels at Kansai in Japan by the Renzo Piano Building Workshop and five levels in the plans for Heathrow's Terminal 5 by the Richard Rogers Partnership) of check-in, lounge, leisure and retail floors serving thousands of passengers an hour. The world's busiest airports now handle in excess of 60 million passengers a year, have considerable economic and environmental impacts and provide one of the toughest challenges for today's architects and space planners.

London Heathrow is a good example. In 1997 over 56 million passengers passed through its four terminal buildings, many using the airport as a hub to other UK or European destinations. Heathrow has enormous economic influence upon the western quadrant of London, employing 62 000 people (more than the City of Oxford) at the airport or in service industries in the hinterland. Of these, half are employed on security in one form or another, about a quarter in serving passenger needs directly and a further quarter in retail. As airports expand (growth rate world-wide is about 6% per annum and 8–9% in the Asian region) they take on the characteristics of cities. Leisure and retail sales at Heathrow now exceed the revenue generated by the airline companies using the airport, leading to the situation where the modern terminal has become rather like a shopping mall with a runway to one side.

The modern terminal is, therefore, a complex structure functionally, socially and aesthetically. As more activities are added to enhance the passengers' experience and to generate additional sources of revenue, the task for the airport designer becomes ever more difficult. The key to good design is flexibility and legibility – the first in order to meet ever changing marketing and operational needs in the terminal, the second to allow passengers to steer their way through the often labyrinthine airport environment.

As the envelope of the terminal becomes larger, there is a growing need for designers to consider user needs as well as those of the client. In contrast to 20 years ago, the majority of the world's airports are now privately owned. They are highly profitable undertakings and airport authorities have become expert at diversifying sources of revenue. In the process, passenger satisfaction levels have declined, especially at airports such as Kennedy, Heathrow and Charles de Gaulle, which developed mainly in the 1960s. Many recently built terminals have been constructed in response to the poor conditions experienced in overcrowded facilities (e.g. Stansted and Chek Lap Kok as relief for Heathrow and Hong Kong's Kai Tak). These new terminals mark a change in approach in which the psychological and physical needs of the passenger are given greater priority. Today's terminals tend to be lofty, spacious, well-lit containers where tranquillity and efficient movement sit side by side.

Characteristics of modern terminals

The 21st-century terminal differs from first generation airport buildings in three major ways:
- Greatly diversified range of facilities, especially in the retail, conference and leisure fields
- More attention paid to the quality of the passenger experience, particularly with regard to legibility, orientation and the creation of tranquil spaces
- Design which accepts the inevitability of internal change and external growth

These three factors have become defining elements of second generation terminals. They reflect changing priorities within the airport industry, especially the need for individual airport authorities to meet global standards of excellence in order to survive competitive pressures. Airport authorities now compete internationally for their share of the air-transportation market and increasingly recognise that the standard of terminal design is a measure consumers use in their choice of airports.

How airport authorities generate income

Airside

Runways and apron areas
- Take-off and landing fees
- Air traffic control charges
- Aircraft parking charges
- Apron services
- Passenger charges
- Freight charges
- Fuel sales

Land side

Terminal building
- Baggage handling
- Rent income from airline companies
- Rent income from franchisers
- Direct retail sales
- Advertising

Peripheral airport areas
- Car parking
- Land development
- Hotels
- Warehousing

Outside airport
Business parks

Non-retail, non-airline facilities in terminal building
- Banks/foreign exchange offices
- Tourist information
- Car rental
- Hairdressing/beauty salon
- Medical services
- Conference/business facilities
- Church/mosque
- Cinema
- Swimming pool/fitness centre

Types of people in terminal building
- Passengers
- Airport employees
- Security staff
- Meeters and greeters
- Leisure visitors
- Business/conference visitors

Criteria for terminal design
- Flexibility and extendability
- Avoidance of passenger cross-flows
- Shortest walking distances
- Minimum level changes
- Easy orientation
- Effective security by design

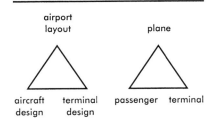

1 Two key interactions upon terminal

2 Stansted Airport, Essex (Arch: Foster & Partners). Elevation of apron area

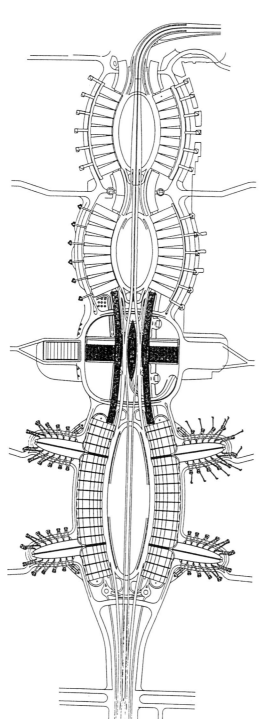

3 Charles de Gaulle Airport, France (Arch: Paul Andrew). Plan of Terminal 2 with railway station

THE AIRPORT

A typical international airport consists of six major physical elements and up to a dozen secondary ones. The major elements are:

- Runway, taxiing areas etc.
- Air traffic control centre
- Passenger terminal
- Car parks and road system
- Freight depot and warehouse areas
- Hangars and aircraft service areas

In addition, there are many secondary elements which can form substantial parts of the airport estate, such as:

- Railway station
- Hotel
- Conference facilities
- Leisure/recreation areas
- Green space and planted areas

Mature airports (such as Chicago's O'Hare or Amsterdam's Schipol) consist of a well-integrated amalgam of major and minor elements sometimes built as a dense collection of closely connected structures. Others have the range of facilities in more widely spaced structures, as at Heathrow where they are joined by an underground railway system and at Gatwick where an above-ground shuttle links the two terminals.

Integration and ease of connection is the key to a successful airport from the passenger point of view. This is particularity true of the means of reaching the airport – whether by car, bus or train. The circulating road system of a typical airport, or the underground railway, tends to disorientate the passenger and is frequently overcrowded. Routes need to be clearly articulated, with buildings and landscaping providing the means by which a sense of direction is established. The progression from car seat to plane seat is necessarily complex (for reasons of security and control) but the experience should not be excessively complicated or at any point unpleasant. Good airport layout and building design should seek to remove ambiguity, to reduce travel length, to maintain a sense of progression towards the destination; and should wherever possible uplift the spirit. Psychological needs are as important as physical ones.

Two clear but divergent perceptions exist – that of the airport authority which wishes to maximise profit, and that of the passenger who wants stress-free travel. Good design consists of reconciling these viewpoints.

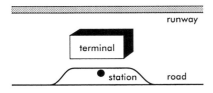

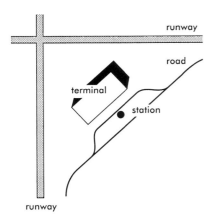

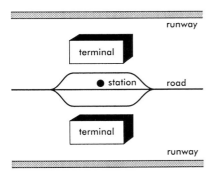

4 Diagrammatic layouts of relationship between terminal, runway and road

In the layout of the airport the determining factor is normally the orientation and length of the runways (see **4**). These are shaped mostly by the direction of the prevailing wind, the size of aircraft to be handled, and external factors such as the position of towns, mountain ranges and power lines. Normally the airport masterplan is prepared by civil engineers working with land-use planners and environmental consultants. Increasingly, environmental impact analysis determines the key elements of the airport plan, especially the resolution of noise, ecological and visual impacts.

As an understanding of the complexities of airport development has grown there has occurred a better balance between infrastructure planning and land utilisation. Most airports today have integrated transport systems which cater for passenger as well as staff needs. This not only serves the airport well but allows for the development of land for non-air transport purposes. Many airports today have extensive warehouse areas at their edge and business parks in the towns nearby. Airport masterplanning and regional development plans need to be well integrated if the full potential of the airport as an investment magnet is to be realised.

Normally architects are appointed after the airport masterplan has been prepared. The task then is one of designing the buildings whose footprint has already been established. However, good urban design is essential if infrastructure planning and building design are to be effectively bridged.

In any airport the terminal building is the key structure physically and aesthetically. Although air traffic control towers may provide welcome points of vertical punctuation, it is the terminal which waymarks the airport and establishes a sense of architectural quality (see **5**). Like a small city, the terminal is the airport's town hall – the place where everybody is encouraged to enter. To fulfil this role the terminal should be the dominant building, with other structures such as hotels and car parks having a secondary role. The visual ensemble of the airport environment needs to be legible, thereby avoiding the necessity for signs. The hierarchy of airport structures for the passenger (terminal, station, car park) is quite different to that perceived by the airport authority (runway, boarding gate, terminal).

Good design allows the terminal building and other structures to be identified immediately for what they are. The role of architectural form is to give meaning to the various buildings. The question of airport character is communicated by reference to aeronautical metaphors or to high technology (e.g. Stuttgart Airport – see **7** and **9**), though there is a trend towards giving airport buildings more of a regional architectural flavour in the belief that terminals are gateways to countries.

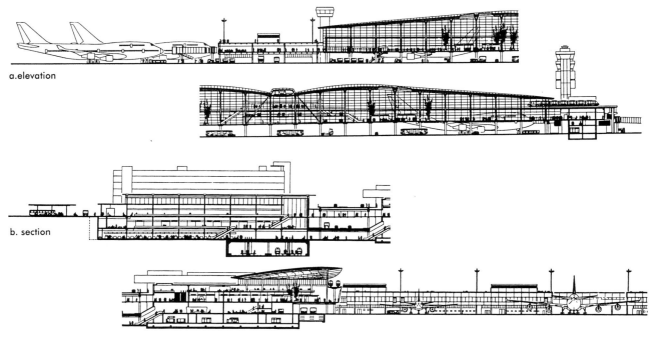

a. elevation

b. section

5 Zurich Airport, Switzerland (Arch: Nicholas Grimshaw & Partners)

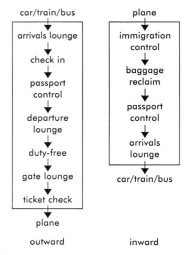

car/train/bus   plane

outward	inward
arrivals lounge	immigration control
check in	baggage reclaim
passport control	passport control
departure lounge	arrivals lounge
duty-free	
gate lounge	
ticket check	

plane   car/train/bus

outward   inward

6 Functional flows through terminal

THE TERMINAL

Legibility and passenger-orientation are important because airports are normally devoid of obvious points of external reference and many travellers are in a hurry (see **6**). Once inside the terminal the problem of identifying routes to check-in, ticket purchase or arrivals lounge can be as great as in the external airport environment. Architectural landmarking is an important adjunct to effective signage. Light, structural form and volumetric orchestration are factors to employ (see **7** and **9**). If the primary architectural language is not strong, the terminal will not survive either retailing pressure or management changes to the use and distribution of space. After the example of terminals at Stansted or Denver, the aesthetic qualities of architectural structure have tended to be the primary elements in establishing airport character. The design of columns and beams, often interplayed with the clever manipulation of roof lighting, provides a memorable experience to aid navigation through complex terminals. It is a philosophy which accepts various degrees of change of structure, enclosure, building services, interior space and finish. With each on a different time-scale, one can be altered without sacrificing the quality of the remainder.

section

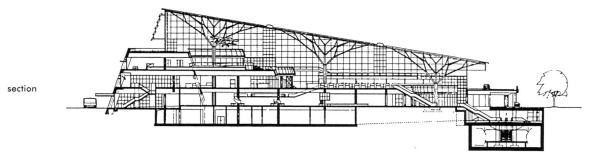

ground floor plan

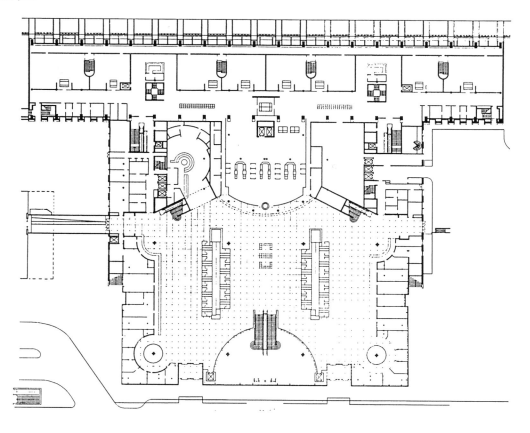

7 Stuttgart Airport, Germany
(Arch: Von Gerkan, Marg & Partners) (See also **9**)

Increasingly terminals are designed with varying layers of permanence attached to the parts. Time-scales from 3 to 50 years apply with the parts detailed so that they can be replaced, renewed or fundamentally altered without jeopardising the operation of the whole. Permanent elements, such as the structural framework, are designed with long life and lasting visual impact. It is these parts, and the social spaces (i.e. departure lounge) which survive the longest and have to be designed to the highest standard. Their enduring qualities depend to a large extent upon the depth of design thought put in at the outset, and the anticipation of change or ease of replaceability of key parts. A well-designed terminal is one which has high and lasting visual impact, yet adjusts readily to interior change, and caters for physical renewal over a 50 or 60 year lifespan.

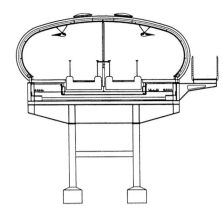

8 Heathrow Airport, London
Transfer satellite at pier 4A: section
(Arch: Nicholas Grimshaw & Partners)
(See also **11**)

section

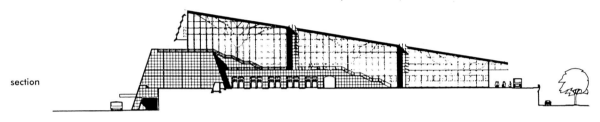

upper floor plan

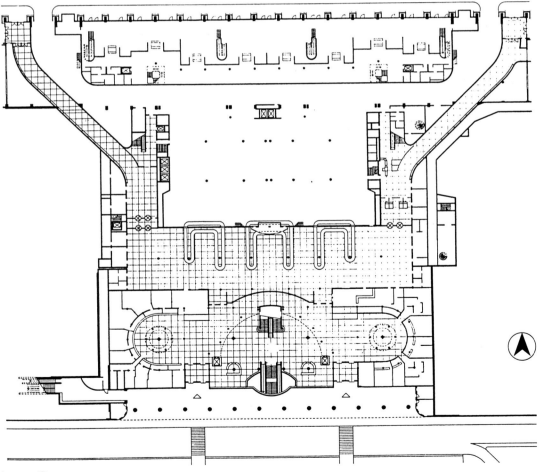

9 Stuttgart Airport, Germany
(Arch: Von Gerkan, Marg & Partners)
(See also **7**)

Terminal facilities

The modern terminal is a complex building with many types of accommodation contained within its envelope and has necessarily to provide for high levels of control. Conceptually, there are public (e.g. departure lounge) and private (e.g. offices) areas, as well as secure and unsecure areas. In addition, there are the barriers to movement needed for ticket and non-ticket holding people, as well as immigration controls. The airport in general and terminal in particular is one of the most intensively managed areas from a security point of view. There are barriers to movement, physical and psychological controls, security cameras and spot checks of passengers and airline staff. Architecture is, therefore, a question of both creating space and helping to control it.

The management of security underpins the plan and section of a typical airport terminal. Different levels of the building are used for different passenger flows (arrivals, transit and departures) with controlled cross-over between them. Different levels also allow baggage to be handled and processed effectively. The growth of the multi-level terminal in the 1970s was in response to growing concern over international terrorism, drug trafficking and illegal immigration.

The complexity in section of a modern large terminal (e.g. Kansai in Japan) places particular responsibility on the design of stairs, escalators and lifts. Changing level is a necessity in current airport design and poses special difficulties for travellers with disabilities. For all, however, the means of moving from one floor to the next needs to be as enjoyable and as possible. Consequently, the escalator and lift have become major visual elements in the interior of a typical terminal. They not only move people effectively but provide points of reference in a waymarking sense for passengers.

Terminals are complex in plan for many of the same reasons. Although passenger space may

Principal function of terminal building
- Facilitates change of transport mode from plane to car, train, bus etc
- Processes passengers (ticket check-in, customs clearance etc)
- Provides services (shopping, conference etc)
- Groups and batches passengers for air transportation

Criteria for effective baggage handling
- Avoid baggage flows crossing passenger flows
- Place baggage sorting alongside apron area
- Avoid turns and level changes
- Keep conveyor slopes below 15°
- Minimise number of handling operations
- Provide for safety and security at each handling stage

Passenger processing in terminal building

Airline function	• Ticket check-in • Baggage handling (part) • Gate check-in
Airport function	• Baggage handling (part) • Security (part)
Government function	• Immigration control • Passport control • Customs control • Health control • Security (part)

Timescale of facilities adaptation

Staircase, escalators, major routes	30–50 years
Passenger lounges	20–30 years
Airport offices	15 years
Airline offices	5–10 years
Shops, bars, restaurants	3–5 years
Carpets, seats, finishes	1–5 years

account for 60% of the terminal volume, the remaining 40% has to provide space for airline staff, airport staff, and governmental and security staff. Four main stakeholder groups have an interest in the terminal, each needing gathering space, secure rooms and connecting routes (see **11**)
- the passengers (lounges, shops etc.)
- airline companies (ticket offices)
- airport authority (administrative areas)
- government (health and immigration control)

Added to this, the essentially public space for the passenger is often surrounded by shops, bars, restaurants and amusement arcades. Reconciling all the different needs is only possible if space planning recognises the inevitability of change and makes adequate provision for it.

Change occurs in the layout of airports terminals in a recognisable and often planned fashion. Different parts of the building are subject to varying levels of usage. Major circulation areas (such as gate corridors) may, therefore, require upgrading more quickly than quieter areas even though the same finishes and furniture have been employed. BAA makes provision for change by entering into long-term 'framework agreements' with manufacturers to ensure that matching components are available well into the future.

10 Kansai Airport, Japan (Arch: Renzo Piano Building Workshop) Sketch of interior of passenger terminal

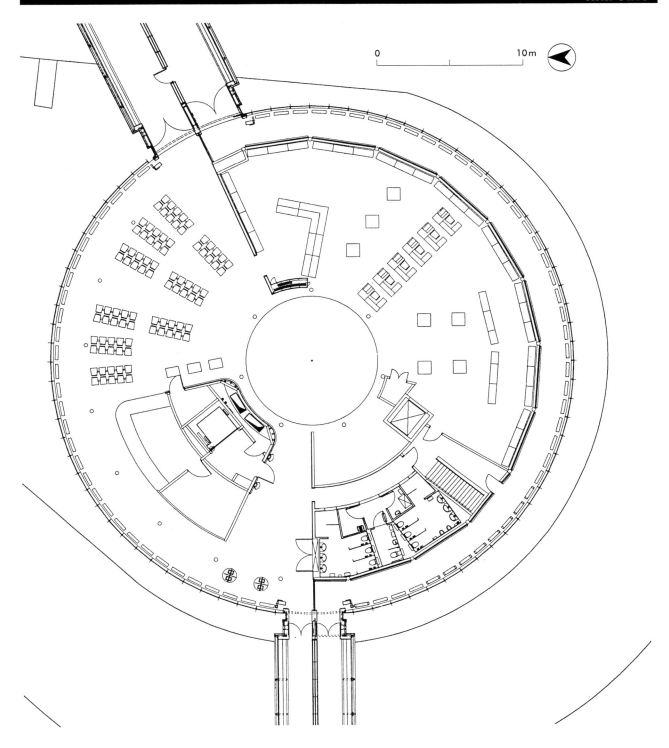

0   10m

11 Heathrow Airport, London
Transfer satellite at pier 4A: plan
(Arch: Nicholas Grimshaw & Partners)
(See also **9**)

movement	activities	space needs
departure passengers	check-in commercial areas customs clearance	departure concourse
	security shopping eating	departure lounge
	gate check-in	gate lounge
arrivals passengers	immigration security	arrivals area
	baggage claim	baggage hall
	customs clearance	customs hall
	meeting refreshment	arrivals lounge
transfer passengers	security customs clearance immigration refreshment	transfer lounge/ departure lounge

12 Activities and space needs in terminal building

13 Rockhampton Airport, Australia (Arch: Bligh Voller)

Planning the terminal

The planning of the terminal building should revolve around passenger needs. In a sense the passenger flow-path from check-in, through ticket and passport control to departure, then gate lounge to plane is a progression through space which needs to be expressed clearly in plan (see **12**). The points of interruption in the flow are where banks of offices of various sorts (airline, airport, customs) need to be located. Passenger needs rather than airport ones need to be given priority in the differentiation of space. Likewise in the opposite direction, the flow from plane to arrivals lounge via baggage reclaim needs to be expressed spatially. Again, the interplay of volume, light and structure needs to articulate key routes not obstruct them.

Balancing retailer needs with passenger needs can be difficult. As terminals become destinations in their own right (i.e. irrespective of further travel) many people present are there for the experience of the building and the chance to shop. Leisure shopping has influenced the terminal as elsewhere yet the passengers' progression through the building should not be overly obstructed by shops and burger bars no matter how profitable for the airline company or airport authority (see **14**).

14 Terminal building: space standards per passenger

check-in area	1.4 m²
departure lounge	1.8 m²
bars/shopping areas	2.1 m²
arrivals lounge	1.5 m²
baggage claim	1.6 m²
customs/immigration	2.0 m²
circulation areas	2.0 m²

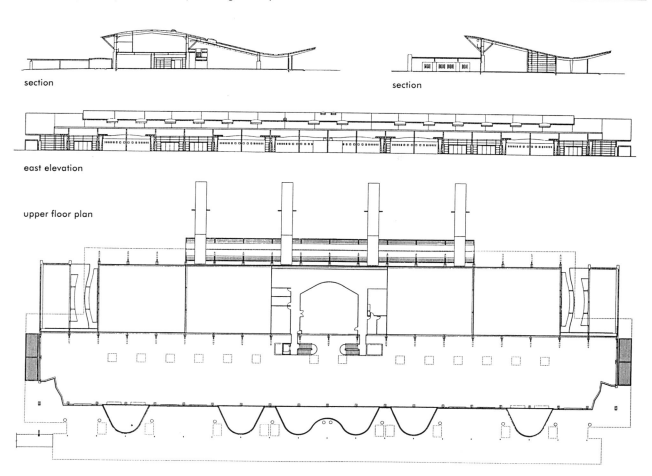

section

section

east elevation

upper floor plan

Terminal layout

The relationship between the terminal and satellites used for boarding planes is an important one for designers. There are four common variations and various hybrids between them (see *15*):

- terminal with linear gate piers connecting the satellites
- terminal with detached satellites
- terminal and satellites closely integrated
- terminal with radiating finger piers with or without satellites

The different layouts reflect the management of the airport, particularly whether it is a hub or destination airport. With larger airports it is common for an airline company to 'adopt' a satellite, thereby giving the ticketing, retail, duty free and movement function a consistent stamp. At O'Hare, Chicago the practice extends to whole terminals being dedicated to the needs of particular airline companies, with the result that the airport consists of a number of terminals each managed and controlled by a different carrier. With smaller regional airports the pattern is usually one of a single terminal with linear piers placed on a parallel alignment to the main runway.

The relationship between ownership, management and shared facilities can be complex. It is common for several airlines to share space in the terminal but to have their own dedicated satellite or gate lounge. But as the life of management systems and that of airline companies is shorter than the life of the buildings, flexibility of use is required.

Just as there are many configurations of terminal and satellite, so too different means are adopted for moving passengers around. Travel distances of up to 300–400 m are acceptable for passengers to walk but over that distance assisted movement is required. Three main methods are employed:

- travellators
- light rail systems
- buses

The first is common for distances of 300–1000 m, the second for distances of 1–3 km, the third for complex multi-stop journeys such as from terminal to satellite via the airport apron. Light rail systems are expensive (at Stansted each AEG train cost around £1 m) and require linear routes and generous radii at turns. At Kansai a mini-train runs through the airside lounge stopping every 200 m or so. At Gatwick and Birmingham Airports there are monorail systems which link together the terminals. Moving people across or below the runways pose obvious safety and logistic problems. The design for Heathrow's Terminal 5 plans to use an underground railway to link the terminal to the four planned satellites. Radiating finger piers with satellites at their end have the advantage of reducing travel distance (and hence use less expensive travellators) whilst maximising the points of access to aircraft standing on airport aprons.

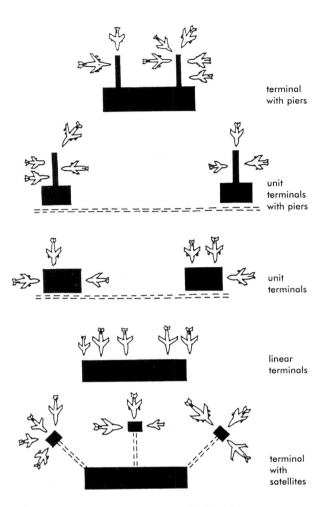

terminal with piers

unit terminals with piers

unit terminals

linear terminals

terminal with satellites

15 Diagrammatic layouts of types of terminal

regional	up to 1 million passengers per year	single deck road, single or 1½ level terminal, apron access to aircraft
national	1–5 million passengers per year	single deck road, double level terminal, elevated access to aircraft
international	over 5 million passengers per year	double deck road, two to four storey terminal, elevated access to aircraft

16 Main configuration of terminal according to size and capacity

17 Aircraft type and gate lounge size

DC-9, BAC 111	60 m²
B 737	100 m²
B 707, B 727, DC-8	140 m²
B 757	190 m²
DC-10, B 767	250 m²
B 747	360 m²
B 777, A3XX series	460 m²

journey type	distance (kms)	typical plane type	passenger capacity	passenger terminal type
intercontinental	over 3000	Boeing 747	450	multi-level terminal with satellites
continental	1500–3000	European Airbus A310	250	multi-level terminal
regional	under 1500	Boeing 737	150	1½ or single storey terminal
commuting	under 300	Saab 340	40	apron loading

18 Relationship between journey, plane and terminal type

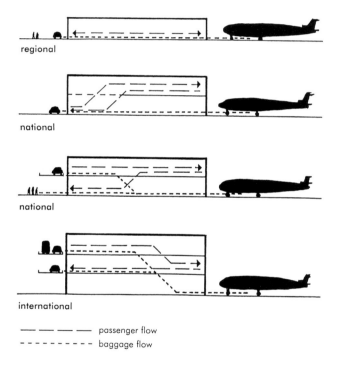

regional

national

national

international

— — — — — passenger flow

- - - - - - - - - baggage flow

19 Diagrammtic sectional layouts of terminal buildings

Design in section

There is inevitably a relationship between the layout in plan and the configuration in section. The degree of complexity of the section reflects the type, layout and capacity of the terminal (see **18**). Simple regional airports are usually single or 1½ storeys high whilst busy international ones may be four to six storeys high. Three main principles shape the design in section (see **19**):

- different levels help provide for smooth passenger movement
- different levels help separate passengers from baggage and public from private areas
- breaks in section help introduce daylight into deep planned terminals and allow for smoke extraction by natural means

Since warm air rises and light falls, the sectional profile of many modern terminals is tempered by the laws of physics (see **20**). Wavy roofs and stepped profiles combine good environmental design with more interesting appearance than is the case with the Cartesian flat-roofed terminals. The use of more natural means of achieving ventilation, smoke extraction and daylight penetration has fashioned the design of some of the world's more interesting recent terminals. Both complex sections and rational plans are required to meet the dual demands of efficient people movement and more natural means of tempering the environment.

Jetty design

The means of reaching the aircraft from the terminal without subjecting passengers to the harshness of the airport environment requires the skilful design of jetties. These are usually telescopic or pneumatic in operation and many types are provided by specialist manufacturers. The rotational geometry of jetties achieves the correspondence between the arms of gate lounges and the various heights and position of aircraft doors.

As new aircraft are introduced great strain is put on the passenger handling facilities, especially in the gate lounge. Although aircraft have standard door cill heights, doors are often positioned at different points along the fuselage. The expected new generation of very large capacity aircraft (800–1000 seater by 2005) will make obsolete current arrangements for passenger handling, not so much in the terminal, but at the airside interface. The need for flexibility and upgradeability is obvious.

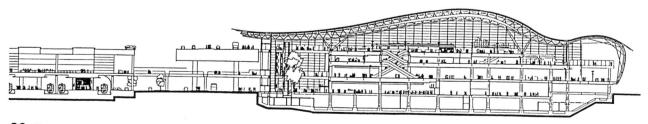

20 Kansai Airport, Japan (Arch: Renzo Piano Building Workshop)

Environmental factors

The airport environment is usually heavily polluted by fumes and noise. As a result most terminals are sealed air-conditioned buildings. Increasingly, however, they are partially open to the elements, with some recent designs using mixed mode ventilation and natural air-current smoke extraction (in the event of a fire).

To make the interior as comfortable as possible two problems have to be overcome:

- solar gain and glare
- noise abatement

Both are largely solved by a combination of interior and exterior measures. External screens and grilles help shade the terminal from direct sunlight and more substantial structures at the building face deflect the noise from aircraft (see **21**). The design of glazing also helps tackle these dual problems. Fritted or solar control glazing helps diffuse both high and low angled sunlight, whilst double or treble glazing reduce external noise to tolerable levels.

Sunlight can add sparkle to the terminal interior and aid the passengers' sense of location or direction. A balance has to be struck between the environmentally neutral interior and dramatic sun-filled spaces. Likewise some contact with external noise can give a sense of being at an airport and a degree of noise is tolerable in busy places. Where noise is unacceptable is in the tranquil areas, such as the transit departure or gate lounges and in office areas.

AIR TRAFFIC CONTROL TOWERS

These are amongst the most prominent and distinctive structures at airports. Their function is to control the skies around the airport, to organise the take-off and landing movements, and to ensure the efficient taxiing of aircraft on runways. Air traffic control towers need height, unobstructed views and good radar communication. Since they address mainly aircraft movement, air traffic control towers are positioned within the air-side zone, with good visibility of the terminal buildings.

Organisationally, there are two main elements: the control room at the top of the tower, and the means of reaching it (lifts, stairs, fire escape) (see **23**). Column free space and glare free visibility is essential for operational efficiency. Angled glass is normally employed to reduce solar gain and sunlight reflection which may interfere with pilot sightlines. Most tracking of aircraft is conducted on computer screens, hence the design of glazing and potential problems with screen reflection need to be carefully considered. The navigational and control systems in such towers have a relatively short life (8–10 years) with the result that three or four electronic refits occur within the life of the tower. Designing for upgrading of equipment with the tower still in operation requires a distinction to be drawn between primary structural elements and secondary fittings such as partition walls, cable systems, floors and ceilings.

Air traffic control towers are useful points of orientation within airports. Their three-dimensional form, shaped by operational needs, helps also to give these buildings the qualities of external landmarks. Many recent air-traffic control towers have used spiral or cascading forms to enhance their visual appeal in the hope of guiding people around the disorientating airport environment. Some air traffic control towers are built as rooftop extensions to the terminal (especially at regional airports) but this restricts their aesthetic possibilities.

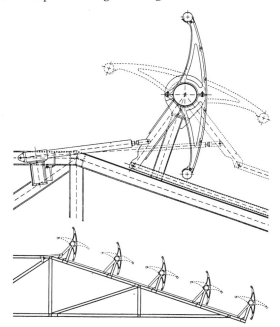

21 Stuttgart Airport, Germany (Arch: Von Gerkan, Marg & Partners)
Acoustic protection

- Determine risk
- Establish smoke patterns
- Establish spread of fire
- Assess success of containment by compartmentation
- Establish 'risk islands' and use local sprinklers
- Assess structural response to fire
- Assess reponse times

22 Fire safety design in terminal building

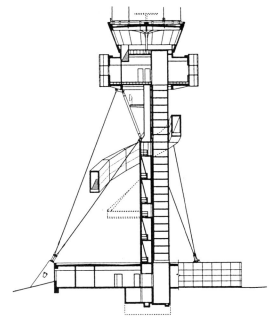

23 Sydney Airport, Australia (Arch: Ancher Mortlock & Woolley)
Air traffic control tower, section

BUSINESS PARKS

See also Industrial Buildings, Offices and Shops

INTRODUCTION

Attempts at the end of the 19th century to separate housing from industry gradually led to the development of purpose-built 'industrial estates'. Some of the most notable of these, such as Trafford Park near Manchester and Team Valley in Durham, were built in the early 20th century on greenfield sites with good connections to rail and (when possible) water networks. Although some office and ancillary facilities were provided (e.g. catering), these were seen as adjuncts to the main purpose, namely providing factory facilities, generally for light industry, in modern buildings.

Over the last 30 years or so, the emphasis has switched away from providing light industrial units to providing a range of buildings suitable for a variety of purposes: offices, light industrial, high technology (e.g. manufacture or assembly of electronic components). The term 'industrial estate' was considered to be unsuitable, although it is interesting to note that this term was itself invented to indicate a better level of provision than the normal Victorian factory premises. The phrase 'business park' therefore replaced 'industrial estate'.

In business parks a high level of building services is often considered essential, together with building designs which can be adapted for a variety of uses relatively easily. Flexible space is required to meet the needs of production, distribution, sales, service and office operations. Soft landscaping, sometimes to a high standard, is often provided, along with related facilities such as quality catering and health clubs. If the developer is also looking for occupation by international companies, extra facilities will be required, such as hotel accommodation. There will be an overall masterplan, but each individual building can have its own design.

Further refinements in terminology have led to 'commerce parks', which attempt to provide facilities between industrial estates (i.e. traditional manufacturing) and business parks (i.e. offices). These sites attempt to provide a greater mix of uses than traditionally available, often resulting from the revolution in information (or 'knowledge-based') technology.

Recent concern by local authorities and planners that greenfield sites can be isolated from local communities have led to attempts to provide a range of uses: for instance, housing arranged to provide a village atmosphere, together with community facilities, shops and schools (see 11).

Good connections to the road network, particularly motorways, are considered essential; it is rare in the UK for there to be connection to the rail network, and even rarer for connections to the canal or river network. Car parking provision must therefore be generous, as bus services may be few. Access will also be required for large lorries (for lorry sizes, see the sections on Vehicle Facilities and Industrial Buildings), which require larger roads and turning bays.

	Size (ha)	Start date	Target markets	Linked universities/institutes		Main sponsors	Special features
				Main	Other		
Existing							
Brunel Science Park	3	1986	Spin-outs Local firms	Brunel University		Brunel University	Accommodates HQ of International Tin Research Council. Waiting list for tenants
South Bank Technopark	1	1987	Local technology and business service firms	South Bank University		Prudential Corporation	Innovation centre
Planned							
Brunel Science Park Phase III	1		Spin-outs Local firms	Brunel University		Brunel University	Aimed at accommodating existing demand for space
Croydon Science Park	13	1996/7	Local service and manufacturing firms Inward investment	Croydon College (University of Sussex)		South Thames Regional Health Authority and private developer	Former hospital site in green belt
Lee Valley Science Park	43	1995	Inward investment Local firms	Middlesex University	University of East London University of North London Guildhall University	London Borough of Enfield Thames Water	Physical regeneration project. Business and Innovation Centre completed - tenants moved in September 1995
Royals Science and Technology Park	10	1998/9	Spin-outs SMEs Inward investment	Royals University College	University of East London Guildhall University QMH Westfield College City University	LDDC LETEC and universities	Regeneration project. Part of Thames Gateway. Close to European Medicines Evaluation Agency
Harefield Medipark	21	1996	Healthcare firms	Harefield Hospital		Trafalgar House	Planning permission restricted to firms in healthcare sector. Private owner unwilling to proceed with these restrictions
Linked to London universities							
London Science Park, Dartford	up to 50	1996	Local and regional firms Inward investment	University of Greenwich	Glaxo Wellcome	Dartford Borough Council SE Thames Regional Health Authority University of Greenwich	Part of East Thames Corridor, and of larger development area including new campus for the university
Imperial Park, Newport	21	1992	Local firms	Imperial College	University of Cardiff	Welsh Development Agency Newport Borough Council	170 miles from related university
Silwood Park, Ascot	2		SMEs	Imperial College			Innovation Centre managed by Imperial College

1 Technology Parks in London (mid-1990s)
(from Segal Quince & Wicksteed Ltd, Technology Parks in London)

Science and technology parks

These sites attempt to provide a mix of uses, often intended for local or 'start-up' firms. They are associated with universities or research centres – there are over 40 in the UK, with an average size of 15 ha (see **1**), but ranging from a few hundred square metres in one building, to over 1000 ha.

Breakdown of activity in science parks

29%	computer related
21%	electronics related
17%	biotechnology related
16%	contract R&D
15%	technical consultancy
17%	business services
17%	engineering design
29%	other

(from Science Park Network survey, carried out by Segal Quince & Wicksteed Ltd in 1993–4 for the EC)

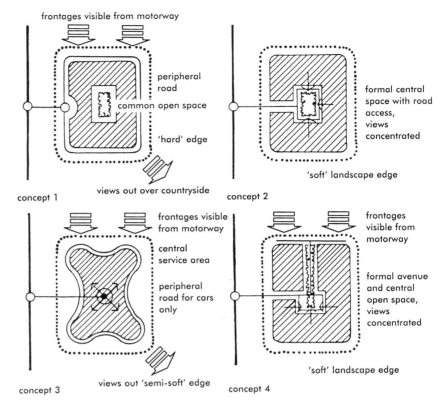

2 Schematic layouts (four variants)
(from English Estates Industrial & Commercial Estates, Planning & Site Development)

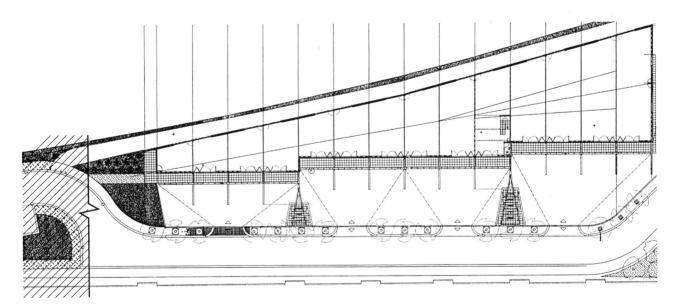

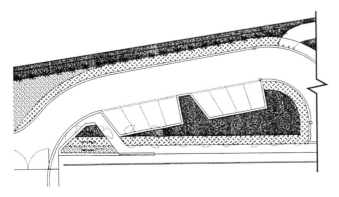

3 Barley Shotts Business Park, Westbourne Park, London
(Developer: North Kensington City Challenge; Arch: Robert Ian Barnes Architects)
An attempt to 'pump prime' an inner-city location (disused railway land) to provide various facilities. A series of B1 units is the first phase and provides affordable, low-maintenance work-spaces, built to a tight budget to a standard commercial brief. A broad range of unit sizes is provided. The steel frame is designed to allow a future mezzanine office area if required. Roof lights provide natural lighting, and combined with wall glazing allow natural ventilation

DETAILED CONSIDERATIONS

Small-scale 'nursery' units meet the need to integrate a group of units into an existing urban or rural community to encourage small local firms. The minimum size is 50 m². Similar terms are 'incubator', 'innovation' or 'seedbed' centres. **5** shows 'nursery' units with a variety of rental areas and grouped goods access. Speculative developments for rental are often built in various forms of terrace to allow flexible space allocation.

Mixture of sizes of unit can be achieved by variable location of cross-walls in the terrace or by providing two or more groups of buildings of increasing size.

Office and amenity accommodation can be either integral within the volume of building (where site area is restricted) or as an attached block (where the developer requires the maximum rental from production/storage area).

Goods access Sufficient heavy goods vehicle manoeuvring and parking areas must be allowed (see also Industrial Buildings – 'loading bays').

Security is important – both physical (mainly theft of high-technology equipment) and intellectual (loss of staff to neighbouring firms).

Car parking Required for occupants and visitors (check local requirements).

Planning permission may need considerable negotiation due to the variety of uses required by developer. Class B1 was introduced to cater for such developments (see the list of classes in the Industrial Buildings section) but the planning authority may attempt to restrict use with a 'section 106' agreement. This is a voluntary agreement by both parties to restrict use to an agreed list, but the real problem is attempting to legally define high-technology or knowledge-based activity.

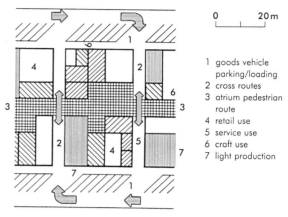

0   20m

1 goods vehicle parking/loading
2 cross routes
3 atrium pedestrian route
4 retail use
5 service use
6 craft use
7 light production

4 Trade mart concept: can be used to revitalise inner city areas; divisible space under a common roof allows a high degree of planning flexibility. Development can mix retail, craft, electronic and light industrial occupancy to stimulate local working community

1 'nursery' units (rental)
2 medium sized divisible units (rental)
3 larger divisible units (rental)
4 purpose-built units (lease back)
5 yard/loading area
6 car parking (grouped)
7 landscaped open space

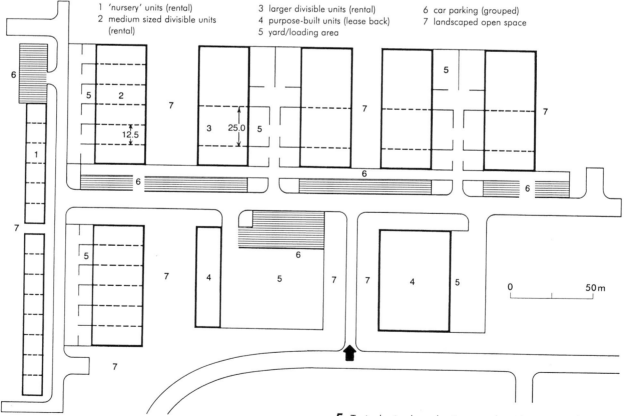

0   50m

5 Typical mixed-use business park, with a range of unit sizes for rental, each having expansion options (by extending into adjoining unit); grouped parking and yards for each property; landscaping is essential to improve what can be a desolate environment

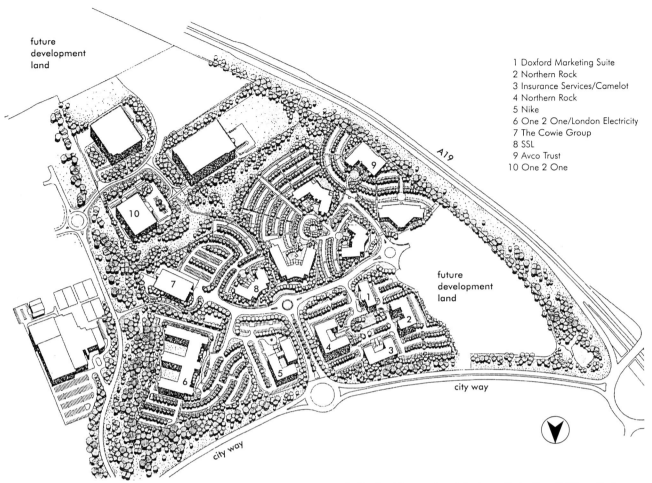

1 Doxford Marketing Suite
2 Northern Rock
3 Insurance Services/Camelot
4 Northern Rock
5 Nike
6 One 2 One/London Electricity
7 The Cowie Group
8 SSL
9 Avco Trust
10 One 2 One

6 Doxford International Business Park, Tyne & Wear (Arch: Aukett Associates)
A 32 ha development in at least five phases by developer Akeler. Buildings are mostly 'loose-fit' to allow for a variety of users

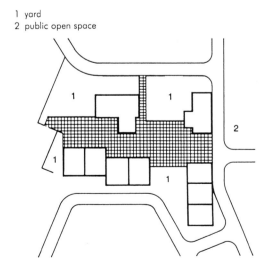

1 yard
2 public open space

7 Nursery units: minimum unit area is 50 m² ; minor access road will not permit heavy goods vehicles. Goods/service access and car park need to be shared (compare **8**)

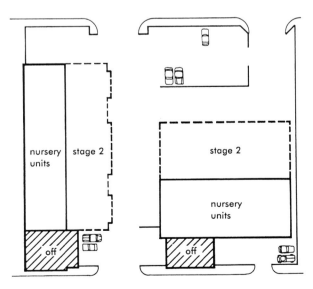

8 Nursery units: layout allows for expansion, but in urban infill sites this may have to be at expense of yard area. Layout provides for heavy goods access: vehicles must enter and leave access roads in a forward direction; goods access is separate from car parking area (compare **7**)

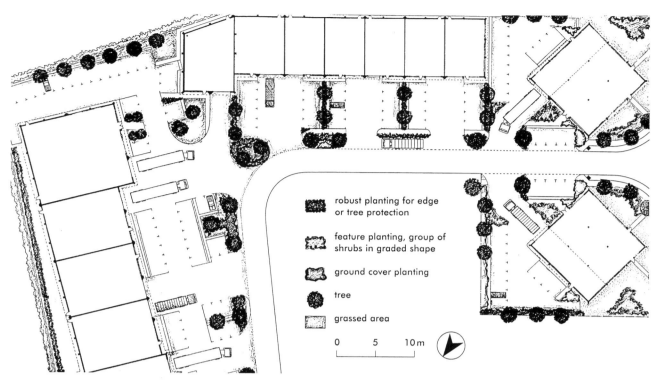

9 Business Park, Letchworth (Arch: Triforum) site plan (part)

Legend:
- robust planting for edge or tree protection
- feature planting, group of shrubs in graded shape
- ground cover planting
- tree
- grassed area

0   5   10m

Business park specification (see 9,10)

Typical specification for speculative light industrial units in a business park location:

Structure Traditional concrete strip foundations to external walls, concrete pads to columns. In-situ concrete ground floor slab. Uniformly distributed load to be $30\,kN/m^2$. Steel frame structure. Height to underside of rafter at eaves to be 5 m.

External walls Traditional construction of facing brick, cavity and insulating blockwork, giving a U-value of $0.6\,W/m^2K$, and a curtain wall system of aluminium sections with a polyester powder-coat finish, double glazed factory sealed units to windows, and composite infill.

Pitched roof structure Profiled galvanised sheeting fixed to galvanised steel purlins with composite insulation, giving a U-value of $0.6\,W/m^2K$. Double-skin roof lights provided to 10% of the ground floor area.

Suspended floors Pre-cast concrete floor planks on steel beams, designed to carry a superimposed load of $5\,kN/m^2$ plus a partition dead-load of $1\,kN/m^2$. First floor office areas: units have either a partial-access floor system, or a screeded floor. Floor finish to be carpet.

Internal walls Party walls of 215 mm concrete blockwork; partitions of 100 mm blockwork at ground floor and metal-stud system with plasterboard finish at first floor.

Ceilings Suspended ceiling of 600 mm × 600 mm tile with modular lighting panels.

Loading doors Sectional overhead shutter doors match the curtain wall system.

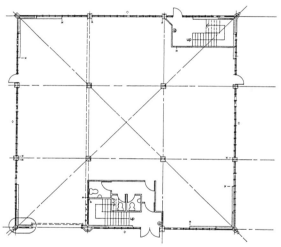

10 Plan of 'diamond' unit (see **9**)

Power Ground floor distribution board for wiring by occupant.

Heating and ventilating A gas-fired boiler and water radiator system. Some units have provision in the roof space above the offices for installation of air-handling equipment by the occupant (including allowance for 300 mm high ductwork and louvres if required).

Access road Set out to local authority adoption standards.

Servicing and parking area Pavior block finish on a concrete base. Footpaths: pavior block.

External lighting Pole-mounted estate lighting. Individual loading-bay lights fitted over the delivery areas.

Landscaping Shrubs, trees and grassed areas; 1.8 m high perimeter fencing.

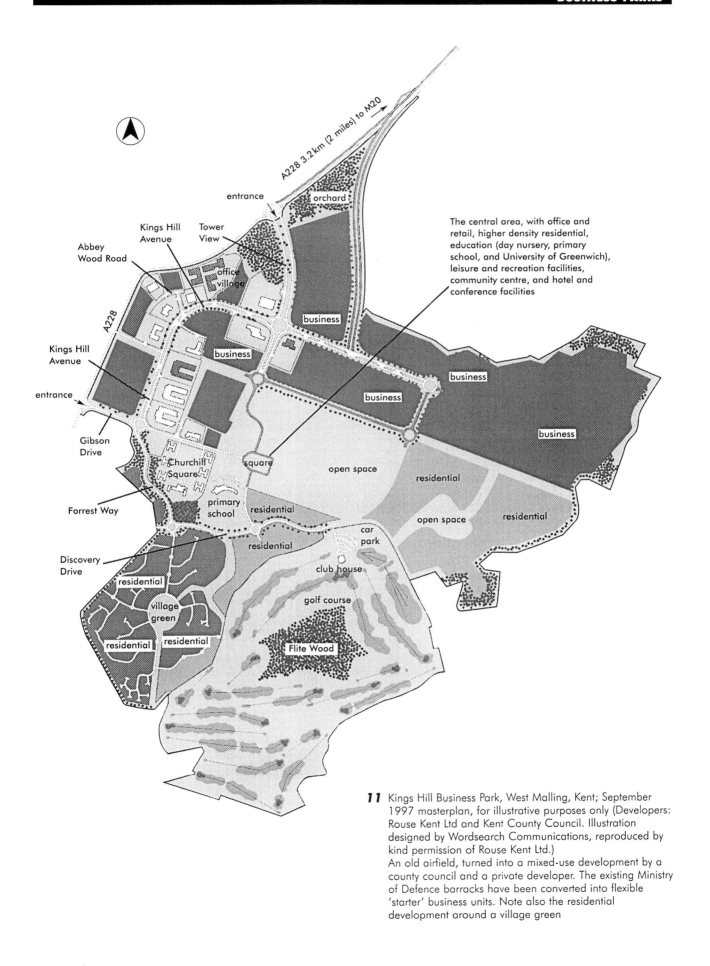

A228 3.2 km (2 miles) to M20

entrance

orchard

Kings Hill Avenue

Tower View

Abbey Wood Road

office village

A228

business

business

Kings Hill Avenue

The central area, with office and retail, higher density residential, education (day nursery, primary school, and University of Greenwich), leisure and recreation facilities, community centre, and hotel and conference facilities

business

entrance

business

business

Gibson Drive

business

square

open space

residential

Forrest Way

Churchill Square

Discovery Drive

primary school

residential

residential

open space

residential

residential

car park

club house

residential

village green

residential

residential

golf course

Flite Wood

11 Kings Hill Business Park, West Malling, Kent; September 1997 masterplan, for illustrative purposes only (Developers: Rouse Kent Ltd and Kent County Council. Illustration designed by Wordsearch Communications, reproduced by kind permission of Rouse Kent Ltd.)
An old airfield, turned into a mixed-use development by a county council and a private developer. The existing Ministry of Defence barracks have been converted into flexible 'starter' business units. Note also the residential development around a village green

CINEMAS

Helen Dallas

See also auditoriums in the Theatres and Sports sections

INTRODUCTION

Despite the advent of videos, cable and satellite TV, cinemas continue to be popular. Generally, commercial cinemas are run by the large film companies although there are still some small independent cinemas (see **1**) and individual club cinemas screening specialised films for members.

The trend in cinema design over recent years has been to offer the public a choice of viewing at individual venues. This has resulted in the conversion of big cinemas into two or more auditoria and the birth of the purpose-built multiplex offering between six and fourteen screens, often on out-of-town sites with ample parking. However, such locations are becoming limited and operators of varying size will be encouraged to maximise existing town-centre sites.

The design of the modern cinema seeks to find a successful balance between the existing site conditions, individual auditorium size, raking of seats to provide an unobstructed view together with good sound and picture quality for the customer. Strong competition has meant operators are increasingly looking to improve comfort for cinema-goers with quality design, particularly in entrance areas, and additional entertainment facilities.

1 Phoenix Cinema, East Finchley, London: originally opened in 1910, this is a good example of one of the few remaining independent cinemas (note access provision for people with disabilities) (Arch: Pyle Associates)

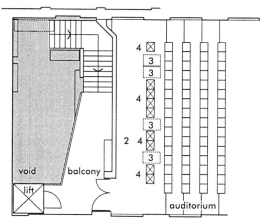

ground floor entrance foyer (as proposed)

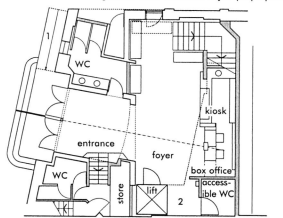

first floor foyer area (as proposed)

1 proposed ramp; 2 wheelchair turning space; 3 wheelchair spaces;
4 all seats in rear row can be removed to create space for wheelchairs

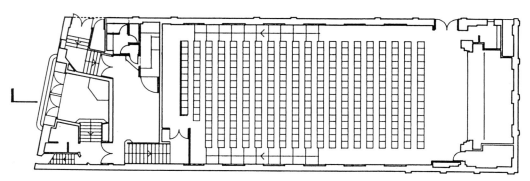

section (as existing)

plan (as existing)

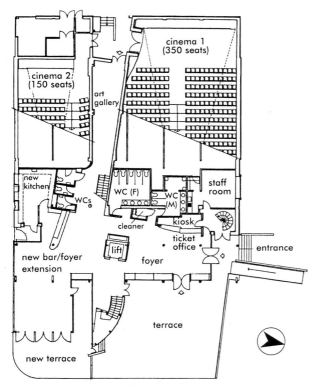

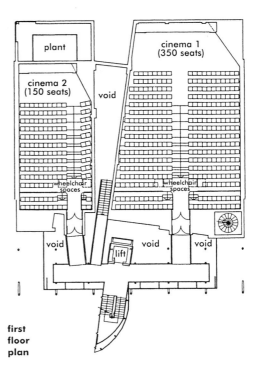

ground floor plan

first floor plan

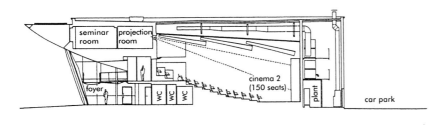

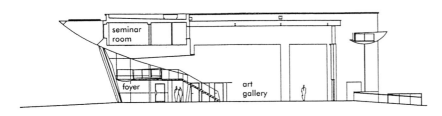

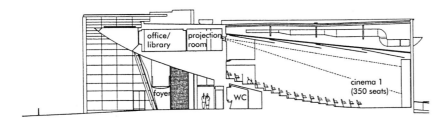

sections

2 Harbour Lights Cinema, Southampton
(Arch: Burrell Foley Fischer)

DETAILED DESIGN

Siting In town-centre locations, open space is required around the cinema to accommodate means of escape, create an identifiable entry and allow for possible queues. New multi-screen cinemas should provide easy access and ample parking to meet Local Authority requirements.

Multiple auditoria These are considered vital in commercial cinemas (see **2**, **4**). Various theories are used to apportion the total number of seats between different auditoria in the same building. In dual cinemas, ratios of 1:2 or 2:3 are used, and 1:2:3 for triple cinemas. Further progressions in seat totals may be used in larger multiples but they rarely exceed a 1:3 ratio between the smallest and largest screens. As well as offering visitors a choice of programme, such venues allow the operator to judge the business potential of each film so as to show it in an auditorium that matches public demand: if the film is playing to half-capacity audiences, it can be switched to a smaller auditorium, and vice versa.

An auditorium width should not exceed approximately twice that of the screen and its length no more than three times the screen width. To achieve the best sound quality the opposite surfaces of floors, ceilings and walls should not be parallel to each other. Where the ideal fan shape is not possible, singular angled walls, raked ceilings or acoustically absorbent features can be used.

Seating   In addition to being comfortable and easily accessible, seating must be designed such that all members of the audience have a clear and unobstructed view of the screen. Seating for customers with disabilities should be integrated within the main body of the seating (see **1**) although this is not always possible because of requirements for refuge points and emergency exits.

Seating areas of auditoria should be within 0.85–1.05 m² per person. The distance between the backs of seats should be a minimum of 900 mm although up to 1.2 m is often used for maximum legroom and comfort. Seat widths vary between 500 and 750 mm, with a suggested maximum of 22 seats per row.

To provide acceptable sight-lines, seating is normally raked, varying between 5 and 10%. Larger auditoria often include stepped seating towards the rear (see **3**).

The distance from the screen to the front row of seats is determined by the maximum allowable angle between the sight-line from the first row to the top of the screen and perpendicular to the screen at that point. The recommended angle is from 30° up to 35° although 45° is used as the maximum in some circumstances. The 35° sight angle limit above the horizontal produces a distance to the screen on the centre-line of 1.43 times the height from the front row eye level to the top of the picture (see **3**).

Gangways   These should have a minimum clear width of 1.05 m. In small auditoria (100–250 seats), a single central gangway is sufficient; for medium size venues, a gangway on either side is acceptable, causing less visual distraction; and in large auditoria (400–600 seats) the preferred solution is to have twin gangways set in 0.25–0.35 of the cinema width from each side.

Public areas   The public areas are important in conveying an image of class and comfort to customers and the decor should therefore be attractive and designed to high standards. The space may include payment booths, advance booking facilities, ticket machines, refreshment kiosks, merchandising stalls, forthcoming film advertising and information on current screenings. There should be sufficient room for queuing comfortably and clear signage to public toilets, auditorium entrances etc. Suitable access, toilets and lifts are required for visitors with disabilities.

Additional accommodation   Other requirements in the design layout of a cinema include: plant room, staff rooms and facilities, cleaners' store, manager's office, film store, kiosk stock room and refrigeration for ice creams, projection booths and a treasury/secure cash room.

Multiplex cinemas may offer a wider range of entertainment. The designer may, therefore, need to consider extending the traditional catering facilities to provide bars and restaurants as attractive integral features. Cinemas are also now combined with other commercial and leisure activities such as shopping malls, computer games arcades, virtual reality centres, bowling alleys etc.

SERVICING FACILITIES

Projection rooms   Traditionally these were divided into separate compartments for rewinding and projecting film, with dimmer room, battery room, spotlight room, workshop and store room, each forming a 6–10 m² suite. Automated systems currently in use include projection areas with rewinding benches, sound equipment, dimmer and switch facilities. To cater for future trends, a minimum area of 5.5 × 4.0 m per screen should be allowed, with a minimum ceiling height of 2.6 m. Continuous playing equipment enables one operator to control several screens.

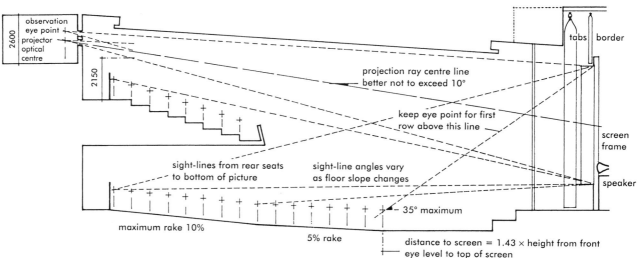

3 Basic requirements for auditorium levels

In multiplex cinemas, a long continuous projection room behind the screens can be installed, or two-way projection rooms for back-to-back screens. Advanced techniques employ variable height and width pictures: the size of arc lamp used is determined by the picture area and the maximum effect is obtained by using different ratios of equal areas.

Projection rooms require a separate system of mechanical or natural ventilation, water cooling facilities, suitable positioned lighting and sufficient heating (or cooling) to maintain a minimum temperature of 10°C.

Screens The aim should be to use as large a screen as possible, up to the limits defined either by given maxima or width of seating. The proportions are 1:1.75 height to width and black masking is used around the edges to preserve the maximum brightness on the screen.

Within large auditoria, curved directional screens were originally developed to overcome problems of dispersion of reflected light from flat screens. Modern cinemas, with better screen material, are able to use the curvature of the screen to reduce the amount of apparent distortion to side sight-lines. However, too much rise of chord can give problems with focus over the whole picture area.

Screen construction is generally pvc or metallised fabric stretched over a metal frame. It should be remembered that the surface will deteriorate over time. (Consult BS 5550 for relevant specifications on screening and projection.)

A minimum depth of 1.35 m is required behind the screens for the installation of speakers, the number and position of which usually depends on the type of sound system and the size of the auditorium. Space must also be left for the tabs (curtains) and mechanical systems to the side of the screen.

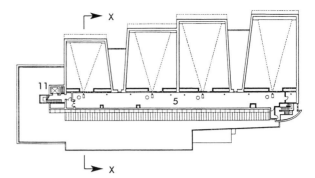

projection floor plan

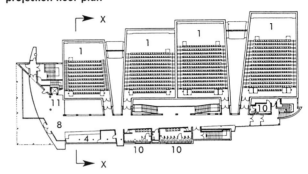

first floor plan

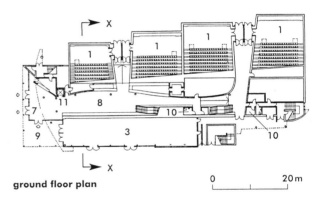

ground floor plan

0   20 m

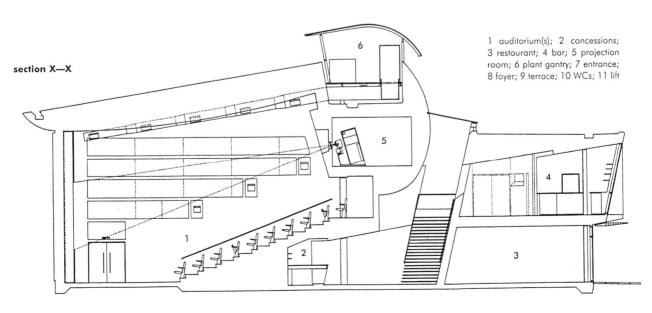

section X—X

1 auditorium(s); 2 concessions; 3 restaurant; 4 bar; 5 projection room; 6 plant gantry; 7 entrance; 8 foyer; 9 terrace; 10 WCs; 11 lift

4 Stratford East Picture House, London (Arch: Burrell Foley Fischer)

Sound systems Considerable developments have been made over the years, with the early problems of handling magnetic sound recordings of film being solved by Dolby encoding optical systems. Digitally recorded sound is now also being used. With both systems the sound is decoded in the projection room to achieve the effect desired for the particular film (e.g. Dolby surround sound for action films or a traditional rear screen transmission). Typically, five speakers are used, one being specifically for bass sounds, and often with a sixth as an auditorium speaker. Very wide screens and side sound sources can produce acoustic problems: generally for cinemas reflected sound paths should not exceed direct paths by more than 15 m.

General servicing

Decorative lighting and any required spotlighting installed in the auditorium must, obviously, be capable of being dimmed when the film is showing. Illumination of seating areas and gangways is required during the film programme but none of the light should fall on the screen or walls. The auditorium system is also used as emergency lighting under management control. Safety lighting is needed to all public, key staff and exit boxes throughout the building. This must be kept on as part of the maintained system and, should the main electricity supply fail, a safety system must be able to provide sufficient light to allow the public and staff to leave the building safely.

A good standard of mechanical ventilation and/or air conditioning is required throughout all public areas, and especially the auditorium, to maintain comfort levels.

Acoustic separation is necessary at entrances to each auditorium and also between the projection rooms and the auditoria. At entrances, this is achieved with lobbies and sound reducing doorsets.

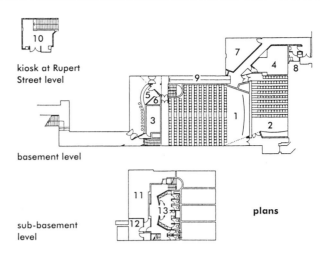

kiosk at Rupert Street level

basement level

sub-basement level

plans

1 cinema 1; 2 cinema 2; 3 projection 1; 4 projection 2; 5 bar; 6 store; 7 viewing; 8 WC (dis); 9 ramp; 10 kiosk; 11 plant room; 12 staff restroom; 13 WCs

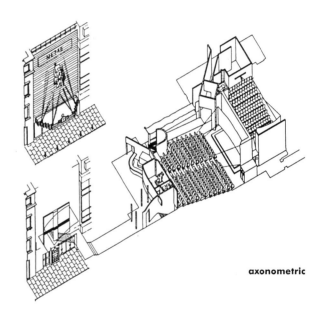

axonometric

6 Metro Cinema, Piccadilly, London: a former theatre converted to a cinema
(Arch: Burrell Foley Fischer)

ALTERNATIVE CINEMA ACCOMMODATION

Drive-in cinemas Popular in the USA, these are designed on the principal of the amphitheatre, with individual speakers for each car. Designs with both single and multiple screens are now used.

The layout should provide a view of the picture at no more than 45° from the perpendicular at the centre of the screen and ramps should be designed so that spectators can see clearly over the cars in front. With large screens the distance from the front row to the screen is often more than 50 m. The typical screen size is 30.4 × 13 m and it should face between east and south to make early evening screenings possible. The height of the screen above the ground depends on the site profile and this in turn determines the angles for the car ramps.

Ticket booths are needed and ample space for queues should be allowed. The design should provide for separate entrances and exits.

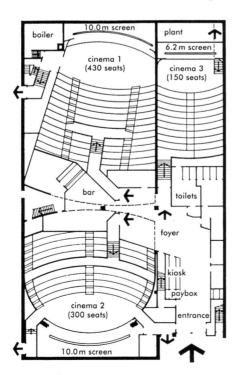

5 Cinema in Putney, London: multiple auditoria with high-level common projection room; part of a commercial building

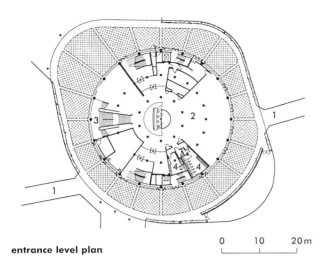

entrance level plan

0   10   20m

Circarama Used successfully in Disneyland, this system uses eleven projectors to give audiences a sense of participation and full involvement. Seating is not practical but handrails are necessary to prevent the viewers from falling over.

Interactive systems These are a development used in theme parks and now in 'Experience' theatres around the world. They use an audio-visual technique of automated multiple projection of still pictures with auditorium effects and multi-track magnetic sound systems. Closed-circuit TV systems are feasible with electronic line enhancement, giving $2.43 \times 1.83\,\text{m}$ pictures. With 'Eidophor' screens, sizes up to $9 \times 12\,\text{m}$ are possible. There have been developments of interactive cinema systems where seating is programmed to move relative to the screen action.

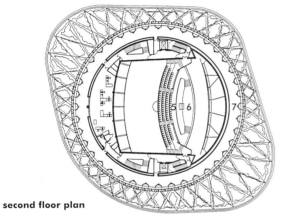

second floor plan

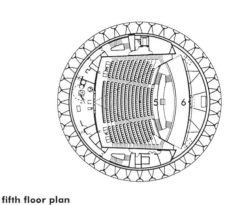

fifth floor plan

1 pedestrian walkways;
2 entrance foyer; 3 stairs;
4 WCs; 5 seating; 6 screen;
7 gallery area; 8 planting;
9 maintenance gantry

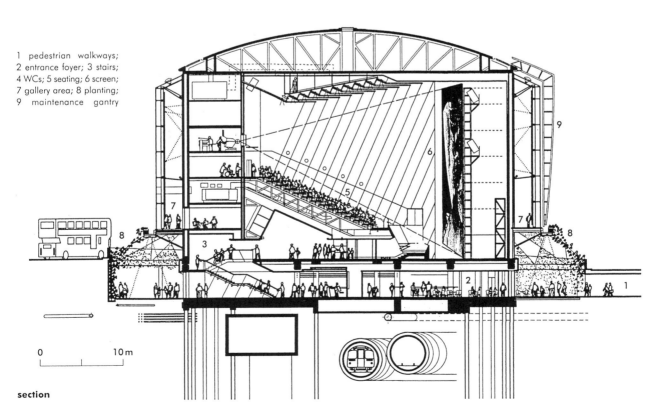

section

0   10m

7 The British Film Institute London IMAX Cinema, Waterloo, London
(Arch: Avery Associates Architects)

COMMUNITY CENTRES

Peter Beacock and Fiona Brettwood

INTRODUCTION AND BACKGROUND

With the decline of the influence of the church and the movement of people from small isolated communities into urban centres, facilities for the local community were initially provided by philanthropists, and were intended as centres for education and public lectures. After World War I a number of different organisations were set up to provide community facilities, such as the Village Clubs Association, which were designed to be 'the centre of communal life and activity'[1]. It was seen as important that 'the foundation of all schemes should be the reliance upon the communal spirit, so that everything which is attempted would not be imposed from the top, but built up from the bottom'[2]. This led to the building of a great variety of village clubs responding to local requirements. Generally, they had a multifunctional main hall, and small meeting room or rooms, but could also include separate boys' and girls' rooms, a gymnasium, rifle range, billiard room, library, or reading rooms. These clubs were mainly self-supporting, with funding for construction of the building supported by the Urban or Rural District Council, or Parish Council[3].

In areas of industrial development, where the majority of the community was directly or indirectly involved in particular activities, resources were provided by employers or unions, as for example in the Miners' Welfare Halls and Clubs in the coalmining areas of the country. These were 'the product of an enforced liaison between miners and their employers resulting from the 1920 Mining Industries Act'[4] (see **1**).

In the 1970s and 80s, communities in Britain 'came to rely on a range of self help activities ... to meet a variety of needs not met by standard Local Authority services'[5]. Finding funding to build and run facilities became increasingly difficult with changes in government policy and society's values. There has, however, been a resurgence in the commissioning of community facilities in recent years, because of funding packages available through European Regional Development Fund, Lottery funding and the setting up of a number of charitable foundations by wealthy private companies. The procurement process has consequently become very protracted, with the early stages of the design process being particularly important.

The need to provide a community centre will usually be generated either by the need to update, modify or replace an existing facility that has genuinely served a need, or to provide a totally new facility intended to encourage the re-establishment of a sense of community. In all cases, funding will need to be sought from a variety of sources, and community groups will have to demonstrate that the proposal is founded on a sound business plan, moving towards financial self-sufficiency. Funders need evidence that the proposed facility and management strategy meet the needs of the local community it is intended to serve. This is best provided by extensive local consultation.

1 Vane Tempest Welfare, Seaham, Co Durham: provision for the needs of a local mining community

Key stages in community consultation are (see **2**):

- working with community organisation or organisations to consult the local population as to perceived needs and requirements
- identifying other local provision to avoid duplication of facilities
- developing a design brief and accommodation requirements from the consultations
- consulting with the Local Authority on funding potential, planning and highways issues.

It is important that the early consultation phase is carried out rigorously if the completed building is to meet the needs of the community and be viable.

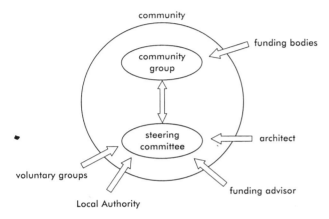

2 Organisations likely to be involved from the early stages of development

COMMUNITY CONSULTATION AND BRIEFING

Local issues

If the proposed centre is to satisfy local needs and satisfy funders that it is viable, early community consultation and data collection is essential to develop the community profile and identify community needs. The community profile will typically consist of:

- demographics
- employment statistics
- existing facilities
- population changes
- geography
- transport infrastructure.

Identification of community needs requires in-depth consultation with existing groups and societies, and broader based dialogue with the wider community. Consultation can be carried out using a range of methods – questionnaires, open days, exhibitions, public meetings, focus groups, themed workshops and similar activities – to give the chance for individuals of all ages to express their opinions and concerns.

SUSTAINABILITY

The idea of community provision, and the encouragement of the community to use local facilities, is very much in the spirit of Agenda 21. There is the opportunity to use the centre to encourage approaches to sustainability, by designing for minimum energy use and water use, choosing locally sourced, or other low environmental impact materials, and involving the community in its

construction. For example, the community centre at Meadow Well, North Tyneside, involved local trainees in its construction, and the Robin Hood Centre in Nottingham adopted a Walter Segal design approach, in which the local community participated in the project (see **3**).

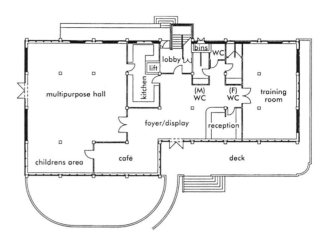

3 Robin Hood Chase Neighbourhood Centre, Nottingham: constructed with community involvement using 'self-build' techniques; ground floor plan
(Arch: Carnell Green Bradley)

DESIGN ISSUES

For community centres to be viable, they must be seen to provide for and be welcoming to the community; they are often a key factor in an area regeneration strategy. Key design issues areas follows.

Image

The centre must be welcoming to all ages, and have a positive impact in the community. Although security is a major consideration, it must not be at the expense of making the building unwelcoming, and well-lit entrance areas can provide an appropriate atmosphere (see **4**). New buildings often have a more noticeable impact but the refurbishment of existing facilities is often more economically viable. If existing facilities are to be retained it is important that the exterior of the building reflects the changes inside the centre, as it is the outside appearance which advertises the improvements within.

4 The New Social Welfare Centre, Choppington, Northumberland: sketch of entrance area, an open and welcoming space
(Arch: WHHLP)

Site and location

Ideally, the centre should be as close to the heart of the community as possible, near other facilities (shops, school, library), and accessible by public transport (see **5**). A flat site is preferable because the construction costs are lower than with sloping plots and it allows for easier access. It should have adequate space for parking cars and bicycles, and may need additional external space for facilities such as play areas, gardens, and sports provision. The profile of the local residents is an important consideration.

Organisation

The building must be easy for the staff to manage. Layout and circulation routes should be clear, and ample storage space is needed. Consider noise, type of activity, likely timing of activities and age groups when locating facilities. A reception area or office at or near the entrance will assist in the monitoring of visitors and provide a focal point for information and organisation (see **6,7**).

5 Bowburn Community Centre, Co Durham, site plan: located at the centre of the village; note relationship to other community facilities, as well as housing and open space (Arch: WHHLP)

Circulation

Economical planning is necessary to keep costs down, so all opportunities should be taken to minimise corridors, and make spaces useable for more than one function. Central circulation space doubling up as a café/informal meeting area is a typical solution. Circulation space must be easily monitored and have robust and hard-wearing surface finishes. Vertical circulation in multi-storey buildings must be visible from a central control point or management office to avoid potential misuse of lifts etc.

Accessibility

The building will need to cater for all age ranges, from children in prams and push chairs to ambulant disabled adults and wheelchair users. Location of bus stops, walking distances from residential areas, provision of disabled parking all need to be considered, as should colour and contrast in the interior design scheme. The implications of sloping sites, changes of level and designs with more than one floor level need careful consideration at the outset. Lifts and chair lifts are expensive to install and maintain, and prone to abuse.

Opening hours and management policies of the building also need to be considered from the earliest stage and can often be subject to planning restrictions to avoid disruption of immediate neighbours.

Flexibility

Consultation with client groups will identify needs, and these will usually encompass a wide variety of uses by a range of age groups. The building design must allow for maximum flexibility of use, which will need to be considered both in the short term to cater for current requirements, and in the longer term, as needs will change with time. For short-term change, moveable walls or partitions to divide spaces may have some applications (see **6**) but there are problems with the poor acoustic performance of some screens and the operational complexity of large systems. Design solutions that give flexibility through planning and space organisation as well as the provision of a range of different sized spaces are to be preferred. For longer term change, designs that can easily accommodate internal reorganisation through appropriate initial structural design and by allowing space for future extension are desirable.

Maintenance

There should be careful consideration of maintenance implications of all specifications to help to minimise running costs and ensure long-term viability of the centre. Specify robust high-quality materials and products wherever possible and avoid unusual fixtures and fittings (such as taps, toilets, boilers and shutters) that may cause maintenance difficulties for the management group through cost, availability of spares etc. Limit external maintenance liabilities by minimising the use of render and other painted surfaces. Consider also vulnerable surfaces; avoid materials and accessible roofs that may be subject to vandalism. It is important, however, to avoid designing a 'fortress'.

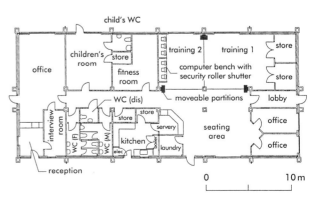

6 Sherburn Road, Durham: plan, showing moveable partitions for flexibility (Arch: WHHLP)

Security

Consider physical measures to protect the building but, to preserve a welcoming image, ensure they are discreet and not overly visible when the building is open. A central, open location for the building encourages self-policing by the local community, and good external and internal lighting is also useful as a deterrent. Planning and internal arrangement should limit access points and allow good overall supervision.

If security shutters are needed, consider installing electrically operated units as they are easier for the management group to operate and avoid the building remaining shuttered even when it is open, which often happens with manually operated shutters. However, maintenance issues also need to be weighed up.

Early consultation with the local police and potential insurance companies will ensure that all aspects of building security are considered and that specifications are to an appropriate standard.

Environment and services

The building should be designed for low energy and water use. Funders are likely to look for evidence of design for high levels of energy efficiency to reduce running costs. Consideration should be given to alternative sources of energy as appropriate: for example, novel forms of energy supply such as solar water heating may be economical, and may be supported by national or local grant aid. Innovative and experimental technology should be avoided, as systems are often expensive to install and need sophisticated controls and specialist maintenance.

Heating, lighting and security systems should be zoned with simple, robust, tamper-proof controls to allow ease of use. Low temperature radiators must be used where elderly people and children are the main users of the space and all supply pipework should be covered or concealed. Consider provision for computers and the future expansion of computer/cable-based information systems.

Consider the maintenance requirements of all systems including boilers, ventilation and extraction systems and alarms. Avoid inaccessible light fittings and unusual bulbs that would be difficult to replace.

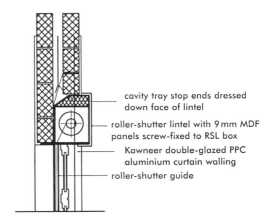

cavity tray stop ends dressed down face of lintel

roller-shutter lintel with 9 mm MDF panels screw-fixed to RSL box

Kawneer double-glazed PPC aluminium curtain walling

roller-shutter guide

8 Concealed shutter system, shutter detail: Eastlea Community Centre, Seaham, Co Durham (Arch: WHHLP)

Typical elements

All community centres will be different, as they are designed to meet the needs of specific local needs but there will be common elements in every building.

Halls Often the main space, the size and shape will be determined by identified activities and uses. Typically the main issue in the design of a hall is whether or not a permanent stage is needed and also the associated changing rooms and storage for chairs and equipment. Floor type is important – if dancing or activities such as aerobics are likely to be popular, hard-wearing sprung flooring, although costly, is essential.

Meeting rooms If more than one is provided, sizes should accommodate a variety of functions, and if they are used for young people's activities, consider location to minimise noise disruption to other areas. There are also privacy issues if these rooms are to be used for counselling.

Computer room Frequently in demand, these provide a good base for college outreach education. Consider the location to minimise heat gain and ensure security. A security mesh may be necessary in wall cavities and roof spaces to provide additional physical security.

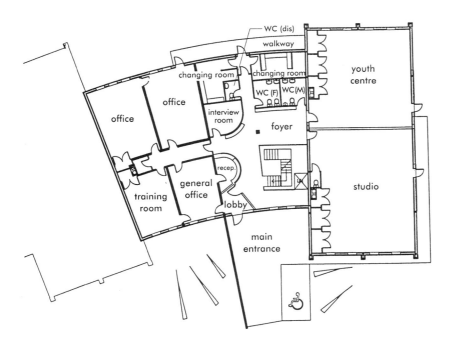

7 Salterbeck Community Centre, Workington: plan; note location of reception and disabled access and circulation (Arch: WHHLP)

Offices The number and type will be determined by the management system in place and the number of organisations using the facility as a base. The management office needs to be near the main entrance for security reasons.

Café/bar Creating an attractive and welcoming social meeting area is often the key to the popularity of a centre. It should be sized and located for maximum flexibility, and to be useable for as much of the day/evening as possible. Providing a licensed facility will be determined by local demand and custom or practice, and will raise many issues of security, staffing, and location.

Kitchen Usually a small servery/preparation area is all that is required, but larger commercial facilities may be called for. The implications of health regulations and costs of storage and space provision must be fully considered when deciding the viability of a catering kitchen.

Changing rooms The size and layout will be determined by the internal/external sports provision and potential for performance use in association with the main hall.

Storage It is vital to have sufficient storage space in appropriate locations, as chairs, tables, and equipment will need to be moved and stored if maximum flexibility is to be achieved. Many user groups will have their own equipment needing on-site storage. Detailed consultation with user groups should identify the exact requirements for each one.

Circulation Cost restrictions will mean minimum circulation space to minimise construction area, but there will need to be enough provision in the entrance area for accommodating different groups of users arriving at the same time (e.g. elderly, infirm, parents with young children).

External facilities These will vary from all weather sports facilities to external play space for toddler's groups. Relation to internal spaces and changing facilities is important.

Unusual elements

There may be need for a number of other elements, according to local demand. These might include:

- Laundrette: this will have implications for water and heating costs as well as space and maintenance; management and payment arrangements must be considered.
- Fitness room: fitness centres are becoming increasingly popular. Consider the space requirements and cost of equipment as well as the insurance implications of specialist equipment, and the relationship to showers/changing areas.
- Sports halls: these large-volume spaces have a major impact on both construction and running costs. Consider requirements of associated storage and changing/showering facilities. Sports halls will need to seen as part of the Local Authority strategic provision if they are to be publicly funded.
- Provision for doctors, nurses, community advisors: space may need to be provided for external users. Consider space provision, planning, security, and privacy.

References

(1) Weaver, L. (1920) *Village Clubs and Halls*, Country Life, London, p. 3.
(2) Ibid., p. 2.
(3) Ibid., pp. 93, 94.
(4) Hanson, D. (1971) *The Development of Community Centres in County Durham (excluding County Boroughs) 1919–1968*, MEd Thesis, University of Newcastle.
(5) Taylor, M. (1983) *Resource Centres for Community Groups*, Community Projects Foundation, London.

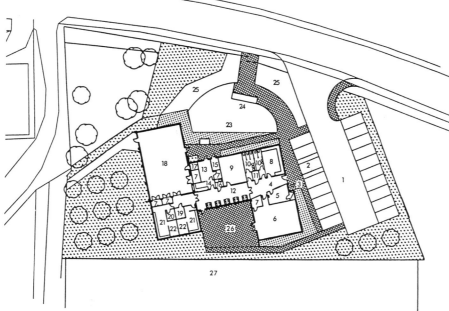

thorny shrubs with low natural height
grass
footpaths

0   20 m

1 car park; 2 disabled parking; 3 cycle stands; 4 entrance; 5 office; 6 youth/games room; 7 store; 8 IT room; 9 meeting/training room; 10 WC; 11 WC (dis); 12 lounge/café; 13 kitchen; 14 servery; 15 plant; 16 cleaner; 17 WC (child); 18 main hall; 19 changing (dis); 20 referee changing; 21 changing room; 22 showers; 23 play area; 24 old colliery wheel; 25 shrubs; 26 terrace; 27 football pitch

9 Thornley Community Centre, Co Durham: ground floor plan; the central circulation space doubles up as a café (Arch: WHHLP)

CREMATORIA

Di McPhee

The disposal of corpses by cremation was being considered in most European cities by the late 1880s because graveyards were overcrowded and thought to be contributing to the frequent outbreaks of cholera. In response to a growing need for an alternative means of corpse disposal the Cremation Society was formed by Sir Henry Thompson in 1876. The first crematorium to be built in Great Britain was Woking Crematorium (1879). Originally just a brick-built flue and crematory, a chapel was added in 1891, all the buildings being designed in a Gothic-revival style. The chimney flue was disguised as a bell-tower. Sir Earnest George's design of Golders Green Crematorium (1902) using an Italianate style was the first to break the Gothic-revival pattern.

It was proposed by the Cremation Society at that time that the design for a crematorium should be a distinctive style of architecture to emphasise the difference between cremation and burial. Albert Freeman in 1904 put forward a design description for crematoria, suggesting that they should include an entrance hall, chapel, vestry, crematory and columbarium. By 1931 crematoria were being designed with an additional room between the crematory and chapel to prevent mourners from hearing the noise of the furnaces.

As the demand for cremation increases, the needs of mourners are gaining more recognition and understanding among those who design crematoria. Care is given to the layout of the crematoria grounds, with views from the chapel to the gardens and sensitive screening of the building from the highway using trees. Circulation routes are also carefully planned so that mourners from different services do not meet. Today's crematoria designs include covered entrances to the chapel or an entrance hallway, toilet facilities, waiting room, offices and covered walkways, chapels of remembrance, and gardens of remembrance.

The comfort of relatives waiting for the ashes of the deceased, the gradual ritualisation of the handing-over of the ashes, and the increasing influence of European legislation will alter the way in which crematoria are designed. Future crematoria design will need to take into account the computerised machinery requirements of the crematory, mourners' requirements (e.g. counselling rooms), as well as the traditional functional aspects of cremation.

In 1889 there was one crematorium in Great Britain and 46 cremations (0.001% of total deaths). A century later there were 231 crematoria in the UK and 445 574 cremations – over 70% of all deaths (1995 figures). It is estimated that in a few years 98% of deaths will result in cremation.

1 Aberystwyth Crematorium, Dyfed; approximately 800 cremations per year (capacity for 2000) (Arch: Critchell Harrington & Partners Ltd)

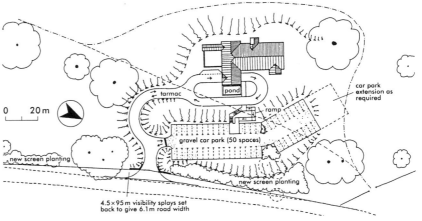

ground floor plan

Crematoria are non-denominational, the chapel being used for services for all religions, as well as for those of no religious faith.

Religions permitting cremation
Most religions, including Roman Catholicism, Anglican, Protestant, Buddhism, Hinduism and Liberal Judaism, permit cremation.

Religions forbidding cremation
Greek Orthodox, Islam, Orthodox Judaism, Russian Orthodox, Parseeism/Zoroastrianism.

SCHEDULE OF ACCOMMODATION

Administrative areas should have separate facilities and access to that of the mourners, and should not overlook the main parts of the grounds. Provision should include staff room, workroom, WCs, fan room, pulverising machinery room, ash storage, cleaners' room, plant room, and an office if required. Noise from these areas must not be audible in the chapel. The superintendent's office can be sited at the main entrance or in another part of the crematorium buildings. A superintendent's house, if provided, should be suitably sited at the main entrance.

Ash   An ash processing room is required and should include space for the storage of ashes. Ash is disposed of by burial or strewing. With the latter, more than one plot is required to prevent souring of the ground.

Car parking   Space for one car should be provided for every two places in the chapel.

Catafalque (historically, the decorated stage for the coffin)   The coffin, usually open, is laid out in an area adjoining the committal room. The catafalque should be about 3 m long and 1 m wide, with the top not more than 1.2 m above floor level. Steps should be avoided.

The coffin is transferred to the committal room either by: (a) lowering it through the floor to a committal room below or (b) moving it horizontally through an opening at the back or side of the chapel. Curtains may be necessary to screen the committal room from view. The catafalque may be placed partly or wholly in a recess across which curtains can be drawn, the coffin then being moved by (a) or (b) above. This layout is now the most common.

Chapel   In addition to a clergy desk and catafalque, accommodation should be provided for up to 80 people, with fixed pews or loose chairs. Plan for an organ or pre-recorded music. The chapel exit should be at the opposite end to the entrance and should connect with a covered walkway where wreaths and flowers can be displayed and viewed by mourners. This walkway should end near the car park, and have access to a WC.

Chapel of rest   If required, this should be sited near, and have covered access to, the main chapel. It should be well-ventilated, unheated, and have an external door to allow delivery of a coffin direct from a hearse.

Columbarium   A room with niches in the walls to hold urns containing ashes.

Committal room   The committal room should separate the chapel opening from the wall of the crematory by a minimum of 3.6 m, or 4.6 m if automatic equipment for charging the cremators is required. Careful furnishing is required as committals sometimes have to be witnessed. Racks are required for temporary storage of coffins. Mourners should not be able to see into the committal room. A warning signal (light or buzzer), with back-up, is required between the clergyman's desk and the committal room.

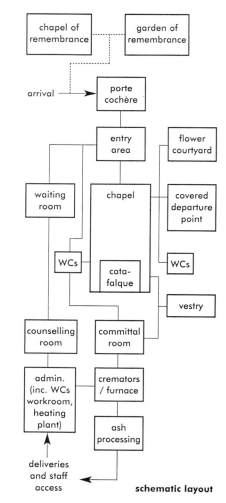

schematic layout

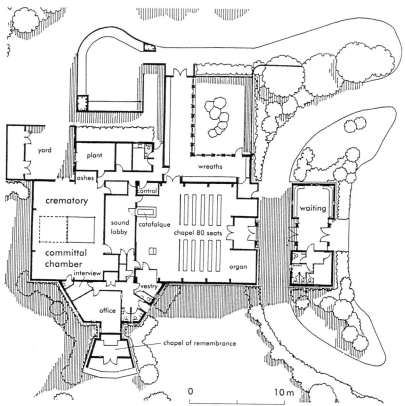

2   Poole Crematorium, Dorset
(Arch: Property Services, Poole Borough Council)

Cremators Provision should be made for at least two and space should also be allowed for the installation of additional cremators to meet future demand. At present the fuel used for cremators is gas. Smoke and odours resulting from incomplete combustion must be avoided and space has to be allowed for the computer equipment that controls the emissions. Instrumentation such as a pyrometer and smoke density equipment, and possibly a view from the crematory to the top of the stack, will help to maintain combustion efficiency.

Crematory The size depends on type of cremator. Normally a minimum clear space of 3.6 m is required from the cremator to the rear wall, and at least 900 mm around cremators. Overhead ventilation and heating are desirable. Mourners must not be able to see into the crematory.

Doorways To give clearance for the coffin and bearers all doorways and passages should be 1.8 m minimum width and 2.3 m high.

Entrance hall Should be connected to the waiting room, chapel and WCs.

Flowers Provision must be made for the display and disposal of flowers.

Garden of remembrance Usually included near the building as a place of quiet contemplation, this should include a lawn, trees and rosebushes. Facilities can also be provided for the scattering of ashes.

Grounds and landscaping The 1902 Cremation Act in the UK requires that no crematorium shall be nearer than 182.8 m to any dwelling (except with the owner's consent) or within 45.7 m of any public highway, or in the consecrated part of a burial ground. The direction of the prevailing wind should be checked in case emissions might cause a nuisance. If mains drainage is not available a treatment plant will be required.

A well-wooded area with natural undulations and good views is an ideal site. It should always be screened from the main highway by trees. A thorough landscaping plan should be developed using both quick-growing trees and shrubs, and long-term planting.

Circulation of traffic should be carefully planned so different groups of mourners do not meet: separate entrances and exits are therefore preferable and there should also be provision for pedestrian access. Sufficient capacity for private cars must be provided, with noise reduction measures included, and good public transport should be available. External walkways should be designed without steps to suit the elderly or users with disabilities.

Memorials These typically include rose bushes, plaques, wall niches and books of remembrance, and appropriate consideration is needed. Plaque space, which is rented, might be on a garden seat or tree, or beside a shrub, crocus or other bulbs. Books of remembrance are housed in a room of remembrance or chapel of memory, a building either set in the grounds or part of the crematorium buildings. They should have a separate entrance as they will generally be used by those paying an individual visit.

Porte cochère A covered setting-down area is needed at the entrance to the chapel or hall (minimum size 3 m high, 5.5 m long to allow room for a hearse and one car), with a 900 mm wide pavement between the kerb and the main door. There should be no steps between the pavement and the chapel.

Service yard Required outside the crematory, suitably screened from the view of mourners.

Stack Containing the flues from the cremators, the dimensions for the stack can be obtained from the cremator manufacturers. It is usually a minimum of 12 m high and not less than 3 m higher than the highest part of the building.

Vestry About 9 m², with separate WC, should be provided for the officiating clergy. The approaching cortège must be visible from the vestry.

WCs Required for both staff and public, provision must include users with disabilities. Several sets of WCs may be needed, suitable for different groups of mourners. Care must be taken to ensure that noise is not transmitted to the chapel, entrance hall etc.

Waiting room Seating should be available for at least 12 people (approximately 18 m²) and WCs should be adjacent. The cortège should be visible from the room, or it can be linked to the entrance hall.

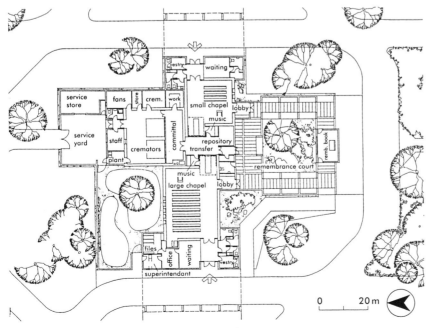

2 Streetly Crematorium, Walsall, West Midlands
(Arch: Department of Architecture, Walsall Borough Council)

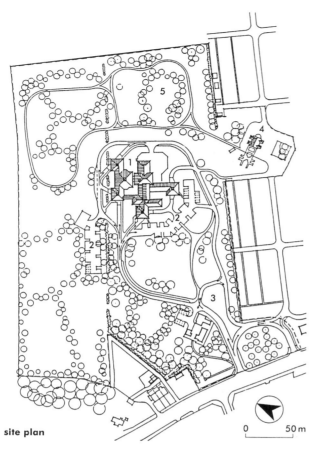

site plan

Air pollution from emissions

Controls on emissions from the cremation of human remains are being tightened and strict sampling and testing is required. In the UK, the objectives are set out in the Environmental Protection Act 1990 (see section 7(2)a) and guidance note PG5/2(95) gives further details. The legislation required existing cremators to be upgraded by 1 April 1998. Guidance is given on design of chimneys and plant, and precautions to be taken in situations where specific emission limits have not been set. Coffins containing lead or zinc should not be cremated, and PVC and melamine should be avoided.

4 Teesside Crematorium: approximately 2800 cremations per year (capacity for 4000)
(Designers: Middlesbrough Council, Transport & Design Services; head of service: Brian Glover)

site plan
1 crematorium; 2 car parking; 3 offices; 4 chapel of remembrance; 5 garden of remembrance

ground floor plan
1 original chapel; 2 crematory; 3 new chapel; 4 transfer room; 5 fan room; 6 pulverisor room; 7 viewing; 8 store; 9 boiler room; 10 flues; 11 cold store; 12 lobby; 13 organ; 14 chapel of rest; 15 waiting room; 16 WC (disabled); 17 vestry; 18 WC (M); 19 WC (F); 20 supervisor; 21 narthex; 22 service yard; 23 floral tributes; 24 pool; 25 covered walkway; 26 chauffeurs; 27 workshop/storage; 28 porte cochère; 29 office; 30 staffroom; 31 cleaner; 32 WC (staff)

ground floor plan

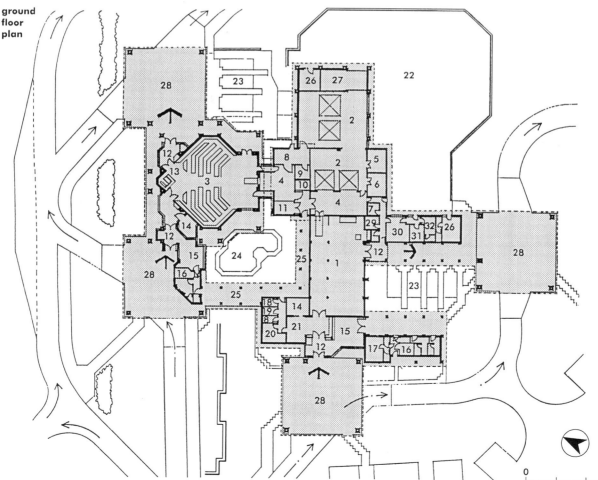

0   15 m

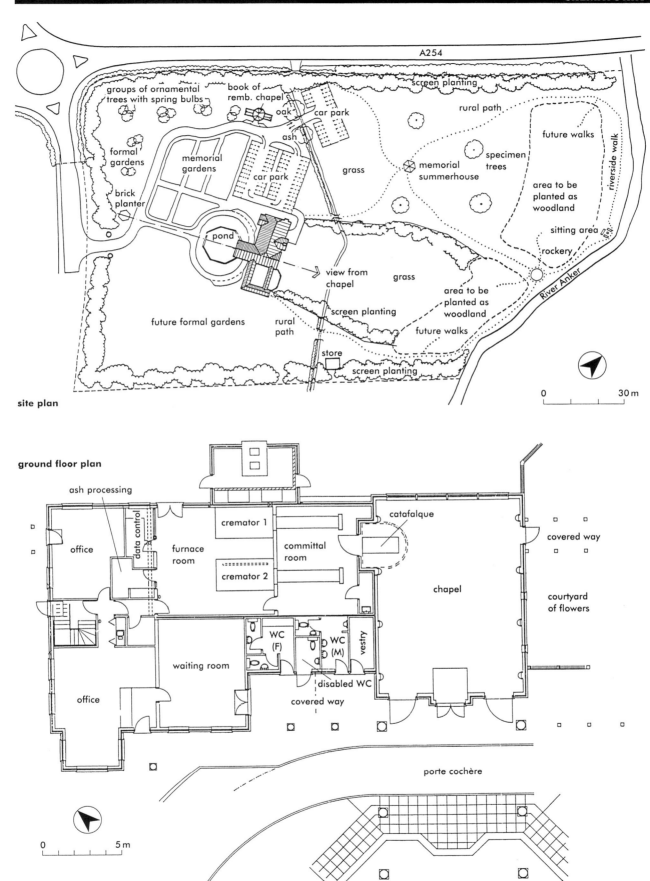

site plan

ground floor plan

5 Nuneaton Crematorium, Warwickshire: approximately 500
cremations per year (capacity for 2000)
(Arch: Critchell Harrington & Partners Ltd)

EDUCATION: SCHOOLS

DfES, Schools Building and Design Unit

Schools and nurseries can cater for a variety of age ranges, depending on the policy of the school or the local authority. The common types of schools, the age range covered and the number in England in 1998 are shown in **1**.

Over 90% of pupils in Britain are educated in the 'maintained sector' (which comprises all schools maintained by a Local Education Authority (LEA)), grant-maintained schools, voluntary-aided and voluntary-controlled schools, and City Technology Colleges (CTCs). Special schools, specialist schools (such as language colleges) and boarding schools are included in the above categories, although most boarding accommodation is found in the 'independent sector' and much is in special schools.

HISTORY

The 1944 Education Act first outlined three stages of education: primary, secondary and further. It also established the need for nursery school provision, and raised the school leaving age to 15 years (postponed until 1947). The latter meant providing for over 400 000 places, about half of which were to be accommodated by the Hutting Operation for the Raising of the School Age (HORSA).

The first urban schools planned on a classroom basis in England had a central hall as a common feature, through which access was obtained to the surrounding classrooms. In the early years of this century the unhealthy nature of urban schools led to recommendations on ventilation, lighting and matters of hygiene and to the emergence of 'open air schools'. Schools became increasingly spread out across their sites.

After World War II, recourse to factory-made components became necessary in order to meet demand, and from the late 1940s to the early 1970s 'system' or 'industrialised' building was intensively used. The 'Raising of the School Leaving Age' (ROSLA) from 15 to 16 in 1971, combined with the increasing population from the 'baby boom', demanded intense building programmes in that period.

In the 1960s, circulation areas came to have dual use as shared teaching areas in order to make the best use of funds available, leading to deep floor plans. Shared areas became as difficult to use as the central hall had been in schools built 100 years previously, and natural lighting and ventilation were often compromised in deep plans.

By the 1980s, school rolls were falling dramatically and many LEAs rationalised school stock to reduce places. Under the 1988 Education Reform Act, city technology colleges and self-governing (grant-maintained) schools were introduced, and by 1995 over 1000 schools (mainly secondary) were grant-maintained (GM), financed directly through the Funding Agency for Schools (FAS).

From September 1999, all maintained schools were in one of three categories: 'community schools' (previously LEA schools), 'foundation schools' (most previously GM schools) and 'voluntary-aided schools'. The 15 CTCs remained outside this structure.

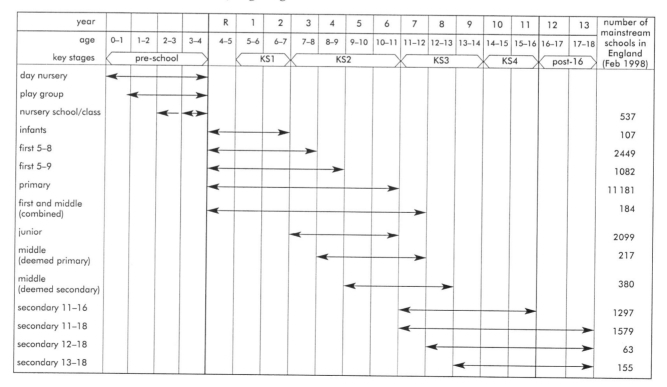

1 Age range and number of common types of school

The education system in England and Wales

The National Curriculum Introduced in the Education Reform Act 1988, this sets levels of attainment that should be achieved in various foundation subjects (see **3**). All maintained schools are required to teach the National Curriculum, which divides compulsory education, from age 5 to 16, into four Key Stages (KS).

As **1** shows, KS1 and KS2 cover the primary age range, known as Years 1 to 6, which also includes reception (R) classes for 4- to 5-year-olds. KS3 and KS4 cover the secondary range, which may also include sixth forms (year 12, 13 and sometimes 14). The reception class group can vary in size over the year if the local authority or school policy is to take 'rising fives' where the pupils start in the term of their fifth birthday, rather than in the year of their fifth birthday.

Nursery education This is an entitlement of all 4-year-olds, if their parents wish it, under recent legislation. In practice, a significant proportion of them are in reception classes, but the rest can be in nursery classes attached to primary schools, separate nursery schools and other pre-school organisations (such as playgroups and day-care centres) which may also involve children between 2 and 4, and often younger. Nurseries inspected by the Government regulator, OFSTED, are expected to organise activities leading towards 'desirable learning outcomes', such as the development of personal and social, physical and creative skills.

Typical subjects taught in the four Key Stages in mainstream schools are shown in **3**. Core subjects are English, mathematics, science and, in Wales, Welsh. The typical schedules of accommodation in this section are based on the proportions of total teaching time likely to be spent on each subject in English schools.

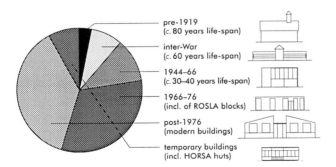

2 Age and type of existing schools in England and Wales

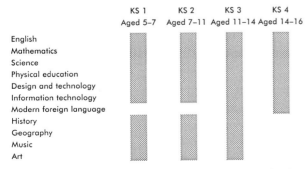

3 National Curriculum foundation subjects taught in the four Key Stages in mainstream schools and pupils' ages

Current design guidance and legislation

The Architects and Building (A&B) Branch of the Department for Education and Skills (DfES, formerly DfEE) publishes priced Building Bulletins (BBs) on a wide range of subjects, giving non-statutory guidance to anyone involved in the design of new schools or the remodelling of existing accommodation. These are the basis of the advice in this section and the relevant BBs are referred to throughout the text as a BB number and in the bibliography with the full title.

BB82 (Area Guidelines for Schools) This gives guidance on appropriate overall gross areas for most types of new schools in the maintained sector (but not special schools), and a measure of reasonableness in existing schools, related to the age range and the number on roll (NOR). Suitable areas for individual teaching spaces and school grounds are also given, on the basis of A&B Branch research. Using the area ranges given, a gross area can be agreed which accommodates the school's particular needs, taking account of the type of curriculum (vocational courses may need more space than purely academic courses), teaching group sizes (smaller groups require more teachers and more teaching spaces), any site constraints and available resources. A curriculum analysis should be used to identify the exact requirements of the school, allowing for possible future changes to the curriculum.

In existing schools, a comparison of the BB82 guidelines (based on the projected NOR and the proposed curriculum) with the existing areas will show if the school is likely to need more building(s) or whether refurbishment, adaptation or even removal of some accommodation is more appropriate. Area standards may be increased by the constraints of existing sites and buildings or by LEA agreed funding allowances.

The Education (School Premises) Regulations 1999 (SPRs) These prescribe standards with which both existing and new school premises of maintained schools are required by law to comply. They supersede previous regulations which stipulated minimum teaching area (MTA), but continue to list requirements with regard to:

- school facilities, including washrooms, medical and staff accommodation
- accommodation specific to boarding schools
- structural, health and safety, and environmental requirements
- minimum areas of playing fields.

In general, maintained schools are exempt from compliance with the Building Act 1984 and consequently the Building Regulations. New school premises in the state sector are expected to comply with the Constructional Standards published by the DfES. The 1997 revision of the Constructional Standards has been closely aligned with the requirements of the Building Regulations and mainly refers to the Approved Documents for guidance. The major exception is Building Bulletin 87, which covers acoustics, lighting, ventilation, heating, water supply and energy rating. There are also minor variations to Approved Documents B (fire), K (stairs) and M (access for people with disabilities, on which design guidance has been produced). Independent schools and non-maintained special schools are not covered by the DfES's Constructional Standards; they must comply with the Building Act, 1984 and the current Building Regulations, and non-maintained special schools are subject to approval by the Secretary of State (they are exempt from Building Regulations).

The exemption of maintained schools from compliance with the Building Act is not expected to continue indefinitely. Designers should therefore always check the current regulations at the time of commencing the design process.

Playing fields Disposal of school playing fields is governed by regulations and generally requires permission from the Secretary of State.

Day-care Accommodation for paid day-care of children under the age of eight should conform to the requirements of the Children Act 1989. The guidance document recommends a minimum area per child of 2.3 m².

Boarding schools Most boarding schools are subject to statutory inspection by OFSTED and Local Authority Social Service Departments. The frequency of inspection and the inspecting body vary with the type of school. Minimum area and other standards are set out in the SPRs. These have statutory force in most types of boarding schools, and are used as a benchmark for inspections where this is not the case.

SEN integration Since 1981 legislation has promoted the integration of pupils with special educational needs (SEN) in mainstream schools wherever possible and in 1984 guidance on suitable accommodation, which is still generally relevant, was provided in BB61.

TYPES OF SPACE (THE BRIEF)

The gross area of school buildings comprises teaching area and non-teaching area. Other facilities for non-school use, such as community areas, may also be included. As a general rule, schools should be aiming for a 60:40 split between teaching area and non-teaching area, although existing site constraints can sometimes make this difficult. In nursery provision, small mainstream schools and all special schools, this is likely to be nearer a 50:50 split.

Teaching area

In primary schools pupils spend most of their time in one teaching area (a single classroom or a smaller 'base' supplemented by shared areas). Some specialist spaces such as a hall are shared by the whole school and, as such, are timetabled for use. In secondary schools, most teaching spaces will be timetabled and used by the whole school. Middle schools have a combination of bases and timetabled spaces. Schools should also have a library resource area and perhaps other local resource areas.

A 'curriculum analysis' can be used to calculate the demand for timetabled teaching spaces based on the school's timetable or a proposed curriculum. The calculations, described in detail in BB82, can be used to demonstrate the effects of curriculum balance, level of staffing, teaching group size and the nature of the subjects taught on the number of spaces required. Once the number of timetabled spaces required has been identified, the non-timetabled and non-teaching areas in the school can be added to give the overall schedule of accommodation. The method is flexible enough to create an area schedule for new school buildings, and also to assess the need for space as the curriculum or the NOR changes. In an existing school it can highlight the areas where refurbishment or a change of use will improve the delivery of the curriculum.

The schedules of accommodation under each type of school on later pages are based on a simple curriculum analysis of a typical curriculum for each type of school, allowing for the needs of the National Curriculum. The number of spaces may differ for individual schools due to the change in percentage of taught time and the number of groups. Class group sizes in mainstream schools are usually assumed to be 30, with smaller groups for optional subjects and some practical subjects. Class sizes in independent schools and some secondary schools are often smaller.

Non-teaching area

Non-teaching area falls into six categories:

(1) *Staff and administration accommodation* will include the head teacher's office, staff work and social space(s), additional staff offices and/or workrooms to suit the type and size of the school, administration areas (including reception, a main office and reprographic facilities), a medical inspection (MI) room and staff lavatories, and may also include changing facilities and showers. The amount of toilet and changing facilities required can be calculated with reference to the Workplace (Health, Safety and Welfare) Regulations, 1992. The head teacher's room will probably be between 10 and 14 m², but in secondary schools may be as large as 30 m², unless a separate meeting room is provided. Staff work and social activities have tended to be accommodated in one space but there is a growing trend, where space is available, towards separate social and work areas in both primary and secondary schools.

(2) *Pupils' storage and washrooms* will include areas for coats and bags (possibly containing lockers) and pupils' sanitary facilities required by the SPRs. These include toilets (one for every 20 pupils aged 5 or over, one for every 10 pupils under 5), changing and showering facilities for pupils aged 11 and over, and a shower or deep sink for every 40 under-fives.

(3) *Teaching storage* will include class storage and walk-in stores for books, materials, equipment (including that for indoor and outdoor PE) and pupils' work in progress. There will also be preparation/storage areas for science and technology departments in secondary schools.

(4) *Catering facilities* comprise dining areas and kitchens, including stores and facilities for catering staff. Many primary schools now only have 'finishing kitchens' to cook or heat convenience food. Dining areas may be available for part of the day as teaching space and in primary schools a multipurpose hall usually accommodates dining, PE and assembly. Dining may occasionally take place in class bases.

(5) *Ancillary spaces* may include a caretaker's office, storage for maintenance equipment, cleaner's, caretaker's and bulk stock, secure storage for valuable items such as examination papers and the boiler or plant room and fuel store.

(6) *Circulation and partitions* including corridors, stairs, foyers and defined circulation routes in open-plan teaching areas, as well as the area of internal walls, can take up a quarter of the gross area of the school, depending on the plan. It is therefore worth trying to make effective use of corridor spaces by making them 'double-loaded' where possible and ensuring that open areas 'off' corridors are designed such that they can be used for small groups, social areas or display without interfering with the natural traffic flow. A minimum width of around 1.8 m in heavily used corridors and 1.2 m in routes to one or two rooms is preferable.

BB82 lists a typical proportion that the above non-teaching functions might occupy in primary and secondary schools.

Facilities for the community

A school can add to the number and variety of facilities available to the community. These amenities may range from a simple meeting place to extensive sports provision. In some locations, especially in rural areas and some inner city communities, the local school may be the only suitable place in which to hold meetings or activities. Community use involves utilising existing school facilities, such as sports halls, ICT suites and general accommodation suitable for adult education, outside school hours. Some extra provision may be needed: for example, zoned heating and security systems, emergency lighting and, perhaps, improvements to the entrance, reception and office areas.

There is now a tendency to widen the range of activities and potential users in favour of more generalised public use during, as well as outside, the school day. This involves more accommodation being available specifically for community use or for shared use during school hours. A separate community entrance may also be needed.

Victoria Infants School, Sandwell (see *4, 18*) has a 'multi-agency centre', at one end of the school building. When not required by the school, it can be used by other departments of the local authority, the community and other organisations providing family support and adult education or training. It is designed to allow independent use outside normal school hours, with easy public access from the road. A range of meeting and other facilities encourages parental involvement in the life of the school, both during and after school hours. Children progress

naturally from the playgroup for toddlers in the multi-agency centre to the adjacent nursery, reception and older classes.

New Leith Academy, Lothian, Scotland (see *5*) has community provision which is integrated with school provision to enable full use to be made of all facilities. It is therefore impossible to identify separate community and school provision. The library area, for example, is planned as a shared access facility for public and school use and incorporates provision for private study and open learning, and there is a 'boulevard café' off the main street.

In the development from school to community learning and leisure centre, it was considered crucial that the building should:

- be warm and welcoming, avoiding the institutionalised visual appearance of some schools
- be easy to read, understand and use
- create a feeling of pride of place in those who use it, through its design and quality
- be a public building.

The pattern of streets and the interest created along them echoes the arcade design of shopping developments from the mid-19th century to date. This gives clarity to the design and reproduces a notable civic sense.

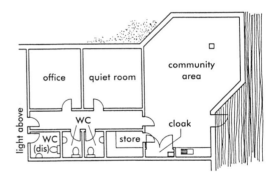

4 Multi-agency Centre, Victoria Infant School, Sandwell (Arch: DfEE A&B Branch for Sandwell Metropolitan Borough Council)

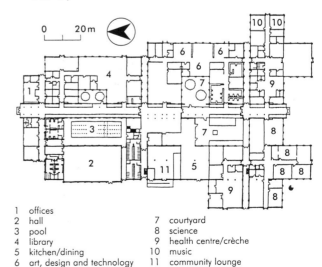

1	offices	7	courtyard
2	hall	8	science
3	pool	9	health centre/crèche
4	library	10	music
5	kitchen/dining	11	community lounge
6	art, design and technology		

5 Ground floor plan, New Leith Academy, Lothian, Scotland (Arch: Architectural Services, Lothian Regional Council)

Provision for pupils with SEN in mainstream schools

Pupils with SEN have attended mainstream schools for many years but there has been a significant increase in both the numbers and the range of difficulties in recent years. Pupils with the most severe and complex difficulties are still usually catered for in special schools (discussed separately) but some, including those with severe learning difficulties (SLD) and profound and multiple learning difficulties (PMLD) now attend mainstream schools.

Provision ranges from 'co-location' (a special school sharing a building or site with a mainstream school) to total inclusion. Some authorities are seeking to provide 'neighbourhood schools' which will take any and every special need in their catchment area but most continue to designate certain schools for a particular range of special needs, which can be expected to have similar resource and accommodation requirements. A combination of in-class support and withdrawal to a SEN base for small group or one-to-one work, in varying proportions depending on the needs concerned, is common.

For some schools the implications of SEN inclusion can be principally a matter of management and timetabling, but for most there will be some additional premises considerations. Depending on the SEN and practice concerned, there are likely to be additional space, planning, design and specification requirements, including:

- space for additional resources and staffing within mainstream classes
- a resource base
- storage space for teaching and mobility aids
- additional washroom and hygiene facilities
- extra medical facilities
- work, storage and parking space for extra teaching and special support staff and for visiting specialists
- additional ICT equipment.

SEN resource bases One, or perhaps two, small classroom spaces are usually appropriate (depending on the number of pupils and the amount of withdrawal), with one or more adjacent small rooms. Ideally, they should be located, in the main body of the school.

Access and escape (Refer to DfES Constructional Standards.) Full and functional access to the whole school curriculum, where the pupil is able to benefit from it, is necessary, including specialist provision and other one-off facilities such as dining and social areas. Timetabling and re-location of subject areas to accessible parts of the building can overcome some problems, especially in secondary schools with separate multi-storey blocks.

Suitable arrangements must be made for pupils who cannot make unassisted escape from upper (or lower) floors. This is principally a management issue, but the usual requirement for alternative directions of escape should apply, with adequately sized refuges to allow pupils to wait in relative safety either within all escape staircases or leading directly into them.

Hygiene For some pupils extensive sanitary facilities will be necessary, including hygiene areas for those who need assisted showering and changing. There may also be a need for a laundry and special waste disposal arrangements. These and other special facilities are described in BB77, which deals with special school requirements.

External areas Pupils are likely to arrive and depart in private cars, taxis and buses. Safe and efficient in/out vehicle circulation is essential.

Other facilities Examples that may need to be considered are covered later under 'Special schools'.

Environmental considerations Pupils with SEN may have particular requirements in terms of temperature, lighting and acoustics (see BB87).

BB61 provides further guidance on mainstream provision for pupils with SEN. Although published in 1984, it is still generally relevant.

Boarding accommodation

(Further information and guidance is available in BB84.) Pupils board for a variety of reasons and may be resident for a few nights per week or up to every day of the year. Expectations of boarding accommodation have changed in recent years, with higher standards and an atmosphere more comparable with home now being expected.

Boarding houses These vary in size from small 'family' houses to larger, more communal houses. They may be on the main school site, sometimes making use of some of its facilities, or on a separate site or sites, but it is important to ensure that within any one school all houses have comparable provision and opportunities. In order to reduce opportunities for bullying and abuse, and facilitate supervision, isolated rooms or areas should be avoided in the design. Because of their small scale, the greater need for adult assistance and supervision, and complex educational and medical needs, many special schools require higher area standards than mainstream schools. They may also have particular requirements in terms of planning, services, storage, finishes, furniture and equipment.

Sleeping accommodation In houses with a wide age range this should be grouped by age. In mixed houses, bedrooms should also be organised by gender. Because of important age-related developmental factors the number of boarders sharing a bedroom, and thus its size, is likely to depend on how old they are. Boarders' bed spaces are one of the few areas that are personal to them. As well as storage for clothes and other belongings, including some lockable storage for private possessions, they should have shelves, a pinboard, a table or worktop and chair.

Social and recreation areas (See 6.) These are an important part of a boarder's life. There should be a choice of activities available, including the possibility of being quiet or of being active, and of being alone or in a group. Where a house has a wide age range there should be separate social areas for younger and older boarders. Any social and recreation accommodation for day pupils should be separate from that used by boarders. Ideally, boarding houses should provide a recreation area, quiet social room(s), TV room, hobbies room, computer room, library and some outdoor social and recreation areas. In small houses some rooms may have to be multi-purpose.

Ancillary facilities In some circumstances, these may be in the main school or shared between houses. The SPRs set out minimum requirements. The main requirements are sanitary accommodation, medical provision, kitchen and dining room, access to a telephone (usable in privacy), laundry, cloakroom(s), drying room(s), and storage. The provision needed for study will depend on the curriculum being followed, boarders' age, and the attitude towards supervision and informal help.

Special schools often require provision to enable older boarders to prepare for independent living. This can range from provision for learning skills such as cooking and care of clothing, to a self-contained bedsitting room or flat.

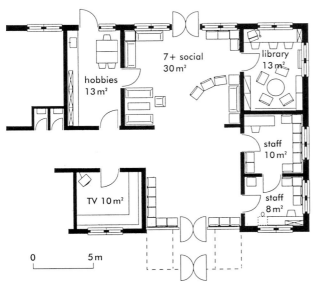

6 Generic layout of a social and recreation suite for twenty 7–9 year olds, with a central lobby. This assumes a shared recreation suite nearby

BUILDING DESIGN ISSUES

Planning strategy: furniture and equipment (F&E)

The size and shape of a space will affect the layout of a room. A regular shape without indentations is generally easier to plan, particularly where large items of F&E are involved. A room with proportions of between 1:1 and 1:1.3 will generally allow for a variety of F&E arrangements. Developing a planning framework will help lay out a space which has the flexibility to accommodate a broad range of activities in safety and comfort. It is useful to consider the possibility of:

- locating services on both external and internal walls but wet services only on external walls where possible
- keeping fixed work surfaces to a minimum and located only around the perimeter

- locating heavy machinery in workshops mainly on external walls
- keeping the centre of the space free of fixed F&E; additional servicing in the centre of the room can be obtained by carrying services through the furniture
- locating the teacher's position to give a good view of the whole space, especially the entrance
- positioning computers and whiteboards at 90° to the window wall to avoid reflection and glare
- avoiding full-height storage: storage units should ideally be mobile and, where appropriate, may be positioned under benching, making more effective use of the space
- accessing store rooms from one end of a space
- providing a storage facility for pupils' coats and bags, adjacent to the room entrance
- providing sufficient clear space around tables, benches and machines to allow for safe circulation and use of F&E.

It is worth preparing initial F&E layouts for each teaching space early in the design process, in consultation with the user and advisors. These can then be used to test the suitability of a building design proposal within the available space, to prepare budget costs and also to decide the location of services. It is essential to consider the particular activities taking place in each subject area – particularly for practical subjects such as design and technology, art, music and science – in order to refine the initial layout. Relevant F&E can then be worked into the plan as the brief is developed.

Specified furniture and equipment

A well selected range of F&E can make a major contribution towards creating an effective and pleasant learning environment. Items should be robust enough to withstand vigorous use, and fit for their purpose. Any items used outside need to be weatherproof and vandal-resistant. Outdoor play equipment must be surrounded by safety surfaces. Furniture, equipment and aids manufactured for special purposes may be needed (e.g. wheelchairs, walking or standing frames). Furniture sizes need to be consistent: for example, the height of a chair should be co-ordinated with the height of a table.

Sizes of tables and benching An important consideration: tables generally follow heights outlined in BS 5873: Part 1, which are based on pupils' ages and average heights. The recommended heights for both standing and sitting activities, using age ranges commonly found in various school types, are shown in **7**.

Fitted benching usually comes in two depths: 600 and 750 mm. The 600 mm depth allows sufficient working space while not encroaching on the central area of the classroom used for main activities; 750 mm is a useful depth where serviced equipment, particularly IT, is used as it allows for a run of trunking at the back of the bench and for a keyboard to sit in front of a visual display unit (VDU).

Most commonly used tables are rectangular in plan (see **8**) and seat up to two pupils, generally side by side. Occasionally pupils will sit at the end of a table although certain frame types may preclude this.

A table length which is twice its width allows for a uniform grouping of tables. Square, circular, semi-circular and trapezoidal tables (see **8**) are sometimes used (particularly in primary schools) to create a less formal feel in a classroom. Square tables are generally suitable for one or four pupils. Small square tables offer layout flexibility but can be easily moved away from adjoining tables, creating a disorganised feel to a classroom. Larger square tables are less likely to be moved around, but four pupils gathered around all four sides is not suitable where a formalised layout is required. Circular and semi-circular tables are more suitable for informal areas such as resource spaces and libraries where pupils may not need a defined table area for formal working. Trapezoidal tables allow interesting table arrangements, particularly in seminar rooms but two pupils may only sit side by side on the longer edge of the table.

Storage units Available in various heights, with a plan size of around 1000×500mm, these usually contain shelves or trays, with or without doors, and can have castors under them. In practical areas it is efficient to place storage under side benching. Some storage units may be wheeled around the classroom and space must be allowed for this in the layout. The maximum reaches for pupils (see **7**) may affect the choice of cupboard height and the position of wall-mounted shelves sometimes used in classrooms.

Polypropylene chairs Mounted on steel frames, polypropylene chairs are commonly purchased by schools because they are considered inexpensive, relatively hard wearing and easy to clean. These chairs generally have a maximum plan size of around 600×500mm. Wooden chairs are sometimes used for their hard-wearing properties. Adjustable VDU chairs are increasingly being used in school IT areas.

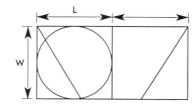

usage	pupil nos.	primary W	primary L	secondary W	secondary L
square					
classroom	1	550	550	600	600
classroom	4	900	900		
classroom/informal area	4	1200	1200		
rectangular					
classroom	2	550	1100	600	1200
classroom	2	600	1200		
specialist (e.g. IT)	2	750	1200		
specialist (e.g. IT)	1			750	1200
specialist (e.g. IT)	1–2			750	1500
specialist (e.g. electronics)	2			750	1800
specialist, small groups	2–3			900	1800
specialist, group gatherings	10–12			1200	2400
circular					
general table, informal use	1	600 dia.			
general classroom table	2	900 dia.			
general table, informal use	2			900 dia.	
general classroom table	4	1200 dia.			
general table, informal use	3–4			1200 dia.	
semi-circular					
general classroom table	2	550 rad.			
general classroom table	2	600 rad.			
general table, informal use	2			600 rad.	
trapezoidal					
classroom	2	550	1100		
classroom	2	600	1200		
classroom/informal area	2			600	1200

8 Sizes of tables generally available and their uses

	E (shelf)
	D (coat peg)
	C (bench)
	B (table)
	A (chair)

age	3–4	5–7	8–11	8–12	9–13	11–14	14–16	11–16	16–18	11–18
A	260	300	340 (380)	340/380	340/380	380 (420)	420 (380)	380/420 (340)	420	380/420 (340)
B	460	520	580 (640)	580/640	580/640	640 (700)	700 (640)	640/700 (580)	700	640/700 (580)
C	555	625	730	730	755	825	830	825	870	825
D	820	920	1095	1095	1135	1275	1385	1230	1450	1230
E	1005	1195	1355	1415	1465	1515	1675	1635	1715	1635

7 Recommended heights for various activities (allow 25mm for shoe height): in certain cases two, or even three, sizes may be advisable; schools may wish to provide larger chairs with footrests for smaller pupils (this is the decision of each individual school)

Adaptability

The activities to be accommodated in schools will change with a variety of teaching methods, and more substantially in the longer term. Only a small proportion of school buildings is likely to remain as designed for the long term. Dedicated specialist spaces, such as kitchens, halls and plant rooms, and primary circulation, including staircases, are unlikely to move and their position should be carefully considered to allow for future change around these areas. Most other areas, from offices and classrooms to highly serviced laboratories or food areas, are all likely to be reorganised over time. Some simple design issues should be incorporated to allow for this change (see **9**):

- Use simple room shapes: rectangular shapes of around 4:5 proportion with a depth of between 7 and 9m are best.
- Use non load-bearing partition

walls, to be removable later, with radiators and major services on outside walls.

- Design fenestration to allow room for new partition walls between window openings.
- Keep plant and service ducts and stairs to external walls wherever possible.
- Limit fixed furniture and equipment, for instance, to fixed benching on one wall only or serviced bollards.
- Incorporate a reasonable distance (22–30 m) between fixed elements such as staircases and external walls.
- Design window openings within 3 m of fixed elements, to allow for small rooms, with natural light and ventilation.
- Design services such that they can be added or removed easily (and limit drainage to near to outside walls, if possible).

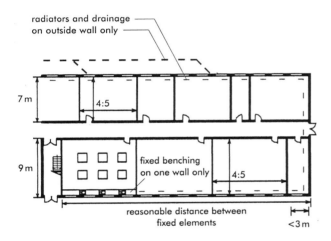

9 Diagram showing important features of an adaptable layout

Djanogly College, Nottingham (see BB72) At this CTC, the planning approach was to group rooms around a central area. At ground level many of the spaces can be subdivided by removable screens, or accommodate activities from the surrounding rooms. A fully demountable science laboratory was developed (see **10**), with 600 mm square serviced bollards designed to fit into a planning grid which allows 600×1200 mm tables to be moved to various layouts. All the services can be 'unplugged' and a pre-finished cover laid to give completely free floor space.

The capacity of the buildings for physical alteration is enhanced at Djanogly by the use of structural frames, the clear separation of the building fabric from the building services and the provision of adequate space for later addition or modification of services (see **10**). The internal walls are separate from the structure and the use of a modular window pattern facilitates a range of potential locations for internal partitions. In each pavilion, only the stair tower and WC block are load-bearing and brace the steel structural frame entirely. All other partitions are of stud construction, most only reaching the suspended ceiling where they locate for bracing and form an acoustic seal.

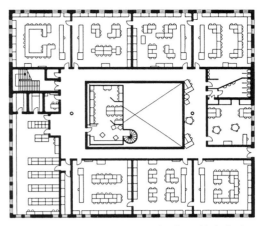

(projects/computer mezzanine; laboratory with relocatable bollards, sinks in 600×1200 mm standard tables, tutor's 600×600 mm bollard with IT network outlets and special connectors for movable fume cupboards, and standing 1200×600×850 mm high laboratory tables (trunking to all walls with wet and dry services); preparation room; demountable storage shelves)

upper floor plan showing furniture layouts of science laboratories

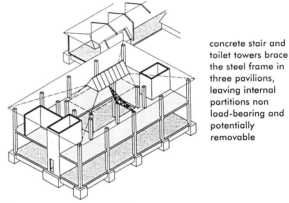

concrete stair and toilet towers brace the steel frame in three pavilions, leaving internal partitions non load-bearing and potentially removable

10 Djanogly CTC, Nottingham
(Arch: DfEE A&B Branch for Nottingham CTC Trust)

Environment
(More detailed consideration of environmental design can be found in BB87.) An environmental strategy will involve looking in detail at acoustics, lighting, heating and thermal performance, ventilation, hot and cold water supplies and energy conservation, particularly with regard to carbon dioxide emissions.

Calculated annual CO_2 production value (See BB87.) This calculates the amount of CO_2 produced per square metre of gross floor area due to the energy consumed. The energy requirements should be estimated at an early stage in the design. The level of CO_2 produced by different fuels varies according to the initial proportion of carbon and the degree of processing required to produce the delivered fuel. Each unit of electricity delivered consumes roughly three times as much primary energy and emits three times as much CO_2 as a similar unit of gas, due to conversion losses at the power station.

Acoustic design The aim should be to enable people to hear clearly without distraction. This is achieved by:
- determining appropriate background noise levels and reverberation times for the various activities and room types

- planning the disposition of 'quiet' and 'noisy' spaces (separating them wherever possible by distance, external areas or neutral 'buffer' spaces such as storerooms or corridors)
- using walls, floors and partitions to provide sound insulation
- optimising the acoustic characteristics by considering the room volume, room shape and the acoustic properties of the room surfaces.

Architectural planning should take into consideration the acoustic conditions required. Particular problems arise where insulation between spaces needs to be high and where there is a desire for open-plan arrangements containing a number of different activities.

Lighting (See BB90.) Successful lighting has a design framework that covers task/activity lighting, lighting for visual amenity, architectural integration, energy efficiency, maintenance and costs. Natural light should be the prime means of lighting during daylight hours, wherever possible. However, supplementary electric lighting will be needed when daylighting recommendations cannot be achieved throughout a space. For most school tasks, a maintained illuminance of 300 lux on the working plane will be sufficient. If the task is particularly demanding (e.g. the task detail content is small or it has a low contrast), then a value of at least 500 lux will be necessary. In some situations, this can be provided by local task lighting to supplement the general lighting. Exterior lighting may be needed for roadways/pathways, floodlighting of the building at night and floodlighting of outdoor sports areas. However, care is needed to avoid light trespass, which causes a nuisance to people in dwellings in the neighbourhood. The types of luminaires and controls available are described in detail in BB78. Emergency lighting should reveal safe passageways out of the building together with fire-fighting equipment, escape signs and any permanent hazards along the escape routes.

Heating A heating installation should be capable of achieving the temperatures recommended in the SPRs.

Hot and cold water Temperatures and supplies are also covered by the SPRs and the recommended Constructional Standards.

Ventilation Ventilation should be natural wherever possible in school buildings. However, supplementary mechanical ventilation may be required in spaces with high functional heat gains. The rates of ventilation required are shown in the SPRs. Measures to limit solar gain should also be considered as part of the ventilation design (see BB79).

John Cabot CTC, Bristol is a two-storey building, arranged along a 'street' running between the sports hall and the main hall. Classrooms are arranged in wings off one side of this street with central facilities such as the library and administration offices arranged in a crescent on the other side. The environmental approach uses systems of proven technology with low-maintenance requirements. (See *11*).

Good daylight levels had to be balanced against excessive heat losses through large areas of glazing.

The external wall of a typical teaching module is 65% glazed, which was believed to be the optimum proportion. However, this ignores the potential problem of glare in the teaching spaces, particularly with the high level of VDU use. In the areas most likely to suffer from glare, various forms of shading are used, including roof overhangs, external roller blinds and internal venetian blinds.

Ventilation is achieved through a mixed-mode approach depending on room type and activity. Concerns about overheating in rooms with heavy computer usage led to a move away from single-sided to cross-ventilation. Rooms are around 7 m wide and have openable windows on one side and ventilating openings, in the form of ventilating 'chimneys' at ceiling level, on the corridor side. Louvres into each classroom are opened manually by the teacher as and when required. A small number of rooms with very high equipment loads and/or those which face south have a small axial fan in the ducting to help the flow through and the workshops have local extract ductwork to remove fumes and dust. Ground floor areas in the street and crescent are side-vented by openable windows while the upper story adopts a cross-ventilation strategy using high-level ventilating louvres.

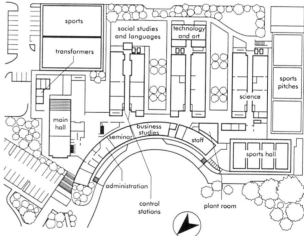

site plan: classrooms are arranged in wings off the central crescent

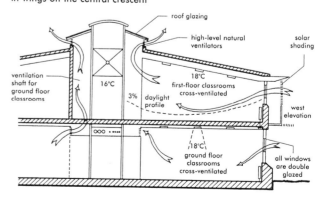

cross-section through the classrooms in one of the wings, showing the environmental strategy

11 John Cabot CTC, Bristol
(Arch: Feilden Clegg Design)

Heating in the classroom wings and the crescent offices is via a straightforward radiator system supplied by gas-fired boilers. Areas have been carefully zoned to allow flexibility (e.g. for use by the community outside 'core' hours) so each of the three classroom wings and the crescent are on a separate heating circuit. The main hall, dining hall and entrance area have underfloor heating to avoid the type of stratification problems that can arise when using radiator systems in relatively large spaces. This is fed with low grade heat from the condensing boiler. A warm air heating system is used to bring the sports hall up to temperature quickly and efficiently for out-of-hours use. The heating plant is located close to the thermal load centre of the building to minimise distribution losses.

Security

(Refer to Managing School Facilities: Guide 4 (DfEE, 1996).) Defensive design – that is, the hardening of the building fabric against possible damage and the installation of security measures such as alarms and CCTV – should not be the only method considered for making schools secure. Planning and design can improve the safety and security of schools in a positive way and requirements to do this should be incorporated into every brief. Pro-active planning strategies, such as crime prevention through environmental design (CPTED), cover issues such as access control, natural surveillance and enhancing feelings of territoriality, which influence how secure buildings will be.

Crime Crimes on school property, especially vandalism and arson, generally occur outside school hours, but of primary concern is the personal safety of pupils and staff during the times that schools are open. Many of the problems related to what might loosely be termed 'day-time' and 'night-time' security have common solutions. For example, measures to protect a school against intruders during the day, such as securing boundaries, will also help protect buildings at night (see 'Site security' below).

New designs The aim for layouts should be that they are reasonably compact and have uncomplicated perimeters. Schools that are spread out on a site with many detached buildings are the most difficult to make secure. If practical, all areas housing valuable equipment (computers, musical instruments etc.) should be located deep within a building complex so that any would-be thief has a higher chance of being detected before reaching them. Simple circulation patterns, avoiding sharp corners and blind spots, enhance vision and therefore improve safety. Cloakrooms and toilets should not be located in isolated places, where they may be perceived as being unsupervised and unsafe. Isolated classrooms, particularly temporary units or mobiles, are most at risk. Multi-purpose use of classrooms reduces the territorial concern for the physical space of both teachers and pupils. When classrooms are used as form bases there is a much greater sense of ownership by the users.

Landscaping, covered ways, drainpipes, canopies and other building features should not be usable as climbing frames, providing access to upper-storey windows, roofs and rooflights. Roofs must be designed so that they are difficult to climb onto or over; one solution being a pitched roof with deep overhanging eaves. Semi-open courtyards, alcoves and recessed doorways provide hiding places for trespassers and are to be avoided in design. If security considerations alone are taken account of there will only be as many external doors as safety demands. Ironmongery should allow fire exits but not entry. Locks to doors and windows should be to the same standard. As windows are particularly vulnerable to damage and forced entry, their numbers should generally be restricted to satisfying requirements for daylight (see 'Environment'). However, strategically placed windows are an aid to security, facilitating natural surveillance of areas such as entrances, gathering areas and car parks. Security lighting may be needed around parts of a building and in parking areas, while good external lighting will be needed for general safety. CCTV may be considered to overlook vulnerable parts of a building and isolated areas, but its specification should be based on whether the intention is to deter or catch offenders. Alarm systems need to be zoned according to how a school will be used after hours.

Access

Where possible the main entrance and reception should overlook the primary pedestrian and vehicular approaches to the school and be clearly visible to those arriving. Good signposting needs to be provided, including signs at other building entrances directing visitors to the main entrance. The reception area should be welcoming and have comfortable seating, but it should not allow free access to the rest of the school. Ideally, once visitors have been admitted through the entrance doors, which may be remotely controlled by a member of staff, they can reach the reception window but no further until their credentials have been checked. Only when they have been signed in and given a badge will the inner door be unlocked. Again this can be done discreetly by remote control.

Access control systems may cover entrances to both buildings and sites. A gate on the school boundary can be remotely controlled by installing a simple entry-phone. A person at the gate can be viewed by a television camera as well as spoken to on the intercom. A gate or door can have a local form of access control to permit entry without the need to contact someone inside. At its simplest this could be a digital code entered on a keypad, or it could require an access card or a card plus a code.

Blenheim High School, Epsom highlights several key design issues for access. For security, there are only two main entrances, one predominantly for visitors and staff and one for pupils. Other doors at the rear offer access from the playing fields/multi-games area, for deliveries and from an enclosed courtyard (see **12**). Ironmongery on external fire doors allows exit only.

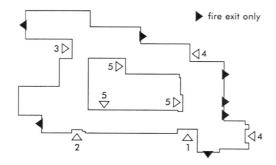

▶ fire exit only

1 main entrance (visitors and staff); 2 main entrance (pupils); 3 from playing fields/multi-games area; 4 deliveries; 5 from courtyard

12 Plan showing the strategy for control of access at Blenheim High School, Epsom, Surrey: see also **28** (Arch: DfEE A&B Branch/EPSL)

Access for physically disabled people Refer to Part M of the Building Regulations and BB91.) Provision should be made which will enable pupils and adults with disabilities to make use of ordinary teaching accommodation, to enter and move around in a building and to have access to WC facilities designed for their use. The seven main areas of provision are: arrival, departure and parking; approach and entrance; doors and doorways; internal changes of level; lavatory accommodation; facilities for medical inspection and treatment; means of escape.

GROUNDS

Types of area

School grounds are a valuable resource. Their size and design, the features they contain, how they are used and the way they are managed can have a significant effect on the ethos of the school and on the quality of education its pupils receive. The overall site area comprises areas timetabled for PE (playing fields and hard-surfaced games courts), untimetabled areas (for informal and social use and for habitats) and the area taken up by the buildings and access. See BB82 and BB85 for details.

Team game playing fields Include summer and winter games pitches, cricket nets and athletic facilities. For primary schools, the area will include one or more (marked) games pitches. A straight running track with six to eight lanes and a length of 60–80 m may be provided for summer use. At secondary level, the area should provide winter pitches for team games chosen by the school, while in summer, cricket pitches, a 400 m running track and facilities for field events may be laid out.

Hard-surfaced games courts These should be of a shape and size suitable to allow courts to be marked out, with appropriate margins. Infants are unlikely to need games courts, as the hard-surfaced portion of the area for informal and social use can be laid out for play, skills learning and small games practice. However, infants can benefit from using the hard-surfaced area for games and having skills practice on grass. At secondary level, the hard-surfaced provision will often include a range of

'multi-games courts': by laying out a variety of courts within a single area, supervision is made easier and the range of games extended. A range of artificial surfaces are available for all-weather pitches and games courts, as well as pitches that can be used more intensively and immediately following rain. The choice of surface should be based on the type of game to be played, performance, safety and durability.

Informal social areas A variety of hard and soft areas should be provided to suit the activities of pupils during breaks and before and after school, as well as any formal curriculum needs. These areas should be conveniently situated and robust, but should also provide shade and shelter. They might include site furniture and a suitable landscape, including smaller, more intimate areas. In primary schools, a patio close to the building will often act as a social area or outdoor classroom, while the more active play areas are beyond it.

Habitat areas These are a valuable resource for all schools. A proportion of the grounds can be developed for a wide range of activities, including amphitheatres, wildlife habitats (such as ponds), gardens and livestock enclosures, to support the curriculum and improve play and recreational spaces (see BB71). Increasingly such spaces are being given a central and accessible location rather than being seen as peripheral extras. Some soft landscape may fall within the area of buildings and access if it is not suitable for other use. Landscape design has a great potential for promoting a sense of ownership of space by pupils and staff, thereby encouraging people to take greater care of their surroundings.

Site security

Sites should have clearly defined boundaries and easily controlled access points. This does not necessarily mean installing fences and gates, and physical barriers should not obstruct views towards or away from school buildings and grounds. When a need for full security fencing is identified, it should be at least 2.4 m high and will need planning permission. Gates should be just as difficult to climb as fencing.

Ideally, there should be only two entrances to the site: one for staff and pupils, but separating pedestrians from vehicles, and perhaps one for deliveries which is only opened when needed. Any further entrances for pedestrians could be opened only at peak arrival and departure times.

The location of buildings on a site should be governed by how visible they will be from public thoroughfares or other occupied buildings. Often this will result in school buildings being within 40–50 m of a street, with the advantage that the main entrance to the site could be overlooked from reception. Paths from site boundaries and parking areas should provide clearly defined routes to the main reception. Informal and social areas, bicycle compounds and car parking should be located so that they are overlooked from school buildings. Hard play areas should also be close to buildings to facilitate supervision, but playing fields and more heavily planted habitat areas can be more remote without being isolated. Landscaping must not provide cover for potential intruders and should not include loose materials that can be used for vandalism. Waste materials and recycling facilities should be accommodated in secure compounds away from buildings.

Layout of the site

The site layout should take account of:
- the nature of the site, including its shape, contours, subsoil, and exposure to wind, rain and noise
- a sensible balance of zones based on practical and curriculum need
- the need for supervision, often over more than one activity at a time
- trespass, vandalism and security
- landscape quality and serviceability
- access for people with physical disabilities
- safety in terms of circulation, and location of activities
- relationship between changing rooms and PE facilities
- community use.

Careful attention should be given to the layout of pitches, courts and practice areas. Their location, size and shape should be based on a number of considerations, including:
- the statutory requirements for playing fields
- layout of winter games pitches and their relationships to summer athletics and cricket provision
- safety considerations, including pitch margins and the direction of play (e.g. for cricket nets)
- orientation of pitches (a north–south direction is desirable for most games)
- gradient
- accessibility for maintenance equipment and water if irrigation is needed.

FACILITIES MANAGEMENT

Capital costs

Funding for maintained schools is invariably strained, so the most effective and efficient use should be made of both capital and recurrent (annual) funding. This can be achieved by:
- keeping the overall gross area low by efficient design
- using materials (and details) that are easy to maintain and are long-lasting
- reducing maintenance costs by considering environmental issues (e.g. heating, insulation and lighting systems)
- incorporating long-term adaptability into as much of the building as possible
- using loose furniture and equipment to allow flexibility of layouts for a variety of activities
- building and refurbishing in line with an overall asset management plan
- designing to the correct brief, based on the demands of the curriculum, the number on roll and the activities or subjects to be accommodated, using curriculum analysis.

Recurrent costs/maintenance

For every square metre of area in excess of real need there will be the capital cost of providing it. Added to this will be a recurrent figure, equivalent to between 4% and 6% of the capital cost, to be paid every year for cleaning, maintenance, heating, lighting, insurance and rates (see the Managing School Facilities Guides).

Asset management plans (AMPs)

AMPs, prepared by LEAs in partnership with schools and dioceses, will be a key element in ensuring that any additional funding, available to the schools sector from Government policy developments, and existing assets are used as efficiently and effectively as possible in helping to raise educational standards. AMPs will provide the means through which likely future needs are assessed, on the basis of
- the sufficiency of the area
- the suitability of the spaces
- the condition of the premises as well as setting criteria for prioritisation and helping authorities to make informed decisions on local spending. Decisions based on AMPs should be more transparent and lead to the more efficient management and improvement of capital assets using innovative, sustainable and energy-efficient building solutions and, ultimately, to improved educational outcomes. (Further guidance on AMPs is available from the DfES.)

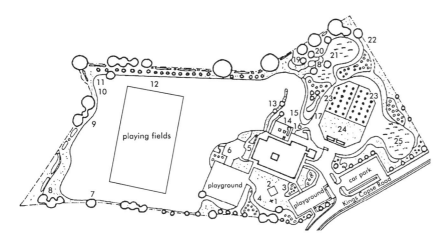

1 wind-driven sculpture; 2 quiet play area; 3 scented garden; 4 living willow withy maze; 5 study patio; 6 meeting place for start of studies; 7 copse (evergreen) 8 log pile; 9 bat walk; 10 raspberry bushes; 11 copse (deciduous); 12 native trees; 13 nuttery and walk; 14 allotments; 15 compost heap; 16 bird-feeding stations; 17 bird hide (bird-on-wing feeders); 18 nature pond; 19 fox walk; 20 butterfly walk; 21 bog/wetlands; 22 secret walk; 23 orchard (apple, pear and plum); 24 paddocks; 25 wild flower meadow

13 Plan of grounds, Kings Copse County Primary School, Southampton

PROVISION FOR UNDER-5s

Types of provision

Settings for under-5s vary greatly, including maintained and independent schools, day nurseries and playgroups. The main factors likely to affect accommodation needs, apart from educational approach, are the age range of the children, the length of their day, the type of management, staffing arrangements and policy towards children with special needs. The programme of activities offered should be supported with appropriate spaces, facilities and equipment. An area of around 2.3 m² per child should allow adequate space for a range of activities. The DfEE publication *Designing for 3 to 4 Year Olds* (1999) offers further guidance on the design of nurseries.

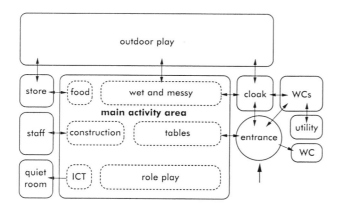

14 Bubble diagram showing a possible arrangement of spaces and activities in a nursery setting

Activities and spaces

General features of the space(s) should include:

- unobstructed floor space for a variety of activities
- distinct zones for a good range of teaching and learning activities defined by furniture, space dividers and (floor) surfaces
- direct access to a range of toys and resources, so children can make independent choices
- displays of resources and finished work
- storage for large, valuable or potentially hazardous teaching resources, out of reach of children or in a secure store (a separate store opening onto the outdoor area is desirable).

Furniture and equipment This should be safe and hygienic, of an appropriate size and scale for the children, robust enough to withstand vigorous use, and mobile or light enough to be moved easily by adults or even children. Tables of modular sizes are most flexible, but fixed worktops or benching may be preferable in small spaces or if a room is an awkward shape. Stools are useful for practical work but they give little postural support. Mobile units and storage units with adjustable shelves or compartments are the most flexible means of storing resources and work. Well chosen furniture and equipment is a major feature of a cheerful and stimulating nursery environment.

Outdoor play space Extremely valuable, this should include a range of experiences, at least some of which should be covered. Approximately 9 m² can be allowed per child. Between half and two thirds of this space should have a suitable surface for wheelchairs, wheeled toys, tricycles and buggies. The rest of the site should have a soft surface, with a variety of different features and habitats. An ideal outdoor space will be easy to access and supervise from inside, protected and safely constructed. It should have enjoyable and challenging apparatus, and varied materials, textures, natural features and habitats.

Parent/community facilities These may be particularly desirable if parents participate in the management. With a few suitably sized and positioned meeting rooms and offices, and careful timetabling, a nursery can be an excellent base for a range of family and community services. It can also form the centre of a fully integrated under-5s or early years care, education and training service.

Environmental issues

Pupils may sit or play on the floor for much of the time so underfloor heating might be considered in new buildings. Radiators and exposed pipes should either be of a low surface temperature or be fitted with guards. Playrooms should have views out and preferably windows with low sills. Because activities can be quite noisy, large areas of hard surfaces should be avoided.

Case study

Nursery class, Victoria Infant School, Sandwell (see **15**) shares some medical inspection, staff and administration facilities with the rest of the school. The main teaching and learning area accommodates a variety of activities and spaces. With the exception of the wet and messy area, these are designed to be flexible during the year, term or even the day. Storage in the space helps to define areas but storage is also provided in a secure store (not accessible to the children) and a separate outdoor equipment store with direct access to the covered outside play area.

The main indoor activity zone is equipped as follows:

- Table work (drawing, painting, model-making etc.): tables, chairs and storage space for games and other resources.
- Role play: a clothes rack and mirror, furniture, props and space for a range of imaginative play.
- Wet and messy work: a waterproof and non-slip flooring, a deep sink and drainer, around which children can gather, and direct access to the outdoor play area. A water tray, sand tray and surfaces or racks to dry paintings and artefacts are useful items.
- Physical activities: preferably take place, weather permitting, in an outdoor play area, protected by a roof overhang of 3 m. Plenty of space is provided for equipment, with safety surfaces, and circulation around it.
- Quiet activity: a circular room with a shutting door, bean bags and comfortable seating, for more concentrated activities, withdrawal and

special needs, but also for story-telling or sharing of books.

- Large-scale construction: plenty of clear floor space for assembly by children, mobile trolleys for small components and space for larger items to be stacked.
- Information technology: floor space for operating programmable toys and a computer table located well away from sink and wet/messy activities.

Areas could also be set aside for musical activities, with some instruments displayed, and for cookery (mixing ingredients, kneading, rolling and cutting out pastry etc.). Cookers and hobs need strict supervision and should be located outside the playroom.

A welcoming entrance/cloakroom area has space for folding and storing prams and buggies as well as the storage of outer garments. Entrances should be accessible for people with a double buggy and wheelchair users. For security, a buffer zone between the entrance and the road, with gates/doors at each end is extremely valuable.

Children's lavatories must be easily accessible from the playroom, the main entrance and the outdoor play areas. Partitions should be designed to retain some privacy for the children, but allow adequate supervision. Space is also needed for adults to give assistance, where necessary, and one cubicle must be large enough for children with physical disabilities. A laundry/utility room is desirable.

Other spaces may also be required. Some will be similar to those in any school, but others, such as adult or health facilities, which in the past would have been provided off-site, may be quite different in character. A small therapy/SEN assessment room is recommended where there are children with identified special needs (or under assessment).

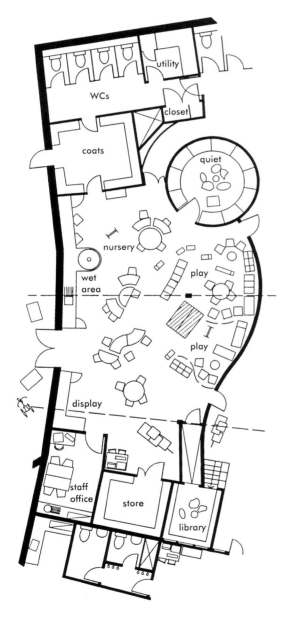

15 Nursery class, Victoria Infant School, Sandwell (Arch: DfEE A&B Branch for Sandwell Metropolitan Borough Council)

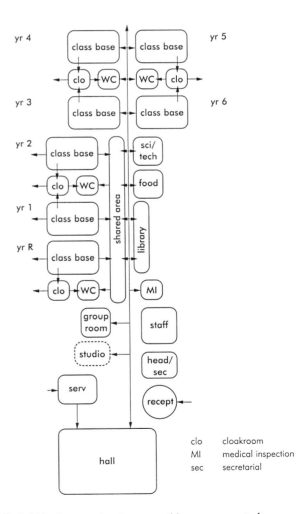

16 Bubble diagram showing a possible arrangement of spaces and activities in a one-form entry 5–11 primary school

PRIMARY

Basic teaching areas

A base is required for every class or group of children within the school, whether in the form of an enclosed classroom, or as part of a more open-plan area. It must be large enough to gather at least 30 pupils together for registration, listening, discussion and for whole-class teaching. An area of at least 35 m² is likely to be needed for adequate table space for every pupil, whether arranged in groups or rows, and the teacher's workstation. Other basic ingredients for class teaching include:

- free floor space, for gathering pupils together and for space-consuming work
- a book corner with room to browse
- computer workstations
- facilities for practical work.

Many teaching activities can also be carried out in shared areas which can, if designed carefully, accommodate different approaches to teaching and foster collaboration.

	likely maximum group size	typical average area (m²) or no. of rooms*	no. of spaces or total area required	
			210	420
classroom	30	54	7	14
small group room	8	12	–	1
small group/SEN support	15	16	1	1
medical inspection/group room	8	10	1	1
studio	30	45	–	1
main hall		1*	145 m²	155 m²
specialist practical including food	8	20	1	3
library	8	1	18 m²	36 m²
total teaching area			**587 m²**	**1090 m²**
admin office		10	1	1
headteacher's office		12	1	1
senior management office		8	–	1
staff/parents'/meeting room		1*	29 m²	42 m²
staff/visitors' and disabled toilets (area/fitting)		3.5	2	4
classroom stores		2.5	7	14
hall PE store		10	1	1
external PE store		5	1	1
drama/music store		6	1	1
central stock room/secure store		6	1	1
pupil toilets (area fitting)		2.5	11	21
classroom cloak bays		4	7	14
kitchen servery (and kitchen staff and storage)		1*	35 m²	50 m²
caretaker's store		1*	5 m²	10 m²
cleaner's store		1.5	2	4
plant room/intakes		–	28 m²	44 m²
circulation and partitions			180 m²	325 m²
total gross area			**996 m²**	**1781 m²**

17 Typical schedule of spaces for a 5–11 primary school

The design of basic teaching accommodation can vary from a collection of entirely self-contained classrooms to a more open-plan system with a high proportion of shared areas and small class bases. Each approach can work well as long as they meet the school's current needs and are flexible enough to allow for changes in the future. An 'enclosed' approach has self-contained classrooms offering a reasonable range of activities. For 30 pupils these would be expected to be in the range of 54 m² to 63 m². An enclosed room allows the teacher to monitor pupils more closely and provides more autonomy and privacy; however, there is less opportunity for co-operation and shared supervision. Another approach is to have 'semi-open' class bases that open onto a shared area to support a variety of teaching methods, though it should be possible for teachers to screen off class bases when more privacy is required. Such arrangements can also give easier access to shared resources and facilities. At the opposite extreme, an 'open-plan' base approach will rely on screens and furniture to create any form of enclosure for each class.

Timetabled supplementary areas

Accommodating specialised facilities in supplementary areas (such as practical areas, studios or small group rooms) can be an efficient use of space and resources.

Subjects which contain a practical element, such as science, technology and art may take place in a specialist practical area. These areas provide opportunities for sustained and often large-scale work, and can be equipped for different activities, from scientific experiment and control technology to cookery and ceramics. Ideally, a specialised cookery space should be fitted out with kitchen furniture of an appropriate height for the age range. Ovens and microwaves can be provided at a height that enables children to watch and participate. A ceramics area should be placed in a self-contained bay or separate room to prevent clay dust contaminating other teaching areas. In addition, an area for wet or messy activities, with a deep sink and suitable floor finish, may be required. A dry practical area for work such as making and testing should have sufficient power points, appropriate furniture (e.g. fixed worktops and work-benches) and access to a range of practical resources. Pupils often prefer to stand to do practical activities, so workbenches should be higher than tables.

A small group room can be used for withdrawing individual pupils or small groups from a class, and can also be used for independent study. Music, drama, movement and dance benefit from a specialised environment with acoustic isolation, 'dim-out' facilities and some stage blocks. In larger schools this could be accommodated in a separate studio but in smaller schools a hall may be suitable if there is appropriate storage space. Most primary schools have a hall for large group activities, such as assemblies and PE, some drama, music, and often for dining. Ideally, the hall should have a range of PE apparatus (both fixed and loose), space for loose apparatus to be left out during the day, and stores for loose PE equipment.

Other supplementary areas

In most primary schools there are spaces that, by their nature as a resource for the whole school, are not normally timetabled. These include the library and resource areas. An SEN support base may also fall into this category but is more likely to be timetabled. Non-teaching areas include staff and administration accommodation, pupils' storage/washrooms, teaching storage and catering facilities.

Case study

Victoria Infant School, Sandwell (see **18**) is a replacement 'three forms of entry' (3FE) infant school for 270 children, with an attached 45-place nursery unit and multi-agency centre, on a site adjoining an existing junior school (see **19**).

Classrooms open off a curved top-lit 'street' containing shared teaching areas, with non-teaching areas mainly on the opposite side of the street. The nursery is at one end of the school, opposite the reception classes and next to the multi-agency centre, which is sited to allow easy public access. This sequence allows zoning for use both during the school day and afterwards, and for good links between the separate elements. Pupils arriving at the school will progress naturally from the toddlers group in the multi-agency centre, to the nursery, reception and onwards, towards the adjacent junior school. A kitchen for 400 meals to serve infants, juniors and staff, and a large space to house dining, music, dance and drama for juniors from the adjacent site are incorporated in the infant school building. Small groups of toilets rather than large blocks, allow direct access to and from the classroom and outdoor areas, easy supervision and a less institutional environment for young children.

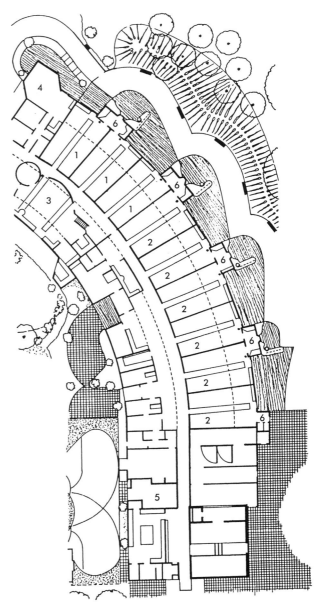

1 reception classes (1–3); 2 classes (4–9); 3 nursery; 4 multi-agency centre; 5 kitchen/servery; 6 WCs

18 Plan, Victoria Infant School, Sandwell
(Arch: DfEE A&B Branch for Sandwell Metropolitan Borough Council)

Case study

Tipton Green Junior School, Sandwell (see **19**) is an adaptation of the existing semi-open plan Tipton Green School, from 2FE (eight classes) to 3FE (twelve classes), with the appropriate increase in related facilities.

The external appearance of the existing building, together with the hall, plant room and WC cores, remain roughly the same as before, but the existing teaching spaces have been rationalised and small extensions added. A new main entrance and reception area improve access whilst the head teacher's and secretary's offices can supervise the main pedestrian approach, reception, and corridors. All classes are in enclosed classrooms, which now average 55.4 m². The classrooms provide for a range of teaching activities and accommodate the bulk of teaching storage. The plan clusters the three classes of each year group together in·identifiable wings of the building. An enclosed science and technology specialist area provides facilities for up to half a class and a food specialist bay is equipped and sized specifically for KS2 pupils. The library is located physically and visually at the heart of the school, and has ample space for individual and group work, two IT workstations, and display space. The ratio of teaching to non-teaching area is improved from 50:50 to 58:42, reasonable for a converted school of this size.

plan

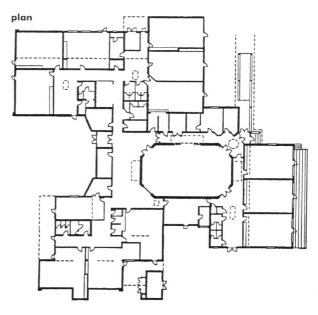

plan layout of the studio

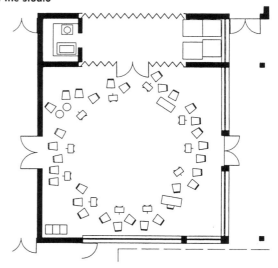

layout of specialist practical areas

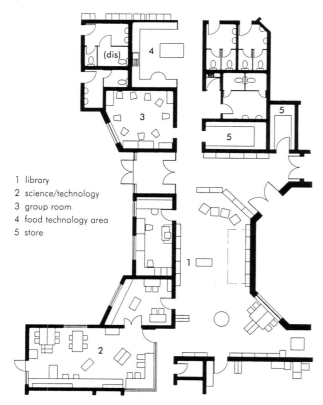

1 library
2 science/technology
3 group room
4 food technology area
5 store

layout of a typical class base

19 Tipton Green Junior School, Sandwell
(Arch: DfEE A&B Branch for Sandwell Metropolitan Borough Council)

Case study

Radbrook County Primary School, Shropshire (see **20**) is a 1½ FE primary school with nine class bases, arranged in a T-shaped plan around a courtyard. The class bases are divided into infant and junior wings, each with its own shared practical and circulation areas. One cluster has two pairs of class bases; the other has one larger class base for the reception class, one pair of bases and two individual rooms. Both clusters have access to the outside through sliding doors in the shared practical areas and through the WC/cloakroom areas (useful when the weather is inclement). Between the two groups of classes, and enclosing one side of the courtyard, are a quiet room and a group room. On the fourth side of the courtyard the hall is surrounded by staff/office accommodation and the kitchen.

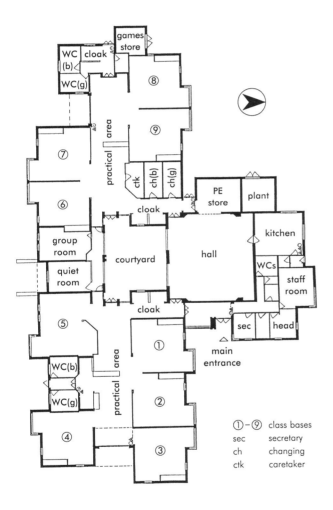

20 Radbrook County Primary School, Shropshire
(Arch: Shropshire County Council)

MIDDLE SCHOOLS

Schools for the 8–12 and 9–13 age ranges were popular during the 1970s but since the introduction of the National Curriculum new middle schools are extremely rare. They are intended to extend the teaching methods and atmosphere of primary schools, while practical activities are backed by more sophisticated equipment and specialised spaces, as might be found in secondary schools. Eleven- and 12-year-olds in middle schools are taught the same curriculum as their contemporaries in secondary schools. As middle schools accommodate work at both KS2 and KS3, the gross area range is determined by a proportion that reflects an allowance for the number of pupils in each Key Stage. Thus, a school for 9- to 13-year-olds is likely to be larger than one for the same number of 8- to 12-year-olds.

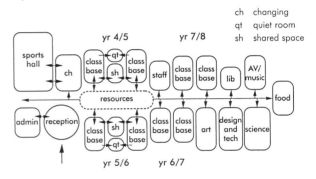

21 Bubble diagram showing a possible arrangement of spaces and activities in a 2FE 8–12 or 9–13 middle school

General teaching areas

The usual format for middle schools is a number of class bases with shared practical areas and/or specialist rooms. In 8–12 schools the mix of spaces is generally akin to that found in primary schools, whereas 9–13 schools are more like secondary schools. Much of the general, class-based work of the 8–12 curriculum can take place in self-contained classrooms, with access to water and some space for practical and investigation work, and pairs of semi-open bases, sharing a small enclosed group room. However, the 9–13 curriculum requires greater use of specialised rooms for certain subjects (science, design and technology, art) which may be used solely by older pupils or may be shared by the whole school.

Specialist spaces

The school hall will not always be appropriate or available for music, so ideally a smaller, acoustically isolated space should be provided which has an uncommitted floor space. Design and technology (and sometimes 3D art) work tends to produce dust and/or noise and should also be isolated from other activities. A workshop space for older pupils should be laid out for work in wood, metal and plastics but may have a less sophisticated range of equipment than in secondary schools. Adequate storage and secure preparation space will be needed near the design and technology space.

One approach to specialist areas for 8–12 middle schools is the provision of 'nucleus' areas, which can be closed off when not needed, adjacent to general teaching spaces. For example, for pupils up to the age of 12, many science activities are compatible with the use of general teaching areas but there are times when the work of the older children involves simple chemical experiments which need a laboratory setting. A nucleus area with gas, electricity and laboratory sinks could provide suitable facilities for a small group of pupils to experiment at one time. This nucleus area should open into a work room for a class group, equipped with extra power points, a large sink and tables and worktops suitable for science but capable of flexible arrangement for other work. Separate storage and serviced science trolleys for demonstration should be provided to enable science to be taught anywhere in the school. In 9–13 schools a fully equipped laboratory and associated preparation room, as might be found in a secondary school, is required for older pupils to undertake practical science experiments.

Provision for learning to prepare and cook food in each type of middle school should follow similar lines to that for science, described above, with a nucleus area in 8–12 middle schools and a fully equipped food room in 9–13 schools.

Layouts of the work tables and equipment to be used in the specialist provision (whether nucleus areas or rooms) for music, design and technology, food and science are the best indicators of the space required (see 'Furniture and equipment' above).

plan

layout of the science nucleus and adjacent class bases

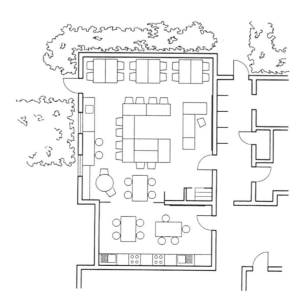

22 St Paul's Middle School, Stoke-on-Trent, Staffordshire
(Arch: DfEE A&B Branch for Staffordshire County Council)

Case study

St Paul's Middle School, Stoke-on-Trent, Staffordshire (see **22**) was designed as a replacement for an earlier St Paul's Middle School, for 300 pupils of 8–12 years. The final plan illustrates most of the design aims for small middle schools, although structural requirements influenced some elements of the design.

The ten class group bases are in the form of four self-contained group rooms and three pairs of semi-open bases, with shared practical areas. The arrangement of bases allows as much flexibility in overall school organisation as possible. All the large group rooms open directly to the outside.

Nucleus areas for cookery and science were provided in conjunction with group bases 1 and 4, respectively. Base 4, which forms a science room with the nucleus when required, is furnished and equipped more appropriately for science than an ordinary class base. Base 1 is treated similarly for food work. The specialist room for clay and design and technology work is situated centrally and can open onto a shared area with facilities for art and light technology.

The other shared teaching spaces, the PE hall and the smaller audio-visual music/drama room are grouped so that they are reached from the communal circulation space, which also opens onto the library area and the small group room. This group of accommodation can be used with part of the dining space for school and parents' functions or community use.

plan

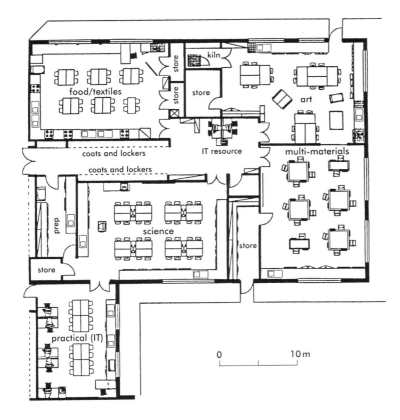

toilets
store
plant
①–⑬ class bases
ch changing
cl cloakroom
MI medical inspection
qt quiet room

layout of the specialist practical spaces

23 All Saints School, Sudbury, Suffolk
(Arch: Suffolk County Architects)

Case study

All Saints School, Sudbury, Suffolk (see **23**) is a 9–13 middle school. It is 4FE in the first year and 3FE thereafter. There is effectively a divide between KS2 and KS3 teaching areas but the younger pupils benefit from access to specialist facilities which include science, art, design and technology and food/textiles rooms (with related storage and preparation spaces), in which three groups of between 16 and 20 are taught at one time. Next to the science room is a less specialised practical room which is used for maths and IT, and as an untimetabled resource. Two groups of four class rooms are clustered around shared resource areas, with their own cloak-rooms and WCs, adjacent to a small hall which is used for dining. On the opposite side of a central courtyard the remaining five class rooms are grouped with the library and staff areas. Ramped changes of level allow wheelchair access throughout the school.

The layout of the practical spaces shows:

- separate rooms are provided for art, food and textiles, multi-materials (including metal, wood and plastics) and science
- each space has a store or preparation area
- an overflow space is available for various simple practical activities requiring no more specialist equipment than a sink and worktops (usually used for maths)
- spaces are organised in a suite for easy sharing of resources and servicing.

SECONDARY SCHOOLS

Staff accommodation

In a typical secondary school today, staff accommodation will include offices for senior teaching staff, some small, local departmental staff work rooms and a central staff room providing work space for the remaining staff and a social area for all teaching staff who wish to use it. The main staff room should preferably be secluded from noisier parts of the school, but centrally located.

Timetabled teaching areas

The secondary school curriculum is normally taught in distinct subjects, using a variety of timetabled teaching rooms which tend to be used predominantly for one subject. Almost half the subjects taught in secondary schools are 'general teaching', normally only requiring standard classrooms. These subjects include English, mathematics, modern foreign languages (MFL), humanities (history and geography), religious education, personal and social education (PSE) and general studies. The remainder usually require specialist spaces which are less likely to be interchangeable, although art and graphics or music and drama may share spaces. IT rooms will be required as a timetabled and bookable resource for most subjects, particularly business studies, GNVQ, MFL, humanities and design and technology.

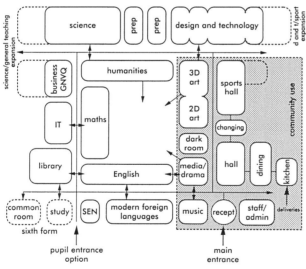

24 Bubble diagram showing possible arrangement of spaces and activities in an 11–16 (11–18) secondary school (design and technology includes multi-materials, pneumatics, electronic and control technology (PECT), textiles, food and graphics)

Size, shape and layout
The size, shape and layout of individual teaching rooms should provide a space which has the flexibility to accommodate a broad range of activities. Keeping fixed furniture and equipment to the perimeter and loose furniture to the centre is recommended. A space which is too narrow may restrict the range of activities and the possible furniture layouts (see pp 40–41), particularly in practical spaces where there may be large items of equipment with minimum space requirements

	likely maximum group size	typical average area (m²) or no. of rooms*	no. of spaces or total area required 600	900	1200
timetabled teaching					
general teaching					
standard classroom	30	50	12	17	22
large classroom	30	62	3	4	6
IT room	30	72	2	3	4
science laboratory	30	84	5	7	9
design and technology					
food room	21	85	1	1	2
multi-materials workshop	21	100	1	2	2
pneumatics/electronics/ control/tech	21	88	1	1	2
textiles (dry, including sewing)	21	84	1	1	1
graphics	21	78	–	–	1
art					
general 2D art room	30	90	–	1	1
3D art (incl. ceramics kiln if req'd)	30	105	1	1	1
wet textiles and 2D art	30	105	1	–	1
music room	30	65	1	2	2
drama studio/music recital room	30	90	1	1	2ᵃ
gymnasium	30	260	1	–	–
sports hall	30	594	–	1	1
non-timetabled teaching					
assembly hall	–	–	240ᵇm²	240ᶜm²	260ᵇm²
SEN classroom	6	22	1	1	1
music group/practice rooms	5	6	3	6	6
music ensemble room (or recording studio)	7	20	1	2	2
small group room	3	6	1	1	1
heat treatment bay	4	16	1	1	1
food technology/testing area	5	15	1	1	1
kiln room or dark room	4	10	1	1	1
IT cluster/resource area	8	24	1	2	3
library resource centre	10% of NOR	1*	128m²	155m²	182m²
total teaching area			2831m²	3956m²	5087m²
non teaching areas					
dining areas	–	–	180m²	232m²	270m²
kitchen (incl. staff and stores)	–	–	90m²	116m²	135m²
lockers for personal storage	0.1		450	675	900
pupils' toilets (area per fitting)	–	3	29	43	57
(area per locker)					
changing facilities incl. showers	1 year group	–	60m²	90m²	120m²
science prep/store room	–	1*	64m²	89m²	115m²
multi-materials prep room	–	1*	46m²	48m²	52m²
walk-in teaching stores:					
general teaching/SEN/IT	–	2.5	40	47	56
off practical spaces	–	6	13	15	24
music and external	–	10	2	3	3
PE eqipment	–	25	1	2	2
head's office/meeting room	–	24	1	1	1
senior management offices	–	8	6	7	8
librarian/SEN offices	–	12	2	2	2
admin/secretaries/reception	–	–	32m²	48m²	63m²
staff room (social)	–	–	32m²	48m²	63m²
staff work room(s)	–	–	40m²	60m²	75m²
reprographics	–	–	12m²	18m²	24m²
staff changing rooms	–	–	4m²	4m²	4m²
staff toilets (area per fitting)	–	3.5	6	8	11
central stock/exam store	–	5	2	3	4
MI room	3	12	1	1	1
cleaner's stores	–	1.5	4	6	8
caretaker's office/maintenance store	–	–	20m²	25m²	30m²
plant	–	–	60m²	85m²	110m²
corridors/circulation	–	–	760m²	1065m²	1320m²
internal partitions	–	–	120m²	167m²	212m²
total gross area			4842m²	6689m²	8479m²

a: 1 of each; b: partially timetabled for PE; c: partially timetabled for drama

25 Typical schedule of spaces for an 11–16 secondary school

between them (BB81, Appendix 1). Good sight-lines are essential and a variety of furniture and equipment will need to fit in the room. The likely required sizes of each room type will depend on the activities accommodated and the maximum group size. Ranges are given in BB82. The size of spaces will also be affected by the extent to which storage and resources such as IT are within the room or in shared areas nearby. Ideally, all teaching spaces should be serviced for the use of computers and audio-visual teaching aids.

General teaching classrooms These accommodate a range of activities which include whole-class teaching and small group discussion, reading, writing, role-playing, and can include the use of computers and audio-visual equipment. There may also be some other activities, such as model making (e.g. in geography or mathematics) so it is therefore desirable to provide one large classroom for every four or five of 'standard' size. General teaching rooms tend to be used for more than one subject to allow a high frequency of use (90%), although they are likely to be used primarily for a single subject so that display and storage can be relevant.

Untimetabled supplementary teaching areas
These may be required in suites of general teaching accommodation: for instance, a room for use by a foreign language assistant to work with small groups or for careers advice. Small clusters of computers may be in a shared area rather than in the class.

Practical spaces
Practically based subjects require a range of specialist teaching spaces. These include science, design and technology, art, music, drama and PE. Business studies and vocational courses, such as GNVQs may benefit from access to practical rooms, and will need ready access to information communications technology (ICT).

Science Generally, science needs to be taught in laboratories, equipped with sinks, gas taps and suitable worktops (see BB80). Central preparation rooms serving a number of general laboratories are economic and offer flexibility.

Design and technology This requires a variety of specialist spaces, depending on the course chosen (see BB81). They are likely to be used at a lower frequency level (70–80%) than other spaces as, for instance, food-related courses cannot be taught in a workshop. The range of timetabled spaces will include:
- multi-materials workshops for designing and making in various 'resistant' materials such as wood, metal and plastic
- pneumatics, electronics and control technology (PECT) areas, including lighter technologies and perhaps CAD-CAM machines
- textiles, as taught in technology, including sewing machines, knitting machines and fabric testing equipment
- food room, including sinks, cookers, fridge/freezer and other kitchen equipment, with suitable worktops and hygienic finishes for preparing food

- a graphics room, which may be included in the suite if the curriculum demands it.

As in any other subjects, ICT will need to be accessed. Untimetabled areas may include a heat-treatment bay, usually part of a workshop, and a sixth form project area.

Art Specialist spaces are required to accommodate activities such as drawing, painting, 'wet textiles' (screen printing and batik) or 3D work (sculpture, pottery, construction). Each room is likely to reflect a particular range of specialist activities (see BB89).

Music A music classroom is needed, and perhaps a larger recital room (see BB86). Untimetabled spaces will include around four small group/practice rooms for every music room (for peripatetic teaching and small group work). A recording studio or control room can also be useful.

Drama Although it can be taught in a large classroom or in a shared music room, this is best accommodated in a drama studio. Performances will require a larger area, or use of the main assembly hall, with appropriate stage lighting and blackout facilities. Fire exits and emergency lighting should be sufficient for evening performances to the public.

PE Physical education requires a gymnasium and a sports hall, as well as various outdoor facilities, including hard courts and grassed pitches (discussed earlier). Although a sports hall is usually more than twice the size of a gymnasium, it is unlikely that it will be timetabled for two groups for more than half the time available. If the sports hall is to be used for competitions or public use, Sports Council recommended dimensions should be used, adding further area (see the Sports Facilities section).

Information technology
The use of information technology (IT) in schools has increased significantly in recent years. Government IT initiatives (such as the National Grid for Learning), combined with the falling cost of equipment, mean that this trend is likely to continue and even accelerate in the future. This has emphasised the need for careful planning and flexibility to cope with future advances. If computers are to be networked across the school, a safe and secure area (an IT technician's room) will be needed to house the network file server(s).

IT facilities may be available in each classroom or equipment may be located in dedicated IT areas, but, more commonly, secondary schools have a mixture of IT resource areas – smaller departmental clusters and individual machines in certain classrooms. Any local untimetabled IT resource areas should be positioned centrally to the area they serve and should be accessible, but secure at all times. Internal glazing allows easy supervision from adjacent spaces.

Environmental conditions Glare and reflections on screens are the most common lighting problems in IT areas. For the best lighting conditions, blinds may be needed to control daylight and direct sunlight, and reflective surfaces should be avoided on the floor, walls and furniture. Computers should be placed with monitors at right angles to the windows and parallel to the light fittings. North-facing rooms will normally provide the best environmental conditions for IT use. A room full of computers and pupils can also give off a lot of heat, which should be controlled naturally. When in use the temperature in an IT room should ideally be between 18°C and 24°C, with humidity between 40% and 60%.

Room size and furniture layout
(See **26**.) Pupils must have space to work comfortably at the workstation. There should be at least 850 mm of clear space in front of the computer table (1200 mm between back-to-back tables). Several pupils should be able to gather around at least one machine or be able to see a large monitor, for demonstrations. The arrangement of computers in a room will affect the activities that can be carried out. At each IT workstation a pupil should be able to sit so that their eye-line is level with the top of the monitor. The ideal dimensions of furniture for different age groups are listed in the A&B leaflet *Making IT Fit* (1995). In most secondary schools, one size of table is used by the entire age range but using adjustable chairs allows each pupil to individually adjust their position to the correct eye level. A useful size for a standard work surface is 750×1500 mm because it enables two children to work comfortably together.

A 'perimeter' arrangement allows pupils to work at computers, with power taken straight off the perimeter trunking, or at tables in the middle of the room. However, glare and reflections can cause problems if the computer screens are parallel to the windows. The 'peninsular' layout (see **26**) allows the centre of the room to be used more effectively, and can give more space next to each computer for written work. Services are channelled through the furniture from perimeter outlets. There are fewer problems with glare as all the computers are positioned at right angles to the windows. An 'island' layout is good for group work and can also give a less formal feel but it can be inflexible if the service outlets or furniture are fixed.

Case study
Emmanuel City Technology College, Gateshead (see **27**) was built as a new school, with a capacity of 900 pupils aged 11–18 years, and opened in 1990. It was built in a linear pattern with the design solution based on a 'necklace' of repeated pavilions. This approach allows considerable economy by repetition of detailing, design and construction, particularly as the blocks are all linked in the same way. Each two-storey pavilion is 800 m², with an atrium area in the centre and great emphasis is placed on easy, flowing access between related subject areas (for example art, design and technology).

To the south, two specialist blocks of similar character accommodate dining facilities and the sports hall and changing area. A suite of conference and syndicate rooms with restaurant and exhibition area at first floor provides a focus for the Centre for Industrial Studies. These facilities are designed to establish links with local business and industry representatives on a commercial and educational basis.

The first of the standard pavilions contains the main double height assembly and drama hall. The remaining four accommodate teaching rooms around central atria. These are lit from above and ventilated by 'stack effect'. The atrium in the central pavilion has an open staircase from the main reception area, with the library adjacent. The last two pavilions house multi-materials spaces, technology and a design studio on the ground floor, with science laboratories on the first floor, together with food and fabric studies and preparation rooms. A series of staff rooms and offices are located within and between pavilions at each level. The characteristics of the planning provide these rooms with natural light and reasonable views into the courtyards, while still being close to the central spine circulation, allowing natural supervision of activities in the pavilions.

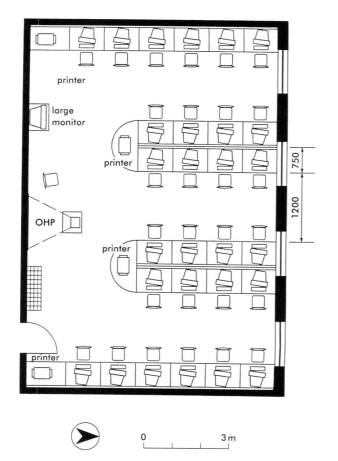

26 Generic layout of an IT room for 28 pupils

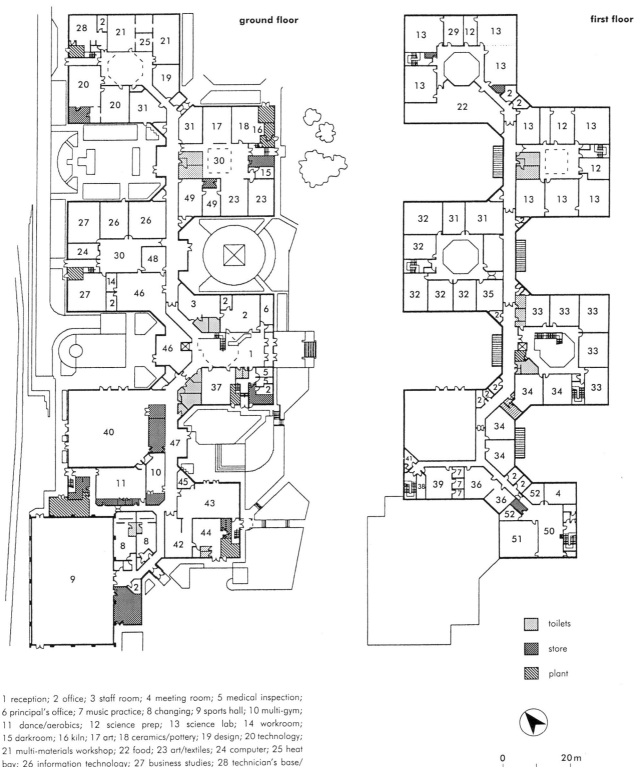

ground floor

first floor

toilets

store

plant

0   20 m

1 reception; 2 office; 3 staff room; 4 meeting room; 5 medical inspection; 6 principal's office; 7 music practice; 8 changing; 9 sports hall; 10 multi-gym; 11 dance/aerobics; 12 science prep; 13 science lab; 14 workroom; 15 darkroom; 16 kiln; 17 art; 18 ceramics/pottery; 19 design; 20 technology; 21 multi-materials workshop; 22 food; 23 art/textiles; 24 computer; 25 heat bay; 26 information technology; 27 business studies; 28 technician's base/materials; 29 tutorial room; 30 shared work area; 31 mathematics; 32 English; 33 modern foreign languages; 34 humanities; 35 religious education; 36 sixth form study/social; 37 lecture room; 38 recording studio; 39 music; 40 assembly/drama hall; 41 control room; 42 food hall (servery); 43 dining; 44 kitchen; 45 wash-up; 46 library; 47 exhibition/tutorial; 48 reprographics; 49 enhanced studies; 50 coffee/exhibition; 51 conference room; 52 syndicate room

27 Ground and first floor plans, Emmanuel CTC, Gateshead (Arch: The DEWJOC Partnership)

Case study

Blenheim High School, Epsom (see **28**) was designed to become eventually an 8FE school (1200 pupils plus sixth form) to teach a relatively vocational curriculum, including sixth form GNVQ courses. The building was designed to take an initial year group of 120, within a year of the purchase of the site, through modest refurbishment of efficiently designed existing buildings in good condition. This allowed the remainder to be replaced by new buildings within the budget.

Features of the design included:

- a phased programme of building
- adaptability to allow for future changes in room numbers, sizes and services
- corridors that are double-loaded, for maximum efficiency, whilst still being a major link between areas of the school
- for security, there are only two main entrances
- buildings grouped around a central courtyard, to afford a secure environment and give a 'sense of place' to occupants
- generally two-storey buildings

- all buildings physically linked to allow internal circulation in inclement weather and to allow access for pupils with disabilities to both floors.

The position of existing buildings and the need to provide a secure environment with limited, controlled access led to a disposition of buildings around a central courtyard, with large spaces and later phases projecting from the main 'circle'. Because of the size of the site, all buildings except halls and gymnasia are two storey. IT is not generally provided in individual teaching rooms, except science and business/GNVQ rooms. Each faculty shares an 'IT cluster' with the equivalent of one computer per room in an open area of the corridor. The sixth form self-study area is close to the library, while a separate common room, for more social activities, is at the opposite end of the site.

There are two main entrances: one for visitors and one for the bulk of the pupils (see **12**). Both can be used by the community: the south entrance for the sports hall and other PE facilities, the north for use of the hall, catering facilities and the amphitheatre in the courtyard.

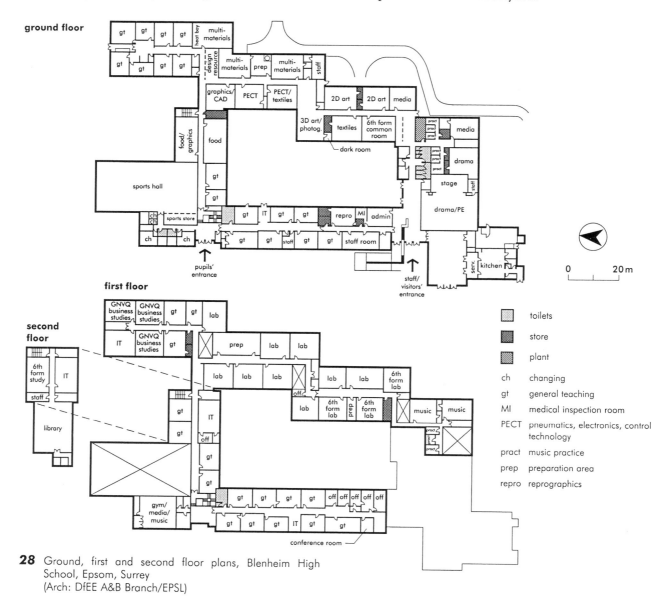

28 Ground, first and second floor plans, Blenheim High School, Epsom, Surrey
(Arch: DfEE A&B Branch/EPSL)

POST-16

An increasing number of 16- to 19-year-olds are continuing to study at school. Sixth form courses are usually predominantly general teaching subjects, with business studies or similar GNVQs and sciences as the main specialist subjects. Other vocational subjects, art, music and other practical courses may also be taught, but these are likely to be in small groups, generally occupying existing (and otherwise under-utilised) practical spaces. Around 20–30% of a sixth former's school time will be spent in private or self-supported study. Depending on the school and student, this may be done in a study area, the library, social areas, IT spaces, at home or in specialist spaces such as art studios, where a sixth form project area may be available for untimetabled work and long-term work or experiments. Extra area for sixth forms in schools (which can be added to the schedule of spaces for an 11–16 school (see **25**) may therefore include:

- general teaching rooms (generally smaller than standard classrooms, to suit the smaller group sizes)
- business studies/GNVQ room(s)
- IT rooms and IT clusters for smaller groups
- science laboratories (suitable for specialist study of chemistry, biology and physics)
- practical areas for vocational courses, such as engineering, if necessary
- specialist supplementary teaching areas, such as a dark room or project areas for art or design and technology
- self-study area and/or extra library resource area to accommodate around 25% of the sixth form at any one time
- common room/social area, comfortably accommodating about 25% of the sixth form
- non-teaching areas, such as head of sixth form's office, toilets, extra catering facilities and stores

In some cases general teaching, business/GNVQ, IT and science rooms may be used by all age groups. The common room, study area and library resource may be linked or separate, depending on the school, to offer shared resources but a choice of quiet or more lively working areas. Sixth form groups are tending to increase in size, so science labs and IT rooms are likely to be the same size as those for 11–16 pupils, but with a larger work area per pupil.

SPECIAL SCHOOLS

(Guidance is provided in BB77.) Meeting the educational needs of many pupils in special schools can require additional teaching and support provision and may place particular demands on other areas of the building. Aspects of the role of special schools, which may involve specific or modified accommodation, can include:

- the need for support from therapists, advisory teachers, medical personnel and other specialists
- increased parental involvement
- case conferences and discussions involving staff, specialists and parents
- extensive hygiene and toilet facilities for some pupils
- greater demands on bulk storage for the large quantities of aids and equipment which may be needed

- circulation planning and design which facilitates ease of movement around the building while avoiding causing distractions or upsets for other pupils.

Generally, the non-teaching area of special schools represents a significantly greater proportion of the overall area than in most ordinary schools. It is likely to be between 45% and 55%, depending on the needs for which it provides.

General requirements for all special schools

Teaching spaces These need to be large enough to accommodate several adults, in addition to teachers, working within the space. Each class should have its own class base. Groups are likely to be from six to ten pupils. Specially equipped teaching accommodation, which includes practical areas for science, art, food and design technology (the extent of which depends upon the age of the pupils), should also be provided.

In smaller schools, provision for pupils to experience physical education, music and drama may be in a multi-purpose hall, but in larger schools separate areas may be needed. Any design brief should take account of the amount of time needed in the hall for curricular and other activities and wherever possible dining should take place in a separate area. Physical education in the hall or gym will require an appropriate range of equipment, and space for courts for games, for secondary aged pupils. Children with SEN can benefit greatly from music and drama. Ideally, separate provision for music should be made and, depending upon the number of pupils, their ages and the difficulties catered for, provision for drama can range from use of the school hall to a separate facility also used for music or, in the largest secondary schools, another hall.

All-age schools In all-age schools positive attempts need to be made to ensure that the environment reflects the age of pupils. Separate and distinct areas should be provided for under-5, primary, secondary and post-16 phases, differentiated in both facilities and character.

Space, storage and display Facilities of a suitable nature need to be provided for books and other resources, and need to be provided both within teaching areas and also in a separate library/resource area.

Accommodation needs at nursery and primary levels

Nursery provision in special schools differs little from that elsewhere, but additional equipment may be needed. Some nurseries based in special schools operate as local neighbourhood nurseries.

At primary level, class bases should allow for a range of activities to be pursued at any one time, with the option of creating a quiet area to support individual or group work. Specially equipped teaching space should be provided for food technology, science and design technology.

Accommodation needs at secondary level

At secondary level the requirement for each class to have its own base remains, although it is likely that pupils will move around different teaching areas. Some bases may also support subject specialisms. Specially equipped teaching areas, together with associated storage and preparation areas, are needed for science, food technology and design and technology and for work in two- and three-dimensional art. These areas should not double as class bases. Where space is limited, a 'nucleus' specialist area adjacent to a class base may be used either for a half group or, in conjunction with the base, for a full group. Pupils at KS4 and beyond need to have access to a more adult environment which facilitates co-operative group work, supports individual study, investigation and research, and encourages independence. More extensive provision for a library and other resource materials with space and facilities for pupils to undertake individual study should be made.

Accommodation for post-16 students

The planning of post-16 provision should include space for work in a more social setting, with facilities for students to take breaks and make drinks and snacks, as well as space for more formal teaching sessions. Small spaces for discussion with tutors and individual counselling should be provided. The accommodation may include appropriately sized independent living areas, where social and independence skills can be practised and developed in an adult setting.

Where post-16 provision is located in a further education, tertiary or sixth form college, it is important that students with SEN should be recognised as part of the student body and have access to general post-16 facilities rather than being provided for as a separate group.

Other accommodation

Sensory curriculum rooms, soft play rooms and pools For many pupils with physical, learning and sensory difficulties there is a need for specialist facilities to help stimulate and develop responses. The three main types of provision are audio-visual rooms, soft play spaces and warm water pools, which can include hydrotherapy and swimming pools.

A pool is an expensive facility and great care must be taken to ensure that an appropriate type of provision is specified. Hydrotherapy pools are of benefit mainly to pupils with physical disabilities. Larger pools for swimming are useful, although additional features may be desirable for pupils with physical, learning and sensory difficulties. Swimming and hydrotherapy are not easy to combine because of the difference in optimum water temperature. However, for multi-purpose warm water pools a temperature of between 30°C and 32°C can provide a compromise. The running costs of a pool may be partially offset by planning so that independent access for use out of school hours is possible.

Hygiene and toilet facilities In addition to the usual requirements, physically disabled pupils will require a number of changing spaces and other hygiene facilities, including shower(s) and sluice(s), dispersed around the school, close to teaching spaces. Separate provision should be made for each gender over the age of 8, with proper regard for privacy and dignity. For child protection reasons, the location of any sanitary facilities for boys, girls and adults should

be considered especially carefully. Where pupils with PMLD are to be fully integrated throughout a school and they comprise around a third or more of the total number, the hygiene facilities in each area will need to be more extensive. A laundry for the washing and drying of clothes may also be required.

Bases for therapists and other visiting specialists Specialists such as physiotherapists, speech and language therapists, occupational therapists and psychologists may be full-time or may visit a number of schools. Therapy now tends to be delivered in the teaching situation but accommodation ranging from a shared office to separate rooms suitably equipped and resourced for work with individual pupils or small groups, will still be required.

Medical facilities All schools require a medical room but some special schools will need more extensive provision for use by clinical and nursing staff.

Technicians' rooms These may be required for the maintenance and repair of technical aids, such as those for pupils with sensory difficulties.

Staff accommodation General requirements are the same as for mainstream schools, but there will be a higher number of staff (a significant proportion of whom may work part-time).

Parents' facilities Most special schools benefit from space set aside for parents to meet, informally and socially. There should be comfortable seating and provision for the making of refreshments.

Kitchen Special schools usually have their own kitchens to cater for the various special diets which are often necessary.

Storage Teaching storage will depend upon the age of the pupils, the nature of the learning difficulties, and the appropriate teaching method. Physical aids and special apparatus can be very bulky.

Heating and ventilation Requirements in special schools may differ from those described for mainstream schools in BB87. Room design temperatures will need to take into account the activity rates of the pupils. As pupils in special schools tend to have more complex needs, special schools generally should be designed so that higher temperatures can be achieved if required. In rooms in which pupils are likely to be unclothed or partially clothed and perhaps wet, comfortable conditions will depend on both temperature and air speed.

Because the occupation density of special schools is lower than for mainstream schools the ventilation rates recommended in BB87 may not be appropriate. In many special schools ventilation should take into account hygiene as well as comfort.

Occupational heating gains are likely to be lower in special schools so that more fresh air needs to be heated, and it is desirable that this air is heated before circulation, especially in schools where the pupils may be vulnerable. These factors, as well as temperature requirements, are likely to result in higher installed heating loads and annual energy consumption values for special schools.

EDUCATION: UNIVERSITIES AND COLLEGES

INTRODUCTION

Most education in the UK after the end of compulsory schooling at the age of 16 takes place in universities and colleges. Students between 16 and 19 years of age attend colleges (and the sixth forms of some schools) studying below degree level, and students over 19 attend universities, undertaking degree and post-degree level study and research; the former sector is known as 'further education' and the latter as 'higher education', but demarcation has become less clear, and the two sectors can be referred to together as 'tertiary education'.

The majority of growth and change in higher and further education is being accommodated through adaptations and refurbishments in existing institutions, whether in buildings designed for education, or in buildings no longer required for their original purpose (e.g. factories, churches, and country mansions).

Higher education: background

After the foundation of Oxford and Cambridge in England (1133 and 1209) and St Andrews in Scotland (1412), the first university not to be tied to the Church was London University, now University College London (1824); during the 19th century the so-called red-brick universities were established in the UK's main provincial cities (Sheffield, Manchester, Birmingham etc.).

A new wave of universities was built in the 1960s as a response to demographic changes, and to the principle spelled out in the Robbins report (1963) that 'courses ... should be available to all who are qualified by ability and attainment to pursue them and wish to do so'. These were the so-called plate-glass universities.

Polytechnics were born at around the same time, to respond to the same pressures, and drew their inspiration from 'A Plan for Polytechnics and Other Colleges', written in 1966; the first were designated in 1968. They were formed from mergers among existing colleges of advanced technology and advanced arts colleges, and were mainly based in city centres, in existing 19th century buildings, with some new teaching buildings.

At that time the UK higher education sector consisted of 42 universities and 30 polytechnics, the former being autonomous institutions and the latter the apex of the local education authority systems. In 1992 the 'binary line' was removed and the polytechnics became autonomous, eventually changing their name to 'university' in order to reflect their new status. In 1997 there were 115 universities in the UK, together with 61 other university sector institutions. In 1966 the age participation rate for higher education for 18–19-year-olds was 10%, but by 1997 it was about 33%, an increase in real terms from around 350 000 full-time students to over 1.1 million today.

Trends In the provision of higher education courses, and therefore in the design of facilities to accommodate them, trends derive essentially from this rapid growth in the age participation rate, coupled with the need to keep costs under control, and this is a world-wide trend. The percentage of GDP spent on

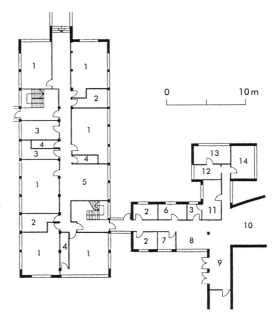

1 general teaching; 2 WCs; 3 office; 4 store; 5 study area; 6 medical room; 7 finance officer; 8 reception; 9 foyer; 10 new drama foyer; 11 general office; 12 principal's secretary; 13 principal; 14 vice principal

1 North Area Sixth Form College: existing layout

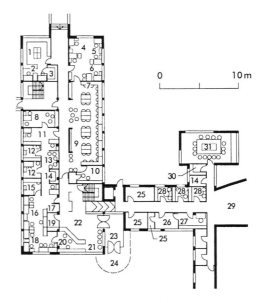

1 reprographics; 2 marketing; 3 reprographics; store; 4 premises management; 5 student support staff; 6 personnel management; 7 student services; 8 principal; 9 resources; 10 student services manager; 11 secretarial support; 12 vice principal; 13 meeting area; 14 store; 15 finance director; 16 finance; 17 tea preparation area; 18 admin and support staff; 19 cash office; 20 reception; 21 waiting; 22 foyer/display; 23 new entrance; 24 porch; 25 WCs; 26 rest room; 27 medical room; 28 counselling and interview; 29 new drama foyer; 30 kitchen; 31 conference suite

2 North Area Sixth Form College: theoretical layout (Arch: Initiatives in Design)

(**1** and **2** from Department for Education, Architects & Building Branch, Design Note 50, *Accommodation for Changes in Further Education*, p. 26, figs 25 and 26. Crown copyright is reproduced with the permission of the Controller of Her Majesty's Stationery Office)

higher education in the UK has oscillated between 0.9 and 1.15% over the last 20 years, but this disguises the fact that the index of public funding per student has fallen from 100 to 60 over the same period (a virtual halving of the real unit of resource).

Therefore the main trends are likely to be an increase in self-directed and distance learning and a better organisation of time and space in existing institutions, with a larger proportion of teaching/learning space given over to resource centres and more wide-spread provision of information technology.

Further education: background

The further education sector in England and Wales by 1997 consisted of 435 colleges, with 2.35 million students, studying for 3.6 million qualifications. Until recently most students were making the transition from school into employment, but now only 28% are under 19, and over half are between 25 and 59 years old.

Colleges include:

- agriculture and horticulture: 7%
- art, design and performing arts: 2%
- general further education and tertiary: 64%
- sixth form colleges: 24%
- specialist designated institutions: 3%.

One thing these colleges do have in common is that they were all made 'independent' in 1993. Before that time they were part of the local education authority system of schools and colleges, and although they did not provide compulsory education and training, their legal arrangements were similar to those of schools, with most of their administrative tasks being carried out by the local authority. Now they have to find the expertise, and the supporting facilities and space, to deal with their own finance, personnel, premises, marketing and student support. This rearrangement can often take place within existing buildings (see *1,2*), or existing buildings can be linked to provide a social centre (see *3*).

Trends In the provision of technical and vocational courses, trends are now reflecting the need for students to be trained in the practicalities of their disciplines; the National Council for Vocational Qualifications in England and Wales is promoting GNVQs (General National Vocational Qualifications) and NVQs (National Vocational Qualifications).

If training cannot be provided in the workplace, under appropriate supervision, colleges will need to provide workplace equivalents, or 'real work environments' (RWEs); at the same time they will need to provide areas within which potential students can be interviewed and assessed, so that existing skills developed through experience can be properly taken into account: this is known as the 'assessment of prior learning' (APL). Plymouth College of Further Education (see *4*) has some of the earliest examples of purpose-designed real work environments for catering courses, designed in such a way that space and equipment can be used in different combinations as requirements change.

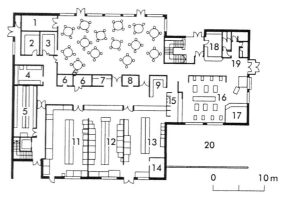

1 furniture store; 2 cutlery; 3 cellar; 4 potwash; 5 store and control office; 6 store; 7 still room; 8 silver room; 9 wash-up; 10 restaurant; 11 production, pastry; 12 production kitchen; 13 production larder; 14 walk-in fridge; 15 servery; 16 coffee shop; 17 bar; 18 reception; 19 WCs; 20 barbecue area

4 Plymouth FE College, Plymouth, ground floor plan

(from Department for Education, Architects & Building Branch, Design Note 50, *Accommodation for Changes in Further Education*, p. 15, fig. 9. Crown copyright is reproduced with the permission of the Controller of Her Majesty's Stationery Office)

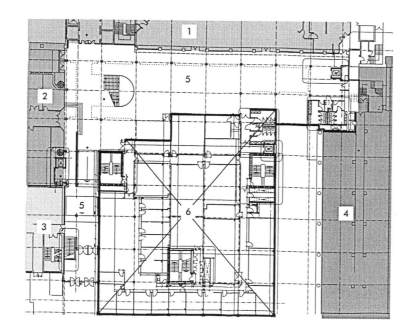

existing buildings
1 12-storey block
2 gym
3 5-storey block
4 8-storey block
new buildings
5 atrium
6 classrooms, laboratories and staffrooms

3 Sheffield Hallam University, Pond Street Campus
(Master plan arch: The Bond Bryan Partnership; arch: Building Design Partnership & Shepherd Design)

SCHEDULES OF ACCOMMODATION

Accommodation categories

Traditionally, educational accommodation at this level consisted of four main types of accommodation: teaching accommodation, learning accommodation, non teaching/learning accommodation, and the balance. However, in the interests of flexibility and adaptability, it is suggested that there should now be more overlap among them.

Equally traditionally, overall space in the different categories was calculated according to the number of space full-time equivalent (SFTE) students to be accommodated, using different space guidelines for different disciplines and levels of work (see Design Notes 33 and 44, and University Grants Committee Notes on Procedure), and using various formulae for turning students into SFTEs. In broad terms, gross figures have ranged from around 20 m² for one advanced level space full-time equivalent student taking drama, building construction or some other course involving large-scale activities (DES Design Note 20, 1979) to 5 m² for one space full-time equivalent student doing humanities in further education in 1996 (Further Education Funding Council, *Guidance on Estate Management*, 1993).

However, with better information on proposed curricula now available, it is suggested that the number of workplaces in each type of teaching/learning accommodation should be calculated according to the level of utilisation it is possible to obtain in that type of accommodation (using optimum scheduling systems, and sharing across disciplines as far as possible). For example, if it is assumed that it is possible to achieve 40% utilisation of general purpose teaching space over a 40 hour teaching week (the accommodation is assumed to be available for 40 hours, not the staff or students), for each teaching hour which needs to be accommodated, 2.5 workplaces need to be provided. When the number of workplaces in different

teaching/learning accommodation categories has been calculated, the appropriate net workplace area standard can be applied, and a percentage addition then can be made to cover non-teaching/learning and balance.

From the total gross area of the buildings:
- 60% approx is teaching/learning area
- 15% approx is non-teaching/learning
- 25% approx is the balance.

The table shows net workplace areas for higher and further education. For recommended breakdown among teaching, learning and other types of accommodation overall (see **5**).

Teaching accommodation is the major component of any institution's total built area and includes general teaching and specialised teaching (large scale and small scale). For very specialised teaching areas, e.g. clinical or manufacturing, see Health Service Buildings and Laboratories sections.

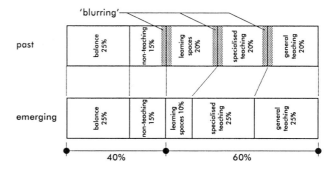

5 Gross floor area: guide proportions

(from Department for Education, Architects & Building Branch, Design Note 50, *Accommodation for Changes in Further Education*, p. 2. Crown copyright is reproduced with the permission of the Controller of Her Majesty's Stationery Office)

---

net workspace areas

higher education: space type used for		further education: space type used for	
general teaching	**workplace (m²)**	**general teaching**	**workplace (m²)**
(1) lecture theatres; close seating arrangements	1.0	lecture theatres; close seating arrangements	1.0
(2) teaching at tables in informal groups	1.8–2.1	teaching at tables in informal groups	1.8–2.1
(3) teaching at tables or desks	2.3–2.5	teaching at tables or desks	2.3–2.5
(4) teaching with demonstration facilities and students seated at large tables	2.5–3.0	teaching with demonstration facilities and students seated at large tables	2.5–3.0
specialised teaching		**specialised teaching**	
small scale		*small scale*	
(5) information technology	2.7–3.2	information technology (commerce and business)	2.7–3.2
(6) science (most science laboratories)	5.6	science (non-advanced)	3.0–4.6
(7) art and design (studios and drawing offices)	4.0–5.6	art and design (studios and drawing offices)	3.2–5.6
large scale (under certain conditions, these figures may be increased)		*large scale* home economics, fashion, trades (carpentry, plumbing, electronics etc.)	4.5–5.6
(8) engineering	5.6	catering, beauty care	6.5–8.4
(9) science and technology	5.6	heavy crafts (e.g. construction, welding, motor vehicle work)	7.5–8.4
(10) art and design (specialist areas)	5.6–8.4		
learning		**learning**	
(11) library/resource centre	2.5	library/resource centre	2.5
(12) terminal room	3.0	terminal room	3.0
(13) project work	as appropriate	project work	as appropriate

Learning accommodation libraries, resource centres and spaces used for untimetabled projects or research (see Libraries section).

Non-teaching/learning accommodation staff areas, administration, catering and communal areas, and the increasingly important student support services.

Balance areas provide for circulation, services, lavatories, storage etc.

Once total areas have been calculated, room sizes should be chosen to respond to group sizes. The range of room sizes should be kept as wide as possible, and the size of forecast groups should be checked as closely as possible (preferably through empirical use surveys); in reality there are always a wider size range and smaller groups than teachers imagine. Spaces designed for one use only should be avoided; stepped lecture theatres should be kept to a minimum.

Building users should be encouraged to treat their space and facilities as adaptable and responsive resources, capable of accommodating a wide spectrum of future demands, so long as current patterns of use and forecast changes and numbers are monitored continuously.

Cambridge Regional College (Kings Hedges campus) phase 3 (see **6**) was designed very much along the lines of the foregoing principles and those in Design Note 50.

OTHER CONSIDERATIONS

An accommodation strategy, as recommended by public funding bodies, should not only suggest how the appropriate amount and type of teaching/learning accommodation should be provided, it should also try to make provision for rapidly changing circumstances, now and in the future, in both the educational field and the field of economic and social expectations.

CHANGING EDUCATIONAL NEEDS

Growth of demand In all advanced countries there is a move towards the 'massification' of higher education, and the development of further education. Between 1994 and 1996 in the UK there was a 16% increase in student enrolments in the further education sector alone, to 3.5 million.

The response to these enormous rates of growth cannot be simply to provide more of the same – more buildings and more teachers teaching more classes. Courses are being delivered in different ways (through information technology, through individualised learning programmes and packages), and buildings are having to work harder (through tighter scheduling, through being open longer, over the day, the week and the year). These demands must be met partly through more robust, more flexible and more adaptable buildings.

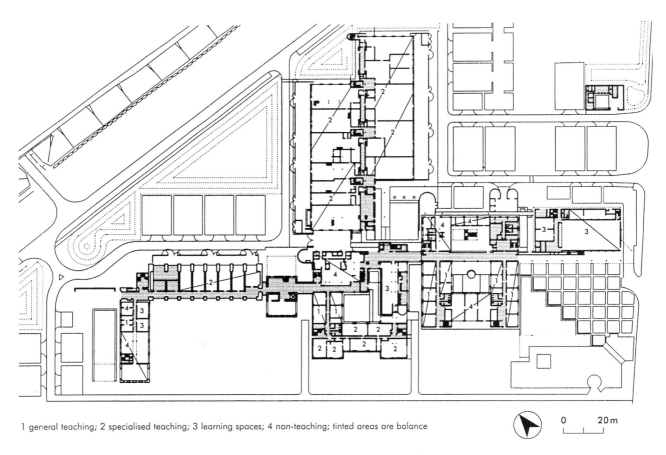

1 general teaching; 2 specialised teaching; 3 learning spaces; 4 non-teaching; tinted areas are balance

0   20m

6 Cambridge Regional College, Kings Hedges Campus, Cambridge: ground floor
(Arch: Bernard Stilwell Architects & Powell Moya Partnership Ltd)

A combination of managerial and physical adaptations can lead to enormous gains within existing buildings. The table shows progress made by Stockton Sixth Form College over 20 years; the building was purpose-built, but together with its users it was able to respond successfully to increased demands, mainly through managerial improvements, improving space utilisation.

Most of the adjustment is from reductions in average gross area per teaching space: reduced from 151 m² to 130 m², and per workplace it has reduced from 8 m² to 6 m². This can represent a fall in premises-related costs per student of £139 a year (at £30/m²/year).

An example of a small-scale but very successful adaptation of a university building from one use to another is that for the archaeology department at Nottingham University (see **7**).

Space management at Stockton Sixth Form College

	1977	1996	increase (%)
area (m²)	6350	6792	10
no. of teaching spaces	42	52	24
no. of workplaces	790	1125	42
no of students	500	840	68
utilisation (%)	44	57	29

New teaching and learning methods Some are moving towards individualised open learning, perhaps using computerised teaching packages. On the other hand, some disciplines insist on permanent, individual workspaces (e.g. architecture), so it is important to realise that different courses lend themselves to different modes of delivery.

The impact of information technology In some institutions there appears to be an insatiable demand for IT; in others it is felt that teachers are too traditional to use it and that the buildings would not be able to cope.

IT will never entirely supplant the need and the desire for interaction between staff and students, and between students and students; it is more suitable for some types of courses than others (e.g. for simulating large-scale or dangerous activities). For medical and para-medical disciplines it may be particularly appropriate therefore, and for other types of high-level training. Good examples are the interactive language laboratory at University of Stockton (see **11**), currently used for work in European Studies, but shortly to be used also by students of geography and chemistry, and the entire conception of Oldham Sixth Form College (see **8**), where for the first time a college in the further education sector was designed and purpose-built to be fully networked.

IT is becoming essential in the running of a university or a college as an organisation and as an organisation within a set of buildings.

IT is also an essential component of open and distance learning, as offered to students wanting life-long learning, at times and in places to suit them: Blackburn College of Further Education, for

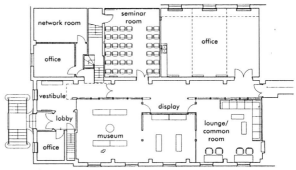

ground floor

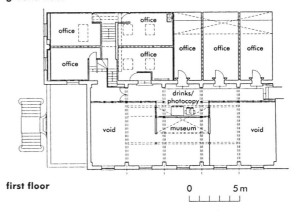

first floor

7 Nottingham University, Department of Archaeology: conversion from old engineering workshops
(Arch: Marsh & Grochowski)

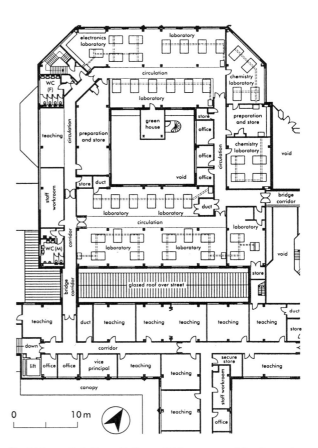

8 Oldham Sixth Form College, Oldham: part of first floor plan, science lab
(Arch: Cruickshank & Seward)

instance, has a purpose-built New Technology Centre, and a Flexible Training Centre in converted premises on an industrial estate, with a local area network for them and all college buildings, with over 500 personal computer terminals.

CHANGING SOCIAL EXPECTATIONS

A new clientèle With the widening of access to non-traditional students, and with more attention being paid to the demands of 'life-long learning', institutions have to answer an ever growing list of needs: some institutions will need to provide very specific accommodation (e.g. for Asian students with different religious requirements), or they may be receiving a growing number of post-graduate students from other European countries (in the context of EU exchange programmes). Part-time and full-time students have very different expectations of what an institution should provide: full-timers in higher education need facilities for every part of their life; part-timers have to concentrate their attendance at classes or other teaching sessions.

Child-care facilities are no longer a desirable add-on, aimed mainly at staff, they are now an essential feature of any institution which wishes to attract mature students, and parents on part-time courses.

The institution in its environment There is a tendency, with the move to greatly increased student numbers, for ever smaller regions and towns each to want its own university (e.g. Lincoln – see **9**), or part university (a trend well advanced in Greece and France). Although greenfield sites are no longer desirable, it is generally agreed that city centres may be too crowded to take on whole new universities, but that suburbs can provide appropriate sites, without becoming isolated campuses.

Institutions can indeed have an important regenerating effect on their surroundings. Docks sites and existing dock buildings make ideal areas for new and developing universities (see University of Stockton (**11**) and the new university going up at Docklands in East London (**13**)), Liverpool John Moores University rationalising the many sites of the old polytechnic.

One of the most impressive new sites is that for Hackney Community College in north-east London (see **12**), where long periods of local consultation, an amalgamation of international, national and local sources of finance, and a design involving existing and new buildings, have all combined to produce a morale-boosting 'flag-ship' project.

Science parks have a mixed impact. They may successfully bring together university and commercial research interests if they are well thought through, and they may provide useful revenue if the university owns the land. They can make use of old, warehouse type buildings, to provide mixed closed, communal and residential accommodation.

Residential and leisure facilities Attractive residential and social accommodation may prove decisive in attracting students and staff. It is important to decide to what standard student residences should be provided, and whether they can double up as part of a conference package.

Access for students with disabilities So far as possible students with physical disabilities should be integrated into the main student body, and where courses are put on for students with special needs, their accommodation should also be integrated into the main student buildings.

Health, safety and security Physical safety and security are big issues among women students and could well play a part in the parental choice of an institution. Closed-circuit TV may need to be installed in some public areas; dummy cameras can be a deterrent.

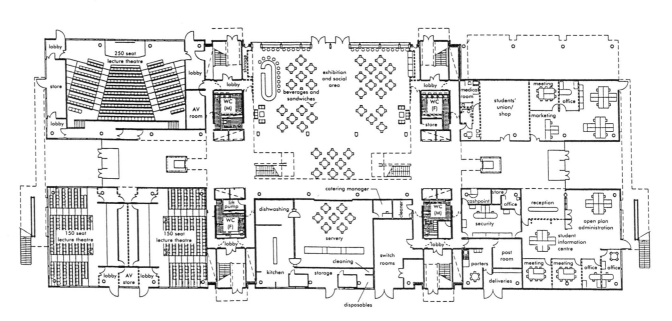

9 University of Lincoln (phase 1): plan of ground floor
(Arch: RMJM/Balfour Beatty)

0   10m

PLANNING NEW FACILITIES

Space norms These are becoming less relevant as institutions have increasingly to find their own finances, and as national funding bodies have less power to impose blanket standards. In very general terms, for planning new buildings and for assessing existing ones, the guidelines suggested in Design Notes 37 and 45 can be applied in further and higher education (see table), but for detailed projects, the institutions themselves need to have accurate information on their space, its allocation and use.

gross area guidelines

buildings used for	further education institution for		further education institution for	
	5000+ SFTEs (m²)	<5000 SFTEs (m²)	5000+ SFTEs (m²)	<5000 SFTEs (m²)
normal spread of work	10.0	10.0	14.5	15.0
small-scale activities	7.0	7.0	10.5	11.0
large-scale activities	13.0	13.0	17.5	18.0

Briefing The briefing process should not lead too quickly to definite solutions; rather it should raise questions as it proceeds. Equally, the architect should enter into dialogue with the users as early as possible (and this should be all users, including the surrounding population and agencies). It is not helpful for the brief to be prepared by an anonymous consultant.

Project management As the project proceeds, under a steering committee to include academic, social, physical and financial interests, there should be a clear decision maker, probably the person with the closest control over the money.

Investment appraisal Some assessment should be made of the whole life costs of a new building, to include running and maintenance costs, although such estimates can be only approximate. Funding bodies which still control the borrowing powers of institutions, such as the Further Education Funding Council in England and Wales, require institutions to prepare an accommodation strategy, with a demand-led (student numbers, new courses, changes in teaching methods) justification for any proposed capital project, including an investment appraisal of its long-term potential, using the Treasury-approved method to find the option with the highest net present value.

Design issues

Flexibility and adaptability Flexibility is the capacity of a building or space to accommodate different activities at the same time, or at least in the very short term; adaptability is their ability to alter over time in order to respond to broader changes in use. Systems of demountable but substantial walls, of heavily serviced shells with plug-in facilities and of free-standing serviced kits help to provide short- and long-term adaptability. From another perspective, 'Flexibility is natural light and natural ventilation' (Bernard Stilwell, architect).

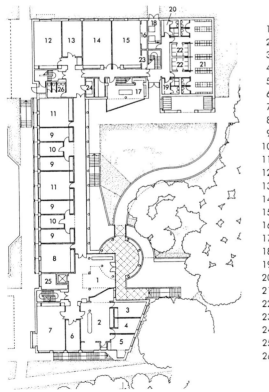

1 entrance hall
2 secretaries
3 school clerk
4 administrator
5 accounts office
6 tutorial
7 classroom/demo
8 research desk room
9 senior tutor
10 meeting room
11 seminar/demo
12 computer
13 technicians' workshop
14 psychiatry
15 classroom/demo (anatomy)
16 anatomy store
17 resource room
18 paladin store
19 staff changing (F)
20 staff changing (M)
21 student changing
22 shower
23 cleaners' store
24 kitchenette
25 plant
26 WC

ground floor

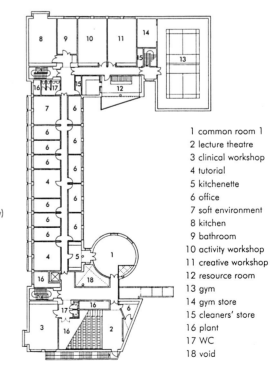

1 common room 1
2 lecture theatre
3 clinical workshop
4 tutorial
5 kitchenette
6 office
7 soft environment
8 kitchen
9 bathroom
10 activity workshop
11 creative workshop
12 resource room
13 gym
14 gym store
15 cleaners' store
16 plant
17 WC
18 void

first floor   0   10m

10 University of East Anglia, School of Occupational Therapy & Physical Therapy
(Arch: John Miller & Partners)

Improvements by design

- Develop sites and buildings so that working links between different faculties can be established easily.
- Surround departments that require an identifiable core or nucleus by spaces which are shared in a way that allows the departments to expand or contract their activities by using shared spaces for more or less time.
- Avoid the use of schedules of accommodation consisting of rooms tailor-made to a single activity.
- Rooms should be grouped into the broadest categories and particular functions should be provided for by furniture and services that can be altered easily to meet likely alternative uses.
- Make sure that buildings contain a variety of room sizes suitable for a wide range of different teaching groups so that changes in courses and teaching methods can be accommodated principally by timetabling.

Improvements by management

- Place as much accommodation as possible in a common pool for timetabling, to be shared between departments or, in large institutions where distances are great, between groups of departments.
- Classify rooms by their basic size, shape and facilities so that all potential uses are revealed.
- Examine carefully the customs that have grown up in the timetabling of events and the use of rooms in order to see which are essential and which may be altered with advantage.
- Spread scheduled activities as far as possible throughout the day, week, term/semester and year so that unnecessary peaking is avoided, bearing in mind that the hours of opening of non-teaching areas such as cafeterias may have a considerable effect on the timetable.

The need to provide for a completely unforeseeable future and to cover other points mentioned above is exemplified by the University of Stockton (see **11**), which is part of a business park, and is a good example of the increasing trend to use a standard office building specification.

first floor

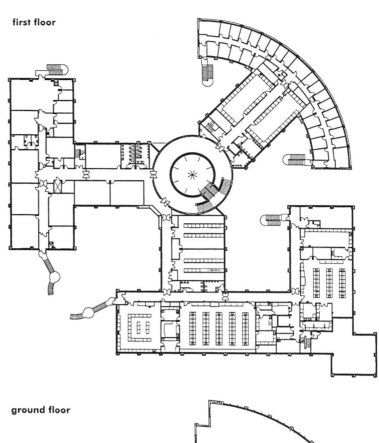

ground floor

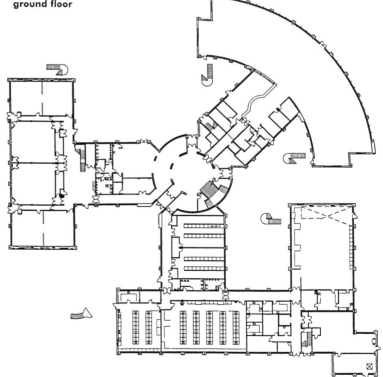

11 University of Stockton
(Arch: Halliday Meecham Architects Ltd)

CONCLUSIONS

Because of the continually changing nature of the educational process, and the need for buildings to be able to respond to change as well as to the sometimes conflicting demands of students, staff, industry and government, the designers of colleges and universities must try to reconcile a series of creative tensions.

Centralisation: decentralisation

Where should the point of decision-making be? If capital funding comes from central authorities, do the building users get enough input into its design? Does an institution have more commitment to its buildings if it has to raise its own money for them? The sorts of consultation procedures undertaken at Hackney Community College, even within the public sector, may obviate these problems (see **12**).

National norms: individual requirements

The use of space norms should be reserved for detailed design work, but they should not be so detailed as to inhibit new approaches.

Long term: short term

Buildings must pay for themselves and be fit for their purpose over the long term; but the students, the buildings' *raison d'être*, inhabit them only in the short term. Academic and administrative staff may use such buildings for 20 or 30 years. In order to respond to this unusually broad range of attendance patterns over time, the designer must include flexibility in the short term and adaptability in the long term.

Independence: cooperation

In the new 'free market', there is the danger that temporarily unpopular subjects will disappear from the curriculum as institutions concentrate on courses which attract students and money. Designers need to make sure that institutions can keep their options open.

Commerce: education and training

There is the danger that some institutions become so involved in raising money that education and training take a back seat to the conference trade or the industrial short course programme. The primary educational function of the building complex must not be forgotten.

Experience: new technologies

Teachers, particularly in the vocational sector, may have come from industry and may not be up to date with modern methods. Buildings and facilities should allow both the experienced practitioner and the cutting-edge experimenter to give of their best to their students.

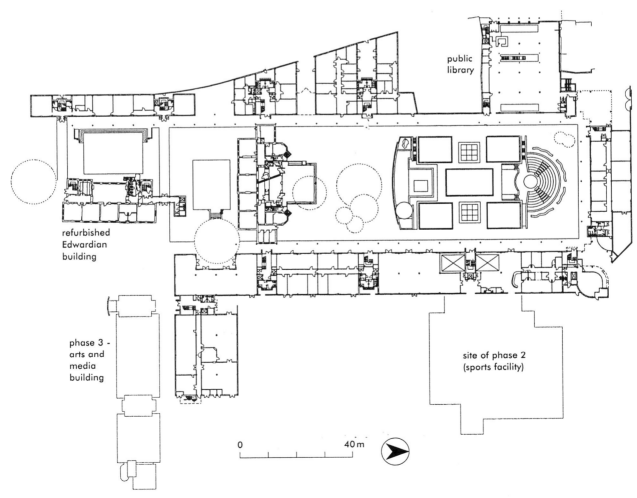

12 Hackney Community College (Shoreditch Campus): ground floor plan
(Arch: Hampshire County Architects/Perkins Ogden Architects)

Teaching staff: support staff

The roles of teaching and technical support are becoming more intertwined; advice and demonstration are made easier when workshops and offices are opened up so that everyone is more accessible, to students and to each other.

Education: training

An institution should offer its students the chance to experience as wide a range as possible of ways of learning, from hands-on to analytical exercises; this may extend beyond the individual establishment.

The individual: the community

More than in any other setting a student is both an individual and part of an intellectual and social community. The buildings must respect and reflect this dual role. Security and privacy must be combined with openness, permeability and corporate interaction with the immediate and wider world. Although universities and colleges should be diverse, and in some senses special, 'special' must not mean 'ghetto'.

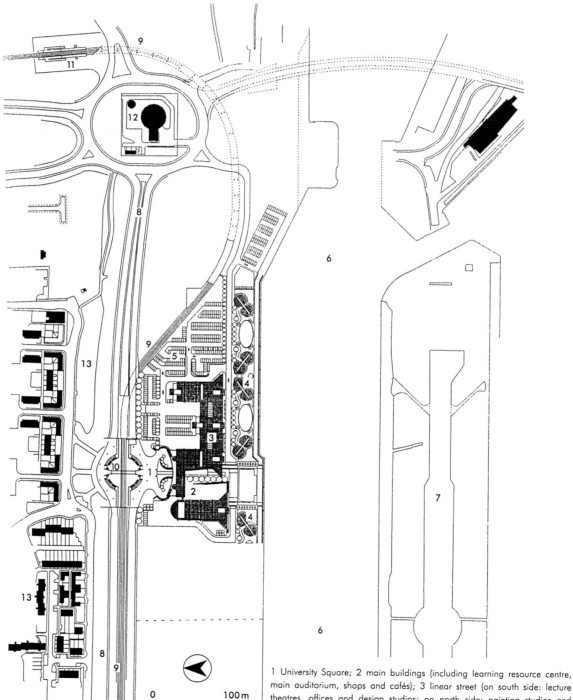

1 University Square; 2 main buildings (including learning resource centre, main auditorium, shops and cafés); 3 linear street (on south side: lecture theatres, offices and design studios; on north side: painting studios and workshops); 4 student accommodation; 5 car parking; 6 Royal Albert Dock; 7 London City Airport; 8 Royal Albert Way (dual carriageway A1020); 9 Docklands Light Railway (DLR); 10 Cyprus Station (DLR); 11 Gallions Reach Station (DLR); 12 Gallions Pumping Station; 13 housing at Cyprus

13 University of East London, Docklands Campus (Arch: Edward Cullinan Architects)

EDUCATION: ART, DESIGN AND MEDIA STUDIOS

INTRODUCTION

Departments in further and higher education are now usually grouped in larger units (e.g. faculties) so that resources can be shared with related disciplines. The layout of any studio is conditioned by type of work being undertaken and type of supervision required. A selection from the following specialist facilities is a likely requirement:

- architecture
- drawing and painting: fine art
- graphic design
- ceramics; sculpture
- media studies: video and film
- industrial design: engineering
- furniture and interior design
- theatre and television design
- photography
- silver and jewellery: metalworking
- textile design, both print and weave
- stained glass.

(See also sections on Schools, Cinemas, Theatres, and Laboratories. Music and drama facilities are not considered here.)

Schedule of accommodation Will generally include:

- design studio and display areas
- technical workshop(s)
- admin office
- storage.

DESIGN STUDIOS

General requirements These should be next to appropriate workrooms or workshops and the exclusion of noise and dust should be considered. Storage is needed for large drawings, models, reference books and clothes/protective equipment; lockers should be included, together with equipment for copying drawings and documents, although the latter may be centralised.

Good lighting is essential, both natural and artificial. Rooflights may provide ancillary light; all windows should be fitted with some form of daylight control (e.g. blinds) to prevent glare and possible damage to materials or colours. All surfaces should be durable and easy to clean.

Display space Traditionally in the studio area, nowadays this space can be varied to include lecture theatres, halls, corridors and entry areas. Note that some specialist display areas will still be required (e.g. for models, which are often fragile, or film and video, which require low light levels or blackout facilities and additional power supplies etc.).

Fine art studios Studios for painting and sculpture require large areas. They must have good natural daylight, with high-level windows equal to at least 25–33% of the floor area, and with north or east aspect.

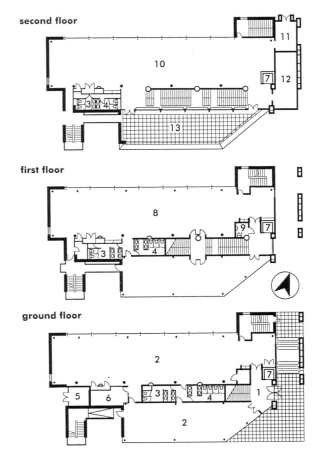

1 entrance; 2 seminar rooms; 3 WC(M); 4 WC(F); 5 boiler room; 6 plant room; 7 lift; 8 graphic design studio; 9 WC(dis); 10 interior design studio; 11 library; 12 staff room; 13 terrace

1 Design studios, Surrey Institute of Art and Design, Farnham, Surrey
(Arch: Nick Evans Architects)

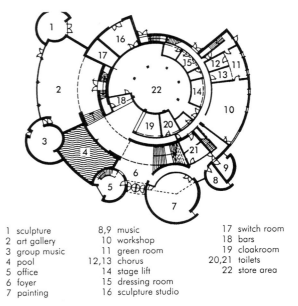

1 sculpture	8,9 music	17 switch room
2 art gallery	10 workshop	18 bars
3 group music	11 green room	19 cloakroom
4 pool	12,13 chorus	20,21 toilets
5 office	14 stage lift	22 store area
6 foyer	15 dressing room	
7 painting	16 sculpture studio	

2 Gardner Centre for the Arts, University of Sussex
(Arch: John S Bonnington Partnership, formerly Sir Basil Spence Bonnington & Collins)

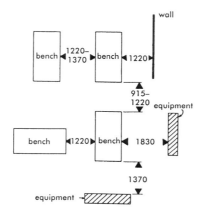

3 Clearances for layouts of metal shops

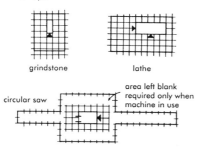

□ 929 cm² ▲ operating position ⊣⊢ run out

4 Working spaces round woodwork machinery

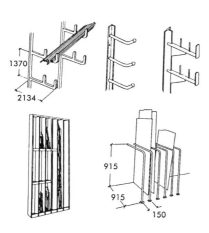

5 Various forms of storage racking

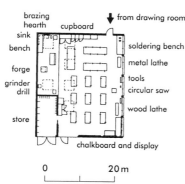

6 Layout for combined wood and metal shop

WORKSHOPS

Siting This will depend on type of work being done. Light work associated with graphics, silver and jewellery, photography and fashion may be placed on a higher floor; metal, wood and plastics workshops, where large machines may be installed, are best sited on ground or basement levels.

Good workshop layout must conform to work flow and safety (see **6**). Provide ample space round machines and for gangways to allow necessary movement without incursion on workspace. Non-slip floor finishes should be specified. A workshop technician should be able to survey the whole area from a partially glazed office.

If each student is provided with sets of tools, space for individual lockers is needed in the workshop area.

For details of equipment, see 'Workshop Equipment Spaces' in the Industrial Buildings section.

Health and safety This is particularly important where machinery is in use – e.g. wood and metalworking (see **3,4**) – or in darkrooms etc. where chemicals are used. Protective clothing, goggles etc. must be available in sufficient numbers and safety procedures must be clearly displayed.

Ancillary accommodation

This will include offices for teaching staff, common room (consider for both staff and students), toilets and possibly showers.

Ancillary areas may include printing and reprographic equipment, either housed in a studio or, if sophisticated or large scale, sited in a separate area. Computer-aided design and drafting equipment is usually located in separate computer areas, use being shared with other disciplines.

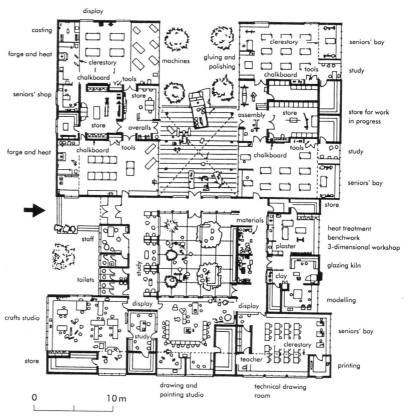

7 Arts centre layout for college

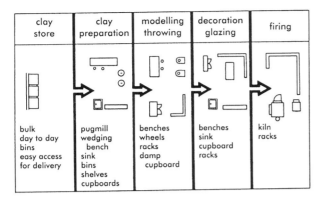

clay store	clay preparation	modelling throwing	decoration glazing	firing
bulk day to day bins easy access for delivery	pugmill wedging bench sink bins shelves cupboards	benches wheels racks damp cupboard	benches sink cupboard racks	kiln racks

8 Sequence of operation: clay modelling and pottery

Storage

Methods of storing a wide range of goods and materials are needed. Areas are required for storing completed works before exhibition or disposal. Some items may be very fragile and/or valuable, and additional security may be required.

All storage should be sited next to the appropriate workshop and satisfy requirements for specific heat and humidity conditions where required for specialised materials being stored (e.g. clay, plaster). External access must be convenient for goods vehicles – see 'Loading Bays' in the Industrial Buildings section.

Special racking is needed for paintings and large canvasses, timber and timber-based board materials, plastics sheets, metal sections, rolls of textiles, glass and paper (see **5**).

Correct archive storage for original drawings, models or other artefacts, which may have to be kept for indefinite periods, must be properly conditioned, and the structure must be fire and flood proof.

DRAWING STUDIOS

Space requirements are related to the type of drawing and allied work, if any, to be undertaken (see **9**).

Workstation Sizes are largely determined by the equipment needed to accommodate the drawing format, based on the 'A' series of international paper sizes (smaller formats being obtained by halving larger dimensions in sequence – see the Drawing Practice and Presentation section). For most industrial, engineering and design consultants, drawing requirements can be accommodated by A1 format; the larger A0 size is rarely required. Note that computer-aided design and drafting is regarded as complementary to traditional drawing skills, which should be taught first.

The simplest form of workstation is: drawing board, equipment trolley (cart) and draughtsman's chair; where drafting work requires reference to details contained on other drawings, either reference tables or vertical screens may be required. Screens have the advantage of keeping the necessary floor area to the minimum, but make group teaching more difficult. Reference tables, which may also provide plan chest drawing storage below the work surface, should either be to the side of the draughtsman in parallel with the drawing board or at right angles to it (see **9**). A further possibility is available with 'back reference', where the reference table also provides support for the drawing board behind. Where the drafting function has to be combined with administration work, the reference area may double as an office desk or the desk may form separate unit.

Referencing may not be confined to information contained on drawings; it is often necessary to have a comprehensive set of reference books or manuals close at hand for draughtsmen.

Setting-out studios A further category of drawing studio is that allied to workshops, where full-size setting-out drawings (or workshop 'rods') are prepared. These are usually found in the construction industry, and joinery shops in particular. Such drawings are prepared on rolls of paper set down at long benches. Draughtsmen work standing up at the drafting surface, which is horizontal and 900 mm high. Rather than the sheets used in other studios, these original drawings are stored in roll form, for which housing may be either horizontal (plan chests with drawers) or vertical (plan file cabinets).

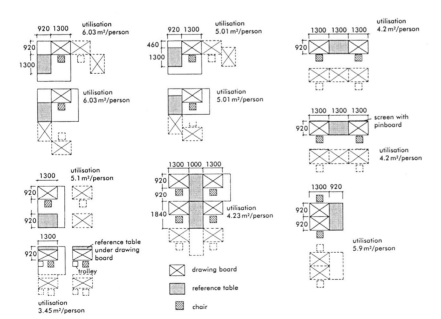

9 Various planning arrangements

FARM BUILDINGS

Patricia Beecham

INTRODUCTION

A farmstead comprises a group of highly specific and inter-related industrial buildings designed to meet a wide and exacting range of agricultural demands. The layout and design of farm buildings have developed out of the farming systems in use, while overall trends in agricultural building activity directly reflect the changing fortunes of agriculture as a whole. In the wider context an interest in farm buildings extends to those concerned with rural amenities, town and country planning and animal welfare.

THE ORIGINS OF THE MODERN FARM

Many farmsteads still incorporate buildings which were put up to meet the new demands of the agricultural revolution of the 19th century. The first systematic information on farm buildings in England and Wales was collected by the Board of Agriculture's surveyors in the series of *County Reports* compiled between 1793 and 1815. The benefits of re-planning the countryside were a common theme, including siting buildings conveniently for the working of the farm. The main criteria of farmstead planning during that period were convenience of arrangement for routine chores, notably the feeding, littering and mucking-out of livestock, and the effectiveness with which manure could be accumulated. Quality and ease of collection of manure, so important to the farming cycle, was affected by the design of the yard and its relationship to the barn and livestock buildings.

With the general intensification of livestock rearing in the late 18th century the prototypes of two of the most familiar of all modern farm buildings first appeared. First, the thatched timber skeleton which later developed into the metallic Dutch barn, replacing seasonally thatched haystacks and cornricks. Secondly the cowhouse, which was improved into a recognisable version of its modern form with sloping standings, chain-ties and divisions between cows, internal water supplies, feeding passages and dung-channels flowing to grated outlets. This differed from its modern equivalent only in its construction.

Mechanisation   It was in this period that the modern concept of the farmstead as an agricultural factory was first consciously established. Machinery was becoming increasingly important for farming processes. The development of a new type of barn to house the mechanical threshing mill and the consequent repositioning of the various buildings acknowledged that farm buildings are coverings for farm processes and that their relationship is determined by the demands of these processes. However, it is generally simpler and cheaper in the short run to put a new machine in an old barn than to plan a general rearrangement of the whole farmstead. So the majority of people fitted the machine to the buildings, not the buildings to the machine.

Efficiency   The farmer delegated many of the traditional responsibilities of design, equipment and erection of complicated buildings demanded by a more exacting farming system to the specialist in terms of knowledge, the engineer for equipment and the manufacturer for building materials. The growing use of expensive purchased concentrates for fattening cattle increased the incentive to provide stock with conditions which encouraged the efficient conversion of feed into meat. Other advances were made by the realisation that better protection of manure from rain significantly improved its value, and that the more intensive systems of boxes or stalls which made possible the individual treatment of stock reduced bullying and allowed each animal to feed and rest undisturbed, while feed could be carefully rationed and manure conserved (see **1**).

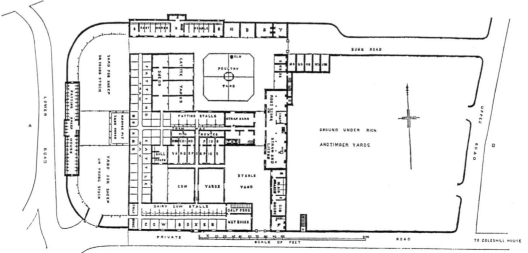

1   Earl of Radnor's model farm (1853) at Coleshill, Oxfordshire
(From *The Builder*, 23 December 1854, p. 654)

Buildings and materials Rising values encouraged expenditure on the protection of farm produce, and implements received greater care and attention. Greater production per acre meant increased reliance on purchased resources, and this, in turn, meant more capital outlay on buildings. The trade in the supply of an expanding range of prefabricated fittings eventually produced prefabricated buildings for assembly on the farm. The future of this system of construction depended on the sale of a standardised product to a large and continuing market. It was first successfully applied to one of the commonest and simplest structures on the farm, the Dutch barn. All the farmer had to do was excavate and prepare concrete foundations.

Farming developments

Towards the end of the 19th century far reaching changes to the traditional farming system of the UK were made by the enormous increase in quantities of imported food. A steady change to livestock farming took place to exploit the cheap imported prairie grain. Above all, the development of the liquid-milk industry, with no competition from overseas, was first made possible by the railways and later encouraged by the development of road transport. In 1933, the Milk Marketing Board was established in the UK, and by the end of the 1930s the income from milk was greater than the total from arable cash crops.

Dairy farming Advances in dairy farming required improvement in detail but no radical change in cowhouse design from Victorian times. Much effort was put into improving conditions and hygiene standards in both cowhouse and dairy, with rules and regulations enforced by government inspectors. The improvement in the milking environment was followed by an improvement in milking techniques. The milking machine allowed one man to milk more than one cow simultaneously. A new and revolutionary type of dairy building was developed with the invention of the 'releaser' milking system, which carried the milk in an overhead pipeline to the dairy. This was developed into the 'milking parlour' based on a milking stall, in which a cow remained only for the duration of the milking. As each stall now served many cows the capital costs were also reduced.

Cattle feeding A very important advance in cattle feeding was the development of the silage-making process, which allowed grass or other green crops to be stored undried in an airtight pit or structural container. The silo tower was one of the first research-based technologies of the 20th century to affect the design and construction of the farmstead.

CURRENT TRENDS

Building

The main boom in agricultural building activity occurred in the late 1950s and the 1960s when yields were increasing dramatically and mechanisation and technological and scientific advances necessitated a change to modern structures. The development of concrete portal-framed buildings also assisted this change.

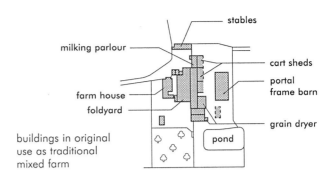

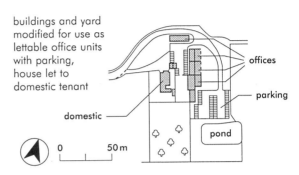

2 New use for farm buildings made redundant through amalgamation: Whinchat Hall, Escrick Park Estate, York (1998) (Arch: Chris Walker RIBA)

In the UK, Ministry of Agriculture Food and Fisheries (MAFF) grant aid during this time was high (up to two-thirds of the cost of a new building). Building activity then continued at a lower level during the 1970s and early 1980s, with buildings generally increasing in size. Since then, MAFF grant aid for agricultural buildings has stopped and, in line with reduced agricultural incomes at the end of the 1980s, agricultural building activity has reduced.

In terms of size of buildings constructed, there has been a continued upward trend for larger buildings, even if actual numbers are decreasing. In the 1990s most new buildings have been erected as a result of changes in the balance of enterprises on a farm (e.g. increase in grain acreage at the expense of livestock enterprise, or the expansion of one particular enterprise). Agricultural need rather than changes in farming practice have produced the demand for more buildings.

Grain stores built in the 1960s are uneconomic to manage: grain handling systems have changed significantly and equipment has increased in size. As grain yields have increased, additional drying and storage facilities have been erected in order to retain a flexible marketing strategy. Whereas additional dairy buildings were difficult to justify, investment in new silos in the early 1980s more than doubled. The move to silage production as a method of conserving grass has continued and pressure is on for lower milk production costs.

Conservation pressures In the past 15 years many new measures have been introduced to reduce the risk of streams, rivers and other water sources being polluted. This has necessitated building work, enforceable by law, to control pollution (e.g. to prevent leakage from silos).

Political and economic background The context in which agriculture is operating continues to change. The current stimuli to agricultural change are Common Agricultural Policy (CAP) reform and the General Agreement on Tariffs and Trade (GATT) agreement. Key components and recent changes in the structure of the agricultural industry can be seen by looking at data for the 1990s. In 1993 the total area of agricultural land was 77% of the land area of the UK, of which roughly 24% was cropped, 36% under grassland and 32% rough grazing. By the end of the 1990s there had been a decrease in the number of dairy cows but almost a 30% increase in beef and sheep. More poultry were farmed, and there was less area under vegetables, fruit and potatoes.

Farm building and fixed equipment grant aid and incentives:

- Government finance is an important factor, and has financed much of the relevant research work undertaken in the UK.
- Advice: various services once offered by MAFF are now only available through private/independent consultants, although DEFRA (successor to MAFF) does still give general advice (i.e. appraisal of land).
- Since 1994 grants have been provided from the EU's European Agricultural Guidance and Guarantee Fund (EAGGF, commonly known by French acronym FEOGA). By offering grants towards capital investments on immovable property and general costs relating to planning, buildings and works, this aims to give assistance to on-farm projects which add value to basic commodities.
- The EU grant aid for 'processing and marketing of agricultural products' is regulated by the Scottish Office of Agriculture, Environment and Fisheries Department (SOAEFD).

Diversification

With major job losses in agriculture, lessening EU support for agriculture, and the decline in real terms in financial support from the CAP, farmers have responded by searching for alternative enterprises.

Reform of the CAP is bringing farmers closer to the market-place, through farm-based enterprises supplying niche markets such as regional and speciality foods, and larger-scale group collaborations such as central fruit and vegetable packing operations and grain stores. These ventures can add value to local produce. Farmers increasingly look to diversify beyond the agricultural industry in order to supplement their income. Much farm-based work is now concerned with activities such as woodland management, farm shops, equestrian businesses, sporting facilities, nature trails, craft workshops and holiday accommodation.

FUTURE TRENDS AND THE NEED FOR NEW BUILDINGS

Trends which affect the need for new buildings are:

Expansion, upgrading This will be driven by the need for more machinery and hay storage, the refurbishment of dilapidated buildings, and legislation relating to waste and slurry handling and animal welfare.

Replacements Numerous buildings erected in the 1950s and 1960s are now nearing the end of their design life (i.e. they are becoming functionally obsolete or structurally weak). Modernisation or replacement will be required, which may mean replacement on the same site or erection of a new, larger or differently shaped building on a fresh site.

Polarisation/amalgamation Many farms will continue to grow in size through the amalgamation of neighbouring units. It is likely that in the future there will be increased co-operation between farm holdings within an area, both in marketing and machinery sharing, allowing group marketing and collaboration. For some, there will be a subsequent consolidation of enterprises into one farmyard, thereby centralising activities and potentially affording greater protection of resources. The advent of the 'fast-track' vehicle, enabling tractors to achieve much greater road speeds, will allow one farmstead to service a much wider area.

It is anticipated that the industry will continue to undergo considerable restructuring which will generate pressure for further building activity.

New entrants/fragmentation These are the purchasers of a bare block unserved by buildings or dwellings, often resulting from the lotting up of farms at a sale, who then erect buildings on the land and establish a farm business. This often results from the increase in part-time farmers with diversification.

Tenancy legislation Restructuring following the reform of the agriculture tenancy legislation in 1995 may potentially necessitate some new building.

Environmental considerations and pollution control The industry will continue to respond to new requirements in respect of the control of water and air pollution. The UK's Control of Pollution Regulations 1991 set minimum standards for new, substantially reconstructed or enlarged facilities for potential pollutants. The Environment Agency (EA) is also empowered under the Regulations to demand improvements to existing facilities in the drive to reduce the agricultural pollution of rivers. New buildings are required to help reduce waste production and to provide for storage of waste materials. Compliance with environmental measures will place increasing demands on livestock farmers.

Animal welfare As a result of the provisions of the current code of recommendations for the welfare of livestock, and encouraged by legislation or by public opinion, a continued move is expected towards keeping livestock in groups rather than individually or on slats (i.e. on slatted floors with no bedding). For pigs, accommodation has needed restructuring following recent legislation regarding stall and tether systems. The Welfare of Livestock Regulations 1994 banned the use of these systems in the UK altogether from January 1999. Farms formerly using these close confinement systems needed to double the space allocation for sows and provide extra storage space for bedding straw and solid manure.

Food hygiene The standard of storage and handling of products destined for human consumption, including milk, vegetables, fruit and grain, is likely to continue to be increased. This may require both building modification and replacement.

STATUTORY CONTROLS

Regulations and planning requirements controlling the siting, design and construction of farm buildings and allied works are contained in various Acts of Parliament as well as in the Building Regulations. Most of these Acts and Regulations are summarised in BS 5502.

Planning amenities and nature conservancy

In addition to the requirements of statutory legislation, other aspects to take into consideration at the design stage are compliance with any local or non-statutory planning requirements, the safeguarding of amenities, general aesthetic values, and quality of landscape; and consultation with the National Park Authority or the local office of the Nature Conservancy Council if the site is in a national park or includes a site of special scientific interest.

The Control of Pollution Regulations (1991) These

have considerably affected methods of disposal of potentially polluting substances on the farm. It is an offence to discharge agricultural waste into any stream, underground water or onto land without written consent from the EA. Among the many side products of normal agricultural activities silage liquor is the most potent natural pollutant, killing fish and corroding steel and concrete. Consideration must also be given to pollution from noise, smoke, smell, chemicals and any specialised buildings and processes.

PLANNING CONTROLS

Background to agricultural planning

A legacy of the power of the farm lobby has been the exemption from planning control over farm buildings. Yet the changes in agriculture, from husbandry to agro-industry, have progressively destroyed much of the unique character of the English countryside. The emphasis of planning policies has shifted since the 1947 Town and Country Planning Act from the need to retain as much land as possible in agricultural use to the diversification of the rural economy. However, farming uses still occupy around three-quarters of the land surface of rural England, and a higher proportion in Scotland, Wales and Northern Ireland. Food production and a competitive agricultural industry continue to be highly important, and provide a basis for many other economic activities in rural areas. At the same time environmental objectives are being integrated into agricultural policies and farmers are increasingly diversifying into other activities to supplement their incomes. Landowners need the flexibility to consider a range of options for the economic use of their land, including non-food crops, planting more woodland, recreation and leisure enterprises, the management of land to provide environmental benefits, and the restoration of damaged landscapes and habitats.

Structure of agricultural planning legislation

The Planning Policy Guidance note of most relevance is the latest revision of PPG No 7, 1991. Government policy is based on 'ensuring rural prosperity and the protection and enhancement of the character of the countryside'. The six principles for the future of the countryside which are stated in the White Paper entitled Rural England: a nation committed to a living countryside, on which the current PPG7 is based, are:

- the pursuit of sustainable development
- shared responsibility for the countryside as a national asset, which serves people who live and work there as well as visitors
- dialogue to help reconcile competing priorities
- distinctiveness, approaching rural policies in a way which is flexible and responds to the character of the countryside
- economic and social diversity
- sound information as the basis for effective policies.

Up to 1991 the majority of agricultural buildings were free from planning control but in June 1995 the Town and Country Planning (General Permitted Development) Order 1995 came into effect. From that time it was stipulated that new farm buildings must be sited on land which is in use for agriculture for the purposes of a trade or business, and must be reasonably necessary for the purposes of agriculture within an agricultural unit which is at least 5 ha in area, as well as meeting other conditions. Since then most developments on farms over 5 ha have been subject to the process of determination by the local planning authority (LPA). The purpose of the determination process is to provide a level of control over developments likely to have a significant impact on their surroundings. It allows the LPA to establish whether its prior approval is needed for the details that the LPA may concern itself with, including the siting, design and external appearance of the proposed development.

Extent of control and responsibilities of the local planning authority The PPG states that

the LPA must determine specific policies for different types of countryside within its area. Regional character is derived from interaction of physical and ecological features with land use and other human activity such as farming patterns, settlement form and building design. The aim is 'to advise on achieving good quality development and respecting the character of the countryside', as well as the protection of good land and the re-use of rural buildings, especially for business rather than residential development.

LPAs are encouraged to prepare design guidelines in association with local farming and conservation interests and MAFF. These are an aid to communication, both with developers and with the agricultural buildings industry.

Planning matters

Details must be given of arrangements for the storage and disposal or spreading of slurry or manure (slurry storage tanks within 400 m of residential or similar buildings also require planning permission).

Planning applications for agricultural developments like intensive pig and poultry units (i.e. more than 400 breeding sows, 5000 fattening pigs; 50000 layers or other poultry, 100000 broilers) have to include an assessment of the effects on the environment and how this can be minimised and controlled.

DETR proposals (From Planning Controls over Agricultural and Farm Developments.) The DETR report states rural areas can accommodate many forms of development without detriment if the location and the design of the development is handled with sensitivity. Rural areas can accommodate many forms of development without detriment if it is carefully related to existing settlement patterns and to historic, wildlife and landscape resources. Building in the open countryside, away from existing settlements or from areas allocated for development in development plans, should be strictly controlled.

Reasons for landscape impact have been identified as:

- development on a bare land plot
- buildings isolated from farmstead
- buildings out of scale/highly visible within existing farmstead
- buildings which have a suburbanising influence.

Remedies suggested are:

- screen planting/avoid isolated skyline or ridge top (high impact); create a landscaped band around building to limit impact in prominent position
- plant trees/relocate near farmstead/modifications to cladding to lessen impact
- landscape treatment/cladding/design modifications/ reduce bulk; use of double rather than single-span roof (see **3**)
- avoid proliferation of small buildings/relocating
- silage clamps, which can be as large as 1.68 m² with 2.4 m high walls, benefit from screen planting
- avoid large areas of hardstanding on a hillside.

DESIGN CONSIDERATIONS

Siting

Farm buildings are a significant component of most agricultural landscapes. Traditionally in their siting and appearance they reflected the farming system, local materials (often underlying geology), local building techniques, and the particular character of the site in the landscape. The siting of a new agricultural building can have a considerable impact both on the site and the surrounding landscape; developments should be assimilated into the landscape without compromising the functions they are intended to serve. The choice of site should respect existing physical features, contours and vegetation as well as existing man-made features, walls, ponds etc.

The aim should be to disturb the landscape as little as possible; the site should be considered from key viewpoints and the relationship between building and site should be enhanced. New buildings should normally form part of a group rather than stand in isolation, and relate to existing buildings in size and colour. The introduction of a new building changes the appearance of the whole group, and can be used to improve existing relationships by choosing the site and orientation with regard to the effect of its scale and shape on the existing buildings. New buildings of modern design may sometimes best be separated from a group of traditional buildings to avoid visual conflict. Sites on skylines should be avoided if possible, and to reduce their visual impact buildings should be blended into the landscape or, on sloping sites, set into the slope if that can be achieved without disproportionate cost.

A single large building may have a greater impact on the countryside than one or more smaller ones, which can be more easily incorporated into an existing group and provide greater flexibility, although the function of the building will be material to shaping its form. Functional and economic requirements can often lead to a large-scale standardised building, generally requiring a flat site and a large area around to allow for access and future expansion. However 'functional' decisions on the position of the building, its shape, materials and the layout of the spaces around the building all help determine the final appearance in its setting. The aim should be to achieve a functionally sound building which also contributes successfully to the landscape.

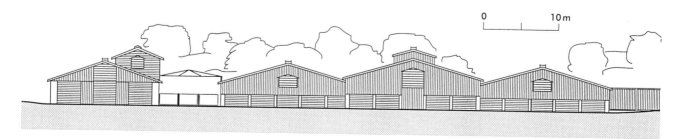

3 Park Farm, Bradninch, Devon (1995): reducing the impact of a building on the landscape; long elevation of a multi-span dairy unit (By Stratton & Holborow)

The landscape

It is important to consider carefully the harmonisation with the existing landscape and buildings by careful choice of materials. Fencing and walling are important visually and for containment. Where earth mounding and banks are used for screening, planting should take account of local landscape and vegetation patterns, and also of existing habitats around the site. The planting should be based on local indigenous trees and shrubs (see BS 5837 and BS 4043). The siting of new agricultural buildings adjacent (but not too close) to existing woods can help to assimilate them into the landscape. Suitable woodland management is required to maintain this effect. Elsewhere judicious tree planting and external work may enhance new buildings. The aim should not be to hide a building from sight, but rather to soften a hard outline, break up a prominent silhouette, and help 'anchor' the new building to the surrounding landscape. Any new planting should reflect the vegetation type already existing in the locality, or be part of an approved Woodland Grant Scheme application.

DESIGN AND APPEARANCE

Feature and form

Planning guidelines may include information on local building design. Traditional building styles may be important in devising local design criteria for modern buildings. It will normally be appropriate to use traditional or sympathetic materials for development taking place in the setting of a listed building or in a conservation area.

Alterations and extensions should not pose the same difficulty as new buildings, but similar considerations concerning design and appearance should be taken into account. Materials similar to the original should normally be used.

Colour ranges and their applications

The colours chosen should be compatible with the rural setting, not to camouflage the building, but to allow it to relate to existing buildings. Careful choice of colour reduces the apparent scale of a large agricultural building. The roof should appear dark when seen from the middle or far distance, and should also appear darker than any vertical side claddings. In general, traditional buildings have roofs that appear darker than the walls, which has the effect of reducing their visual impact on their surroundings. The natural growth of lichen on some roofing materials reduces reflectivity and so helps the building to be visually acceptable in the landscape.

A survey of landscape colours has identified weight as being of major importance in achieving a visual relationship between a colour and its background. This has limited the colour range to be selected (see BS 5252) from weight columns 21 to 29, 37 to 39, 44 and 45; greyness has been limited to groups B, C and D; and the hues found to harmonise with the countryside were identified as 04 red, 08 yellow-red, 10 yellow, 12 green and 18 blue. The colour range has been divided into a separate range for walls and roofs, so that the weight difference achieves this effect.

Main wall areas and roofs When selecting colours, consideration should preferably be given to any local colour characteristics, and should be selected from those given in BS 5252.

Other wall areas While in the majority of new farm buildings, factory coloured cladding will constitute the major external surface area which determines the general colour appearance of the building, there are other external surfaces, such as brickwork, blockwork or stone, forming plinths and the lower areas of walls or gables, which may be site coloured for various reasons.

Door and window frames etc. All other building items such as doors, window frames, gutters and downpipes also involve colour choices. In general, narrow linear features are most suitable in a neutral colour such as white, grey or black (see BS 4576: Part 1). Window frames painted white or light colours draw attention to the openings, while those painted black or dark colours tend to draw attention to the spaces between or around them. Doors can be painted in brighter colours, selected from BS 4800, such as those in the D and E groups, provided that the contrasting hue or weight is not excessive in relation to the adjacent wall colours. The following BS 4800 colours are suggested as suitable for doors relative to wall and roof cladding colours: 08 B 29, 08 E 51, 18 B 25, 20 D 45. Factory applied colours should be matched accordingly.

TYPES OF FARM

- Mixed livestock: mostly mixed beef and sheep, with some including a small area of arable land or a modest pig/poultry enterprise.
- Dairy: where the principal or sole enterprise is dairy farming.
- Pigs/poultry: where the principal enterprise is either intensive or outdoor/free-range pigs/poultry.
- Arable with pigs/poultry: a number of large farms contain both enterprises.
- Arable: where the principal enterprise is cropping.
- Other: horticultural, mushroom etc.
- Principally non-agricultural: equestrian etc.

Building types

- general purpose agricultural buildings
- stock housing (pig, stables, sheep housing, cattle sheds, stock pens, field shelters)
- poultry houses
- storage facilities (agricultural implements and grain/hay)
- slurry and manure stores; dirty water lagoon.

General design considerations

The function of the farm building should be established and its design should draw together both functional and aesthetic requirements within the constraints of statutory legislation. Every farm building should be designed in accordance with one of the four classes as described in BS 5502 CP for design, construction and loading. Part 20 (1990) of the Code of Practice covers general design considerations and the specific recommendations in livestock, crop, and ancillary buildings series.

Part 21 discusses the selection and use of construction materials, and mentions special aspects of use which may affect the durability of materials, such as animal body pressure, kicking, chewing, routine hygiene, damage by farm vehicles, presence of aggressive atmospheres and/or corrosive chemicals, fertilizers and effluent.

Planning the building Various factors have to be considered, such as:

- Aspect: open-fronted stock buildings need to face south or south-west.
- Services: may need special provision for collection of silage effluent, provision for isolation of new stock and diseased animals and separate disposal of their waste.
- Optimum size: wide spans can make ventilation difficult in livestock buildings and in grain/potato stores, as lateral ventilation ducts are not so efficient.
- Water supply: it is important to avoid back siphonage (i.e. with sheep-dip, pesticides and other contaminants).

Access and circulation The space in and around farm buildings is important. Flow, volume and type of traffic should be organised in the most economical way, taking into consideration material handling and weights involved. For some typical turning circles, see **4,5,6**.

Allow sufficient space for ease of vehicle movement while keeping to a minimum the distances livestock have to move, to save time and reduce stress and injury to the animals.

Mechanisation The importance of eliminating wasteful manual handling of materials to increase efficiency has led to their being mechanically carried, scraped, dragged, blown, sucked or floated around the farm. It has been estimated that for every acre farmed at least 8 tonnes of material are handled every year. As mechanisation and the control of microclimate in livestock houses has increased so has the demand for electricity and the need for bulk fuel storage. Bulk delivery and storage has replaced the sack as the handling unit.

Races, crushes, treatment areas Regular weighing is required for pigs and beef cattle. Loading and unloading of animals, ramps and weigh-bridges all have to be considered.

ENERGY REQUIREMENTS

These include fossil fuels, alternative energy sources, etc., and also feed energy. In livestock enterprises, particularly of monogastric animals such as poultry and pigs, there will often be a trade-off between the use of heat energy and feedstuff. Attention should be paid to benefits and penalties that might be incurred by using one or the other. In addition, attention should be paid to the conservation of the waste heat from animals by the use of thermal insulation and control of ventilation in buildings, to reduce the consumption of either heat energy or feedstuff (see BS 5502: Parts 40, 41 and 42). Solar and ventilation heat gain may have to be considered in buildings used for crop storage at reduced temperatures.

Thermal insulation The approximate standards of thermal insulation required in buildings for different livestock housing and commodities are given in BS 5502: Parts 40 to 43, 49, 60, 61, 65, 66, 72, 73, 80, 81 and 82.

Internal environment
Natural and artificial lighting The levels of illumination both from natural and artificial sources should provide sufficient light for the efficient and safe execution of work being done by an operative in any part of that building. In the case of livestock housing, the level should be sufficient for the proper welfare of the animals and be satisfactory for inspection.

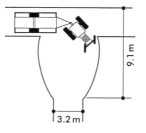

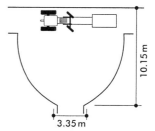

4 Reverse turn with large forage box

5 Big bale handler on front-end loader

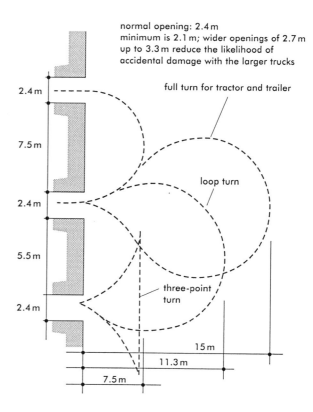

normal opening: 2.4 m
minimum is 2.1 m; wider openings of 2.7 m up to 3.3 m reduce the likelihood of accidental damage with the larger trucks

full turn for tractor and trailer

loop turn

three-point turn

6 Turning into buildings

Daylight A nominal daylight factor of 5% should be provided in all buildings except where natural light is to be completely excluded. In most totally enclosed buildings natural lighting is most economically provided by rooflights and in other cases wholly and partially by unobstructed side openings.

Note: when planning and calculating the lighting of buildings by daylight, an outdoor illumination of 5380 lux is used. (This figure is reduced inside the building by structural obstructions and the daylight factor is the percentage of external level of illumination achieved at a particular point inside a building.) Thus the illumination by natural sources from rooflighting in agricultural buildings, taking the nominal 5% daylight factor is:

$$\frac{5380 \times 5}{100} = 269 \,\text{lux}$$

lamp type	luminous efficiency (lumens/watt)	life (hours)	colour rendering	lumen range	application
filament	13	1000	perfect	200–2200 (25W–150W)	general lighting
compact fluorescent	52	5000	deluxe	200–1400	amenity lighting
mercury fluorescent	52	7000	fair	1700–110000	grain dryers; cattle sheds; large enclosed areas
metal halide	55	6000	deluxe	13600–166000	large enclosed areas; external area lighting
high-pressure sodium	96	8000	poor	3000–123000	sheep buildings; workshops; area lighting
low-pressure sodium	200+	7000	none	1800–26000	security and amenity lighting

7 Lights and their relative performance

Artificial lighting Follow recommendations of BS 8206 (see **7**); emergency lighting to BS 5266: Part 1. The choice of lighting must take into account safety, such as in grain installations where heat from lamps could ignite dust, conditions of high humidity, or corrosive conditions caused by ammonia.

Heating and ventilation
The working environment should, as far as possible, satisfy the needs of both humans and livestock/stored crops. Ventilation is important; if there is too much moisture, bacteria thrive, and poor animal performance results. Baffles can be installed to avoid draughts. Poor ventilation allied to wide temperature variations may result in loss of efficiency and an increase in the levels of both accidents and sickness.

Ventilation and infiltration
Certain buildings, particularly those used to house livestock, will require a minimum rate of ventilation at all times. To reduce the incidence of respiratory disease in cattle and sheep it is better to provide too much ventilation rather than too little, although the airflow immediately above the backs of housed stock should not exceed 1.2 m/s. The building should be orientated across the prevailing wind to avoid gable end ventilation (north–south axis), and the ventilation openings normally positioned at the ridge and below the eaves. Very wide or multi-span structures may require a 'breathing roof' with gaps or slots at intervals along the building. Ventilation openings should be designed so that even in calm conditions the stack effect created by warm air rising from the stock brings in fresh air at a lower level (e.g. 1 m depth space boarding inlet or 400 mm gap in conjunction with an open or ventilated ridge outlet). (See **8**.)

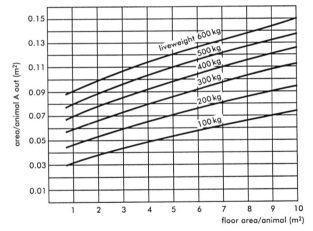

outlet area for height difference of 1 m: thus A out for 400 kg animal at 4 m²/head is 0.093 m²/head

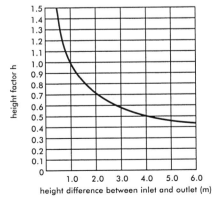

height factor: for a height difference of 3 m, height factor is 0.58; outlet area required is thus 0.093 × 0.58 = 0.054 m²/head; inlet area is twice outlet area

8 Ventilation areas for cattle buildings

In buildings which need to be kept at temperatures above the outside temperature the reduction of ventilation heat losses requires careful attention. Pressures due to external wind or internal heat sources (i.e. natural ventilation) can cause high rates of air infiltration in buildings. Such infiltration can be a major source of heat transfer and may greatly outweigh the structural heat losses or gains. Forced ventilation systems which cannot be accurately controlled or which are wind prone can also give rise to the same problem. The design of a ventilation system can also influence the internal temperature distribution. Temperatures at ceiling level which are higher than those at the occupancy height can cause excessive roof heat losses in buildings. The designer should consider the internal air distribution and internal air mixing if such heat losses are to be contained.

EXAMPLES OF TYPES OF STOCK HOUSING

CATTLE

Housing cattle in the UK does not significantly improve their growth or milk yield, but does allow more stock to be kept and managed. It reduces waste of feed, and improves the working conditions for stockmen. Accommodation for adult cattle is normally limited to dairy cattle, suckler cows and bulls. Space requirements for cattle vary with size of breed and age of animal; allowance has to be made for increase in size of growing animals during the housing period. If cattle are housed all year round the movement of machinery around the unit is of vital importance as feed has to be brought from the fields in the summer months as well as from silage clamps during the winter.

Waste handling

Housing systems can be classified by method of collecting and handling waste products, bearing in mind that each animal may produce about 57 litres of waste per day. In slatted floor systems waste passes through perforations in the floor to be collected and periodically removed from a cellar beneath (see **9**). In bedded pens straw is added daily to absorb liquid waste and the resultant farmyard manure must be removed periodically, while in cubicle systems waste is deposited into the cubicle passage, which is scraped regularly, or may be slatted (see **10**).

Slatted floor systems

These eliminate bedding and save labour. A high stocking density, twice that for bedded yards, has to be maintained to ensure sufficient animal treading action to push the waste through the slats. Totally slatted floors are normally only used for beef cattle or suckler cows. For dairy cows the use of slats is limited to cubicle passages, feeding stances and circulation areas.

Bedded yards

When cows are housed in wholly bedded yards a raised central tractor passage and feed trough allows the bedding to build up for some time and so reduce the frequency of mucking out. Much larger quantities of bedding are required in yards than in cubicles or cowsheds, and the depth and weight increase of built-up litter has to be designed for.

Slurry store This is required for waste from scraped areas in cubicle units or as an extra store for slatted units with shallow channels. The method by which the slurry or manure is transferred from the building to the store depends on the housing method: this is often done using a tractor mounted scraper at least twice a day. The distance the slurry has to be scraped should be as short as possible with the least number of turns. Various designs of automatic scrapers can also be used.

The slurry storage (and silage effluent) container must be well ventilated and preferably not below ground. Where slurry is to be disposed of by land application a minimum of four months storage is required under the Control of Pollution Regulations unless safe year-round disposal can be proven. The slurry tank depth can vary depending on whether it is linked to a lagoon (1.2 m), or tanks adjoining the building, or is to hold the slurry build-up over a complete winter period (3 m). Slurry cellars should be flat floored with draw-off points or receiving pits for vacuum tankers or pumps at gable ends or perimeter walls. Sluice gates are lifted or pushed down allowing slurry to fill the receiving pit; an overflow lip system can also be used. It may be necessary to provide access points for agitation of the slurry before emptying.

Rainwater run-off from open cattle yards becomes contaminated and thus a potential pollutant. In order to avoid rainwater dilution, and therefore minimise the amount of waste stored, it is best to roof all cow accommodation, including collecting, dispersal and handling areas, and deal with clean water separately.

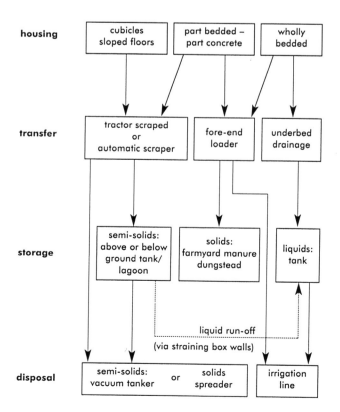

9 Slurry transfer system

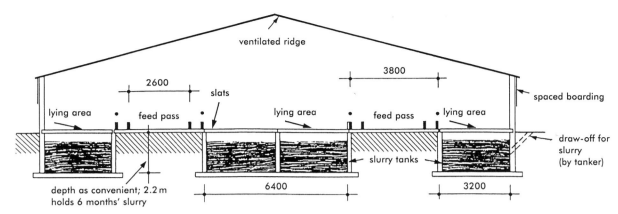

10 Slatted system

Feeding

Housing layout is affected by the feeding system; and determining factors include the type and quantity to be fed to each class of stock on the unit, the method of presenting feed to stock both in terms of machinery involved and method of distribution (i.e. manger, trough etc.), whether feed distribution and slurry/bedding clearance must take place when cows are in the feeding area and the feed storage method and capacity. There are basically three feeding systems: self-feed, easy-feed or complete diet.

Self-feed This can mean feeding silage, self-fed-feed from a storage area, manger or feed troughs. When cows have unlimited access to silage where it is stored, storage height, drainage and floor finish are important. Good cow flow and access are essential. The width of silage clamp accessible to cows has to be based on the space required for mechanical handling equipment as well as total number of stock that will feed at once.

Easy-feed system This allows more control over type and quantity fed to the animals. Yoke-type barriers control intake. The system relies on a feed barrier separating the cows from the feed, which is placed in troughs, mangers, or on the floor against the barrier

either by tractor or mechanically along a conveyor. Management is easier when the tractor passage is on the opposite side of the barrier to the cow stance, but where space is limited double-sided troughs can be used, accepting the restrictions of cow and tractor access at certain times. Feed stance and barrier design is important in preventing aggressive behaviour and injury (see **11,12**). Excessive feed wastage is avoided and a feeding space for every cow makes grouping easy and improves total management flexibility.

Complete diet feeding With complete rations fed to cows as with the easy-feed system, there is a potential reduction of feed trough length compared with that of the self-feed system, providing the trough can hold a whole day's ration and the cows have unrestricted access (see **13,14,15**). When feed is rationed or restricted, sufficient trough space must be provided for all animals to feed simultaneously. When feed is continuously available (ad lib feeding) not all animals require feed at once. Trough width per animal depends on type of feed as well as size of animal, and feeding barriers are essential to prevent feed wastage. Self-trapping feeding barriers (yokes) are designed to prevent animal having access to feed, or restrain or release selected animals.

Less space is required for cereal feed than for forage. For grain or concentrates, 75–100 mm trough width per animal; self-feed silage, 100–175 mm/animal; mechanically filled trough maintained full, 175 mm/animal.

Watering Troughs or bowls may be used. Provision to prevent cattle fouling the water drinker is required: install a floor curb 200 mm high or rail about 300 mm from drinker; or drinkers can be recessed into the wall or covered with cattle operated flaps. Water bowls or troughs are usually installed at a height of 700–1000 mm and should be located where they do not obstruct other animals feeding or moving to and from feeding area, and where spillage will not wet bedded lying areas.

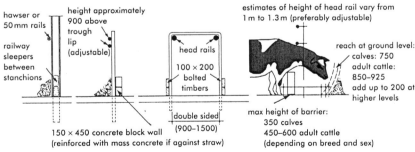

11 Feed barriers

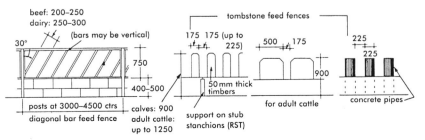

12 Feed fences

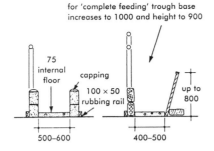

13 Single-sided feed troughs

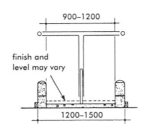

14 Double-sided feed trough

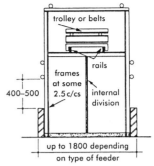

15 Automatic feeder

Types of cattle housing

The housing type varies depending on the class of animals to be accommodated.

Beef cattle housing For several reasons, cubicles are not often used for beef cattle. Keeping the cubicle bed dry is more difficult with male animals and the problem of providing the right size is accentuated by the fact that the animals are growing: the cubicle system is therefore not suitable for bull beef production. Beef cattle are normally housed in slatted, bedded or part-bedded pens. Linear plans are usual, with pens arranged either side of the feeding passages.

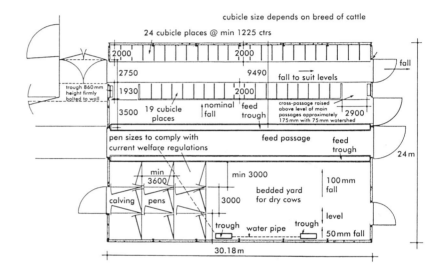

16 Cow and calf house

Suckler cow and calf housing Dairy cows have to produce a calf every year so calving pens and calf pens form part of the accommodation required. If heifer calves are reared as replacements they may have to be accommodated separately for at least 2 years (see **16**). The cows are housed in cubicles, bedded pens or slatted pens. Provision should include calf creep pens where calves can pass through gates to receive food without competition from cows and each other. There should be visual contact between cows and calves in the creep, and inspection of and good access to the creep pen is necessary for supervision, feeding, the cleaning of water bowls and mucking out in bedded pens. If cows are to calve indoors, a separate calving area is required, preferably a straw bedded pen.

Calf pens Divisions for individual pens can be constructed from demountable and adjustable rails, or boards where complete separation required (see **17**). They must be easy to clean and disinfect. An alternative to individual pens is a tethered feed fence. In group pens with bucket feeding the pen front is often equipped with a simple manual trapping yoke. An alternative to buckets is a cascade trough which

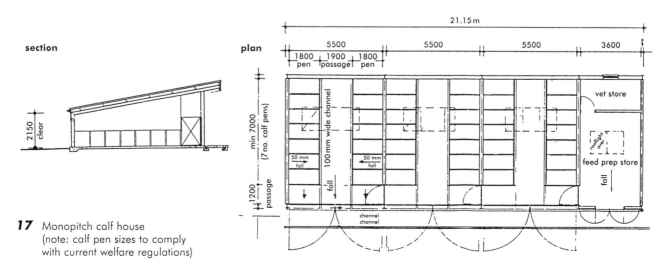

17 Monopitch calf house
(note: calf pen sizes to comply with current welfare regulations)

allows simplified pipeline delivery of milk with individual rationing. The system is suitable for larger scale operations where labour spent on feeding tasks is often reduced to a minimum. Self-trapping yokes are installed to control calves during feeding, which reduces subsequent cross-suckling. Automatic feeders mix and supply milk substitute feed to groups of 10 to 15 calves on an ad lib basis: this allow more flexible labour routines but feed consumption (and hence cost) is higher.

Bull pens Wall, gates and feeders must be of substantial construction and the feeding and watering of the bull must be carried out from outside the pen. The feeder should be provided with a strong trapping yoke to restrain the animal for routine veterinary treatment or restriction during cleaning. A 'refuge' should be installed in each corner of the pen. An unroofed exercising yard is often provided next to the bull pen.

Dairy farms

Although changes in farming practice dictating the need for new farm buildings are very rare, one such change was the move from in-byre or cowshed milking parlours in the 1960s. Essentially the milking parlour is a housed mechanical process; a building planned around a machine and in accordance with the routines it dictates. The 'tandem' parlour, in which cows stand at shoulder height to the cowman, was developed in the post-war period. This was then developed into the highly efficient herringbone parlour, reducing the distance between udders by 'angle-parking'. A refrigerated tank was developed enabling the milk producer to cool and store the milk in bulk. Refinements to dairy farms have been demanded by the requirements of the Milk and Dairies Regulations, administered by DEFRA. Certain aspects of design and management are set separately by the requirements of the Milk Marketing Board, such as turning areas and roads in association with vehicle collection.

Cubicles

The development of cow cubicles in the 1960s did not need new buildings, just alteration and/or modification. Litter was in increasingly short supply; straw was less abundant, and the cost of moving it high. Generally communal cow yards have been superseded by the cubicle system. Cows have individual stalls but freedom of movement and access to a common feeding area; a 'loose-housing system' in which cows and machines do more work, and people less (see **18**). The advent of milk quotas, together with research on cow behavioural systems, has assisted in promoting animal orientated design.

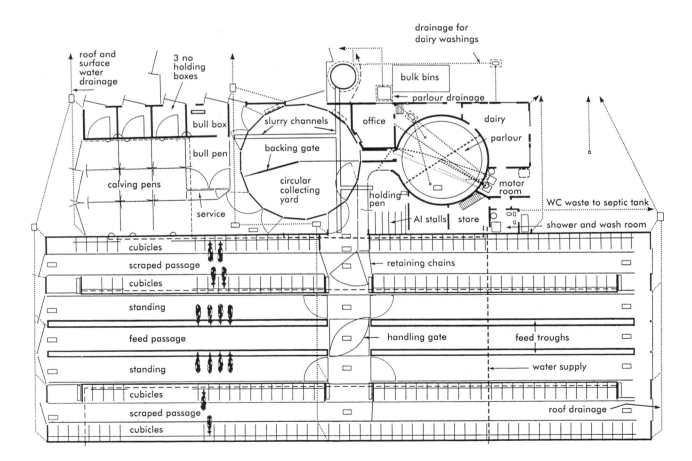

18 Dairy cubicle layout

Cubicle design   Important factors are adequate space, the provision of lunging space to assist the cow when rising, and bed comfort. In the UK, for practical and legislative reasons, a concrete bed, or equivalent material, is standard practice with small quantities of bedding and matting as appropriate. Many farmers install cubicle mats to improve cow comfort. Rubber and even water-filled mattresses are being experimented with to justify claims of higher milk yields and reduced veterinary bills.

Cubicle divisions should not hinder lying or rising movements of animals, or allow them to get trapped or entangled in the cubicle frame. The cubicle must not be so wide that the smallest animal to use it can turn round and dung in it; but it must be wide enough to allow animals to lie comfortably. Cubicles must be short enough to ensure dung falls in the passage; but cubicles too short will not be used as animals will lie over the heelstone or curb. Adjustable head or knee rails are used to reduce the effective length of the cubicle; adjustable side rails accommodate different sizes of beast.

The cubicle bed is set above the level of the passage to allow it to be scraped daily. Many types of cubicle available (e.g. free-standing mushroom divisions allow cows more headspace when using cubicles and more freedom when lying down).

Cow movement and handling   Efficient cow movement without stress or injury depends on good planning. Unexpected changes in floor level, sharp turns or projections, and dark and narrow passages must be avoided. Simple straight run layouts with wide passes, sensible gating and easy grouping can help achieve the highest standards of cow management. Gate swings and cow movement need careful planning to avoid time wastage as cows have to be shut in one area of the building while another is being cleaned.

The cubicle access passage should not be less than 2.4 m wide and should be slatted, or capable of frequent cleaning by automatic scrapers in long straight runs. Access to the parlour should be visually direct and easily cleaned. Facilities must be designed to enable one person to move cattle alone.

Recent pollution legislation   Minimum storage periods for farm waste are now required. To avoid rainwater dilution of slurry, and therefore minimise the amount of waste stored, it is best to roof all cow accommodation, including collecting, dispersal and handling areas.

Milking parlour   With at least twice-daily milking all year round, the layout of the parlour and associated facilities is critical, and should allow efficient movement. Cleanliness to food producing standards is of great importance, and daily access of a bulk milk tanker may be necessary.

Various alternatives are available, but most new installations are of the herringbone type (see **19**).

In many situations the milking parlour will be contained within the main structural frame of a new dairy complex, but designed so that it can be completely sealed off between milkings.

With such high humidity, internal finishes need to be impervious and capable of withstanding regular thorough cleaning.

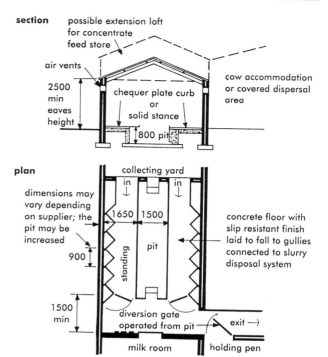

19   Herringbone milking parlour

Ancillary facilities

- Collecting yard: required to hold the maximum number of cows which may spend up to 6 hours a day in the yard so water, light, ventilation, shelter and good drainage are needed.
- Dispersal area: enables cows to be held before returning to the fields. This facilitates the separation of individual animals requiring treatment, after the routine inspection during milking, and so treatment facilities need to be adjacent to this area (see **20**).
- Foot-bath: 3 m long, position far enough away from parlour exit to prevent slow flow of cattle leaving parlour.
- Handling: calving pens, holding pens, isolation pens for veterinary treatment, artificial insemination (AI), disease diagnosis etc. should be provided. Feed should be delivered to troughs from outside pens. For dairy cows a milking line should be installed. Drainage should be separate from other animal areas.

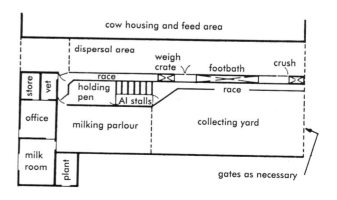

20   Dispersal area

- Funnel shaped forcing pen: leads from collecting pen to race.
- Race: (chute) catwalks should be provided on both sides of race.
- Crush: (squeeze chute) race terminated by crush to provide good access to all parts of animal. Crush should be under cover with good daylight and artificial light and provision for hosing down whole area.
- Shedder gate: should be installed after crush, wherever there is a need to sort animals for weighing, separate pregnant cows, for loading etc. Gates should be installed at the far end of all holding pens, allowing the recirculation of groups or individual animals.
- The dairy: normally attached to the milking parlour to reduce the length of pipe runs. Should be sited so that the rear of a milk tanker can be parked within 3m of the door; adequate tanker turning space must also be provided. 900mm clear space should be left all round bulk milk tank(s). Space must be provided for working and for equipment as required: washing troughs, water heater, cupboard, cleaning products etc. The internal finish of the dairy must be smooth and easily cleaned; non-slip concrete floor draining to trapped gully; roof lined on underside. The dairy must be light and well ventilated with fly-proof openings.
- Milkroom: holds the bulk tank which is sized to hold one or two day's production at peak yield. There should be no direct communication between the dairy and cow housing areas (see **21**).
- Motor room: houses vacuum pumps and motors and possibly a stand-by generator, or provision for a tractor to operate the vacuum pump in power emergencies may be required. It should be separate from the dairy.
- Office or records room: should be sited with a clear view of the parlour and the area next to the unit.
- Staff facilities: toilet, shower, and rest room.
- General chemical store.
- Central switch gear room.

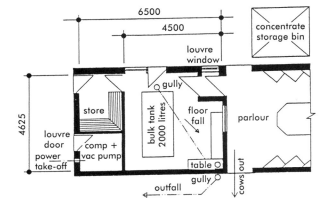

21 Milkroom layout

Feed storage

Concentrates are stored in bulk bins or a loft area above the milking parlour. Access for machinery and delivery lorries is essential. Imposed loads of stored materials and loaded vehicles in yard areas must be considered.

The Control of Pollution Regulations 1991 cover siting, design and construction of all silage and silage effluent stores.

Siting and orientation

Siting and layout should allow for future expansion or possible changes in management systems. Covered yards and cubicle houses maintain a more balanced internal environment when ridges run north–south. Open-fronted buildings should face south-east for protection against westerly winds and to admit winter morning sun. Exposed hill tops and sheltered valley bottoms should be avoided.

Dairy farm layout

The main blocks are: milking parlour complex, cow housing, slurry store, feed store, and ancillary accommodation.

The milking area is the most important. The parlour block should be positioned next to the main access point of the unit so that the collection of milk is speedy and efficient. The access road has to be designed to take a fully laden milk tanker, and to be as short as possible. The milking parlour must be easily accessible from winter cow housing and summer grazing, and cow buildings must be within easy reach of the slurry store.

Wherever possible, routes for material, stock and personnel should be kept separate with crossings avoided. Clean and dirty activities should be separated. Vehicles such as forage boxes impose design constraints such as passage widths and turning areas. Reduction of manoeuvring space can lead to increase in the time taken to perform tasks. Layout and location are important also to enable easy access and operating conditions for emergency services (see **18**).

Requirements of a good dairy layout:
- The layout must suit the ultimate size and potential of the enterprise in terms of land, livestock and management skills.
- It must be strategically sited in relation to the farm to suit grass transportation, grazing and summer milking, slurry spreading etc.
- It must integrate with the diverse elements of the enterprise associated with cow feeding, movement and handling, milk collection, waste storage and collection and ancillary accommodation in such a way as to ensure efficiency in working towards the full potential of the animals housed without imposing undue stress or an obvious health risk to those animals.
- It must have a feed system compatible with the grazing and feeding policy of the farm, with an in-built flexibility to cope with changes in that policy.
- It must suit the stages in the development of the unit towards full potential, taking into account existing buildings, capital available, herd expansion policy and continuity of existing production, if applicable.

- It must be visually and environmentally acceptable with careful attention paid to minimising the risk of pollution.
- It must meet all the relevant legislation appropriate to the farm circumstances, including all safety legislation.

PIGS

Pigs were traditionally fattened on dairy waste products but cheap grain and imported concentrates encouraged new types of pig farming requiring a new type of piggery. By the 1930s pigs were concentrated in larger numbers on fewer farms. Also, the 'Danish' house was adopted, which kept the pigs warm by conserving their body heat and thus reduced the food bill, which was the main item in their production cost.

The planning of pig units This process is based on the periods and accommodation required at various stages of production. An enterprise may specialise in one of the following stages or incorporate the whole production cycle:

- The farrowing unit – keeping sows for production and sale of weaners
- Fattening/finishing unit – taking weaners through to sale of fat pigs, usually baconers (see **22,23**).

Piglet mortality rate is a crucial factor in the economics of pig farming. Deaths are reduced significantly by the use of a specialist farrowing house, where the sow is confined to the centre of the pen to avoid crushing the piglets and heating is provided for the piglets. Farrowing sows need artificial heating, generally by infra-red lamps. Although the provision of a high level of environmental control is expensive it can ensure a much higher survival rate of piglets. For fattening houses, insulation and artificial ventilation are important to conserve the pig's natural heat. Underfloor heating or good insulation is necessary, as pigs are lying down for much of the time and they convert food into heat rather than body weight if temperatures are too low (see **24**).

Pig buildings These are required to incorporate boar pens and sow yards, which accommodate in-pig sows for 3–4 months before farrowing. A service building combines sow and boar pens with a service area. Pig production costs are kept to a minimum by the use of automated feed systems and slatted floors in conjunction with mechanised waste disposal.

Farrowing accommodation

There is a need to review the care and welfare of pigs as a result of the new legislation banning the use of sow stalls and tethering systems. A redesign and evaluation of buildings and associated space standards is required for dry sows. The criteria for design briefs must be defined and ranked using quantitative data, sympathetically balanced with general opinion regarding animal welfare. The emphasis is towards freedom of movement, and progress has already taken place with the innovation of the 'freedom farrowing crate'. Trials are being carried out to develop a system of pig units allowing a modified version of normal pig behaviour. The

'family pen' system indicates improved maternal behaviour in farrowing sows and a reduction of anomalous behaviour, such as the chewing of pen fittings and other pigs. General freedom of movement for dry sows can be achieved with straw yards, but the associated problems are unknown food allocation, animal welfare (including protection from peer group aggression), aerial integrity and appropriate space standards.

The management objective for pig farming is to produce a high-quality product from a relatively low priced unit of production, at a profit. Feed costs represent 70–80% of the total costs for producing pigs, and building costs around 10%. The pig expends energy on three main functions – maintenance, protein accretion and fat disposition – and the metabolic utilisation of gross energy will in part be influenced by the quality of housing.

Criteria for evaluating housing These will therefore include:

- thermal performance of building elements
- the design and control of the aerial environment
- space standards
- feeding systems (i.e. installation and integration of equipment)
- husbandry, including access and observations by stockmen.

Pigs regulate their behaviour in order to maintain their body temperature and a controlled thermal environment is required to optimise metabolic energy utilisation. The building, therefore, has to provide a controlled internal environment which will operate efficiently within optimal temperature ranges. The energy demands of the environment are influenced by: air temperature, mean radiant temperature, relative humidity, air velocity and conduction through body contact with floor and walls.

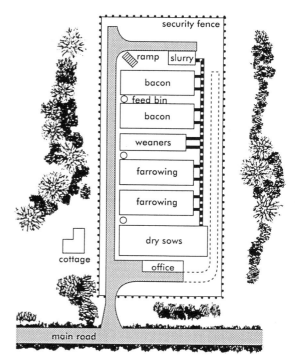

22 Pig unit layout

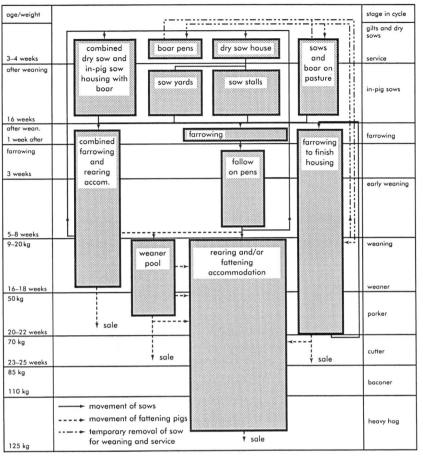

23 Pig production systems

Ventilation This is important for the well-being of pigs and working personnel. There is a need to design a maintainable environment which inhibits growth of pathogenic micro-organisms, reduces the probability of respiratory infection and so promotes pig performance and development. The Welfare of Livestock Regulations requires that all farmers with automatic ventilation systems:

- have an alarm system that will warn of system failure
- provide alternative ventilation in the event of primary failure
- have alarms and equipment tested by a competent person at least every 7 days.

Temperature and humidity are affected by pig and group size, type of food and intake, access to water, floor space and construction, and air ventilation.

typical age (days)	weight (kg)	description	trough length for 10 pigs (m)	floor space (for 10 pigs)			critical temperatures* (range given in code of recommendations for welfare of livestock – pigs) (°C)
				lying (m²)	dunging (m²)	total (m²)	
0	1.5	piglet	0.5	(litter 1.3)†			25–30
20	5	early weaner	0.5	(litter 1.75)			27–32
35	9	weaner	0.6	0.7	0.3	1.0	
65	20	weaner	1.75	1.5	0.6	2.1	21–24
115	50	porker	2.75	3.5	1.0	4.5	15–21
140	70	cutter	2.75	4.6	1.6	6.2	
160	85	baconer	3	5.5	2.0	7.5	13–18
185	110	heavy hog	4	6.7	2.3	9.0	10–15
210	140	overweight	5	8.5	3.0	11.5	
		dry sow	5	15.0	5	20	15–20
		in-pig sow	5	15.0	5	20	15–20
		boar	(500 mm)	(8 m²/boar)			

notes: †creep size: 0.8 m² to 35 days, then 1 m²
* perforated/slatted floors or solid concrete floors and low feed levels increase temperature requirements while straw bedding, high feed levels and high body weights decrease requirements

24 Space requirements and critical temperatures for pigs

Design aspects covered by BS 5502 Code of Practice (Notes on Part 42: 1990) (1) Scope (2) Definitions (3) Animal welfare considerations (4) Design and construction (5) Environment (6) Dimensions and space (7) Feeding and drinking arrangements (8) Services (9) Ancillary accommodation (10) Fire precautions (11) Safety signs and notices.

Tables are given covering: (1) recommended maximum thermal transmittance (U) value for pig building structural components; (2) environmental conditions for pigs; (3) maximum allowable gas concentrations in occupied buildings; (4) minimum floor areas for pigs loose-housed in groups; (5) minimum trough lengths for simultaneous feeding; (6) waste storage for pigs; (7) minimum areas for warm environment creeps; (8) typical dimensions of sow stalls and cubicles.

POULTRY

Development of the industry

Like pigs, poultry also benefited from the new supply of cheap concentrates. The poultry industry, based on egg production, expanded between the wars and ultimately far exceeded any other line of farm expansion. The discovery that cod-liver oil could provide sufficient vitamin D to enable the birds to survive permanently indoors without direct sunlight meant only buildings, hens and food were needed, and no farmland. Batteries of up to five tiers of cages were experimented with in the 1920s to control feather-pecking and cannibalism, and these allowed easy feeding, egg collection and recording, and manure removal, with the sale of manure as a side product. This was a major step in the intensification of the livestock husbandry. The duration, periods and extent of light are crucial to egg-laying, and the intensive battery cage system allows substantial control over the environment in general.

Deep litter system This is an alternative in an enclosed building, enabling control of light to maintain winter egg production but allowing hens free movement. Both housing systems require a closely specified environment: a temperature of 18–21°C, subdued lighting for predetermined periods, and clean air free from excessive moisture. Specialist firms produce standardised prefabricated houses, windowless, to enable light control of mechanically fed and watered flocks, with tall hoppers to receive bulk deliveries of foodstuffs.

Poultry buildings Regulations (e.g. BS 5502: Part 43: 1990) give the scope and definitions, and then cover such aspects as animal welfare considerations (e.g. avoidance of sharp projections which may injure birds), design and construction (to be sited away from other buildings as poultry buildings pose an increased fire risk – high temperatures and arid conditions), environment, dimensions and space (giving minimum headroom requirements for people but no dimensions for poultry cages). Feeding and drinking arrangements, ancillary facilities, services, fire precautions and safety signs and definitions are also covered. The Code gives tables for: (1) recommended illumination intensities for 'light' periods in poultry houses with a controlled environment; (2) daily provision of feed and water for poultry; and (3) volume of waste produced by poultry.

SHEEP

Housed sheep are still not common; sheep pass on disease when clustered together, so cleaning is important. In the early and mid-1980s there was a move towards the winter housing of sheep, in unsophisticated simple low-cost buildings, often conversions, the economics demanding a low-cost solution. It has proved difficult to identify any benefit from using anything other than the cheapest building.

STORAGE BUILDINGS

Storage is an important element of the farm processes, for machinery, feedstuffs, crops and fuel. As mechanisation and the control of microclimate in livestock houses has increased, so has the demand for electricity and the need for bulk fuel storage.

New uses can often be found for old barns: combine harvester and grain drying installations need shelter for an 11 month inactive period each year. Although a combine harvester is too big for original hay-wagon entrances, the blank end wall can be knocked out and fitted with new wooden doors while largely retaining the original appearance. Fork-lift trucks are useful for barn storage, and can utilise space up to 6 m high.

Crop storage buildings These are required to accommodate the anticipated quantity of material for the storage period required. The quality of storage (i.e. airtight, covered or open) and the rate of drying depends on the material. Temperature, moisture content and oxygen may need to be controlled, and there is a constant risk of infestation and fungal diseases. Grain is stored by retarding biological activity to a minimum. It is dried by air blown through circular bins inside a general purpose building or a purpose-built bulk grain store (see **25**). The grain drying storage plant, a 'ventilated bin', which dries grain in the building in which it is stored, replaced the barn by the 1960s as the dominant feature of arable farmsteads. Grain grown for cattle feed can be stored undried under a system using airtight silos or acid treatment.

Each crop needs either adapted or special-purpose buildings, scientifically designed for optimum conditions. For example, bulk potato stores need retaining and insulating walls, and a ventilated floor is also required for drying or conditioning crops such as grain, seeds, and onions.

The buildings also have to provide acceptable working conditions for the people loading and grading inside them.

Chemical storage The aim of recent legislation is to reduce risk of contamination of personnel and the environment by controlling the construction and day-to-day management of pesticide stores. In addition to general legislation there may also be other requirements imposed by the local authority, the fire service and the crime prevention officer. (See **26**.)

Central grain stores

Large agricultural buildings are used as collection and distribution points for the produce of several farms. The UK is a net exporter of grain and it is important that the harvest is handled and marketed to the best advantage nationally. The advantages of central grain stores for the farmers are that equipment for drying, cleaning and preparing grain may be operated at lower cost than on individual farms, that different types or qualities of grain can be assembled separately, and that they are suitably located relative to the main grain growing areas and/or docks. Such buildings also enable grain to be stored near where it is to be processed. As older on-farm stores are due for replacement, some growers may wish to use centralised storage that meets modern marketing requirements. In view of their potentially obtrusive appearance, they should be designed and located with particular care to minimise their effect on the landscape.

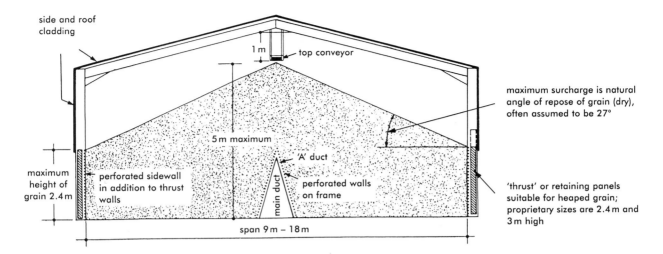

side and roof cladding

1 m

top conveyor

maximum surcharge is natural angle of repose of grain (dry), often assumed to be 27°

5 m maximum

'A' duct

maximum height of grain 2.4 m

perforated sidewall in addition to thrust walls

main duct

perforated walls on frame

'thrust' or retaining panels suitable for heaped grain; proprietary sizes are 2.4 m and 3 m high

span 9 m – 18 m

25 Bulk grain dryer

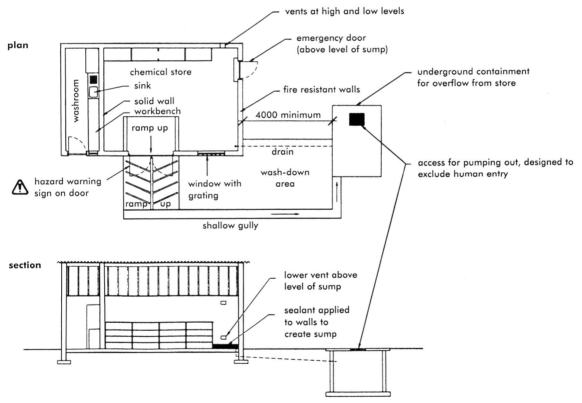

plan

vents at high and low levels

emergency door (above level of sump)

washroom

chemical store

sink

solid wall

workbench

ramp up

fire resistant walls

4000 minimum

underground containment for overflow from store

drain

wash-down area

access for pumping out, designed to exclude human entry

hazard warning sign on door

window with grating

ramp up

shallow gully

section

lower vent above level of sump

sealant applied to walls to create sump

26 Chemical store

FIRE STATIONS

The London Fire Engine Establishment was formed in 1833 and 19 fire stations were built in London during the following 30 years. Being a private service, with costs covered through insurance premiums, the stations tended to be built in the wealthier areas of central London. A publicly funded body, the Metropolitan Fire Brigade was first established in an Act of 1866, and resulted in 26 new stations being built between 1867 and 1871 (plus Mobile Street Stations, consisting of one fireman and a ladder). For the first time, dormitories were incorporated, as well as a mess room, a watch room (for firemen on duty) and washing facilities. Self-propelled, petrol-driven engines were first introduced in 1903.

Early stations in London were designed by the Metropolitan Board of Works, and later by the London County Council's Architects Department (Fire Brigade Section). While the plan form and functional requirements remained the same for many years, the elevational treatment reflected the stylistic design of the day. Many examples of the 'free gothic', neo-classical and arts and crafts styles remain in use today. Towards the end of the century, standard provision in new stations included facilities such as quarters for married staff, telephones, electric lighting, a gym and laundry.

By the end of the Second World War, many of London's fire stations had been damaged or destroyed, while others were out-moded. At first, the policy adopted was generally to renovate and improve existing stations, rather than build new ones.

Of the 114 London Fire & Civil Defence Authority fire stations (including Lambeth river station), 22 are less than 20 years old, while 26 are over 80 years old – although some stations have had a major refurbishment in the last 20 years. National standards for station design were first established in 1966 (Fire Services Building Note 1) and were further refined by the GLC in 1971: Holloway, New Malden and Kentish Town are typical examples. However, this resulted in a fairly standard two-storey design which was sometimes not considered suitable in many urban areas with much higher surrounding buildings. By the end of the 1970s, there was a move towards more individual designs (and also, for the first time, facilities for female fire-fighters). In 1986, the GLC was abolished, and fire services were transferred to a new organisation, the London Fire & Civil Defence Authority (LFCDA), composed of elected councillors seconded from the London boroughs.

Until recently, requirements have remained fairly constant, areas such as the appliance-bay, watch room and dormitories always being required. This typical layout is sometimes referred to as the 'T' plan, with the staff and support areas being at right angles to the appliance areas. Newer stations have a much wider range of facilities, such as a gymnasium and lecture/conference rooms. At Ormskirk Fire Station, Lancashire, (see *14*) a glazed display room adjacent to the main appliance-bay houses an old horse-drawn fire appliance; the overall design is in three distinct zones: appliance bays, operational support, and catering/recreation areas.

Bathgate Fire Station, Lothian, (see *16*) was strongly influenced by a re-assessment of functional requirements. The building is strategically located at the junction of a number of important trunk roads, which improves its potential response times. More radical is the radial layout, resulting from specific functional requirements to facilitate the rapid assembly of the fire crew; all activities related to fire-fighting (including dormitories) are located on the ground floor. Detail design – such as the elimination of right-angles in passageways – can also help to reduce response times.

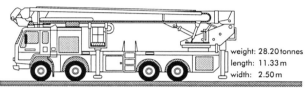

weight: 28.20 tonnes
length: 11.33 m
width: 2.50 m

aerial ladder platform

weight: 11.16 tonnes
length: 7.70 m
width: 2.32 m

pump ladder

weight: 15.30 tonnes
length: 9.32 m
width: 2.46 m

hydraulic platform

weight: 11.08 tonnes
length: 8.29 m
width: 2.50 m

fire rescue unit

weight: 5.92 tonnes
length: 7.70 m
width: 2.50 m

heavy demountable chassis

weight: 10.72 tonnes (max)
length: 7.70 m
width: 2.50 m

with bulk foam unit pod

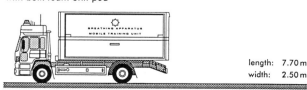

length: 7.70 m
width: 2.50 m

with mobile breathing apparatus training pod

1 Fire appliances

Risk categories The Greater London area has been divided into half-kilometre squares, each allocated a risk category from A to D. Category A is 'high risk', for instance Heathrow Airport and the West End; category D is the lowest risk areas. Where necessary, individual buildings are then further categorised (e.g. hospitals would normally be category A, even if in a lower category area).

Accommodation Owing to the adoption of the four-shift system, dormitories and flats for married men are no longer required. This has resulted in redundant space at older stations, which can sometimes be converted for suitable fire brigade use, or other uses where separate access and services can be provided.

The watch Each shift is known as a watch, and is coded red, white, blue or green. Fire engine crews are expected to be able to turn out for any call in an approximate average time of 36 seconds.

(Note: much of the detailed information that follows is based on the LFCDA brief; fire station requirements outside Greater London may differ.)

SCHEDULE OF ACCOMMODATION

The intention of the LFCDA design brief is to provide a guide and does not require rigid adherence; it is a guide to current philosophies, and it will be continually updated. The following descriptions are an indication of areas and uses generally required, but which may vary depending on requirements of specific sites.

Site planning generally

Stations are broadly divided into three groups:

Station with minimal training facilities (see **2**) Restricted site, two appliances; 945 m² minimum site area. Training facility of three floors with the ability to test equipment (particularly ladders); small yard with single hydrant and some parking space (approximately 400 m² residual area). Internal training provided by gym and lecture facilities.

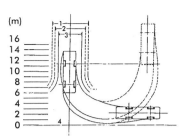

3 Turning circle of pump ladder appliance

1 bay width (no forecourt): 6.5 m
2 bay width (forecourt): 5.5 m
3 minimum door width: 4.2 m
4 centre-line of road

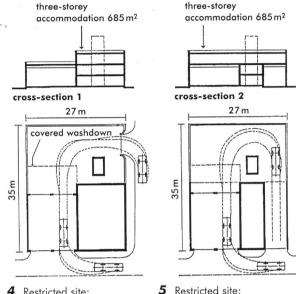

three-storey accommodation 685 m²

three-storey accommodation 685 m²

cross-section 1

cross-section 2

27 m

covered washdown

35 m

27 m

35 m

4 Restricted site: schematic arrangement (rear/side access)

5 Restricted site: schematic arrangement (front return access)

36 m

covered washdown

drill tower

two-storey accommodation (640 m²)

50 m

single storey (45 m²)

36 m

two-storey accommodation (640 m²)

50 m

single storey (45 m²)

front return access

6 Limited site: schematic arrangement (side return access)

7 Limited site: schematic arrangement (front return access)

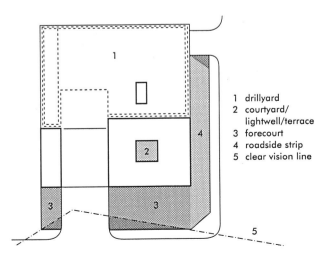

1 drillyard
2 courtyard/lightwell/terrace
3 forecourt
4 roadside strip
5 clear vision line

2 Recommended site layout

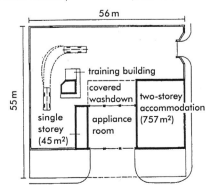

56 m

training building

covered washdown

single storey (45 m²)

appliance room

two-storey accommodation (757 m²)

55 m

8 Full site: schematic arrangement

Station with basic training facilities Limited site, two appliances; approximately 1800 m² site area. Purpose-built training facility for use with a full range of standard ladders; drillyard sufficiently large to allow testing of ladders and hoses, with single hydrant and pumping well (approximately 700 m² residual area). Internal training provided by gym and lecture facilities.

Station with full training facilities Where there is a demonstrable strategic area training need; full site, three appliances; approximately 3100 m² minimum site area. Training tower of four floors, incorporating a dry rising main and additional breathing apparatus training facilities. Drillyard (approximately 1400 m² residual area) with two hydrants, pumping well and space for comprehensive drills (e.g. water relays); large enough for turning circle of largest appliances, testing of equipment and execution of combined drills. Roof ladder training facilities, separate lecture room, larger gym, derv pump and underground tank.

Dual access sites These are preferred (i.e. secondary access is available from minor road at the side or rear).

Ingress/return Appliances should be able to navigate a clear return to the covered wash-down area.

Open external areas (see **2**) Normally divided into two parts: the forecourt, in front of appliance bays and ancillary accommodation, and the drillyard at the back of the site. The forecourt is used for direct access for appliances from the appliance bays to the roadway; the drillyard is for drills, training tests, returning appliances, and deliveries etc.

Vehicle turning circles (see **3**) Critical and often difficult to achieve (e.g. a 9 m deep forecourt is desirable to allow appliances to pull out without crossing the centre of the road).

Traffic obstructions Ideally, the site should avoid obstructions like traffic lights, access to schools or hospitals, one-way streets etc.

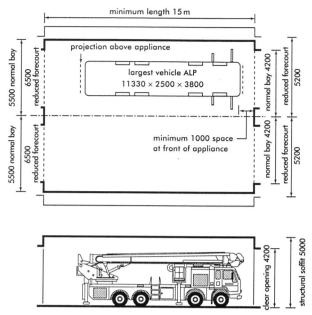

12 Appliance room layout

For planning purposes, the station is organised into five zones:
(1) Operational: essential to operational readiness and performance
(2) Training and drill
(3) Control and administration
(4) Amenity: ancillary support activities
(5) Services: engineering plant and controls
For flow diagrams, see **9**, **10**, **11**.

(1) Operational

Appliance room (see **12**) The operational base for fire appliances, allowing a 24-hour response to emergency calls. Also used for roll call/muster, equipment storage, minor vehicle repair and training in inclement weather. Minimum length 15 m.

Appliance bays 6.5 m wide (if no forecourt); doors to be 5.5 m wide by 4.2 m high to allow access for appliances.

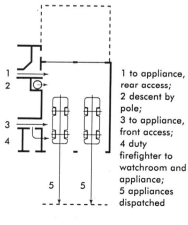

1 to appliance, rear access; 2 descent by pole; 3 to appliance, front access; 4 duty firefighter to watchroom and appliance; 5 appliances dispatched

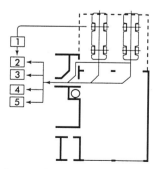

1 external rear access; 2 breathing apparatus room; 3 operational equipment wash; 4 operational equipment store; 5 lockers and washroom

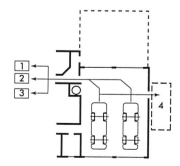

1 operational equipment store; 2 operational equipment cleaning; 3 breathing apparatus room; 4 alternative operational equipment store

Schematic arrangements:

9 Mobilisation   **10** Return   **11** Cleaning and maintenance

Breathing apparatus (often abbreviated to BA) Area for cleaning, servicing and testing of breathing apparatus and protective suits. Must be directly ventilated to open air, or have mechanical ventilation (area: 13 m²).

Covered wash-down Area for washing of vehicles under cover; possible emergency extra appliance space. Minimum length of canopy cover is to be 9 m.

Drying room Area for simultaneous drying of operational clothing (area: 10 m²).

Fire gear uniform store 30 m² (two appliances); 40 m² (three appliances). Note that on-duty personal gear is put into appliance at watch changeover.

Forecourt Deep forecourts are recommended (see **2**) to allow adequate sightlines for appliances entering or leaving the station. Minimum depth 9 m.

Fuel storage/pump Tank capacity of 5 000 l derv, to be positioned externally near boundary wall, under drillyard.

Oil/paraffin/propane store Area for general storage and maintenance. Propane gas location must be agreed with local authority.

Operational equipment and general store A subdivided storage area with separate facilities for non-mobile specials, hoses, sand and foam, work bench and general use (area: 18 m²).

Operational equipment cleaning Space is needed for storing equipment and for washing appliances, dirty uniforms, and small items of equipment (area: 8 m²).

Slide poles Means of quick vertical descent for call-out crews. Must have direct access to appliance room, and must conform to strict design criteria.

(2) Training and drill

Drillyard Vehicle return access to covered wash-down area and appliance bays. Space required for drill tower and drill/practice/instruction; also for deliveries of fuel, and for essential car parking. Volley ball is a traditional game in fire stations, and is generally played in the yard.

Drillyard wall Used for testing equipment, often involving considerable amounts of water. Structurally, it must withstand water pressure from hoses up to 40 bar. Height: 2.7 m minimum.

Drillyard pumping well Located under the drillyard, this supplies static water for use in water drills; reservoir to have capacity of 36 000 l.

Drill tower Used for training firefighters, there are two types: 'integrated' towers, within the structure of the station, and free-standing ones in the drillyard. The tower has a minimum of three drill platforms (i.e. equivalent to a building of three floors) and is triangular, square or cranked in plan. Plan for a dry riser and numerous special requirements (e.g. line cleats and dummy haulage devices).

Fire hydrant One or two hydrants to BS 750, fed from unmetered supply.

Training roof (see **13**) Area of roof for training purposes.

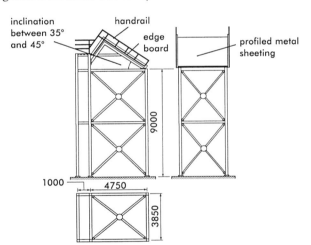

13 LFCDA training roof (when freestanding steel structure)

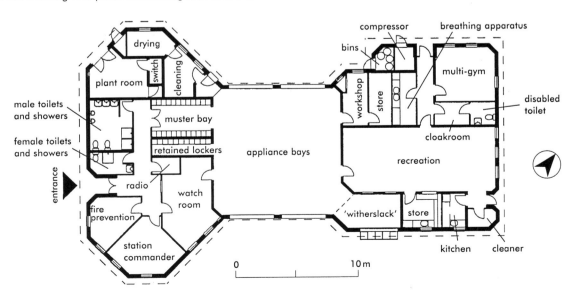

14 Ormskirk Fire Station, Lancashire (Design and procurement: Lancashire County Property Consultancy)

(3) Control and administration

Commander's locker and washroom Shared by station commander and watch commander (area: 15 m²).

Fire safety officer Room for fire prevention officer and his meetings with the public; space for one officer and four visitors (area: 10 m²).

Station commander's office Accommodation for the person in overall charge of station, with space for up to five visitors (area: 20 m²).

Station office Place for records and staff matters, and a point of contact with the public (area: 15 m²).

Stationery store Area: 1 m².

Waiting and reception Space for three visitors (area: 8 m²).

Watchroom (see **15**) Room which receives emergency calls and other messages (phone and teleprinter); also contains maps, duty rosters etc, plus a fold-down bed (area: 10 m²).

Watch commander's room Area: 15 m².

(4) Amenity

Note: changing facilities and lockers must be adequate since staff no longer live-in; female facilities are also required.

Cleaners' store Area: 6 m².

Consumables store Bulk storage (area: 2 m²).

Dining/TV Allow for general recreation, such as playing darts, cards etc. (area: 40 m², three-bay appliance; 35 m², two-bay appliance).

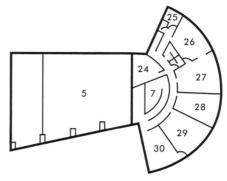

first floor

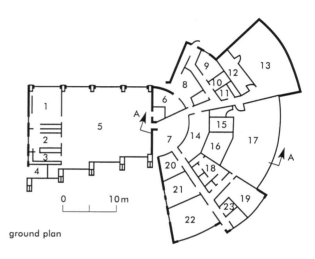

ground plan

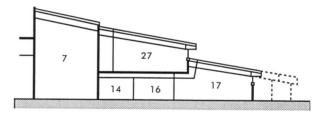

section A–A

1 workshop/garage; 2 general store; 3 breathing apparatus cleaning room; 4 breathing apparatus; 5 appliance bay; 6 drying room; 7 muster bay; 8 gear clean; 9 study; 10 switch; 11 WC (F); 12 officers' rest room; 13 firefighters' rest room; 14 fire gear room; 15 showers (M); 16 WC (M); 17 locker room; 18 showers and WC (F); 19 fitness room; 20 station store; 21 station office; 22 administration; 23 WC (disabled); 24 boiler room; 25 office; 26 kitchen; 27 dining; 28 TV room; 29 lecture room; 30 recreation

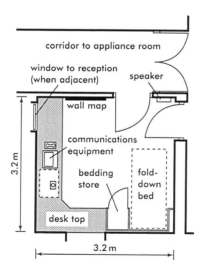

15 Watchroom (LFCDA)

16 Bathgate Fire Station, Lothian
(Arch: Lothian Regional Council, Property Services Department, now City of Edinburgh Council Architectural

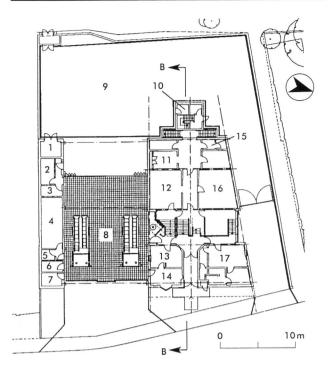

ground floor plan

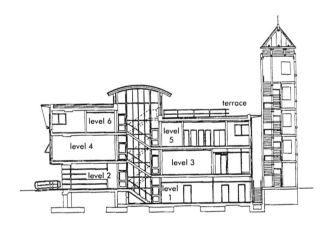

section B–B

1 emergency generator; 2 appliance wash store; 3 sand and foam store;
4 breathing apparatus; 5 hose store; 6 non-mobile and small gear store;
7 consumables store; 8 appliance bay; 9 drillyard; 10 drill tower; 11 gear
cleaning; 12 fire gear store; 13 station office; 14 watch room; 15 civilian
clothing; 16 multi-gym; 17 officer in charge

17 LFCDA Leyton Fire Station, London E10
(Arch: Rock Townsend)

Firefighters' locker and changing room Area: 81 m², three-bay appliance; 58 m², two-bay appliance.

Firefighters' WC and washroom Area: 41 m², three-bay appliance; 32 m², two-bay appliance.

Gym Area: 38 m².

Junior officers' study/quiet rooms Area: 39 m², three-bay appliance; 26 m², two-bay appliance.

Junior officers' WC and washroom Area: 39 m², three-bay appliance; 26 m², two-bay appliance.

Kitchen Area: 25 m².

Lecture and rest room Capacity for 30 people; converts to rest area for night watch: 12, three-bay appliance, or 9, two-bay appliance. Area (depending on circulation routes): 75 m² for three-bay appliance; 45 m² for two-bay appliance.

Lecture store Area: 10 m².

Quiet study Should include a library etc.; secondary use is to receive members of the public. Area: 15 m².

(5) Services
Boiler room Area: 15 m².

Communications Area: 5 m².

Electrical intake Area: 3 m².

Gas meter Area: 1 m².

Refuse chamber Area: approximately 4.5 m².

Standby generator In case of power failure (area: 12 m²).

Water meter No fixed area requirement.

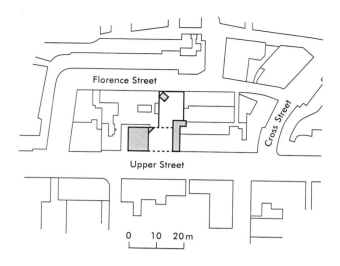

location plan

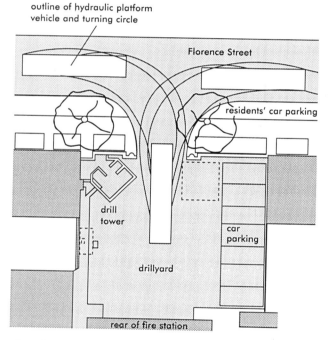

outline of hydraulic platform
vehicle and turning circle

Florence Street

residents' car parking

drill
tower

car
parking

drillyard

rear of fire station

plan of drillyard

18 LFCDA Islington Fire Station, London
(Arch: LFCDA Architect's Dept)

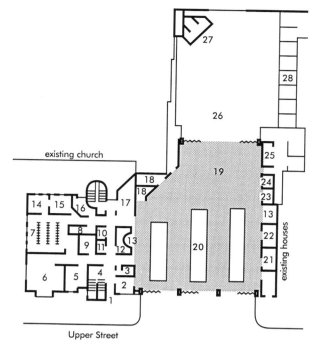

existing church

Upper Street

ground floor plan

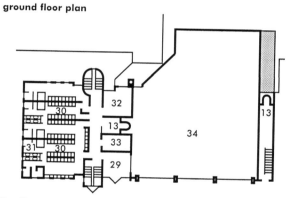

first floor plan

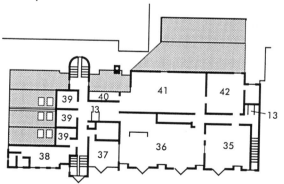

second floor plan

1	entrance	12	BA room
2	watch room	13	pole
3	store	14	drying room
4	reception	15	gear clean room
5	fire prevention office	16	cleaners
6	breathing apparatus room	17	boiler room
7	fire gear store	18	electrical services
8	consumables store	19	appliance wash area
9	stationery store	20	appliance bays
10	civilian clothes store	21	maintenance and non-
11	laundry store		mobile specials store

22	sand/foam store	33	officer's locker room
23	hose store	34	appliance bay
24	appliance wash store		(upper level)
25	refuse	35	kitchen
26	drillyard	36	dining and TV room
27	drill tower	37	station commander
28	car parking	38	junior officers' lockers
29	officer in charge	39	junior officers
30	lockers	40	equipment store
31	WC	41	lecture room
32	station officer	42	gym

HALLS OF RESIDENCE AND HOSTELS

University and college accommodation for students; hostels for the homeless, and foyers. See also Youth Hostels section.

HALLS OF RESIDENCE

Traditionally, halls of residence have been provided for most first year university students, being considered an important part of university life. In the older universities, halls have often been designed in quadrangles (see **1**), and rooms could be spacious, particularly at Oxford and Cambridge where they were very much associated with college life. After the first year, students have usually been allowed to find their own accommodation, although some places in halls have always been reserved for a few second and third year students wishing to remain.

However, the great growth in student numbers after the Robbins Report of 1963 resulted in many students having to find their own accommodation, as places in halls were very limited. This problem has become particularly acute with the second great expansion in student numbers in the 1990s, resulting in many of the newest universities only being able to provide accommodation for students coming from outside the UK. It is therefore important to ensure that such accommodation has regard for moral or religious requirements that may not have been considered important when designing for UK students (e.g. separate eating facilities or diets, and segregation of male and female students).

Halls of residence are expensive buildings, and although some accommodation is still being provided in the traditional way, finance and space constraints continue to increase. Rental charges to students may absorb much or all of their funds; university and college administrators are well aware of this and have to maximise use of this accommodation by letting it out to conference delegates and the like when the students are away. The layouts must therefore cater for more discerning users as well as basic provision for students, which can result in conflicting demands. For instance, conference delegates usually require rooms with showers and all meals to be provided; students are usually happy with communal washing facilities and self-catering kitchens.

In traditional halls, several hundred students are accommodated in single rooms with shared washing and sanitary facilities, a kitchenette, and a central refectory and communal facilities. Nowadays, however, smaller groupings of six to eight students (often with self-catering facilities) are considered more satisfactory (see **14**). Twelve or more do not form a cohesive group: a shared kitchen, with dining room used for other activities, could lead to problems, and smaller groups of up to four students can be satisfactory, but need to be self-selected.

Current trends are to provide a range of accommodation suitable for all categories; many students prefer small independent units sharing some variety of accommodation to more expensive full-board halls. Independent housing or hostel units favoured by final year and postgraduate students can be in purpose-built groups, located in the urban community or converted houses (see **18,19**).

Single students generally need accommodation for 30–36 weeks a year; research students and married couples usually for 50–52 weeks. Accommodation may also need to cater for children (e.g. by providing outside play space) and be placed near shopping, social services and other amenities.

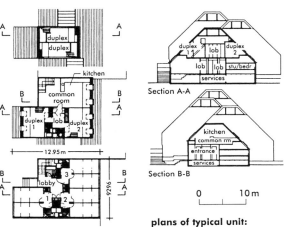

plans of typical unit:
second, first and ground floor

three pairs of study/bedrooms with separate lobbies

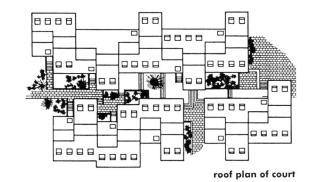

roof plan of court

Student residence, Guildford, Surrey
(Arch: Robert Maguire & Keith Murray)

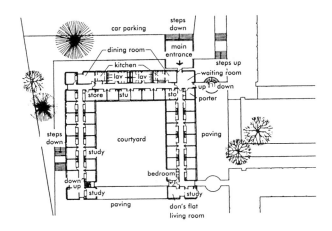

Halls of residence, Southampton University: typical floor plan
(Arch: J S Bonnington Partnership)

1 Typical types of student accommodation

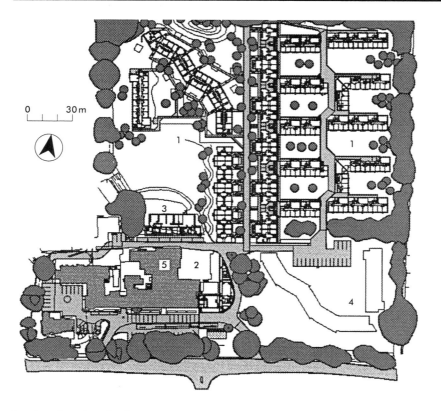

1 student village; 2 ancillary facilities (student union, bar, shop etc.); 3 nursery; 4 proposed phase II student housing; 5 former West Downs School, undergoing conversion to provide student accommodation, conference facilities and centre for performing arts

2 West Downs Student Village, King Alfred's College, Winchester: site plan (Arch: Feilden Clegg Bradley Architects)

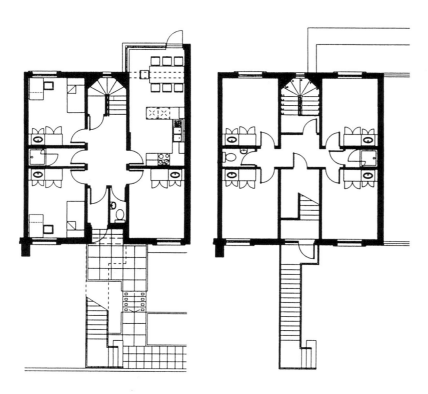

3 Plan of a typical seven-person maisonette

Funding arrangements Universities wishing to encourage foreign students realise that they have to provide halls, and have developed a variety of funding methods. Some of the older universities, particularly Oxford and Cambridge, are able to fund halls from their own resources. Other universities have in the past often been able to take advantage of government grants or loans, but this is now increasingly difficult. Open market loans (or sometimes loans or grants from benefactors) are often the only route. This can be supplemented by letting for conferences, educational courses and holiday visitors. Accommodation provided therefore depends on the uses the building can be put to, and on any annual income obtained.

Design standards There are no national standards and requirements vary considerably, depending on the client (university, college, local authority, health trust etc.). Hostels on the other hand are defined under the 1985 Housing Act (see p. 105).

The overall layout will be determined by the room type (see plan types, **4–12**) and the dining and communal facilities. There may also be a room or flat for a lecturer, in order to provide assistance and supervision.

Conference use This requires a minimum of a washbasin, and preferably a shower, in each room, with good nearby car parking, lecture, seminar and dining rooms. Alternative accommodation is necessary for the few students in residence during vacations/conferences, and storage for possessions is needed.

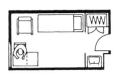

4 Single study/bedroom with washbasin: 10 m²

5 Single study/bedroom: longer plan gives more economical use of space

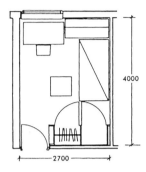

6 Single study/bedroom without washbasin

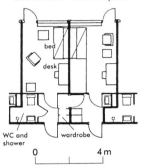

7 Unit for two students (shared WC and shower)

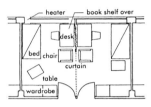

8 Double study/bedroom

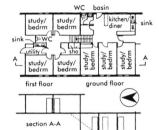

9 Typical staircase access

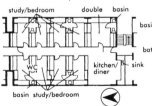

10 Typical composite access (corridor access similar but continuous between staircase): note position of kitchen/dining area and shared washroom/toilet

11 Corridor access around service core (e = lift)

12 Composite access

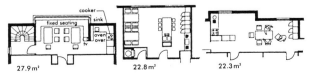

13 Typical amenity area

ACCOMMODATION REQUIREMENTS

Plan types The traditional layout (see **4–12**) includes: single rooms, study bedrooms along a corridor, rooms for two/three/four people, sets of rooms (often served from a single stair, but now rare). Now more popular are: flatlets, not fully self-contained (see **3**), self-contained shared flats (for two or more people), self-contained flats (possibly sharing some communal facilities, such as a common room, laundry etc.). Two or three people sharing a kitchen and bathroom is often referred to as a cluster. Above three floors, lifts are required.

Areas For one-bed/study space, 9–15 m²; two-bed/study space, 13–19 m²; self-catering unit, total area 16–20 m². Areas may be slightly reduced in family flats to allow more room for amenity space. A shower and WC, if included within individual rooms, will increase the area by approximately 2.5 m². Some rooms should be larger to provide for entertaining and meetings. A variety of layouts is important to avoid an institutional atmosphere. Married student accommodation should comply with normal housing space standards: some students will have families. All accommodation should be suitable for people with disabilities, but the proportion required for full wheelchair access should be agreed in the brief.

Furnishings Rooms should have bed/divan, desk and chair, chest of drawers, wardrobe or shelves and hanging space for clothes, open adjustable shelving and pin board, easy chair, small table, bedside table, mirror, bin, room light and desk/bed lamp, socket outlets, room heater, and curtains/blinds. If computers are to be used, additional desk area and socket outlets will probably be needed. If a washbasin is included provide a towel rail, mirror, cupboard or shelf and shaver point.

Background heating is generally provided, supplemented by a room heater controlled by the occupant. Ensure good sound insulation (note that banging of doors can cause considerable annoyance, and is often the result of fitting cheap door closers to fire-resisting doors, or poorly maintained ironmongery). Good local lighting is needed for close study work at desks.

Sanitary provision Provide one WC per five students; one bath/five students, or one shower/ten students (preferably 50% baths); one washbasin/ three students if not provided in the rooms. For conference delegates etc., a higher level of provision is required.

Amenity space For dining kitchens, where not intended for full meal service with utility space, allow 1.2–1.6 m²/student. With full meal service allow 1.7–2.0 m²/student (or less for more than six students).

Where halls are close to other university buildings and communal services, the dining kitchen may be the only shared social space. Cooking and dining areas should be separated, with the dining room located where all students pass it. (For refectories, see Restaurants and Catering Facilities.)

New accommodation is more likely to be self-catering. Self-catering equipment should include: cooker, fridge, freezer and microwave, single or double bowl double-drainer sink, a 2.0–3.0 m worktop with cupboards under and over (include individual food lockers), refuse storage with capacity for 1 day's use. Laundries: provide a sink and coin-operated equipment for washing, drying and ironing for each group of rooms. Ensure good ventilation, and suitable location to avoid disturbance to others (smell, flooding and especially noise can be a problem, particularly if used during the night; flexible mountings to machines and additional sound protection may be needed).

Further accommodation may be required for: coffee bar/shop, ante-room/coffee lounge, place for debates and society meetings, television, music practice, WC for visitors.

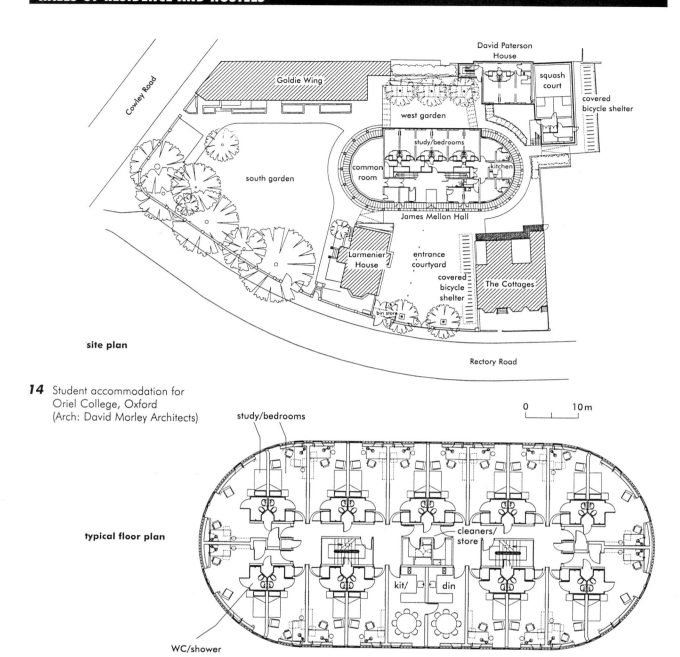

site plan

14 Student accommodation for
Oriel College, Oxford
(Arch: David Morley Architects)

typical floor plan

Offices/administration Large halls away from
campus need some office accommodation (areas are
approximate): warden/supervisor* 20 m², secretary/
archives 20 m², management committee room 30 m²,
housekeeper* 9 m², cleaner's changing room* 9 m²,
porter* (next to entrance) 9 m², students' union
20 m².
(*Also needed when the hall of residence is on
campus.)

Staff Design to suit single, married and family
categories. Separate accommodation in houses or
flats may be more economical. Approximate areas:
warden, 67–93 m²; single academic staff and
housekeeper, each 56–67 m²; single supervisory
staff 46–56 m²; single domestic staff as for
students.

Storage Allow baggage storage of 0.3 m²/student.
Provide adequate central storage for household and
cleaning equipment, linen, and furniture; and, on each
floor, storage for cleaners and equipment, with sink and
water supply (a laundry chute may also be required).
Refuse stores will be sized according to student
numbers and frequency of collection; ensure they are
suitably located and easy to maintain and clean.

Circulation areas and ducts Allow for 2.0–
5.7 m²/student. Ensure passages are wide enough for
trolleys and people carrying suitcases and trunks.
Provide an entrance hall, supervised by the porter,
with space for notices, telephone kiosks and milk
and mail delivery. A public announcement system
may be required. A security-entrance system may
also be required (especially in urban areas).

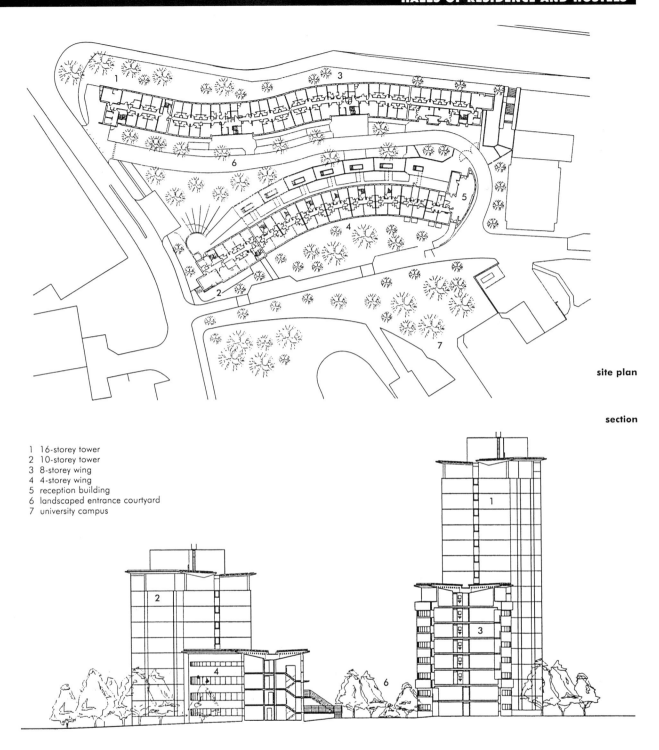

site plan

section

1 16-storey tower
2 10-storey tower
3 8-storey wing
4 4-storey wing
5 reception building
6 landscaped entrance courtyard
7 university campus

15 Lakeside Residences, Aston University, West Midlands
(Arch: Feilden Clegg Bradley Architects)

Finishes All materials should be durable, hard and need little maintenance.

Fire regulations These are complex. Under the Building Regulations Part B (table D1), halls of residence and hostels are normally classed as 'residential (other)'; a fire certificate may also be required if the premises are used for conferences etc. Hostels, but not halls of residence, are normally considered to be 'houses in multiple occupation', and further regulations apply (see below).

Car parking/cycles A minimum ratio for cars is one space/three students; space is also needed for motorbikes and bicycles, preferably with secure storage or in easily supervised areas. For conference use, a much higher provision is required (one car space/delegate), particularly if the campus is away from town centre or public transport.

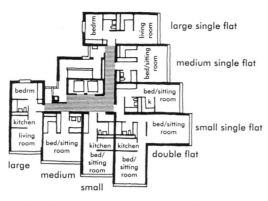

16 Housing for single people, Leicester: typical floor plan (Arch: DoE)

17 Variant of part of **16**, which provides large shared flat for four people instead of large, medium and small single flats

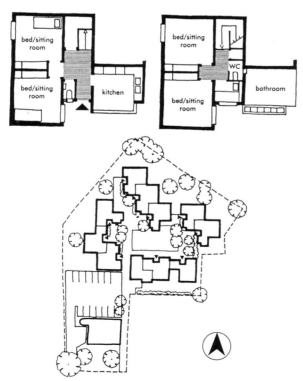

18 Bed-sitting accommodation with kitchen common room in small four-person houses: note WC separate from bathroom (Arch: Manning Clamp & Partners)

HOSTEL AND SHARED ACCOMMODATION

In many ways, accommodation is similar to halls of residence. Traditionally, hostel accommodation was provided for the destitute or peripatetic (e.g. Salvation Army hostels in the poorest urban areas, seamen's hostels in ports). Social and economic changes since World War II have resulted in many of these traditional hostels closing completely; many were also considered too institutional and lacking in modern facilities. However, the growth in homelessness in the 1980s and 1990s has led to the realisation that much greater provision was required. Many of the young, single homeless do not wish to fit into the traditional provision of local authority housing, and they tend to congregate in the centres of the large urban areas where housing provision is often already quite inadequate. Many of these people also require help and counselling – for problems such as disruptive family background, drug or alcohol abuse – and these hostels are often linked with counselling centres.

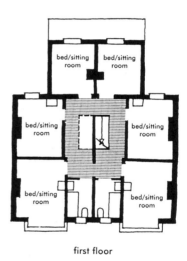

first floor

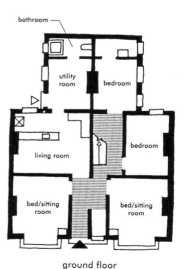

ground floor

19 Two Victorian terraced houses adapted for sharing (Arch: York University Design Unit)

Definitions and standards

The 1987 Planning Use Classes Order groups hotels and hostels in class C1; however, if personal care and treatment is involved, the development will be considered as class C2 (residential institutions). If not more than six people live together as a single household (and who do not consider themselves to be a family), the development can come under class C3 (dwellinghouses).

The 1985 Housing Act defines hostels in a different way, as:

- residential accommodation otherwise than in separate and self-contained sets of premises, and
- either board or facilities for the preparation of food, or both.

The Act also defines houses in multiple occupation (HMOs) as 'a house which is occupied by persons who do not form a single household', and this normally includes hostels. A 'single household' is open to different interpretations, but it seems to be accepted that a single household does NOT exist when kitchen and dining activities are not undertaken together or are carried out on a business scale. If a HMO exists, the local authority Environmental Health Officer should be consulted as additional recommendations, particularly concerning means of escape in case of fire, may be applicable.

Under the 1996 Housing Act, local authority registration schemes for HMOs were strengthened, and 'fitness works notices' and fire precautions (as opposed to means of escape) were introduced.

DoE Circular 12/92 This gives guidance on standards of fitness when local authorities require work to be carried out. These are very broadly based:

- Each 'unit of accommodation' should have adequate kitchen facilities within the unit, or shared facilities on the same floor.
- Dining facilities should not be more than one floor from the kitchen.
- Shared facilities should be a minimum of a sink, full-size cooker and worktops per three small households, or in a house occupied on a shared basis by a maximum of five (e.g. students).
- Storage: 0.13 m³ fridge space/person
                   0.30 m³ dry goods storage/person
- Each unit (or up to five people) should have a WC, washbasin, bath or shower; if outside the unit, the facilities should be on the same floor up to a maximum of 30 m away, or not more than one floor away.
- There are general recommendations on health and safety, and ventilation.
- To clarify the position relating to means of escape in case of fire, it is stated that work complying with the Building Regulations will normally be satisfactory for the 1985 Housing Act/HMO provisions.

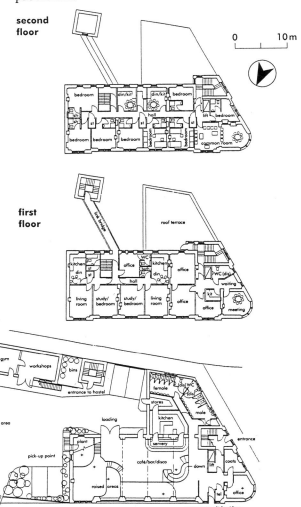

20 'New to London', hostel in converted vicarage, Marylebone, central London: hostel provides short-term accommodation for young homeless people, in seven double rooms plus single room for warden
(Arch: Triforum)

21 The Firehouse, Paisley, Renfrewshire: an existing fire station converted to hostel accommodation (note provision of other facilities, e.g. café and disco, gym and workshops)
(Arch: AADD Partnership Ltd)

FOYERS

Foyers offer accommodation for disadvantaged young people between 16 and 25 years old (particularly the homeless and jobless), and also provide training and social space for residents and other young local people (see **22,23**). The average stay is between 6 and 18 months and rents are low. Residents have to participate in job-seeking and counselling; training will also be offered, to tie in with the government's 'work culture' policy, and self-sufficiency is encouraged. The government is aiming to provide a foyer hostel in every town with a population greater than 40 000 (around 100 were operating at the end of the 1990s, with over 400 being the eventual aim).

Some foyers also incorporate lettable space (planning class B1 – office/light industrial use) to generate extra revenue, which will allow alternative use if the hostel does not succeed, and hopefully also provide an opportunity for work experience for those in the hostel. Commercial operations could include: restaurants, shops, sports facilities, nurseries, medical surgeries, information centres, and business start-up facilities. Private sector involvement is encouraged, particularly for initiating and funding schemes.

Funding Financial support can be from central or local government, housing associations, voluntary sector or private organisations. Requirements and standards therefore vary widely.

Location To help overcome feelings of isolation, schemes should be located in areas with shops and other communal facilities, and good public transport.

Accommodation Provision is straightforward (see also halls of residence layouts, **4–12**) and three layouts are used:
- Bedroom, with all other facilities shared (recommended areas: single 6.5 m² minimum; double 10.2 m² minimum).
- 'Clusters', where two or three people share a kitchen and bathroom.
- Self-contained, including bedroom, kitchen and bathroom.

Double rooms may be required, not only for reasons of economy, but to ease the transition from hostel to more individual living. Communal living is encouraged by the provision of large kitchens and lounge areas. It is important to clarify whether cooking is permitted in rooms or not. Washing should generally be discouraged in rooms – adequate laundry and drying facilities must be provided.

Sanitary facilities One WC, washbasin and bath/shower are required for each cluster or self-contained unit, or up to five people. If five people share a WC it should normally be separate from the bathroom. A WC and washbasin should not be further away than one floor or 30 m horizontally. If there are washbasins in the rooms, other sanitary facilities should not be more than one floor away.

Kitchen A communal canteen is often provided: commercial cooking facilities are therefore required (see Restaurants section). Kitchenette facilities may

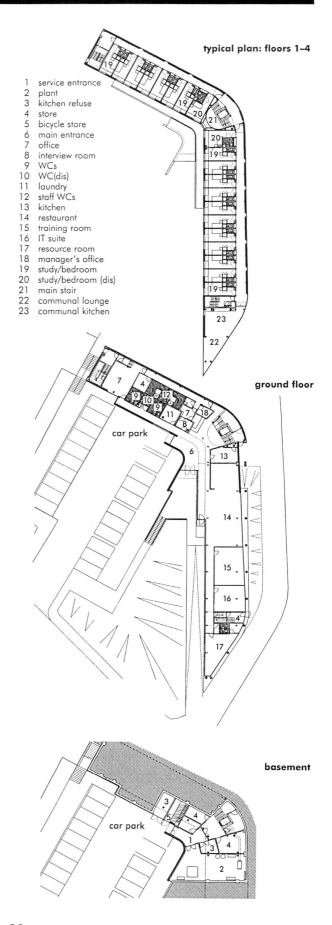

1 service entrance
2 plant
3 kitchen refuse
4 store
5 bicycle store
6 main entrance
7 office
8 interview room
9 WCs
10 WC(dis)
11 laundry
12 staff WCs
13 kitchen
14 restaurant
15 training room
16 IT suite
17 resource room
18 manager's office
19 study/bedroom
20 study/bedroom (dis)
21 main stair
22 communal lounge
23 communal kitchen

22 Focus Foyer, Birmingham
(Arch: Ian Simpson Architects)

be provided for individual use. Alternatively, if self-catering facilities are provided, provision will be as in halls of residence (see earlier pages).

Communal areas, storage, circulation The requirements are similar to halls of residence.

Car parking/cycles Provision for car parking should be discussed with the local authority. In theory, little or none is required, but some staff provision may be necessary; also allow for possible future increase. Secure cycle storage should be provided.

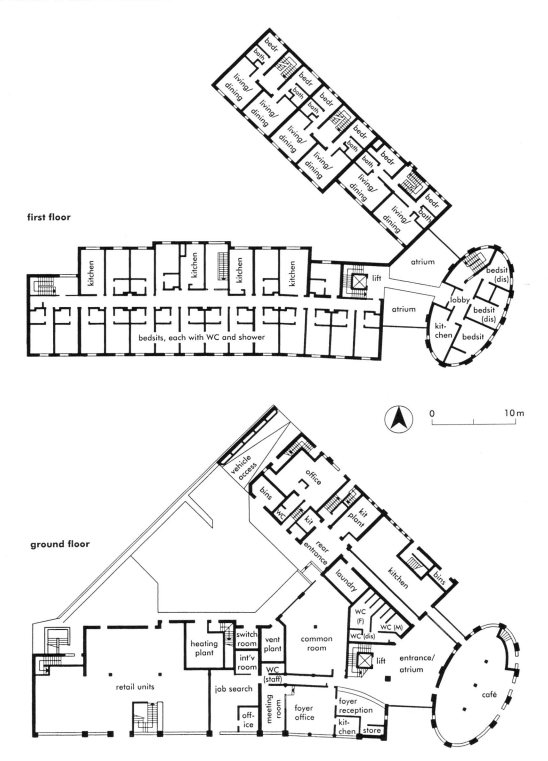

23 Tyneside Foyer, Newcastle upon Tyne
(Arch: Ian Derby Partnerships)

HEALTH SERVICE BUILDINGS

Roger Dixon, Howard Goodman and Tony Noakes

See also Laboratories section

SECTION CONTENTS

1 Older adult acute unit (mental health), Highcroft Hospital, Birmingham
(Arch: MAAP)

INTRODUCTION

Building types and recent history

Health services require a wide range of buildings of very different sizes and types. The basic components of the total health building estate and the means by which they are procured vary from country to country. Everywhere the balance is shifting away from in-patient care, with consequent changes in the location and content of new buildings, and increasing modification of existing buildings to serve new needs.

In 1948, Britain's new National Health Service (NHS) inherited two main kinds of 'acute hospital' – the local authority infirmaries that incorporated former workhouses and voluntary hospitals, some of which had a medical teaching role and associated medical schools. There were also fever hospitals, tuberculosis sanatoria and small local cottage hospitals, as well as clinics that were operated by local authorities. General medical practitioners (GPs) were mainly sole operators and owners of their own premises.

A few major hospital developments were started in the 1950s, but it was the Bonham Carter Report which led to the 1962 Hospital Building Plan that consolidated the concept of the 'district general hospital' (DGH), typically serving a population of 200 000 to 250 000. Some of these were on new sites, and many of them amalgamated the functions of former infirmaries and voluntary hospitals. Cottage hospitals tended to disappear, but some re-emerged as 'community hospitals' in the 1970s; some of these were associated with health centres combining general medical practice and health authorities' preventive medicine services. Hospitals for a single speciality, such as maternity, ophthalmic and orthopaedic, tended to be incorporated into DGHs. Some private hospitals exist outside the NHS, but most are quite small and provide mainly elective surgical services.

In Britain, specialist physicians and surgeons are mostly salaried employees of the Hospital Trusts. In the USA they are mainly independent practitioners and their consulting facilities are usually in specialised office buildings where they have extensive diagnostic equipment. This means that American hospitals do not need the large out-patient departments that characterise British hospitals. Eastern European polyclinics have something in common with these American so-called 'medical arts buildings'.

Traditionally, long-stay hospitals provided for the infirm elderly and those with mental illness or learning disabilities. The large remote asylums that housed the majority of these patients are being phased out in most developed countries. In Britain, from the 1950s, they began to be replaced by psychiatric departments of between 50 and 120 beds in DGHs. Smaller units, some free-standing, are becoming more common as part of a move towards providing 'Care in the Community' services, thus obviating the need for hospitalisation. However, some special units for longer stay patients, or those with needs of greater security, are still required. Learning disability is seen as a social rather than a medical matter, and is provided for mainly by educational, social and housing services. Long-term care of frail elderly people requiring more than domiciliary nursing and support care, including those with problems of senility, is generally in nursing homes provided mainly in the private and voluntary sectors.

Future trends

Changes in healthcare are having a greater and more radical effect on major hospitals than on the smaller healthcare buildings, which are generally simpler and more adaptable. Costs of healthcare everywhere are rising at a greater rate than inflation. An ageing population not only means a relatively higher percentage of people living in an age bracket with a higher incidence of illness, but also a smaller percentage of the population earning the money from which, by taxation or otherwise, care must be funded. Added to this is the ability of medical science to cure or treat conditions that were previously untreatable, which has increased public expectations.

The consequence of these factors is a rationing of services – either mainly by the ability to pay directly for services, as, for example, in the USA, or by more indirect means such as national health service funding limitations, as in the UK, thus limiting the type and amount of service available. Hospitals have been forced to seek every available way of economising, with as little deleterious effect as possible on their patients. Reduced length of stay is generally welcome, provided that domiciliary nursing and support services are adequate; the same applies to day surgery. Minimal access therapy (MAT) techniques such as laparoscopic (keyhole) surgery and new forms of anaesthesia have enabled a large proportion of elective surgery to be carried out on a day basis. This proportion is currently about 70% in the UK, and still rising.

District general hospitals in the UK provide general medical, surgical and maternity services; in addition, most provide some specialist services (e.g. ophthalmology, ENT). When the National Health Service was more centrally planned and coordinated, these services could be allocated to DGHs in such a way that a balance could be maintained between these hospitals. The NHS reforms of the early 1990s

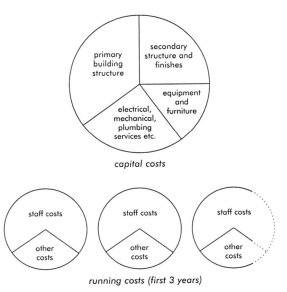

capital costs

running costs (first 3 years)

2 Capital versus running costs

with the establishment of Hospital Trusts and a competing market have tended to destabilise this tradition. Medical specialisation is growing, as is the range and cost of diagnostic and treatment equipment. The form which rationing is taking here is a concentration of the super-specialists and high-technology equipment in the larger hospitals. These tend to gain prestige and become more attractive places for junior doctors, nurses and others to seek work, thus depleting the less specialised hospitals.

In the USA and other countries where much hospital care is privately funded and provided, rising running costs and reduced length of stay have led to mergers and to the closures of many hospitals. The same kinds of pressures are evident world-wide. The key to ensuring good and accessible treatment for all kinds of illness depends on high-quality services not only in the acute hospital but also closer at hand for those functions that do not need to be on the acute hospital site.

In the provision of healthcare facilities it is important to be conscious of life-cycle costing and the relationship between the initial capital costs of providing the built facility and the ongoing running costs. Typically, the running costs will exceed the capital costs within 2 or 3 years of operation (see **2**). Clearly, one of the aims of design should be to reduce the running costs.

Another major factor that will influence future trends in the way public healthcare services and facilities are provided and operated in the UK in the future is the introduction of public–private partnerships in the NHS. There are various models of partnership but, typically, once a health service need that requires a new facility has been approved by the Health Service, the private sector will be invited to tender for a contract to finance, design and build the facility and subsequently operate it over a number of years (typically around 30) with the non-clinical services being provided by the private contractor and clinical services by the Health Trust. The assessment of tenders has to include a comparison with publicly financed alternatives.

Future strategies

A number of different strategies have been proposed to address the delivery of healthcare to meet changing needs and circumstances. These are not generally mutually exclusive.

One strategy involves the provision of an enhanced and larger acute hospital serving a population of between 1/2 and 3/4 million, with a major accident and emergency (A&E) department. That is twice the population served by current mainstream UK acute hospitals. (In the interests of clarity, the term 'major acute hospital' will be used in this text for this enhanced facility.) Peripheral to this major acute hospital, but organisationally integrated and linked to it by the latest information and communications technology, would be a series of 'locality hospitals', each serving a population of about 100 000. The major acute hospital would take all or most of the patients brought in by ambulance. Most of the self-referrals would be to a minor accident unit at the locality hospitals. Triage at the latter, and close communication with the major acute hospital, would be needed to ensure immediate transfer to that hospital of any patient whose condition proved to be more severe than first appeared to be the case. However, for most patients, emergency care would be provided closer at hand than at the current typical acute hospital serving 1/4 million people.

In this model (see **3**) the locality hospitals would also provide most out-patient clinics, a day surgery unit, maternity services (except where difficulties are predicted), a rehabilitation department and a small number of medical beds. The major acute hospitals would provide all the other functions of a traditional DGH, with enhanced opportunities for teaching and research.

This particular alternative model is not a new idea but it illustrates how changes in the economic climate, in health service organisation and in medical, information and communications technology produce both pressures and possibilities that may combine to generate practical solutions in response to changing circumstances.

Another strategy involves the development of specialist centres addressing a particular group of healthcare needs and located either on existing hospital sites or as 'stand-alone' units. The aim of these centres is to better manage the diagnosis and treatment of elective cases by separating them from the unpredictable emergency cases and thus increase throughput and reduce waiting lists. Recent examples of these are 'ambulatory care and diagnostic services' centres (ACADs) and 'diagnostic and treatment centres' (DTCs). ACADs typically provide a diagnostic service backed-up by treatment for booked patients who may also use associated hotel facilities (see **4**). Because

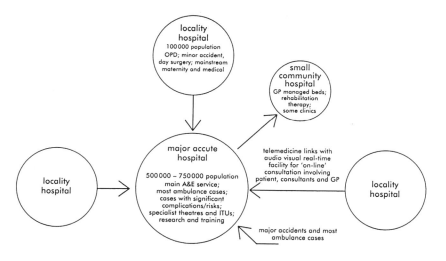

3 Future strategy option: major acute hospital

they do not handle the unpredictable emergency cases they are able to deal efficiently with the booked elective cases, where the patient is able to move around the centre for consultation, diagnosis and treatment in one visit. The DTCs also only deal with elective cases and typically will deal with mainstream procedures that may involve in-patient stays such as hip and knee replacements. These units are in their infancy and issues over precisely what services should be included, where they should be sited and how independently they are best used and managed are still subject to debate.

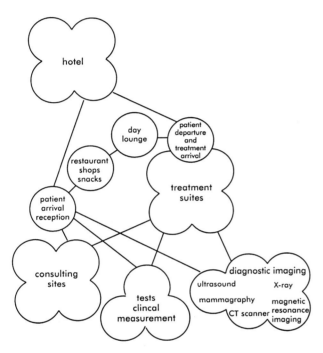

4 Ambulatory care and diagnostic centre (ACAD): functional clusters

THE ACUTE HOSPITAL

The differences between the traditional general hospital and the larger more centralised major acute hospitals described in 'Future strategies' above are of scale rather than of kind. The latter will tend to have more beds, and will have a greater proportion of high-technology elements – e.g. more specialised operating theatres and 'intensive therapy units' (ITUs). Both, however, comprise a large number of functions; the following sections are generally relevant to both.

A major hospital shares several characteristics with universities and airports. All these building types are complexes of diverse functions, with a high level of technical complexity, and frequent and unpredictable functional changes. All tend to resemble villages or small towns rather than single buildings. All must be designed for future growth and change; this means that accommodation for new functions must be easy to provide by physical extension, internal conversion or the introduction of new technology. The high level of adaptability needed requires the easy ability to modify building services, as well as spaces. The aesthetic implications are different from those that apply to a building of more finite form.

In the 19th century, 70% or more of a hospital's accommodation would consist of wards. The introduction of anaesthetics led to the increased provision of operating theatres. Then, as more complex methods of diagnosis and treatment were developed, X-ray, pathology, pharmacy and rehabilitation departments came to occupy increasing amounts of space. These supported not only the in-patients, but also the out-patient and accident and emergency departments. Service departments included supplies, disposal, catering, sterilising, and boiler house. Workshops were needed for building trades, as well as for electrical, mechanical and biomedical engineering services. Administration, health records, mortuary, staff residences and dining rooms are further components of the hospital 'village', of which wards, or in-patient accommodation can now occupy less than 25%.

The means by which this diverse range of accommodation is physically linked for the circulation of people and things are usually referred to as hospital streets (see **5**). The size and complexity of hospitals can be daunting to staff and visitors, and can be overwhelming to ill and anxious patients. Simplicity of access to and between the areas generating most traffic is essential. Although fire-risks in acute hospitals (except in a few areas like stores and kitchens) are low the means of escape criteria are stringent. This is because of the high proportion of people who are unfamiliar with the detailed building layout and include the bed-bound, sick and those with disabilities. It is good advice that 'the way in should also generally be the way out': in other words, evacuation will be most effective if it is by well-known and well-used routes.

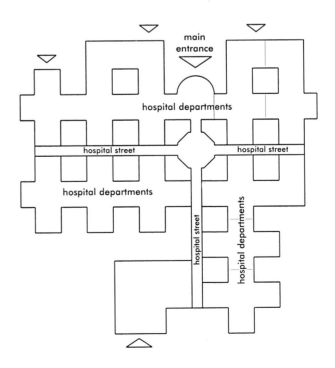

5 Hospital streets and departments: typical main circulation configuration

High or low?

Acute hospitals will inevitably occupy more than one level, so vertical circulation is another crucial element. It raises the controversial issue of how tall hospitals can sensibly be built. The designs of the 1940s mineworker hospitals in the USA were very influential: driven by logistics of materials handling, Gordon Friesen devised a plan form which consisted typically of a basement of supply and service functions, diagnostic and treatment facilities on the ground floor, and a tower of wards, all connected with ingenious lift and conveyor systems. These were, however, quite small hospitals. When this constructional form was expanded for large hospitals they became very tall, often inhuman in scale, and inflexible; as the in-patient content diminished, these ward floors were generally hard to convert to other uses. The taller the building, the more inherently expensive, especially as the proportion of floor space occupied by stairs, lifts and shafts increases with height, as does the need for total artificial ventilation. Lately, the lifts in some tall hospitals have proved inadequate to cope with the greater volume of vertical travel caused by shorter and more intensive in-patient stays.

Against this background, the issue of 'high- or low-rise' was addressed in the 1960s in the UK when the Health Ministry launched an extensive national hospital building programme. Already there were hospital planners opting for low-rise solutions. At Greenwich in south-east London, a major redevelopment project provided a 'test bed' for a number of innovative ideas in hospital planning and design that would inform those charged with implementing the national programme. The Greenwich Hospital was a deep-planned, air-conditioned, 800 bed scheme on a 3 hectare existing urban hospital site. It had a maximum of four storeys and was planned as a model for the replacement of urban hospitals, well located for the communities served, on small existing sites. Subsequently, the hospital building programme led to a greater demand for hospitals on rural or suburban sites. These could be somewhat more spread out, of two or three floors with ample courtyards providing daylight and natural ventilation. From the Greenwich Hospital onwards, the norm in the UK has been a fairly compact low-rise form. (See **6**.)

Because of their location, these hospitals required more car-parking, and much bigger sites, thus establishing a vicious circle: these sites tended to be further out of town, and so increased travel distances to them and generated more car use as the out-of-town location made them less accessible on foot or by public transport. This seriously disadvantaged the elderly and people with disabilities, and their visitors, who are less likely to have access to cars. These locations also encouraged rather than discouraged the use of cars and building on greenfield sites so are no longer compatible with current national UK energy, environmental or land-use policies.

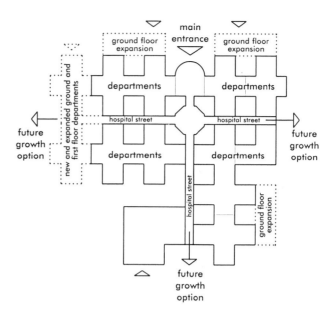

6 Planning for future growth and change

Built form

The typical British hospital since the 1970s has been fairly compact but of low rise. Horizontal contiguity of functionally related departments has been a guiding principle. That is, functionally related departments should if possible be close to, and on the same level as each other. This avoids time wastage, especially when moving supplies, equipment, and patients on trolleys and in wheelchairs.

The horizontal layout also takes account of fire safety and evacuation procedures. The principle of progressive horizontal evacuation of in-patients is generally applied where patients are moved away from the fire to adjacent accommodation within a different fire protected compartment, and so on, with final evacuation down escape stairs to outside the building being a 'last resort'.

There is also evidence that social and professional interaction between staff works better where they are on the same floor level, as long as they are not too far apart. The post-Greenwich, 'best-buy' hospitals and the subsequent 'Harness' and 'Nucleus' hospital planning systems characterised this approach, which also provided a built form that could cope with expansion and change in response to future demands (see **6**).

Examples of departmental clusters that benefit from horizontal contiguity on the same floor are illustrated in **7**.

Some departmental inter-relationships require less proximity than formerly owing to developments in information technology and materials handling techniques. Computer linkages have reduced much of the need for moving information between hospital departments. Pneumatic tube systems can be effective in moving pathology specimens and pharmaceutical items; robotic trolleys are used widely in American hospitals for moving supplies; and there is now remote monitoring of blood pressure and other bodily functions.

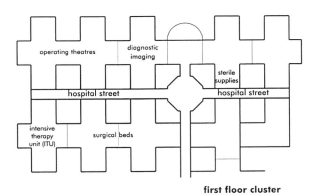

first floor cluster

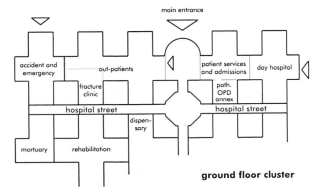

ground floor cluster

7 Typical functional clusters of hospital departments

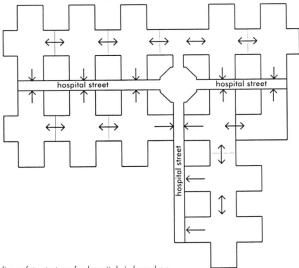

fire safety strategy for hospitals is based on:
(1) progressive horizontal evacuation moving away from fire to adjacent fire compartments (usually coterminous with hospital department interfaces) and each compartment linked back to 'fire safe' main circulation hospital street
(2) limiting maximum travel distances between fire compartments and to final fire exits; this limits the distance any part of the upper floor accommodation can be from the hospital street (ground floor accommodation with direct escape to outside does not have the same restrictions)
(3) limiting the area of each fire compartment
(4) avoiding putting 'life risk' departments, such as in-patient beds, over high fire/load risk departments
(for full guidance, see NHS 'Firecode' suite of documents)

8 Fire safety strategy

'Telemedicine' has had the effect of reducing hospital activity. For example, high-quality images can be electronically transmitted from one hospital to another or to a GP's consulting room in real-time mode, thus enabling consultations and patient examinations to take place between general practitioners, consultants and patient, and often obviating the need for a hospital visit. An increasing number of service functions can now be provided off the hospital site: more food is prepared off-site, as are sterile supplies; an increasing number of pathology investigations can be carried out in free-standing laboratories serving several hospitals. (See **9**.)

The whole hospital: development control plans
While some complete hospitals are built on new sites, in a great many cases the architect is asked to undertake the phased redevelopment of an existing hospital, or to add one or more departments to it. A hospital resembles a living organism, in that what is done to one part of it is likely to have direct or indirect effects on other parts. The strategic plan indicating the options for future growth and change is commonly called a 'development control plan' (DCP). Important elements in the DCP include the pattern of movement of people or materials, as well as an energy strategy and the organisation of mechanical and electrical services.

For a new hospital, the DCP will include a description of the hospital's logistics and circulation routes, as well as indicating where and how subsequent extensions can be made. Where an existing hospital is being redeveloped, it is essential first to chart the present circulation and service routes. Such a traffic survey is needed to ensure that the way the hospital functions is fully understood, and to minimise disruption to its activities during the construction process. Even relatively small additions to a hospital can have unforeseen repercussions on the existing functions.

When any work on an existing hospital is envisaged, the DCP should be examined, and modified if necessary. If there is no DCP, one should be produced. The DCP will also have the effect of preventing, or at least limiting, the spread of temporary huts and short-life buildings that have turned many hospital sites into expensive chaos. The temptation to solve an urgent overcrowding problem,

general practitioner with patient in GP local practice premises

audio-visual link giving real-time communication between GPs, consultants and clinical technicians, including options for multi-person case conferencing between scattered locations; promoting patient participation in the GP–consultant conferencing and encouraging 'one-stop' approach for increased throughput

specialist consultant in acute hospital with 'telemedicine' audio-visual link

9 Telemedicine: links between general practice and acute hospital

to make use of unexpected capital finance, or to accommodate a new item of medical technology by means of a proprietary tack-on can be overwhelming. Such mostly single-storey additions are often unsightly, and frequently poor long-term value for money: if single storey they are poor in terms of land-use and are liable to be in the way of larger properly planned extensions. As the proverb says: 'There is nothing so permanent as a temporary measure that works.'

The DCP should identify in advance those departments where growth and change is likely. There are a number of ways of planning to accommodate growth and change. One of the most fundamental is by planning horizontal buildings rather than vertical. With a generally horizontal building a simple way of providing for growth is by locating those departments likely to grow at ground level with space to build outwards along with the ability to provide, if necessary, for easy emergency exits direct to the outside rather than having to plan within the travel distance restrictions of internal escape routes (see **8**). Accommodation of small-scale growth and change might be anticipated by the careful choice of juxtaposed departments such that one might expand into the other which in turn might expand outwards on the periphery of the hospital. A department on one level that needs to expand may be provided in a permanent two- (or more) storey extension that makes space for other, temporary or long-term uses, on the floors above or below.

Interdepartmental relationships

The DCP must seek to optimise the location of various departments and functions of the hospital. Examples of clusters of functionally related departments are illustrated previously under 'Built form'. A basic problem is that a number of these that together require a disproportionately large floor area usually need to be on the ground floor, and as near as possible to the main entrance. Of these the most important is the 'out-patient department' (OPD), as it is the destination of the largest volume of patients, many of whom are elderly or have disabilities. If the site and its access routes permit, it may be best for the hospital's main entrance to have the OPD opening straight off it. Then the out-patients will be able to share the associated facilities (enquiry point, shops, cafés) with visitors, staff and other users, and thus to improve the economy and viability of these facilities. This main entrance needs particular attention to detailed design, artworks and planting in order to give a reassuring first impression.

The pharmacy, or at least a dispensary, should be nearby, as should a phlebotomy base (or pathology laboratory annex) for taking blood samples (and possibly for some laboratory work on them). Diagnostic imaging should also be easily accessible from the OPD. Rehabilitation services (physiotherapy, occupational and speech and language therapy) need to be nearby with an easily accessible ground level location, but these services, together with day hospitals for elderly people, could, on a sloping site, be on another level with its own ground level entrance from outside. However, from the point of view of security and economy of manning, the fewer entrances the hospital has, the better. Against this must be set the

need for reducing patients' travel within the hospital. Such journeys as they have to make should be well signposted, pleasantly eventful and attractive.

If the operating theatre floor is on the same floor as, and reasonably close to, enough beds to accommodate all surgical patients, it will function more efficiently than if lift journeys, and the likely consequent delays, are involved. There are practical but not overwhelming arguments for a top-floor location on account of the extensive air conditioning and other engineering services. Surgical patients will also need to visit other locations, particularly diagnostic imaging. If a diagnostic imaging service is to be provided on the same level as the surgical beds, it may need to be divided to also serve the OPD and A&E department on the ground level, thus leading to duplication of equipment and staff – an arrangement that may be justified as part of a 'patient-focused' regime, as outlined under the next heading.

Other key interdepartmental relationships are referred to in the descriptions of hospital departments.

Some relationships will inevitably be sub-optimal, particularly where an existing hospital is being redeveloped. In new hospitals, that are planned to be built in phases, consideration needs to be given to the possibility of a project being halted before all the phases are complete. In some cases there may be a significant degree of uncertainty about the prospect of the later phases being funded or completed within a reasonable time scale. The bitter experience of cancelled later phases and resultant inefficient and incomplete hospitals was one of the driving forces behind the Nucleus hospital concept. As the name implies the functional content and design strategy was aimed at achieving a complete and efficient hospital in a fully funded single phase but with the potential for planned expansion with later phases. This 'fail safe' or 'risk management' approach to phasing may influence the degree of sub-optimal departmental relationships that will be acceptable even in the case of a new hospital.

Patient-focused care (PFC)

This concept originated in the USA as a reaction to the impersonal nature of much hospital care: the carers, and their equipment, should, where possible, come to the patients rather than the patients trailing from one hospital department to another. Along with it went the idea of multi-skilling such that nurses, for example, should develop competence in basic physiotherapy and radiography: this has significant effects on professional training.

The effect of PFC on hospital design is fragmentation rather than centralisation of some departments. This may mean that some radiology functions may be associated more closely with wards or groups of wards than all in one place (usually near the OPD and AED) in the hospital. The balance must be struck between the traditional arguments of economies of scale and the convenience and more holistic care of patents. PFC will often mean that several of the clinical services (e.g. those for women and children) may take the form of a pavilion with its own entrance and organisation, albeit linked to other parts of the hospital.

Engineering services

Apart from the provision of medical gases, the services in hospitals are different from those of most other building types in their extent rather than in their fundamental nature. Control of infection requires special attention to air filtration, especially in operating theatres where orthopaedic and other very sensitive procedures are carried out.

A critical factor is that large areas of hospitals are in use continually every day and every night. This means that, where possible, access to services for maintenance and repair should be provided without disturbance to clinical activities. One means of achieving this is to include 'interstitial engineering spaces' or 'walk-in' service sub-floors between each functional floor (see **10**). This approach was pioneered at Greenwich, and has been refined in the building system developed for the USA Veterans' Administration. It is only justifiable for compact low-rise buildings in which all or most areas require artificial ventilation.

The engineering services design philosophy needs to be compatible with the overall aims of functionality, economy and flexibility for the healthcare facility. The positioning and sizing of major plant and the engineering services/energy distribution strategy will need to take account of the immediate and future needs of the facility, including risk factors and programming regarding any future development proposals. Key factors are the choice of economic service runs in life-cycle costing terms and the need to provide vertical service routes that occur within the main circulation areas rather than within departments. A 'building and engineering management system' (BEMS) is an essential component of the engineering installation.

The requirement for 24-hour use, and the presence of energy dependent life-support systems creates a need for a high level of emergency electrical generation. It follows from this that major hospitals are potential candidates for combined heat and power systems.

Standardisation

The design requirements of any one acute hospital are not in most respects unique. Due to the amount of technical complexity there have been strong pressures to standardise the design of parts of hospitals, or even in a few cases, of whole hospitals. Any architects' office with wide experience in this field will tend to develop standard solutions to frequently encountered problems, or at least modify and update previous designs in the light of experience. All too often where hospitals or parts of hospitals have been too precisely tailored to the demands of particular users, their successors have found these designs a hindrance to their different method of working. The production of standard designs can warrant more functional research than could be justified for a one-off design. However, the greatest danger is the use of a standard solution in an unimaginative or bureaucratic manner, when it is inappropriate to the needs of the project, or when it has become functionally obsolete.

Whole hospital standardisation was adopted successfully for the 'best-buy hospitals' built in the 1970s. These required a generally flat, fairly square greenfield site. These site limitations led to the development of the Nucleus system, consisting of standard departmental plans, based on standard operational policies and designed so that they can be assembled to form unique hospitals with differing functional content requirements and site constraints. The Nucleus system provided a complete and efficient hospital in a single phase with the capability of growth and change in response to needs and funding. The system could also provide for phased development of existing sites. A large number of Nucleus hospitals were built: the Maidstone General Hospital in Kent, the St Mary's Hospital on the Isle of Wight and the additions to the North Staffordshire City General Hospital were among the most successful hospital projects of the 1980s. The Nucleus programme was controversial, but provided an excellent case-study of the merits and snags of relative levels of standardisation.

Nucleus was a planning tool, not a total package. Total standardisation may sometimes be appropriate for small buildings, but the most common and effective application of standardisation is to room layouts and assemblies of furniture and equipment, such as the NHS Estates Activity Data Base. Another successful approach is in the USA Veterans' Administration building system, which is a dimensional strategy for the coordination of structural, mechanical and electrical engineering services design.

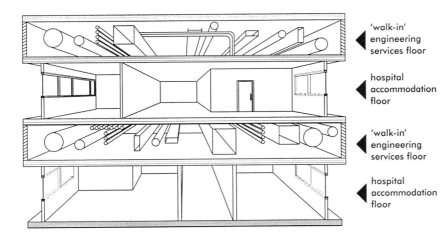

'walk-in' engineering services floor

hospital accommodation floor

'walk-in' engineering services floor

hospital accommodation floor

10 Interstitial engineering services floors

Property assessment

A major hospital is a very valuable piece of real estate, to which principles of sound estate management must be applied. Assessment of existing buildings is often a first stage in the rebuilding or ongoing development of a hospital. Each department or element may be graded on a number of criteria such as:

- condition of building fabric and engineering services
- energy efficiency
- safety (fire etc.)
- functional suitability (i.e. how well it is suited to its current function or a specific alternative function)
- whether it is being used to its full capacity (or indeed in excess of its capacity)
- whether it is appropriately located, with respect to functionally related departments, and is easily accessible, including to people with disabilities
- the cost of bringing sub-standard buildings up to a satisfactory condition and of any upgrading, or necessary alterations
- the potential life of the upgraded facility.

The results of such an assessment should indicate which buildings should be retained, whether for their present function or for some other purpose, and which are no longer worth retaining.

HOSPITAL DEPARTMENTS

The following descriptions of departments and functions of hospitals do not claim to be comprehensive. They aim to point out some key functional and design issues, and in these illustrations to give some useful examples. Changes in medicine and the organisation of healthcare occur more frequently and unpredictably than the updating of books. Architects should refer to other sources of design guidance, such as the latest editions of *Health Building Notes*, *Hospital Technical Memorandum* and other design guidance documents from NHS Estates and other sources.

In-patient beds

Even though in-patient bed areas are diminishing as a proportion of the whole hospital's accommodation, they are still generally the largest single element, and the one that causes most public interest. The experience of being an in-patient is in itself traumatic and disturbing, quite apart from the anxieties about outcome, and the pain and disability associated with the illness and its treatment. In the past 50 years, there have been enormous social changes, and thus increased expectations among those destined for a stay in hospital.

The single-sex, 30-bed open wards espoused by Florence Nightingale provided excellent observation together with natural lighting and ventilation. For over 100 years, they were every Briton's idea of the hospital experience. Even with curtains replacing the original screens, they lacked privacy, but for many, a mutually supportive camaraderie was a real benefit. In recent times some hard-pressed managers started using these as mixed-sex wards, which was acceptable to some, but anathema to others.

From the 1950s, an alternative pattern emerged, one that eventually became the norm. Typically this consisted of wards with four six-bed rooms and four single-bed rooms. Since then the number of singles has been growing.

The optimum size of 'ward', defined as the territory of a sister or charge nurse, has been much debated. For a long time, 25–30 beds was the preferred range, but as the average length of stay shortened, consequently leaving an increasing proportion of patients who are more ill and disabled, a smaller number is now preferred.

There are many advantages to having an en suite WC (preferably with shower) to each single or multi-bed room. In view of the uncertainty of future demand for single rooms, some schemes now opt for four-bed rooms instead of six-bed – quieter for patients, and also more easily convertible into two single rooms at a later date.

When wards have been very precisely designed for a particular number of beds (the extreme situation being the ward floor in a vertical hospital), they can be very hard to adapt or alter. There is a case for planning bed areas in continuous bands, so that different sized groupings may be made, as required by changing medical needs and patterns of management. This works best if linen, drugs and other supplies are held as close as possible to the patient's bed. In America, Gordon Friesen devised 'nurse-servers' or pass-through cupboards for this purpose. The Millennium Hospital plan (see **11**) shows mobile storage, in the form of trolleys, close to the single and multi-bed areas. These are within a band of ancillary rooms whose function and layout can be varied according to the needs of particular specialities (e.g. the requirements of orthopaedic wards for storage of large equipment). These rooms can also be easily altered to meet subsequent changes in function.

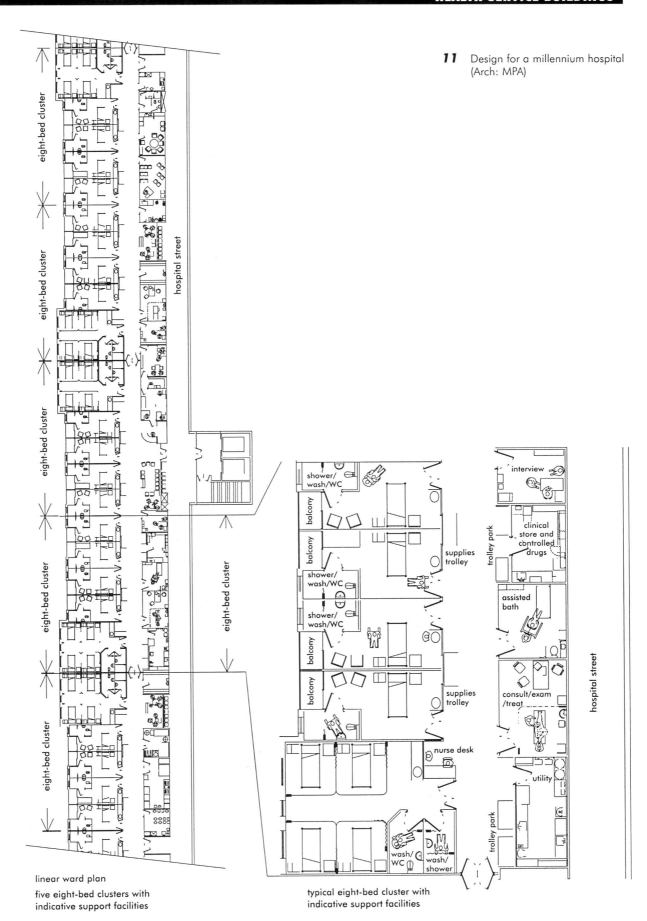

11 Design for a millennium hospital
(Arch: MPA)

hospital street

eight-bed cluster

eight-bed cluster

eight-bed cluster

eight-bed cluster

eight-bed cluster

eight-bed cluster

linear ward plan

five eight-bed clusters with
indicative support facilities

shower/
wash/WC

balcony

balcony

shower/
wash/WC

shower/
wash/WC

balcony

balcony

supplies
trolley

supplies
trolley

nurse desk

wash/
WC

wash/
shower

typical eight-bed cluster with
indicative support facilities

interview

trolley park

clinical
store and
controlled
drugs

assisted
bath

hospital street

consult/exam
/treat

utility

trolley park

Intensive therapy, coronary care and high-dependency units

(These are generally referred to as ITU, CCU and HDU.)

The term intensive therapy unit (rather than intensive care unit) denotes active medical as well as nursing treatment of those most at risk, either following surgery, accidents or sudden illness such as strokes. The unit should be in close proximity to operating theatres and easily accessible from the accident and emergency department and in-patient areas generally (see **12**). A large space is required for each bed, together with extensive services that need to be located in such a way as to allow free movement of staff around the bed and to the patient. Various methods have been used for providing these services and experience suggests they are best delivered from overhead by swivelled pendant or service beam, which leave the floor around the bed free for staff and resuscitation and other equipment. Patients are continuously monitored and the monitoring apparatus must be in clear view. Supplies may be held on mobile shelf units of sufficient height between adjacent beds to provide some screening and privacy between beds while also allowing standing staff to have a generally clear view around the multi-bed area. A few beds should be in single rooms to cater for cases needing isolation because of infection or other reasons (see **13, 14**).

A CCU can be similarly equipped for patients who have suffered coronaries. In very large hospitals, the CCU may be associated with the cardiac medical and surgical departments. In other hospitals, the ITU and CCU may be a twinned unit sharing facilities such as supplies, on-call accommodation for staff and waiting areas for relatives. More single rooms are required for CCU beds in order to provide a minimum stress environment.

An HDU may be a part of a group of ordinary wards with higher staffing for the most ill patients, or may be associated with the ITU, providing a 'step-down' from that unit. However, with shorter stay, most hospital in-patients can be regarded as high-dependency, and thus distinction is becoming less valid.

ITUs and CCUs are accepted as suitable for male and female patients being located in the same bed area. However, in hospitals with a large children's unit, a separate children's ITU is desirable and justified.

There is evidence that patients who appear to be semi-conscious may be aware of their surroundings and remember their experiences to a surprising degree. In spite of the inevitable omnipresence of high-technology equipment, much care must be given to making the environment as pleasant as possible. Good external views are important in order to help ease patient anxiety and relieve the stressful nature of the work for the staff.

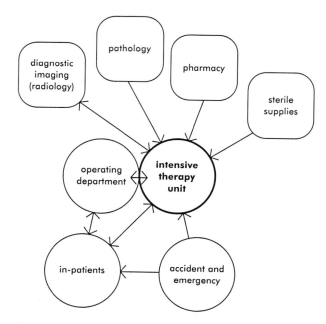

12 Intensive therapy unit (ITU): interdepartmental relationships

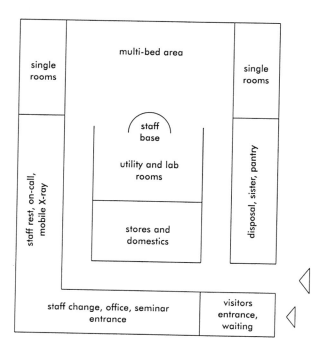

13 Typical intensive therapy unit layout

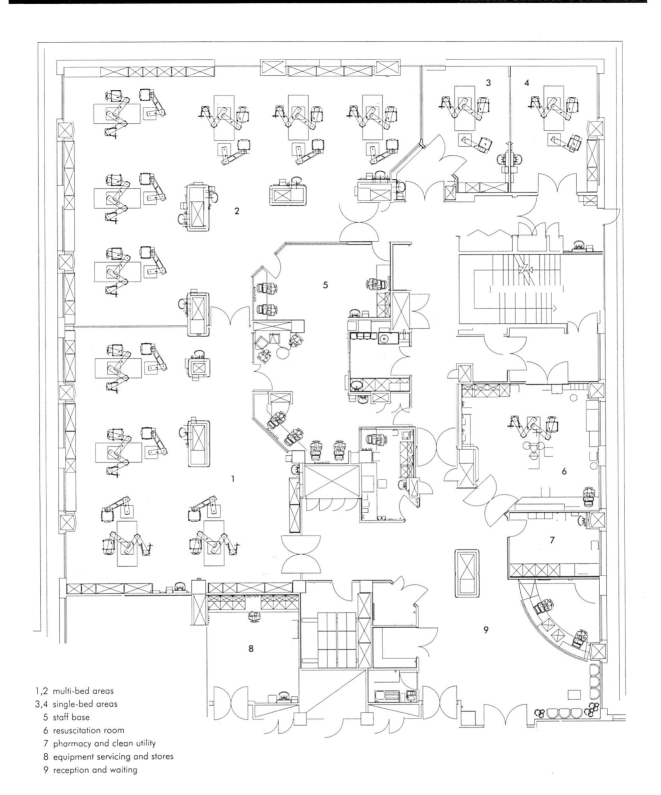

1,2 multi-bed areas
3,4 single-bed areas
  5 staff base
  6 resuscitation room
  7 pharmacy and clean utility
  8 equipment servicing and stores
  9 reception and waiting

14 Intensive therapy unit, Charing Cross Hospital, London
(Arch: Tangram Architects & Designers)

Accident and emergency (A&E)

Various studies in the UK have indicated that only around 1% of those attending an accident and emergency department are suffering from major trauma needing a high level of multi-disciplinary care and, at the other end of the scale, around 50% of attendees could more appropriately have been treated by their GP. This has led to a move to provide a wider range of A&E facilities from regional major trauma centres, through departments in local hospitals down to enhanced facilities in local GP-based centres. Because the term 'trauma centre' has a number of different interpretations, the term A&E is used here used to describe all types of facility. Much of the accommodation required for a 'minor accident unit' (MAU) in a local hospital is of a similar nature, but is smaller, simpler and with less specialised equipment.

For all types of A&E or MAU the entrance provides the first impression of the hospital for the most ill and anxious patients, and their equally anxious family and friends. While they may not be consciously aware of the appearance of the building it is likely to be one factor that will increase or lessen their anxiety. Also very important is the signposting both to the hospital and within the hospital's grounds. In most cases, and certainly for trauma centres, a helicopter landing pad will be needed, as close as possible to the A&E's entrance.

Traditionally, two entrances are provided, one for the 'walking wounded' and one for ambulance cases. For an MAU, only one is needed; the same may be argued for a trauma centre-type A&E. In all cases, a substantial draught lobby is required, with automatic doors at each end. These should preferably be at right angles to each other, to prevent both opening together and thus causing a through draught; this requires generous space for turning. In areas where violence or disturbances are common the inner doors from the draught lobby may be locked from the reception point, to keep out those who may be trying to continue an affray. A single entrance reduces ambiguity or confusion as to where people should go. If the draught lobby is overlooked from the reception point, those entering may be directed either to the waiting area, or immediately to the resuscitation and treatment areas.

The sorting of patients according to the urgency of their need is referred to as 'triage'. Initial triage is usually undertaken by an experienced nurse, whose base should enable him/her to observe everyone entering and to make a preliminary assessment of their condition. A small room adjoining both this base and the reception counter will facilitate confidential interviews.

Registration usually takes place after the patient has been seen by the triage nurse; in the case of seriously ill or injured patients, it will take place later.

In cases where there is a single entrance, once inside the A&E's draught lobby the two streams of patients should be separated. The serious emergency case will go straight to the resuscitation room (with medical gases and X-ray facilities) or major treatment room (sometimes referred to as a minor theatre). In the case

of the A&E of a traditional DGH, the number of places in the resuscitation room will depend on the population served, and this is reflected in the annual attendances; a range of 30 000 to 70 000 is typical, although a number of large urban hospitals now have attendances of more than 100 000. In the instance of trauma centres backed up by MAUs, the resuscitation room will be sized according to the number of serious emergency cases.

Patients with less urgent conditions will go after triage and registration to a waiting area that must be as quiet, comfortably furnished and attractive as possible. Children and their parents should be directed immediately to a separate waiting area with associated examination, treatment and consulting rooms. All other patients will be called forward to one of a range of cubicles or rooms. Most will need to be examined and treated on a couch. For some, a smaller cubicle for seated treatment is adequate. Separate rooms will be needed for eye injuries, for distressed or noisy patients, or those with alcohol or drug problems. A room for the application of plasters may be shared with the fracture and orthopaedic clinic (see 'Out-patient services'). Emergency X-ray facilities may form part of the A&E, but are more economic if they can form part of a nearby imaging department.

The size of the main waiting room will depend on the extent to which patients are called forward to sub-waiting areas. It needs public telephones, and some facilities for refreshments, unless it is close to the cafés at the main entrance. Such proximity makes for ease of operation at night, as the A&E entrance may well then be the only one open. Outside the building, there must be sufficient separation of traffic routes, so that the A&E access route is not blocked – a few parking spaces are needed nearby for cars bringing emergency patients, but parking and unloading space for ambulances takes priority. (See **15**.)

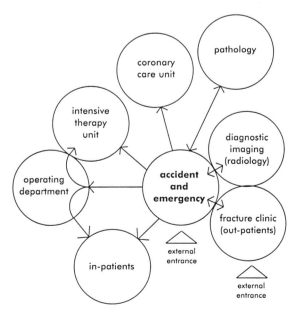

15 Accident and emergency unit: interdepartmental relationships

Out-patients department (OPD) and services

The OPD provides consultation, investigation and diagnoses for patients who require little or no recovery services afterwards; they generally attend by appointment. There is usually a main waiting area, with registration and enquiry point, but, preferably, it should be relatively small, with patients sent onwards to sub-waiting areas near the clinic they are to attend. Those clinics with little specialised equipment (e.g. general medicine, general surgery, gynaecology, urology) can use multipurpose consulting and examining facilities. Although traditionally many doctors preferred a purpose-designed clinic, with designated consulting rooms, each with one or more examining rooms, a more flexible and economical arrangement is a long row or string of combined consulting and examining (CE) rooms, in which the patient remains in one room, but the doctor may move between two or three adjoining rooms. Each should be 14–15 m², with sound resisting intercommunicating doors. Each clinic will use as many CE rooms as its staff and patients need. (See **16,17**.)

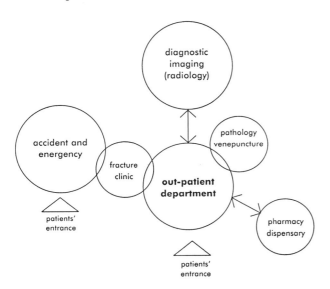

16 Out-patient department: interdepartmental relationships

The key to economy in construction and efficiency in use is to plan for 85 or 90% occupancy. This is easier to achieve in multipurpose OP suites than for clinics like ophthalmology, which require much specialised equipment, and which are not easy (and not usually appropriate) to use for other purposes. Associated with each group of CE rooms should be a sub-waiting space, nurse's treatment room, with clean and dirty utility rooms, toilets and weighing and measuring facilities. A toilet adjoining a dirty utility room can have a pass-through hatch for specimen testing.

Some clinics can use CE rooms for most purposes, but also need some special accommodation to serve cardiac clinics (e.g. electrocardiography (ECG)), audiology (a soundproof room – often a prefabricated booth) for ear nose and throat clinics, and treatment baths and ultra-violet light equipment for dermatology. Genito-urinary clinics deal with venereal diseases and used to be discreetly located away from all other hospital functions, although this is not now generally deemed necessary, and they may be part of a general OPD. They are often open at evenings and weekends, and so access must take this into account. They also keep extensive records and they can share facilities with the dermatology clinics, and may be adjacent to them. Fracture and orthopaedic clinics are often planned in association with the A&E department, for sharing of plaster room and of staff. Both in waiting areas, toilets, CE and other clinical rooms, the space required by people with disabilities and those with limbs in plaster will be greater than in most other areas.

Children may attend any of the clinics at an OPD, but as far as possible they should have separate provision. This may be combined with a child assessment centre for investigating possible anomalies of development; this requires facilities for testing sight, hearing, speech, mobility and intelligence. Antenatal clinics may be associated with (but distinct from) those for gynaecology, or form part of a maternity department. In some hospitals with a patient-focused emphasis, both may form part of a 'women's and children's unit'.

Rehabilitation

This describes both a process and a department. There is some element of rehabilitation in the care and treatment of most hospital in-patients. They must, on leaving, be as fit as possible to resume such activities as their condition permits. This is very important for elderly patients: for example, those with fractured femurs. Once their urgent surgical care has been undertaken, their longer term rehabilitation may best take place in a community or locality hospital; otherwise beds in the orthopaedic ward can be blocked. There are similar rehabilitation needs for patients who have had strokes.

The rehabilitation (or physical medicine) department includes facilities for physiotherapy, occupational therapy (OT) and speech and language therapy. It serves mainly out-patients and day patients, and should thus be at ground entrance level and conveniently placed for parking, including spaces for people with disabilities, at least one of which should be under cover to provide a degree of protection from rain for wheelchair transfer.

Acute medical and surgical patients are generally in hospital for too short a time to make visits to the rehabilitation department worth while. Increasingly, physiotherapists, and to a lesser extent occupational therapists, visit and treat the patients on the wards. A ward day room may contain some physiotherapy equipment. An exception is the case of stroke or other rehabilitation wards which should preferably be close and on the same level as the rehabilitation department. Both can then benefit from the use of courtyards and gardens for additional exercise and activity.

Physiotherapy is the largest part of the department (see **18**). Its main components are a gymnasium, hydrotherapy facilities and rooms and cubicles for individual treatment. The gymnasium may be in two parts, one for more active games and one for group exercises. Fixed equipment includes wall-bars. Storage is needed for equipment and floor mats. The active games for patients do not usually require a full height (6–7 m) gymnasium although this may be justified if it is also used for staff recreation, in which case explicit policies for joint use must be established. Otherwise, a height of 3.3 to 3.6 m may suffice. The two parts of the gymnasium may with advantage be divided with moveable partitions: both need changing rooms and showers for staff and patients. The treatment cubicles need generous socket outlet provision for electrical equipment and metal grilles for support of limbs during treatment. One or two rooms are needed where treatment can be given with more privacy: one will be used for wax bath treatments, which involve fire risk. The relative amount of individual as against group treatment may vary with time: the treatment cubicle area and the group activity gymnasium can with advantage adjoin, in the interest of long-term flexibility.

Hydrotherapy pools will be needed in most rehabilitation departments: they are expensive to build, to maintain and to staff. They should only be provided if it is certain that staff and other resources will be available. The main decision required is whether the pool edge will be at general floor level, or above it; in the later case, therapists can, if they wish, work from outside the pool. WCs, showers, changing and utility rooms are all required, as is a rest area – if possible with a pleasant outlook – with beverage facilities. Occupational therapy was traditionally geared to 'heavy' and 'light' craft workshops. Although these are still used, more of

the emphasis is now on the 'activities of daily living' – a kitchen with some variable height equipment, typical bedroom and bathroom situations – so that patient's ability to cope may be assessed, and aids for use in their homes may be prescribed. Orthotics, including the making of plaster splints, the selection or design of appliances, and wheelchair practice are areas involving both occupational therapy and physiotherapy.

Speech and language therapy in hospitals is most often for the purpose of recovering speech lost because of strokes, head injury or tumours. There are both one-to-one and group sessions. Rooms that are quiet but not necessarily sound-proofed may be used for other interviews, and other professions involved in rehabilitation, such as clinical psychologist and social workers.

Geriatric day hospitals allow elderly people to continue a slower rate of rehabilitation, often subsequent to hospital admission, either attending for a whole day or part of a day. An area for lunch and other refreshments may also be used for some table-based occupational therapy, but these patients will in many cases be able to use the facilities of the rehabilitation department. Due to age and infirmity, they will usually use them at different times from younger patients.

18   Rehabilitation department: diagrammatic functional layout

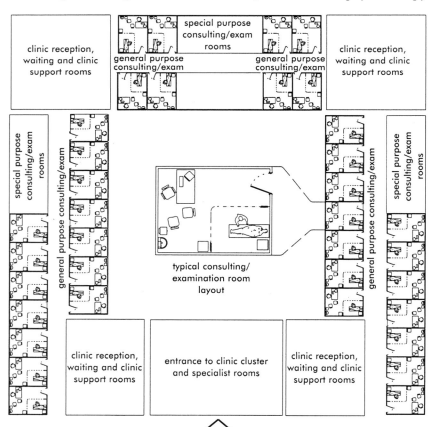

17   Out-patient department: diagrammatic layout with combined general consulting/examination rooms

Maternity (see *19*)

Childbirth is a natural process, but one that may occasionally threaten the life or health of both mother and child, and this presents dilemmas for designers of maternity units. For the great majority of cases, a stay of only a day or two is enough. Traditionally the components of a maternity unit are the antenatal clinic, wards (mainly post-natal, but also for the few who need observation before birth), the delivery suite, and the neonatal (or special care baby) unit. With ever shortening lengths of stay, the logic of separation of delivery suite and post-natal ward has been questioned. The alternative, pioneered in UK at Kingston Hospital, is the LDRP (labour, delivery, recovery, post-partum) room. This room – fully equipped as a normal delivery room, but with domestic decor and equipment located out of sight, and toilet and small sluice en suite – is accepted by the mother for the whole of her stay. An abnormal delivery room and full operating theatre are still needed for Caesarian and other more difficult births. There is also likely to be demand for one or more water-birthing rooms. The LDPR arrangement has the disadvantage of a lack of the company of other mothers, which is more important for some than for others, so a day room is needed. Waiting facilities for the expectant fathers pose an acute problem that arises in many parts of the hospital: here, above all, the dangers of smoking need emphasis, but this is a stressful situation and one particularly difficult for smokers. Groups of smokers are often seen huddled outside entrances to many hospitals. A possible solution is a small well-ventilated room with a separately ventilated lobby between it and any other corridor: this lobby might be approached directly from the draught lobby at hospital entrances.

The antenatal clinic in a large hospital will be fully utilised throughout the week, and may usefully be sometimes open outside normal hours. The traditional design with three-sided examining rooms open to a shared corridor, is no longer acceptable: convenient for doctors, it denies to the expectant mother the necessary privacy for confidential talk. A combined consulting/examining room, such as is found in OPDs, is the preferred solution. In smaller hospitals, the antenatal clinic could take place in the general OPD, provided that the waiting and other ancillary spaces are for exclusive maternity use during these clinics.

A neonatal unit is needed for any major maternity department. There is controversy about the required size – many have been built larger than has ever been needed. Very high levels of engineering services – particularly of socket outlets and temperature control – are required: many babies will be in incubators, some (where isolation is needed) in single rooms. Every facility must be given to maximise parents contact with their babies. Some longer stay babies, and those needing surgery, will have to be transferred to more specialised units.

In a hospital with a patient-focused emphasis, the maternity unit may form part of a 'women and children's hospital'. In any case, it is an advantage for the children's wards and services in the hospital to be near the maternity unit, for ease of access by paediatricians. The obstetricians are usually also responsible for gynaecology wards and out-patients.

In the context of a service provided by a major acute hospital with related locality hospitals, as described under 'Future strategies' in the introduction to this section, the general maternity units would form part of the locality hospitals, providing sufficient medical cover is available. The major acute hospital would then only take those cases where difficulties are expected, or where transfer from the locality hospital proves necessary.

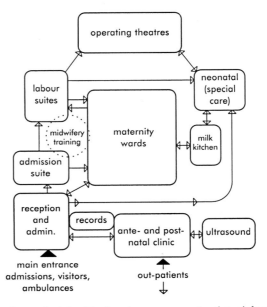

functions and relationships based on women moving through from admission to poist-natal recovery in a sequence of rooms or spaces

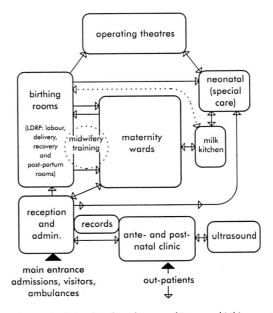

functions and relationships based on a multipurpose birthing room where women remain for labour, delivery, recovery and post-partum (LDRP)

19   Maternity: interdepartmental relationships

Diagnostic imaging

This term embraces diagnostic investigations using X-rays (either as plain films, or making use of contrast media) and the non-X-ray modalities using ultrasound and magnetic resonance to produce images.

The essential feature about planning 'imaging departments' is that, apart from ultrasound, imaging modalities require specialised protective arrangements, either from radiation or from magnetic fields.

Protection in X-ray rooms may be provided by lead or by barium plaster which prevent the emission of radiation beyond the room. Where control positions are within the room, operators may be protected by lead screens. During investigations staff who must work in close proximity to the patient, may additionally wear lead aprons, and patients themselves may require specific shielding from radiation to sensitive zones such as gonads.

Patients on entry to the imaging department need tranquil reception and waiting areas before moving to the diagnostic rooms. The layout of the department should ensure that frequently used rooms and those whose investigations are brief (e.g. plain X-ray, chest rooms) are sited closest to the waiting areas. All rooms will require patient changing facilities, with fast-throughput rooms requiring a higher proportion than those servicing longer procedure rooms. Changing rooms may be either 'stand-alone' or 'pass-through'. In this latter category, the patient accesses the room from the sub-waiting space, and enters the diagnostic room directly from the changing room. These rooms have the advantage that, once undressed, the patient does not have to traverse any general circulation and so benefits from greater privacy. However this pattern

is often found to be very claustrophobic for patients, and can generate anxieties that one has been placed in this isolated space and forgotten. It is also a pattern which, because of the more numerous doorways into the X-ray rooms, creates additional problems in achieving radiation protection. The greater flexibility of the stand-alone pattern usually makes it the preferred option.

X-ray rooms which make use of contrast media need some facility for preparation. With the simple applications, such as computerised tomography or intravenous pyelogram, a simple utility/preparation is needed; for barium studies, a barium kitchen where the medium can be made up is needed; and for barium enema studies a WC en suite with the radiography room is vital.

Protection from magnetic fields in magnetic resonance imaging studies initially depended on the provision of sufficient area around the magnet for the strength of the field to fall off. However, current trends are for the use of lower tesla magnets and for protection from the magnetic field to be built into the machine (see **20**).

In radiology departments, considerations of radiation protection demand that the diagnostic rooms are internal. In those circumstances it becomes particularly important that the more general spaces, offices, sorting and reporting rooms and staff rest rooms have natural light.

Most X-ray processing now makes use of daylight processing, and processors can be sited within the staff areas or within general circulation space, which can help to simplify circulation and to create a more compact staff working area. However, some specialist investigations may make use of cine film, and for these a small dark room needs to be provided.

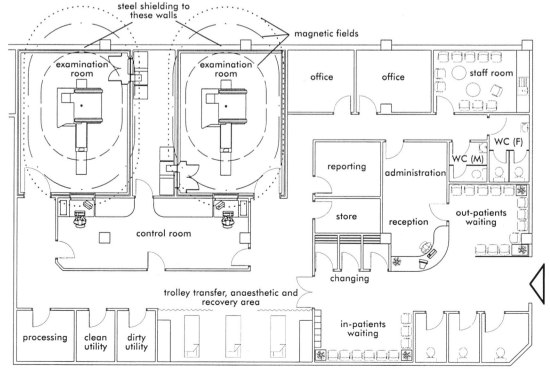

20 Magnetic resonance imaging suite: example layout
(Scheme: Siemens Medical Solutions)

Radiotherapy and nuclear medicine

The treatment of patients with radiotherapy – mostly, but not exclusively, cancer patients – requires specific provision of protected facilities. The general departmental requirements are not dissimilar to those of diagnostic imaging departments, with the need for reassuring reception and waiting spaces and, as all the treatment rooms are internal, for as much of the general departmental spaces to have daylight and outlook.

In radiotherapy of the 'conventional' type, irradiation levels are much higher than in diagnostic work, so that the physical provision for radiation protection is greater and imposes limits to future change and flexibility within departments.

With the more complex modalities, such as linear accelerators, the physics requirements are highly specific and complex, such that these very high-powered machines usually are given their protection by housing them in a massive concrete bunker with maze entries to prevent irradiation leakage.

The essence of planning radiotherapy departments is the housing of the therapeutic irradiation machines and, apart from the 'soft' areas, is mainly an exercise in housing the machinery and ensuring radiological safety. Therefore, the process begins with the identification of the machinery to be housed and the very specific requirements it will have for protection.

Nuclear medicine involves the use of radio isotopes in diagnostic or therapeutic mode. The process embraces:

- the preparation of the isotopes
- their injection into the patient
- tracking them in the body
- measuring the rate and degree of their uptake using gamma cameras.

Therefore a nuclear medicine department must contain a radiation protected isotope store, a laboratory for manipulation and preparation of the isotopes, and a gamma camera room or rooms where the procedures will take place.

Following the conduct of the procedure, the patient, in the recovery phase, may have to be in a protected environment and specific precautions about the disposal of urine and faeces should be made because, following examination, the patient may be excreting radioactive waste (See **21**.)

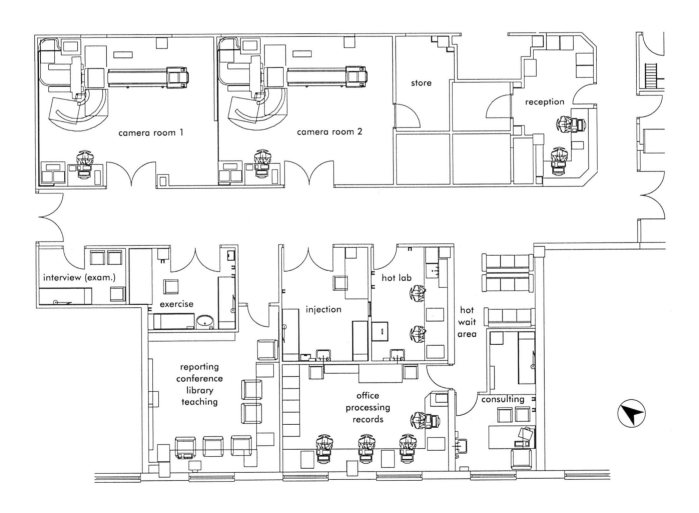

21 Nuclear medicine suite, Charing Cross Hospital, London
(Arch: Tangram Architects & Designers)

Operating department

The essential feature of an 'operating department' is the provision of a 'sterile' operating room for the performance of major surgical procedures, so that they may be carried out without risk of infection to the patient. This end is achieved by the operating room being positively pressurised in relation to the surrounding rooms, and the air supply to it being passed through filters. In standard theatres an air change rate of 20 changes per hour is effective. However, a number of surgical procedures require a higher standard of sterility. These are procedures where any degree of infection would result in the operation being unsuccessful. Typical of this group is hip replacement surgery, but the 'ultra clean' conditions are also called for in any joint replacement procedure or when any 'foreign' implant is being introduced into the body (e.g. stents).

Provision of 'ultra clean' conditions is achieved by the use of so-called 'sterile enclosures', within which a vertical laminar flow of high volumes of filtered air is achieved. It should be noted that while laminar flow has been shown to be very successful in minimising infection rates in joint replacement surgery, it has shown no such benefits in the broader range of general surgery. In view of the large volumes of air that need to be pumped through enclosures to ensure an effective laminar flow pattern, this is also a costly ventilation option.

The remaining areas of the operating theatre suite, in addition to the operating room itself, may be categorised into three zones:

- an inner 'high sterility' zone where conditions akin to those in the operating room are required, and which contains the preparation room where instrument trolleys are laid up, the anaesthetic room, and the scrub-up and gowning room
- an outer zone, still within the protected confines of the theatre suite, consisting of staff changing rooms, showers, toilets, staff rest rooms where breaks during operating lists may be taken
- the entry zone which may also contain offices, stores and laboratories.

The entire operating theatres suite must be tightly controlled at the entry point, at which transfer of the patient from bed or trolley should take place to prevent contamination of the theatre environment.

Theatre planning in the UK has been dominated by the desire to separate 'clean' and 'dirty' environments, and this desire gave rise to the typical 'double-corridor system' used in UK hospitals (the second corridor generally being used solely for the 'dirty' function of removing used material and clinical waste via a 'back door' from the theatre). This produces difficult circulation patterns and is arguably not necessary and wasteful of space. By contrast, in the USA and many other countries the appropriate separation of 'clean' and 'dirty' is achieved by clinical waste etc. being bagged in the operating room after which it is moved through the single corridor system without risk of contaminating the theatre environment. (See **22,23**.)

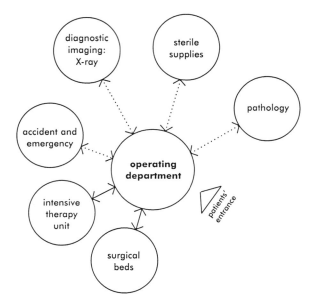

22 Operating department: interdepartmental relationships

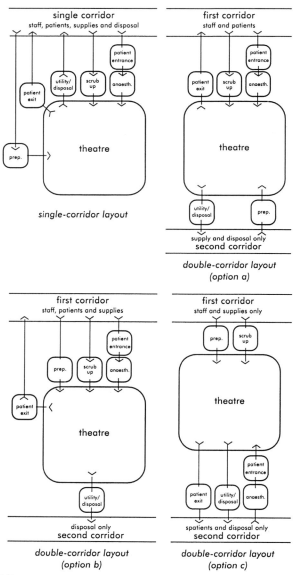

23 Theatre suite: double- and single-corridor alternatives

Day surgery

Already 70% of elective surgery is in many places being carried out on a day basis, and this proportion is still increasing. In the USA, day surgery units are often provided as completely free-standing units but for safety's sake, as well as for the ability to share back-up services, there is a case for them being located in a hospital.

Where all surgical services are centralised at the DGH, there is a dilemma as to whether the main operating theatres should cater for day surgical patients or whether a separate day surgical unit (DSU) should be provided. The latter may be conveniently located near a hospital entrance and car park. However, as day surgery patients are often more ambulant than many out-patients this location should be balanced against the possibly stronger needs of other departments to be readily accessible from car parks.

From a utilisation point of view, there is an advantage in the use of main theatres for day surgery: as day surgery grows, in-patient surgery will generally decline. There are also economies in staffing, supplies and other back-up services, and in air-conditioning and other engineering plant. Where the main theatres are used for day surgery there must be separate day surgery facilities – reception, consulting, preoperative waiting and post-operative recovery – which should be easily accessible from an external entrance.

If larger acute hospitals are linked to and supported by locality hospitals, as outlined in the 'Future strategies' example, then day surgery would generally take place in units at the locality hospitals.

One or more endoscopy rooms will generally be provided as part of the day surgical unit. They may have their own recovery area. The operating theatres need to be designed to the same size and standards as those provided for in-patients. In some DSUs, anaesthetic rooms are omitted, and anaesthetic is (as is generally the case in the USA) administered in the theatre.

It is important to know whether patients will go to a bed area, change and leave their clothes there, and return there after surgery, or whether they will go straight from a changing room to the theatre suite. In the latter case their belongings will be taken to the bed area where they will recover.

HOSPITAL SUPPORT SERVICES

A wide range of functions is briefly described here. Many of these are not entirely specific to hospitals; for others, the technology changes rapidly, and reference to the NHS Estates Health Building Notes and other frequently updated guidance is recommended.

Pharmacy

A dispensary is needed, close to the out-patient department and with a comfortable waiting area. If the main hospital pharmacy cannot be so located, pneumatic tubes from it to the dispensary and some other user areas may be justified. More and more pharmaceutical items are commercially produced; where manufacturing is undertaken at the hospital, increasingly stringent sterility requirements prevail. Security is of the highest importance, especially associated with the entrance used for deliveries.

Pathology

The four main laboratory disciplines in hospitals are (see also the Laboratories section):
- histology
- microbiology
- haematology
- biochemistry.

The last two may be grouped together as they can share much automated equipment. The whole department will generally have a shared receiving area for specimens and records. Ventilation and other safety standards must meet current legislation.

There is a tendency for large hospitals or commercial laboratories to take in work from smaller hospitals; economies of scale may increase this tendency. Laboratories in the past were mainly spaces with benches with equipment on them. More and more equipment now takes the form of floor mounted cabinets. Change is endemic, and flexibility in access for engineering services is crucial.

Mortuary

It is desirable, but not essential, for the mortuary to be near the pathology department, as the histologist is responsible for post-mortems. The main elements are the body store, post-mortem rooms, and facilities for visitors. The access route into the mortuary for bodies from the hospital should be separate from that taken by visitors, although mortuary trolleys are discreet enough that separate lifts and circulation routes through the hospital are not needed. Particular care is needed for the furnishing and outlook of the visitors waiting and visiting areas; a toilet and kitchenette unit is required. Access by hearses should be out of sight from windows of wards and other patients' areas.

Religious facilities

Depending on the nature of the local community, this may need to satisfy the needs of different faiths whose representatives should be consulted. It must be easily found – preferably near the main entrance – and be easy to reach and use by patients in wheelchairs.

Health records

Computerisation of records is coming, but how soon is hard to predict. At present, health records occupy much space. Although they may be remote from patients' areas, ease of access to records, especially to and from the OPD, is important. The work of manually filing and retrieving records can be monotonous and the working environment must be carefully considered in order to compensate for this. It should be comfortable, attractive and should provide adequate visual relief, preferably with a good outlook.

Administration

The extent of offices provided in the hospital depends on whether they are also the headquarters of the Trust. Main functions include Trust Board and Secretariat, finance, personnel, supplies, and senior nursing and other professional staff. Ancillary spaces include computer facilities, stationery and other stores. The post room and telephone exchange are often associated with the main entrance. Other administrative functions do not need priority locations, and may be on an upper floor. Clinical Directorates' offices are generally near their clinical areas. Offices for consultants (shared if not full-time) may be centralised or near clinical areas.

Catering

The most common systems for in-patients are centrally processed – often off-site – with local regeneration on the wards. Pantries are needed for preparing snacks and beverages outside normal meal times. It has been traditional to provide a large central dining room for staff, but in some hospitals the development of 'shopping clusters' near the main entrance, incorporating fast food and other speciality cafés, has reduced the use of staff dining rooms. It is possible to envisage all staff meals provided from such outlets – and shared with out-patients and visitors – as long as services for night and evening staff are maintained. The dieticians, whose main role is advice to out-patients and in-patients, may have an advisory role in catering services, especially concerning special diets and the promotion of healthy eating generally.

Education

Undergraduate nurse training is now in the education sector rather than part of the hospital function. However, continuing post-graduate training of doctors, nurses and other health professionals has a vital role, and provides an interface forum between GPs, community nurses and others. Accommodation is required for these functions, as well as for conferences and meetings. Catering facilities are required and these may be supplied from the regular staff or patients' catering sources.

Staff facilities

The extent of central changing rooms needed will be determined by the whole hospital and departmental operational policies. A crèche may be justified for the children of staff, as may a staff club. Sports and recreational facilities may be warranted if they are not available nearby in the community and they are thought likely to help in staff recruitment.

Staff residency

In the past, nurses homes and a variety of other residential buildings were provided specifically for hospital staff. Occupancy was very variable and it has been found to be more practical to arrange with the Local Authority or Housing Association for accommodation for hospital staff to be located within the local community, thus avoiding being 'in a ghetto'. On-call bedrooms, with en-suite toilets and showers are needed for a few staff.

Supplies

A 'just-in-time' approach to delivery is tending to reduce the quantity of stores held in hospitals. However, a central receiving point is needed for food, linen, bulk sterile and other supplies. The distribution system must be determined at an early planning stage: its efficiency is crucial to all aspects of the running of the hospital. This applies also to the collection of items for disposal or reprocessing. For horizontal journeys, tug and trolley systems are often used; in this case, special attention to the design of floors and their finish is needed. A sterilising and disinfecting unit is required to prepare sterile packs and items for theatres and other departments. This is best located with other service and quasi-industrial functions; it generates much heat.

Energy centre and workshops

The energy centre – boiler house, emergency generator, calorifiers – may, for efficiency of energy distribution, be as centrally located as possible in the hospital. Electrical and mechanical workshops should be nearby: other workshops are for carpentry and other building trades (depending on how much work is to be done in-house) and for maintenance of bio-medical engineering equipment. A delivery yard and garages for some essential transport is required.

COMMUNITY AND LOCALITY HOSPITALS

In Britain, the term 'community hospital' is used for a wide range of smaller hospitals subsidiary to DGHs. In America, the term may refer to a facility that equates with the UK's DGH. In this section, the term 'locality hospital' (LH) will be used for the wide range of subsidiary hospitals as well as for the more specific role of locality hospitals described previously in the introduction to this chapter under 'Future strategies'.

A locality hospital must be easy to access, including by public transport. Many of its patients and their visitors are elderly and may not have cars, or the ability to drive. However, car parking near to the main entrance is needed. It is very important to present a homely and non-institutional appearance. Many LHs have been formed by conversion or adaptation of existing buildings, or as additions to old cottage hospitals or health centres.

The content of the LHs varies according to its location (urban or rural), distance from the DGH and population served. The LH envisaged under the introductory 'Future strategies' heading might comprise the following services and departments:

- A minor accident unit.
- An out-patient department, including a full range of clinics.
- Imaging service centred on a radiodiagnostic provision but excluding computerised tomography, magnetic resonance imaging and angiography, which would be located in the acute hospital.
- Rehabilitation service, with the extent of facilities dependent on the relative roles of the LH and DGH: in the 'Alternative strategy' example, most rehabilitation services would be at the LH, and thus might include hydrotherapy. Associated would be day hospital facilities for elderly people, including those with mental incapacity.
- A maternity unit which, for a LH servicing a population of about 100 000, would provide for most normal delivery as well as antenatal care. (In other situations a small maternity unit is only usually provided in remote rural locations.)
- Low-intensity care beds providing for a number of categories in simpler, more friendly surroundings than the DGH; they are also generally more economical, if a good level of occupancy can be maintained. The types of care that would be provided include:
  - care of those with non-life threatening medical conditions
  - pre-convalescent care of post-operative patients from the DGH
  - day-to-day nursing care
  - respite care for those with serious disability or long-term illness
  - terminal care (closer at hand for most than a hospice) provided that staff have suitable training.
- A day surgical unit for all or most day surgery.
- Ancillary functions, including administration, supplies, catering, energy centre and workshops.

LHs may be provided together with health centres or other GP premises, with which some sharing of facilities may be achieved (see **24, 25**).

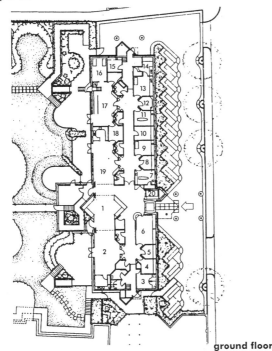

ground floor

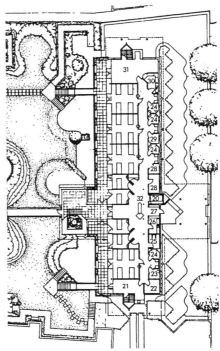

first floor

1 sitting room; 2 dining room and servery; 3 staff change; 4 administrator and evaluator; 5 community link worker; 6 reception and records; 7 dentist; 8 social worker; 9 speech therapist; 10 office; 11 podiatry; 12 hairdressing; 13 clean utility; 14 dirty utility; 15 kiln room; 16 passive physiotherapy; 17 physiotherapy; 18 assessment bedroom; 19 occupational therapy; 20 bed lift;

21 staff room and kitchenette (night duty); 22 boiler room; 23 cleaner; 24 clients' WC (dis); 25 bathroom; 26 delivery and disposal; 27 clean utility; 28 store; 29 shower; 30 servery; 31 sitting, drinking and relatives' overnight rest; 32 nurse base; plus four four-bed rooms and four single-bed rooms

24 Lambeth Community Care, London
(Arch: Edward Cullinan Architects)

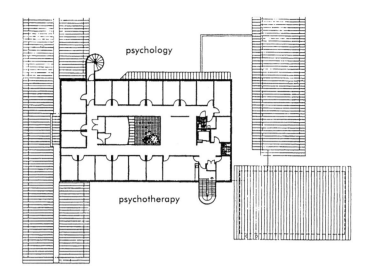

psychology

psychotherapy

first floor

25 The Hove Polyclinic
(Arch: Nightingale Associates)

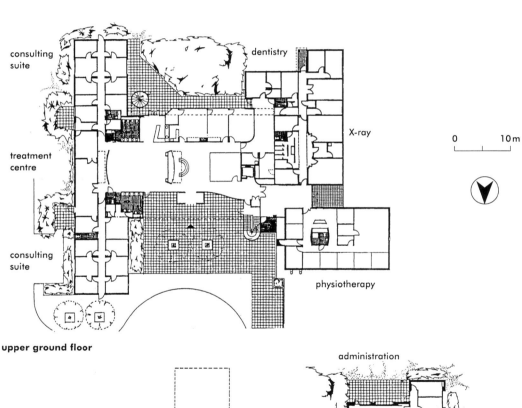

consulting
suite

dentistry

treatment
centre

X-ray

consulting
suite

physiotherapy

upper ground floor

0   10 m

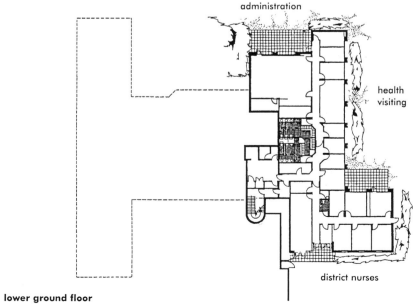

administration

health
visiting

district nurses

lower ground floor

HEALTH CENTRES AND GENERAL MEDICAL PRACTICE PREMISES

These have sometimes been provided together and sometimes separately. In the UK, GPs are independent practitioners who traditionally provided their own premises. Local authorities provided maternity, child welfare and other services in community clinics. The bringing together of these elements in 'health centres' was accelerated by the 1974 health service reorganisation, but slowed down 5 years later by a change of government policy which again encouraged and assisted GPs to build for themselves. Since then, the distinction between the publicly owned health centre and the GP provided premises has been blurred, as more GPs have recognised the need for other health professionals to work alongside them. These include nurse-practitioners, counsellors, physiotherapists, and in some cases providers of alternative medicine.

These buildings may conveniently be described as having public zones (waiting spaces, toilets), staff zones (offices, records, stores, rest and seminar rooms) and zones where staff and patients interact. For GPs, the latter usually comprise combined consulting and examining rooms of 11 to 12 m² each. At least one such room is needed in excess of the number of GPs likely to be working at any one time so that, for example, a possibly infectious patient may be temporarily accommodated. A range of rooms of this size for use by other clinical staff will provide the most flexible layout. A designated treatment zone, with supplies base and one or more treatment bays, cubicles or rooms is needed. Space for patients' records is often underestimated: computerisation may eventually radically alter this. (See **26**.)

The entrance to the building must be welcoming, as must the reception area. Anxiety about violence has often led to protective glazed screens to the reception desk; if this need is inescapable, they must be devised so that human contact between patient and receptionist is not jeopardised. A small interview room is needed where a receptionist can talk privately to a deaf, disturbed or disabled patient or when confidential matters may be raised. Wheelchair access is essential; and a lower part of the reception counter (and public phone) should be suitable for wheelchair users.

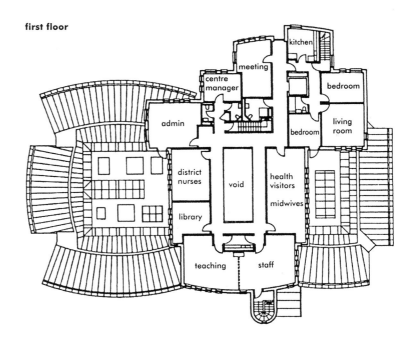

first floor

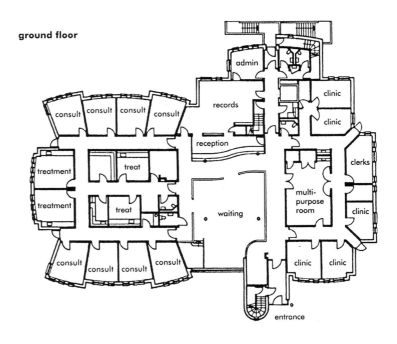

ground floor

section

0   5 m

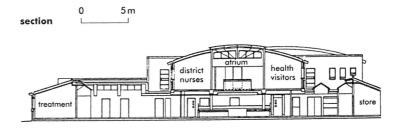

26 The Fairfield Centre (primary care), Charlton, London (Arch: Peerless & Noble Architects)

MENTAL HEALTH SERVICES AND THEIR BUILDINGS

The development in the 1950s of drugs which could cure, or at least relieve, conditions such as depression changed the care of mentally ill people from mainly custodial to a mainly curative or palliative nature. From long-stay asylums where many mentally ill people remained until their death, the required building type became instead a department of a general hospital, to which patients were admitted, treated and discharged. This 'medical model' was challenged not only by traditionalists but also by those with an orientation towards individual or group psychotherapy rather than medical means such as drugs and electro-convulsive therapy (ECT). The traditionalists at best provided a caring refuge for those for whom life 'outside' was intolerable, or for those whose behaviour was a threat to themselves or others; however, all too often the old asylums only institutionalised patients and, even after their recovery from acute phases of illness, left them unable to function independently. The psychotherapists, and particularly the proponents of the 'therapeutic community', regarded the whole pattern of the life they devised for their patients as an educational one, giving them insight into their condition and retraining them for 'normal' life.

The typical mental health buildings of the 1950s and 1960s were 'psychiatric departments', added, usually as a discrete but linked block, to the DGH. Links with the local population were also emphasised, so that GPs and community health workers could liaise closely with the mental health team psychiatrists, psychiatric nurses, occupational therapists and social workers to provide better treatment and aftercare. Most people presenting symptoms of mental illness to their GPs can be treated as out-patients or day patients. The size of the psychiatric department depended on that of its parent DGH, ranging from 60 to 150 beds; they comprised wards of 25 to 30 beds, not unlike those for medical patients, together with day hospitals, where in-patients as well as day patients underwent individual, group and occupational therapy.

Some of these units functioned in whole or part as therapeutic communities, but increasingly they came to be regarded as too medically orientated, and too big so smaller institutions replaced bigger ones. An even closer working relationship between the psychiatric team and community health services is being demanded. A pioneering scheme in East Birmingham has led to units of 15 or 20 beds, in one case planned adjoining a health centre. Larger units can claim economies of scale, but smaller ones can more easily be designed to a domestic scale, and to be of a less stigmatising nature. This is especially important for out-patients, or those attending for the first time. (There is a strong case for psychiatrists to hold clinics in GP clinics and health centres – locations without connotations of abnormality.)

Most units of whatever size now favour single bedrooms throughout. Much smaller units for the majority of patients with mental illness have many benefits, but are less suitable for those who, in spite of all means of treatment available, still need to stay for more than a few weeks, or those whose behaviour is seen as dangerous. A hierarchy of units for a minority of patients with special needs ranges from one or more longer stay unit serving perhaps a population of 500 000, by way of regional medium secure units, to the 'specialised hospitals' (e.g. Broadmoor, Rampton and Ashworth). In the two latter categories, the problems of combining the security normally associated with prisons with a therapeutic environment are considerable. The NHS Estates' design guide on medium secure psychiatric units is a valuable reference. (See **27**.)

The care of elderly patients with mental illness presents several problems. Initial assessment or diagnosis is essential to see whether psychological symptoms or generally deteriorative diseases such as Alzheimer's are evident. This assessment process may be done on an out-patient basis or on a medical ward for elderly people. Elderly patients with depression or other mental illnesses may well be cared for in general psychiatric units. Those with advanced forms of dementia need a protected nursing home environment; as they are generally ambulant, they need secure indoor and outdoor walking space.

The day areas of all these mental health buildings need as wide a range as possible of rooms of different sizes, planned to be highly adaptable. Activities include one-to-one therapy or interviews and group therapy, for which comfortable sitting areas can be used. For training purposes, one of these rooms may have observation through a one-way window. Heavy workshops, various craft facilities, physiotherapy and outdoor activities (e.g. games, gardening etc.) are needed more in larger or longer-stay units. ECT suites are seldom used enough to warrant the considerable space they occupy unless much of the space can also be used for other functions.

Learning disability (previously designated as 'mental handicap') is now regarded as a matter for social and educational rather than health services. Nevertheless many health service personnel are involved in the care of people with learning disabilities, whether in special schools, residential hostels or their homes.

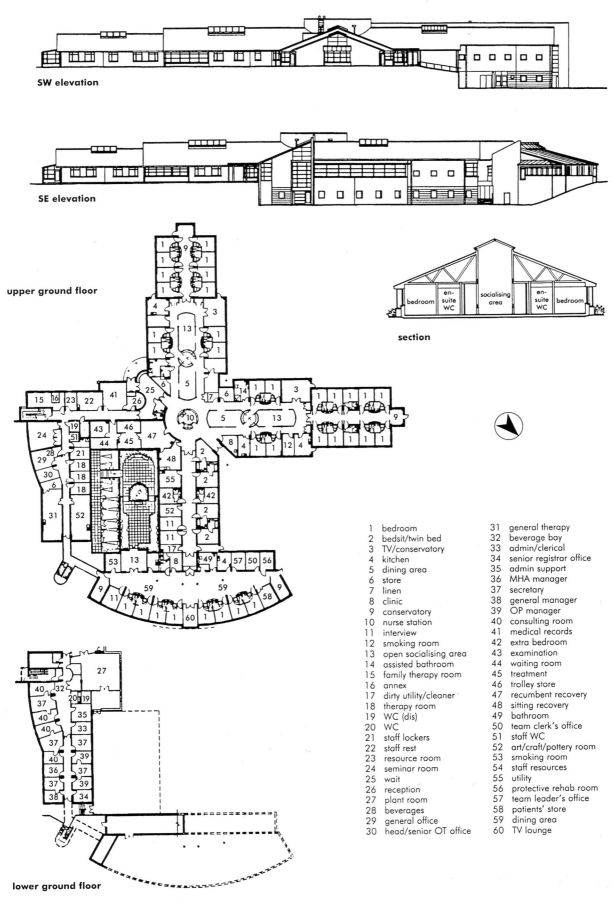

SW elevation

SE elevation

upper ground floor

section

bedroom | en-suite WC | socialising area | en-suite WC | bedroom

lower ground floor

1	bedroom	31	general therapy
2	bedsit/twin bed	32	beverage bay
3	TV/conservatory	33	admin/clerical
4	kitchen	34	senior registrar office
5	dining area	35	admin support
6	store	36	MHA manager
7	linen	37	secretary
8	clinic	38	general manager
9	conservatory	39	OP manager
10	nurse station	40	consulting room
11	interview	41	medical records
12	smoking room	42	extra bedroom
13	open socialising area	43	examination
14	assisted bathroom	44	waiting room
15	family therapy room	45	treatment
16	annex	46	trolley store
17	dirty utility/cleaner	47	recumbent recovery
18	therapy room	48	sitting recovery
19	WC (dis)	49	bathroom
20	WC	50	team clerk's office
21	staff lockers	51	staff WC
22	staff rest	52	art/craft/pottery room
23	resource room	53	smoking room
24	seminar room	54	staff resources
25	wait	55	utility
26	reception	56	protective rehab room
27	plant room	57	team leader's office
28	beverages	58	patients' store
29	general office	59	dining area
30	head/senior OT office	60	TV lounge

27 Mental Health Unit, St Mary's Hospital, Isle of Wight
(Arch: Nightingale Associates)

NURSING HOMES

Nursing homes may cater for residents of all ages, from children to the elderly. Currently in the UK by far the majority of residents are in this latter category. Nursing homes provide for a wide variety of nursing and related needs that are of a type or severity that do not need permanent hospital care and yet cannot be catered for in residential care homes.

Some homes cater for general nursing needs whereas others focus on particular types of nursing such as care of the young; the severely physically disabled; those with learning difficulties; the mentally ill; respite care; the chronic sick or others requiring specialist nursing. A few homes may have acute medical or surgical facilities. In terms of accommodation and service, nursing homes bridge the gap between hospitals and residential care homes – that is, between health services and social services.

Registration and inspection

Nursing homes are mainly provided by the private and charity sectors. In the UK, to qualify for compulsory registration, they are required to meet nationally drafted minimum standards set out in Regulations and reviewed from time to time. These standards cover accommodation, staffing and levels of service.

Some establishments are registered as both nursing and residential homes. This dual registration reflects the frequent progression of residents from needing basic residential care to becoming increasingly dependent and needing nursing care. This is especially the case with the elderly. Residential homes in the UK must also be registered and meet minimum national standards.

In the UK funding for nursing care generally comes under the NHS. On the other hand, residential care is either paid for by the resident (usually elderly) or partly or wholly by the local authority depending on the resident's assets. If the care is partly nursing and partly residential then the costs are shared between the health authority and the resident or the local authority, or both, this latter aspect again depending on the resident's assets. The method of funding the care of the elderly is a matter of current debate.

Design and accommodation

In all cases the design of nursing homes should aim at providing as relaxed a domestic atmosphere and environment as possible, within which the necessary level of nursing care can be safely and efficiently provided. Even the most frail or heavily dependent residents should be able to maintain their dignity. The current trend is to provide individual personal space for residents. Hence, individual rooms with toilet facilities en suite backed-up by communal lounges and dining areas along with shared treatment and assisted bathing rooms are the norm. Special attention is required to making sure the facilities are suitable for the physically disabled and frail. (See **28**.)

Typically, the following facilities are required:

- A reassuring and welcoming entrance and reception facility for arriving visitors and potential new residents.
- An office for the 'head of home' and a general administration office, both close to the main entrance.
- A staff base or bases in central positions relative to bedroom clusters. This is particularly important at night.
- Bedrooms, each of which should be for a single resident except for one or two double rooms for married couples. Rooms should be capable of accommodating some personal possessions and furniture. Space must be provided for wheelchair manoeuvring, the use of walking aids and hoists, and assistance by staff. A choice of positions for beds and furniture is desirable. Provision for clothes, both hanging and in drawers, must be made. Space is required for one or two easy chairs, a moveable table and a dressing table that can be used as a writing desk. Each bedroom should have direct access to a room with a WC, washbasin and a bath or shower.

In addition other rooms are required within easy reach of bedrooms. The include the following:

- An assisted bathing room (with access to three sides of the bath) and assisted showering. These rooms should have hair washing facilities and be capable of accommodating wheelchairs. The number of these rooms should be determined by the number of residents and the location of the rooms in relation to the bedrooms they serve, especially if the bedrooms are on more than one floor.
- A secure treatment/clinical room with associated secure storage for clean linen, drugs, medicines, sterile and disposable supplies.
- A room for emptying, cleaning and disinfecting bedpans, for urine testing samples, for temporary holding of items for disposal or reprocessing, and for the parking of wheelchairs and/or commodes.
- Rooms for communal dining and sitting, and alcoves or similar for more private conversation.
- Beverage preparation bays convenient to the bedrooms so that residents can entertain visitors in their rooms.
- A kitchen located and designed to easily receive deliveries and for rapid serving and distribution of food to the dining areas and bedrooms.
- A laundry, including provision for receiving and sorting heavily soiled linen, for washing, spin and tumble drying, pressing, folding and sorting, marking and repairing.
- One central domestic services base and outstations as necessary on each floor to accommodate cleaning equipment, trolleys and materials.
- A disposal room near a service entrance for sealed containers for refuse and reprocessing items.
- A small room to serve as a mortuary, convenient for discreet access by hearse.
- Staff facilities, including separate toilets for male and female staff, dining and rest areas, changing rooms, lockers and staff showers.
- General storage and maintenance provisions.

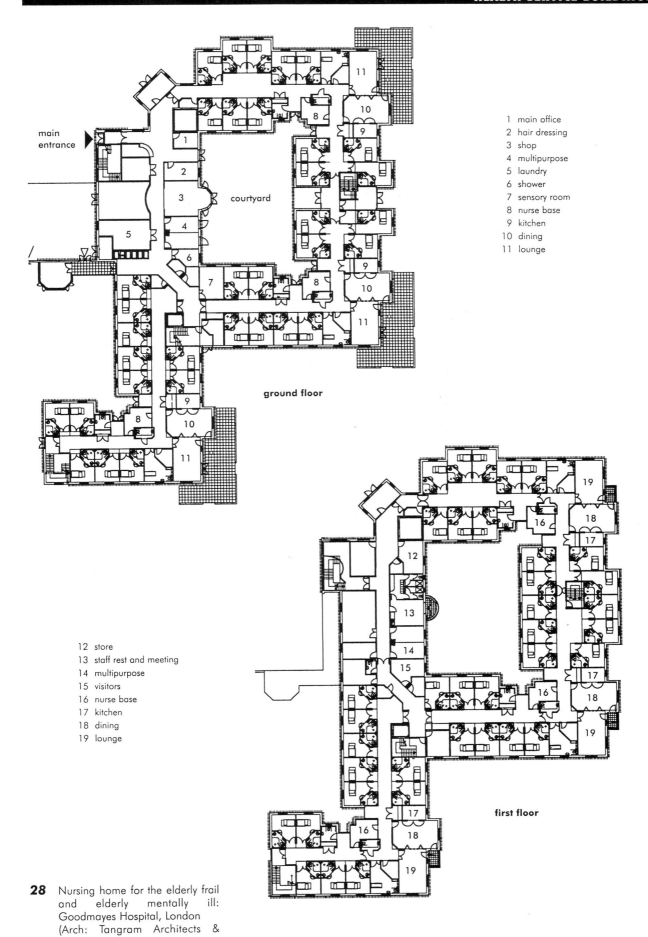

main entrance

courtyard

ground floor

1 main office
2 hair dressing
3 shop
4 multipurpose
5 laundry
6 shower
7 sensory room
8 nurse base
9 kitchen
10 dining
11 lounge

12 store
13 staff rest and meeting
14 multipurpose
15 visitors
16 nurse base
17 kitchen
18 dining
19 lounge

first floor

28 Nursing home for the elderly frail and elderly mentally ill: Goodmayes Hospital, London (Arch: Tangram Architects & Designers)

GLOSSARY

Abbreviations

A&E Accident and Emergency Department (or AED)
ACAD Ambulatory Care And Diagnostic centre
BEMS Building and Engineering Management System
CCU Cardiac Care Unit
CSSD Central Sterile Supply Department
CT Computer (-aided) Tomography
DCP Development Control Plan
DGH District General Hospital
DSU Day Surgery Unit
DTC Diagnostic and Treatment Centre
ECG Electro Cardiography – a scan of electrical heart activity
ECT Electro Convulsive Therapy – electric shocks administered for some kinds of mental illness
EEG Electro-encephalography – a scan of electrical brain activity
ENT Ear, Nose and Throat
HBN *Health Building Notes* (previously *Hospital BN*) – a series of guidance documents published by NHS Estates
HDU High Dependency Unit
HSDU Hospital Sterilising and Disinfecting Unit
ICU Intensive Care Unit (alternative to ITU)
ITU Intensive Therapy Unit
LDRP Labour, Delivery, Recovery and Post-partum – referring to the birth process and used to describe the activities in a 'birthing room'
LH Locality Hospital
MAH Major Acute Hospital
MAT Minimum Access Therapy
MAU Minor Accident Unit
MIT Minimum Invasive Therapy (same as MAT)
MRI Magnetic Resonance Imaging
OPD Out-Patient Department
PFC Patient-Focused Care
PFI Private Finance Initiative – the policy of inviting the private sector to contract to finance and operate health buildings
PPP Public–Private Partnership – a form of PFI (see above)

Clinical and technical terms

Angiography – X-ray imaging of heart and blood vessels after introduction of a radiopaque contrast medium into bloodstream.

Biochemistry – the chemistry of living organisms and life processes; a discipline within a hospital pathology laboratory.

Cardiography – graphically recording the movement of the heart by means of a cardiograph.

Diagnostic imaging – all the types of imaging used for diagnosis: e.g. Radiodiagnosis (X-ray); Ultrasound; Magnetic Resonance Imaging (MRI).

Endoscope – an illuminated optic instrument for viewing the interior of a body cavity or organ.

Endoscopy – use of an endoscope inserted via either a natural orifice or an incision for internal examination and/or treatment.

Haematology (hematology) – study of blood and blood-forming tissues; a discipline within a hospital pathology laboratory.

Histology – the study of microscopic identification of cells and tissue and the structure and organisation of the same; a discipline within a hospital pathology laboratory.

Laparoscope – type of endoscope consisting of an illuminated tube and used to examine the peritoneal cavity.

Laparoscopic surgery – 'keyhole' surgery using, for example, endoscopic penetration either through a natural orifice or via an incision.

Microbiology – the study of micro-organisms; a discipline within a hospital pathology laboratory.

Nuclear Medicine – use of a gamma camera and injected radioactive isotopes to acquire images of body parts such as the liver and kidneys.

Orthotics – provision of orthopaedic appliances such as braces for limbs.

Phlebotomy – the incision of a vein (venipuncture) for taking blood for samples etc.

Pyelogram – (or intravenous pyelogram) an X-ray picture of the kidneys, ureters and bladder taken after the injection of a radiopaque dye.

Stent – A mould or device made of stent (a compound used for making medical and dental moulds) used for supporting body openings/cavities during grafting of vessels and of tubes of the body during surgical joining of ducts or blood vessels.

Telemedicine – medicine practised at a distance by use of communications technology such as videoconferencing, multimedia communications, internet and intranet.

Triage – process of assessing, prioritising and directing a number of patients for appropriate treatment according to the relative severity of the injury and urgency of treatment; historically, in the case of accidents and emergencies, but the term is now applied more widely to the initial assessment and care management of a group of patients needing treatment.

Ultrasound (imaging) – use of high-frequency sound to produce an image of internal structures that differ in the way they reflect sound waves.

HOSPICES

INTRODUCTION

The general philosophy should be to create a caring atmosphere for those who are terminally ill; institutional buildings are to be avoided. Many hospice designs are intended to have a domestic character: single storey where possible, using traditional materials, and set in carefully landscaped areas or gardens. All patients should have a good view of the garden area and, preferably, have easy access to it. The location should be away from noise, heavy traffic, smells and other pollution. The wards should be for no more than four patients, to avoid an institutional atmosphere, although single-bedded wards are generally limited to one or two per hospice to avoid any feeling of loneliness or isolation. Good natural lighting and ventilation is required to all patient rooms; finishes should have a domestic (rather than medical or institutional) character. Avoidance of glare is important.

Communal areas (e.g. sitting rooms, dining rooms, hobby areas etc.) are very important to allow patients to join in the community of the hospice if they wish. A chapel or quiet room is usually considered essential. The location of the laying-out room or mortuary, and associated facilities, is very important. Death is a constant factor in a hospice, and patients often wish to be more closely involved than is usually the case in hospitals. Some may wish to use the hospice on a day-centre basis, where they can meet in-patients, and obtain expert attention. Others may wish to stay for only a week or two while their families have a rest. Provision of children's accommodation needs to be considered, both in terms of ward provision and crèche or nursery facilities.

A hospice is short-stay: the average stay is 7 days, the longest is 2 months. Many hospices are organised and funded by locally based charities, without a great deal of central control, and therefore the amount of provision can vary widely. The minimum size is eight beds; maximum 25 beds.

The following is taken, with permission, from the philosophy prepared by the Hospice of St Francis, which is part of an internationally recognised movement:

As far as possible life for those who will not recover from their illness should be purposeful, acceptable and fulfilling. Staff should help patients to retain their self-esteem and self-integrity, so that their approach to death may be peaceful and dignified. The environment should be conducive to these aims, promoting an atmosphere of love and security.

Each patient should be cared for as a person with his/her own unique, individual needs, which may be physical, psychological, social, intellectual, spiritual and emotional (holism).

Patients should be treated with compassion and humility, kindness, gentleness, sensitivity and honesty.

Nursing will be based on the principles of individualised care planned in partnership with the patient and based, as far as possible, on the patient's normal routine and life-style. Patients should be enabled to do what they can for themselves, nursing intervention replacing only that which they are incapable of doing.

Patients should be included in decisions regarding the management of their own care, and goals set bearing in mind the patient's own priorities of need.

1 Schematic layout

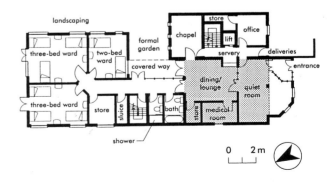

2 Harlington Hospice, Middlesex: design for hospice for eight patients, ground floor plan; tinted area represents existing house, the rest represents proposed new building; some accommodation is in the basement and first floor of house (not shown)
(Arch: Triforum Ltd)

DETAILED DESIGN

Note that room sizes can vary considerably, depending on local provision; where none has been given, it is because there appears to be no consensus on an optimum size.

Although the client is usually a voluntary or religious organisation, careful liaison is needed with the local health authority (NHS Trust). This organisation has the responsibility (delegated from the government) for registration and inspection of independent nursing homes in their area, and also registration of proprietors and managers. Registration may also be required with the Local Authority (Social Services Dept) as a Residential Care Home.

Registration requirements include that the hospice must provide an adequate standard of care, that those owning or working at the premises must be 'fit persons', and that the building must be fit for its purpose.

Typical hospice accommodation could provide for
- 15 to 20 patients/residents
- 1 single respite bed (for chronic illness)
- 50 out-patients
- day-space of 2.3 m²/person should be provided.

Patient accommodation should normally all be on the ground floor but if accommodation on more than one floor is unavoidable, a lift (suitable for people with disabilities) must be provided.

Patient/resident facilities

Wards/bedrooms   One-, two- or three-bedded wards (single rooms should have an area of 10 m² minimum; double rooms 16 m²) with en-suite bathrooms where possible. Not all bathrooms need to have disabled facilities. Additional separate WCs and shower rooms may be required.
Entrance area/patient reception   (16–30 m²)
Day room/sitting room   (20–35 m²)
Guest room   (10–20 m²) with adjacent WC and washing facilities; can also serve as quiet room.
Meeting room   (13 m²)
Lounge/dining room   (20–50 m²)
Storage room   Needed, for example, for wheelchairs.
Chapel   (15 m²) or non-denominational quiet room.

Support facilities and administration

(Some areas need not be on ground floor):
Administrator's room   (10 m²)
Staff room   (12–25 m²) to have fridge and desk; the nurse-call system panel is often located here.
WC and changing room
Matron's room   (10 m²)
Secretary's office
General office
Meeting room   For 12–15 people.
Jumble room   Also for use of volunteers and fund-raising groups.
Storage space
Medical treatment room   (10–20 m²)
Drug store   Adjacent to the medical treatment room, this must be of substantial construction (to prevent forced entry), must be kept locked, and should be in a cool location. It should provide separate compartments for various categories of medicines and drugs, and it may need to be large enough to

first floor

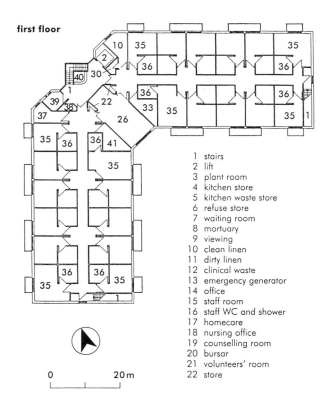

1 stairs
2 lift
3 plant room
4 kitchen store
5 kitchen waste store
6 refuse store
7 waiting room
8 mortuary
9 viewing
10 clean linen
11 dirty linen
12 clinical waste
13 emergency generator
14 office
15 staff room
16 staff WC and shower
17 homecare
18 nursing office
19 counselling room
20 bursar
21 volunteers' room
22 store

0   20 m

ground floor

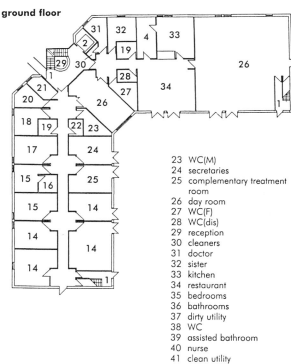

23 WC(M)
24 secretaries
25 complementary treatment room
26 day room
27 WC(F)
28 WC(dis)
29 reception
30 cleaners
31 doctor
32 sister
33 kitchen
34 restaurant
35 bedrooms
36 bathrooms
37 dirty utility
38 WC
39 assisted bathroom
40 nurse
41 clean utility

basement

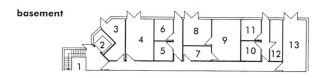

3 Brighton Aids Hospice, Brighton, Sussex
(Arch: Colwyn Foulkes & Partners)

accommodate a drug trolley. A separate lockable fridge may also be required. The key must be the personal responsibility of the nurse in charge.

Kitchen (15–35 m²) large domestic pattern cooker with gas hobs and two electric ovens; three fridges (to separate meat, cooked puddings, and other food); dishwasher; walk-in storage; separate pantry preferable.

Laundry and waste disposal (12–15 m²) to have washing machine(s), tumble drier(s) and ironing unit. Dirty linen should be stored in containers which are disposable or which can be regularly disinfected.

Sluice room (6–15 m²) to have bedpan washer.

Workshop

Boiler room/plant room There must be back-up equipment for heating and electrical generation in the event of failure of primary equipment.

Staff Could comprise: one full-time secretary; one full-time

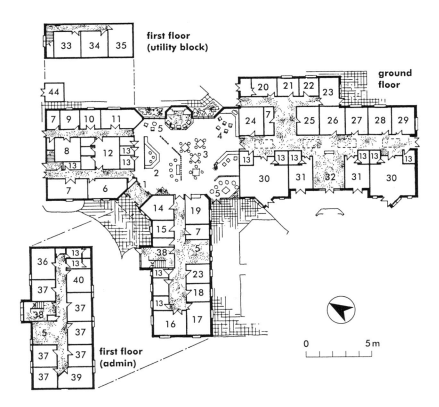

ground floor
1 entrance; 2 reception; 3 dining area; 4 TV area; 5 sitting area; 6 staff dining/conference; 7 store; 8 laundry; 9 utility; 10 hair salon; 11 physiotherapy; 12 kitchen; 13 WC; 14 home care office; 15 unit office; 16 assisted bathroom; 17 consultant/treatment; 18 interview; 19 activity kitchen; 20 viewing room; 21 sister; 22 doctor; 23 quiet room; 24 linen and equipment store; 25 pantry; 26 dirty utility; 27 treatment/clean utility; 28 assisted shower and WC; 29 assisted hairwash and WC; 30 four-bed ward; 31 one-bed ward; 32 day sitting room

first floor (utility block)
33 plant; 34 changing (M); 35 changing (F)
first floor (admin)
36 seminar/conference; 37 office; 38 stair; 39 library
site layout
40 terrace; 41 lawn; 42 informal garden; 43 parking; 44 refuse; 45 possible future extension to a 20-bed ward

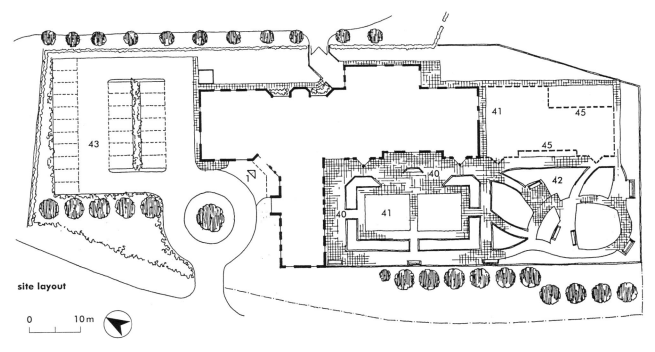

4 Dartford Hospice, Kent
(Arch: Architects Design Partnership)

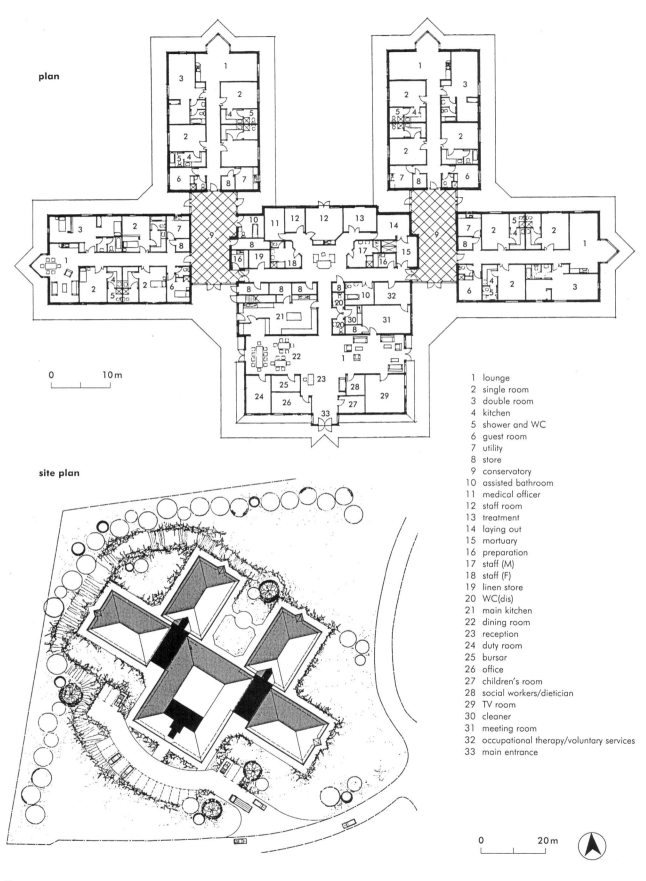

plan

site plan

0   10m

1   lounge
2   single room
3   double room
4   kitchen
5   shower and WC
6   guest room
7   utility
8   store
9   conservatory
10 assisted bathroom
11 medical officer
12 staff room
13 treatment
14 laying out
15 mortuary
16 preparation
17 staff (M)
18 staff (F)
19 linen store
20 WC(dis)
21 main kitchen
22 dining room
23 reception
24 duty room
25 bursar
26 office
27 children's room
28 social workers/dietician
29 TV room
30 cleaner
31 meeting room
32 occupational therapy/voluntary services
33 main entrance

0   20m

5 Milestone House Hospice, Edinburgh: layout arranged as four 'bungalows' attached to central block by conservatories; each bungalow has one double and three single rooms, and one guest room; each room has WC and shower, and simple kitchen (Arch: David Boyle Associates)

admin/fund-raiser; one full-time medical director; one matron; nurses (part and full-time); one part-time social worker; volunteers and fund-raising groups.

A registered general nurse must be on duty or resident at all times, plus at least one other member of staff (minimum staff ratios for each 24 hour period are one whole-time equivalent to two patients). There must be a qualified cook and adequate kitchen support staff.

Possible additional provision

This could include:
- physiotherapy room (15–30 m²)
- laying-out room/mortuary (12 m²), with associated viewing area (8–14 m²); undertaker must have unobtrusive collection point
- separate dining room
- interview/counselling room (8–12 m²)
- vestry for chapel
- quiet room (15 m²)
- crèche
- staff teaching/study area (12–19 m²)
- utility room (10–20 m²), for hairdressing/beauty care etc.
- day centre/clinic facilities
- hobby or seminar area (20–25 m²)
- family room (20 m²)
- separate WCs for guests.

Other specialist equipment

This will include:
- special beds
- phone to each bed-space

- nurse call system, required for each bed-head, bathroom, WC and dayroom, with the call-board located at a base room with 24-hour staffing.

Indicator lights are required outside the entrance to each room. Single doors of 900 mm nominal width (to allow for full wheelchair access) are preferable to double doors. Bathrooms with disabled facilities may require island baths (i.e. not placed against walls).

Storage and disposal of waste

This must be carefully organised: incineration is the most effective solution, but local incineration may not be permitted. The Local Authority and local health and safety department must be consulted. All waste must be collected in colour-coded bags (e.g. black bags for normal household waste, yellow bags for waste for incineration, and red bags for infected linen from, for example, hepatitis B and AIDS patients).

Medical gases

Suitable storage will always be required. Cylinders are normally secured in trolleys or with chains.

Heating and power
- all patient areas: 18°C minimum
- day spaces: 21°C minimum.

Radiators may be required to have a surface temperature of 50°C maximum or a substantial fixed guard. Emergency heating (e.g. back-up boilers) must be provided to ensure the above temperatures are maintained in the event of a breakdown.

Adequate local lighting is required and sufficient power points should be provided to prevent trailing leads.

HOTELS

F. Lawson

CATEGORIES OF HOTELS

Hotels may be categorised in terms of location, market orientation and standards, the latter affecting the levels of tariffs charged. Individual hotels may also be operated independently or as part of a chain, the latter usually specifying standards to meet brand requirements. The residential areas of a hotel normally account for at least 65—70% of the total built space, and the number of bedrooms is critical in relation to hotel operation (see table below).

rooms	
family run hotels, guesthouses	< 25
independent hotels, country houses	50–80
budget inns, lodges	80–120
suburban hotels, airport hotels	120–200
resort hotels	200–300
luxury hotels, boutique hotels	150–250
city-centre convention hotels	300–500
integrated resort villages	300–800
mega-resorts, casino hotels	500–1000+

National systems of classification may be compulsory or voluntary and vary in requirements and designation (stars, crowns, figures, letters). Most are based on the World Tourism Organisation (WTO) model but customised to suit local requirements.

LOCATIONS

Site selection and decisions on hotel facilities are largely dictated by town and country planning and other conditions, market feasibility and investment appraisal. The range of new developments covers the types outlined below.

City centre hotels

High costs of land in cities restrict prime sites to higher grade hotels and justify expensive conversions. These include large 'convention hotels', which are mainly operated by international chains and are characterised by high plot ratios, often with high-rise construction, and extensive facilities for business visitors, including large meeting and function rooms. Club leisure centres and shops are commonly included to increase viability. 'De luxe (5★) hotels', including intimate 'boutique hotels', provide the highest standards of quality and service, and are invariably confined to select areas overlooking parks or water and near elegant shopping avenues. 'All-suite hotels' cater mainly for business users requiring separated living rooms, while 'serviced apartments' offer self-contained accommodation with the benefit of other hotel services.

Suburban hotels

Hotels on suburban sites and in urban redevelopment areas are mainly mid-grade, catering for business and other visitors to the locality as well as travellers en route. They are best sited near major road intersections, business parks and major institutions. Facilities typically include standardised rooms, one or two restaurants, some meeting/function rooms, a gymnasium and extensive parking.

Motor hotels

Accommodation for travellers en route includes budget chains of 'lodges', 'inns' and 'motels', with highly standardised blocks of bedrooms sited alongside service stations on motorways and highways, 'motor hotels' and 'suburban hotels' near major road junctions, and 'airport/seaport hotels'. Hotels must be conspicuous and easily recognised, with easy access and a high ratio of parking spaces. Facilities are similar to suburban hotels but higher grade 'convention hotels' are also sited near major airports and other prime places easily accessible to travellers.

Resort hotels

New hotels in destination resorts are generally high standard with extensive leisure facilities plus large meeting rooms for out-of-season conventions and banquets. Locations include high rated seaside and mountain resorts. There are also 'country hotels', with associated golf courses, sports and equestrian facilities, and 'marina hotels' with sailing harbours.

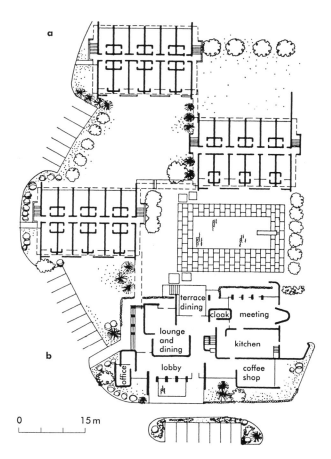

a units in blocks of 12 with access to parking at each end of building;
b catering and admin building provides entertaining, dining and meeting facilities

1 Motor hotel, Revere, Massachusetts, USA
(Arch: Salsberg & Le Blanc)

Related developments

'Resort villages' are large integrated complexes of tourist accommodation clustered around swimming pools and other leisure attractions, which may be glass enclosed for all-weather, year-round attraction. Self-owned properties in 'condominiums' share common central amenities and management services. Other resort properties may be in individual or multiple ownership, such as 'timeshare' arrangements. More specialised 'executive conference centres' combine residential accommodation with high-quality conference and fitness facilities.

FUNCTIONAL RELATIONSHIPS

Four distinct types of areas are involved: guest rooms, public areas, administration offices and 'back-of-house' facilities. Relationships between these areas must be planned to provide separation of customer and back-of-house areas but also allow efficient service without cross-circulation or distraction (see **2,3**).

Layouts depend on the location and surroundings, the area, contours and cost of site, plot ratios and other planning conditions, and the required size (number of guest rooms) and sophistication of hotel. Three examples of conceptual approaches are shown in **4**.

Guest rooms are sited to take advantage of the best views and orientation while minimising noise and disturbance. This also applies to those public areas in which daylight is essential: from restaurants, small meeting rooms and foyers or lounge areas to larger convention halls.

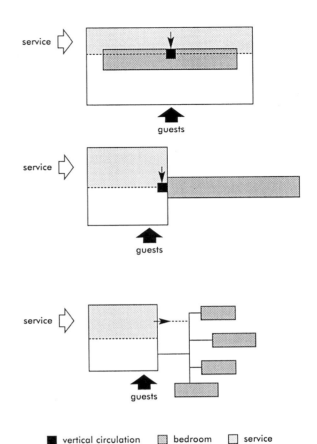

- ■ vertical circulation
- bedroom
- □ service

3 Three basic arrangements for relationship of bedroom block to public room areas

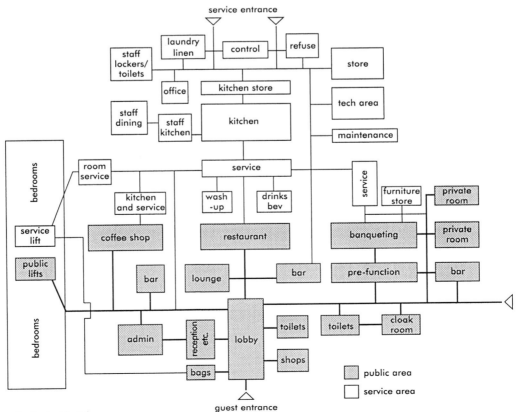

2 Flow diagram for typical hotel

high-grade city hotel

based on 280 guest rooms on eight floors above ground floor

public areas include: lobby lounge, theme bar, main restaurant; coffee shop; banquet hall (divisible) with adjacent foyer and meeting rooms; large leisure club

back-of-house services are on the ground and basement levels with access to service lifts

 back-of-house and service areas

 administration

1 stairs, emergency exits
2 meeting/committee rooms
3 front offices
4 admin/executive offices
5 kitchen/food preparation
6 main stores
7 employee changing, etc.
8 housekeeping with adjacent laundry areas
9 technical areas, engineering offices

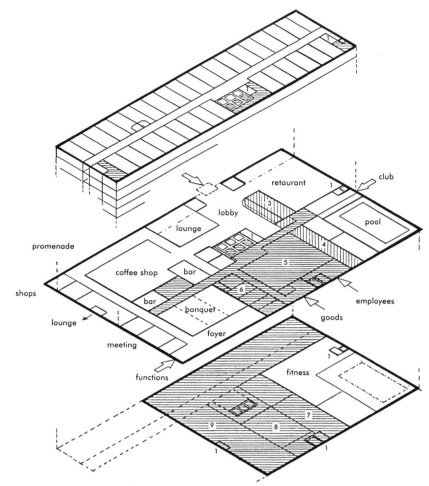

suburban hotel

144 standard guest rooms occupy three floors over the extended ground floor, which provides public areas, back-of-house and 14 guestrooms (total 158 rooms)

one restaurant area with adjacent bar and lounge

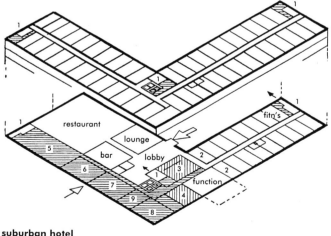

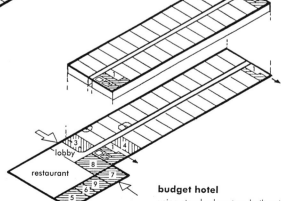

budget hotel

using standard, system-built units and designed for minimum service, this may have 52 rooms (two floors), or 79 rooms (three floors)

guest rooms have en suite shower rooms

4 Functional relationships: stylised examples of hotel layouts
(F. Lawson)

Space allocation

Typical allocations of the total built space are indicated for hotels of 1★ (budget) to 5★ (deluxe) classification. With increasing sophistication, guest room areas become larger and a greater proportion of space is allocated to public and back-of house-facilities (see **5**). The latter will depend on the scope for attracting non-residential custom, functions and conventions as well as the extent of services contracted out (particularly laundry, central food preparation, and maintenance).

A more detailed analysis of space in two types of hotel illustrates the range of facilities provided. These will vary with each site and particular requirements (see **6**).

Structural design

Guest rooms are invariably designed to standard repetitive modules facilitating system building and prefabrication, rapid construction, bulk purchasing and efficient housekeeping and maintenance. Dimensions and gross factors are critical.

Public areas generally require larger spans and may extend into podium or atrium spaces.

Ballrooms used for conventions must have large column-free areas and are often divisible with movable, sound-proofed partitions.

standard category	economy ★	moderate ★★	good ★★★	high ★★★★	Deluxe ★★★★★
gross areas (m²/room)					
residential	22[4]	27	33	44[2]	53[2]
public/support	5.5[5]	8	12	18[3]	22
total	27.5	35	45	62[3]	75

[1] mid-range: may vary by ±3%
[2] includes 5% suites (two rooms)
[3] increase by 2–4 m²/room for large convention, spa or casino facilities
[4] with en-suite shower rooms; others have en-suite bathrooms
[5] minimum catering

5 Typical allocation of built areas: hotels[1]
(F. Lawson)

typical provisions	500 room ★★★★ city-centre hotel		200 room ★★★ suburban hotel	
guest rooms and suites	32		25	
circulation, services, etc.	12		7.5	
total residential areas	44.0	71.0%	32.5	72.2%
lobby with lounge area	1.0		1.0	
shops	0.2	1.9%	0.1	2.4%
coffee shop	0.8		0.8	
main restaurant	0.7			
speciality restaurant	0.4		0.7	
lounges, bars	1.1		0.8	
circulation, cloaks etc.	0.6	5.8%	0.6	6.7%
pre-function area, foyer	0.5			
ballroom/banquet hall	1.5			
conference/function rooms*	1.9	6.3%	1.3	2.9%
leisure pool areas*	0.6			
club facilities/fitness room*	0.6	1.9%	0.4	0.9%
front office, administration*	1.6	2.6%	1.4	3.1%
main and satellite kitchens	1.1		0.8	
stores, circulation, etc.*	0.5		0.2	
receiving/garbage areas*	0.3		0.3	
general stores*	0.4		0.4	
housekeeping, laundry*	1.2		1.4	
engineer, stores, equipment*	1.8		1.3	
employee/control/personnel*	0.2		0.1	
changing, lockers, canteen*	1.0	10.5%	0.8	11.8%
total built area	62.0	100%	45.0	100%

* gross areas, including circulation and ancillary areas

6 Space allocations
(F. Lawson)

GUEST ROOMS

Internal room dimensions are dictated by the market requirements, standards of hotel, number and sizes of beds and furniture. Twin beds (1000×2000 mm) or one double (1500×2000 mm, for single or double occupancy) are most common, with queen size (1650×2000 mm), king size (2000×2000 mm) or double used in higher grade hotels, particularly in America. In studio rooms, a convertible settee provides a third bed for family use.

Floor-to-ceiling heights are usually 2.5 m (minimum 2.3 m), lowered to 2.0 m in the room lobby to allow for mechanical services. The most critical plan dimension is room width: 3.6 m (12 ft) is efficient, allowing a wardrobe in the lobby and furniture along the party wall (see **7a**). With staggered wardrobes and minimum space, width can be reduced to 3.4 mm (see **7h**). For a narrow frontage, the minimum room width is 3.0 m (see **7c**). Increased room width allows more spacious impression and alternative bed and bathroom layouts (see **7c,g**). Room length is usually more flexible and may extend to a balcony or angled window for directional view (see **7f**). Executive rooms have a workstation/lounge near the window. Larger and multi-room suites are usually limited to corner areas and the top residential floor, where changes in the module are practical.

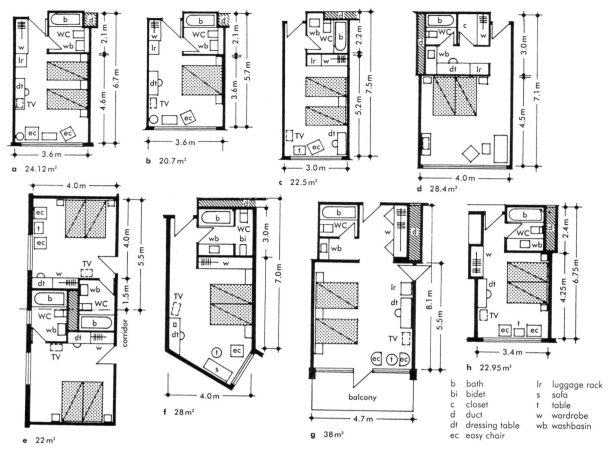

7 Guest room dimensions

a standard twin guest room: 3.6m (12 ft) optimum width for efficiency; wardrobe in lobby and furniture on party wall

b double bed (single/double occupancy) allows shorter room or space for work area

c narrow frontage: minimum width 3.0m

d increased width 4.0m: allows bed rearrangement and separate dressing area

e central bathroom: one with natural light

f high-class room with separate WC and bidet areas; in any scheme, an angled window gives less light but extra sitting area and directional view

g spacious room with external balcony; separate washbasin

h minimum dimensions for twin rooms with staggered wardrobes

b	bath	lr	luggage rack
bi	bidet	s	sofa
c	closet	t	table
d	duct	w	wardrobe
dt	dressing table	wb	washbasin
ec	easy chair		

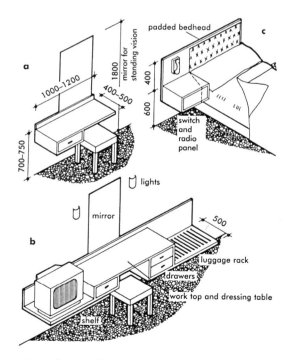

a minimum dressing table unit

b combined unit: firmly cantilevered to facilitate cleaning or frame supported; durable, scratch/stain proof surfaces with back upstand; balanced wall lighting

c bed head with side table (may be splayed for bed movement): telephone, radio and lighting controls installed; individual reading lamps

8 Guest bedroom fittings

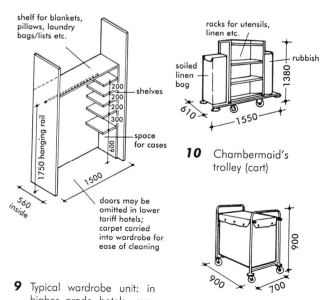

9 Typical wardrobe unit: in higher grade hotels, may be fitted with drinks cabinet and wall safe

10 Chambermaid's trolley (cart)

11 Linen trolley (cart): fabric

En suite bathrooms

Bathrooms are mainly sited on interior walls, using mechanical ventilation. For minimum building width, bathrooms may be one behind the other between rooms. Luxury bathrooms or economy shower rooms may be against external walls. Adjacent pairs of rooms are arranged mirror image to share common vertical ducts and isolate bathroom noise transmission. (See **12**.)

Typical fitments: 1500mm bath, with grab bars, shower spray, retractable clothes line and curtain/screen; WC and washbasin. High-grade hotels use 1700mm bath, twin basins set in vanitory surrounds, WC and bidet. Luxury units include separate dressing area and shower. Safety considerations are critical.

Requirements: non-slip, drained surfaces; tiled walls; acoustic ceiling; mirror over basin; screened, moisture-proof lighting; panel access to services; controlled warmed air inflow/extraction; mixer valve and thermostat control of hot water; shelf space, towel racks, toilet roll holder, coat hanger, electric shaver point, lidded waste bin, tissue dispenser, toiletry tray/basket. In higher grade hotels: telephone, music relay.

Resident circulations

Gross residential areas add circulation and floor service spaces to the net room areas (see **13**). Gross factors can range from less than 5% for chalet and lodge type buildings with external entrances, through 20–30% for 'double-loaded' central corridors accessed by lifts and stairs, up to 35–45% for single-loaded side corridors and tower buildings.

As a rule emergency stairs must be sited at or near the ends of each corridor. Lengths of corridors are limited by travel distances to protected fire escape stairs as specified in local codes. For corridors with sprinkler systems and fire exits at/near opposite ends allowing two directions of escape, maximum distances usually range from 45 to 60m (with smoke doors at 30m). Dead-end corridors with one exit are limited to 7.6m and travel distances within suites of rooms to 9m.

Minimum fire resistance periods for separation of exits such as staircases are normally: 1 hour for buildings up to three storeys, 2 hours for four storeys or more. Combustible material and surface flame ratings of linings in exit routes are controlled. Large hotels use automatic sprinkler systems, fire mode ventilation switching with alarm, lift and smoke door activation. Fire alarm, indication panel and hydrant systems must be installed, together with portable and CO_2 extinguishers (for electrical equipment), in specific areas as required.

Apart from atrium scenic lifts, guest lifts are best located off the main lobby within control of the front desk. Guest and service lifts, normally in the ratio 2:1, 3:2 or 4:3, are often sited back to back for economy, the service lifts rising from back-of-house areas and opening into a separated service lobby on each floor (see **3,14**). Large and high-grade hotels often require specific provision for luggage handling.

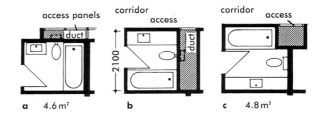

12 Typical arrangements of bathrooms and ducts: (a) is best for access to duct but (b) and (c) provide more space for vanity top

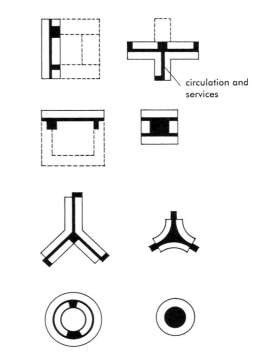

13 Plan forms for bedroom accommodation

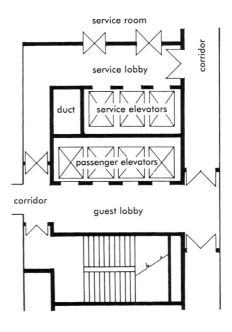

14 Typical vertical circulation core for 500 bedroom hotel

Guests with disabilities

Statutory provision must be made to enable easy access for users with disabilities to designated rooms, usually 1–2% of the total, as well as to the public areas. Requirements include: ramps 1:20; corridors at least 915 mm wide; doors 815 mm clear opening with lobbies 460 mm wider than the door on the latch side. Bathrooms require: 1.52 m central turning space and 2.75 m width, specially designed fittings and grab bars. Between beds and furniture, 910 mm space is required; 685 mm for knee space; switches set 1.2 m high. For window cills, mirrors, etc., note that wheelchair eye level is 1.07–1.37 m high.

ENTRANCES

The main entrance must be conspicuous and attractive. Forecourt space should allow for: pedestrians; persons alighting from vehicles, vehicles waiting and passing without hazard; coach waiting and baggage storage for large tourist groups. Revolving doors or a draught lobby with automatic doors are used in larger hotels. Alternative baggage entrance, disabled access and fire escape routes need to be considered.

Car parking space depends on the location, transport modes and the availability of public parking close by. Motor, suburban and airport hotels typically provide 1.1 spaces/room, city-centre hotels 0.3 spaces/room plus 0.2 spaces/convention or banqueting seat. Resort hotels used by tour groups may require less than 0.2 spaces/room plus coach waiting areas.

LOBBIES

The main lobby is the hub of circulation, a place for assembly, waiting, registration, account settling and information services. Ranging from high-grade city hotels (about 1.0 m² per room), often spectacular in design, to budget designs (about 0.3 m² per room or less), the lobby includes a front desk, lounge-waiting area, public telephones, cloakrooms and facilities for luggage handling and safe deposit. In larger hotels, this may extend to individual or arcades of shops, concierge, currency changing, telephone exchange, bell-captain, group registration and other services. (See **15–18**.)

The front desk is set back at least 1.2 m from circulation routes and is supported by a front office. Planned around 1.5–1.8 m vdu workstations, it has reception, cashier and information (concierge) sections and is adjacent to the telephone switchboard, meter and alarm indicator panels. Working space behind the desk: 1.2–1.5 m. Desk lengths: 50 rooms, 3 m; 100/150 rooms, 4.5 m; 200/250 rooms, 7.5 m; 300/400 rooms, 10.5 m. A separate area for convention reception/information may be required.

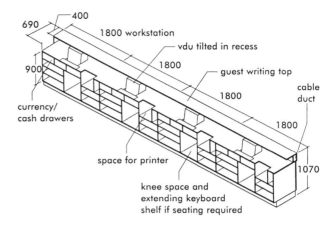

15 Typical reception desk for 300–400 rooms: four to five stations with reception, cashier and information sections; central stations are flexible for check-in/cash-out to allow for peak arrival/departure flows; working heights are for standing; writing tops 300–400 mm wide; concierge desk may be sited separately; key and message rack may be sited behind the counter, but preferably screened (Fred Lawson)

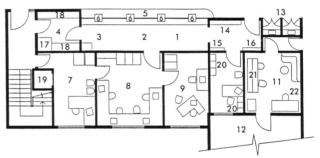

1 reception; 2 information (general); 3 cashier; 4 safety deposit; 5 front counter; 6 vdu monitor (printers below counter); 7 front office manager; 8 front office; 9 cashier/accountant; 10 security manager; 11 telephone operators; 12 business centre; 13 public telephones; 14 key/letter rack; 15 indicators (fire); 16 meters; 17 desk; 18 deposit boxes; 19 safe; 20 monitors (cameras, entry); 21 switchboard consoles; 22 rest area

16 Compact arrangement for front desk and office for 300 room hotel: executive offices on another floor; first aid room located near by; separate computer room; located within clear view of main entrance; set back 1.2–2.0 m from main circulation, on route to guest rooms and lifts (Fred Lawson)

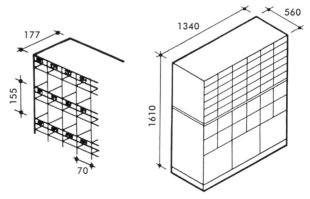

17 Key and letter rack

18 Typical bank of safety deposit boxes; various sizes should be provided

breakdown of public areas

restaurants	m²	occupancy	
main lobby:			
main restaurant	595	425	
coffee shop	280	400	
lobby bar	185	185	
mezzanine:			
gourmet restaurant	370	200	
lower lobby:			
snack bar	175	185	
ice cream bar and café	93	75	
night club	520	375	
convention space		**meeting**	**banquet**
small ballroom 1	520	800	400
small ballroom 2	390	600	300
grand ballroom	3750	5785	2900
guest of honour room	540	758	880
total 3 adjoining ballrooms	4660	7148	3580
pre-convention foyer space	740		
total area contiguous meeting room	5390		
21 additional meeting rooms:			
average size 75–100 person	70		
exhibition space (convertible to parking)	7930		
shops			
main lobby floor	58		
mezzanine	520		
lower lobby	432		
total	*1010*		

main lobby floor

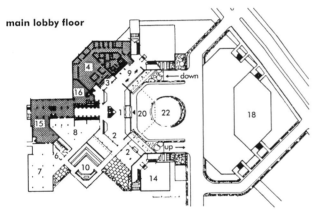

lower lobby floor

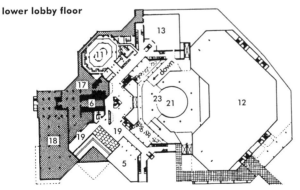

1 main lobby; 2 lobby lounge; 3 registration; 4 admin; 5 shops and agencies; 6 check room; 7 restaurant; 8 coffee shop; 9 news stand; 10 bar/cocktail lounge; 11 discotheque; 12 grand ballroom; 13 meeting room; 14 receiving kichen; 15 main kitchen; 16 room service; 17 kitchen; 18 mechanical; 19 snack bar; 20 main entrance; 21 convention foyer; 22 open light-well; 23 convention entrance

19 Phoenix of Atlanta Hotel, USA: total of 2058 guest rooms (Arch: Anan Lapidus)

ground floor

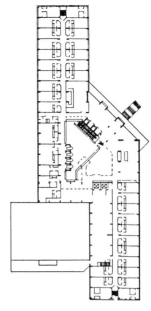

typical guest room floors

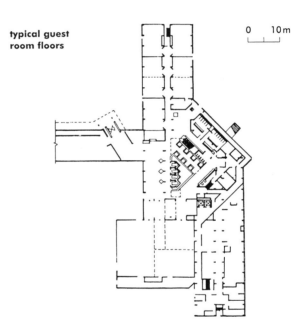

0   10m

20 Hyatt Hotel, Boston, USA: atrium design with added feature of orientation over river providing view from public spaces and guest rooms (Arch: John Portman)

RESTAURANTS, BARS, FUNCTION ROOMS

More than one food outlet is offered by high-grade hotels, typically designed as the main restaurant, a coffee shop, theme, ethnic or speciality restaurant and a café-bar for more casual day or leisure area use. The largest restaurant or coffee shop is adapted for more concentrated breakfast service. Usually the public facilities include a sophisticated cocktail bar, adjacent to the main restaurants, and a separate main bar designed to create social interest. Refreshments are also served in the lobby lounge.

The ratio of covers (seats) provided per room depends on the extent of non-residential demand, group travel and room service. As a guide: city-centre hotels, 0.8–1.2 seats/room; resort hotels, 1.8–2.0

In mid-grade hotels one restaurant with an adjacent bar is usual; in budget hotels this is usually limited to simple continental breakfast counter service or operated independently in a separate unit.

High-grade hotels usually offer separate banquet halls and function rooms for conventions and group events. Group access is via foyers or pre-function rooms which provide cloakroom facilities and temporary refreshments service. Large ballrooms are usually divisible with removable sound-proof partitions. Each of the separated areas must have its own independent access and service entrance, air-conditioning, lighting, power, audio-visual aid services and controls.

typical areas	(m²/cover)
high-class restaurant	2.0–2.4
coffee shop	1.6–1.8
banquet	1.1–1.3
smaller function	1.6–1.8
foyer	0.3–0.5
service areas	**(m²/cover)**
main kitchen	0.9–1.0
banquet kitchen	0.2–0.3
satellite service kitchen	0.3–0.4
furniture stores (ballroom)	0.2

Food service planning in a large hotel is often complex. Control systems for food received, in storage and used is necessary. Main and satellite kitchens must be level with and adjacent to the restaurants served. Transport of food to outlets on a different floor requires dedicated goods lifts.

Apart from standard continental breakfasts ordered in advance, room service is expensive and limited to high-grade hotels. Service pantries, with basic equipment, on each floor are used in conjunction with food prepared in the main kitchen, having access to the service lifts (see **21**).

Leisure facilities

Enclosed leisure areas range from a fitness room to a fully equipped health club with pool and spa facilities attracting local fee members. In resorts, leisure facilities are crucial and buildings are planned around landscaped pools and attractions.

Built areas: high (urban), 1.3 m²/room; mid-grade, 0.3 m²/room; resort, 0.3–0.5 m²/room (+ large external areas).

LAUNDRY AND HOUSEKEEPING

Collection of soiled laundry may be by trolley or chute. In small or economy hotels most laundry is contracted out. A standard laundry room for a 200 room hotel takes up about 160 m², plus separate linen storage and housekeeping areas of 80 m². Requirements include ventilation giving rates of 15 to 20 air changes/hour, separate extracts from steam and dry cleaning equipment, high lighting (160 lux), moisture- and fireproof electrical systems, non-slip flooring and drainage, and storage for chemicals.

Housekeeping areas are 0.4 m²/room. Separate areas may be required for sewing work, uniforms and guest valet services (see **22,23**).

Other stores

Separate secure storage with controlled issue required for:

- furniture (with repair and paint shops adjacent)
- cleaning materials
- glass, china, silver
- drinks – red wines (14–16°C), white wines (10–12°C), spirits, beers, etc. and soft drinks.

Overall area: high-grade, 0.8–1.2 m²/room; budget, 0.3–0.5 m²/room

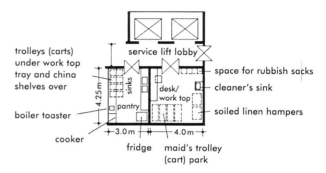

21 Typical service area for 50–60 rooms/floor: note provision of pantry depends on class of hotel and room service arrangements in kitchen; local linen store or cupboard may be required depending on method of control

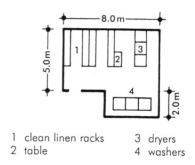

1 clean linen racks 3 dryers
2 table 4 washers

22 Non-iron laundry for 120 bedroom hotel

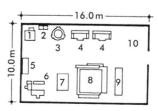

1 tumbler 6 press and board
2 tubs 7 shake-out table
3 extractor 8 four-roll ironer
4 washer 9 folding table
5 table 10 soiled linen area

23 Laundry for 200 bedroom hotel

EMPLOYEE FACILITIES

- Employees per room: luxury, 1.5; high-grade, 0.8–1.0; mid-grade, 0.5–0.6; budget, 0.2–0.3.
- Requirements: controlled entry with time recording; personnel offices; lockers (one per employee); changing rooms, showers and toilets with separate facilities for men and women.
- Staff canteen: to accommodate about one-third of staff numbers in shifts.

Area: luxury, 1.8 m²/room; high–mid-grade, 1.1 m²/room; budget, 0.5 m²/room.

Administration

Include the front office (located adjacent to the reception desk), executive, accounting, sales and catering offices, and personnel and engineer's offices (the last two being near the work areas). Group administration may be largely centralised. (See **24,25**.)

Area: high-grade, 1.6 m²/room; mid-grade, 1.2 m²/room; budget, 0.4 m²/room.

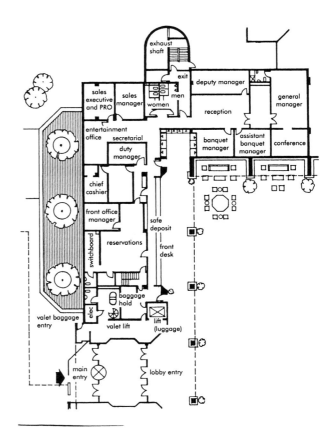

25 Example of admin offices for a large hotel: except for front desk, reservations and cashier, these may also be sited elsewhere (e.g. on mezzainine)

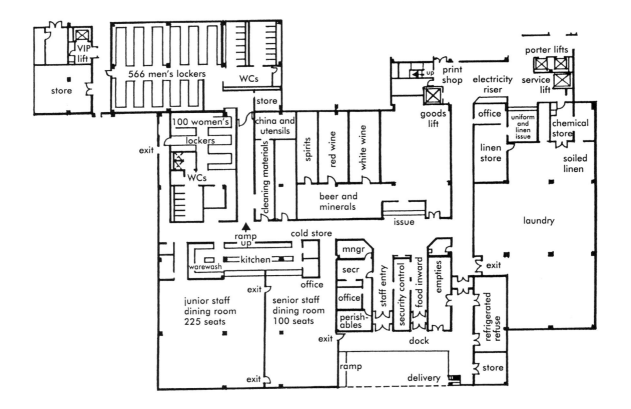

24 Service area and staff accommodation for large hotel

TECHNICAL AREAS

Space provisions depend on the extent of workshops on site: most phased maintenance and specialist repair work is contracted out. Technical equipment may be sited in back-of-house, on higher technical floors, roof or ceiling mounted or/and external to the building. (See **26**.)

Requirements in high-grade hotels: engineers' offices; security office; computer rooms; meter and switchgear room; electrical transformers; standby generators; telephone exchange equipment room; public address system; water storage, treatment, and pumping equipment; boiler plant and calorifiers; airconditioning plant and coolers; swimming pool treatment plant; workshops and equipment stores.

Total built areas: high-grade, 1.8 m²/room; mid-grade, 1.2 m²/room; budget, 0.6 m²/room.

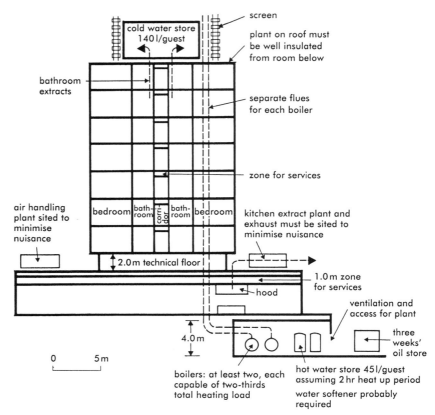

26 Section showing salient features of building services design for hotel

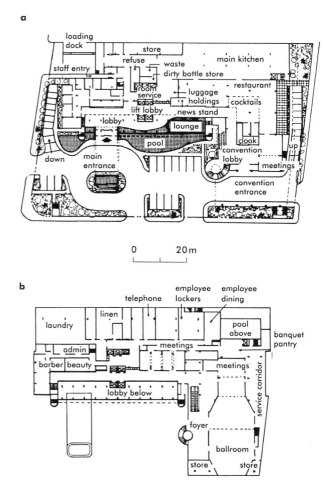

27 Small convention hotel (400 room): (a) ground floor; (b) upper floor, showing segregation of hotel and convention business vehicle traffic and tight control of service and personnel traffic inside

a

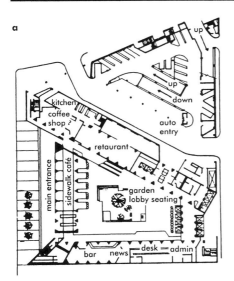

b

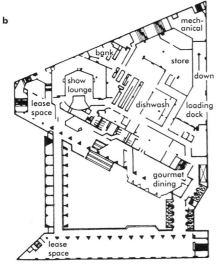

c

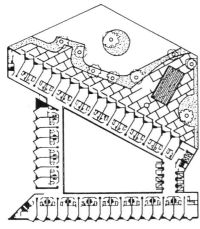

d

a lobby floor
b first floor
c typical guest room floor
d examples of bedroom suites showing provision of meeting space (note possible use of dividing walls to create smaller rooms

28 Hyatt Regency Hotel, Houston, Texas, USA
(Arch: JVIII)

section

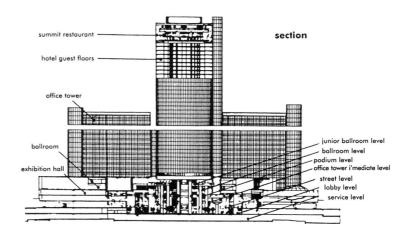

street level

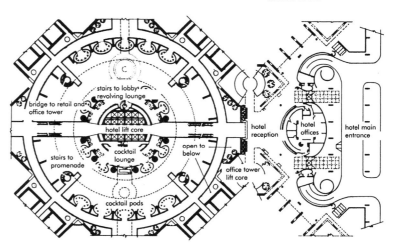

29 Renaissance Center, Detroit, USA: convention centre and 1400 room hotel with 2650 m² hall, 13 restaurants, office space, commercial retail space and rentable flats (or condominiums)
(Arch: John Portman)

HOUSING AND RESIDENTIAL BUILDINGS

See also sections on: Halls of Residence and Hostels, Hospices, nursing homes (in Health Service Buildings), Youth Hostels, Design for Accessibility

This section is arranged as follows:
- introduction
- public sector (social housing)
- private sector
- current trends: PPG 3, brownfield sites
- site topography, layout, access and garages
- relationship to other buildings (privacy etc.)
- dwelling design standards
- plan types (single storey, houses, flats)
- internal function: general factors, main entrance, living/reception, dining rooms, study, specialist rooms, kitchens, laundry/utility, bedrooms, bathrooms and WCs, storage
- safety and security.

Note: throughout this section, the word 'house' is often used, as it is a generally recognised term, to describe what is more correctly termed a dwelling.

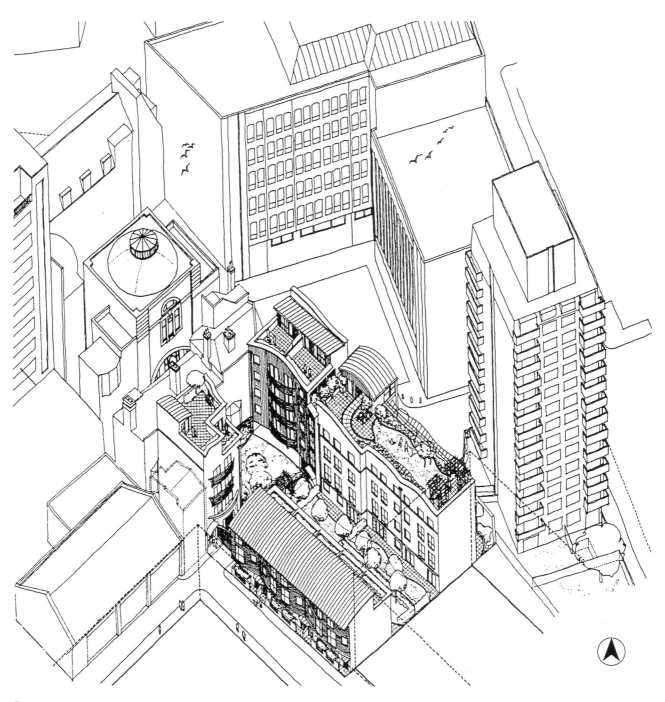

1 Social housing in the city: Green Dragon House, London WC2 (see also **7,138**)
(Arch: Monahan Blythen Architects)

INTRODUCTION

Historical context

Many designers look back to the Georgian terrace house as providing the finest urban housing ever produced in the UK, although its contribution was perhaps more in terms of its townscape value than internal arrangement, which was traditional, with the main floor on the first floor and the kitchens in the basement. However, by the second half of the 19th century, the kitchen and service facilities had been moved to the back addition, giving the typical Victorian L-shaped layout which has never been surpassed for its flexibility. Both the 18th and 19th century house have proved very adaptable to both changes in family size, the internal environment, and the provision of modern services and other amenities.

The poor quality of much Victorian housing, the lack of planning, and the related social conditions resulting from increasing urbanisation, led to the involvement of charitable trusts (e.g. the Peabody Trust) and philanthropic individuals, who developed the concept of model settlements (e.g. Saltaire, near Bradford (begun 1851), and Bournville, Birmingham (begun 1895)). These ideas were developed by Ebenezer Howard and others into the concept of the garden city. One of the earliest and most successful of the early developments, Hampstead Garden Suburb, north London (begun 1906) (see **3**), established a pattern copied throughout the UK and abroad. The layout remains remarkably successful – and has been a victim of its own success, as the original idea of a mix of social groups has given way to the present occupancy by middle-class professional people. The ideal of the semi-detached house set in its own garden seems to appeal to a very deep instinct within the British (or, more precisely, English) character. The garden city concept has been repeated an endless number of times in debased layouts, and although often criticised by designers for visual poverty and over-centralised planning, in social terms it is rarely unsuccessful.

Until the 1920s, provision of housing was generally by the private sector and charitable trusts; it was not until the 1909 Housing and Town Planning Act that all local authorities were required to establish housing and public health committees. By 1914, there were only some 20,000 local authority houses.

Low-rise layouts, based on the traditional grid layout or street pattern, were the norm, and applied equally to both private and public schemes, and it was not until the 1960s that high rise blocks in public-sector developments began to seriously challenge the traditional layout. The new ideas largely stemmed from the designs of Le Corbusier, who in the 1920s promoted the concept of the 'vertical garden city', and who had an enormous influence on British planning and design in the post-war period. One of the few outstanding examples of pre-war high-rise flats is High Point 1, Highgate, north London, by Lubetkin (1935).

The past 50 years

Probably more than any other building type, housing is influenced by factors outside the architect's control: for instance, by town planning constraints, socio-economic factors, and political considerations. Many consider these factors to have had a greater influence on the development of the layout and design of housing over the past 100 years than pure design considerations.

It is therefore essential to consider housing in its wider context. Attempting to identify some of the more important aspects of housing policy over the past 50 years or so, is a near-impossible task, but it will hopefully enable the designer to produce solutions applicable to current demands.

It is interesting to speculate on when, and why, housing came to be designed by architects. The individual house has always held great fascination for architects, but as far as mass housing is concerned, prior to the 20th century, perhaps only the Georgian terrace (and a few other rare exceptions) could be held to have been designed by architects. Only with the advent of socialist governments did general housing development become of real interest to architects.

It is also interesting that housing is one of the very few building types with a physical form that can remain largely unchanged for decades – in some instances, even for centuries (religious buildings are another example). The Victorian house (see **2**) is still a remarkably flexible unit; and the irony is that many would argue that the modern home is less flexible than many of its predecessors.

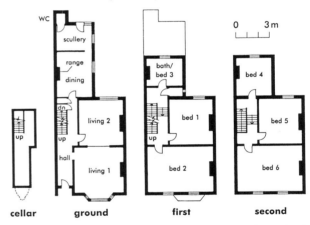

2 Typical late-Victorian L-shaped terrace house (note: back-addition has superseded 18th century basement and small cellar is now coal store; services (including range for cooking) generally grouped in back-addition, improving hygiene and minimising smells; bathroom on first floor was optional (could be bedroom); servants confined to back-addition and second floor bedroom; main rooms have direct access to garden)

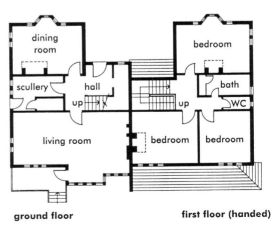

3 'Cottage' design at Hampstead Garden Suburb (Arch: Parker & Unwin)

In the UK, the traditional division has been into rented local authority accommodation, and private-sector housing, usually purchased with a building society mortgage. The private rented sector has been in decline since the rent restrictions imposed at the time of World War I, resulting in this sector becoming an insignificant part of the market (under 10%). Only in certain areas – such as renting for students, at the very top of the market (e.g. for those working for international companies) and also to some extent in Scotland – does the rented sector retain any significance. Current predictions are that around 150,000 new homes are required annually, or about 4 million by 2021.

Low-cost rural housing is an area traditionally neglected. Planning restrictions and the popularity of rural housing within higher-income groups has resulted in a severe shortage of straightforward housing, either to rent or for purchase, in the countryside. Two schemes designed to provide low-cost housing are at Abbotsbury and Broadwindsor (by Ken Morgan Architects) and The Apple House, Lytchett Matravers, Dorset.

PUBLIC SECTOR
Social housing
For much of the 20th century, until the mid-1980s, public-sector rented accommodation provided a huge amount of the housing stock. It was intended to cater for a social need; that is, to provide straightforward accommodation for lower-income groups who would normally have been unable to obtain a building society mortgage to purchase their own home. Of course, there were many exceptions to this – some people did not wish to buy, some considered it socially wrong, some wished to be able to move regularly, and so forth. Unfortunately, it has become a mark of social position to be purchasing one's own home, and a tremendous social division has arisen between those who own and those who rent.

Whereas the private sector was, on the whole, allowed to develop largely to satisfy market forces, the public sector was subject to constant involvement from many different groups (all no doubt with good intentions), and all attempting to offer solutions to two apparently intractable problems: firstly, what level of amenities to provide, and secondly how to finance the cost through the public purse.

Of the numerous guidelines produced, one of the most influential was the Parker Morris Report (1961) – see later, under Design Standards and Regulations.

This report proposed a set of minimum standards, which were made mandatory for public sector housing from 1967 to 1981, but never adopted by the private sector although this had been the original intention. From the 1980s, government policy has been to relax proscriptive standards wherever possible, with the result that there are at present only 'guidelines' on space standards for social housing, with very few mandatory requirements.

From the 1960s, an attempt was made to provide a 'third way' with the development of housing associations. These are semi-autonomous organisations, able to obtain public-sector finance via the Housing Corporation, a public body established by the Housing Act 1964. Housing associations have expanded to the extent that by the 1990s they were providing most of the public-sector housing in the UK (see **5**).

For a variety of factors, which many consider to be politically motivated but which were also financial, the provision of housing by local authorities has now slowed to a trickle (see **5**). There was also increasing concern about the whole concept of major redevelopment in urban areas, and the apparent deterioration, in visual and social terms, of many of the large developments of the 1960s and 1970s. High-rise developments (see **4** and pp. 183–4), considered essential in many post-war schemes, gradually gave way to low-rise, two- and three-storey housing. The 'right to buy' legislation, introduced by the Conservative Government in the

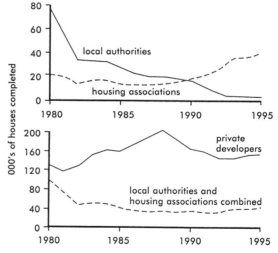

5 House-building trends in Britain, 1980–95 (from Goodchild, diagram 6.3)

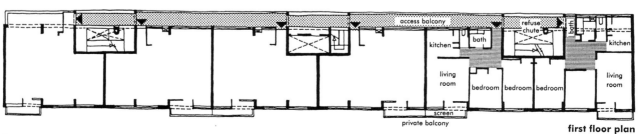

4 Slab block: nine-storey flats with balcony access, built 1953 at Pimlico, London; in situ reinforced concrete construction; note use of storage to insulate bedroom from stairwell (Arch: Powell & Moya)

early 1980s for the first time attempted to encourage local authority tenants to buy the accommodation in which they lived. Fiercely resisted when first introduced, it now appears to have become an accepted part of the housing scene: by 1986 over 1 million dwellings had been sold. There can, however, be considerable problems if unforeseen structural defects become apparent, or if the owner finds the property is difficult to sell.

Rehabilitation

Another aspect which must be mentioned is the move away from comprehensive redevelopment towards rehabilitation of existing dwellings. In the late 1970s it was realised that rehabilitation of existing dwellings had several advantages – it was quicker than rebuilding, it appeared to be cheaper, and it preserved the existing townscape pattern. However, it also became apparent that rehabilitation and conversion of existing dwellings needed a different approach to that of large-scale new building, and dealing with the structural problems of poorly constructed Victorian housing was often considerably more expensive than originally anticipated. Nevertheless, some local authorities were able to compulsorily purchase whole streets of housing, and rehabilitate to an acceptable standard in a few years; in many instances, the flexibility of the original dwelling layout enabled conversion to a ground-floor flat, and a first- and second-floor maisonette.

Social housing at the end of the 1990s

The 'New Labour' Government, first elected in 1997, is committed to considerable increases in local authority housing budgets (roughly one-third being provided from the release of capital receipts from the sale of over 1.5 million council houses). Whether this increase in funding will continue on a long-term basis is too early to say. Considerable funds are also allocated to regeneration projects in 50 of the most deprived areas of the UK (not only to housing schemes, but also to town-centre refurbishment and community buildings). It has been estimated that local authorities could soon be providing around 80% of social housing. Note that local authorities are to some extent regarded as 'enablers' who co-ordinate national government, housing corporation and private sector efforts, in order to produce a viable scheme. One intention is that private house-builders are given incentives to build low-cost housing, which will then be handed to the local authority or a housing association for management. Some of the more innovative housing organisations are attempting to provide a mix of dwellings in one development.

As part of the move away from the overall concept of public-sector housing, new terminology has been developed to cater for a more fragmented market. Public-sector housing is now often described as 'social housing'; the concept of designing accommodation which can be easily adapted to provide also for elderly people (those in the 'third age') or people with disabilities is known as 'lifetime homes'; the whole concept of accommodation for the 'disabled' is being questioned, and terms such as 'mobility housing' and 'design for disability' have been coined to cover these new areas.

Another encouraging development is the resurgence of the private rented sector; this is almost entirely due to the relaxation in controls as a result of the 1988 Housing Act.

There is evidence of a change in attitudes towards some high-rise developments – for instance, in 1998 some post-war housing was 'listed' (e.g. Trellick Tower, Golborne Road, west London, by Erno Goldfinger (1971), and Park Hill flats in Sheffield, by Jack Lynn and Ivor Smith) – and previously unlettable dwellings can become sought-after when the whole development is refurbished and properly maintained; recladding of the exterior can transform the visual appearance and also improve energy efficiency. Installation of door entry systems at ground level can reduce vandalism dramatically.

A recent endeavour is to establish Local Housing Companies and Joint Venture Companies, involving both local authorities and private developers. Government investment is available.

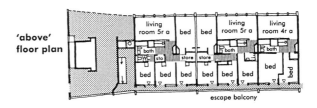

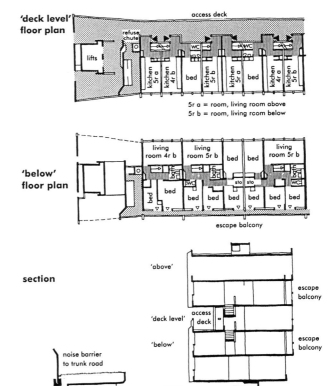

6 Robin Hood Gardens, east London: wide access balcony or deck housing; one of the most influential UK examples; partition walls (shown as open lines) can be arranged to permit a wide variation of dwelling sizes (Arch: A & P Smithson)

Private finance initiative

Another attempt by government to finance housing development is through introducing private finance to public-sector schemes; this idea, introduced by the Conservatives, has been continued by the Labour Government. Covered by the acronym PFI (private finance initiative) it is intended to cover all aspects of public finance, not just housing. At present, it has had little success, but it is at least in theory an important part of the government programme, of all main political parties. The problem with PFI is how the risk taken by the private sector can be covered within the rules of public accountability; in housing, the costs of the loans are intended to be repaid from rents, but it is difficult to know whether this can be achieved in practice.

Ownership in the mid-1990s

68%	owner occupied (up from 56% in 1979)
18%	local authority/public sector
10%	private rented sector
4%	housing association

(from DoE, *Our Future Homes*)

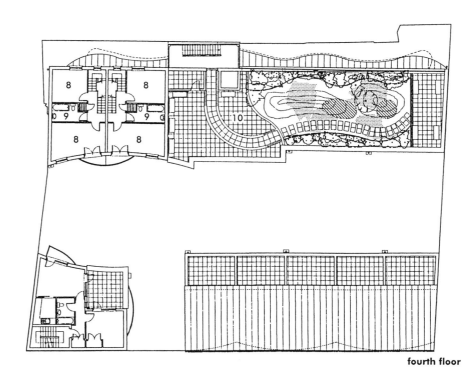

0   5m

1 entrance gates (see **138**)
2 disabled parking
3 landscaping
4 private gardens
5 yard
6 living room
7 kitchen/dining
8 bedroom
9 bathroom
10 communal roof garden

fourth floor

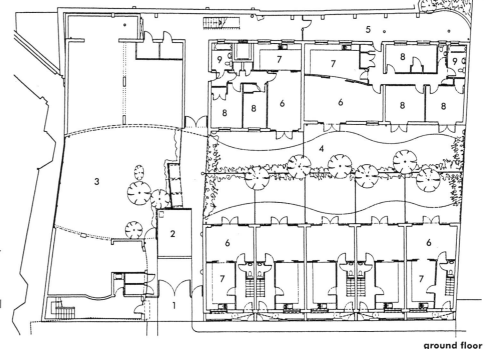

an inner-city, high-density scheme, seven-person housing, one- and two-bed flats, and accommodation for people with disabilities (see also **1,138**).

7 Green Dragon House, social housing, London WC2. (Arch: Monahan Blythen Architects)

ground floor

PRIVATE SECTOR DEVELOPMENT

The design of an individual house has always had a great fascination for architects (see **8,13,14**), but a design of mass private-sector housing for developers has rarely been successfully achieved. Eric Lyons' designs for SPAN (for instance, at New Ash Green, Kent) are one of the notable exceptions.

Most developers have to work with a limited range of plans and elevational treatments, depending on the market in which the dwellings will be sold. Layouts have not changed much over the years (see **12**), the main changes coming in constructional techniques or in economy of labour or materials. Despite attempts by builders to promote faster forms of construction – for instance, timber frame – this is not popular and has received much bad publicity. Some housing is now built as timber (or steel) frame with an external brick skin, which appears to satisfy house buyers, but traditional brick and block construction remains the overwhelming favourite.

It has been said that changes in living patterns tend to precede design changes, which are then forced onto the market by demand; it is also true that most house purchasers are more conscious of design aspects, and more choice is demanded. The old truism of 'you get what you pay for' is very applicable to the private housing market, while the designer must also have the ability to visualise the house through the layperson's eye, and not necessarily through that of the architect or planner.

Elevational treatment For private sector dwellings, this almost always has a traditional appearance. An attempt at so-called Georgian styles is often made, which appear to be continually popular with purchasers but rarely considered successful by designers; a situation that has caused endless debate over many years. More recently, attempts at vernacular (or 'cottage') styles have been more successful. There is an interesting paradox in that many purchasers appear to want traditional and reproduction styles, while also requiring many of the conveniences of modern living – for instance, double garages and fully equipped kitchens. Attempts by designers to combine both demands can result in unsatisfactory solutions unless handled with considerable competence. A sense of proportion and human scale is essential to any design.

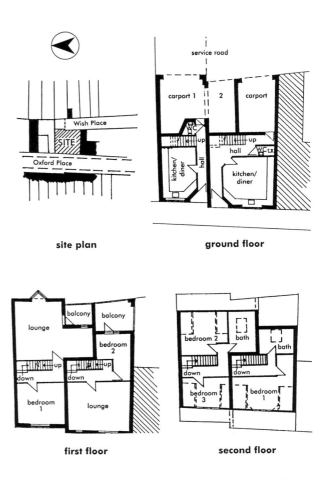

8 House at Halland, Sussex (1938)
(Arch: Serge Chermayeff)

9 Urban regeneration scheme, Southsea, Portsmouth: an extremely confined and difficult site, needing careful internal planning to maximise its use
(Arch: Rex Hawkesworth)

Car ownership Growth in car ownership has resulted in two- or even three-car families, a situation considered inconceivable in the 1950s. The resulting overcrowding on many estate roads has had seriously detrimental effects on the visual quality, and no solution is yet in site. Public transport is often expensive, woefully inadequate or even non-existent.

Current trends Current trends include a revival of interest in decoration, particularly in the use of different colours of brickwork. Pitched roofs are invariably required, except for garages, dormer roofs etc., although even here pitches are sometimes used. Smaller windows are necessitated by energy requirements, often resulting in better overall proportions. Changing social habits – particularly requiring smaller units of accommodation – have resulted in a greater variety of dwellings than has been the norm in the past.

A recent development has been the promotion of 'urban villages' (mixed-use developments for up to 5000 occupants, in both urban areas and smaller towns); one intention is to try and ensure good public transport. Poundbury, on the edge of Dorchester (Dorset) is the first example, but many more are envisaged.

The present pattern of low-density, largely traditionally built housing seems likely to continue for the foreseeable future. One of the few innovations, that of timber framing, is now being used more frequently, generally with a brick skin to conceal the timber framing.

The private sector regularly complains that a major constraint is assembling of sites of a suitable size – sites allocated are often too large.

One UK national house-builder has suggested that its own future developments should attempt to concentrate on:

- ensuring that developments are designed as identifiable neighbourhoods, with boundaries, centres and focal points ('think public first, private second')
- providing better quality external space
- wherever possible, linking development to better public transport
- providing narrower roads, reducing the depth of front gardens and building nearer to the road
- dispensing with cul-de-sac layouts
- designing 'hide and disguise' garages (i.e. garages incorporated within, or under, the house whenever possible, rather than designed as large, separate buildings).

PPG 3 (HOUSING)

Planning Policy Guidance Notes are government guidance documents concerning planning policy; PPG 3 (housing) has recently been revised and suggests several changes in direction. Many local authorities will be required to review their development plans.

PPG 3 suggests that housing development should have more regard to:

- higher density development (less than 30 dwellings/ha should be avoided; between 30 and 50 dwellings/ha should be encouraged) in town centres and with good public transport
- lower car-parking standards
- 'sequential testing' of sites (considering inner-urban sites first, then urban edges, then village infill, then new settlements)
- offering more choice, both within sites and buildings (e.g. flats over shops, a greater mix of dwelling types)
- fewer planning restrictions on conversions to residential use
- providing more affordable housing (also for renting)
- re-using previously developed land and buildings
- improving quality of design (local authorities are to actively promote good design)
- co-ordinating transport and land use
- promoting sustainable development.

BROWNFIELD SITES

Recent developments have included attempts by the government to encourage new building on so-called 'brownfield' sites (i.e., generally, urban sites suffering from some ground pollution). This approach suffers in particular from two problems – the additional cost of building on polluted sites, and the difficulty of persuading private-sector purchasers to live in inner-urban areas previously avoided. The first problem has been alleviated to some extent by government grants – the Derelict Land Grant and the City Grant. There is some evidence of a long-overdue return to city living in the UK: a number of regeneration schemes have been completed (see **9,16**) utilising small urban sites, but these are the exception rather than the norm. Another possible resurgence of interest in living in inner city locations is epitomised in marketing terms as 'loft living' (see **97**).

LIFETIME HOMES

A concept developed in a study for the Joseph Rowntree Foundation, to develop dwelling layouts that are 'flexible, adaptable, and accessible', and able to meet the varying needs of a family, from young children to the elderly or disabled. The layouts allow easily adaptable internal arrangements, and incorporate 16 specific design features. It is considered that the additional costs are minimal. Many of the suggested features are linked with those in the Housing Corporation standards, and are arranged in three areas: access, inside the home, and fixtures and fittings. The section on 'inside the home' suggests that the family room should be at ground level, there should be a ground floor WC, and that in dwellings of more than one storey there should a space on the ground floor suitable for a bed. Most of the suggestions cover access for the elderly or people with disabilities. For typical examples see **10,11** (note: b = bedrooms, p = people).

key (*10* & *11*)
1 dotted circle indicates 1.5 m turning area for wheelchair; 2 removable panel; 3 possible shower; 4 bed position; 5 area that could be used to fit a lift; 6 possible carport

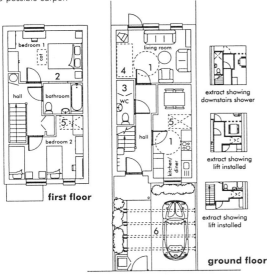

10 Lifetime homes: 2b/4p narrow-frontage dwelling (76 m²); ground floor can be open plan or partitioned; note possible lift position
(Arch: Wright & Wright Architects)

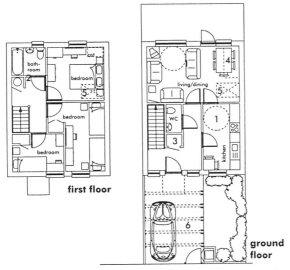

11 Lifetime homes: 3b/5p medium-frontage dwelling (82 m²)
(Arch: Wright & Wright Architects)

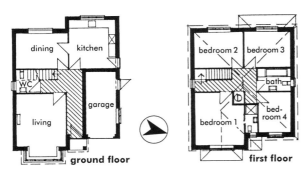

12 House at Bedhampton, Hampshire: typical plan for speculative housing, in use with little alteration from 1930s to present
(Arch: Rex Hawkesworth)

CONCLUSION

Few people would regard the housing provided over the last 50 years to be a great success. Despite the well-intentioned efforts of many professionals – architects, planners, housing managers, sociologists and others – we seem to be as far away as ever from being able to provide adequate and affordable housing for the whole population. High-rise accommodation is generally derided, some having been demolished after only 20 years' life. Living in town centres is impossible for many as suitable accommodation no longer exists, while at the same time thousands of flats above shops lie vacant. Many large housing estates are unfriendly, unpopular places; some have severe social problems. At the other extreme, the private sector shows an enormous lack of imagination in terms of design and flexibility, and a notable unwillingness to provide urban housing (although, as noted above, it is possible that this could be about to change). Energy-saving measures, and better quality standards have only been incorporated after pressure from successive governments. Against this supposed lack of innovation, however, some would say private-sector housing cannot anticipate public preferences and must swim with the tide; houses which do not sell will soon bankrupt the developer. It is a curious reflection on the current situation that a study commissioned by government at the end of the 1990s (*Housing Quality Indicators*, see p.173) considered it necessary to say that 'dwelling design should be related to the way people wish to live and the surrounding context'.

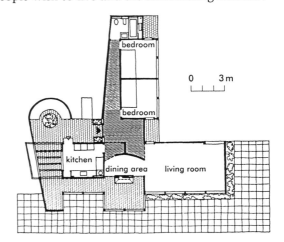

13 House at Whipsnade, Beds (1935)
(Arch: Lubetkin & Tecton)

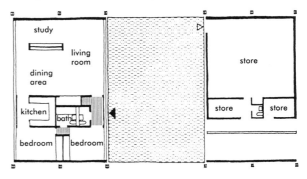

14 House for an artist
(Arch: Rogers)

15 Bungalow at Bedhampton, Hampshire: note large kitchen, separate utility and room used as office
(Arch: Rex Hawkesworth)

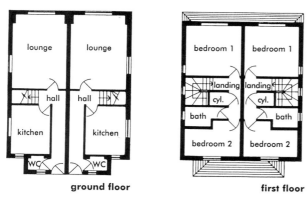

ground floor

first floor

good example of 'minimum layout' 2b/4p starter homes in the private sector, also an urban regeneration scheme on the site of a removal firm yard; house area is 70 m² (750 ft²); compare with public-sector layouts

16 Starter homes at Cosham, Portsmouth, Hampshire:
(Arch: Rex Hawkesworth)

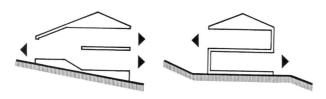

17 Split level

18 'Upside down' section

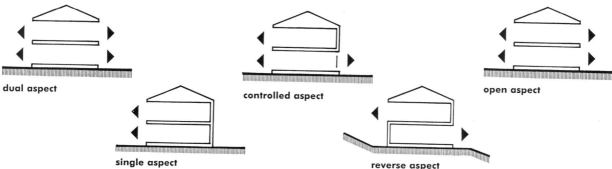

dual aspect

controlled aspect

open aspect

single aspect

reverse aspect

19 Possible aspects

SITE TOPOGRAPHY

Effect of gradient

Where slopes are moderate, the choice of plan is affected little by gradient; on steeper slopes some forms of plan can be used to greater advantage than others. Where houses run parallel to contours the use of wider-frontage houses minimises the need for under-building or excavation. Savings thus made can counterbalance the usually adverse equation between wide frontage and greater servicing and development costs. Very steep sites can, however, present opportunities for imaginative use of split-level plans or entry to upper floors (see **17**). Houses running across contours, especially in terraces, should employ narrow-frontage plans, stepping at each house or pair of houses.

North slopes

North slopes aggravate problems of maintaining density while providing adequate sunlight to each house and garden. A simple solution is to reverse the usual rule and place each house at the lower end of its plot, with access on the north side. However, on severe slopes the spacing required might be excessive; the solution then might be to employ an 'upside-down' section, placing the living room on upper floors where occupants can enjoy sun from south and views in each direction (see **18**). Houses running across contours can be particularly advantageous on north slopes, since no garden need be immediately overshadowed by houses and all rooms will get sunlight.

Aspect

Aspect is an important characteristic which relates the plan to the conditions of its site. Four basic layouts can be identified (see **19**):

- *Dual aspect:* rooms look out in both directions, to access and garden sides.
- *Single, blind-side, or controlled aspect:* rooms other than kitchen and service room look out in one direction only, usually garden side.
- *Reverse aspect:* rooms on ground storey and upper storeys look out in opposite directions.
- *Open aspect:* ideal detached or semi-detached condition where rooms can look out in three or four directions without constraint.

Prevailing wind

Wind directions (usually westerly in UK) must be considered for each site in planning heat and cold protection measures.

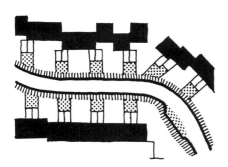

20 Residents' and visitors' parking within boundary of property; note service vehicle parking area

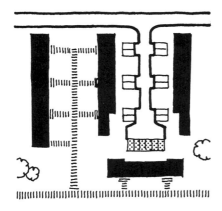

21 Residents' parking partly within boundary of property and partly communal

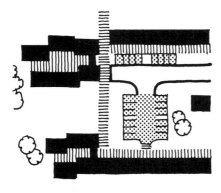

22 All parking communal

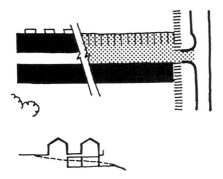

23 Parking area off covered access below pedestrian deck

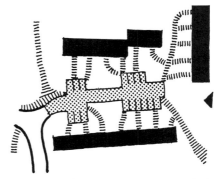

24 Access area shared by pedestrians and vehicles

SITE LAYOUT AND ACCESS

Access to dwelling

Terrace accommodation has greatest access problem; detached houses the least, although deep and narrow front gardens can result in costly service routes. Five basic systems can be distinguished:

- Houses and footpaths along road with no segregation of vehicular and pedestrian traffic. Implies no through traffic; no on-street parking (see **20**).
- Road and footpath on opposite sides of house. Implies house design permitting access either side without loss of privacy; requires children's play area other than in road (see **21**).
- Vehicular access stopped short of houses. Limited by access distance (45 m maximum for fire appliances, about 25 m for refuse collection); requires particularly well-designed and maintained parking and garaging (see **22**).
- Vertical segregation of vehicles and pedestrians. Expensive; suits high density of steeply sloping sites (see **23**).
- Primarily pedestrian access to small groups of houses shared with private cars and light delivery vehicles. Requires careful design to enforce low speeds and restrict use to legitimate access (see **24**).

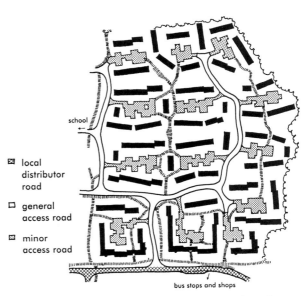

⊠ local distributor road

▢ general access road

⊠ minor access road

25 Road hierarchy within housing area; example makes use of shared pedestrian/vehicle courts as minor access roads

Densities

(Note: hr/ha = habitable rooms per hectare.)

- 125 hr/ha: low-density layout (e.g. four-bed detached houses with front and rear gardens)
- 200 hr/ha: highest density possible utilising two-storey housing with a traditional street pattern
- 250 hr/ha: three-storey flats required; street pattern still possible
- above 250 hr/ha: blocks of flats required; street pattern no longer possible.

See also proposed density matrix (see **52**).

Access roads

Access roads to houses can be subdivided into two groups (see **25,26**). Traffic calming measures (road humps etc.) may in place; see Vehicle Facilities section.

- General access roads: for service vehicles, cars and (depending on layout system), frontage access or occasional visitor parking. Design to limit speed at junction with local distributor road.
- Minor access roads: designed to allow slow-speed vehicle penetration of pedestrian priority area, serving up to 25 houses, with speeds kept low by width, alignment, speed humps, surface texture and visibility provision. May be a cul-de-sac with turning at end, short loop, or leading to restricted vehicle/pedestrian mixed courtyard.

Car parking provision   Guidelines vary – the local authority average appears to be about 1.2 spaces per unit; current government proposals (draft PPG 3) suggest that provision 'should not exceed an average of 1.5–2 spaces per dwelling'. Some planning guides ask for a second garage or car space for larger houses (e.g. above 110 m²), as well as a car space for visitors. Parking spaces should be within 20 m of the dwelling. See 'Private Garages' below for details of individual garages.

Design standards

Local authorities often have stipulations or guidance relating to access requirements (e.g. regarding frontages, footpaths, road widths and construction, etc.). Usually these have to be promoted through planning departments, and their legality has often been questioned. These guides attempt to improve standards, particularly relating to roads and footpaths; the Essex Design Guide (1973, new edition 1997), for instance, is one of the most highly regarded.

Privacy: public and private spaces

Among the most difficult problems in housing layout is striking the right balance between the need for privacy and the need to avoid social exclusion. The balance obviously varies according to individual character, temperament and age so no perfect solution is possible, but good layout will at least allow some degree of individual choice. Designs which opt strongly for either a 'social' or 'private' approach may not satisfy the majority of occupants.

Dwellings opening directly onto busy public spaces and access decks designed to encourage social contact and neighbourliness may also suffer intolerable intrusion, while screening designed to provide 'defensible space' may result in roads and footpaths bounded by blank walls and fences. Either approach is likely to lead to feelings of insecurity and dissatisfaction amongst residents.

In high-density layouts, in particular, user satisfaction is likely to be enhanced, and the incidence of vandalism reduced, by sub-division of large anonymous public areas into smaller spaces related to identifiable groups of dwellings.

For houses, a public access road may lead to a mixed-use pedestrian/vehicle court (see **24**), with psycho-logically restricted entry, related to a group of 20 or so houses and then to a further transition zone provided by a front garden to each individual house. For flats, the transition can be by a semi-private lobby zone (see also the security issues at the end of this section).

26   Barnetts Wood
(Arch: Hazle McCormack Young)

site layout, using one design forming cluster arrangements; a through-lounge gives flexibility in siting; a detached double garage either in front or to one side provides an entrance courtyard;

development was brought closer to the road to improve the streetscape and to give more emphasis to front gardens and driveway spaces, which are different form house to house;

the site was fully landscaped, with shrubs near plain gable ends and front courtyards, and trees on the larger spaces;

houses 10, 7, 19 and 20 keep the eye within the site and help containment

27 Layout plan, 25 houses, Havant, Hampshire (Arch: Rex Hawkesworth)

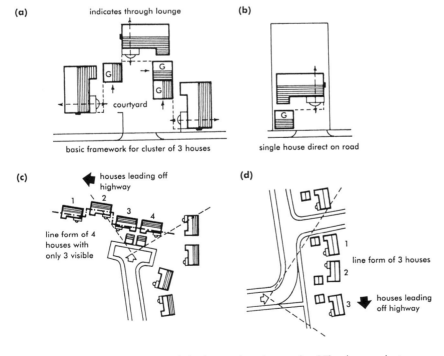

28 Cluster arrangements (a and c) of up to three houses (→ **27**): where a cluster was not feasible, garages were placed in prominent positions near the pavement (b), with two or three houses visible in a line form; where line forms occur, they were placed not directly on the highway, but leading off from that viewpoint (d)

29 House plan (→ **27**)

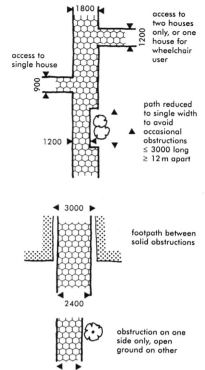

30 Pedestrian access and traffic routes

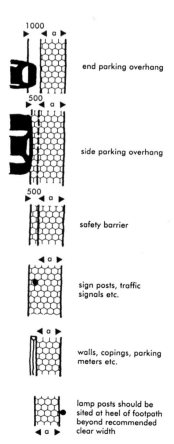

a = minimum clear width

31 Footpaths: minimum clear widths

PEDESTRIAN ACCESS

Primary access

Footpaths should run as directly as possible to major attractions (schools, shops, bus stops) away from heavy traffic roads. They should be well-lit and overlooked (for security), sheltered and avoid steep gradients. Use ramps rather than steps, or ramps as alternative routes where steps are necessary. The design width should allow prams and wheelchairs to pass clearly round obstructions: minimum 1.8 m, but on pedestrian traffic routes generally allow 2.4 m on open ground and 3.0 m between buildings and fences. Footpaths between a road or pedestrian traffic route and small groups of houses can be 1.8 m; 1.2 m for two houses, 0.9 m for a single house (see **30,31**). The maximum distance from the road to the door of a house should be 45 m.

Secondary access

Additional paths to or within gardens, garage courts etc. can be 0.7–1.0 m between fences, 0.3–0.6 m on open ground (see also **60**). Their use as through routes should be discouraged. (See also Landscape Works section.)

SERVICES

Statutory utilities (e.g. gas, water, electricity, telephone) should be supplied with details of any proposed housing development at an early stage in order to agree service routes between different interests and avoid later adjustment, which can be both time consuming and costly. Mains services will generally be laid within the public road, as this gives certain automatic statutory rights of access; but in segregated layouts or those designed with narrow road widths this may prove inconvenient or uneconomic and alternative routes may need to be agreed. An alternative solution might be rear-of-block service strips, easily accessible and surfaced with materials which may readily be removed and reinstated. (For mains services entries to individual dwellings, see **32**.)

Television Master aerials for television signal boosting often require a licence or permit. Satellite dishes may require planning permission, depending on the location on the building or if it is in a conservation area: check with the local planning authority.

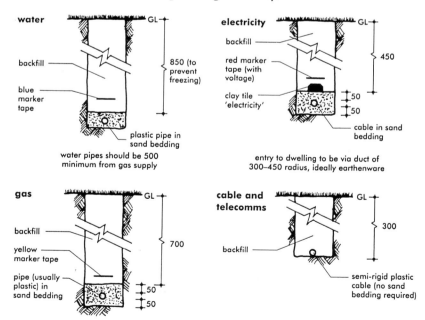

diagrams are for single dwellings, and are for general guidance only; bedding sand must be washed (i.e. salt-free); specified depths for electricity and cable/telecomms are to prevent damage from spades and forks etc. when digging domestic gardens; for water, the depth is to prevent freezing
(NB: requirements change from time to time, and also vary between different authorities across the UK, and the relevant authority must always be contacted at the appropriate time)

32 Mains services entries to dwellings

PRIVATE GARAGES

Siting garages Ideally, the garage should be located adjacent to, or within, the dwelling. However, this is often not possible: lack of space and the provision of garages lags far behind levels of car ownership, resulting in much car-parking on the roadside or on drives. In the public sector (see earlier), provision of garages has often been in rows opening off a communal parking area; garages adjacent to dwellings are rare. In many high-rise developments, parking is often in open-sided, open access multi-storey car parks. This can give rise to many social problems such as vandalism. In the private sector, garages are usually close to the house entrance, though not necessarily the front door, with easy access (see **34**). Boundary and shared arrangements are options (see **36,37**).

Size Avoid under-dimensioning garages (see **33**). Clearance between the car and the side walls should be 200–300 mm minimum, with minimum 500 mm margin in front. For getting out allow at least door width between car and wall or between cars, and never less than 700 mm. For car cleaning, walls or other cars should be a minimum of 1.2 m away.

Within house Direct access to the garage from the entrance hall or lobby via a half-hour fire-resisting door is usually permissible; internal floor level must be 100 mm minimum above garage floor. Otherwise access to garage can be provided under a common canopy with the entrance door to the house (see **39,40**).

Access driveway This should have a suitable surface (see **38**). An apron in front of the garage should have a full-width surface, and be 5–6 m long and drained for car washing and to provide occasional off-street parking for another car. The garage floor should be raised slightly above the washing area and slope towards it. (See also Landscape Works section.)

Building regulations Garages are subject to building regulations, even when considered as open carports, particularly concerning roof coverings and distance from boundaries. For basement garages for more than three cars, the local authority can impose additional requirements relating to access, ventilation and safety.

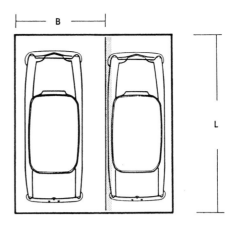

33 Typical garage plan (B: 2.5–3 m; L: 5–6 m)

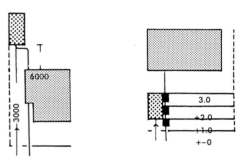

34 Usual siting

35 House on slope; garage on road below

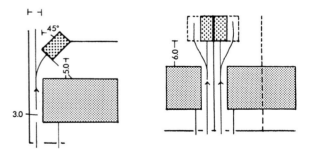

36 Boundary in close proximity to house so garage at angle

37 Combined garages where distance from boundary not stipulated

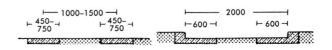

38 Access driveway wheel runs

second storey

first storey

ground storey

39 Three-storey house with integral garage; can be sited directly behind pavement as garage and central porch provide privacy; access to garden through utility

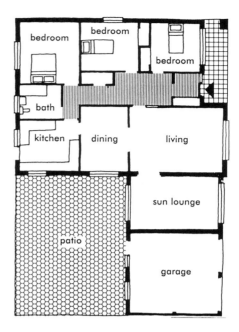

41 Double garage used to extend one-storey house to screen patio; low-density solution

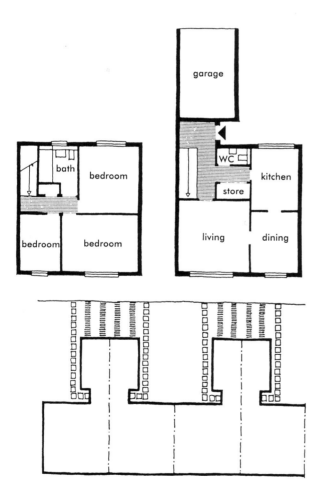

40 Two-storey terrace house with attached garage in front, screening semi-private entrance court; generally more economical and attractive than layout with integral garage (see **39**), but results in lower density

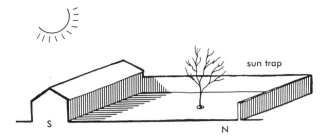

42 North face of house in shade and immediate foreground overshadowed but longer prospect on to sunlit garden and wall forming sun trap

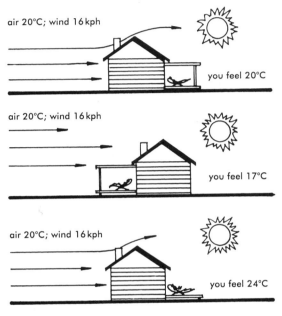

43 Wind effects

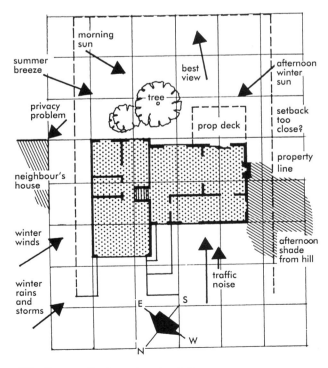

44 Factors affecting external activities

RELATIONSHIP TO OTHER BUILDINGS

Daylight and sunlight

Consult relevant regulations and codes for daylighting standards in habitable rooms; these also provide for the protection of residential buildings and undeveloped sites from obstruction of daylight by new development. These provisions are normally adopted in England and Wales by the planning authority in development control (and are to some extent mandatory in Scotland). A proposed building can be tested for both distance from its own boundary and distance from other buildings by using permissible height indicators.

So far as possible, principal rooms should receive sunlight at some part of day throughout most of year but this not generally enforced by regulations or development control. Angles and direction of sunlight can be established hourly for any time of year at any latitude.

Private open space

All dwellings, and particularly those for families, require some kind of related open space – whether garden, patio (see **45**) or balcony – which is sunny and sheltered from wind. It should ideally be large enough to allow space for clothes drying, (see **119**), toddlers' play, out-door hobbies and sitting out. For factors affecting location of outdoor living areas see **44**.

Gardens

(See also Landscape Works section.)
An enclosed garden enhances privacy. Walls, hedges and, to a lesser extent, trees can provide natural protection from noise, wind and dust. It is an advantage if a private garden can open out of the living area, providing an outdoors extension of the living space. The best locations are generally on the south and west sides, but an enclosed garden on the north side can provide a sunlit view if deep enough (see **42**).

Visual privacy

Many planning authorities seek to prevent houses being overlooked from neighbouring houses or across the road (this being controlled by building regulations in Scotland). Rule of thumb minimum distances of 18 m (front of dwellings) and 22 m (rear) are often stated but this is restrictive and ineffective since visibility is affected by the types of windows involved and their respective levels, and the incidence to one another – for instance, for diagonal sight-lines, distances can be reduced to 10 m.

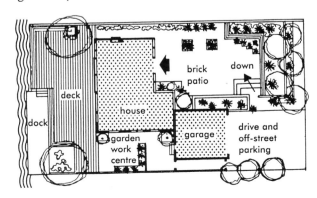

45 Patio and deck on water's edge
(Arch: Lawrence Halprin)

As with other environmental factors privacy must be considered in relation to competing benefits; in high-density developments it is a matter for careful consideration in design and layout.

Use of blind side or single-aspect house designs will help (e.g. on sloping sites or where footpaths pass close to houses) and effective screening of private gardens is also important (see **46,47**). However, privacy should not be achieved at the cost of isolation: ideally a degree of screening for visual privacy should be within the control of residents.

Privacy from noise

Houses built near distributor roads, or main highways, are best protected from noise nuisance by embankments or other land formations (see **48**). Privacy can, however, be improved by use of suitable house plans with rooms facing away from noise sources. There is increasing realisation that noise is a growing problem; noise within or between dwellings, or from refuse chutes etc., can be an equal problem. The Housing Corporation *Good Practice Guide* recommends that living rooms and bedrooms should be orientated away from footpaths and vehicle areas. The problem of aircraft noise is very difficult to alleviate: although engines are becoming quieter, flight frequencies have increased dramatically.

Spread of fire

Building regulations generally restrict distances between dwellings built of combustible materials, such as timber, shingles or thatch, and their own plot boundaries; where non-combustible materials are used the extent of window and door openings in walls close to a boundary might be restricted to prevent the spread of fire to adjoining property by radiation.

See also 'Flats: privacy and fire' later in this section.

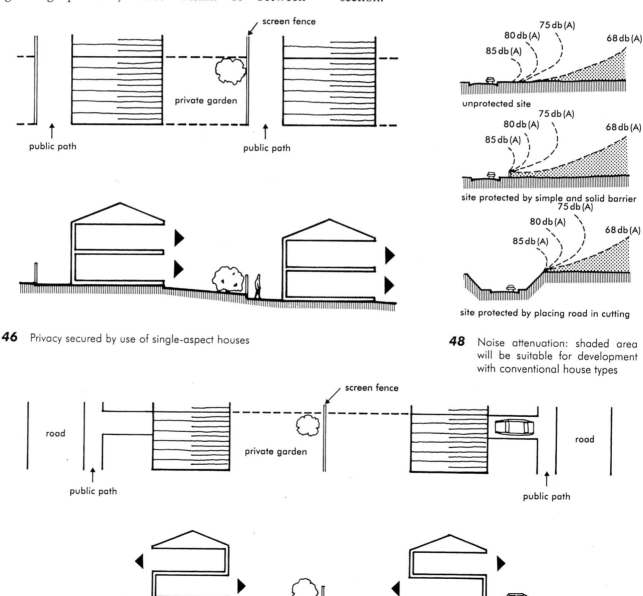

46   Privacy secured by use of single-aspect houses

48   Noise attenuation: shaded area will be suitable for development with conventional house types

47   Privacy secured by use of reverse-aspect houses; best orientation E–W

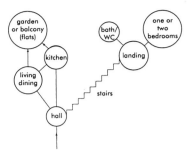

49 Dwelling flow diagram: minimum provision for starter home or small flat; sometimes also found on expensive sites in city centres (stairs and landing not applicable to flats)

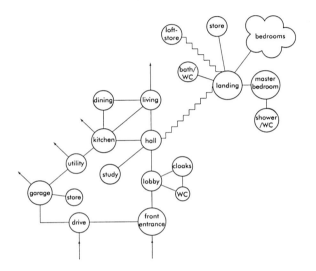

50 Flow diagram for larger dwelling

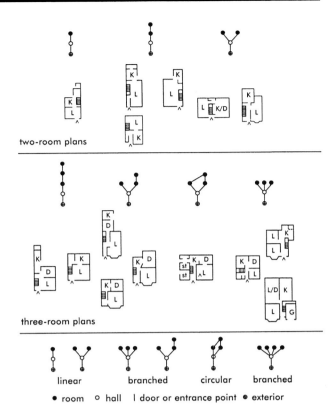

two-room plans

three-room plans

linear   branched   circular   branched

● room   ○ hall   l door or entrance point   ◉ exterior

linear arrangement: rooms arranged one off each other from the front door
branched arrangement: rooms arranged around a hallway
circular arrangement: rooms can have a double point of entry from other rooms

classifies layout in terms of 'depth' (doors or access points between a room and front entrance), 'linearality' (whether a room opens off another or a central hall), and 'circularity' (multiple relationships between rooms)

51 An attempt to analyse dwelling space in terms of 'space syntax' (from Goodchild, diagrams 2.7 and 2.8)

		option 1	option 2	option 3
car parking provision		high 2–1.5 spaces per unit	moderate 1.5–1 space per unit	low less than 1 space per unit
predominant housing type		detached and linked houses	terraced houses and flats	mostly flats
location accessibility index	setting			
sites within town centre 'ped shed' 6	central			650–900
	urban		200–450	450–700
↕ 4	suburban		150–250	250–350
sites along transport corridors and sites close to a town centre 'ped shed' 3	urban		200–300	300–450
↕ 2	suburban	150–200	200–250	
currently remote sites 2 ↕ 1	suburban	150–200		

density nos: habitable rooms/ha
location: relates to public transport and facilities
setting: urban fabric
shading: combinations which result in inappropriate densities
(note also suggested variations in car-parking provision)

52 A density matrix (from a report by Llewelyn-Davies Architects on sustainable residential development): an attempt to relate the site location with the setting and housing type, to give a variety of housing densities (compare with densities commonly adopted: see p. 164)

entrances	1 is protection from weather provided at entrances? 2 is there space in hall for receiving visitors? 3 is there convenient storage for outdoor clothing and pram? 4 can meters be read without entering living area? (NB. outside in USA)
living area	5 is there space for required furniture in sensible arrangement? 6 is there sufficient space to seat guests in dining area? 7 does living area face private garden?
kitchen	8 is there direct access, on same level, from kitchen to dining area? 9 is work surface adequate, free from interruption and obstruction? 10 is 'work triangle' (sink – cooker – fridge/larder) compact and free from cross-circulation? 11 has possible use of kitchen by elderly or disabled people been considered? 12 is there space for additional equipment, or larger items, likely to be used in furniture? 13 has kitchen view of outside world – for callers, toddlers' play etc?
bedroom	14 is there space for required furniture in sensible arrangements – consider use of single beds? 15 can bedroom be used for child's homework, entertaining friends and hobbies?
bathroom	16 is bathroom convenient for bathing baby? 17 has use of bathroom by elderly people or invalids been considered? 18 is there space for appropriate bathroom equipment, hanging towels etc?
storage and accessibility	19 are refuse bin and fuel storage accessible, conveniently placed for collection and delivery? 20 can bicycles be taken outside, pram put in the garden, and garden refuse removed without passing through living area?

53   User requirement checklist

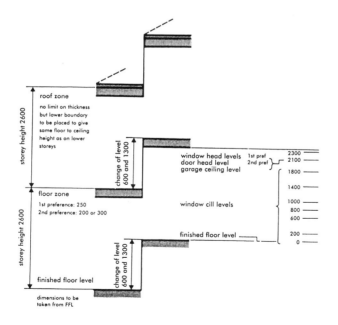

54   Recommended vertical controlling dimensions

DWELLING DESIGN STANDARDS AND REGULATIONS

User requirements

Where the dwelling is not designed for a known client, user requirements are generally summarised in terms of number of people to be accommodated and agreement of number and use of rooms.

User requirement checklist   If the client or user is not known, the layout of a dwelling should be tested by a list of questions that might be asked by a user. It will probably be impossible to meet all the requirements – the designer has to judge which priorities should be achieved. (See **53**.)

Controlling dimensions

Recommendations for horizontal and vertical controlling dimensions have been developed in order to make use of dimensionally co-ordinated standard components.

Horizontal dimensions (plans)   A 300 mm grid is used, with a 100 mm grid as second preference and a 50 mm grid as third preference.

Vertical dimensions   These are more closely defined (see **54**).

Housing standards (public sector)

In 1961, the Parker Morris committee published *Homes for Today and Tomorrow* (HMSO, 1961). Public-sector dwellings were expected to comply with the fairly generous Parker Morris areas (see **55**), which were based in many ways on those of the 1944 Dudley committee. Areas were generally larger than equivalent private-sector dwellings, and Parker Morris areas, and although stated as minimum standards in fact became maximum ones. Plans also had to show layouts of furniture and domestic equipment based on layouts shown in *Space in the Home* (HMSO, 1968). Parker Morris area requirements lasted until they were abolished by the government in 1981; since then, there have been no national requirements for public housing design standards. However, in 1983, the Housing Corporation established basic standards in its Design and Contract Criteria, which had in many ways a similar approach to Parker Morris, and applied to all housing association projects. These criteria were first relaxed in the *Procedure Guide and Good Practice Guide*, and then in the *Scheme Development Standards* issued in 1993 and revised in 1995.

In 1983 the Institute of Housing and the RIBA published *Homes for the Future*, which emphasised the importance of factors other than just floor areas – for instance, energy conservation, increased emphasis on costs-in-use, and the need for quality of external space. Layouts should be assessed in relation to activities rather than just floor areas. It was felt that three principal aspects where changes in lifestyle required a change to Parker Morris standards related to general storage, kitchen accommodation, and heating systems.

Housing Corporation 'Scheme Development Standards' (SDS), (1993 and 1995)

Section 1: quality of housing Criteria are divided into essential and recommended items; for rehabilitation schemes, the criteria may be relaxed if disproportionate costs are likely to be involved. Housing for sale does not necessarily have to meet the criteria. The main headings are as follows:

- external environment
- internal environment (including elderly and special needs accommodation)
- accessibility (mainly concerning access for people with disabilities)
- safety and security
- energy efficiency
- building practice and maintenance (services, components and materials).

The 1995 revision includes an appendix listing furniture and fittings for various areas.

Sections 2 and 3 These cover procurement and administration.

The SDS are very broadly based and set out principles rather than firm standards: for instance, '(housing) associations should produce good quality housing to meet identified need' and 'designs should be safe and secure and should minimise accidents'.

Relating to services, equipment and finishes, 'designs should reflect good building practice and ease of maintenance'. The SDS are much less prescriptive than the earlier Housing Corporation *Guides and Contract Criteria*. Space standards and room sizes are no longer specified.

Energy efficiency Schemes should incorporate cost-effective energy efficiency measures, generally using the Standard Assessment Procedure (SAP).

Housing Quality Indicators

In 1999 the Department of Environment, Transport and the Regions (DETR) and the Housing Corporation published information on 'Housing Quality Indicators' in an attempt to develop a system to assess quality in housing. It is suggested that housing quality can be evaluated in three main areas: location, design and performance. These are enlarged to produce ten 'quality indicators', to which are assigned various percentages to give an overall quality score:

- location
- site: visual impact, layout and landscaping; open space; routes and movement
- unit: size; layout; noise, light and services; accessibility; energy, green and sustainability issues
- performance in use.

A very detailed analysis is given (see **56,57**) which could indicate a return to some form of national standards.

Disabled access See Design for Accessibility section. Note that Parker Morris minimum standards would not be suitable in some instances for wheelchair access.

N = net space[1] S = general storage space[2]		number of persons (i.e. bed spaces) per dwelling						
		1	2	3	4	5	6	7
					(m²)			
houses								
one-storey	N	30	44.5	57	67	75.5	84	
	S	3	4	4	4.5	4.5	4.5	
two-storey (semi or end)	N				72	82	92.5	108
	S				4.5	4.5	4.5	6.5
(mid terrace)	N				74.5	85	92.5	108
	S				4.5	4.5	4.5	6.5
three-storey	N					94	98	112
	S					4.5	4.5	6.5
flats	N	30	44.5	57	70*	79	86.5	
	S	2.5	3	3	3.5	3.5	3.5	
maisonettes	N				72	82	92.5	108
	S				3.5	3.5	3.5	3.5
		*(67 if balcony access)						

[1] net space is area of all floors in dwelling measured to unfinished faces; includes area of each floor taken up by stairways, by partitions and by any chimney breasts, flues and heating appliances and area of any external WC; excludes floor area of general storage space (S), dustbin storage, garage, balcony, any part of room less than 1500 high because of sloping ceilings, and any porch or covered way open to air; in single-access house any space within storage required for passage from one side of house to other, taken as 700 wide, shall be provided in addition to area in table

[2] general storage space to be provided exclusive of any dustbin storage, fuel storage or pram space within storage area, and in single-access house, space required within storage for passage from one side of house to other; in houses some storage space may be on upper floor, separate from any linen storage or cupboard, but at least 2.5 m² shall be at ground level; in flats and maisonettes up to 1.5 m² may be provided outside dwelling; in some circumstances part of garage integral with or adjoining dwelling can count towards general storage space

55 Areas for public sector dwellings, as set out in Parker Morris report of 1961, and as used in public sector housing until late 1980s; originally intended as minimum areas, but in fact regarded as maximum areas; still often used today, but without any statutory backing

UNIT LAYOUT

Units by layout – Table of furniture to be accommodated in units of different sizes
All sizes in mm
See previous pages for illustration of the way in which furniture and access, passing and activity zones are shown on plans.

Living space	1p	2p	3p	4p	5p	6p	7p	+
arm chair 850x850 – combination to equal one seat/person	2	2	3	1	2	3	4	+1
settee – 2 seat 850x1300 (optional; as above)								
settee – 3 seat 850x1850 (optional; as above)				1	1	1	1	
TV 450x600	1	1	1	1	1	1	1	1
coffee table 500x1050 or 750 diameter	1	1	1	1	1	1	1	1
occasional table					1	1	1	1
storage unit 500x1000 (or combination to reach length)	1	1	1					
storage unit 500x1500 (or combination to reach length)				1				
storage unit 500x2000 (or combination to reach length)					1	1	1	1+
space for visitor chair 450x450	2	2	2	2	2	2	2	2
Dining space	1p	2p	3p	4p	5p	6p	7p	+
dining chair 450x450	2	2	3	4	5	6	7	8+
dining table 800x 800	1	1						
dining table 800x1000 – and incrementally larger	1000	1200	1350	1500	1650			
sideboard 450x1000 (+ larger) (but not in dining/kitchen)	1000	1000	1000	1200	1500	1500	1500	+

Bedrooms	1p	2p	3p	4p	5p	6p	7p	+
Double bedroom	n/a							
Double bed 2000x1500 or 2 singles 2000x900		1	1	1	1	1	1	1
bedside table 400x400		2	2	2	2	2	2	2
chest of drawers 450 x750		1	1	1	1	1	1	1
table 500x1050 , and chair/stool		1	1	1	1	1	1	1
double wardrobe 600x1200 – could be built in		1	1	1	1	1	1	1
occasional cot space 600x1200 for family dwelling								
Twin bedroom								
single bed 2000x900			2	2	2	2	2	
bedside table 400x400			2	2	2	2	2	
chest of drawers 450 x750			1	1	1	1	1	
table 500 x 1050, and chair/stool			1	1	1	1	1	
double wardrobe 600x1200 (or two singles) could be built in			1	1	1	1	1	
Single bedroom			1	1	1	1	1	
single bed 2000x900								
bedside table 400x400	1		1	1	1	1	1	2+
chest of drawers 450 x750	1		1	1	1	1	1	2+
table 500 x 1050 and chair/stool	1		1	1	1	1	1	2+
single wardrobe 600x600 – could be built in	1		1	1	1	1	1	2+

Kitchen	1p	2p	3p	4p	5p	6p	7p	+
1 sink top and drainer 600x1000	1000	1000	1000	1000	1000	1000	1000	1000
2 cooker space 600x600	600	600	600	600	600	600	600	600
3 washing machine position / worktop 600x630	630	630	630	630	630	630	630	630
4 other base units 600 x length	1200	1200	1600	1600	1600	2700	2700	+
5 ancillary equipment space 600x length					600	600	1200	1200
6 fridge/freezer space 600x600(space above not in VOL)	600	600	600	600	600	600	600	600
7 broom cupboard 600x560x600x1950 (or adjacent in area)	600	600	600	600	600	600	600	600
8 tray space 600x150	inc.	inc.	inc.	inc.	inc.	inc.	inc.	inc.
9 Length of fitments = 1+2+3+4+5+7+8+9	4630	4630	5030	55030	5630	6730	7330	+
10 VOL- min capacity (cu m.) (MUST include drawers)	1.3	1.5	2	2.1	2.2	2.4	2.6	+
* (any wall units 300 deep + 450 above base units)								

Bathroom	1p	2p	3p	4p	5p	6p	7p	+
WC + cistern 500x700	1	1	1	1	2	2	2	2
Bath 700x1700	1	1	1	1	1	1	1	1
Wash hand basin 600x400 - 2nd one can be 250x350	1	1	1	1	2	2	2	2
shower tray 750x750 optional								
Storage	1p	2p	3p	4p	5p	6p	7p	+
General normal (300x1500ht) Min shelf area 1.5 sq m	1.5	1.5	2.25	3.0	3.75	4.5	5.25	+.75
General tall (ht over 1500) min floor area 0.5 sq m	0.5	0.5	0.5	0.5	0.5	0.5	0.5	0.5
Airing cupboard - shelf area 0.4 sq m(included in above)	0.4	0.4	0.4	0.4.	0.4	0.4	0.4	0.4
Lockable external min 2.5 sq m (except flats w/o gardens)	2.5	2.5	2.5	2.5	3.0	3.0	3.0	+
TOTAL storage shelves: general + floor: tall/external	4.5	4.5	5.25	6.0	6.75	7.5	8.25	+
For unit types that comply, tick in this line								

In addition to listed furniture each room requires a heat source - nominally a minimum 1100mm x 75mm

Source: adapted from 'Standards and Quality' National Housing Federation/Joseph Rowntree Trust

56 Unit layout: table of furniture (from DETR *Housing Quality Indicators*, reproduced with the permission of the Controller of Her Majesty's Stationery office)

UNIT LAYOUT

6.2 Additional desirable features (50%)
please enter the number of units to which any of the following apply

	Number of units	n/a
Living space		
6.2.1 living room not an essential part of circulation		
6.2.2 space for future focal point fire installation in living room		
6.2.3 essential storage space not accessed only in living room		
6.2.4 two separate living rooms or areas are possible		
6.2.5 direct access from living to private open space is possible		
Dining area		
6.2.6 dining room is separate (not in kitchen)		
6.2.7 casual eating for 2 people in kitchen (not the household dining area)		
Bedrooms		
6.2.8 space for occasional cot in main (double) bedroom		☐
6.2.9 beds (in all rooms) can be in more than one position		
6.2.10 beds (in all rooms) have one position with bedhead NOT under window		
6.2.11 all single bedrooms can accommodate double bed		☐
6.2.12 double room can accommodate twin beds		☐
6.2.13 one or more twin or double bedrooms can subdivide into two singles		
6.2.14. one or more bedrooms has direct access to washing/WC		☐
Bathrooms		
6.2.15 shower over the (main) bath with necessary wall tiling and screening		
6.2.16 a separate shower cubicle is provided		
Kitchen		
6.2.17 view from kitchen of outdoor area suitable for plants, toddler play, sitting		
6.2.18 direct access from kitchen to private open space		
6.2.19 kitchen sequence storage/prep: cook/serve: waste/wash-up		
6.2.20 kitchen worksurface not interrupted by circulation or tall fittings		
6.2.21 Min 1200 run between cooker and sink in kitchen		
6.2.22 drawers of varying depth provided in kitchen units		☐
6.2.23 facing kitchen units 1200mm apart or more		
6.2.24 space for auxiliary equipment, such as microwave,dishwasher etc, provided		
6.2.25 500mm min. clear work top each side of cooker - wall units set back 100mm		
Circulation and storage		
6.2.26 halls, corridors compactly planned, naturally lit and good proportions		
6.2.27 hanging for outdoor clothes by external doors		
6.2.28 large item(e.g. push chair, wheelchair) 'park' by external doors		
6.2.29 recyclable materials store in kitchen , hall, or external lockable		
6.2.30 tall storage in or adjacent to kitchen (or to utility room if this is provided)		
6.2.31 Provision of fitted storage - eg in bedroom, under stairs etc		
Safety		
6.2.32 slip resistant floors in 'wet' areas (bath/shower rooms, Wcs, kitchen, utility)		
6.2.33 restrictors on upper floor casement windows		☐
6.2.34 reversible childproof hinges on casement windows to allow safe cleaning		☐
6.2.35 hard wired smoke alarm on every floor		
6.2.36 secure storage for harmful substances, eg medicines, cleaning/gardening items		
6.2.37 laminated glass on internal glazed doors		☐
6.2.38 laminated glass on any single glazed ground floor windows		☐
General		
6.2.39 Glazing line in living/dining/bed rooms no higher than 800mm from floor level		

COMMENTS: Have any comments been entered on the comment page at the end?

Yes **No**
☐ ☐

57 Unit layout: additional desirable features (from DETR
Housing Quality Indicators, reproduced with the permission
of the Controller of Her Majesty's Stationery office)

Housing standards (private sector)

The private sector has no national required standards, other than the normal constraints of planning permission and the Building Regulations. The planning authority often attempts to exercise control over external appearance or general layout, but has no control over internal planning (unless it is an existing building). The Building Regulations are primarily intended to cover health and safety matters, although they also lay down standards concerning conservation of fuel and power (note that the Scottish Building Regulations tend to have more specific requirements on several areas).

The National House Building Council (NHBC) The NHBC exercises some control over private-sector standards. It is an insurance company providing a guarantee (currently 10 years) against structural failure or poor workmanship, and most builders are registered with it, although there is no requirement to do so. The NHBC has published a set of standards, which are regularly updated; until early 2000, the standards were in ten parts giving technical information about materials and site works but there were also short sections on security (see 'Safety and Security' at the end of the section), siting of dwellings and 'accommodation and services'. Some sections of the standards were mandatory for NHBC registered builders; others were for guidance only. The NHBC standards did not set space standards and were fairly basic, and have in several instances been relaxed during the 1990s (e.g. guidance on the provision of storage space was withdrawn in 1992). 'Whole-house' heating was not a requirement; the main living room 'should' have an adequate heat source. Builders were expected to provide 'correctly dimensioned plans' to purchasers, showing furniture layouts in, for example, kitchens, bathrooms and bedrooms (see **122**), although freestanding furniture except beds did not need to be shown.

The NHBC standards had a short section on design standards which stated that 'the siting of dwellings shall take account of those aspects which could affect the satisfactory performance of the dwelling and associated works'. The guidance included information on the need for:

- planning approval
- highway, refuse and fire brigade agreement with the relevant authorities
- the need to retain existing rights of access
- access provision, including gradients: for roads, 1:14 is recommended, 1:10 maximum; paths to dwellings should not have a gradient in excess of 1:6
- access to dwellings, including steps and thresholds
- precautions against flooding
- formation levels.

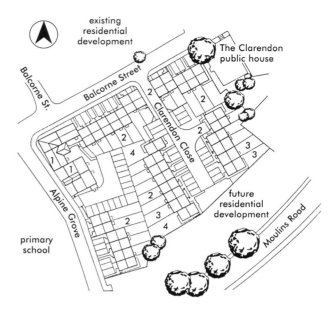

note traditional names of dwelling types: type 1: the Alton and the Oakdene (two-bed apartments); type 2: the Fitzroy (two-bed house); type 3: the Gladstone (three-bed house); type 4: the Riversdale (four-bed house); dwellings have 10 year National House-Building Council guarantee; at least one car parking space is allocated per dwelling

58 A good example of private-sector development in an inner-city location, utilising a variety of dwelling types: Victoria Place, Hackney, east London, by Copthorn Homes Ltd

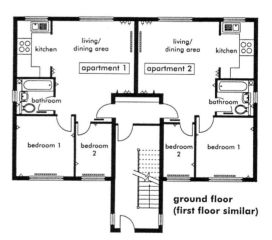

ground floor (first floor similar)

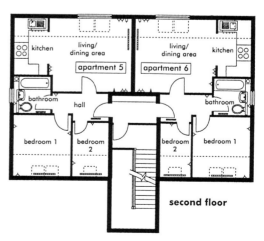

second floor

59 Two-bed apartment (the Oakdene (**58**))

CLASSIFICATION OF PLAN TYPES

There are surprisingly few variations in types of housing plan (see **60–66**).

Determining factors The main internal factors affecting selection of house plan are:
- user requirements
- mode of horizontal circulation within house
- site orientation and climate
- standards and regulations.

House plan: horizontal circulation

Circulation within the dwelling is determined primarily by the type of access appropriate to external conditions and layout (see **60**). Circulation space should be kept to a minimum, whilst also allowing the maximum flexibility in use of rooms, and making due allowance for the elderly, disabled and children. The following five or six modes of horizontal circulation are possible.

Through circulation (see **61**) This provides circulation from entry to garden side by-passing all living and working areas. No secondary access to garden side is needed. Through circulation is suitable for all forms of entry, and is particularly appropriate where entry is possible from only one side.

Through-storage circulation (see **62**) In small terrace houses through circulation although desirable can require an excessive proportion of whole ground-floor area. Modification permits circulation from entry to garden side through hall and store area. This arrangement is suitable for all forms of entry.

Through-kitchen circulation (see **63**) Provides circulation from entry to garden side through the hall/lobby and kitchen. It is appropriate in layouts which provide secondary access to garden side, although it can be used where there is none.

Single circulation (see **64**) From point of entry, the garden can be reached only by passing through the living room. This plan should only be used in layouts which provide secondary access to the garden side. Secondary access will normally be necessary only in mid-terrace houses but layout situations can arise when the siting of other buildings imposes similar conditions on end-of-terrace, detached and semi-detached houses.

By-pass circulation (see **65**) The garden side can be reached from outside the house but within the property limits (e.g. by a path or through a garage).

Through-atrium circulation (see **66**) This is only applicable to the very largest, individually designed houses. The plan has its origins in the Roman villa and hot climates.

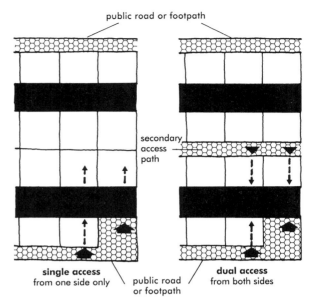

60 Access to property

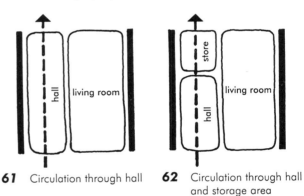

61 Circulation through hall

62 Circulation through hall and storage area

63 Circulation through hall and kitchen

64 Circulation through hall and living room

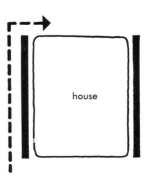

65 By-pass circulation

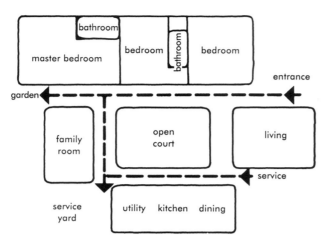

66 Traditional atrium arrangement, often found in Mediterranean countries but rare in UK for climatic reasons

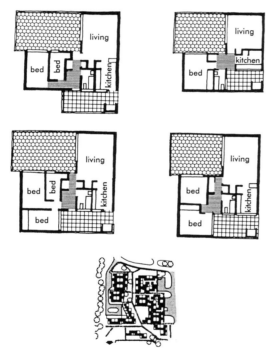

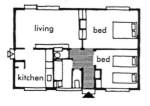

67 Houses at Dundee, Scotland: variations in simple basic plan (Arch: Baxter Clark & Paul)

SELECTING PLANS

Classification of plans

From external and internal determining factors set out in previous pages, the basic characteristics of the plan can be stated under the following headings:

- levels: one, two, three storeys or split-level
- aspect: dual, single, reverse or open (see **19**)
- horizontal circulation: through, through storage, through kitchen, single, by-pass, or through atrium (see **60–66**)
- number of rooms and size of household (e.g. four room, five person).

These characteristics provide the basis for classification of all house plans. To them is added vertical circulation when dwellings of more than one storey are considered.

Plan development

Plan selection is not initially affected by the household size or specialised user requirements. The first three heads of classification (levels, aspect and circulation) give a narrow choice to various plan arrangements at this stage, expressed in the simplest possible terms (see **67**). This example shows how single-storey dwelling plans are basically similar, developed to accommodate different household sizes.

SINGLE-STOREY DWELLINGS

The single-storey house (bungalow) gives the greatest planning freedom, the only planning determinants being aspect and horizontal circulation. Consequently, both the simplest and the most luxurious dwellings are often planned on one storey (compare **13,14,15** with **68,69**). Single-storey dwellings are particularly suitable for the elderly or people with disabilities.

Due to services requirements, the relationship between the kitchen and bathroom is ideally horizontal and adjacent, rather than vertical or dispersed: there are economies in placing them together, but savings in cost may not be advantageous when weighed against user convenience.

68 'Arcon' prefabricated house (Arch: Arcon)

69 Bungalow suitable for elderly people

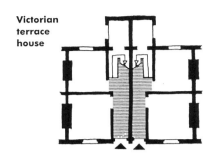

Victorian terrace house

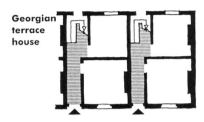

Georgian terrace house

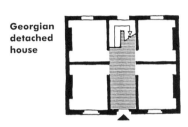

Georgian detached house

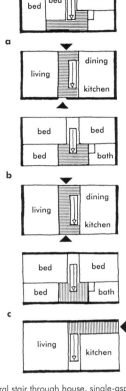

(a) central stair through house, single-aspect plan
(b) central stair through house, dual-aspect plan
(c) central stair across house, dual-aspect plan

70 Dog-leg stair has great planning advantages and is much used in traditional English houses; note in terrace house how access to small rooms and services can be provided at half-landings

71 Straight flight at right angles to horizontal circulation is often attractive in saving circulation space but divides plan rigidly; not a disadvantage in some circumstances, particularly in blind-side planning

MORE THAN ONE STOREY

New planning determinants are introduced: vertical circulation, relationship between kitchen and bathroom (which becomes vertical as well as horizontal), and balancing of ground- and upper-storey accommodation.

Vertical circulation: the stair

In all houses of more than one storey, the plan is influenced by the position and design of the stair. The stair and its location tend to affect the constructional system to be employed: in repetitive house design, this is often the most important single standardising component.

Stairs differ in design (straight flight or dog-leg) and in position. These, in combination, impose different planning constraints. To provide the best circulation, the aim is to arrive on the first floor at a point as close as possible to the middle of the house; the best choice of position and type of stair to achieve this is related to the plan shape (see **70**).

Kitchen and bathroom

These comprise the most heavily serviced parts of the house; economy in plumbing and water supply systems and the problems of accommodating unsightly soil and waste stacks make it preferable to place one above the other (see **73**).

72 Simple and economical design of terrace house with 'farmhouse' kitchen and bathroom on ground floor

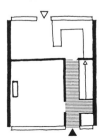
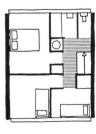

73 Economy achieved by placing bathroom over kitchen

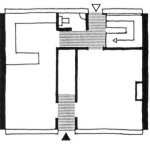

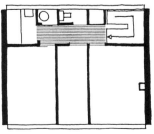

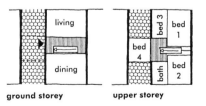

ground storey   **upper storey**

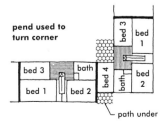

pend used to turn corner

path under

74 Bedroom over pend (passageway) allows provision of extra room

Balance of ground- and upper-storey accommodation

In some house types, designed for both small and large households, the total area required for bedrooms and related accommodation does not balance the living, kitchen and other areas usually placed on ground floor: this is because, unlike the number and size of bedrooms, the space allotted for common use does not increase proportionally with family size. Economic design for small houses, say for three or four persons, employs a 1¼-storey arrangement, basically of one-storey construction with an open roof truss to enable roof space to be used for bedrooms. Such a roof on a one-storey house can also facilitate future extension of small houses.

The opposite problem occurs in two-storey houses designed for more than six persons, where house plans can be adapted by providing a bedroom over a passageway, linking houses across pedestrian routes (see **74**).

Room functions

Functions are generally self-evident, and will be linked by common circulation space (see **49, 50, 51**). In some layouts, stairs and circulation can be within living/dining area, but this is rarely satisfactory (due to fire precautions, noise, lack of privacy and energy conservation). (See also Halls of Residence and Hostels section for examples of minimum layouts, bed-sitting rooms etc.)

Dwellings should be designed to provide flexible spaces, but layouts with, for example, small bedrooms or open-plan living/dining areas often make this impossible. Use of loft space for storage is often restricted (or even prevented entirely) by the timber roof truss system. Bedrooms particularly should be regarded as flexible rooms, not just a space for a bed.

HOUSE PLANS

Plan ranges

By classifications of type outlined (see p. 177), many organisations, in both the public and private sectors, have compiled sets of related house designs called plan ranges. Designs comprising a plan range have basic constructional features in common, such as staircase type and location, kitchen/bathroom relationship and upper-floor construction. House designs in such ranges can be varied to meet differing requirements while retaining a useful degree of standardisation (see **77**).

The first-floor plan of a three-bedroom, wide frontage house can be adapted to allow the house to be used where a controlled aspect is required (i.e. the first floor has a view out only on one side – see **19**). This is possible because the critical elements remain unchanged (in this case, plumbing, heating and stair). Use of the same first-floor plan as the narrow frontage house is possible (turned through 90°), but would impose dual-aspect conditions on its use in layout (i.e. views out are required on two sides).

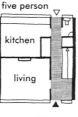

five person

ground floor   first floor

ground floor   first floor

75 Two 'through-hall' type plans: note how wider frontage provides one extra bedspace but results in long circulation space on first floor; layouts originally planned for solid-fuel heating and chimney
(Arch: National Building Agency)

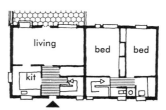

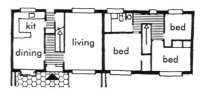

76 Houses at Moulton, Yorkshire
(Arch: Butterworth)

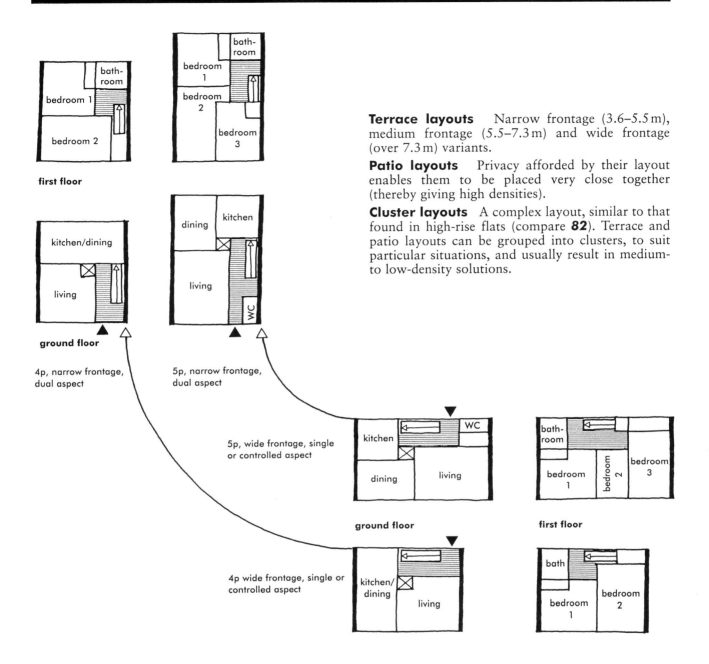

first floor

ground floor

4p, narrow frontage, dual aspect

5p, narrow frontage, dual aspect

5p, wide frontage, single or controlled aspect

4p wide frontage, single or controlled aspect

ground floor

first floor

Terrace layouts   Narrow frontage (3.6–5.5 m), medium frontage (5.5–7.3 m) and wide frontage (over 7.3 m) variants.

Patio layouts   Privacy afforded by their layout enables them to be placed very close together (thereby giving high densities).

Cluster layouts   A complex layout, similar to that found in high-rise flats (compare **82**). Terrace and patio layouts can be grouped into clusters, to suit particular situations, and usually result in medium- to low-density solutions.

77   Range of house types for four and five people, wide and narrow frontage layouts
(Arch: National Building Agency (Scotland))

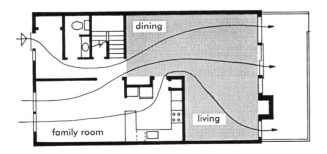

78   Combined room: natural lighting and ventilation

Combined rooms: natural lighting and ventilation

Unless separately lit and ventilated, the required area should be based on the total area of combined spaces, provided degree of openness, relationship and planning of adjacent space allow adequate natural lighting.

In a terrace-house plan (see **78**), the shaded area should be used in calculating required amounts of natural light and ventilation for combined dining and living space. Assuming the total floor area of the dining and living room is 41.8 m², the minimum amount of glazed area required would be 41.8 × 10%, or 4.18 m² in the living room exposed wall. Ventilation should be located to provide circulation of air throughout the area. Because of the distance of the dining area from a source of natural light, the size of glazing is critical.

FLATS: BUILDING TYPES

This part of the section describes buildings divided horizontally to provide separate and self-contained dwellings which need not necessarily be on one floor only (e.g. maisonettes – see **79**).

Types can be distinguished as follows.

Low-rise or high-rise

In the UK the accepted maximum height of entrance doors to dwellings normally reached by ramp or stairs is four storeys from ground level or from the main entrance to the building. Beyond that limit, lift access must be provided; and a building containing such flats is regarded as high-rise. In practice, low-rise flatted buildings are often provided with lifts; in public sector housing these are required where more than two storeys have to be climbed to any private entrance door. Such a building, from three to five storeys, is generally called medium-rise.

Point block or slab block

In a point block, all dwellings share a single vertical access system (see **80**). Vertical access must always include the stairway; according to height and layout, the building might also have one lift or more and secondary escape stairs. Slab block is a continuous building in which dwellings are reached by 2 or more separate vertical access systems (see **4**).

Maisonettes

Separate dwellings in low- or high-rise blocks having rooms arranged on more than one storey are known as maisonettes: they have been built in the UK in four-storey blocks (see **79**), in slab blocks and in combination with flats (see **81**). Such arrangements can show savings over flats of similar accommodation because there is less common access space.

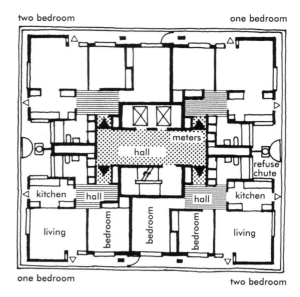

80 Twelve-storey point block, Battersea, London: typical upper-floor plan, with balcony escape routes between flats (Arch: George Trew & Dunn)

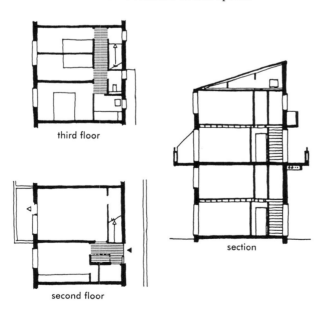

79 Maisonettes in four-storey blocks in London: high-density development; site levels allow access at second floor but require single/controlled access plan; note screening of stair and escape balcony at bedroom floor in upper maisonette (Arch: Yorke Rosenberg Mardall)

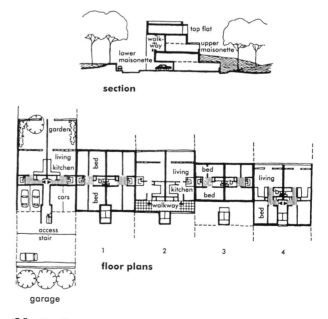

81 Dwellings at Runcorn, Cheshire: on five levels; layouts show two × two-storey maisonette (lower entered from ground level, upper from second-storey walkway) and top-storey flat (entered from stairs from ground or walkway); ramps and bridge connect to main shopping area (Arch: James Stirling)

FLATS: TYPES OF ACCESS

Access can be classified as stairway, balcony or corridor.

Stairway access

Stairway access, with two, three or four flats per landing, allows grouping of services and can provide a high degree of privacy – the standard solution in point blocks. In slab blocks, however, there are disadvantages where more than two flats are served from each landing: this usually involves back-to-back planning and consequently some form of artificial ventilation (see **80**).

Balcony and corridor access

Balcony and internal corridor access, usually employed in slab blocks, permit savings in common access space. Exposure to weather is the obvious disadvantage of balconies, particularly in high-rise, and internal planning is constrained by the potential lack of privacy on the balcony side; window design can modify this constraint. Internal corridors escape weather problems, but introduce new problems of sound insulation, lighting and ventilation, and require high standards of management in use. Open corridors or roof-streets avoid most of these difficulties. In medium-rise development, open corridors and sheltered balconies giving access to small flats over larger dwellings can accommodate a wide variety of household sizes at high densities (see **83**). Balcony and corridor access have been much used in conjunction with split-level flats and maisonettes (e.g. see **6**).

European development

The development of flats in Europe between 1919 and 1939 was largely dominated by the concept of the 'minimum dwelling'. In a period of extreme housing shortage, dwellings of small floor area and few internal amenities were used to provide high-density housing in inner-city areas (see **85,86,87,88**). More generously planned flats were used in suburban situations and for middle-class occupation (see **90**).

82 Three × two-room flats; landing achieves good daylighting and cross-ventilation but extra length of wall has to be weighed against economy of circulation
(Arch: E Gutkind)

Standards for flats and maisonettes

Modern flats should not be regarded as 'second-best' but should provide accommodation similar to houses for equivalent household sizes. In fact, space standards for flats in the public sector in the UK have been slightly more generous than for houses, recognising the difficulties of providing for internal circulation and escape in the event of a fire.

site plan

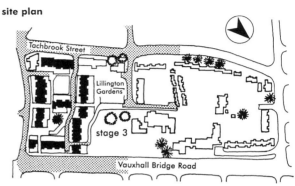

floor plans

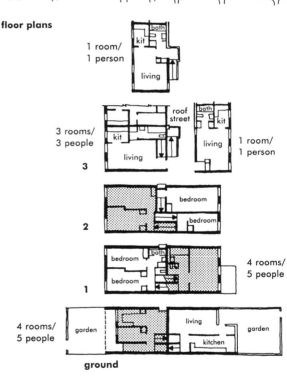

typical section

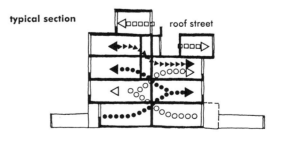

83 Medium-rise dwellings, Lillington St, London: high-density (618 bed-spaces/ha); each family dwelling is entered at ground level through private garden; smaller maisonettes and flats have access from open corridor or 'roof streets', which bridge between blocks and are served by lifts
(Arch: Darbourne & Darke)

  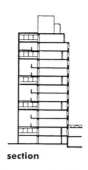

section

84 'Triplex' arrangement, Cambridge, USA: access corridor every third floor; flats above and below access corridor have private stairs
(Arch: Kock-Kennedy)

  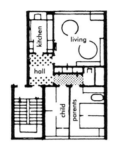

85 Small German flat with WC on inner wall; living area 28 m²
(Arch: Märkische Wohnungsbau)

86 More generous three-room flat with WC and shower

87 Dutch three-room flat with internal bathroom; compacted plan with separated service
(Arch: H. Leppla)

DUPLEX AND TRIPLEX SECTIONS

Designs for split-level flats and maisonettes, with access balconies, decks or corridors every second (duplex) or third (triplex) storey, have been developed over many years. While some design problems have been solved, (e.g. visual privacy and cross-ventilation), others, such as sound insulation, have increased.

FLATS: DETERMINING FACTORS

SERVICES

Attention should be paid to grouping of services and provision of adequate service ducts, especially where buildings incorporate a variety of dwelling sizes and plans are not repetitive. Standard location and arrangement of bath, WC and kitchen fittings facilitates the design of ducts and service stacks. Internal bathrooms and WCs require mechanical ventilation, either individually or by common ducting. Shared ventilation systems require smoke-stopping by fire dampers and stand-by fans to ensure continuous operation.

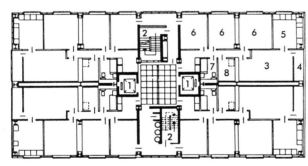

1   lift
2   staircase
3   living
4   loggia
5   kitchen
6   room
7   bathroom
8   heating and water tank

88 Flats in high-rise block, Balornock, Scotland
(Arch: S Bunton & Associates)

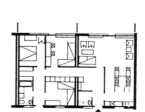

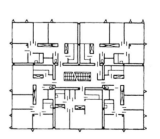

89 Convertible flat in day and night use, with fold-away beds and screens; area 40 m²
(Arch: C. Fieger)

90 Five-bedroom flat in system building, Stora Tuna, Sweden
(Arch: Y. Johnsson)

91 Apartment-size floor in block of flats, Rouen, France
(Arch: Lods Depondt Beauclair Alexandre)

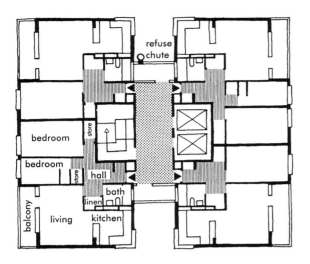

92 Point block at Thamesmead, London: 12-storey system-built structure provides four flats per floor
(Arch: GLC Architects' Department)

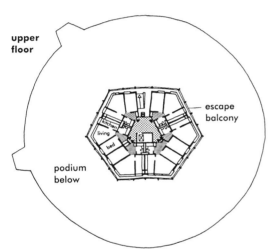

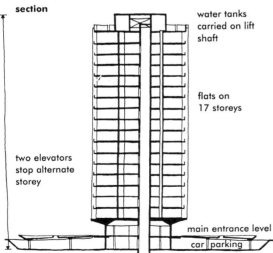

93 Point Royal, Bracknell, Berkshire: in continental Europe some designs achieve up to ten flats/floor served from central access, but fire regulations make this rarely possible in UK; this hexagonal plan achieves six flats/floor with minimum circulation space and escape distances; car space is provided for each flat under circular podium
(Arch: Arup Associates)

PRIVACY AND FIRE

Privacy

Privacy is best secured by stairway access, where only the entrance door opens onto the landing. In balcony access, the bathroom, WC and kitchen can be placed on the access side, but it can be difficult to provide sufficient natural light where high windows are below balconies. (See also pp. 169–70, 195.)

Sound insulation presents greater difficulties in flats than in houses, and privacy is best secured by planning. Avoid long separating walls to bedrooms, and avoid bedrooms beneath access balconies or adjoining lifts, stairs or refuse chutes. Where possible use cupboards to increase sound insulation of separating walls.

Fire escape

Bedroom doors opening into a private entrance hall should wherever possible be nearer to the entrance door than the living room or kitchen. All doors other than bathroom and WC should be self-closing and fire-resisting; walls enclosing the entrance hall should have half-hour fire-resistance. In most other conditions, plan for alternative escape routes from bedrooms above two storeys.

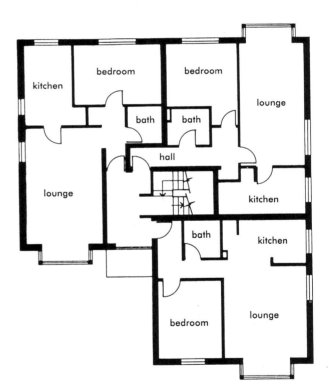

94 Flats at Cosham, Portsmouth, Hampshire: on three floors (typical floor shown); note bedrooms nearer flat door than kitchen, to comply with fire officer's recommendations
(Arch: Rex Hawkesworth)

upper floor plan

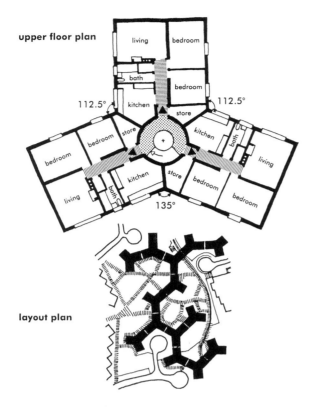

layout plan

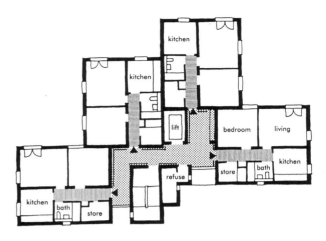

97 Three-storey sheltered dwellings, London: low point-blocks or 'stub blocks' with lifts can provide suitable accommodation for elderly people
(Arch: Yorke Rosenberg Mardall)

95 Y-blocks have been developed in several countries, particularly in low-rise forms where they can be joined together without overshadowing; this example, built 1957 at Cumbernauld, Scotland, has arms at different angles giving greater variety of layout arrangements and avoiding closed courts
(Arch: Cumbernauld Development Corporation)

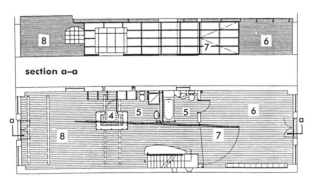

section a–a

lower floor

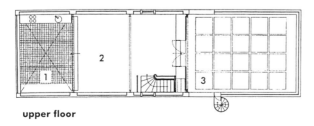

upper floor

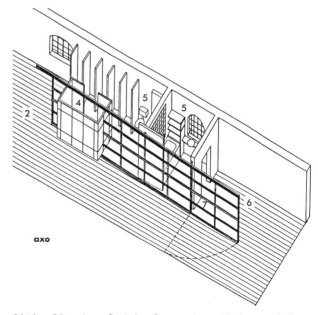

axo

1 kitchen; 2 living (upper floor); 3 roof terrace; 4 store; 5 bathroom; 6 bedroom; 7 screen (to close bedroom); 8 living (lower floor)

96 A loft conversion, Derbyshire Street Residence, Bethnal Green, London: interesting example of recent trend to reuse old industrial premises, often in inner-city areas, to provide residential accommodation (remainder of building not shown)
(Arch: Fraser Brown MacKenna Architects)

INTERNAL FUNCTION

Note that layouts in social housing schemes should conform to *Space in the Home* and other DoE Design Bulletins where relevant.

MAIN ENTRANCE

Although it is stating the obvious, it is sometimes forgotten that the main entrance should be easily visible from the approach; if there are other adjacent doors (e.g. to a study or living room) the main entrance should be easily distinguishable.

The entrance threshold and lobby is often one of the most difficult areas for disabled access: a ramp or level threshold should be considered (see Design for Accessibility section). If part of the dwelling is also used as an office or workroom, this should have either a separate front entrance, or be easily reached from the main entrance. For halls and lobbies, and circulation, see **61–64**.

LIVING/RECEPTION ROOMS

The purpose of these include:
- relaxation, social activities and entertainment
- children's play area
- possibly, occasional dining (depending on the size and atmosphere of other dining spaces).

A friendly, informal atmosphere is generally required, with good natural light and views, preferably over a garden and away from noisy areas such as the front road etc. In larger dwellings, more than one living room may be provided, possibly both self-contained, or alternatively divided by double doors. The circulation route should not be through a living area, except in the smallest dwellings. A door to the garden is desirable. A good deal of wall space is required, for bookshelves, pictures, ornaments etc. A fireplace is often regarded as providing a focal point: it may not need to be a traditional solid-fuel fireplace.

DINING ROOM

The purpose is self-evident; this area is often combined with the living room in smaller dwellings. Traditionally, if intended as primarily a breakfast room, it has faced east to get the morning sun; if primarily a room for lunch or evening meals, it has faced south or west to take advantage of the sun later in the day. A reasonable layout for eight people (allowing for storage and circulation) occupies about 12 m² (see **98**).

Dining-kitchen It may be acceptable to provide an area opening off or adjacent to the living room, rather than a separate dining room (see **113**). Separation can be achieved by arranging fitments to provide a degree of screening, by a change of floor finish, or by a change in level (usually undesirable unless skilfully designed).

Farmhouse kitchen The kitchen may also be enlarged to contain an eating area and chairs, without separation, to form a breakfast bar or 'farmhouse kitchen'. This is more economical in space than either a separate kitchen and dining room or dining-kitchen, but offers less flexibility in use (see **99,112**).

STUDY

A study is increasingly required due to growth of home-working. The availability of cheap computers, Internet links, and fax machines etc. have made it possible for many people to work at home in a way inconceivable in the 1980s. While it has been traditional for some people to work from home (e.g. vicars and authors) it is now becoming possible for many others; it has been estimated by the late 1990s that about 70% of all small-business start-ups were home based (i.e. about 350 000 pa). A separate room is essential, preferably on the ground floor; for reasons of privacy, noise and security it is necessary for this room to be apart from the general living area (see **15**).

Facilities required   (see **100**):
- desk (with space for computer, positioned to avoid glare)
- comfortable chairs, sufficient for small meetings
- adequate communications links (e.g. power points, phone sockets)
- space for photocopier, fax, filing cabinet, books etc.

SPECIALIST ROOMS

Rooms that may be required in more expensive private dwellings include: library, music room, playroom, games room (e.g. for billiards, darts, table tennis: see Sports section), breakfast room, dance room.

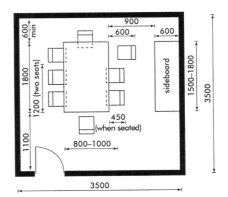

98 Dining room

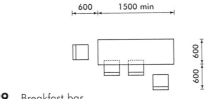

99 Breakfast bar

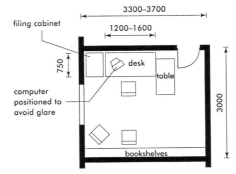

100 Study

KITCHENS

The kitchen should have direct access to the dining area (a serving hatch may be sufficient).

Facilities are required for:
- meal preparation and serving
- eating: occasional meals; perhaps breakfast
- washing up
- food storage
- utensil and crockery storage.

Ancillary activities can include:
- clothes washing
- general household mending and cleaning
- young children's play (must be supervised and adequately protected).

Working sequence

The sequence of activities (see **101**) relates to sequence of fitments (namely, worktop–cooker–worktop–sink–worktop), which is the basis of modern domestic kitchen planning (see **102**). This should never be broken by full-height fitments, doors or passageways.

Work triangle The distance the user has to walk between sink, cooker and refrigerator or store is critical in kitchen planning. Lines joining these three elements form what is known as 'work triangle' (see **103**). For the normal family house, the combined length of the sides of the triangle should be between 5.50 and 6.00 m. The distance between the sink and cooker should not exceed 1.80 m, and should never be crossed by through-circulation.

Sinks These are usually best placed under windows; a double bowl is often considered essential. Sinks should be 3.00 m maximum from the waste stack or external gully, with adequate standing room in front, and should be kept away from corners. However, in small kitchens the sink may need to be placed near a corner.

Cookers and worktops There is no ideal location for the cooker: if in a continuous worktop, the work flow will be interrupted; if outside the work triangle, there will be extra travel distance. Cookers should never be placed in front of windows and should, where possible, be provided with a ventilating hood. They should not be placed below wall cupboards, and a gas cooker should be away from locations where draughts might blow out burners. Worktops should be provided on each side; where a cooker adjoins a corner fitting a return of at least 400 mm should be allowed for easy standing and access space. Low-level cookers require a space of at least 1.20 m in front for access. Adjacent worktops should be at the same level as a cooker top: if a change of level is essential, it should be at least 400 mm from the cooker. Split-level cookers with separate hob and wall oven are sometimes popular. (See **109–113**.)

Refrigerator This is the most difficult item of kitchen equipment to position. An important component of the work triangle, it should be adjacent to a worktop space. The fridge door should open away from the work area for easier food access, and should not block passageways or hit another door when opening.

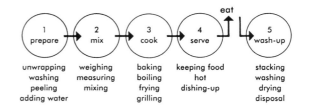

101 Sequence of activities

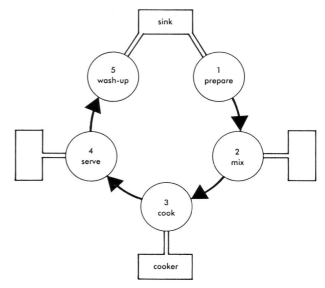

102 Sequence of fitments

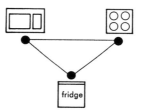

103 Work triangle (sink–cooker–refrigerator)

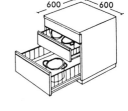

104 Dish cupboard with drawers

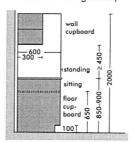

105 Section through worktop and storage

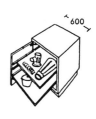

106 Equipment cupboard

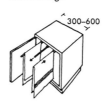

107 Cloths and towels

108 Space-saving vertical storage of dishes

Kitchen storage

Space is required in or adjacent to the kitchen for storing food and cooking equipment. Storage is also need for general cleaning and laundering equipment. Dry goods should be enclosed and readily accessible from the cooker and sink positions.

Floor units are best used for storing heavy or infrequently used articles. Wall units are economical in space and provide convenient storage for smaller and frequently used items: they should be shallow enough to allow full use of worktops below (see **105**), and should have a clearance of at least 450mm above worktops.

Larders are now rare, but if provided they should be ventilated to outside air (the vent being protected by fly-proof screen), and they should not contain heating or hot water pipes, nor receive direct sunlight.

The freezer need not necessarily be in or adjacent to the kitchen, but if placed in an outside storage area it may need to be locked to prevent theft.

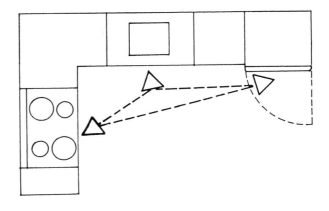

111 L-shaped kitchen

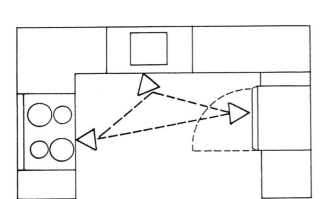

109 U-shaped kitchen

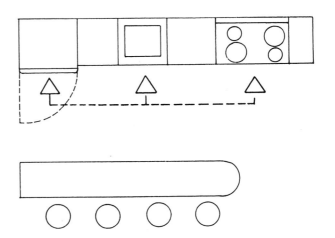

112 Straight-plan kitchen, with breakfast bar

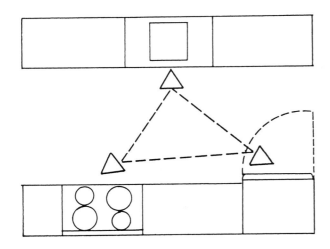

110 Corridor-plan kitchen

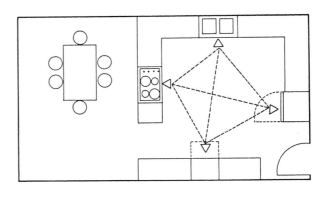

113 Square-plan kitchen with dining area (dining-kitchen)

PROPRIETARY KITCHEN UNITS

Most kitchens are fitted with a range of standard proprietary kitchen units, although purpose-made designs are available. Special worktop surfaces include hardwood timber, marble, stone and slate.

Note the industry standard co-ordinating dimensions:
    depth   500 or 600 mm
    height   900 mm
    width   300, 400, 500, 600, 800, 1000, 1200 mm
tall units:
    height   1950, 2250 mm

wall units:
    depth   200 or 300 mm
    height   300, 600, 900 mm

There is also a huge range of special fittings: for example, hob units, corner units, open shelf units, fridge and dishwasher fronts, wine-rack units, and pelmet, plinth and other decorative sections.

Ranges generally have the same basic carcass construction, and are differentiated by door fronts and worktops. Worktops are usually supplied in standard lengths, including L-shaped.

 base unit
full height door

 base/hob unit
one drawer

 base/sink/hob unit
full-height doors

 base/sink/hob unit
two dummy drawers

 base unit
one drawer

 base/sink/hob unit
one dummy drawer

 base/hob unit
two drawers

 sink unit
one drawer
one dummy drawer

 base unit
full height door

 pan drawer
hob base unit

 base/sink/hob unit
two dummy drawers

 base/sink/hob unit
full-height doors

 base unit
one drawer

 pan drawer
hob base unit
one drawer

 base/sink/hob unit
full-height doors

 base/hob unit
two drawers

 base unit
three drawers

 pan drawer
hob base unit
one dummy drawer

 base/hob unit
two drawers

 base/sink/hob unit
two dummy drawers

base units

 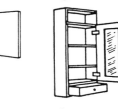

wall units

 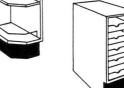

dresser units

larder units   appliance housings

wine rack

114 Typical range of standard kitchen units:
(Reproduced by permission of by Moores Furniture Group Ltd)
note that only some typical units are shown, whole range
not reproduced (not to scale)

end base units

LAUNDRY/UTILITY SPACES

The laundry area needs space for a sink and worktop, washing machine and drier, and storage for cleaning materials and, possibly, dirty washing; it may also have to accommodate an ironing board or ironing machine and a working surface for sorting. An external door, or easy access to one, is preferable. Although mobile washing machines are available, most models, automatic machines in particular, are best plumbed in with permanent connections to the water supply and suitably trapped waste. Where a washing machine is not used, or in large households where much hand washing is done, a sink 500×350×250mm deep is required and a second bowl or tub is desirable. Tumble-driers (see **118**) are best placed against outside walls to allow the direct extraction of water vapour; removable lint traps are required by some models. Even where a tumble-drier is provided, a rack or line is needed for some clothes. In small houses or flats this can be fixed above the bath or shower; otherwise it should be in a ventilated drying cupboard or over a trapped draining tray. Open-air drying is preferred by many and makes no demands on energy resources. Open-air drying space (see **119**) should be easily accessible from the laundry area and preferably visible from the kitchen.

BEDROOMS

Bedrooms should be seen as more than just a place for a bed; they should allow space for leisure and study facilities – activities which often cause problems if undertaken in living spaces.

Facilities are required for:
- sleeping
- relaxation
- leisure (e.g. computers, music)
- studying
- storage (clothes, personal items and linen).

Ancillary facilities might include:
- washbasin
- adjoining separate dressing room or shower/WC/bath.

The Housing Corporation Good Practice Guide states that layouts should conform to DoE DB6 Space in the Home. Bedrooms should not be located under or adjacent to circulation areas or rooms of a different function in another dwelling.

Position of bed
Bed-making requires clear space of at least 400mm (preferably 700) beside bed. In most smaller houses, therefore, the choice of bed position is restricted by the shape and size of the bedroom. To free as much floor space as possible single beds are usually placed along walls and double or twin beds placed head-to-wall. Nevertheless, the relation of the bed to the walls, and to the room as a whole, can also be important in contributing to a feeling of security. While a stable, self-reliant person may prefer a bed positioned away from walls, others may prefer a bed against a wall regardless of the amount of space available.

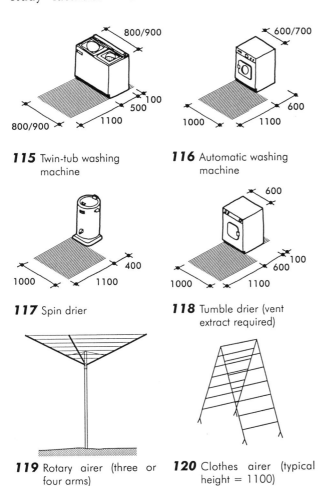

115 Twin-tub washing machine

116 Automatic washing machine

117 Spin drier

118 Tumble drier (vent extract required)

119 Rotary airer (three or four arms)

120 Clothes airer (typical height = 1100)

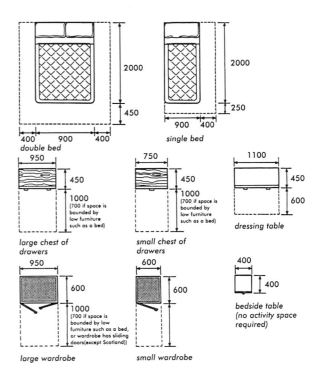

121 Furniture and activity spaces for bedrooms (not to scale): broken lines around beds indicate the activity space and not room size; activity spaces can overlap
(From NHBC Standards: not mandatory and no longer a current publication)

A sense of restfulness depends on wall coverings and colours, shape of bed, orientation (head towards north), relation to daylight (looking away from window) and relation to door (looking towards door). Ideally, different positions for bed(s) should be possible, especially where the bedroom is intended for two single beds.

If a water bed is required, it should be borne in mind that, fully loaded, it may impose a floor load of up to 2 or even 3 tonnes.

BATHROOMS

Facilities are required for:
- washing and bathing
- WC (or may be in separate compartment)
- storage.

Additional facilities possibly required:
- space for bathing young children
- elderly or disabled equipment
- separate shower
- bidet
- consider also if en-suite facilities are to be provided for master or other bedrooms.

The space required is shown in **122**. However, a minimum space layout may be undesirable, particularly in private sector where larger layouts give an impression of luxury. Also, the layout of the dwelling plan may result in a larger bathroom layout than strictly necessary, in order to correspond with structural layout etc. Economy in services arrangement (particularly waste and hot pipes) may be more important than the overall plan. The length of waste and soil pipes is limited by building regulations (unless vent pipes or special designs are used); hot supply is limited by the water authority and the need for energy efficiency.

Showers generally use less water than baths (but note that power-showers can use more water), are more hygienic, and take up less space. Fixed shower arms should be mounted at a height of 1.9 m; alternatively a rail with an adjustable hand shower should be used. Bidets are still rare, but are more common in higher priced dwellings.

Where possible, space should be available for at least one item of bathroom furniture, such as a stool or laundry box. Fittings such as towel rails and toilet roll holders should not obstruct activity spaces. Consider also the problem of noise where bathrooms/WCs are adjacent to bedrooms.

Windows above baths can be difficult to open or to clean without standing in bath (a potential cause of accidents); they may also limit privacy and cause draughts unless well insulated. Windows behind washbasins can also be difficult to reach; the wall above a washbasin is best used for a mirror or medicine cabinet (which should be fitted with a safety lock to prevent access to children).

Electrical sockets are not permitted in bathrooms other than a specially designed shaver point, which should be out of reach of bath. Switches to light fittings must be outside the bathroom or cord-operated.

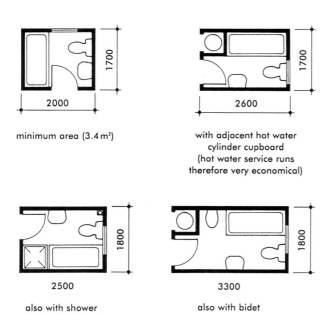

122 Typical bathroom layouts (including bath, WC and washbasin)

minimum area (3.4 m²)

2000 / 1700

with adjacent hot water cylinder cupboard (hot water service runs therefore very economical)

2600 / 1700

also with shower

2500 / 1800

also with bidet

3300 / 1800

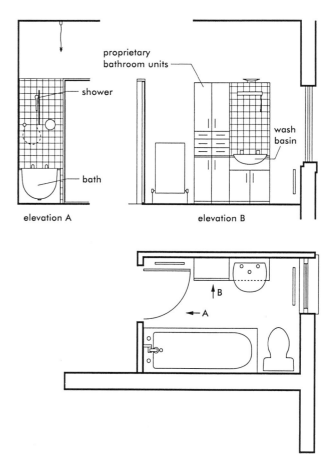

123 Bathroom plan and elevation, with over-bath shower and washbasin in vanity unit

elevation A

elevation B

proprietary bathroom units

shower

bath

wash basin

WC

Facilities required are:
- flushing lavatory
- washbasin
- consider ground-floor location – preferable for elderly or disabled visitors (door locks to be openable from outside).

Possible additional requirements:
- consider linkage to bathroom
- keep service routes as economical as possible
- pump extracts for wastes allow WCs in previously unacceptable locations (but note that noise of the pump may be a problem)
- possible noise problem if adjacent to study etc.
- bidet (see under Bathrooms).

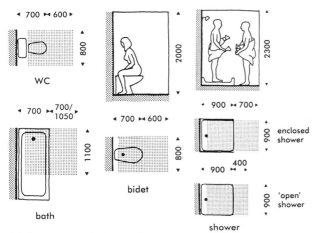

124 Recommended areas for use

STORAGE

Requirements:
- differentiate between internal and external storage
- general or specific storage (e.g. linen)
- for kitchen storage, see under Kitchens.

Shape and position of storage space is as important as its capacity. Storage should be provided within easy reach of activities to which it is related, and its shape should allow maximum use of wall area for shelving (see **129,130**). Storage is generally more useful at ground level than on upper storeys, and should be accessible form a circulation area. A family house will require at least 5 m² of general storage, of which at least half should be on the ground floor.

General storage

Storage rooms require ventilation and those providing part of the passageway through a house should also permit natural lighting. In such cases, allowance must be made for the loss of usable space to circulation requirements (see **130**).

Storage in roof space should ideally be reached from a door at first-floor level (i.e. into the roof space over a extension above the ground floor or garage).

Garden tools, bicycles etc. are usually best kept in external storage or, if within house itself, in storage with direct access from outside. If there is no garage, bicycle storage requirements should be as shown in **125**.

Coats and hats

Space is required in or adjacent to the entrance hall for hanging hats and coats and storing outdoor footwear. This should preferably be in a wardrobe or with racks to take hangers **131,132**). Additional space may be needed for storing working clothes and equipment.

Prams/buggies

Although now used less frequently, a pram or large buggy will be required for infants; the space requirement is considerable (see **126**). It should be easy to manoeuvre the pram or buggy indoors so that it can be used as a cot during the day if required.

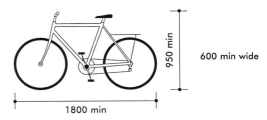

125 Bicycles: minimum dimensions for storage

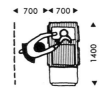

126 Prams: dimensions

127 Internal storage accessible from garden without passing through living area of house

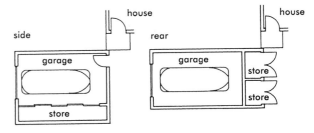

128 Garage and storage

Linen

Separate storage should be provided for linen and bedding. At least 0.6 m³ (or 1.5 m²) is required, fitted with slatted shelves. It must be heated and dry and therefore preferably not accessed from the bathroom or kitchen, and is often combined with a hot water cylinder cupboard (but not with 'combination' water unit as condensation might occur).

Wardrobes

For clothing in particular, ease of access is more important than storage capacity as such. The effective depth of built-in cupboards for clothes hanging is 600 mm, but deeper cupboards can be more fully utilised by attaching accessories to backs of doors. As loads are not great, normal blockboard doors on strong hinges are adequate; shelves can be supported by adjustable ladders and brackets.

Meters

Meters should preferably be capable of being read without entering the house. This may be a requirement or simply a recommendation of the supply authority: check for local area. Remote reading devices may become available in the near future, thus removing the need for external meters. Many meters are large and visually ugly: care is needed in design to provide suitable enclosure or concealment. Water meters are usually installed below ground and are therefore not a problem. Prepayment meters must be easy to reach from floor level, but all meters must be out of reach of small children, or in a lockable enclosure. Fire precautions may require a fire-resisting enclosure.

Wine and beer

Wine and beer cellars should be clean, dark, dry, well ventilated (but avoid cold draughts) and in a quiet position free from vibration and away from direct heat. White wines are best kept at a constant temperature between 10 and 12°C; red wines at between 14 and l6°C; beer at about 12°C.

Fuel storage

Solid fuel bunkers should have a capacity of 0.5 t minimum. The store should be accessible from within the house or from porch or other shelter. To avoid the spread of dust, arrange it such that bags can be tipped from outside, without entering house.

Oil storage tanks should have capacity of 2700 l for family dwellings. Fuel tanks up to 2000 l can generally be located adjacent to houses without restriction; if enclosed they should be separated from remainder of the building and provided with catch pit. Fuel inlet points should be positioned within 30 m of the place where delivery tankers can conveniently stop. Tanks should be screened, under cover or below ground. Under-cover access should be provided from the house to the fuel store.

Refuse

The Building Regulations, Part H4, covers solid waste storage. Requirements are very general: provision is to be of adequate size for storage, suitably sited for users and collectors, and facilities must not present a health risk. Provision is therefore largely dependent on the collection methods of local councils, which should be consulted for guidance.

Alternatively, provision can be based on BS 5906: 1980 (1987): Code of Practice for the storage and on-site treatment of solid waste from buildings (which also gives full details of refuse chutes).

Storage capacity should be:
- up to four stories, based on weekly collection: individual containers of 0.12 m³, or communal containers of 0.75–1.0 m³ capacity

- above four stories: a refuse chute should be provided, or a suitable alternative.

If collections are not weekly, the local authority should be consulted.

Refuse storage should be outside the dwelling and easily accessible from the kitchen door. Simple, easily cleaned, covered enclosures are required (see **134**); doors are often a hindrance and are easily broken, but help to keep out vermin and prevent an unsightly view. 'Wheelie bins' are an alternative (see **135**). Communal refuse storage should be provided with washdown facilities and artificial lighting.

Refuse chutes need careful design, particularly with regard to sound insulation (see Building Regulations, Part E). Carry-distance to a chute or bin for householders should be 30 m maximum; from bin to collection vehicle, the maximum distance should be 25 m.

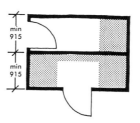

129 Entrance on long side of storage area allows maximum use of shelving

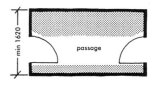

130 Allow space for passageway in 'through' storage area

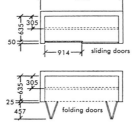

131 In-line wardrobe

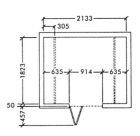

132 Walk-in wardrobe

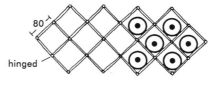

133 'Lazytongs' racking to fit available cupboard spaces (80×80×80)

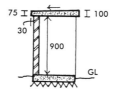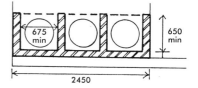

134 Typical small refuse store: often used where large house has been converted into flats; careful siting is needed to avoid unsightly view, but also to allow easy access for refuse collectors; doors to front are usually a hindrance

Waste recycling initiatives are resulting in additional containers for domestic waste, from small boxes (size 500×350×300mm deep) to larger 'wheelie bins' (see **135**). The collecting authority often requires waste to be separated out into separate containers (e.g. for glass, paper, metal, card and plastic) and providing adequate room for such containers can be a problem.

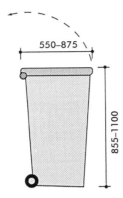

135 Two-wheeled polyethylene refuse container ('wheelie bin'); capacity 90, 120, 240 or 330l; larger communal bins (1100l) have four wheels and can be braked

550–875

855–1100

SAFETY AND SECURITY GENERALLY

(See also Privacy, p. 185.) Free detailed advice, based on expert local knowledge, is available from all UK police forces through their crime prevention officers. See also BS 8220 (Guide for security of buildings against crime) and BS EN 5013.

Domestic safety

Statistically, it is in the home that most personal accidents occur. Many aspects are covered by statutory requirements (mainly building regulations) or quasi-legal recommendations (e.g. IEE regulations), but additional items need to be borne in mind, such as the height of window cills, particularly in children's bedrooms, opening windows and restrictor mechanisms, glazing in doors, stairs (especially retractable steps to lofts), unexpected changes in level, heating appliances and cookers, electrical equipment, temperature controls (to hot water and radiators). Situations to which the immediate family may be accustomed could present unexpected danger to visitors, particularly young children, the elderly and people with disabilities. Medical cabinets should be located in the master bedroom (not the bathroom) and should be out of reach of young children; they may also need to be kept locked, in which case sticking plasters and other treatments for minor ailments need to be kept elsewhere and easily accessible to children. All tools should be kept in a secure location. Doors to kitchen units and alcohol cabinets should have restrictor fastenings to prevent easy opening by young children. However, remember that safety devices for young children may also make access difficult for the elderly.

External and site security

This is best served by good lighting and visibility. Access routes and entrances should never be dark or concealed, however romantic this might appear, and should if possible allow sufficient space to avoid difficult encounters. Video cameras are now common and appear to have good deterrent effect,

but many consider them to be an infringement on privacy. They are expensive to maintain properly, and they add considerably to visual clutter. Avoid dense planting round entrances and ground-floor windows (or use prickly shrubs or roses etc.).

In blocks of flats entry is now often controlled by entryphones (see **136**) but this may be inconvenient where small children are involved. For single people or working couples some provision is needed for daytime deliveries (usually by a tradesman's button, operative up to 10.00).

For flats, the transition between the fully public street zone and the entirely private zone of individual flat may be by way of both a semi-public zone shared by all flats in a block (lift and staircase hall etc., possibly with some form of supervised access) and a semi-private zone shared by two or three flats with access under the control of occupants (see **137**).

The NHBC Standards mentioned earlier also suggested that:
- layouts should be organised so that general public access is discouraged
- good street and background lighting should be provided

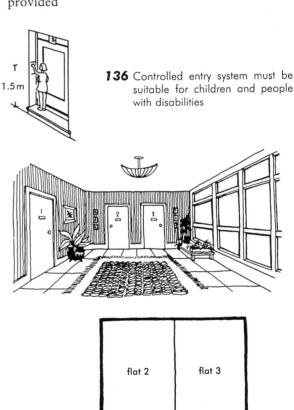

1.5 m

136 Controlled entry system must be suitable for children and people with disabilities

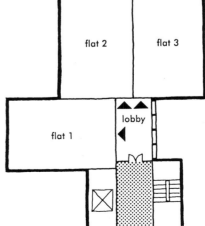

flat 2

flat 3

flat 1

lobby

137 Semi-private entry zone for flats

- dark corners etc. should be avoided
- footpaths away from vehicular routes should be avoided, as should those allowing unobserved through-routes
- the fronts of dwellings should generally be in open view, and walls etc. should be kept to waist height, although there is a potential conflict between visibility and privacy
- rear gardens should back onto one another, and should not abut open spaces such as parks, railway embankments etc.

Security for dwellings

This is now essential to help prevent petty crime, which has increased considerably over the past 40 years. Relatively simple devices help to prevent much minor crime (70% is quoted); more sophisticated systems are rarely needed. For thieves, ease of exit is as important as ease of entry. Some may be prepared to break glass to secure access but will be unwilling to rely on this as a means of exit. Most illegal entry to dwellings is by forcing windows or bypassing poor-quality locks.

Windows All openable windows should have key-operated security locks, with the key kept in a safe location away from the window. Ideally, the security device should allow slight opening for ventilation (opening of 100 mm max). Louvre windows must have panes permanently fixed into the frames (special adhesives may be acceptable). Small glass panels are particularly vulnerable. All putty must be in good condition, or it can be easily broken out and the glass removed.

Final exit doors These should have a five-lever mortice deadlock or lock conforming to BS 3261: 1980 (fitted about one-third of the way from the bottom, but not adjacent to a stile), a door viewer and security chain. There should be one and a half pairs of 100 mm hinges and a pair of hinge bolts. A cylinder rim latch is normally fitted about one-third of the way from the top of the door, but this must not be regarded as a security fitting. A 22 mm wide metal

strip (often known as a London bar) can be fitted to the frame to cover the lock box plates, although this looks unsightly. The door itself should be solid timber (i.e. not hollow core), at least 45 mm thick, with a good frame securely fixed to the surround (there is no point in a good quality door and security devices if the frame can be pushed out of the surround). Thinner door panels should be avoided, and glazed panels should be reinforced with plastic film or sheet or decorative grilles (remember that Georgian-wired glass is a fire-resisting glass, not a security glass).

Other doors Single doors should have five-lever mortice locks or key-operated security bolts at top and bottom; double doors should be rebated and fitted with security bolts. There must be secure bolt housings in lintels and thresholds. Other requirements are as for final exit doors, as appropriate. Sliding patio doors may need special protection to prevent them being lifted off the running track.

PVCu doors and windows These need to be checked with manufacturers to ensure that security fixings can be securely housed in the frames, and that the frames themselves are robust and adequately fixed into the surrounds.

Security and fire If doors are required to be emergency exits (e.g. in flats and dwellings converted into flats) care must be taken to ensure that any locks are suitable for emergency exit: locks requiring key operation from the inside are usually not acceptable. There is no entirely satisfactory solution.

Alarm systems Numerous proprietary alarm systems are available, giving audible or/and visual warning. The master control unit needs to be carefully located to allow suitable access by the occupiers, while avoiding an obvious or easily visible location for an intruder. Systems can be linked to police stations or commercially run centres. Systems include pressure mats, and sound and vibration detectors. Wire-free installations are becoming increasingly popular.

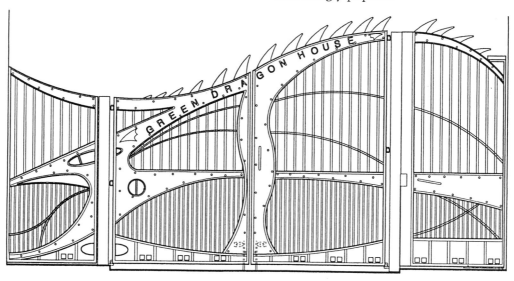

138 Entrance gates: Green Dragon House, London WC2
(Arch: Monahan Blythen Architects)

INDUSTRIAL BUILDINGS

Including factories, warehouses and workshops
See also Business Parks section

INTRODUCTION

The industrial revolution of the 18th century introduced the large-scale, organised collection of industrial processes into specific buildings. Purpose-made machines for industry required larger buildings capable of taking heavier loads. Integral with this were improvements in transportation (first canals, then railways) and materials. Cast iron, then steel and reinforced concrete created the 'factory aesthetic'. Sir Owen Williams designed some of the best early 20th-century industrial buildings in the UK; e.g. the Boots Factory at Nottingham (1930–32). The Firestone Factory (Brentford, 1930) and Hoover Factory (Perivale, 1932), both by Wallis, Gilbert & Partners, demonstrated that industrial premises could be bright and enjoyable buildings. During the past 30 years further structural developments and the introduction of lighter cladding materials have allowed design of large clear-span sheds which can be adapted to a variety of uses.

SITE SELECTION

Assess area requirements from client's brief, including:
- expansion potential
- parking (visitors, employees, trucks)
- external storage area
- landscaping
- road or rail access.

Check EU, national and local legislation for:
- permitted site densities
- use of public utilities such as water, power, gas, effluent disposal for both process and personnel use
- access on public and private roads for employees, goods vehicles and trucks

Assess the environmental impact of heavy industry, light manufacturing and warehousing on the surrounding community. Consider:
- noise (machinery and vehicles), particularly at night
- vibration
- light (external circulation, marshalling, shipping and storage areas at night)
- fume and dust pollution (Clean Air Act, 1993)
- effluent into waterways or ground water (Water Industry Act, 1991)
- hazards of possible explosion or radiation exposure.

Investigate assistance for development finance from EU, central government and local authorities, etc.

Legislation Unsurprisingly, there is a considerable amount of legislation concerning industrial premises. The Factories Act, 1961 imposes some practical controls over constructional matters, but most requirements are covered in other legislation (e.g. planning and building regulations) and the

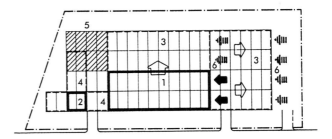

1 manufacturing area; 2 office area; 3 factory expansion options; 4 office expansion options; 5 area of potential planning conflict; 6 goods vehicle access

1 Buildings must be located to allow for expansion, preferably in more than one direction; consider vehicle provision affected by expansion

Offices, Shops & Railway Premises Act (see References section for a fuller list). The Fire Precautions Act, 1971 (SI 1989/76) imposes a general duty of care to provide adequate means of escape, but if more than 20 persons are employed on the ground floor (or 10 persons above or below the ground floor), a fire certificate is required.

DEVELOPMENT OPTIONS

These include: rehabilitate existing site/building; infill and rehabilitate (including town sites); new building on existing site (including phased redevelopment); new building on new site. Each will be defined by:
- planning use class (see below)
- suitability of site size/shape, boundaries
- suitability of building size/type/shape (as briefed)
- geology
- topography
- public utilities
- statutory permissions
- access for industrial vehicles and private cars
- rail or water access
- airport proximity to site
- labour resources of area
- finance (development costs or subsidies, operating costs including taxes/tax relief, loan interest).

Planning use classes

This can only be a brief summary: the SI Town & Country Planning (Use Classes) Order, 1987 must be consulted for the precise wording. The Order introduced revised use classes, and class B1 (business) in effect merged two old classes of office and light industry and is therefore of particular relevance as far as industrial premises are concerned. Provided the premises pass the 'environmental test' of not being likely to cause excessive nuisance in a residential area (even if the premises are not in fact located in a residential area), use can be for office or light industry without the need to obtain planning consent (subject to certain other safeguards). Class B1 was introduced particularly due to changing industrial processes (e.g. 'hi-tech' assembly), which could hardly be differentiated from office use, and would not cause the pollution normally associated with industry.

Class B1: business Use for: office (not within class A2 (financial & professional services)); R&D; any industrial purpose (which can be carried out in any residential area without causing excessive noise, smell, fumes, dust etc.).

Class B2: general industrial Use for any industrial process not covered elsewhere.

Class B3: special industrial group A Use for any work registrable under the Alkali Works Regulation Act (1906) and not included elsewhere.

Class B4: special industrial group B Use for any of the following processes (except where ancillary to mine or quarry works): smelting ores etc., metal casting and similar work, scrap metal recovery, and similar metal working.

Class B5: special industrial group C Use for any of the following processes (except where ancillary to mine or quarry works): brick or lime burning, cement and pulverised fuel ash production, and similar work.

Class B6: special industrial group D Use for distilling, cellulose-spraying (other than in vehicle repair workshops), various chemical processes involving rubber, bitumen, resins, etc.

Class B7: special industrial group E Use for boiling blood, bones, tripe, skins, fat, rag and bones, and other decayable animal or vegetable matter.

Class B8: storage or distribution Use for storage or distribution centre.

SITE LAYOUT

Site layout for factories and warehouses is determined by:
- shape and size of building
- expansion potential
- services running through site (e.g. gas mains, power cables)
- topography, which will affect access for heavy vehicles and building economics (cut and fill)
- energy conservation, including exposure to prevailing and storm winds
- ground conditions and drainage (e.g. to avoid piling or potential flood areas)
- surrounding neighbourhood, keeping noisy external plant and loading bays away from residential area
- vehicle (road and rail) manoeuvring and marshalling area in relation to loading bays (see pp. 222–4).

Economics

Comparing alternative site layouts will usually result in trade-off between conflicting factors. Alternatives for siting distribution warehouse are shown in **2,3**: important cost factors here involve the expansion potential and linked mechanical handling equipment investment decision.

The first option (see **2**) minimises excavation by exploiting the fall of the land to provide a raised loading dock at input; distribution vehicles would need to be side loaded from ground level. But the goods inwards loading bay would face the prevailing wind, affecting the energy cost, and circulation around the site is required, necessitating relocation in the event of expansion.

The second option (see **3**) accepts some excavation for the raised dock, which is sheltered from the prevailing wind, and exploits the fall of the site to sink part of the high-bay stacking area, providing less environmental intrusion and increased handling efficiency. The revised axis of the bulk storage area allows much increased expansion potential without affecting the operation of the existing installation. This, combined with improved storage and handling economics, more than offsets any increase in the capital cost of construction.

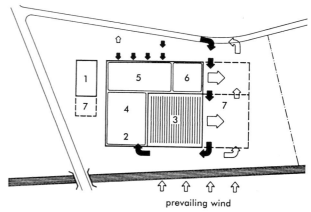

prevailing wind

1 office; 2 goods inward; 3 racked bulk pallet store; 4 order picking area; 5 order and dispatch assembly area; 6 repackaging and processing area; 7 expansion

2 Option 1: low-rise conventional layout; minimal site works

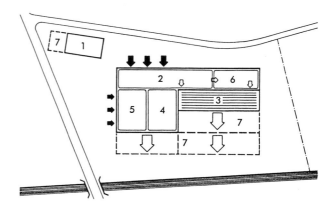

1 office; 2 goods inward; 3 racked bulk pallet store; 4 order picking area; 5 order and dispatch assembly area; 6 repackaging and processing area; 7 expansion

3 Option 2: narrow aisle high-bay storage; trade-off is cost of site works against increased operational flexibility and lower energy loss

Structural planning grids

To co-ordinate the building's structure, services and circulation in the formulation of the siting and expansion strategy, and to integrate these elements during building design, impose discipline on their disposition by employing a planning grid (see **4**).

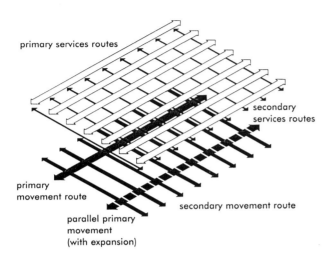

primary services routes
secondary services routes
primary movement route
secondary movement route
parallel primary movement (with expansion)

4 To coordinate structure services and movement in development strategy work to master grid; note three-dimensional implications

BASIC BUILDING TYPE SELECTION

Factories and warehouses are building types which are economically and operationally interchangeable where the structure will not conflict with requirements of mechanical handling equipment, and can accept the loading of production and environmental services.

Many companies have mixed manufacturing and storage uses on site, and rapid interchangeability may be required: flexibility must be built into the structure and services.

	structural type	1	2	3	4	5	6
factory type	light duty	● C S T	● S	● C S T	● A S	● A S	●(a) A S
	medium duty	● C S	● S	○ (b) C S	● S	● S	
	heavy duty		● S	○ (b) c S	● S	● S	●(c) A S
	high technology		● S		● C S		● A S
warehouse type	small scale	● C S T		● C S T			
	general purpose	● C S	● S	● C S	● C S		
	intermediate high bay	● C S	● S	● C S	● C S		●(c) A S

● appropriate structure; ○ appropriate structure in noted case only; **A** aluminium; **C** concrete; **S** steel; **T** timber; **a** multi-divisible spaces; **b** with overhead gantry cranes only; **c** wide spans on irregular site

5 Factories: structural options

		factors affecting fabric design											required room sizes (m)			floor loading:			floor to ceiling height (m)			corridor width (m)			service requirements			water services needed:			waste disposal:					
		process produces noise or vibration	process affected by noise from others	normal security	high security	N light	natural	artificial	self-contained	open plan	partly enclosed	5.0×3.75–5.0×7.5	10.0×3.75–10.0×12.5	15.0×7.5–10.0×12.5	up to and including 3 kN/m²	up to and including 5 kN/m²	over 5kN/m²	2.7 (min)	3.3 (min)	4.2 (min)	2.0 (min)	2.5 (min)	3.0 (min)	16–19	19–22	cold	hot	sink(s) cannot be shared	domestic drain	industrial drain	solid material	paper packaging	electricity: three phase needed	gas normally used
A	Pottery			●		●					●	●	●		●			●			●			●		●					●		●	
	glass blowing			●						●		●	●		●			●			●			●		●						●		●
	timber furniture	●		●				●			●	●	●		●			●			●			●		●					●			
	film production		●		●		●		●				●		●		●	●			●			●							●	●	●	
B	furs, skins			●		●					●				●			●		●					●			●			●			
	film processing	●	●	●				●	●			●			●			●		●				●		●		●		●	●	●	●	
	electronic recording	●		●				●	●				●		●			●		●				●						●			
	engraving	●		●	●		●	●		●			●		●			●		●			●		●		●			●	●		●	
C	toys, musical instruments	●	●	●				●			●		●		●			●		●				●						●		●		
	metalwork, plating, casting	●			●			●	●			●				●		●		●				●		●	●	●		●	●	●		
	clothing	●		●			●		●			●	●		●			●		●		●		●						●		●		
	shoes	●		●			●		●			●	●		●			●		●		●		●						●		●		
D	light engineering	●		●				●		●		●				●		●		●				●						●		●	●	
	valves, tools	●		●				●		●		●	●			●		●		●				●						●			●	●
	desk accessories, plastics	●		●				●	●	●			●		●			●		●		●			●					●	●	●	●	
	food processing	●		●				●	●		●			●				●		●		●		●	●				●	●		●	●	●
E	printing	●		●	●		●	●			●	●	●				●			●	●			●						●			●	
	manufacturing stationery	●		●	●		●							●			●			●	●			●					●	●		●		
	brewing	●		●				●	●			●				●		●		●		●		●	●		●	●		●			
	spinning	●		●		●						●				●		●		●			●	●				●					
F	electronic repairs		●	●	●		●		●				●			●				●				●			●					●	●	
	motor car repairs	●		●				●			●		●	●			●			●				●					●	●	●		●	
	bicycle repairs	●		●				●			●		●				●			●			●	●			●			●		●		●
	theatrical props	●		●				●				●		●			●			●			●	●			●			●		●		●

6 Design and services requirements for industrial and workshop premises

SITE DEVELOPMENT

Building plot ratio and site coverage

A plot ratio of 1:1 should be regarded as the maximum on all sites, inclusive of industrial and ancillary office building. Site coverage should not exceed 75% of site at ground level; coverage of approximately 50–60% should be achieved. The site area for plot ratio calculation purposes excludes any part of adjoining streets (except where these are to be closed).

Car and truck parking

Typical car parking requirements for industrial accommodation are as follows (but check for local standards):

	m²	spaces
less than	92.90	4
"	232.26	5
"	371.61	6
"	510.96	7
"	656.32	8
"	789.67	9
"	929.92	10
"	1021.92	11
"	1114.83	12

Lorry parking requirements will depend on the needs of particular users and local regulations.

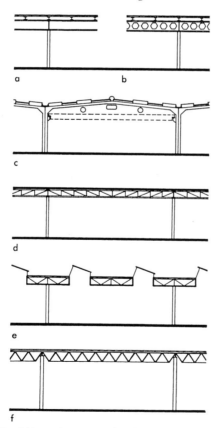

(a) single axis solid beam, long-span purlins; (b) single axis castellated beam; (c) portal frame for use where service loading is minimal or with gantry craneage (typical pitch 6°, rooflights built into pitch or ridge); (d) flat or cambered truss, one or two axes; (e) monitor roof, evenly distributed light, single axis; (f) space frame, for very wide spans, or where columns cannot be at equal spacing, or where high degree of servicing freedom is required

7 Structural types

SELECTION STRATEGY

Single or multi-storey development

Modern production and storage techniques make full use of the building cube, with inherent multi-level characteristics.

Multi-storey development (or conversion) can be efficient for light- and high-technology industry, particularly where land is costly, such as in urban areas. Consider personnel circulation and escape, national and local regulations, fire control, goods circulation and process, services routeing, lorry and private vehicle access and parking, and, particularly in dense developments, consider cost and environmental impact.

Key factors in building type selection

For factories (see also p. 202):

- Operational flexibility for rapid response to changing production demands: clear height, column spacing, roof and floor loading, roof construction to allow for services routeing for type of manufacturing process involved.
- Energy and environmental control: natural or artificial light, environmental needs of/from process, good working conditions for labour.
- Durability and fire control: selection of materials for structure and envelope related to fire risk and any corrosive effects from process.
- Resale potential.
- Promotional value for user company.
  For warehouses (see also p. 207):
- Structure to suit storage demands: structural spans to suit pallet-and-rack system, and height and floor strength to allow more than one arrangement of energy and environmental control.
- Envelope to keep stored products in good condition: insulation and cooling in some cases, ventilation in others.
- Good working conditions for labour (e.g. avoiding loading docks facing into prevailing wind).
- Fire control: compartmentation to minimise fire spread to be assessed against hindrance to storage and handling and cost of sprinklers.

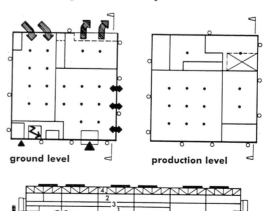

ground level   **production level**

1 ground level: goods in, dispatch, parking; 2 production level; 3 intermediate process plant level; 4 principal environmental plant level

8 Multi-storey factory: suitable for process-based industries (e.g. food, and pharmaceuticals)

Areas for some industrial occupancies

For feasibility studies before a detailed brief from the user, the following can be used as approximate building areas.

Service industries

Smallest, 15 m²/person; medium size, up to 30 m²: electrical repairs; builders; engineering contractors (e.g. machine tool movers); appliance repairs; instrument repairs; reprographic services; printers; machine tool repairs.

Manufacturing industries

Average 28 m²/person (range 23–33 m²); 33 m²/person under 664.5 m²: anodising; sheet metal work; polishing; furniture manufacture; shop-fitting manufacture; clothing; textiles (made-up).

Distributive trades

Average 80 m²/person: builders merchants; timber supply; books and magazines; machine spares; electrical goods and spares; antiques/furniture; upholstery/textiles.

Average area/worker

The following areas (m²) are typical

clothing	11
research and development	13
electrical components and assembly	17.5
surgical instruments/appliances, scientific instruments	19.25
miscellaneous manufacture (e.g. plastics products, musical instruments)	23.5
leather work	24.0
metal goods, cutlery, jewellery, forging, small tools	24.25
made-up textiles (e.g. bags)	28.75
packaging, stationery, printing	32.5
pottery and glass blowing	36.75
motor repairs, reprographic services	45.5
joinery, furnishing upholstery, shop fitting, timber goods	46.75

Typical area distribution

Including circulation space:

Manufacturing
production 60–70% (decreases as size increases)
storage 20% and less (increases as size increases)
office 10–15% (increases as size decreases)
amenities 5–9% (increases as size increases)

Distribution
storage 80% and above
office 10–20%
(greater need in some types of distribution)
amenities 0–5%

Plan selection

The selection of plan shape is a function of:
- demands of production or storage system
- expansion potential of process in relation to site (see **2,3**)
- climate
- topography and geology of site
- location of utilities.

The majority of industrial uses can be efficiently installed in rectangular plan with proportions from 1:1 to 1:4, typically 1:2/2:3. Modern mass-production methods capitalise on mechanical handling techniques. Multi-storey factories can be economic for process-based industries (e.g. food, pharmaceuticals, tobacco) where gravity can be used in the process and energy can be conserved by compact planning: see **11**. On the other hand, some production processes require a long, narrow building:

- intensive line production methods (e.g. metal rolling, paper manufacture)
- factories using overhead gantry cranes (e.g. heavy engineering)
- multi-storey development, flatted workshops for natural light and ventilation.

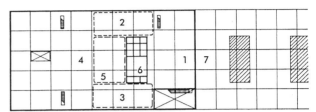

1 office area; 2 lab area; 3 amenity area; 4 production area; 5 testing and inspection; 6 wet service core; 7 expansion

9 In light- and high-technology industry production, research and admin areas are becoming less distinct; departments will need to expand or contract freely

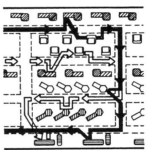 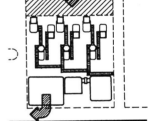

traditional batch production lines of similar machines, may need to be reorganised as opposite

integrated cell exploiting modern mechanical handling techniques

10 Factory structures must have sufficiently wide spans (in both directions) to allow optimisation of the production layout

 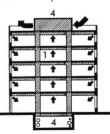

1 vertical service risers; 2 goods elevator; 3 access and escape stairs (check local regulations for maximum distances); 4 plant area

11 Multi-storey development or conversion can provide efficient accommodation for light- and high-technology industry, particularly where differences between production, laboratory and admin are hard to define; example shows potentially divisible space

There is increasing demand for buildings which will not restrict the location of production, storage and administration to clearly defined areas, but which permit rapid re-allocation within the building envelope.

Just-in-time delivery processes, direct from component supplier to production line, are dramatically reducing the amount of storage capacity required within buildings.

An industrial building designed to be closely matched to the initial process or layout can prove as inflexible and costly to operate in the long term as those designed to minimise capital cost (to exclusion of consideration of operating costs and operational flexibility).

FACTORIES

Factories should be designed to serve a variety of uses within their life and production sector. A frequent problem is inefficiency of factory buildings through obsolescence, whether structural (including short spans and capacity of roof structure), insufficient services support and inadequate headroom. The function of 'how' the product is manufactured or stored may well be more important than what the product 'is'.

Buildings should not be considered merely as weather-proof envelopes around the production process. Form and disposition of their structure fundamentally influence essential freedom to optimise production layout, and to route services equally freely to serve that or any future production layouts, without demanding long periods of down-time for alteration. Selection of the structure, particularly the bay size, is the key factor in providing efficient and flexible operation. There is a range of structural types that have proved efficient and adaptable, and technological innovation may add to these types (e.g. stressed-skin construction, requiring only minimal frame support for the envelope).

The roof structure should be assessed for:

- service-carrying ability in each direction and easy access for relocation
- ability to accept point loads and flexible location for materials handling equipment (e.g. overhead hoists, conveyors)
- natural lighting (consider glare and insulation/ heat loss)
- durability and maintenance (performance in fire and the need for cleaning/repainting, particularly in clean areas).

FACTORY BUILDING TYPES

Light duty

This implies small scale (see also 'Workshops', p. 212) industrial building where operational demands of production or storage process place few demands on the structural frame or floor. They are interchangeable between light production and distribution duties, and typically up to 2000 m². Examples include light metal work, packaging, clothing, consumer durable repairs, small printers, distribution of electrical goods, builders' materials, sub-depots for local retail distribution.

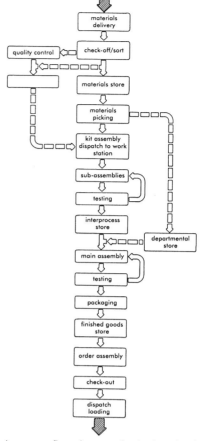

12 Typical process flow diagram for high-technology industry (e.g. electronics material)

13 Light-duty industrial building mainly for storage purposes: portal framed structure, typically 4.5 m to eaves, spans 12 m (9 m minimum), roof loading 0.35 kN/m² (no hoisting), floor loading 16 kN/m²

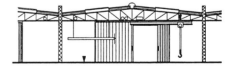

14 Mainly light production: trussed frame, eaves height and spans as **13**; roof structural loading for services 0.5 kN/m² (up to 2 t hoist loads distributed per structural bay)

Medium duty

Principally, these are for batch production or storage duties where process and supporting services imply some demands on the design of building structure, shape and floor, allowing potential flexibility of production and storage layout. Storage and production building types are not interchangeable unless the roof structure is designed with production services support capacity.

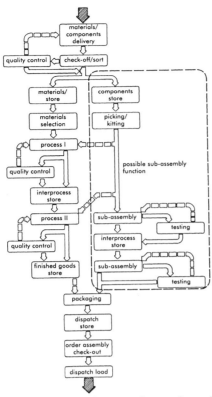

15 Typical process flow diagram for traditional batch production organisation (e.g. engineering components)

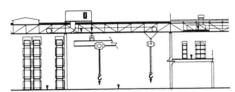

16 Medium-duty industrial building: 6.5 m preferred eaves height (to allow mezzanine), 5.5 m minimum; spans typically 12 × 18 m; roof structural loading to accept point loads of 2t monorail hoist/bay or up to 5t suspended crane loads distributed over bay; floor loading 25 kN/m² for stacked storage

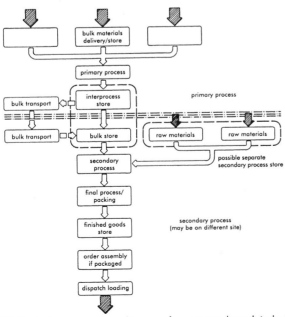

17 Typical process flow diagram for process-based industry (e.g. petrochemical, rubber)

Heavy duty

Designed to accept large-scale batch or mass-production systems, which have intensive demands for overhead production and environmental service and materials handling, and dense floor layouts with some heavy production machinery and inter-process storage areas. A high building may be needed to exploit multi-level ability of materials-handling equipment. In the heavy engineering sector, some special types exploit heavy-lift overhead gantry cranes.

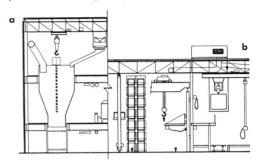

18 Heavy-duty industrial building: 7 m minimum general purpose eaves height, 9 m for racked storage and overhead handling systems
(a) 12 m for bulk processing plant
(b) spans typically 12×18 m but can be less for heavy roof loadings (9×12 m) or greater for lighter loads (20 m); roof structural loadings of 5t point loads and 10t beam loads distributed over bay (heavier loads need gantry cranes and additional structure); floor loading 15–30 kN/m² with some special bases for heavy machine tools

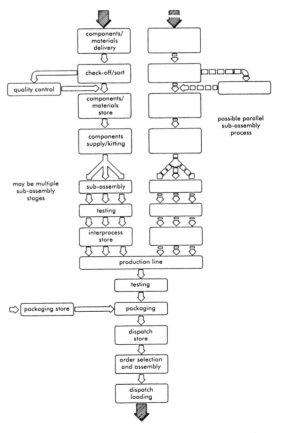

19 Typical process flow diagram for traditional mass-production line: modern developments tend to split assembly function off line into teams

Hi-tech

These factory types demand a high-quality process and/or personnel environment and have similar design demands for small- or large-scale enterprises. Provision is required for intensive services in the roof zone and under-floor. There is a high content of bulk handling (e.g. powders, liquids, gases). Inter-changeability is required between production, laboratory and administration areas, to allow for rapid change, technological innovation and volatile markets.

site plan

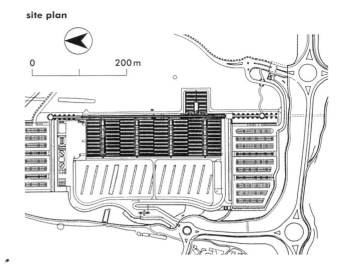

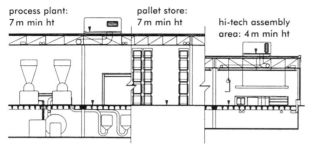

process plant: 7m min ht   pallet store: 7m min ht   hi-tech assembly area: 4m min ht

20 High-technology industrial building: may require basement for bulk process access and services routeing; roof structure up to 1.2 kN/m² distributed load (for services); hoist loads up to 5t distributed load per bay for plant removal; floor loadings 15–20 kN/m² for large plant, 10–15 kN/m² for high labour use assembly

ground floor

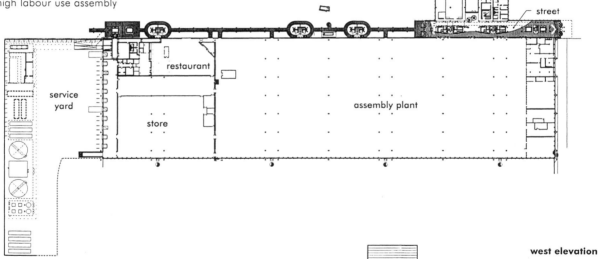

offices

street

service yard

restaurant

store

assembly plant

21 Manufacturing and administrative offices for Motorola, Swindon: design had to be flexible and capable of expansion; the core elements are all in the 300 m long 'street', containing service ducts at high level; manufacturing area is 24 500 m² in four bays formed of A-frame structures (Arch: Sheppard Robson)

west elevation

south elevation

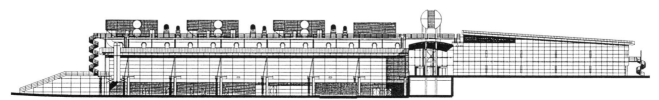

ground floor

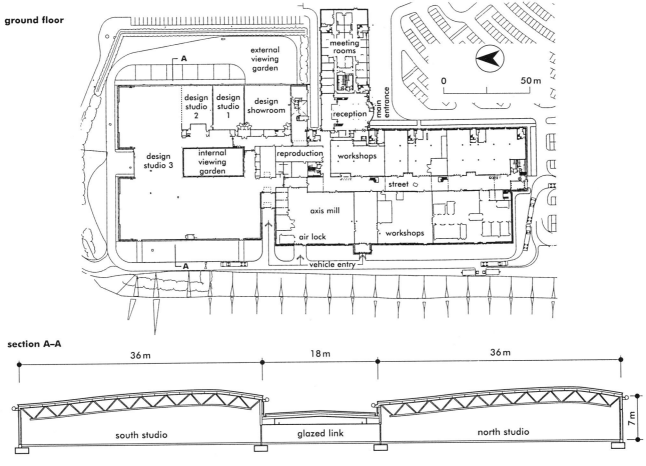

section A–A

22 Rover Group Design and Engineering Centre, Gaydon, Warwickshire: complex comprises: design studios, workshops (where design sketches are converted into full-scale mock-ups), showroom, viewing garden, office accommodation (for 400–600 engineers); deliberate aspect was an open engineering environment to stimulate as much creative interaction as possible; studios, workshops and offices are arranged around an internal 'street', which includes informal areas and a café; structure is based on a 9 m steel grid
(Arch: Weedon Partnership)

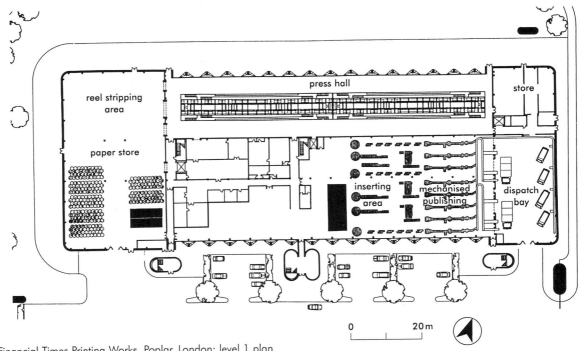

23 Financial Times Printing Works, Poplar, London: level 1 plan
(Arch: Nicholas Grimshaw & Partners Ltd)

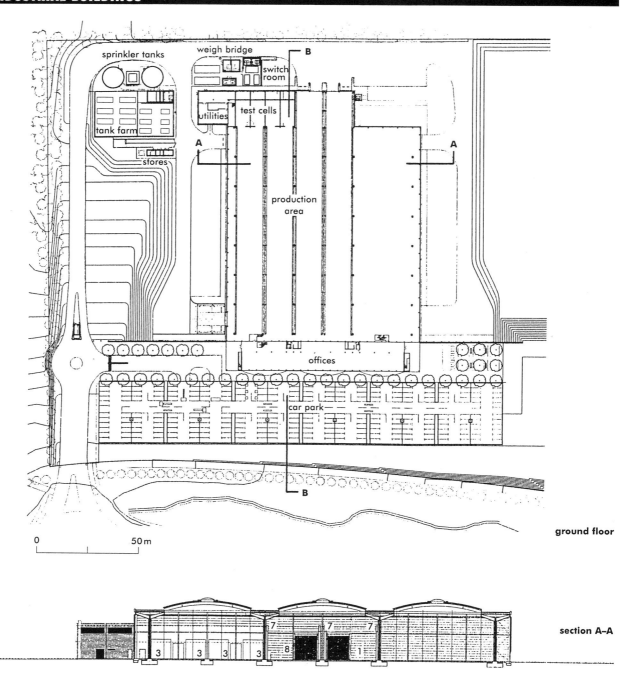

sprinkler tanks

weigh bridge

switch room

utilities

test cells

tank farm

stores

A

A

production area

offices

car park

B

B

0   50 m

ground floor

section A–A

7   7   7

3   3   3   3   8   1

section B–B

5

2   4   7

2   4   1   7

4   3   6

24 New Cummins Production (CPG) Unit, Manston, Kent: heavy-duty industry building producing power generators; additional bays can be added as production expands (Arch: Bennetts Associates)

1 production area	5 roof-mounted plant
2 offices	6 service duct
3 test cells	7 60t crane rail
4 WCs	8 dispatch area

WAREHOUSES

The traditional warehouse was a relatively straightforward storage facility, designed to contain as many goods as possible in a structure offering protection from the weather and a certain degree of security. The structure was required to have as large a span as possible to allow flexibility of storage. All goods were either loose or in small units (e.g. sacks or barrels) to allow ease of transfer between ship, canal narrow boat, railway wagon or cart etc., and had to be small enough to be man-handled. In effect, the goods fitted the enclosure, rather than the other way round.

As unit sizes became larger, particularly after World War II, and containerisation became the norm, purpose-designed warehouses became essential. The typical 19th-century general-purpose warehouse has become redundant, as containers can be mechanically transferred directly from, for example, ship to road vehicle. Modern warehouse buildings should be regarded less as storage areas, and more as automated, computerised transit points which are an integral part of the distribution chain.

LAYOUT

Layout depends on scale and type of storage operation. Different methods of storing unit loads give varying levels of efficiency in filling the building volume and accessibility for loading. Ideally equipment should be in standard modules, but sufficiently flexible to allow future change. Layout will be defined by:

- capacity: storage and rate of reception and dispatch
- capacity and flow: defined in terms of units handled
- unit load: e.g. pallets (commonest form in UK), hanging garment rails, ISO containers etc.; will influence equipment and use of space.

Key design criteria should include:

- *Goods handled* – dimensions, sizes; packaging and unit loads; stock levels and throughput; growth trends.
- *Order characteristics* – e.g. distribution and frequency of stock.
- *Goods arrival and dispatch patterns* – e.g. size and frequency of vehicles.
- *Warehouse operations* – e.g. product flows, quality assurance and level of automation (see p. 211).

Warehousing operation usually involves bulk storage and order selection functions. These tend to have dissimilar storage and materials handling demands except with small-scale installations: typically high, dense storage for bulk stock to exploit handling techniques with lower 'active stock' areas for order picking. A typical proportion divides warehouses: one-third high-bay area, two-thirds lower area for order picking and assembly and loading bay zones (see **25**). Because of density of stock the bulk storage area may not need to expand so rapidly as processing zones.

25 Typical proportions of high- and low-bay area for distribution warehouse

Quantity of goods This is important for space and storage design:

- large quantities and few lines: use live storage or drive-in packing
- small quantities and many lines: use conventional pallets.

For FIFO (first-in, first-out), block stacking or drive-in racking is not suitable.

Clad rack versus traditional Structural clad-rack warehouse buildings are widely used in Europe, but less so in the UK. They offer lower construction costs, and operational and financial benefits can be significant, but note that large undivided areas can be a problem under fire regulations. A clad-rack 'hybrid' has the benefits of the latticed-framed and structural clad-rack building; the main supporting structure uses conventional heavy-duty adjustable pallet racking, and can reach 20–30 m high.

Arrival and dispatch bays These should allow all-weather operations (using air-locks, with body seal and overhead canopy), preferably on the lee side of the building. Adequate vehicle manoeuvring areas are essential (see p. 223).

Unit loads The benefits include:

- standardisation of equipment
- minimum movement
- improved security
- less loading/unloading time.

Wooden pallets These can be single-sided, reversible, two-way entry, etc. The commonest size in the UK and USA is 1200 × 1000 mm; in most of Europe (excluding the UK and Holland), 1200 × 800 mm. Incompatible sizes must be borne in mind if international operations are envisaged.

Picking requirement The frequency with which goods are handled will determine type of equipment (e.g. fast-moving product lines must have easy access).

Storage and access The layout should facilitate:

- access to stock for input/output movements and checking
- balanced traffic flow pattern
- minimum travel distance for stock movements
- systematic identification of stock locations
- grouping of products with similar storage characteristics (e.g. cold store, ambient temperature, open air).

Staff and amenity areas Provide for general managerial, clerical and site staff, and also perhaps for drivers and maintenance engineers. Amenity and support areas will include: locker rooms, toilets, canteen, rest area, reception, training rooms, medical room, cleaners' stores, workshop.

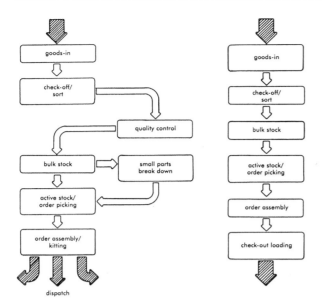

26 Typical storage flow diagram: repository, component store for adjoining production process

27 Typical storage flow diagram: repository, e.g. cold store, steel stockholding

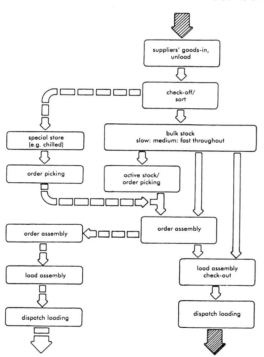

28 Typical storage flow diagram for distribution warehouse, e.g. retail food distribution

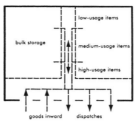

inverted 'T' warehouse flow

goods inward and dispatch are on the same side of the building

advantages include
- [ ] high-, medium- and low-usage areas minimise movement (i.e. low-usage has longer travel paths and is in least accessible areas)
- [ ] better utilisation of loading docks and associated mechanical handling equipment
- [ ] reduced area compared with separate loading and unloading areas
- [ ] the same docks may be used for the different functions at different times of day
- [ ] integration of goods inward and dispatch allows unified management of merchandise flows
- [ ] unified bay operations allows better security control
- [ ] building can be extended on three sides
- [ ] easier to place bay on lee side away from prevailing winds
- [ ] better utilisation of yard areas for vehicles

disadvantages include
- [ ] central access aisle may become congested in high-throughput situations
- [ ] expansion will require modification of flow
- [ ] travel paths for bulk areas can become excessive
- [ ] common docks need unified management

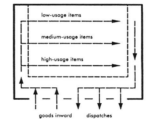

cross-flow warehouse layout

similar to inverted 'T', but with rearrangement of internal storage and picking areas

advantages include
- [ ] benefit to stock management due to integration of bulk and picking goods

but note
- [ ] segregation into high-, medium- and low-usage items may not always be possible (e.g. if product catalogue is organised by type of customer order)

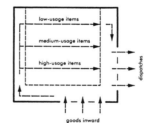

corner warehouse

similar to inverted 'T', but inward and outward flows are on different but adjacent sides of the building;

advantages include
- [ ] goods in and out are segregated to allow for situations where there could be conflict if they are too close
- [ ] expansion can be on the two sides without doors

disadvantages include
- [ ] less appropriate where expansion is probable (major changes to internal layout are likely)
- [ ] prevailing winds etc. need careful consideration
- [ ] higher security and surveillance costs

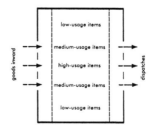

through-flow warehouse

note: inward and outward flows are on opposite sides;

advantages include
- [ ] use where there is a natural flow with other facilities
- [ ] use where goods in and out have different requirements (e.g. platform heights)

disadvantages include:
- [ ] all materials have to travel the full length of the building
- [ ] separate goods in and dispatch requires two yards; internal bay area is doubled
- [ ] expansion can be difficult
- [ ] prevailing winds etc. need careful consideration

29 Diagrammatic warehouse layouts (from *Principles of Warehouse Design*; diagrams courtesy of the Institute of Logistics and Transport)

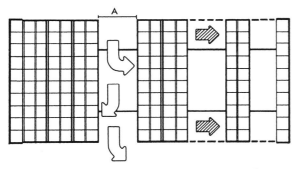

30 Where storage area is limited and throughput speed is not top priority, intense use of volume can be made with mobile racking; with double-sided racking mounted on rail-borne carriers, racks nest face-to-face, only one aisle opening at a time; width A is related to type of fork-lift used (see p. 210)

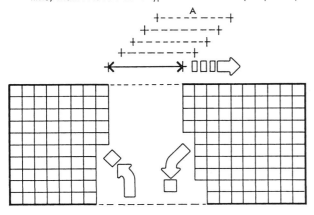

31 Block stacking, three or four pallets high; aisle moves through stack to provide first-in, first-out rotation; aisle width A is related to type of fork-lift used (see p. 210)

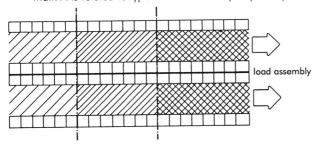

32 For bulk pallet storage in long aisles, stock should be arranged in notional areas so that fastest throughput stock is closest to assembly area; note rack orientation at 90° to assembly zone

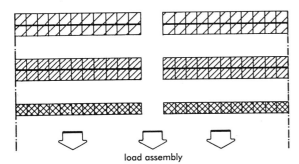

33 For order picking diverse stock, racking arranged parallel with load assembly zone, with rack area devoted to stock with various throughput speeds (fastest nearest to assembly zone); reduces slow-moving picking machinery blocking movement of others

WAREHOUSE BUILDING TYPES/HANDLING

Small scale   See earlier description of the light-duty factory and **5**.

General purpose   These are designed for fork-lift, reach truck and narrow aisle stacker operation. The building acts as a weather-proof envelope to the storage operation. It is important that the spans, height and floor strength allow for flexible installation of storage methods (see **45–50**). See also earlier description of medium-duty factory types and **52**.

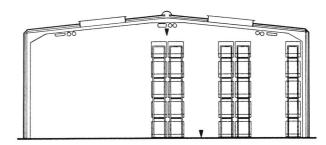

34 General purpose warehouse, typically for 7.5 m stack height: 8.0 m height to eaves; spans 12–18 m; floor loading 25 kN/m² minimum

Intermediate high-bay   An independent building structure for intermediate height narrow-aisle storage systems. Building height can be up to 14 m (12 m storage height), which allows variations in storage layout and the possibility of other later uses. See also earlier description of heavy-duty factory types.

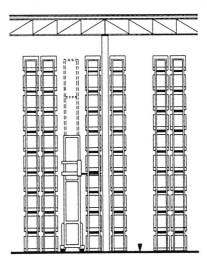

35 Intermediate high-bay warehouse, typically 14 m to eaves; spans 11.1–20.5 m, depending on aisle width and pallet size; floor loadings 50 kN/m² distributed

High-bay   With integral rack structure, for storage heights up to 30 m, these exploit automated handling techniques (see **36**). They can be economic where land costs and labour costs are high, but expansion potential is limited. Storage racking forms the building structure, with roof and wall cladding attached to it. Floor loadings can exceed 60 kN/m² distributed load, so very strong floor and foundations are required; poor ground conditions can preclude the concept.

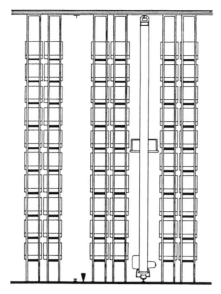

36 High-bay warehouse, building structure integral with pallet racking; height 30 m; floor loadings can be more than 60 kN/m² distributed

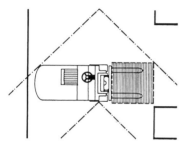

37 Counter-balance fork-lift, capacity 3000 kg: stacking aisle 90° with 1220 mm square pallet, length 3670 mm; intersecting aisle (dotted) 2.0 m; without pallet, length 3150 mm, width 1100 mm

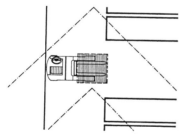

38 Reach fork-lift, capacity 1500 kg, pallet carried within wheelbase: stacking aisle 90° with 1220 mm square pallet, length 2400 mm; intersecting aisle (dotted) 1.9 m; without pallet, length 1600 mm, width 990 mm

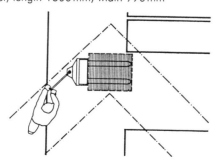

39 Powered person-controlled pallet fork-lift; stacking aisle 90° with 1220 square pallet, length 1750 mm; intersecting aisle (dotted) 1.5 m; without pallet, length 1820 mm, width 787 mm

Fork-lift dimensions

In designing for the best use of storage space, note the interaction between aisle spaces and fork-lift dimensions: the decision on stacking may decide the size and make of fork-lift, or choice of fork-lift may determine the stacking. For details of some fork-lift types and pallet sizes (see **37–38**).

Fork-lift maintenance and battery-charging areas This area must be provided apart from rest of warehouse because of health and safety requirements. The floor should be able to withstand heavy impact and battery acids (e.g. heavy-duty epoxy resin). Battery chargers should be mounted on external walls with extractor fans. An equipment store may also be needed.

type of fork-lift	dimensions (mm)	weight (kg)
counter-balanced fork-lift: load capacity 2500 kg at 610 load centre		
length without pallet	3246	
width without pallet	1118	
height mast lowered	2286	
weight without load		4500
wheel loads laden[1]: front (drive)		6000
rear (steer)		750
90° stacking aisle (1200 pallet)	3480	
turn-out aisle (1200 pallet) (dotted) see **37**	2000	

[1] for distributed rolling loads divide by wheel contact area, available from trade literature

40 Counter-balanced fork-lift dimensions and weights

type of fork-lift	dimensions (mm)	weight (kg)
extending mast reach fork-lift: load capacity 2040 kg at 610 load centre		
length without pallet	1930	
width without pallet	990	
height mast lowered	2667	
weight without load		2722
wheel loads laden[1]: front (mast extended)		4282
rear (mast extended)		481
90° stacking aisle (1200 pallet)	2362	
turn-out aisle (1200 pallet) (dotted) see **38**	1905	

[1] for distributed rolling loads divide by wheel contact area, available from trade literature

41 Extending mast reach fork-lift dimensions and weights

type of fork-lift	dimensions (mm)	weight (kg)
powered person-controlled pallet fork-lift: load capacity 1815 kg		
length without pallet	1854	
width without pallet	762	
height mast lowered	not applicable	
weight without load		372
wheel loads	not applicable	
90° stacking aisle (1200 pallet)	1752	
turn-out aisle (1200 pallet) (dotted) see **39**	1498	

42 Powered person-controlled pallet fork-lift dimensions and weights

43 Fork-lift in block stack: 3.5 m aisle; 3.6 m stack height; 4.5 m building height (dotted)

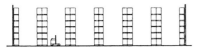

44 Fork-lift in pallet racking: 3.5 m aisle; 7.5 m stack height

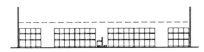

45 Reach fork-lift in block stack: 2.6 m aisle; 3.6 m stack height; 4.5 m building height (dotted)

46 Reach fork-lift in pallet racking: 2.6 m aisle; 7.5 m stack height

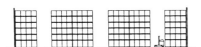

47 Reach fork-lift in drive-in racking, drives into stack between frames: 7.5 m stack height

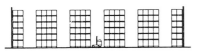

48 Reach fork-lift in double-deep racking, has extending fork attachment: 2.6 m aisle

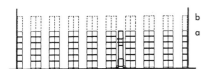

49 Narrow aisle stacker, moves parallel with rack: stack height (a) 7.5 m, (b) 10.5 m (dotted)

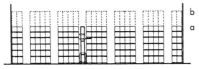

50 Narrow aisle stacker in double-deep racking: 1.6 m aisle; stack height (a) 7.5 m, (b) 10.5 m (dotted)

Storage efficiency with various handling methods

Taking typical stacking areas of 33×33 m, volume efficiency assessment includes a repositioning aisle at the end of rack runs. See examples shown in **43–51** (pallet size: 1200×1000×200 mm tall). Figures in column two of **52** relate to illustration numbers. Note that high-bay narrow aisle designs have stringent requirements governing level floors, rack alignment, and guidance systems.

Automatic handling techniques

'Automated handling' is the direct control of handling equipment producing movement and storage of loads without the need for operators or drivers – i.e. equipment is controlled by computer systems with little or no human input. Automation can be from information level only, to complete automation of all operations and flows. It is generally viable when:

- repetitive tasks are performed regularly
- lift-height is above 10–12 m
- very high storage densities are required (e.g. high-bay).

Automated equipment categories

Warehousing involves two main categories:
(1) processing at a fixed location (equipment includes vehicle off-loading, weighing, palletising, etc.)
(2) movement of goods between fixed processes.

The equipment used can be grouped within the same two categories:

- processing equipment (e.g. vehicle off-loading)
- transport equipment, which includes
  - fixed equipment (e.g. conveyor systems)
  - mobile equipment (usually AGVs (automated guided vehicles) guided by cables buried in floor – so there are no physical barriers – which replace lift trucks, or storage and retrieval machines – usually stacker cranes, storing up to 30 m high).

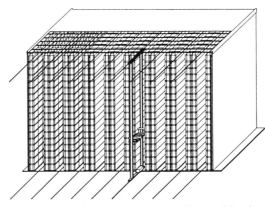

51 Automated fixed-path stacker crane: 1.4 m aisle; 24 m stack height; integral rack structure

equipment	type of storage	stack height	pallets stored	volume efficiency (%)	access (%)	storage increase over fork-lift equivalent (%)
fork-lift: building height 8 m to underside of structure	43 block stack[1]	3	1452	24	poor	
	44 beam pallet racking	5	1200	20	100	
reach fork-lift building height 8 m to underside of structure	45 block stack[2]	3	1584	28	poor	9
	46 beam pallet racking	5	1400	35	100	17
	47 drive-in racking	5	2400	58	1st in last out	
	48 double deep racking	5	2400	49	50	
narrow aisle-stacker	49a beam pallet racking[3]	5	1800	46	100	50
	49b beam pallet racking[4]	7	2520	46	46	110
	50a double deep racking[3]	5	2400	59	50	
	50b double deep racking[4]	7	3360	60	50	
automated high bay stacker crane, rail guided: building height 24 m to underside of roof structure (can be 30 m+)	51 beam pallet racking	15	5400	32[5]	100	

[1] volume efficiency increases if lower building used (4.5 m min) [2] volume efficiency increases if lower building used [3] building height to underside of roof structure 8 m [4] building height to underside of roof structure 11 m [5] as section of longer aisle: typically 100 m+

52 Storage efficiency with various handling methods

WORKSHOPS

There is great variety in the shape and size of workshops; here, they are classified by location, circulation requirements, tenancy types, and the technology they can accommodate (see below). Most of the detailed standards and examples given in the following pages are those required for a typical inner-city flatted factory (rental unit).

Location

For most common locations, see **53–57**.

domestic

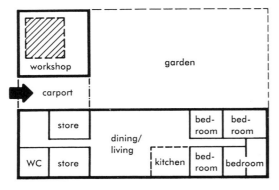

53 One or two people carrying on hobby or part-time occupation in home extension

educational institution

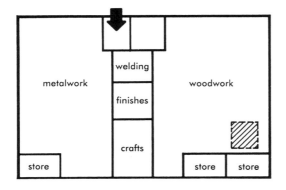

54 Repetitive provision for class or group of 20–40 people

small industrial estates

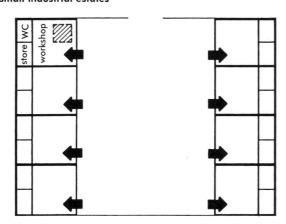

55 Group of non-specific units for range of very small businesses

rental unit

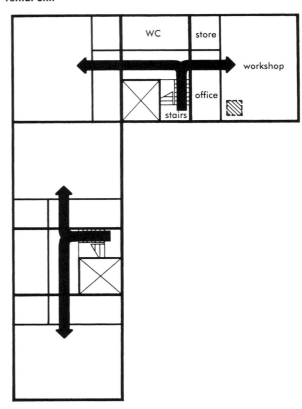

56 Standard units with shared access in a multi-storey building

ancillary to large factory

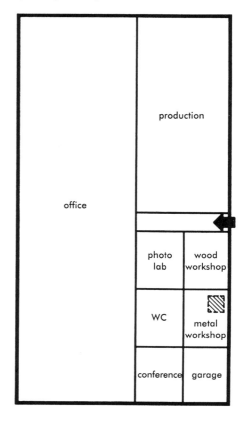

57 Specialist workshops for use by staff maintaining company's plant or building itself

spaces/floor area	inner-city	suburbs and rural
distribution	(m²)	(m²)
heavy goods vehicles	1/1000	1/500
light commercial vehicles	1/1000	1/500
cars	1/400	1/1000
light industry		
heavy goods vehicles	1/4000	1/2000
light commercial vehicles	1/1000	1/500
cars	1/200	1/50
office space		
light commercial vehicles	1/1000	1/500
cars	1/150	1/30

58 Parking guidelines

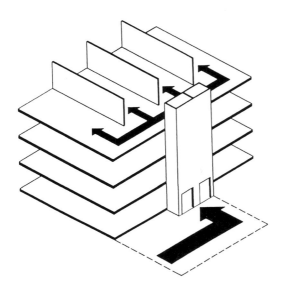

59 Goods lift serving large group of tenancies: peak load may cause problems and central coordination may be required

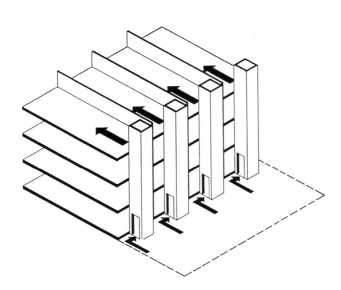

60 Several lifts, each serving several tenants: some cooperation needed, but less than **59**

Workshop circulation

- *Parking outside building*: standards depend on location as well as on type of use (**58**).
- *Lifts inside building*: related to external parking and to tenancies (**59,60**).
- *Circulation within workshop*: derived from the technology used as well as type of tenancy (**61–64**).

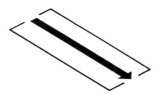

61 Straight line: goods in and out at opposite sides of plant; requires building with good access at both sides; common in medium-size firms

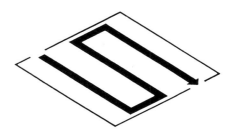

62 Overlapping: similar to **61** but for much larger type of firm

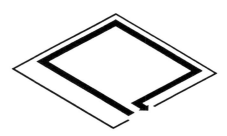

63 U-shape: goods in and out at same side of plant; possible in buildings with only limited access; common with very small firms

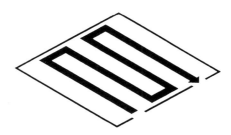

64 Convoluted: goods in and out on same side of plant; sometimes necessary for large firms when accommodated in buildings with restricted access

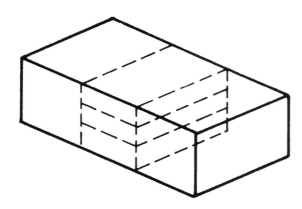

65 Indirect access

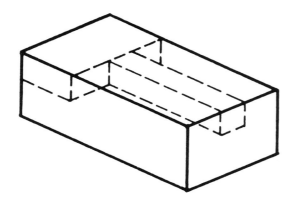

66 Open plan

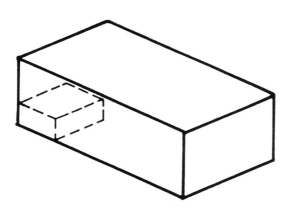

67 Shared space

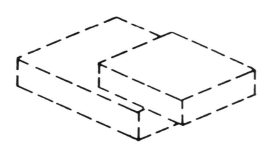

68 Shared space

WORKSHOP TENANCIES: BUILDING TYPE

Indirect access (65)

- *Type of building*: shallow or medium depth with cross-walls to create vertical compartments.
- *Type of management*: individual firm's name displayed and each has a unit with its own services. Management could occupy one unit for its own use.
- *Type of user*: small well-established firms requiring their own identity.
- Subdivision: units have street (or yard) frontage, they may receive visitors directly and have their own stairs, or lift.
- *Compartmentation*: each building contains several tenancies divided by fire resisting walls.
- *Escape routes*: each tenant has a fire-resisting stairway; if there is an area of high fire risk, an alternative means of escape is required.

Open plan (66)

- *Type of building*: shallow or medium depth with central corridor on each level.
- *Type of management*: common receptionist; lifts/stairs/corridors from intermediate space to be maintained.
- *Type of user*: small firms needing some security but less concerned with presenting an individual identity.
- *Subdivision*: units are reached through internal stairs or corridors common to several users.
- *Compartmentation*: each tenant is separated from adjacent tenants by fire-resisting floor.
- *Escape routes*: each individual tenant has a door to shared fire resisting escape corridor which leads to fire resisting stairway; a second means of escape is normally also needed.

Shared space I (67)

- *Type of building*: deep plan.
- *Type of management*: tenants share services and participate in management of the accommodation.
- *Type of user*: small expanding firms with compatible uses; this allows for rapid changes in size and staffing.
- *Subdivision*: units as such do not exist but tenants take space within a large envelope having a single front door.
- *Compartmentation*: each open area is surrounded by fire-resisting walls and floors.
- *Escape routes*: each compartment has direct access or two or more fire-resisting stairways; it may be necessary to protect relevant doorways with fire shutters.

Shared space II (68)

- *Type of building*: any building type.
- *Type of management*: head lessee relinquishes no responsibility for space; may provide telephone, secretarial services on time-sharing basis.
- *Type of user*: newly established, very small firms (one to five persons) requiring low overheads and minimum commitments.
- *Subdivision*: space rented from another firm, usually on some kind of licence.
- *Compartmentation*: separate subdivision only required if sub-tenant represents high risk of fire or explosion.
- *Escape routes*: considered the same as for main tenant, unless there is a special fire risk.

type	passengers	heavy goods	light goods	machine room	pit	external fittings	access
electric lift	yes	yes	yes	yes	yes	yes	3 sides
hydraulic lift	yes	yes	yes	no	yes	yes	3 sides
manually operated lift	yes	no	yes	no	yes	yes	3 sides
platform hoist	no	yes	yes	no	no	yes	2 sides
electric service lift	no	no	yes	no	no	yes	3 sides
scissors lift	no	yes	yes	no	yes	no	4 sides
dock leveller	no	yes	yes	no	no	yes	2 sides
electric belt conveyor	no	yes	yes	no	yes	no	2 sides
gravity conveyors	no	yes	yes	no	no	yes	2 sides
electric winch	no	yes	yes	no	no	yes	4 sides
manual winch	no	no	yes	no	no	yes	4 sides
manual floor crane	no	no	yes	no	no	mobile	mobile

69 Suitable handling equipment for small premises

Workshops: equipment space

The requirements for some suitable handling equipment for small premises are given in **69**. Typical spaces needed per machine in a tightly planned layout are shown in **70,71**: note, this does not necessarily allow for general circulation, process storage or initial installation of machinery. The percentages of total area required for operations in various types of workshop are illustrated in **72**.

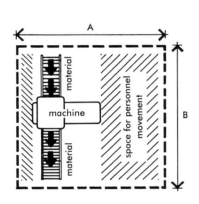

70 Equipment space: read with **71**

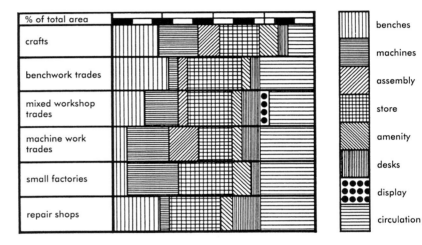

72 Space budgeting by technology types

equipment in common use	A × B (from 70) working space per item (m)
metalwork	
machining centre	6.0 × 4.0
jig boring and milling machine	3.0 × 3.0
turret drill	2.6 × 3.2
surface grinding machine	2.6 × 2.2
capstan lathe	3.0 × 4.0
bar and billet shears	2.5 × 3.0
press brake	3.0 × 6.0
engraver	2.2 × 3.0
die sinker	1.8 × 2.2
welding plant	2.8 × 2.5
tool grinder	1.1 × 1.2
shaper	1.7 × 2.1
power hack saw	4.0 × 1.2
punch press	1.5 × 1.3
slip roll	1.1 × 2.1
nibbler	2.3 × 1.2
shear clamp head	2.1 × 1.5
band saw	2.3 × 3.1
workbench	2.7 × 1.9
plastics	
extruder	2.8 × 2.8
vacuum former	2.8 × 2.8
blow moulder	3.0 × 4.5
acrylic saw	3.0 × 5.0
heating oven	0.6 × 1.1

woodwork	
band saw	3.0 × 5.0
circular saw	4.8 × 7.9
surface planer	2.6 × 5.0
knot hole drill	2.2 × 4.2
milling machine	4.0 × 5.0
slot boring machine	2.2 × 5.0
dove-tailer	2.2 × 4.3
jointer	1.4 × 8.3
scroll saw	1.6 × 1.9
drill press	1.6 × 1.6
wood shaper	2.9 × 1.6
radial arm saw	6.5 × 1.8
belt sander	4.4 × 4.8
veneer press	5.0 × 4.2
lathe	2.0 × 3.0
polisher	2.2 × 2.6
carpenter's bench	3.0 × 4.5
printing	
lithographic press	2.5 × 5.0
plate maker	1.5 × 1.8
folder	1.2 × 1.5
drill	1.2 × 1.5
guillotine	1.5 × 3.0
glueing belt	2.0 × 4.2
photographic	
developing tank	2.4 × max length print
enlarger	1.5 × max length print/2

clothing	
laying up machine	7.0 × 14.0
sewing machine	1.2 × 2.2
steam press	2.0 × 2.0
ironing bar	2.0 × 2.0
steam boiler	1.2 × 1.2
footwear	
nailer	1.5 × 2.2
sole press	1.5 × 2.2
heel press	1.5 × 2.2
shaping machine	2.0 × 2.5
leather cutter	3.0 × 3.5
pattern stamper	1.5 × 1.7
electronics	
instrument bench	1.5 × 4.5
motor repairs	
each bay	3.0 × 6.0
general	
compressor	0.75 × 1.2
dust collector	1.5 × 2.0
furnace	1.5 × 3.0
hot dip tank	1.7 × 2.2
drying cabinet	3.0 × 7.0
upholstery press	2.5 × 3.5
forge	0.9 × 2.1
kiln	0.9 × 2.1
potter's wheel	1.8 × 1.7

71 Typical space required per machine in tightly packed layout

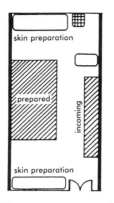
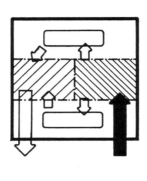

73 Benchwork shop: fur skins, employs two, approximately 75 m²

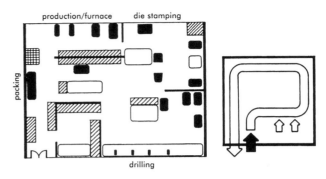

77 Mixed workshop: die casting, employs 15, approximately 150 m²

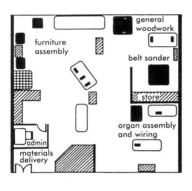
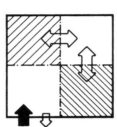

74 Craftwork: organ making and wood furniture, employs two, approximately 175 m²

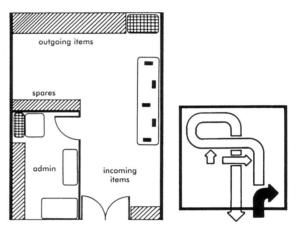

78 Repair shop: electronics repair, employs two, approximately 47 m²

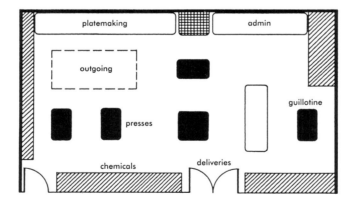
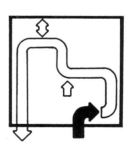

75 Machine workshop: lithographic printing, employs three, approximately 93 m²

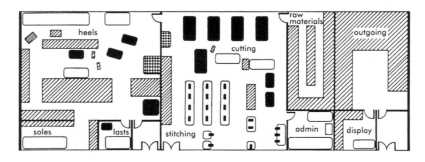
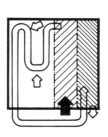

76 Small factory: women's shoe manufacturer, employs 47, approximately 370 m²

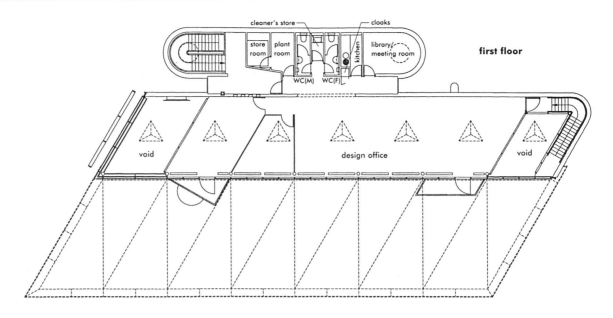

first floor

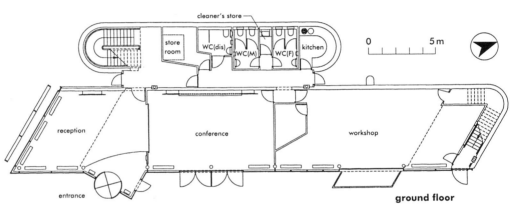

79 Design and Research Centre for More Group UK, Adshel, Earls Court, London: expansion by one further bay is possible on NE side; externally, the company's advertising designs can be displayed in a 'street-scene' setting (Arch: Apicella Associates Ltd)

0   5 m

ground floor

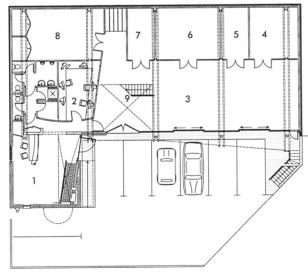

ground floor

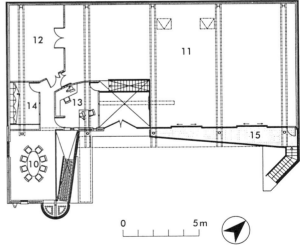

first floor

0   5 m

80 Workshop premises for Thorpe Architectural Modelmakers, Windsor, Berkshire
(Arch: Corrigan + Soundy + Kilaiditi Architects)

1 reception
2 CAD/video animation
3 modelling studio
4 lathes/mill/CNC
5 store
6 band saws/sanders
7 spray booth
8 wood-working machinery
9 double-height space for making large-scale models
10 conference room
11 first-floor modelling studio
12 photographic studio
13 office
14 common road
15 balcony

BUILDING ENVIRONMENT

Rising energy and labour costs make the building environment an increasingly important contributor to operating costs and productivity. Factors to be considered in providing good conditions at the workplace include:

- dust and fume extraction
- ventilation in hot weather
- heating in cold weather
- natural and artificial lighting
- noise control.

Ventilation and heating

As a rough guide for ventilation, 5 l/s/person can be used. The conventional air change rate of 1–1.5 air changes per hour may result in more than 50 times this requirement, wasting much energy.

Recommended temperature levels are:

sedentary work	19°C
active (bench) work	16°C
very active work	13°C

For many companies with processes involving heat, energy can be recovered and waste heat transferred to contribute to workplace requirements: considerable cost savings are possible. Warehouses with refrigerated or chilled areas can also benefit, heat being recovered from the chiller's compressors to warm areas where people work.

Heating and ventilation demands are also a function of the standard of insulation and quantity of glazing provided. Exposed walls and flat roofs of factory and warehouse buildings are to have a max U-value of $0.7\,W/m^2K$ (1994 amendments to the Building Regulations – check for current position; note that alternative calculation methods are possible), with openings limited to 20% of exposed roof area and 15% of exposed wall area. These areas are still high for energy conservation: 10% of wall and roof area is usually considered appropriate.

Natural lighting

Demand for natural roof lighting influences the selection of roof structure. Compared with the insulated roof without any openings, 20% glazing will increase both heat loss (by up to four times) and ventilation demand through solar gain: in highly serviced environments uncomfortable glare can result from pipe runs crossing bright roof lights. Outdoor illuminance varies between 5000 and 25 000 lux from overcast to sunshine conditions in temperate climates. Therefore, a 3% daylight factor (DF) will provide the equivalent of 150–750 lux at the workplace; 10% roof glazing will result in an average DF of about 5%. Flank glazing must be carefully designed to avoid glare, particularly at high level. Natural lighting in warehouses can be a positive disadvantage, sunlight raising the temperature and causing package fade.

Artificial lighting

Typical requirements are shown in **81**.

Noise control

Noise is a major pollutant and limit on working

place	light requirement (lux)
engineering machine shops	
manual work	200
bench work	300
careful bench work	500
precision work	1000
engineering inspection and testing	
medium detail	500
fine detail	1000
minute detail	1500
sheet metal	
bench work	750
stamping, pressing	500
spot welding, general	500
precision welds	1000[1]
assembly	
medium detail	500
small detail	1000[1]
very fine detail	1500[1]
stores issue counter	300
paint shops	
paint dips	300
spraying	500
colour matching	1000
warehousing	
loading bays	150
pallet picking	200
order picking small items	300
packing stations	500
[1] also needs task lighting	

81 Artificial lighting: typical requirements

sound pressure level dBA	maximum exposure time
	(hr)
85	24
87	16
90	8
93	4
96	2
99	1
	(minutes)
102	30
105	15
108	7.5
111	3.75
continuous levels over 85 dBA should be avoided	

82 Maximum exposure to noise

efficiency: it can cause damage to hearing. There is also human sensitivity to vibration: when vibration frequency exceeds approximately 20–30 Hz it passes into the audible range (i.e. the vibration will be heard as sound). For maximum levels in the workplace, see **82**.

Reduce noise at source by design of equipment, screening and enclosure.

Reduce vibration at source by mounting machinery on resilient pads or special foundations.

Reduce noise before it reaches the workplace by absorption (walls, roofs and pendant absorbers) and/or by modifying background noise.

Reduce noise effect by isolating workers in noise-reducing enclosures.

Escaping noise can also be troublesome outside the building so place external plant away from direct lines with surrounding users and screen/suppress the source.

WASTE REMOVAL

Contact the local authority or specialist firm to agree optimum method of disposal. Materials can include: paper and card; plastic bags and foam infill; metal containers; glass. Some materials may need to be sub-divided (e.g. plastics and aluminium/steel cans). A compactor may be required. Waste collection must be near where the materials are generated. Contaminated or toxic materials may require a licence from the local authority.

Waste disposal can be:
- high grade to waste processor
- low grade
- contaminated (specialist collection needed).

PLANNING FOR FIRE CONTROL

Designing factory or warehouse buildings to meet potential fire hazard involves the following:
- Measures to limit the spread of fire within and outside building by compartmentation, detection devices, sprinklers and choice of materials for structure and cladding.
- Providing readily accessible and identifiable means of escape with alternative route(s) in every situation.
- Providing ventilation in the roof to reduce heat and smoke build-up, to prevent fire 'leap-frogging' under roof cladding and to enable the fire service to rapidly vent smoke (**83–84**). Typically one vent per structural bay, with curtains of non-flammable material forming smoke reservoirs in roof space.
- Extinguishing fire or at least controlling the seat of fire until the fire service can extinguish it, by means of sprinklers, high expansion foam or gas drenching.

83 Factories without smoke vents can become rapidly smoke-filled, with fire spreading under roof surface

84 With vents and smoke reservoirs fire can be quickly contained and controlled

Fire design decisions involve consultation with:
- Users: compartmentation may significantly affect the layout of process or warehouse. Building Regulations (Part B) – see below – apply; note that the Building Regulations are designed to protect human health and safety whereas the protection of property is the responsibility of insurers.
- Fire officer: involving local regulations and practice, particularly on fire appliance access, water supply and means of escape.
- User's insurance company: this can be a significant influence on fire control. Most companies have their own, unofficial, rules.

The Loss Prevention Council (LPC) was established in 1986 and took over the responsibilities of several other organisations involved in fire safety. LPC technical advice should be incorporated in the design at the earliest stage (see LPC publication Code of Practice for the Construction of Buildings).

LPC Rules for Automatic Sprinkler Installations, first published in 1990 and subsequently extended, specify minimum standards:

Light hazard: usually non-industrial premises.

Ordinary hazard: industrial and commercial premises unlikely to develop instant fires; four groups, each with the same requirement for water density, but as risk increases, the requirement for more sprinklers increases.

High hazard: industrial premises with high fire loads, either because of piled storage or rapid-burning materials.

Statutory controls

Building Regulations affect the maximum cubic capacity of compartments for single and multi-storey buildings and the fire resistance of elements of structure and finishes for factory and warehouse buildings of certain floor areas. The provision of emergency escape routes and exits, fire mains, and access for fire appliances, can also affect the design.

Other legislation will probably also apply (e.g. BS 5588 and the Fire Precautions Act, 1971).

Note that in large and complex buildings, and some existing buildings, particularly those of historical interest, it may be impractical to apply a strict interpretation of the Building Regulations, and an alternative approach of a fire safety engineering or fire risk assessment may be preferable.

Warehouses

Warehouses with pallet racking can present a particularly acute fire hazard, the aisles acting as flues. Regulations define sprinkler installation, including frequency of outlet and flow rates based on the degree of hazard for the stored material.

Site planning

Control of fire spread can also affect the location of a factory or warehouse on site, particularly in relation to adjoining users. This can affect building costs as the Building Regulations limit materials and fire resistance of walls when adjoining another property, depending on distance from the boundary.

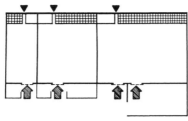

85 Speculative units for renting: office and amenity accommodation is positioned in strip, allowing for flexible space allocation

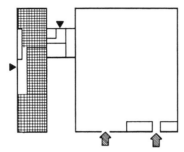

86 Environmental factors can be considered for purpose-designed factories: with noisy and dirty processes, office and amenity accommodation can be segregated from production zone

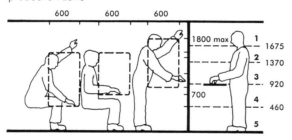

1 light material: low usage, infrequent operation; 2 frequent high-level controls or light positioning; 3 convenient control zone: standing manipulation; 4 seated control zone: light and medium-heavy location; 5 infrequent zone of heavy material

87 Manual work and storage involve some critical dimensions: most common working and manipulative zone is in 2–4 band

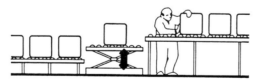

88 Simple handling aids such as scissor lift can improve working conditions and productivity

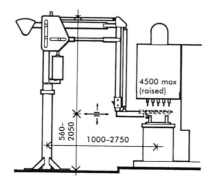

89 Counter balanced manipulator can enable operator to place heavy loads accurately

ENVIRONMENTAL COMPARTMENTATION

Compartmentation, so long as it is compatible with the handling and services demands of the production and storage process, can be used to reduce both energy loss and certain harmful environments, such as fumes, heat, noise and dust, as well as limiting fire spread.

Hot, dirty processes can be grouped to exploit energy and material recovery techniques. The proportion of factory area/volume affected by the process will indicate the strategy; if a high proportion of the area is affected, group processes into compartments; if a low proportion, then enclose separate elements of the process with local extraction and controls. Alternatively, segregate those who work in the production area into an environment enclosure, exploiting automation, and only minimally temper the majority of the area (this is an increasingly attractive option with high energy costs). Where parallel with warehouses, automate the main storage section, limiting environmental controls to zones of high labour use for order picking and assembly.

WORKPLACE DESIGN

Equipment, layout and operating procedures should constitute a safe system of work as defined in the Health & Safety at Work Act and manual handling legislation. Design of the workplace is fundamental to achieving high levels of productivity: this also influences labour relations and absenteeism. The workplace considerations include the following.

Ergonomics
Workers' relationships to machinery and work actions must be designed to reduce fatigue and increase safety.

Mechanical handling
Equipment includes the most basic, low-cost handling devices, scissor lifts, hoists and counterbalanced manipulators, which can revolutionise manual work, up to accumulating conveyors, automatically routeing mobile workstations and robot assembly machines.

Work organisation
This may entail grouping people for certain tasks. The traditional isolation of machine operators and line assembly organisation is under review in many countries in Europe and the USA; team organisation can offer greater communication and production flexibility.

Environment
Positive demands:
- temperature suited to activity
- air flow and air cleanliness
- lighting: background and task (see **81**).

Defence against:
- glare
- noise
- vibration
- harmful gaseous or dust products: explosions.

AMENITY AND HYGIENE

Washing, changing, WC and smoke/rest provision is related to the workplace. Location and scale depend on work organisation (see **93**): traditional line production will require centralised services accessible to numbers of people; team organisation implies amenity accommodation close by, or local to team operating area. With changes in production organisation depending on manufacturing methods and volume, both are likely to change with increasing frequency.

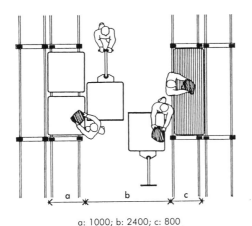

a: 1000; b: 2400; c: 800

90 Typical manual order picking from pallets and shelf, replenished by reach trucks; simultaneous picking from each side for high throughput installation

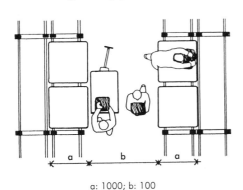

a: 1000; b: 100

91 Slower throughput picking operation with one-way trolley access: replenished by narrow aisle stacker or from behind rack

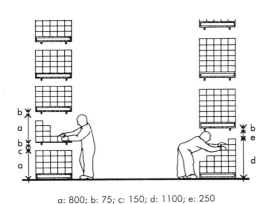

a: 800; b: 75; c: 150; d: 1100; e: 250

92 Typical rack and shelf heights for floor-level order picking

Washing and toilet facilities

Legal requirement is simply that adequate and conveniently accessible washing facilities are provided and maintained. BS 6465 gives general guidance.

Lockers

For clean trades, one locker/person must be provided; for dirty trades one double locker/person, to keep work and street clothing separate.

Changing areas

The minimum changing area is 0.5 m²/person.

Ambulance rooms

Floor space to be not less than 9.29 m², with natural light and ventilation. Separate male and female rooms are required.

Rooms should contain: sink with hot and cold supply, table with smooth surface, facility to sterilise instruments, adequate supply of suitable dressings, bandages and splints, couch, and stretcher. A qualified nurse should always to be available.

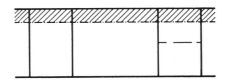

small divisible units as strip along boundary

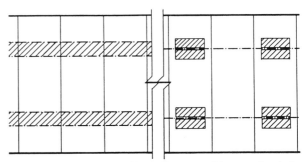

medium and large factory building with two possible zones for placing wet services, either allowing free location in each zone or grouping into flexibly positioned but distinct wet service units (e.g. for team access)

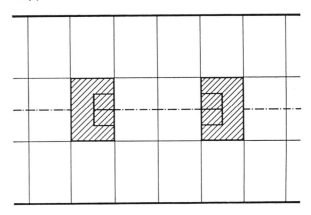

for large-scale factories another option is island wet services and amenity areas; advantages: single underground services run and accessibility from all sides

93 Wet services, washing and rest area

LOADING BAYS

These are the link between production or storage process and the distribution system. Much effort to reduce production costs can be wasted through delayed vehicle turn-round and increased manning if loading areas are not carefully designed. Particularly in mixed developments (e.g. shops, offices and small factory units), careful planning is needed to prevent delays in finding the correct delivery location; for instance, the provision of an internal phone in the loading bay area can save considerable time.

Purpose-designed bays are not required for some vehicles (e.g. containers or swap-bodies, aggregate lorries top-loaded from hoppers or dump trucks, and car-transporters).

Planning

Generally, for end-loading containers and box-bodies vehicles, as in retail distribution, raised decks are preferred. For side-loading curtain-sided and flat-bed vehicles, a covered, ground level dock is suitable; specific bays are not usually required – loading/unloading is by fork-lift truck, and a working clearance around the vehicle of 2.5–3 m is required. Long loads, such as pipes, need special consideration. Wheeled pallets are sometimes used, in which case the layout must therefore avoid any stairs. Doorways should be 1.5 m wide; internal passages should be 2.0 m wide. Floors, walls and corners need to be hard-wearing.

Layout criteria include

- pre-assembly of loads
- load units (e.g. pallets, bins, cages)
- unloading procedure (e.g. roll-in, roll-out or fork-lift truck)
- loading to sea/aircraft/rail containers
- timing of dispatch
- type of packing required (and storage of pallets etc., and waste)
- any specific environmental conditions
- any special security or legal requirements.

Separate loading bays

Should be provided for incoming and dispatch (see **94**). Separate bays, together with vehicle marshalling areas, are required where the manufacturing system involves different characteristics between raw materials and finished products – raw materials needing side-handling at ground level, and palletisation for dispatch needing end-loading. It is similar for a large distribution warehouse (e.g. bulk loads of a single product are delivered and mixed loads of orders are dispatched, in distributors' own vehicles) so segregation is needed for traffic management and materials flow in the warehouse, particularly as vehicle handling peaks may coincide. Traditionally, income and dispatch were located at opposite ends of buildings, but modern layouts may need loading bays at strategic locations around the building. This results in higher construction costs, but should mean lower production costs in the long-term, and is worth careful examination at the design stage.

Number of bays, spacing and layout

Loading bays must never be considered in isolation; they must be related to the circulation and check-off area behind them. Decision on numbers is a question of throughput patterns and available area next to the dock for load preparation (see **95**). Clearly if vehicles can be handled faster with pre-assembled loads, less loading docks are required than for slower turn-round with material being assembled as loading operation continues.

Loading bay spacing and layout are influenced by the depth of the manoeuvring area available and depth of the load accumulation space behind the dock (see **97**).

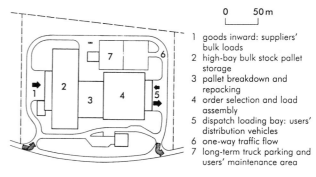

1 goods inward: suppliers' bulk loads
2 high-bay bulk stock pallet storage
3 pallet breakdown and repacking
4 order selection and load assembly
5 dispatch loading bay: users' distribution vehicles
6 one-way traffic flow
7 long-term truck parking and users' maintenance area

94 Large retail distribution centre with separate goods inward and dispatch loading bays

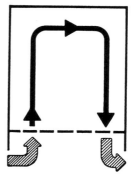

95 Many warehouses can use dock for incoming and dispatch goods; in factories, sharing type of loading bay may not be possible but goods vehicle manoeuvring area can be common

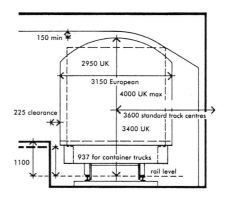

96 Rail gauge (container outline dotted)

Vehicle spacing

Spacing is directly related to yard depth (frontal clearance). The conditioning factor is the distance that closely parked vehicles have to pull out before turning (see **97**). Angled (usually 45° or 60°), raised docks reduce yard depth at expense of the number of vehicles handled at one time; drive-through bays reduce circulation width but increase length. Angled docks increase construction costs, complicate the internal layout, and require a one-way traffic system as the driver should not reverse blind. The finger dock (10° angle) is a compromise for side- and end-loading where the manoeuvring area is limited.

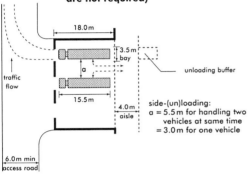

90° enclosed bay (flat floordeck) (note that specific vehicle bays are not required)

18.0 m

3.5 m bay

a

unloading buffer

15.5 m

4.0 m aisle

side-(un)loading:
a = 5.5 m for handling two vehicles at same time
= 3.0 m for one vehicle

traffic flow

6.0 m min access road

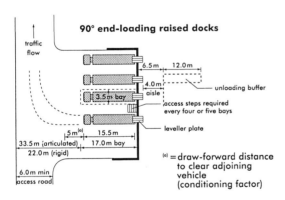

90° end-loading raised docks

traffic flow

6.5 m   12.0 m

4.0 m aisle

unloading buffer

3.5 m bay

access steps required every four or five bays

leveller plate

5 m (a)   15.5 m

33.5 m (articulated)   17.0 m bay
22.0 m (rigid)

6.0 m min access road

(a) = draw-forward distance to clear adjoining vehicle (conditioning factor)

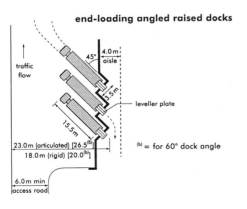

end-loading angled raised docks

traffic flow

45°   4.0 m aisle

3.5 m

leveller plate

15.5 m

23.0 m (articulated) [26.5]
18.0 m (rigid) [20.0 (b)]

6.0 m min access road

(b) = for 60° dock angle

97 Loading dock layouts

A bay width of 3.5 m is usually sufficient, but the width of the bays is also directly related to frontal clearance:

bay width (m)	frontal clearance (min) for 15.5 m articulated vehicle (m)
3.5	16.4
4.5	10.4
5.5	9.6

(NB 2.0 m should be added to frontal clearance if adjacent to wall)

Load check-off/accumulation space

This should be located behind the cross-circulation aisle load handling zone and should have a capacity of 1.5 vehicle loads. Allow space of at least one load area for broken pallets, rejected loads and rubbish. A cross-circulation aisle 4 m wide allows space for two fork-lifts to pass and for turnout from dock levellers.

Raised docks

These should be equipped with dock leveller plates to accommodate both changes in vehicle bed height as they are loaded and different types of vehicle (see **98**). The standard loading dock height is 1.2 m, but medium-size vans require 1 m and refrigerated vehicles may require 1.35 m; the highest can be 1.65 m. The dock should preferably be slightly lower than the vehicle platform (to prevent a moving load trapping anyone inside the vehicle).

Dock levellers These are usually built into the dock, with a length between 2 and 4.5 m, and giving height adjustments of approximately 0.5 m above and below the dock level; the gradient should not exceed 1 in 10. Straight lifts are rarely a suitable alternative. Note that many vehicles are now fitted with tail lifts.

Dock shelters

Dock shelters form a hermetic seal between the vehicle and building; a segmental or roller shutter door closes onto the leveller when the vehicle leaves. Dock shelters may be essential for cold store transfers. Ground level or finger docks can be completely enclosed (straight through flow or tail in). Alternatively, hot or cold air curtains can be used but these are not a substitute for enclosure. Bay widths need to be wider when shelters are used: 3.7 to 4.5 m wide.

Security/health and safety

Drivers should not be able gain access beyond the dock, except in some distribution operations with the company's own vehicles where the driver arranges the order of loading. Generally, raised docks with dock shelters provide inherent security: separate lavatories and access to traffic office should be provided for visiting drivers. A high percentage of accidents occur in the loading area: careful design is crucial.

Weather protection

If dock shelters or an enclosed dock cannot be installed, a canopy is required over the loading area: allow at least 4.5 m clear height (see **98**); sometimes 5 m may be required (note that there is no legal restriction on heights of goods vehicles in the UK). If clearance above the vehicle is required (e.g. for access to manholes etc.) a minimum height of 6 m should be allowed. Do not face loading bays into prevailing winds.

Gradients

Ground should be flat (except for local drainage fall) for the length of vehicle in front of the dock, or for a minimum of the length of the vehicle trailer.

Large goods vehicle marshalling and circulation

- Segregate light vans from large goods vehicles: different docks or parts of the dock should be used.
- Provide heavy vehicle waiting bays before loading bay area and clear of manoeuvring space.

98 Section through raised loading dock with dock shelter for energy retention: canopy (dashed) only needed if shelter omitted

- Provide parking bay(s) before exit for drivers to check load security.
- Traffic flow should be one-way clockwise so that reversing into loading docks is on the driver's side (if anti-clockwise and reversing blind, a second person may be needed).

LABORATORIES

Walter Hain

INTRODUCTION

This section is intended as an introduction to the requirements of those laboratories in which the scale of activity is associated with benches and with equipment of a similar size, covering the vast majority of labs. With the increased rate of change today, most labs except those for teaching need to be designed for maximum flexibility, so for the designer's purposes the traditional distinctions – chemistry, physics, biology, wet or dry – are seldom relevant.

Teaching labs Consisting usually of a large lab area of island benches which seldom changes, teaching labs remain distinctly different.

Routine and research labs These share similar space, servicing and furniture requirements, so for initial design purposes they can be taken as one lab type. The spatial information given here applies particularly to them, but much of the other data applies also to teaching labs.

For layouts of two existing lab buildings, see **1** for plan using the rectangular lab module and **2** for plan with the square module.

SPACE STANDARDS

In the UK most official organisations publish tables giving their area allowances, see **3**. While those for teaching provide firm information, the figures for research should be used for guidance only. Public organisations and private firms usually have their own standards and these will normally be included with their brief. For accepted space requirements between benches for various traffic conditions, see **11**.

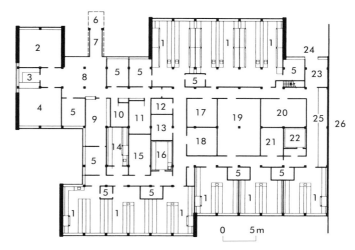

1 standard labs; 2 seminar; 3 kitchen; 4 lounge; 5 office; 6 entrance; 7 lobby; 8 entrance hall; 9 reception/secretarial; 10 female; 11 male; 12 store; 13 dark room; 14 radioactive lab; 15 instruments; 16 cold room; 17 MRI room; 18 wash-up; 19 equipment; 20 central store; 21 balance room; 22 behaviour suite; 23 goods lobby; 24 deliveries; 25 WCs and shower; 26 existing building

1 Pharmaceutical research laboratory building: rectangular module (3.3 × 7.2 m), double corridor naturally ventilated, single storey; all vertical services distribution direct to and from roof plant room into labs, without ducts

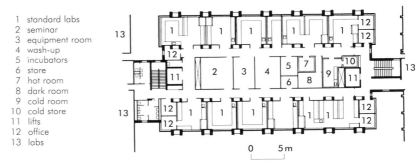

```
1   standard labs
2   seminar
3   equipment room
4   wash-up
5   incubators
6   store
7   hot room
8   dark room
9   cold room
10  cold store
11  lifts
12  office
13  labs
```

2 Wellcome Trust/Medical Research Council Building, Cambridge: square module (4.8 × 4.6 m), double corridor naturally ventilated, six stories; corridor ducts – piped services distribution from roof plant room to labs; external ducts – fume cupboard extracts to plant room; ducts at each end of core – ductwork to and from plant room for mechanical ventilation to core; fume cupboard make-up air supply from air-handling unit in lab ceiling void
(Arch: Cusdin Burden & Howitt)

1 Schools	Level of work	Area per workplace		Scale of work	Area per workplace	
		(m²)	(ft²)	(m²)	(ft²)	
	General science	2.8	30	Bench scale	3.2*	34*
	Individual projects	3.6	40	Workshop scale	4.6*	50*
	*These allowances include storage and preparation.					
2 Colleges of further education	Level of work	Area per workplace		Addition for ancillary rooms (%)	Addition for balance area (%)	
		(m²)	(ft²)			
	General science	4.6	50	15	40	
	Advanced science and engineering	5.6	60	25	40	
3 Research (government and commercial)	Likely range	Area per workplace				
		(m²)	(ft²)			
	Chemistry	8–12	86–130			
	Physics	6–8	65–86			
	Biology	6–8	65–86			
	Area requirements can vary considerably, depending on individual requirements and equipment.					

3 UK space standards

THE LABORATORY SPACE

The vast majority of activities that take place in routine and research labs can be accommodated within a standard room size and shape – the 'lab module' – or in multiples of that module, with differing requirements of individual labs met by modifications to the servicing or fitting-out. The module most used is rectangular and experience has confirmed the 1961 Nuffield research, which found a space 3–4m wide by 6m long would be satisfactory for most requirements. Some research activities are better served by a square module which allows squarer bench arrangements (see **4,5**). The length of the module chosen should preferably be a multiple of the chosen lab furniture module to facilitate bench rearrangement.

Standard labs These are continuously occupied and should be naturally lit and, where mechanical ventilation is not required, naturally ventilated. The minimum floor to ceiling height is 2.7m. See **6** for some typical standard lab layouts.

Special labs These may not be suited to the basic module, may have non-standard servicing, environmental or safety requirements, may not be continuously occupied and, as mechanical ventilation is often a performance requirement, can be positioned in core areas. They are better separated from the standard lab areas to avoid inhibiting the latter's flexibility. They include 'radioactive labs' (Radioactive Substances Act, 1993), 'biohazardous labs' (Categorisation of Pathogens According to Hazard and Categories of Containment – Advisory Committee on Dangerous Pathogens, 1990), 'tissue culture suites' and '+4°C cold rooms' (essentially low-temperature labs which can only be occupied for limited periods at a time). See **7,8** for some typical non-standard lab layouts.

Planning principles

To provide natural lighting plus flexibility in size and layout, standard labs should be planned in a bank along the external wall, uninterrupted by other accommodation. The bank will usually be one module deep, but where larger lab areas are required can be deeper. In a single-corridor width building any special labs, back-up facilities and offices will occupy the bank of accommodation on the opposite side of the corridor. In a double-corridor building, the standard lab banks usually occupy the space on the outside of each corridor, with the core area between corridors housing special labs, back-up facilities, stores, etc. The choice of plan configuration will usually be determined by the amount of accommodation required and the site area available for it.

For the designer the two requirements which most distinguish lab buildings from other building types are the need for a variety of engineering services at each workstation, together with the presence of fume cupboards. Both need vertical services drops/risers at frequent intervals which can require space-consuming vertical ducts that should be allowed for at the outset. Both also generate extensive plant room areas, usually at roof level, which should be borne in mind when initial design work is undertaken.

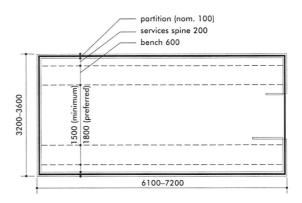

4 Rectangular lab module

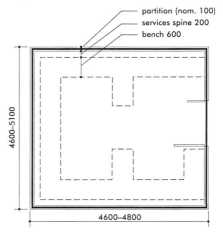

5 Square lab module

The ducts carrying the vertical supplies to the bench services run-outs in each module, and/or the extract ductwork from fume cupboards, may occur along either the corridor side of a bank of labs, the window wall side, or both. In single-storey labs with extensive roof plant rooms, the vertical services can be taken direct from plant room into lab beneath, obviating the need for these ducts.

For Building Regulations in the UK, laboratory buildings are usually included in the 'Offices' purpose group classification.

OFFICES

Research activities usually require more office space than routine work and this should be provided separate from the labs, but as close to them as is practicable.

BACK-UP ROOMS

These are used by the occupants of more than one lab. They are not used continuously and are therefore best provided separate from the standard lab areas. Teaching labs usually require only a 'preparation room' and a 'wash-up room'. Other labs are likely to require one or more of the following:

- wash-up room
- equipment room for floor-standing equipment
- instrument room for bench-mounted equipment
- -20°C cold store, usually entered from the cold room or an insulated lobby

- hot room (+37°C is usual)
- dark room
- constant temperature room
- electron microscope suite, including preparation room, microscope room and dark room
- MRI room, housing magnetic resonance imagers
- clean room (BS 5295).

See **9** for some typical back-up room layouts.

Research procedures often require the use of animals but 'animal houses' are a separate building type not covered here. The most relevant regulation for designers is the 1989 Code of Practice for the Housing and Care of Animals used in Scientific Procedures.

LAB STORAGE AREAS

In addition to the storage requirements of most building types, the following are specific to labs:

- central store (for bulk storage of equipment and apparatus)
- solvents/inflammable liquids store (usually external)
- special gases cylinder store (either a central bank of cylinders with piped supply to lab outlets or a store from which cylinders are trolleyed into the labs – usually external); prefabricated modular gas houses complete with all the necessary fittings are available
- chemicals store (for bulk storage); requires permanent ventilation and for chemistry labs may be required adjacent to labs
- radioactive store (may be required for holding radioactive waste material until it is collected for disposal; however, radioactive material – such as isotopes – is usually delivered and kept in lead-lined containers, in which case no store will be required).

FITTING OUT

The only items common to all lab work that need to be fixed are the engineering services, so for maximum flexibility these should be restricted to the sides and possibly the ends of the module, with their outlets mounted on fixed services spines or bridges. All else – benches, underbench units, wall cupboards, etc. – are best movable and interchangeable.

Partitions The best partitions between modules are the post and panel type, with posts at the same centres as the lab furniture module to provide support for shelves and wall cupboards, as well as services run-outs. Panels may be opaque, glazed or omitted altogether and can be changed as the function of the lab module changes. This system also provides space within the partition thickness for pipe and conduit vertical drops where the supply is from above. Partition posts supporting the various engineering services run-outs, waste, services spine and laboratory furniture wall fittings are shown in **10**.

Services spines These are fixed ledges or shelves on which outlets for the piped engineering services and dripcups are fixed; 200 mm back to front, usually level with bench tops and of solid laminate on brackets off wall channels. In island/peninsula positions they may be mounted about 200 mm above the bench with a solid panel between spine and bench for power outlets.

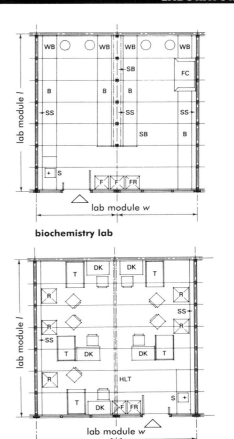

biochemistry lab

electrophysiology lab

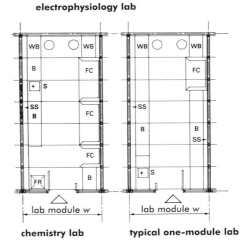

chemistry lab   **typical one-module lab**

6 Standard labs
(Reproduced, with permission, from *Laboratories: A Briefing and Design Guide*, by Walter Hain, published by E & FN Spon (an imprint of Taylor & Francis), 1995, page 14)

key to symbols **6–9**

A	autoclave	INC	incubator
B	bench	LF	laminar-flow cabinet
C	centrifuge	R	rig
CO	counter	S	sink
D	dryer	SB	services bridge
DF	deep freezer	SC	safety cabinet
DK	desk	SH	shelves
DS	drench shower	SHK	shaker
DT	dunk tank	SHR	shower
EW	eye wash	SS	services spine
F	refrigerator	T	table
FC	fume cupboard	TR	trolley
FD	freeze dryer	W	washer
FR	freezer	WB	writing bench
HLT	high-level trunking	WHB	wash-hand basin

Services bridges These are often used in island/peninsula bench positions and consist of a box mounted above and clear of the bench, with services outlets projecting from both sides or on the bottom, and power trunking fixed to both sides.

Laboratory furniture (BS 3202: 1991) This should be movable and modular. It is usually supplied and fixed by specialists, who offer their standard ranges but will quote for variations to these to suit individual projects. Common modules are 900, 1000 and 1200 mm. The furniture module chosen will determine the centres of partition studs and will also affect the overall length of the lab module. Movable benches comprise a worktop on a tubular steel underframe. Solid laminate is a common worktop material; for radioactive lab benches, which require a joint-free raised edge to contain spillage, epoxy resin is suitable. The common benchtop depth is 600 mm, with a height of 900 mm, but other depths and heights are obtainable. Lengths of one or one and a half modules are usual. Balance benches are of heavier construction and some suppliers produce them with vibration dampers incorporated.

Underbench units should be half or one module wide, floor standing or suspended from the bench underframe (for easy removal), and are available in cupboard and drawer configurations.

Wall cupboards and shelves should be one module wide, and hung on wall bars for easy removal.

Sink units are bowl-and-drainer combinations in acid-resisting 316S16 grade stainless steel on bench-type underframes, and are one, one and a half or two modules long.

In addition to their furniture, some suppliers also supply services spines and bridges on fixed frames, with run-outs and outlets pre-fitted.

Fume cupboards (BS 7258:1990) These are ceiling-height cabinets with openable glass fronts and work surfaces at bench level, supported on a steel underframe or underbench unit and with an outlet at the top for connection to an extract system. The glass front is usually vertically sliding and the work surface should have a raised lip around the periphery, and a waste outlet. Services outlets are mounted internally on the side walls, which are usually of double-skin construction about 150 mm thick (making the smallest practical fume cupboard width 1000 mm), with remote controls on the outside of the cabinet together with power outlets and the cupboard controls. Walk-in or full-height cupboards for tall apparatus extend to the floor, which usually forms the work surface.

Most fume cupboards are about 950 mm deep, are available in widths of 1000, 1200, 1500, 1800 or 2000 mm, and can be accommodated within a 2700 mm floor-to-ceiling height. Services spines usually terminate against the cupboard sides, with the piped services run-outs and wastes continuing through below the work surface, with connections to the cupboard outlets. Many lab furniture suppliers also supply fume cupboards.

The activities within these cupboards are potentially hazardous and they should preferably not be sited near escape routes, high traffic areas or doors, and should be at least 300 mm from return walls or columns, for airflow reasons.

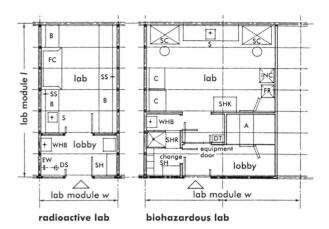

radioactive lab   **biohazardous lab**

7 Special labs
(Reproduced, with permission, from *Laboratories: A Briefing and Design Guide*, by Walter Hain, published by E & FN Spon (an imprint of Taylor & Francis), 1995, page 15)

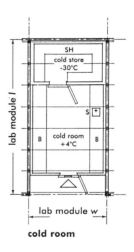

cold room

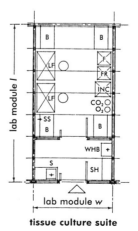

tissue culture suite

8 Special labs
(Reproduced, with permission, from *Laboratories: A Briefing and Design Guide*, by Walter Hain, published by E & FN Spon (an imprint of Taylor & Francis), 1995, pages 15 and 24)

ENGINEERING SERVICES

'Bench services' are the services required at the workstations and include piped services (for water, fuel gas, special gases, etc.), power and communications.

Piped services The piped services outlets may be mounted on the services spines or on services bridges. They are usually supplied from small bore piping run-outs, either run in a horizontal band below the spine or enclosed within the bridge itself. The outlets (lab taps) are supplied by specialist firms in two forms – 'bench outlets' for spines and 'wall outlets' for bridges – and should be specified with removable nozzles to enable users to connect piping to them. Handles are colour coded to identify the gas/liquid conveyed.

Power and communications These are usually provided in trunking, either mounted above the spine or on the side of the bridge.

Supply The horizontal run-outs may be supplied from their main circuits by:
- vertical drops from overhead
- vertical risers from underfloor
- vertical drops at the corridor or window wall into the end of each run
- horizontal runs along the window wall into the end of each run, supplied from widely spaced vertical ducts
- in single-storey buildings with extensive roof plant rooms, direct through the plant-room floor into each run.

Underfloor supply is a potential source of leaks through the floor and any modifications will affect the floor below, inhibiting flexibility and causing disruption.

Dripcups These are waste outlets on services spines into which fluids can be tipped and equipment drained.

Wastes These are usually moved by means of gravity from dripcups, sinks, fume cupboards, etc., but pumped or vacuum-assisted systems are also available. It is usual for each run of lab waste to discharge into a dilution recovery trap or catchpot before connection to a floor outlet or stack. Radioactive and biohazardous wastes have more onerous requirements for discharge.

General mechanical ventilation/air-conditioning systems

For labs these are similar to other building types, but each fume cupboard usually has its own separate extract ductwork and fan with the discharge vertically above roof level, together with a make-up air supply to the room, which is activated with the extract system when the cupboard is switched on. In mechanically ventilated/air-conditioned labs the make-up air will usually be from the central ventilation system. In naturally ventilated labs it may be ducted to the lab from a central air-handling unit (AHU) in the plant room, or may be from an individual AHU mounted at high level in the lab and drawing fresh air direct through the external wall. The extract ductwork can be in the range of 250 to 300 mm diameter, depending on the size of cupboard, so in multi-storey buildings with many fume cupboards the vertical duct space required is considerable.

Central heating systems for labs do not differ in principle from those of other building types but the presence of benches inhibits the choice of radiator positions.

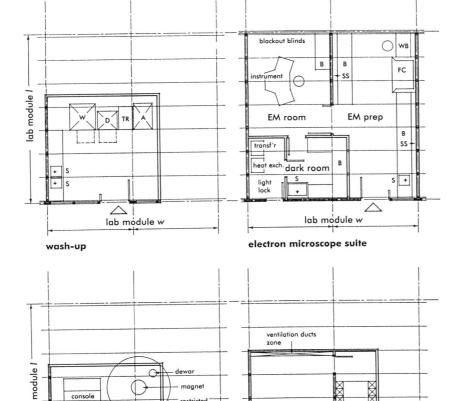

wash-up

electron microscope suite

magnetic resonance imager room

clean room

9 Back-up rooms
(Reproduced, with permission, from *Laboratories: A Briefing and Design Guide*, by Walter Hain, published by E & FN Spon (an imprint of Taylor & Francis), 1995, page 26)

BUILDING FABRIC

The structure and external finishes of lab buildings do not normally differ markedly from those of other comparable building types, but some provision in the external wall to enable the future insertion of make-up air louvres, such as high-level fixed window panels, should be considered.

For most standard labs a vinyl emulsion finish on plastered or wallboard walls or ceilings will be acceptable. Some labs and back-up rooms may require gloss paint or sprayed plastic finishes.

Lab doors should be one and a half leaves wide to enable bulky equipment to pass, with a main leaf being 900 mm wide and having observation panel.

The usual floor covering is sheet PVC with welded joints, with epoxy resin in rooms that are regularly washed down. The machinery in plant rooms is a potential source of leaks, so the floor covering should be waterproof and taken up into coved skirtings, epoxy resin being a suitable material.

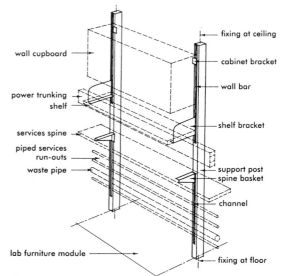

10 Support system
(Reproduced, with permission, from *Laboratories: A Briefing and Design Guide*, by Walter Hain, published by E & FN Spon (an imprint of Taylor & Francis), 1995, page 36)

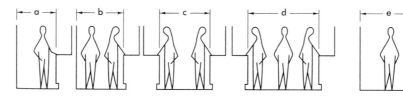

a	one worker, no through traffic	975–1200 mm
b	one worker plus passage way	1050–1350 mm
c	two workers, back-to-back, no through traffic	1350–1500 mm
d	two workers, back-to-back, plus passage way	1650–1950 mm
e	gangway only, no working spaces either side	900–1500 mm

11 Space between benches

LANDSCAPE WORKS

Helen Dallas

INTRODUCTION

Landscape design has increased in significance in relation to buildings over recent years. While its importance has traditionally been associated with the historic country house and then expanded through Victorian public parks and tree lined avenues, it now extends to current trends for internal and external landscaping to complement commercial and public buildings and the greater interest shown in the small private garden. It is common for Authorities to require landscaping schemes for all new developments.

This section covers the subject from hard landscaping elements, planting and soft landscaping to planning of the private garden and public park. It includes garden structures and buildings associated with landscape works.

DESIGN FACTORS

When designing any form or extent of landscape works its purpose should be determined (e.g. to soften or enhance buildings, as an outdoor living space or for leisure and enjoyment). Detail design should consider the following.

- Orientation has an important bearing on the amount of sun received during different seasons or times of day (see **1,2**) and any adverse wind effects: this dictates plant type and the need for sheltering (see **3**).

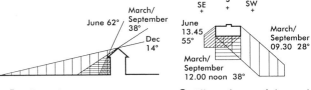

1 Effect of season on shadowing

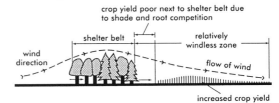

2 Effect of time of day and season on shadowing

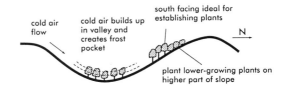

3 Effect of shelter belt on crop production

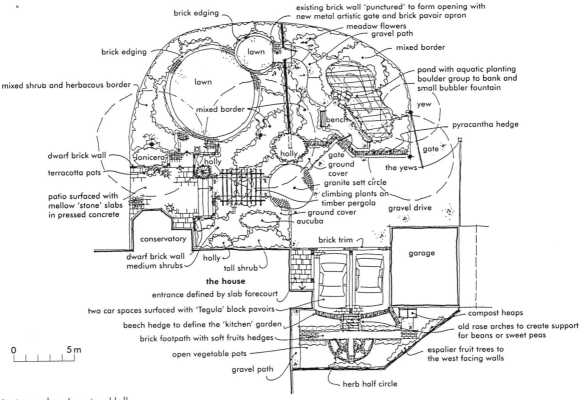

4 Effect of slope and exposure on establishment of plants

- Ground contours not only affect the degree of solar radiation and exposure but also the stability of planting and irrigation patterns (see **4**). The elevation affects sight-lines and visual impact.
- Access and circulation to and within landscaped areas must be considered in relation to adjacent buildings, entrances, paths and roads (see **5**).

5 Private garden, Langton Hall
(Landscape Arch : Don Munro)

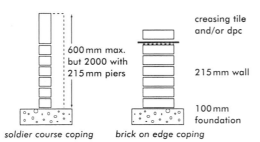

6 Masonry walls: 102mm width with piers and 215mm brick wall

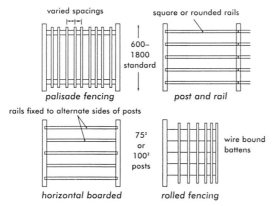

7 Traditional timber fences

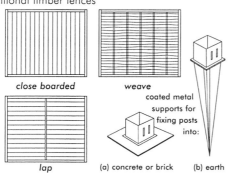

8 Typical timber fence panels and post supports

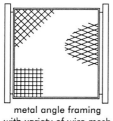

9 Metal mesh fencing with concrete posts

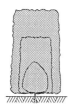

initial hedge plants (eg. privet) planted 300–400mm spacings regularly pruned to form shape

11 Hedging enclosures

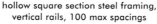
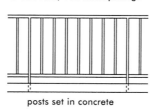
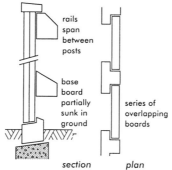

12 Timber boarded acoustic barrier

GENERAL FEATURES OF LANDSCAPE WORKS

Enclosures

These are used for demarcation, privacy, security, level changes and acoustic barriers. The design of a fence and the materials used in its construction should harmonise with the surroundings.

- Walls may be of brick or stone and should blend with the materials used to construct adjacent buildings (see **6**).
- Wooden slatted, panelled or railed fencing (see **7,8**) is commonly used in residential areas, while metal mesh fencing is often favoured to enclose commercial developments (see **9**).
- Railings, usually of metal, are often used in public spaces (see **10**).
- Hedges: clipped foliage (formal) or flowering (see **11**).
- Acoustic barriers of wood and derivatives should be considered to separating busy transport links from residential areas (see **12**).

The best side (fair side) of a boundary fence or wall should face outwards with posts visible from within the site. On sloping ground, fencing should follow contours. Fences to guard against animal movements should be extended 100–200 mm below ground, especially where hedges are planted. Allow sufficient space for the ultimate width of hedge when fully established. Most timbers used for fencing require protective treatment (e.g. pressure impregnation). Concrete plinths, bases and metal shoes help prolong life of most timber fences. Retaining walls at level changes using concrete, stone or brick (see **13**) often require specialist design.

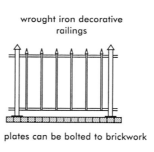

10 Typical metal railings and securing fencing

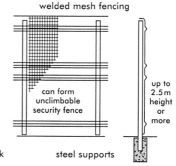

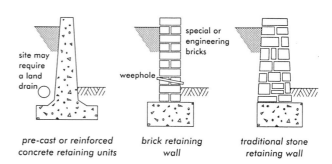

13 Concrete, brick and stone retaining walls

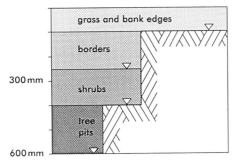

14 Recommended depths of topsoil

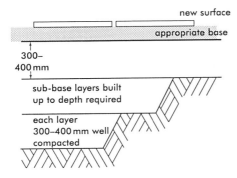

15 Build up of soil under hard landscaping

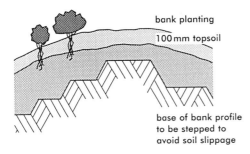

16 Earth profiling to banks

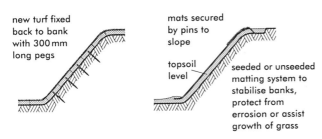

17 Laying turf and matting systems to steep banks

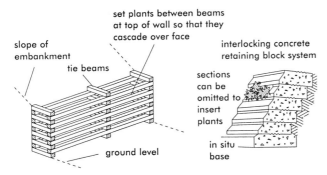

18 Examples of timber and concrete crib structures

Soil preparation

Topsoil Topsoil is essential for the healthy growth of plants. If the quality is reasonable, separate from subsoil and retain for use wherever possible. Recommended depths of topsoil vary (see **14**).

Soil compaction Soil used as fill for hard landscaped areas should be spread in layers 300–400 mm deep and well compacted (see **15**); not all soils are suitable for this. Materials of different character should be deposited and compacted separately. Sub-base material will vary from region to region but ideally be a mix of small stone and firmer material. Old brick and rubble should only be used if well broken up and blinded with fine materials.

Banks To prevent soil movement, fill along slopes should be placed in layers. Form cuts in existing ground surface to create serrated profile to retain fill material (see **16**). On higher banks, ground profile should be stepped to prevent sliding of fill material.

Angle of slope should be considered in relation to the maintenance operations required, and the top and bottom of the bank gently rounded off. Provide drainage at both the top and bottom of a bank so that soil only receives moisture falling on its surface. Maximum gradients are: for mowing grass 1:3; for planting 1:2 (or 1:1 where no maintenance required). Precautions need to be taken when laying turf to banks (see **17**). Earth can be protected and stabilised for planting using biodegradable matting systems (see **17**).

Apart from retaining walls, crib structures can be utilised and can incorporate planting (see **18**).

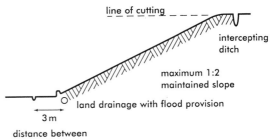

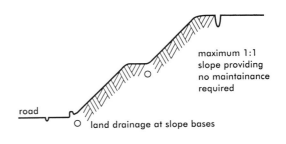

19 Typical sections through road cuttings

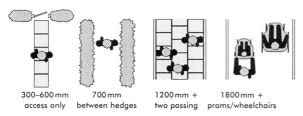

20 Recommended widths of paths

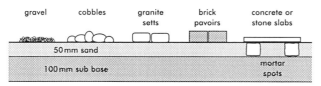

21 Typical range of path constructions

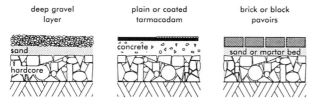

22 Typical range of driveway constructions

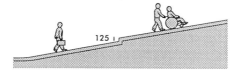

23 Profile of ramp with step

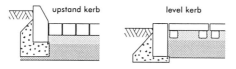

24 Kerb details to paths

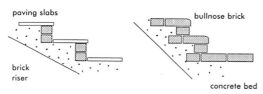

25 Typical step constructions

Paths and steps

Paths Width of paths (see **20**): minimum for access, 300–600 mm; single-file between hedges and shrubs, 700 mm; two people passing, 1.2–1.8 m, allowing extra for prams.

Selection of material subject to appearance, cost and performance required; base dependent on usage (see **21,22**).

Ramps Maximum gradient of 1:12 for negotiation by wheelchairs; minimum width 1.2 m. If stepped, maximum step height is 125 mm (see **23**).

Kerbs Kerbs and edge trim construction depends on the adjoining surfaces (see **24**).

Steps Tread depth not less than 300 mm; risers 90–150 mm high (see **25**). Detail of the finish to the end of steps is important, especially where set in a grass bank.

Handrails These are required for public steps with more than one riser. Divisional rails are desirable when the flight width is greater than 1.8 m. Specialist design may be required to ensure structural stability and adequate fixings, particularly where changes in level are involved.

Planting

Planting areas must be adequately prepared using appropriate fertilizers and composts to provide balance and stimulate growth, and these should be applied at a suitable interval prior to planting. Grass grown from seed is planted early autumn or spring, using a seed mix suited to the soil type or appearance. Alternatively, turfing can be considered for quicker establishment of grass area.

A topsoil depth of 150 mm is needed for grass areas and seed beds; 300 mm for shrub beds (see **26**); 500 mm for climbers; and 600–1000 mm for tree planting. Seedlings can be brought on in greenhouses or under cloches for later transplanting.

Tree pits are formed with a minimum 750 mm diameter and 350 mm deep (larger for mature trees), and filled with subsoil, compost and topsoil. Staking may be required for young trees (see **26**). Obtain specialist advice if planting mature trees. Larger specimens should not be planted within 6 m of buildings, further if subject to root formation.

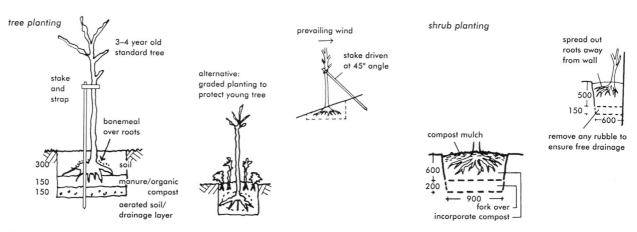

26 Recommended details for planting shrubs and trees

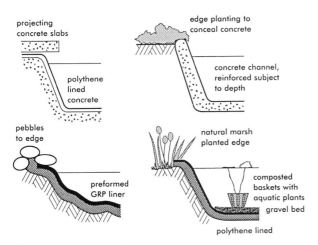

27 Range of edge details to garden pools

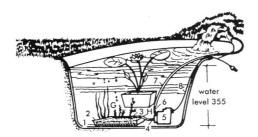

1 filter plate
2 filter tray
3 pipe fittings
4 pump fittings
5 under water pump
6 pipe fittings
7 hose to waterfall
8 cable with ground wire
H hose connection to pump
G filter mat and gravel

28 Filter system installed in prefabricated glass fibre pool

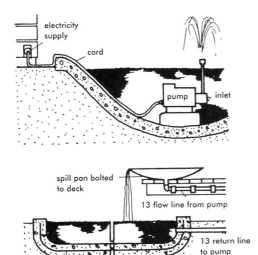

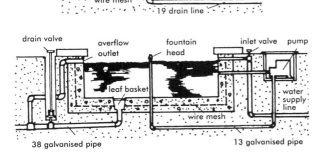

29 Plumbing and pumping systems

Water supply and features

Ensure adequate water supply for planting and features. Consider mains supply (may be metered), own well or rainwater retention.

Shallow wells   Sunk directly into water-bearing strata, the yield likely to fall off in dry weather. To prevent contamination risk, they should be at least 10 m from any septic tank or sewer main and constructed with water-tight lining.

Pools   Small pools may be constructed in variety of ways, depending upon site conditions and economics. The shape can be formal or natural. Prefabricated pools are usually plastic or glass fibre. Built-in pools using reinforcing concrete (125–150 mm thick) are cast in wooden forms or shaped excavations in firm soil lined with vinyl plastics before pouring. Pool edges need to be concealed: paving flags or coping stones are more suitable for formal shape pools, and grass, marsh plants or rocks for informal layouts, according to final effect desired (see **27**). Pools must be sited for maximum sun, high enough to ensure ground water does not enter during heavy rain, and near the water supply if it is not automatic. Depth of water should be no less than 300 mm so aquatic plants (e.g. water lilies) may be planted in open-sided containers for ease of removal. To prevent build up of algae, incorporate a recirculating pump system. Provide an overflow pipe and filters, removable for draining and cleaning (see **28,29**).

Fountains   A variety of waterfall effects and fountains can be created using pumped systems (see **31**).

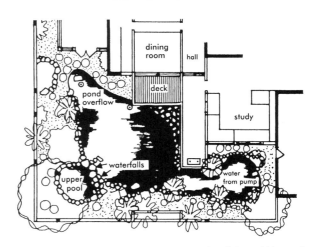

30 Garden arrangement largely devoted to fish and lily pool

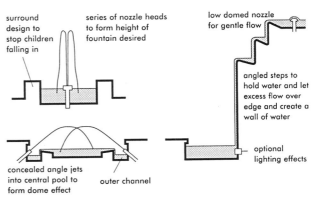

31 Range of fountain and waterfall effects

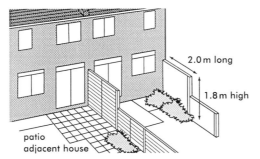

32 Recommended privacy screening and terracing

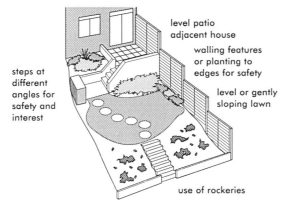

33 Suggestions for treating steeply sloping gardens

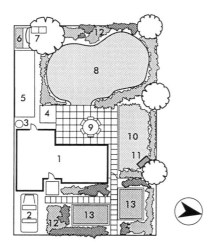

1 house
2 car parking space
3 refuse area
4 herb garden
5 vegetable garden
6 shed
7 compost area
8 garden lawn
9 seating area and terrace adjoining house
10 children's play area
11 seating area in shade
12 mixed flower borders
13 ponds

34 A garden layout incorporating typical requirements

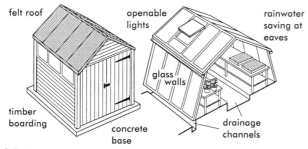

35 Typical garden shed and greenhouse

PRIVATE GARDENS

The preferred minimum size is 20 m² per habitable room of the dwelling. For privacy, a minimum length of 2.0 m, 1.8 m high screening is recommended between dwellings (see **32**). Adequate flat terracing to the immediate rear of property is desirable and steep gradients to the remainder should be avoided; if necessary split the garden into flatter terraces (see **33**).

Detailed design must consider orientation, user type, ratio of paving to planting to grassed area, garden furniture, storage of furniture and tools, compost disposal, play equipment, existing and proposed trees, vegetable and fruit growing and facilities for maintenance (see **34**).

Garden structures

- **Sheds** for storage of garden equipment and tools range in size from 1.2×1.8 m to 1.8×2.4 m as standard and are usually of timber construction (see **35**). There are no restrictions to siting unless within sensitive conservation areas.
- **Greenhouses** vary in size from the small lean-to of 600×1500 mm to larger independent Dutch light style (see **35**). There can be limitations on size, location and height of the structure. They may need to be heated (subject to type of cultivation) and ventilation is essential. Smaller hot or cold bed frame lights or cloches, which can be set on sliding tracks, may be considered. Automated watering systems are available.
- **Pergolas** are decorative wooden structures for terraces, walkways and supporting climbing plants (see **36**).
- **Gazebos and arbors** are decorative, folly like structures set in positions for effect and for occasional seating (see **37**).
- **Conservatories** are glazed structures attached to dwellings to create a semi-outdoor room (see **38,39**). A large range of sizes, styles and qualities is available. Limitations may prevail on size and height of structures, and the design should always be sympathetic to the existing property. Consider heat gain and need for shading, the type of internal finishes and environment to allow extensive use throughout the year.

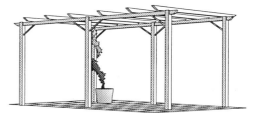

36 Construction and arrangement of pergolas

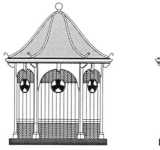

37 Decorative garden structures (as available from several manufacturers)

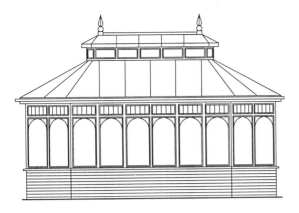

38 Typical conservatory elevation (as available from several manufacturers)

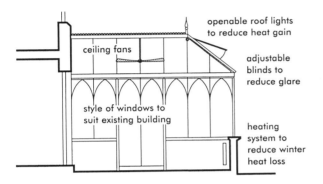

openable roof lights to reduce heat gain

ceiling fans

adjustable blinds to reduce glare

style of windows to suit existing building

heating system to reduce winter heat loss

39 Section through conservatory showing detail considerations

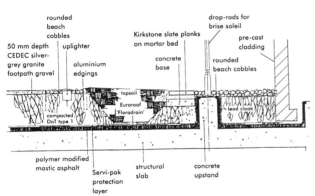

rounded beach cobbles

50 mm depth CEDEC silver-grey granite footpath gravel

uplighter

aluminium edgings

Kirkstone slate planks on mortar bed

drop-rods for brise soleil

pre-cast cladding

concrete base

rounded beach cobbles

topsoil

Euroroof 'Floradrain'

lead cloak

compacted DoT type 1

polymer modified mastic asphalt

Servi-pak protection layer

structural slab

concrete upstand

40 Detail section through roof garden, Wellcome Trust Genome Campus, Sanger Centre Courtyard, Hinxton, Cambridge (Landscape Arch: Elizabeth Banks Associates)

Roof gardens

The need to make better use of limited space has resulted in an increasing number of roof gardens. In their design, consider shade from nearby buildings, wind and pollution when choosing the location and plant types for roof gardens. Weight of soil is a factor in roof garden design: if the structural strength of the roof is in doubt, consider hydroponic gardening using a lightweight holding medium such as perlite or vermiculite (see **40,41**). It is desirable to set plants in containers or hanging baskets rather than beds for ease of replacement and weight reduction.

Larger commercial roof gardens are becoming common for reasons of appearance, provision of leisure space and insulating properties (see **42**). Concrete supporting structures must be designed to suit earth and plant loadings. It is important to consider the selection of the irrigation system at design stage.

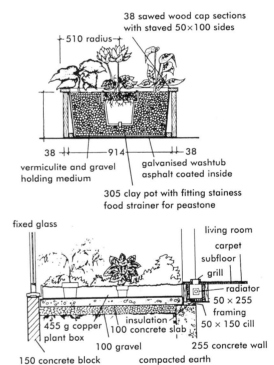

38 sawed wood cap sections with staved 50×100 sides

510 radius

38

914

38

vermiculite and gravel holding medium

galvanised washtub asphalt coated inside

305 clay pot with fitting stainess food strainer for peastone

fixed glass

living room

carpet

subfloor

grill

radiator

455 g copper plant box

insulation

100 concrete slab

50 × 255 framing

50 × 150 cill

150 concrete block

100 gravel

255 concrete wall

compacted earth

41 Sections through contained hydroponic and internal gardens

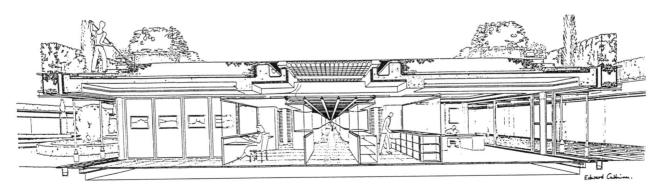

42 Section through roof garden, international headquarters of RMC Group PLC, Chertsey, Surrey (Arch: Edward Cullinan Architects)

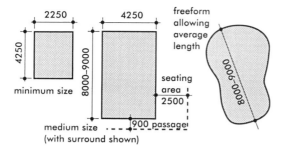

43 Standard dimensions of external and covered pools

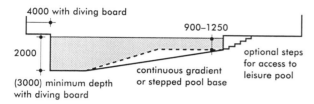

44 Typical section through standard private pool

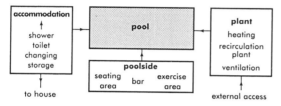

45 Typical pool accommodation requirements

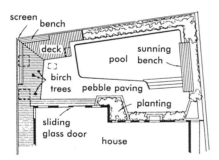

46 Deck at level of paving conceals filter equipment and heater below
(Designer: Armstrong & Sharfman)

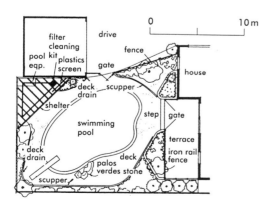

47 Perimeter fence at property line property line provides safety and background for plant materials, and shelter

Garden swimming pools

The shape and size of pools can vary (rectangular, curved end, circular, kidney or free form – see **43**) although rectangular shapes are more cost effective. Irrespective of shape, incorporate an 8 m minimum clear length for straight, regular swimming. Minimum water depths are: 900 mm for swimming, 1.25 m for standing, unless it will be used by young children (see **44**). Pool bases may be raked or level. Allow for shallow built-in steps or combined rail/step structure fixed to side.

The pool should be in a sheltered and sunny position, either adjacent to the house with combined terracing plus access to facilities or in a secluded area with its own patio, pump and changing areas (see **45**). Consider the position relative to trees to minimise problems with leaves.

Construction   Pool construction is usually of in situ concrete if excavated, but can be of steel if built-up. GRP basins with concrete backfill are also common. Internal surfaces are non-slip ceramic mosaic or terrazzo, or paint on waterproof lining.

Automatic covers are available for maintenance and reduction in heat loss. Water is kept clean via recirculation systems, skimmers, filters and chemicals.

Consider position of heating, circulation pump and filter systems for their protection and access for control (see **46,47**).

Indoor pools   The requirements are generally similar to outdoor pools. Water temperature should be 26–27°C, air temperature 30–31°C. Relative humidity can cause problems, so partial opening of the enclosure is desirable; and/or use a dehumidification system. For ventilation, use a system with either fresh or secondary air, with ducts in the ceiling and floor, or a simple ventilation box and extractor. Heating may be by radiators, convector heaters or warm-air heating, combined with air conditioning, or possibly a solar collector system. Underfloor heating provides extra comfort.

Consider energy saving by means of a heat pump or heat recovery using a heat exchanger in the air-conditioning plant, by covering the pool, or by raising air temperature in between use.

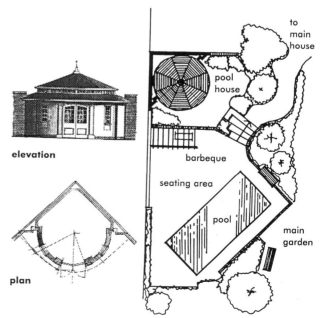

48 Decorative private pool house, Wimbledon, London
(Designer: Alan Cable)

PUBLIC AND COMMERCIAL LANDSCAPE WORKS

Landscape works to new public and commercial developments can enhance their appearance and provide an attractive setting. Larger schemes are often developed using a primary:secondary:tertiary strategy.

- **Primary** – or structural landscape: the predominant form and patterning intended for the overall site.
- **Secondary** – or framework landscape: the creation of development cells within the larger site, into which the buildings are located.
- **Tertiary** – landscape works of human scale in the immediate vicinity of the building (i.e. entrances, seating areas and parking).

Commercial schemes should consider capital and running costs, allowing for maintenance. Careful planning is required to suit construction phases and planting seasons.

A management programme using new techniques can develop good ecological balance of planting to encourage complementary pest avoiding growth (Injurious Weeds Act), limit weed problems and sharing of nutrients; the problem of early maturity and fast-growing planting against future maintenance can be considered, as can policies on thinning, pruning, replanting, level of ground cleaning and positive use of herbicides and mulches. 'Management plans', which take into account the above, may be required under the Planning Acts.

Designers also need to be aware of the implications of the Wildlife and Countryside Act, Tree Preservation Orders and the Environmental Agency edicts (including the Rivers Authority) which may affect their proposals.

The types of scheme can include:

Business park Use of existing and natural features or artificially created elements (e.g. copses, banks and lakes) to provide surrounding environment for commercial buildings (see **49**).

0 — 300m

1 northern meadows and woodlands, main entrance sequence; 2 Blythe Valley Countryside Park, SSSI with footpath network; 3 Hawkeshead Brook and Wetlands, SINC and natural water treatment; 4 eastern meadows, natural land art to motorway frontage; 5 plot landscapes, building perimeters and environs; 6 Greenways, existing hedgerows with paths and cycleways; 7 Central Boulevard, sculptural landscape spine; 8 Park Centre Lake, setting for the complex; 9 ha-ha, park perimeter statement and flood retention; 10 landscape features, character statements

49 General landscape layout to business park, Blythe Valley Park, Solihull, West Midlands (Landscape Arch: Munro & Whitten)

Industrial parks Emphasis generally rests on softening extensive parking and service areas by tree lining, planting divisions and screening to separate zones.

Office buildings Subject to space available, the emphasis is generally on enhancing the entrance area, both internally (see Atriums) and externally with planting immediately adjacent to or on the building.

Medical facilities and sheltered accommodation Adjacent spaces can be landscaped to form private gardens to improve the well-being of patients and residents. Differing surfaces, features and furniture are used for people with disabilities (see **50**)

Private housing Use of landscaping to provide an attractive setting for new dwellings or flats.

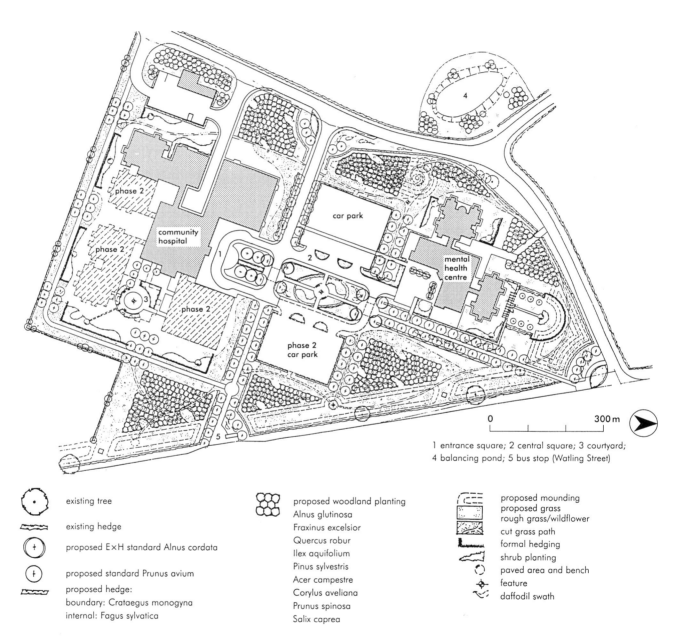

1 entrance square; 2 central square; 3 courtyard;
4 balancing pond; 5 bus stop (Watling Street)

existing tree

existing hedge

proposed E×H standard Alnus cordata

proposed standard Prunus avium

proposed hedge:
boundary: Crataegus monogyna
internal: Fagus sylvatica

proposed woodland planting
Alnus glutinosa
Fraxinus excelsior
Quercus robur
Ilex aquifolium
Pinus sylvestris
Acer campestre
Corylus aveliana
Prunus spinosa
Salix caprea

proposed mounding
proposed grass
rough grass/wildflower
cut grass path
formal hedging
shrub planting
paved area and bench
feature
daffodil swath

50 General landscape layout to Sir Robert Peel Hospital, Tamworth, Birmingham
(Landscape Arch: Jamie Buchanan)

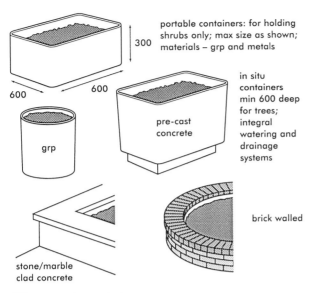

portable containers: for holding shrubs only; max size as shown; materials – grp and metals

300

600   600

grp

pre-cast concrete

in situ containers min 600 deep for trees; integral watering and drainage systems

brick walled

stone/marble clad concrete

51 Range of typical planters

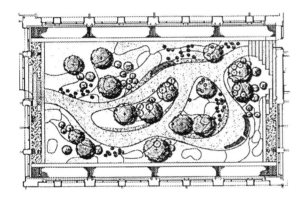

52 Plan of internal courtyard, Wellcome Trust Genome Campus, Sanger Centre Courtyard, Hinxton, Cambridge (Landscape Arch: Elizabeth Banks Associates)

Internal planting

The internal environment of buildings, from private houses to offices, shopping malls and civic buildings, are increasingly being enhanced by the incorporation of planting on a scale varying from window cill pot to elaborate atriums. All require careful maintenance of an appropriate temperature (15–20°C), plenty of light but not too much direct sunlight, regular watering, feeding and cleaning. Only specialist planting may require additional humidity control.

Planters   These range from free-standing decorative ceramic pots, glass reinforced plastic moulded containers, plated or coated steel planting troughs to in situ brick or concrete containers (see **51**) and are available in range of shapes and sizes, often with integrated automatic and semi-automatic watering systems.

Atriums   Usually large, central circulation spaces or entrance areas these act as visual enhancement to deep-plan cored buildings, as communication space or as prestige features (see **52,53**). Larger ones are often glazed at roof level, requiring automatic venting systems in case of fire.

Planting   Planter depth is important: 300–400 mm for 600 mm high plants, 600 mm for 2 m plants, 1500 mm plus for 10 m trees (see **53**). Large areas of planting will require increased structural allowance to cope with soil levels and drainage systems. Central building planting can suffer from insufficient light but can be assisted with artificial fittings. In public places, low-maintenance hydroculture systems can be used, especially in conjunction with water features, and are now available in synthetic form. The choice of plants (see **55**) is critical, as failures are common and costs can be prohibitive. Displays using a minimal range of species, ecologically balanced, have been successful.

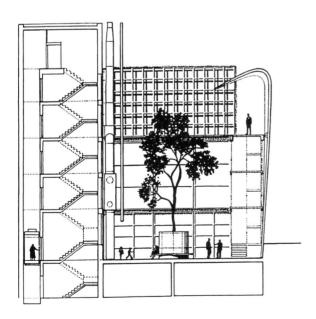

53 Cross-section through landscaped court, Artezium Arts and Media Centre, Luton (Arch: Fletcher Priest; image: Gerry Whale)

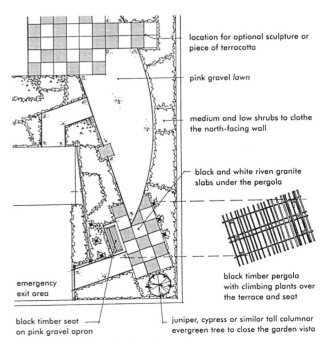

location for optional sculpture or piece of terracotta

pink gravel *lawn*

medium and low shrubs to clothe the north-facing wall

black and white riven granite slabs under the pergola

black timber pergola with climbing plants over the terrace and seat

emergency exit area

black timber seat on pink gravel apron

juniper, cypress or similar tall columnar evergreen tree to close the garden vista

54 Plan of enclosed external room, Royal Jordanian Embassy, London (Landscape Arch: Munro & Whitten)

Latin name	common name	form
Ficus benjamina	weeping fig	tree
Arundinaria nigra	bamboo	tree
Phoenix roebelinii	pygmy date palm	tree
Brassia actinophylla	umbrella tree	tree
Bucida buceras	shady lady,	
	black olive	tree
Ficus pumila	creeping fig	shrub
Cibotum chamissoi	tree fern	shrub
Cycas revoluta	sago palm	shrub
Helxine soleirolii	baby's tears	ground cover
Hedera helix	common ivy	ground cover
Philodendron scandens	sweetheart plant	ground cover
Spathiphyllum 'Mauna Loa'	peacy lily	ground cover

55 Commonly used plants for interior commercial project

STREET FURNITURE

Every street and public open space incorporates some form of street furniture. The designer or planner needs to consider co-ordination of the different elements, appropriateness of style, suitability of material and robustness of construction.

Seats Design to be comfortable, stable, vandalproof and immovable with low maintenance. Height 420 mm, depth 480–600 mm. Materials: timber and metal, occasionally concrete or grp. Bench formation, straight or curved for three or more people, or individual modular sections linked together (see **56**).

Bollards For divisions between vehicle and pedestrian areas; collapsible ones provide occasional access. Available in range of styles and materials (concrete, cast iron, steel or timber). Heights 550–900 mm, depending on use (see **57**).

Litter bins Design to be easily emptied and maintained, immovable and robust. Capacity 50–100 litres. There can be a conflict between security (keeping contents visible) and need for concealment to avoid odours (see **58**).

Railings For protective divisions between vehicle and pedestrian areas and level changes. Structural performance and fixing is important so as to resist laterally applied forces, especially around steep drops. A range of styles and materials are available (steel, cast iron and timber). Height 900 mm minimum; security barriers 1100 mm plus (see **59**).

Lighting Street lighting needs to serve pedestrians and vehicles, and provide security to pathways, indicators for steps or other obstacles and floodlighting of buildings. A range of styles, heights and bulb type exist for different locations and effect: pedestal, bollard, wall-mounted or bulkhead type with single or multiple fittings (See **60**).

In addition, the design of other street elements can be co-ordinated (tree grids, street signs, planters, bus shelters and canopies) – see **61,62**.

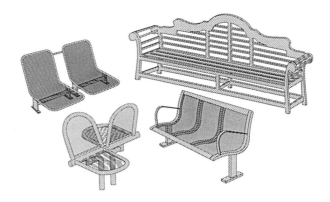

56 Range of typical external seats/benches

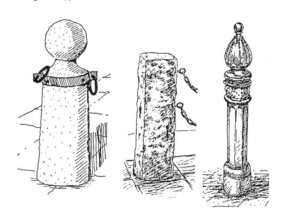

57 Range of typical bollards

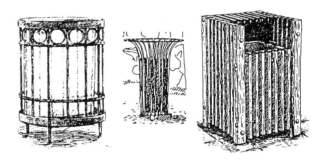

58 Range of typical litter bins

59 Range of typical railings for public places

60 Range of typical town centre street lighting

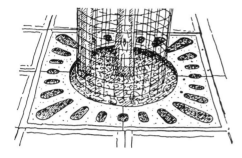

61 Typical tree grid

62 Typical public shelters

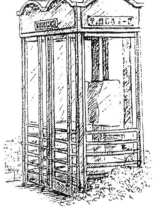

PUBLIC OPEN SPACES AND PARKS

The majority of towns and cities retain their public parks created up to a century ago whereas premium land values and lack of space usually preclude the formation of large new parks. Instead, smaller community based areas of open space are often created, in conjunction with housing or commercial developments.

Amenity spaces should be designed to suit the likely users: play equipment for young children, adequate seating for older residents and appropriate activity and leisure facilities for mixed use (see **63**).

The landscape architect considers the overall layout of the space or park to provide logical access and an interesting environment. There is a need for the following facilities:

- General: car parking, conveniences, refreshments, information and events areas.
- Leisure: hard and soft training areas and pitches, tennis courts, bowling greens and children's play equipment.

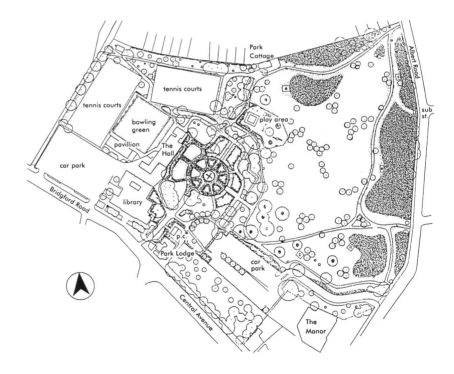

⊙ existing trees	— existing hedges	● hexagonal seats repaired
⊙ proposed trees	grass areas	– park benches
proposed woodland planting	footpaths fibre-dec surface	▦ trim trail equipment
☐ existing shrub/rose beds	brick paving	
proposed shrub planting	⊙ pool and fountain	

63 Landscape masterplan, Bridgford Park
(Landscape Arch: Ian Stemp Landscape Associates)

Also, discrete gardens for passive leisure activity, plant displays, picnicking and even barbecues.

- Water based: sailing and boating lakes, ornamental ponds and fountains.
- External artwork: sculpture, forms and spaces add to the landscape to give an interesting and exciting experience for the visitor.

New larger open spaces are moving away from the traditional public park, with examples including environmental and educational landscapes, nature reserves and amusement/theme parks (see **64,65**).

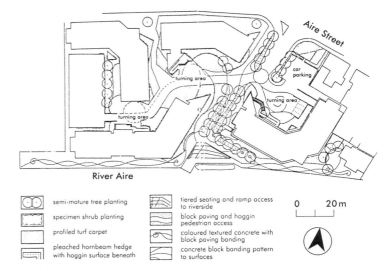

semi-mature tree planting

specimen shrub planting

profiled turf carpet

pleached hornbeam hedge with hoggin surface beneath

tiered seating and ramp access to riverside

block paving and hoggin pedestrian access

coloured textured concrete with block paving banding

concrete block banding pattern to surfaces

0   20 m

64 Riverside walk, Leeds
(Landscape Arch: Horsman Woolley)

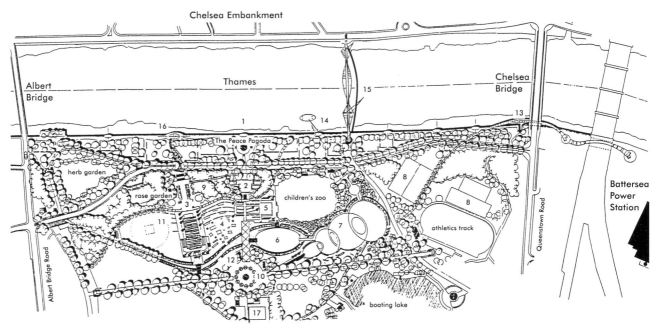

1 river promenade; 2 central plaza; 3 grand vista; 4 Queen's garden; 5 artists' garden; 6 events arena W; 7 events arena E; 8 tennis courts; 9 fire garden; 10 central avenue; 11 transverse paths; 12 pleached plum avenues; 13 the walkway; 14 landing stage; 15 Millennium Bridge; 16 restaurant; 17 bowling green

0   200 m

65 Landscape masterplan, Battersea Park competition, London
(Landscape Arch: Munro & Whitten)

Garden centres

With the growth in landscape works and gardening activities, there has been an increase in the number of garden centres. These vary between small town-based ones supplying house plants, smaller shrubs and containers, to extensive nurseries selling a wide range of plants, including trees and shrubs, equipment, furniture, sheds and greenhouses. The larger centres require ample parking, facilities for loading and transporting plants, display areas for a full range of plants, tools, equipment and outdoor structures, glasshouses for cultivation and open nursery beds.

Landscape engineering works

Landscape works also involve the planned improvement or alteration of existing areas of land. Large-scale engineering schemes include the landfilling of disused industrial works (e.g. mines), together with waste management sites, reformation after major services installations, treatment of slopes adjacent new transportation routes, reclamation of coastal or marshland areas and diversion of water courses.

LAW COURTS

Patricia Beecham

INTRODUCTION

Law courts are public buildings which are part of the long and complex history of the legal system, with roots that go back to Anglo-Saxon Britain.

The Lord Chancellor's Department has existed in various forms for over 900 years. Since 1972 it has existed as a major government department with wide responsibilities for the administration of justice in England and Wales. Following the Courts Act, 1971, it was made directly responsible for running a new system covering all courts above the level of Magistrates' Courts. In 1995 the Court Service, an executive agency, was created to manage the Crown and County Courts. Magistrates' Courts remain the responsibility of the Lord Chancellor's Department.

The court system

- The House of Lords (the highest Court of Appeal).
The Lord Chancellor's Department embraces:
- The Court of Appeal (two divisions, criminal and civil; normally never sits outside London)
- The Royal Courts of Justice
- The High Court
- The Crown Court
- The County Court
- The Magistrates' Courts (policy only)
- Various tribunals (e.g. VAT).

section

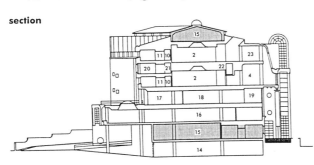

third floor

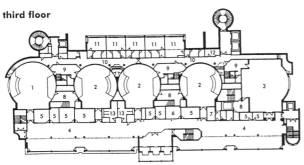

1 medium court; 2 small court; 3 large court; 4 lower concourse; 5 consultation; 6 witness support; 7 special witness; 8 defendants' waiting; 9 jury waiting; 10 judges' corridor; 11 judges' retiring room; 12 exhibits; 13 toilets; 14 car parking; 15 plant; 16 crown and county general office; 17 judiciary dining; 18 barristers' dining; 19 justices' dining; 20 jurors' retiring room; 21 jurors' corridor; 22. defendants' corridor; 23. upper concourse

1 Newcastle Combined Courts Centre: principal public concourse level to courtrooms on third floor
(Arch: Napper Architects)

TYPES OF COURT

The Crown Court Until 1972 criminal trial by jury was carried out by the Assizes and the Quarter Sessions. These courts had their origins in the medieval government of the kingdom. Originally, the Assizes were held in great halls in royal castles, while the Quarter Sessions were usually held in local town halls. Purpose-built courthouses began to appear in the 17th century, but it was only in the second half of the 18th century that they began to assume a distinctive plan.

The increasing complexity of the law, the higher status of the legal profession and rapidly growing urban populations during the 19th century led to the Assize and Sessions courts becoming larger and more complicated. In 1972 the creation of the Crown Court prompted a wave of construction that transformed the building type.

The Crown Court is a national court which sits continuously in major towns and cities in England and Wales. Practically all its work is concerned with cases committed for trial or sentence from the Magistrates' Courts, or appeals against their decisions.

County Courts These came into existence to meet the need for the resolution of civil disputes in a more accessible or cheaper forum than the High Court.

In 1846, County Courts replaced the previous ad hoc system of Courts of Request and Courts of Conscience for dealing with small debts. County Courts deal with private disputes between individuals and are quite separate from Magistrates' Courts and Crown Courts. They are now usually located in modern city-centre office buildings, frequently alongside other government departments.

The Combined Court Centre Since 1972 nearly 40 Combined Court Centres have been created to accommodate both County Courts and Crown Courts. They contain accommodation for the Crown Court and a smaller suite of rooms for the County Court. Both share a common central entrance and main public spaces.

Magistrates' Courts These are the people's courts and their fundamental basis is justice delivered not by professional judges or lawyers but by appointed representatives of the local community. The Magistrates' Court developed from The Petty Sessions, which were developed to deal swiftly with minor criminal offences and were held when required in the private houses of Justices of the Peace, in town halls and frequently in public houses. By the mid-19th century, reforms led to a regular pattern of sittings. Town halls continued to be the most common venue but purpose-built courthouses also developed. Since 1949, when the name 'Magistrates' Court' was adopted, they have been independent of the police. Consequently, new buildings have been separate from, though frequently adjacent to, a local police station.

Coroners' Courts These courts are specifically for the holding of inquests into the cause of death. Inquest accommodation provided since 1965 has been in the form of court rooms in other buildings.

The future

A current review examines the Crown Court and Magistrates' Courts as a single entity for the first time. The possibility of a single Criminal Justice system would be made more efficient by introducing a single procedural code and unified information technology. A combined Crown Court and Magistrates' Courts system could share court buildings. This would lead to the closure of many Magistrates' Courts and extensions to many Crown Courts. It would probably lead to the development of a new type of court building housing all criminal and civil courts.

THE COURT BUILDING

The majority of new court buildings occupy a prominent site in towns and civic centres and are often physically and symbolically closely related to other historic civic buildings. However, although an important civic building, the courthouse function is strictly utilitarian so the aim is to produce a civilised building that functions well and gives good value for money.

The building should have 'an aura of calm and quiet dignity, security, durability and permanence; a feeling of quality of materials, workmanship and design; an imposing edifice and an enhancement of the local environment.' The building needs to be simple and efficient to use and sympathetic to the tensions and pressures generated within a court.

The courthouse should 'be seen less as a symbol of authority than as an expression of the concept of justice and equality before the law'. It should express tradition, but acknowledge that the law is constantly evolving. The expectation is that the building will have a long life: courtrooms built 200 years ago are still able to satisfy their original function, and it should be anticipated that present-day courts could also operate well into the future given sufficient flexibility in ancillary accommodation in which changes will inevitably occur.

Entrances

Law court buildings have to be recognised externally and understood internally. 'The designer should aim through architectural style and symbols to clearly show the visitor where to enter the building.'

There are normally three entrances, one for defendants in custody via a very secure vehicle lock, a secure route for judges, magistrates and vulnerable users and a main entrance for all other users, staff and public, screened by building security. (Special cases such as the Bournemouth Court, which is designed to handle sensitive issues such as child cases, can be provided with four – see **5**.)

Access for people with disabilities

Unimpeded wheelchair access must be provided both to the public area via the public entrance door and also to the well of the court via the main entrance.

section

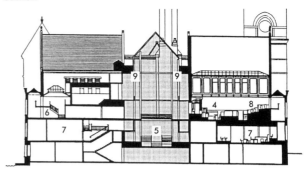

ground floor

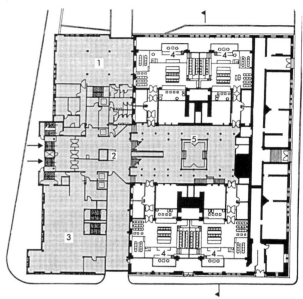

▨ new extension

1 advocates' lounge; 2 information desk; 3 administration; 4 original courtrooms; 5 public concourse and atrium; 6 public concourse; 7 new courtroom; 8 public gallery; 9 original ventilation ducts adapted for modern air-conditioning

2 Crown Courts, Minshull Street, Manchester: renovation of four Victorian courtrooms, with four new courtrooms inserted at ground level; two new courtrooms and ancillary accommodation in new extension; new concourse, formed from the original courtyard, is heart of the building; providing segregated circulation for public, jury and judiciary on four levels, it connects old and new parts of the building, both literally and architecturally
(Arch: Hurd Rolland Partnership)

Planning relationships/circulation

The plan has to balance the conflicting demands of separating different users within the building while allowing them to meet for the trial or hearing. It is the culmination of hundreds of years of development in the layout of courtrooms.

Each category of participant has to enter court at their designated seating area which can be reached from the area of the building they are allowed to visit. As a consequence law courts inevitably have a complex plan to balance the conflicting demands of separation prior to all parties meeting up in the courtroom.

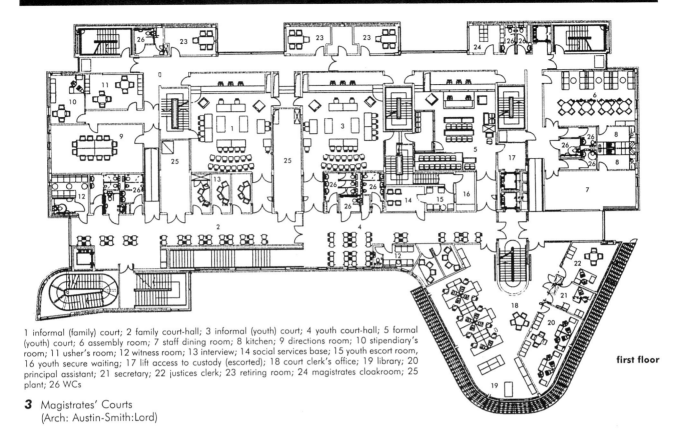

first floor

1 informal (family) court; 2 family court-hall; 3 informal (youth) court; 4 youth court-hall; 5 formal (youth) court; 6 assembly room; 7 staff dining room; 8 kitchen; 9 directions room; 10 stipendiary's room; 11 usher's room; 12 witness room; 13 interview; 14 social services base; 15 youth escort room, 16 youth secure waiting; 17 lift access to custody (escorted); 18 court clerk's office; 19 library; 20 principal assistant; 21 secretary; 22 justices clerk; 23 retiring room; 24 magistrates cloakroom; 25 plant; 26 WCs

3 Magistrates' Courts
(Arch: Austin-Smith:Lord)

Symbols An important supplement to the architectural form, symbols reinforce the recognition of the courthouse. A figurative interpretation of 'justice', one of the four 'cardinal virtues', often appears. The Royal Arms are prominently and permanently incorporated in the fabric of the building and are mandatory features in all courts. In addition to Royal Arms, civic coats of arms may appear on the exterior of court buildings and even in courtrooms.

Signs These are important to ensure that court users enter by the correct door and occupy the appropriate seating in the courtroom.

Information technology The introduction of IT hardware is likely to have tangible effects on existing court buildings. In the future, computers are likely to be used increasingly during trials. Computers are already being used for giving evidence, and the increasing use of video links allows sensitive witnesses to give evidence without entering the courtroom.

Infrastructure for IT is needed. Raised floors permit flexible arrangements of trunking beneath floors, and appropriate electrical supplies and furniture suitable for electronic equipment are required.

The Design Guides Every aspect of court design is closely prescribed and is subject to the detailed requirements laid out in the design guides issued by the Lord Chancellor's Department. There are two guides, the *Combined Courts Design Guide* and the *Magistrates' Court Design Guide*, and they contain sections that deal with the procedures, costs and the functional relationships between different users. Very detailed specifications of each element of a courthouse are given.

THE CROWN COURTROOM

Courtroom layout

The design parameters of the courtroom are continually evolving, subject to the continuous adjustments dictated by changes in attitudes to such matters as child witnesses, the need to protect witnesses and jurors from possible intimidation and developments in technology. Courtroom design has recently been modified to accommodate more flexible furniture layouts and the implications of information technology, aspects which will continue to change.

Although it occupies under 10% of total building area, the courtroom is the primary workspace and focal point of a courthouse, which is developed around it. It is the only place where all parties in a case are intended to meet. Of paramount importance is the need to segregate judge, jury, defendant and others in the courtroom and within the courthouse.

Relationships within the courtroom

Courtroom layout incorporates specific and well-defined relationships between the various participants by means of carefully arranged sight-lines, distances and levels. Lines of sight must be complied with to enable the court to function satisfactorily and for the judge to maintain full control of the proceedings.

There are four main elements in Crown Court cases:
- judge
- jury
- witness
- counsel (barristers and solicitors).

Relationships are all-important – e.g. witnesses are asked questions by the counsel but they are expected to address their answers to the judge. When

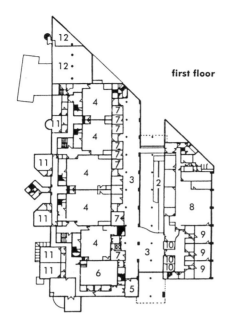

first floor

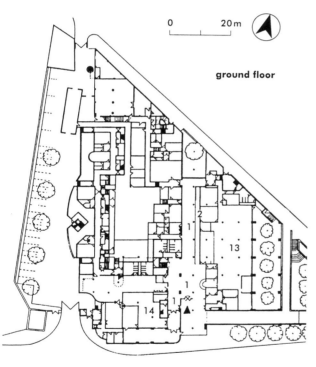

```
0        20m
```

ground floor

1 public concourse; 2 ramp, stair and lift; 3 waiting area and long gallery; 4 crown courtrooms; 5 waiting area for children beside the County Court separated from gallery by glazed screen; 6 County Court; 7 consultation rooms for barristers and solicitors, between them are the lobbies to the courtrooms; 8 Crown Court offices; 9 registrar's suites; 10 consultation rooms; 11 judges' suites; 12 plant; 13 County Court offices; 14 public dining

4 Northampton Crown and County Courts: design is composed of three major elements – court building containing high, naturally lit courts at first floor level and ancillary accommodation at ground floor level, the office building containing administrative functions and district judges' chambers, and between them a two-storey public concourse with glazed roof
(Arch: Kit Allsopp Architects)

answering the questions their responses should be visible to the jury.

Defendants do not take part except as witnesses. Each element must be closely related, and be able to see and hear each other clearly at all times without mechanical or electrical aids, and without excessive turning from side to side.

Factors determining the position of the main courtroom elements

The judge presides over the courtroom, and should be able to observe the whole of it to see clearly the principal participants as well as the defendant in the dock and, when called, the antecedents and probation officers.

The court clerk administers the case and needs to keep a watchful eye over the court. He or she often advises the judge and should be able to stand up and speak to the judge without being overheard.

The exhibit table is in front of the counsel benches for the display of exhibits put forward for evidence.

Counsel are barristers and solicitors who represent the defendant or prosecution. They need to be able to see the jury, judge and witness to whom they address their remarks. The barrister at each end of the front bench should be able to keep every jury member and the witness on the stand in view within about a 90° angle to obviate too much turning and to ensure that the judge, the other main party, shall have at least a partial view of his or her face. The counsel benches are wide enough to hold the large and numerous documents and books that are often in use.

The defendant is assumed to be innocent until proved guilty and current practice is to reduce any prison-like appearance of the dock by lowering the barriers enclosing it as much as possible and compatible with security. Defendants sit in separate fixed seats and if they are thought to be a security risk a prison officer will sit on a seat immediately behind, or at each side of them. The dock is controlled by a dock officer and situated at the back of the courtroom.

The jury comprises 12 members of the public whose duty it is to reach a verdict based on the evidence presented. The jury sit opposite the witness stand and must be able to see the defendant in the dock, as well as the judge and counsel. They must have a writing surface and a place to put documents.

The witness waits outside the courtroom, and when called gives evidence from the witness stand near to the judge's bench. The stand faces the jury who must be able to observe the witness's face. The witness is questioned by the barristers and occasionally by the judge. If the judge directs that a witness should be retained, he or she can wait seated within the courtroom.

The shorthand writer keeps a transcript of the trial and consequently must be able to see and hear everyone who speaks.

Probation and antecedents officers give evidence from their seats after the jury have reached a verdict. This evidence is used to assist the judge in passing sentence

The press are not party to the proceedings but they should be able to see the participants.

The public are in court to see that justice is done. They are placed at the near end of the courtroom and have a general view of the proceedings, but with the minimum possible direct eye contact with the jury to reduce the risk of intimidation. A public gallery over the jurors is the most effective method of eliminating possible intimidation but security problems of access to such a gallery and the increase in height of the courtroom has to be considered. In the most recent courts the public seating faces the bench and a screen impedes the public's view of the jury to reduce possible intimidation of jurors.

The glass screen between the public and the dock is partially obscured to prevent members of the public from seeing the defendants(s) (and vice versa) while seated.

THE COURTROOM ENVIRONMENT

There is constant pressure to improve environmental standards both within the courtroom and in the many and varied spaces within the complex layout of the court building.

Lighting
After the controlled environment courthouses of the 1980s, many users expressed a preference for more traditional designs incorporating natural light and high ceilings.

Daylight is now a requirement for all courtrooms but direct sunlight must be controlled and security risks avoided. Supplementary artificial lighting in the form of a combination of uplighters and downlighters reduces glare and contrast, and enhances the character of the courtroom. Lighting levels and colour should ensure correct colour rendering and that all participants, exhibits and written evidence can be clearly seen without strain or dazzle.

Ventilation
Well-balanced and easily managed environmental conditions within the courtroom are essential to the smooth running of the court. They keep the participants comfortable and interested, and prevent distractions. The current trend, supported by most users, is to move away from full air-conditioning and provide natural ventilation with openable windows. This will subject the courtroom to wider temperature fluctuations but this can be minimised by integrated automatic control systems.

Mechanical assistance (or, in extreme cases, full air-conditioning) will be necessary where there would be unacceptable noise intrusion or where the courtroom cannot have the height to induce air flow by the natural stack effect. It is normally more economical and energy-efficient to have separate air-handling units for each courtroom, managed by time switches and occupancy sensors.

Acoustics
The acoustics and noise levels should ensure that the proceedings can be heard in all parts of the courtroom, while avoiding distraction and annoyance from movement by the public, press or others. There may be a need for reflective or absorbent surface treatment to walls and ceilings.

THE COURTHOUSE
Functional relationships
Within a courthouse there are at least eight groups of people each requiring a range of accommodation within a separate area, each with its own self-contained circulation. These are the judiciary, jury, public, custody, barrister/solicitor, catering, courthouse staff, building services.

Movement between areas is limited and restricted. Even those who need to move freely can only enter certain restricted areas by passing through manned control points or other secure doors.

Four segregated circulation routes are provided so that the judge, jury and defendants in custody make their way to the courtroom without meeting each other or any other users such as members of the public.

Some prosecution witnesses have to be protected from intimidation; a separate secure waiting room for them is often situated with its entrance off the vestibule provided between the public entrance and the courtroom itself. An alternative arrangement has a separate access from the secure waiting area into the courtroom adjacent to the witness box.

The public enter the court behind or to the side of the public seating at the rear of the courtroom; neither public nor witnesses pass areas dedicated to other participants (e.g. jury or defendants in custody) on entering or leaving the courtroom.

Judiciary The judiciary (judges, recorders, etc.) arrive at the court building and enter through a manned or otherwise restricted entry directly into their own secure area of the building. This contains the judges' retiring rooms and all areas devoted to judicial use.

The only other users of this area in 'working hours' are the staff (i.e. ushers, court clerks, security staff and invitees, e.g. legal representatives), guests and some members of the public invited to a judge's room. Invitees will always be escorted, and access for all will be either via the judges' entrance into court or through staff areas. Each entrance will be via a self-locking, secure door.

Jurors Jurors enter through the main public areas until they reach the reception area to the jury assembly suite, where they are booked in. They then wait in the lounge or dining area, where refreshments are available, until called upon to form a jury panel. The period of waiting is variable and can be all day. Once jurors have entered the jury assembly suite they remain there, in court, or the jury retiring room until sent home at the end of the day, or on dismissal.

Egress from the assembly area, other than back past reception, is into jury-restricted circulation, which leads to court and jury retiring rooms. These should be adjacent or close to related courtrooms, and all capable of supervision by one jury bailiff.

5 Bournemouth Combined Courts: linear plan, dictated by the site, splits into nine main components;
entered centrally there are flexible open-plan offices to the left with jury assembly, general dining and police to the right;
behind the reception are cells accessed from the secure rear;
public generally use the first floor waiting/consulting rooms along the front of the building;
five main and two ancillary courts form the core with civil courts to one end for privacy and there is also a child case court room designed to deal with the sensitive needs of children in legal procedures;
behind the courts are judges and jury retiring rooms on two levels with views out;
judges, jury, defendants and public have separate entrances to court rooms, while defendants and candidates for victim support have separate waiting areas;
this is the first new-build court to have naturally ventilated courtrooms, utilising the stack effect to draw in cool external air through underground ducts
(Arch: Stride Treglown)

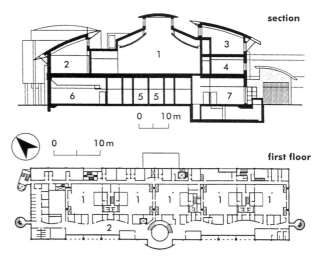

1 courtroom; 2 waiting; 3 jury retiring; 4 judge retiring; 5 cell; 6 arrival/meeting; 7 jury dining

Defendants The custody area is a self-contained compartment within the court building designated for the temporary use of prison governors in the discharge of their duties to the court to produce and retain prisoners in custody. It consists of the following principal parts, each separate from its neighbour and all non-custody uses:

- the custody core
- the vehicle entrance
- the visitors' entrance
- the courtroom entrance
- three independent secure connecting routes:
  – custody core to vehicle dock
  – custody core to courtroom entrance
  – custody core to visitors' entrance.

While courts are sitting, the custody area is staffed and administered by prison officers. A principal or senior officer is in charge, supported by number of officers according to the number of courts and the level of risk.

Custody areas are designed and constructed to contain defendants, and to produce them to the court. Containment requires the meticulous and consistent application of passive security measures. Confinement and attendance at court for defendants is stressful, and this is compounded by natural frustration and anxiety. The designer must therefore:

- Devise a layout that will achieve maximum control, make the best use of staff resources and maintain an acceptable level of safety and security.
- Use the building fabric and the facilities within it to provide a secure envelope.
- Deny the public direct view or contact with defendants while they are inside the custody area, except during authorised visits.
- Pay careful attention to all aspects of the design from the overall plan and its approaches, down to fixtures, fittings, finishes, alarms and communications to prevent the possibility of any fixtures and fittings being used as weapons, with detailing to minimise injury in an affray and prevent self-harm.

Public The public areas, with their associated circulation, form the central core or axis from which most non-judicial functions of the court building radiate.

Except for the judiciary and specified car-park users, all users enter the building by the main entrance door where space and facilities for security checks are provided. The arrival concourse contains the information/enquiry point and the case-list display, both of which should be clearly seen on entering.

Public circulation then leads to court waiting areas. These may be combined with associated circulation to form concourses off which are located the courtrooms and consultation/waiting rooms. Waiting areas should be visually interesting, preferably with external views. Public circulation also gives access to private and semi-private accommodation occupied by Court Service (CS) staff, non-CS staff, the probation service, custody visits and to refreshment facilities. Access must also be available to the Crown Court office counters. Direct access from the arrivals concourse to the jury assembly area is desirable.

The Crown Court office This is occupied by executive and administrative staff engaged in the general administration of Crown Court business.

The general office counter must be conveniently located to allow easy access for the public and for the legal professionals. There should be separate circulation to other staff areas and for direct access to the judges restricted circulation by ushers. Within the Crown Court offices, accommodation is provided for some more specialised groups (e.g. court clerks, ushers and listing staff).

Non-courts service users Such users include police, Crown Prosecution Service, probation service and shorthand writers, all concerned with the running of the court.

- The police area consists of two sections:
  – The Police Liaison Unit offices for police staff attached to the courts and providing antecedents,

etc. Included is a room where police witnesses can assemble and change if necessary.

- The Police Law and Order Unit offices for police who maintain security or 'law and order' in the building (currently under review).

■ The Crown Prosecution Service needs an office.

■ The probation service: the probation suite is a separate individual unit and where night reporting facilities are required and must be able to operate in isolation while full security to the remainder of the court building is maintained.

Catering

Catering within Crown Courts involves self-service facilities together with waitress service for the judiciary. The catering area should be sited on one floor with easy access for all court users.

DESIGN VARIATIONS WITH NON-CROWN COURTS

Magistrates' courts

Magistrates' courts deal mainly with criminal matters but they have some civil jurisdiction, including licensing, youth cases and family cases.

The Lord Chancellor's Department would like the design to reflect their position in the courts hierarchy and their unique position as places where justice is administered by representatives of the local community. The building should be seen less as a symbol of authority than as an expression of the concept of justice and equality before the law.

The principal zones

(1) the court hall and public areas; may be divided into adult and youth areas
(2) the courts
(3) the clerk to the justices department
(4) the magistrates' area
(5) the custody area.

Also a small zone is required for the welfare suite, and plant areas.

Two-storey options are generally preferred for courthouses of up to 12 courts. Where practicable a single-storey solution should be considered for courthouses housing six or less courts.

Courtrooms should be on one level if possible.

Courthouse users

These include: magistrates, clerk to justices and staff, ushers, custodial staff, applicants and complainants, defendants; adult and youths, witnesses, police witnesses, probation and aftercare staff, welfare services staff, Crown Prosecution Service, advocates, public and press.

The courtroom

The docks are at the side of the courtroom as there is no jury. These courtrooms are usually smaller and have less furniture than Crown Courts.

The *Magistrates' Courts Design Guide* (1991) increased emphasis on security, both in and around the building and also within the courtrooms. The convenience of the court users was considered to be secondary to security within the design.

section: upper levels of courtrooms are entered on bridges across void of concourse

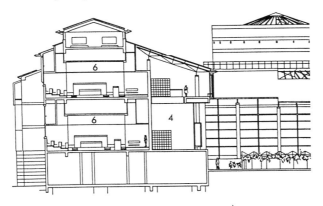

1 security
2 arrival/meeting area
3 court waiting
4 glazed concourse
5 medium court
6 small court
7 county court
8 registrar waiting
9 bailiff
10 listing office
11 general office

6 Preston Combined Court Centre: two linear blocks of accommodation are linked and ordered by an entrance rotunda and arranged around a new public open space; court building relates to adjacent, modern law-and-order buildings (police headquarters and magistrates' court), providing a new public campus; courtrooms are stacked on three levels above secure areas; daylit courtrooms are 'twinned' to economise on vertical circulation; each courtroom is treated as a self-contained entity, giving recognition to the importance of processes taking place within (Arch: Austin-Smith:Lord)

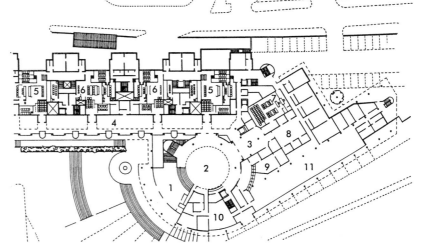

lower-level floor plan: rotunda provides access to one wing of courtrooms and another of offices

Family proceedings courts These courts, where family matters are heard, are held in informal courtrooms within the magistrates' courts building and are usually physically separate from the criminal courts.

County courts Cases concern disputes between parties, individuals asserting claims against other individuals, bodies or the state. Therefore there is no dock but there are two witness stands, at opposite sides of the room, occupied by the defendant and the claimant. Furnishings are sparser and less expensive than in Crown Courts. They are generally less formalised, with a more balanced layout. There are only two entrances; the judge's secure entrance and that for all other participants. Freed from the constraint of needing separate access for the defendant and jury, the planning of the court within the building is more flexible – however, it is customary to locate all county court functions in reasonable proximity to each other either horizontally or vertically.

Areas immediately associated are:

- A sound lobby to insulate the courtroom from the noise and disturbance of court waiting/public areas.
- Court waiting to connect to the public concourse.
- Consultation/waiting rooms located off waiting area or contiguous circulation.

- Restricted circulation for judges, leading to:
  - judges' retiring suites and district judges' chambers
  - public circulation.

Accommodation required
Judiciary, district judges, jury and defendants require similar accommodation to the Crown Court.

Advocates' suite
- area for solicitors and barristers to prepare for court
- court waiting areas to provide access to legal areas where advocates meet their clients to discuss cases and gain access to courtrooms
- advocates' dining room.

Combined court office This has a number of functions, many of which involve direct contact with the public.

The public counter should be as near as possible to the main entrance.

The combined court centre The county court usually has a separate waiting area for people waiting to see the district judges in their chambers. There are normally separate offices for the two courts. The civil courts differ from the criminal courts in having no dock and often they have moveable, rather than fixed, furnishings.

LIBRARIES AND LEARNING RESOURCE CENTRES

INTRODUCTION

The concept of the 'public library' evolved from the Guildhall Library in 15th century London. In the 17th and 18th centuries, most libraries were created by gift or endowment, but by the beginning of the 19th century, these had generally been superseded by either institutional (e.g. those attached to mechanics' institutes or literary and philosophical societies) or subscription libraries. The Public Libraries Act of 1850 was one of several social reforms of the mid-19th century, and was generally intended to create 'free libraries', available to all classes of society throughout the country. The first two purpose-designed public libraries were Norwich and Warrington, in 1857.

The Public Libraries Act of 1919 further extended library provision. Besides the lending library and the reading room, most libraries now had a reference department, and many had separate children's departments. After 1918 there was a considerable increase in technical and commercial libraries (over 115 by 1924). By the 1930s, most libraries had adopted open access (as opposed to books being available over a counter via the library staff), which required more sophisticated classification and cataloguing systems – the Dewey system was generally adopted.

After World War II, the creation of the welfare state had a great influence on library provision, and this led particularly to an increase in reference and study facilities. Libraries for the first time extensively began to offer material other than books – for instance, gramophone records, then music cassettes, videos and CD ROMs. Invariably, however, these were regarded as complementary to books, rather than as a replacement for them.

The Public Libraries & Museums Act of 1964 incorporated several recommendations. Finance became available for many library authorities: in the early 1960s, over 300 new library buildings were built in the UK. The buildings tended to reflect 'modern movement' ideals (the last of the typical old-style neo-classical designs probably being Kensington Central Library, London, 1960). The new buildings were large urban central libraries (e.g. Holborn, London (1960), Hampstead, London (1964) and Hornsey, London (1965)), county libraries (e.g. Stafford (1961), Durham (1963) and Maidstone (1964)) and branch libraries (e.g. Jesmond, Newcastle (1963)). The latter was round in plan, and there were many other experimental shapes: e.g. triangular (Eccleshill, Bradford, 1964) and octagonal (e.g. Selsey, West Sussex, 1964). The use of modern materials, particularly glass, was seen as complementary to changing organisational patterns and a blurring of distinctions between different departments; open planning was seen to have many advantages. The problems of storage were alleviated with the development of microfilm, and then computers.

Increasing literacy and leisure time plus the 'information explosion' make it important to plan for maximum flexibility and for future expansion.

New techniques are changing methods of control, indexing and retrieval. The growing availability of computerised information (particularly on compact discs and on-line electronic systems) means there is a change in emphasis from book storage to information exchange utilising computer equipment. These require additional ventilation and secure power supplies, and suitable lighting levels for users. The wide availability of computers means that the problem of space, and particularly the location of a library in a single building, may no longer be critical.

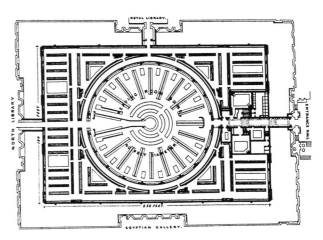

1 British Museum Reading Room (1854–7)
(Arch: Sydney Smirke; illustration © British Museum Central Archives)

Types

- *Community*: primarily lending books to adults and children, and with a general reference section. Current trend is towards larger central libraries with branch satellites; rural areas are often served by mobile units.
- *Specialised*: primarily used for reference, with small loan section.
- *University*: used for reference and research; collections continually growing.

Note that there are many other types of specialised library, which are not covered here – for example, in hospitals, prisons, schools, learned associations (e.g. the British Architectural Library at the RIBA), and national libraries (e.g. the British Library).

Several new learning resources centres (LRCs) have been completed, often at the newer universities (e.g. Brighton, Hertfordshire, Teesside, Manchester Metropolitan, and Sheffield Hallam). By the mid-1990s, over 60 universities and colleges were intending to provide new LRCs, aiming to serve an extra 200 000 students.

Preferred space standards, from the Follett Report, are:

- one space for 6 full-time-equivalent students
- 2.39 m² per reader (subsequent research indicates that 2.5–3.0 m² may be required)
- reader modules to be minimum of 900 × 600 mm
- information technology (IT) spaces to be 1200 × 800 mm. (See **2**.)

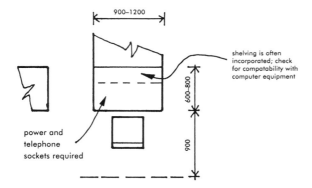

2 Study desk/open carrel (2.39 m² but 2.5–3.0 m² preferred): note (1) research workers traditionally require enclosed carrel or small room, area 3.5 m² approximately; (2) larger dimensions are for where computing equipment is required

Note that planning must allow for noisy areas. It is also important for libraries to be easily accessible for those with disabilities (including sight- and hearing-impaired people).

A public library should encourage the following uses: browsing, seeking, studying, meeting, and borrowing. Major trends likely to influence library design in the foreseeable future include: a 30% increase in pensioners by 2025, and a significant diminution in those of working age; a significant increase in those with a higher education; more part-time work; more jobs in knowledge-based areas, and fewer in manufacturing.

SCHEDULE OF ACCOMMODATION AND DETAILED DESIGN

Public services
A central library may serve in the region of one million customers per year, with a peak daily count of approximately 5000 to 6000 people and a peak hourly count of up to 400. The following service areas may be provided (see schematic layouts in **3,4**).

Branch library May be included as a discrete section of a central library, probably near the entrance, and cater for more popular books and related material. There will be only a few thousand volumes, acting as a 'taster' invitation to what is available elsewhere in the library.

The library may be divided into subject areas (see below), perhaps with defined enquiry points. Study spaces, browsing areas, and publicly available computer terminals can also be provided in each subject area. The various areas may be open plan, but must be visually defined (possibly by variations in lighting, different finishes and planting).

Older teenage section An area for this group is desirable (fiction and non-fiction) and should be located between the children's library and main lending library (literature and humanities sections).

Children's library Occupying approximately 300 m², with roughly 12 000 volumes for ages up to 14 and their carers, this area should have its own identity, and demonstrate to all children that visiting the library is a safe and enjoyable experience. There must be good visibility to maximise child security

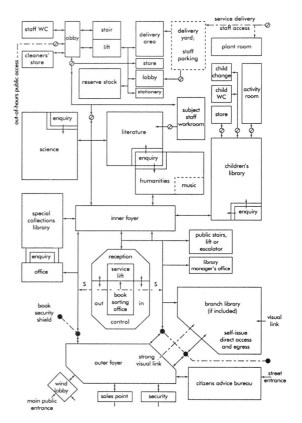

→ access route between different activity

● book security point (i.e. to prevent theft)

⊘ security point (separation of public and staff, or isolation for out-of-hours use)

3 Schematic arrangement: ground floor

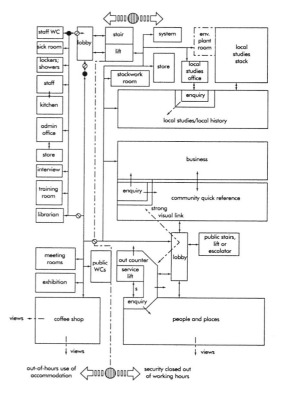

4 Schematic arrangement: upper floor(s)

(**3** & **4** reproduced from information provided by NPS Architectural Services and Library and Information Service, Norfolk County Council)

and safety; it should also be difficult for children to wander out of this area.

There should be a sequence of information books for all ages and sections for:

- pre-school (there should be 'kinderboxes', shelves with picture books, novelty cushions, child chairs)
- early school years (easy-reader books, with appropriate shelves and browser units)
- primary school years (stories, with appropriate shelves and browser units)
- young teenage (novels, with appropriate shelves and browser units).

Spoken-word cassettes and other media should also be available. In addition, provide ten study places, eight browsing seats and an enquiry desk for two staff.

Children's activities room A room for up to 35 children may be required for a variety of activities (63 m²).

Exhibition area Easily accessible from the main entrance, but with a distinct identity and with suitable security, an area for exhibitions is desirable (40 m²).

Lavatories The requirement for customers is 38 m² and also 15 m² for the children's library, which should include a nappy changing room. Depending on the overall plan, one or two sets of staff lavatories will be required (each of 32 m²).

Meeting rooms Include one room for 100 people (200 m² in total), with divider to separate the room in a proportion of 60:40. Chair storage and simple catering facilities are also required. A small room for about six people is also required. Access may be required when other parts of the library are shut; good access from entrance(s) is therefore required.

Special collection library This area may be required in larger or specialised libraries. An adjoining librarian's office is necessary.

Refreshments/coffee bar For 50 customers maximum, providing drinks, snacks and light meals (105 m²).

Sales point An area to promote sales is required (this may be no more than a display case): the strategic location is important, but it may be combined with another area (13 m²).

Study desks These (see **2**) should be suitable for use with personal computers (which may be the customer's own machine, necessitating simple plug-in compatibility). The integration of PCs with study furniture is very important. Two power sockets are also required.

Art in architecture Libraries are often considered excellent places in which to display local (or national) art, either in the form of permanent murals or sculpture, designed as an integral part of the building, or in facilities for temporary exhibitions.

Subject departments

Organisation of a library into subject departments has always been a consideration; a possible arrangement of a central library could typically be as follows:

Business At 184 m², this department contains 2100 volumes covering all aspects of business information (local, national and international). Customers will include: those hoping to set up their own business, those undertaking research to develop their existing business, and students. Some queries may come via fax or phone. Computerised information resources will probably be more prevalent here than in other departments. Includes 40 study places and an enquiry point for two staff.

Community With 9000 volumes (300 m²), this holds social sciences and all quick-reference works (e.g. directories, yearbooks, timetables, etc.). Includes 30 study places and an enquiry desk for three staff. Customers will be coming for both quick fact-finding and for longer-term study: any potential conflict therefore needs to be resolved.

Humanities Department for arts, recreational pursuits (e.g. gardening), religion, music (books and scores), sound recordings (music cassettes and compact discs), and videos for hire. With 495 m², 22 000 volumes, 9000 recordings (including videos), and 10 500 sheet music. Includes 12 study spaces, four browsing seats and an enquiry desk for three staff.

Note that there is a noise problem with customers browsing through music cases, which can be distracting in the study areas.

Literature and language Department for adult fiction (9000 volumes), large-print fiction, spoken-word cassettes, multi-media, drama (9000 volumes), single copies and playsets (286 m²), covering English and foreign languages. Includes 12 study spaces, four browsing seats and an enquiry desk for two staff.

Local studies/history 3000 volumes on public shelves (230 m²); 50 study places; enquiry desk for three staff. This area will be used by short-term browsers (e.g. tourists) and for long-term study (students and researchers). It will also be used by those wanting information about local statutory agencies, and those looking for a quiet study area. Environmental conditions for this area must be designed in accordance with BS 5454: 1989.

People and places For information books on travel (guides and travel/adventure), biographies, and human geography. 15 000 volumes (240 m²); 15 study places; four browsing places; enquiry desk for two staff.

Science and technology Area with 11 000 volumes (200 m²), covering computing and pure and applied sciences: 20 study places; no browsing seats; enquiry desk for two staff.

Access and circulation areas generally

As mentioned above, generally all public and staff areas should be accessible to people with disabilities, particularly those with sight or hearing impairments.

Other considerations are as follows.

Customer services/reception An informal and welcoming atmosphere is required, as this is the first major point of contact for new customers and where existing customers can resolve queries (e.g. about availability and overdue books); space is required for three staff (51 m²). Estimated peak daily level of registrations/updates is approximately 200; estimated peak level of enquiries, approximately 600. The area should allow for satisfactory queuing arrangements. (See also 'Counters' below.)

The general layout requirements are for: a professional, inviting and efficient reception area; clear layout and instructions for customers; maximum flexibility in staff resources; suitable supervision of customers; and suitable staff security.

Internal circulation The flow of people and materials (particularly the two-way flow of trolleys) should be made as easy as possible. Note that circulation areas provide opportunities for vandalism and concealment of theft, and should therefore: be kept to a minimum; follow a logical route; allow visual control by staff (closed-circuit TV may be installed); allow segregation of staff and public areas; allow segregation to enable secure out-of-hours use to specified areas; and allow easy emergency evacuation.

Internal vertical circulation This should be by lift and stairs, and possibly escalator. Lifts should: allow movement of staff, books and materials to all floor levels; be linked with the book sorting office; provide public access to main lending floors; provide suitable access for out-of-hours use. No more than four lifts should be provided.

Security generally The key considerations concern the control of access between staff and public areas (both during and outside opening hours), and prevention of theft. These issues can be addressed by: strategic location of staff enquiry points, with line-of-sight control; CCTV cameras; electronic book sensors at exit points; and security personnel.

Trolleys Allowance must be made for trolleys: for instance, by providing suitable protection to prevent damage to wall surfaces, adequate door widths, and suitable flooring (studded and ribbed flooring is not suitable).

Entry/access areas
One main entrance and two others are required, preferably separate:
- *Main entrance foyer/lobby*: (190 m²) should be clear and inviting, and be sufficiently spacious to cater both for visitors who have a specific destination and those who may wish to wander around.
- *Public out-of-hours entrance*: must provide a short and secure access route from the street to the meeting rooms etc. It could be combined with the main entrance, but a lift solely for out-of-hours use is not acceptable.
- *Staff/service entrance*: to be a safe and secure area, particularly for staff leaving after dark. (See also 'Delivery area' and 'Counters'.)

Queuing space should be allowed for 40 people to wait (at 0.5 m²/person, 20 m² is required).

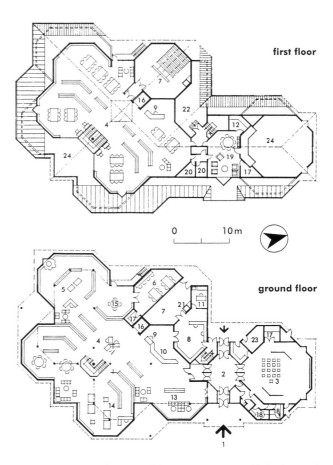

first floor

ground floor

0   10 m

1 main entrance; 2 foyer; 3 exhibitions/meetings; 4 adult lending and reference; 5 junior library; 6 junior activity; 7 book store; 8 workroom; 9 enquiry; 10 counter; 11 librarian; 12 kitchen; 13 periodicals; 14 audio-visual; 15 story area; 16 lift; 17 store; 18 WCs; 19 staff room; 20 staff WC; 21 hoist; 22 plant room; 23 boiler; 24 void

5 Chipping Barnet Library, Barnet, London
(Arch: Architect's Dept, London Borough of Barnet (Marshall Amoa-Awua and Alan Graham))

In-counters (51 m²) There will be one central counter for the whole building, after which customers will either move to other departments, move to customer reception, or leave. Peak hourly levels of customers are approximately 250–300, with a peak hourly level of returns of approximately 1000 items. Space is required for three staff plus computer terminals for customers. The layout must allow for clear and direct flows.

Out-counters (38 m²) All items issued or renewed will be from the out-counter and there may be more than one, depending on overall layout. Note that some customers may wish to return to other areas of the library (e.g. the coffee bar) after visiting the out-counter. Peak levels are as for the in-counter. Space is required for two staff plus computer terminals for customers. The layout must allow for clear and direct flows: in particular, customers not wishing to borrow items must be able to avoid becoming involved with this area.

Library returns bin This is required in the entrance area for returns during times when the library is closed. It must be a secure unit.

Self-issue terminals The space required is 3 m²/terminal and at least three terminals are required at various points in the library.

Smartcards The inclusion of a 'smartcard' system is increasingly likely, to allow customers to pay for services (e.g. photocopying, overdue charges, borrowing videos, etc.). The machines will be located throughout the library.

Admin and staff accommodation

In addition to a general admin office space of roughly 53 m², provision will also include the following.

Enquiry desks These should ideally be located so that they can service more than one department at quiet times or during staff shortages.

Librarian's office (20 m²) The base for the manager in charge of the whole building, the room must be close to the administrative support and interview rooms. Apart from everyday managerial tasks, the room will be used for small discussions with up to two people and project work.

Library manager's office (13 m²) This includes one office for two assistants, shared desk, and also room for small meetings of one to three people. Privacy is necessary, although easy access/overview is required for counters and customer services. The office should be located near the branch library.

Delivery area (16 m²) There will be a daily 'in' delivery of boxes containing: books from this library, but returned to other libraries; books requested from other libraries; and new books. The 'out' delivery will be of books sorted in the sorting office, and books requested by other libraries. This area will also act as a short-term reception and dispatch area for other equipment, furniture, exhibition equipment, etc., and sufficient space should be allowed for this.

Interview room (14 m²) To be used by all staff for private meetings, appraisal interviews, meeting the public and recruitment interviews, the room must accommodate up to four people and ensure confidentiality is maintained.

Local studies reserve stack (150 m²) Most local studies stock will be reference only, in closed-access storage areas, obtained by staff on customer request: access systems therefore need to be quick and simple. (Book stacks must be designed in accordance with BS 5454: 1989.)

A local studies workroom (38 m²) will usually be required adjacent to the local studies area.

Reserve stacks (155 m²) Certain sections of stock will be housed in closed-access rolling stack storage, including: seasonal overflow (fewer items are borrowed during the summer and over Christmas); reference stock; music sets; playsets. The weight of rolling stack storage is substantial and will need to be taken into account in structural calculations.

Secure area for exhibits A secure storage area is required, with easy access to both the delivery area and the exhibition area.

Security control room (17 m²) This acts as the base for control attendants, and for the closed-circuit TV system.

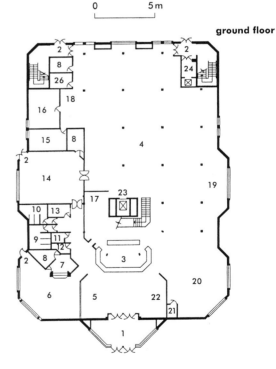

first floor

0   5 m

ground floor

1 entrance lobby; 2 emergency exit; 3 control desk; 4 adult lending library; 5 community information; 6 coffee area; 7 bar; 8 store; 9 WC (F); 10 WC (M); 11 WC (dis/staff); 12 baby changing area; 13 caretaker; 14 multi-purpose room; 15 librarian's office; 16 general office; 17 music library; 18 waiting area; 19 teenage library; 20 children's library; 21 WC (children/dis); 22 exhibition area; 23 lift; 24 trolley lift; 25 line of first floor above; 26 cleaners' store; 27 local history room; 28 WC (dis); 29 WC (staff); 30 kitchen; 31 staff room; 32 workroom; 33 reference store; 34 plant room over; 35 roof trusses over ground floor

6 Hartlepool Central Library, Cleveland
(Arch: Property Services Division, Cleveland County Council)

Shelf storage

Typical examples (see **7**) based on 900 mm shelf module are:

adult non-fiction	37 vols/900 mm run of shelving
adult fiction	30
sheet music	60
junior fiction	44
junior non-fiction	74

All shelving units should be four shelves high except:

local studies	6	shelves high
music scores	3	(overall height to be as four-shelf unit)
children's non-fiction	ditto	

Note that floor loadings must be given careful consideration: lending floors must be designed to take specified loads for books and shelving (e.g. a floor-plate loading of 6.5 kN/m²).

Sorting office (63 m²)   Required for sorting all returns. The main divisions are: for return (by trolley) to the various departments; for return to other libraries; for special requests (e.g. customer reservations); and for particular processes (e.g. book repair). Wall shelving for 1000 items is required for temporary storage during peak flows or staff shortages. This area also acts as a supervisory area for the counters and the customer reception, allowing the easy allocation of additional staff when necessary and for general troubleshooting duties.

Staff room (115 m²)   With a total staff of approximately 50, the staff room should accommodate seating for 30 and also be suitable for relaxation, social gatherings and informal meetings. During special events, staff will work outside normal working hours so there should be an adjacent kitchen area suitable for making light meals and drinks; a dishwasher may be desirable. Staff lockers (25 m²) are ideally located in a separate room and storage for wet clothing is also required.

Stock workroom (127 m²)   For four to five staff, its functions are: processing books from the delivery area; repairing stock; binding requirements; stock exchanges; inter-library loans for music sets. Wall shelving is required for approximately 2000 books.

Subject staff workroom (152 m²)   Required for processing complex enquiries and selecting new stock, these rooms are needed in humanities, literature and science libraries; for six librarians and support staff (maximum). Wall shelving will be required.

System room (38 m²)   Needed to house computer equipment for library circulation and other information systems.

Training room (58 m²)   Required for meetings and training sessions, facilities must be suitable for current technology and equipment.

Other areas

- sick room (10 m²)
- stationery store (25 m²)
- general stores (four; approximately 100 m² in total)
- cleaners' room/store (29 m²)
- WCs; shower if possible.

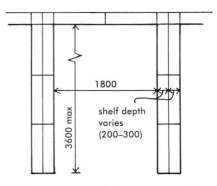

7   Open-access shelves, arranged in alcoves (based on 900 mm shelf module)

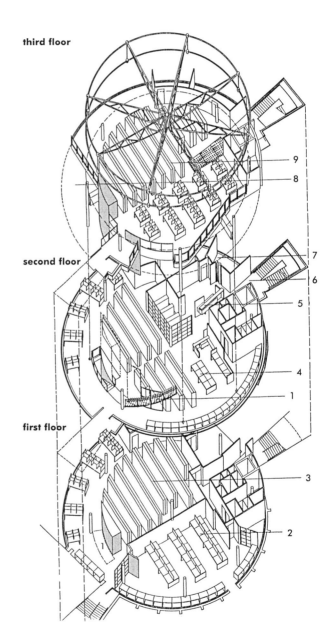

1 stairs; 2 drop-in computer centre; 3 book stacks; 4 reader tables; 5 reception and check-out desk; 6 entrance from existing building; 7 offices for library staff; 8 void over reading area; 9 magazines and periodicals

8   Hollins Faculty Library, Manchester Metropolitan University (Arch: Mills Beaumont Leavey Channon)

BUILDING SERVICES

Heat reduction is a major problem, and is exacerbated by the use of computers. Air-conditioning is expensive and environmentally undesirable and should therefore only be used where essential, natural ventilation being the preferred option (traditional window ventilation, however, can be a security risk).

Service zones are required above ceilings and below floors: ventilation systems, heating and electrical fittings, and information technology units, must be designed to allow flexibility of layout, and must allow for movement of shelving without causing disruption. Distribution cabling for networked computer systems and terrestrial/satellite aerials also needs to be allowed for.

Noise in libraries is a problem, both from external sources and between different activity areas within the building. Acoustic considerations must therefore be carefully considered.

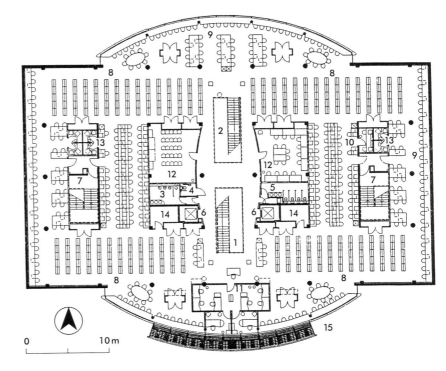

1,2 central stair core; 3 WC (M); 4 WC (dis); 5 WC (F); 6 lift; 7 emergency stairs; 8 book stacks; 9 study areas; 10 IT workstations; 11 library staff office; 12 seminar room; 13 private study rooms; 14 wiring closet; 15 external solar shading

9 Teesside University Learning Resources Centre, Middlesbrough: typical floor plan (Arch: Faulkner Browns)

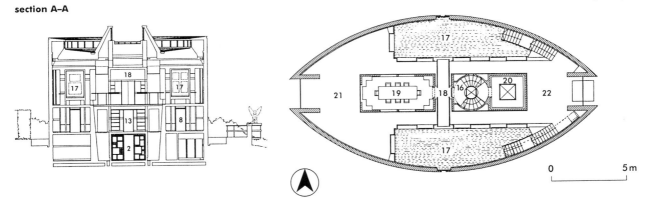

section A–A

gallery level

ground floor

1 entrance; 2 archive; 3 reception; 4 stairs to gallery; 5 entry to cloakroom; 6 WC (dis); 7 stairs to cloakroom below; 8 curator's office; 9 deputy curator's office; 10 assistant's office; 11 reading room; 12 invigilation desk; 13 archive (books, letters and photos); 14 archive lift; 15 wheelchair stair lift; 16 stairs; 17 gallery; 18 bridge link; 19 meeting room; 20 archive (letters and photos); 21 void over reading room; 22 void over entrance foyer

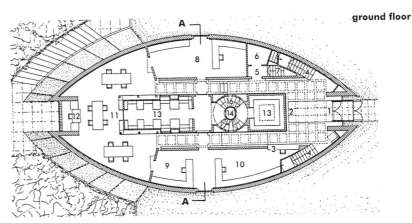

10 Ruskin Library, Lancaster University (Arch: MacCormac Jamieson Prichard)

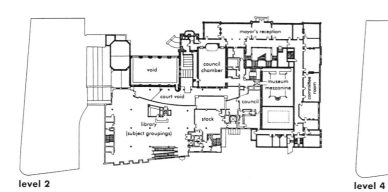

level 2

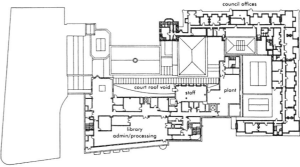

level 4

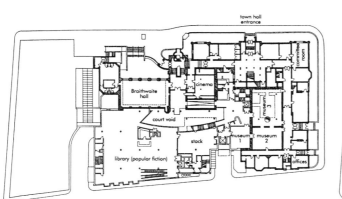

level 1

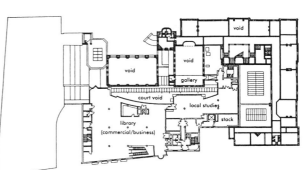

level 3

level 0

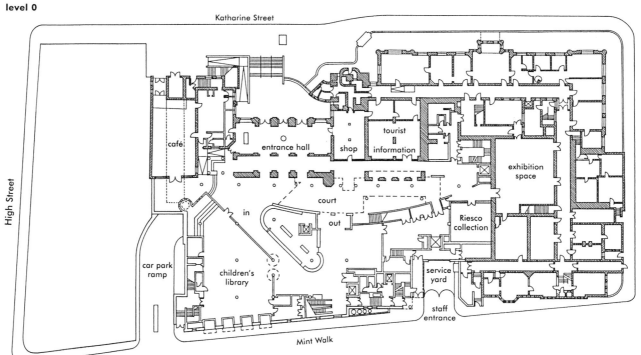

11 Croydon Central Library, Greater London
(Arch: Tibbalds Monro)

MUSEUMS AND ART GALLERIES

Patricia Beecham

The information in this section generally relates to art galleries as well as museums unless specifically mentioned.

INTRODUCTION

Origins of the museum and gallery Although records of collections of precious objects go back to Greek and Roman times, art collecting in the modern sense began with the Italian Renaissance, when enthusiasm for the products of classical antiquity and a sense of history first developed. The first formal setting for the display of antiques was provided by Bramante in the Vatican around the beginning of the 16th century, and the special display rooms of wealthy, private individuals in 16th-century Germany and Italy formed the architectural models for the 17th- and 18th-century art galleries, which became almost a standardised element of palace planning.

The term 'museum', first used during the Renaissance, was a different experience from what we now know. In a 'cabinet of curiosities' natural and art objects were jumbled together on the walls and ceilings, cupboards and drawers of one or two rooms. Their purpose was to surprise and delight; viewers had to find what attracted them and then make their own connections.

Public museums and galleries After the opening of the Uffizi in Florence to a select public in 1591, other museums followed later in the 17th century, among the first being the Tower of London, the University museum at Basel and the Ashmolean at Oxford University in 1683.

In 1753 Parliament established the British Museum to house the private collection of the monarch, perhaps the first art museum supported by public revenues. The opening of the Louvre in 1793 was a thoroughly republican event; the revolutionaries commonly referred to the Louvre as an institution dedicated to the glory of the nation. Public participation became an important aspect of museum policies; a socio-political organism.

The 19th century The dramatic rise of the museum in 19th-century Europe was closely allied to industrialisation, a concern to gather up and preserve artefacts from the past which provided a sense of continuity. At the same time, the new collections served to illustrate and reinforce the ideology of linear progress which underpinned and sustained the whole industrial revolution. Collections of pieces of material culture provided public evidence of the progress of human rationale and man's control over the environment. Industrial philanthropists provided money to build museums and also aimed to display the products of national skill for the edification of the public.

The 19th-century museum was designed as a piece of ceremonial architecture in which the idea of the sacred was translated into secular or national or civic terms.

The present While the 19th-century museum was supported by an educated and refined, although limited audience, now there is a much broader audience. With this comes a need to make a collection as visible and readable as possible.

The unusual aspect of the present Lottery-funded buildings in Britain is that they are all required to have majority public approval as a condition of funding. Decision-making regarding the content and presentation is opened up to a much wider sector of society than formerly, when the state or private patrons close to the sources of political power made the decisions. As a result the architecture of the museum is being reinterpreted.

Five functions of the museum:
to collect, store, conserve, research and present

THE ORGANISATION OF THE COLLECTION
development of layouts

Many early museums were organised on rigid plans, the daylit galleries set out as symmetrical corridors, with a wide central aisle for 'the promenade' and cases arranged strictly, by taxonomy, on the grid plan. Collections were organised to appeal to the connoisseur, collector or scholar, and the displays were either arranged 'aesthetically' or by classification or chronology.

During this time other forms of display were developing whose techniques have now been incorporated in the museum repertoire. By the 19th century a host of diverse entertainments and exhibitions had arrived, and it had been accepted that one could inform, educate and entertain all at the same time.

The Great Exhibition of 1851 was a milestone in the cultural and industrial life of Britain. This first great international exhibition established a style of display and an organisation of the floor plan, starting a tradition of 'world fairs' that have been vehicles for experiment in architecture and design ever since. From that time all the factors that influence the modern concept of the museum came together. To the original objects had been added 'the organisation of the fair, the entrepreneurial skill of the showman, the simulation of the waxwork tableaux, and the right of the general public to access'.

Rigid layouts do not facilitate thematic treatments. A more fluid style was to follow, making use of the whole area and with sub-areas devoted to aspects of the topic. In the 1920s, new ideas emerged with design philosophies of the Bauhaus. In the *Deutscher Werkbund Exhibition* in Paris in 1930, Gropius and Bayer placed exhibits in a predetermined sequence to express an organic flow. Curved walls and changes of level were implemented to present the information.

Aspects of style and technique of the 1951 Festival of Britain were to be absorbed into museum

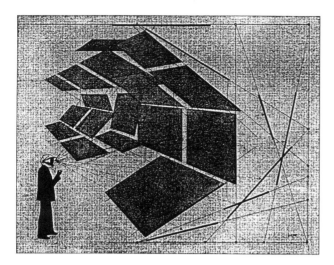

1 *Deutscher Werkbund* exhibition catalogue: diagram of field of vision by Herbert Bayer (1929)

exhibitions of science, archaeology and decorative art. During the 1950s and 1960s, exhibition design developed along two distinct lines: the Italian-influenced style, where a minimum number of objects were carefully displayed in beautifully detailed settings, with the intent of enjoyment rather than instruction, and that which presented the exhibition as theatre, in the 'evocative' style.

THE ROLE OF THE MUSEUM *duty and aim, objective*

Up to the middle of the 20th century a museum was a place of learning, in which notions of cultural dominance were reinforced visually through an imposing and often severe approach in the design of the building. The museum now has to represent a much more welcoming, all-embracing image, as it can no longer afford to present a single establishment view of society and must reflect a diversity of cultures and expectations. The most important task of the contemporary museum is to communicate to the widest possible audience the breadth of collections and accessibility of learning facilities.

Museums today are complex buildings housing different activities for people with diverse interests, containing collections and accommodating general and specialist staff dedicated to providing a service to the public as well as caring for their collections. They have to be designed for both client and local community, and to connect people of all types with museum objects.

THE MUSEUM TODAY *general, current policies*

The museum reflects how a society sees itself as well as being a symbol of commercial and cultural achievement for the outside world. For many, the new cathedrals are the shopping malls and the museums, the latter combining family entertainment with self-improvement. Galleries or museums are among the most popular visitor attractions in the UK. Increased mobility, more leisure time and the growth in global tourism are important factors.

The contemporary museum is a place with a multiplicity of functions, which has to combine traditional roles of interpreting and conserving a wide range of artefacts with requirements for large-scale retail areas, complex new technologies and the circulation needs of the public. In competing with other forms of entertainment, museums are looking to the architecture and techniques of theme parks, themselves an outgrowth of the 19th-century international exhibitions.

The Pompidou Centre in Paris (1977) by Piano & Rogers, an important trend-setter, turned its back on the conventional role of the museum as a sanctuary for serene contemplation and supplied a civic institution providing education and entertainment. Galleries and museums now have to be equipped for people wishing to relax, shop or have a meal. They have to be able to accommodate seminars and postgraduate courses. At the same time they are monuments that identify and differentiate cities.

Galleries act as art markets, promote certain artists and anticipate fashions by organising temporary exhibitions. Art has also become theatre, with its expansion to a variety of media that includes installation, video and performance.

Existing galleries and museums have to continually adapt to reflect current feelings on exhibition areas; areas where objects are not displayed in static form, but which offer itineraries through which the explanatory panels, computer screens, and the atmosphere of the area invite the visitor to participate. The ultimate aim is, therefore, not merely to classify and divulge the contents but to incorporate the museum into the type of place where people will readily spend their leisure time.

ACCESSIBILITY *relationship with surrounding area*

A museum or gallery can serve an important function in the context of its location. The museum can be the focus of urban regeneration in a depressed area, either as a new building or by making use of an existing redundant building. The construction of the Walsall Art Gallery (1999) by Caruso St John is regarded as an essential element in the regeneration of the town as a whole. The gallery provides a tall landmark, visible across the town. It has a heavy emphasis on educational areas for children and adults, with social areas and existing public civic space around the building.

The proposed Manchester Imperial War Museum by Daniel Libeskind is also planned to have a regenerative role: in common with the Bilbao Guggenheim, it is on a waterside site in a depressed industrial port. In such cases, the building's value is not simply as a container for artefacts but as a representation or aspirational symbol of its host city's changing identity.

The museum can also have an important role by becoming an integral and approachable part of its neighbourhood. The Tate Modern (2000) by Herzog & de Meuron is described as 'not at all precious'. It 'gives the sense that the building ... would be one that young and old people would want to use, ... and that groups from the neighbourhood would not be intimidated by.' At the Great Court, British Museum (2000) by Foster and Partners, replanning, which involved the demolition of accretions in the great court and the creation of a lightweight umbrella of fitted glass, has created a huge new public space (see **2**). Placed on a proposed 'cultural route' for London, it has been designed as a thoroughfare.

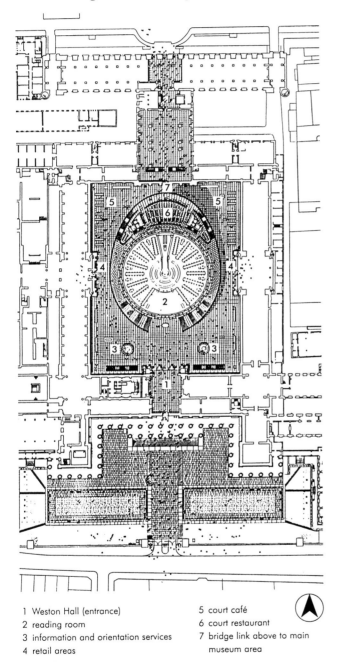

1 Weston Hall (entrance)
2 reading room
3 information and orientation services
4 retail areas
5 court café
6 court restaurant
7 bridge link above to main
   museum area

2 British Museum Great Court: site/circulation plan
(Arch: Foster and Partners)

The museum can be physically integrated into the life of a town, as in Falmouth, where the National Maritime Museum (1994) by Long & Kentish mediates the change of scale between working harbour and town, and provides public open space. The buildings define a new square which can be

covered and serviced for mixed-use, with a perimeter board-walk and public marina intended to integrate the museum with the life of the town. A new museum gives an opportunity to create a coherent place in a town. It can give definition to a square, which if well-placed can become a natural fulcrum for both residents and visitors. It can also be a place to learn about the town, its history and places of interest. In Stuttgart, the Neue Staatsgalerie (1984) by James Stirling Michael Wilford & Associates has its entrance approach as a progression across terraces and sloping ramps, with the incorporation of a public right of way; the visitor can either enter the museum's tall entrance lobby or follow a ramp along the periphery of the courtyard's drum and emerge in the street on the other side. The building is woven into the historical urban fabric by means of a pedestrian path.

THE MESSAGE OF THE BUILDING *symbolism, determinism, character of the building*

The contemporary museum is an art object in itself. The Bilbao Guggenheim (see **3**) illustrates the contentious container versus content conflict. Architects have previously attempted to include different kinds of space to accommodate various art forms; only here are such disparate spaces brought together into a synthetic whole. Six rectilinear classical rooms are positioned so as to facilitate comparisons with work in the adjoining sculptural spaces, and thereby linkages can be made. In each of five other rectilinear larger spaces there are variations in shape, ceiling treatment and light.

The Museum of Scotland in Edinburgh by Benson + Forsyth is designed to be 'suitably monumental and assertive for a national museum'. The building makes reference to the Scottish heritage of castles and brochs. The Staatsgalerie in Stuttgart is both a rejection and an affirmation of the established pattern: Stirling remarked '... we hope that the Staatsgalerie is monumental, because that is a trend for public buildings, but we also hope that it is informal and populist, hence the anti-monumentalism of the meandering footway and the voided centre. The formal route can be altered at will by individuals who may leave it at many points to make short cuts.'

The Royal Armouries, Leeds, by Derek Walker Associates, aims to inspire an interest from visitors who respond more naturally to an emotional approach than an intellectual one. The building is regarded as a vessel which contains the displays and allows them to succeed. The architect was appointed as head of the whole display design process, employing a holistic approach to the building. The collection is fundamental to the whole process and dominates every aspect of the museum.

The emotional message is strongly represented in the Jewish Museum, Berlin (1998) by Daniel Libeskind. The brief was to convey the historical and cultural background of the city and to house an extensive collection of Jewish cultural objects. This powerful building uses dramatic architectural forms to address the relationship between Berlin and its Jews.

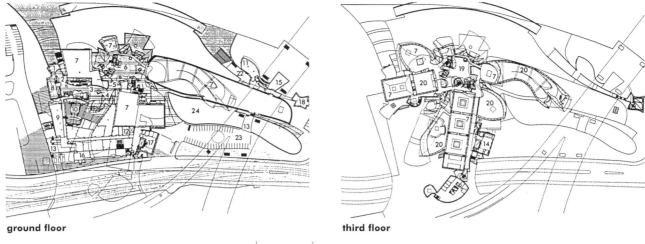

ground floor   third floor

section through the wing running east containing a curvilinear gallery 130 m by 30 m

1 foyer; 2 tickets; 3 lobby; 4 main entry; 5 admission line; 6 atrium; 7 gallery; 8 retail; 9 retail storage; 10 auditorium; 11 café/bookstore; 12 storage and workshops; 13 loading dock; 14 conservation; 15 storage; 16 plant rooms; 17 workshop/ maintenance; 18 tower; 19 void above atrium; 20 void above gallery; 21 kitchen; 22 fan room; 23 car park; 24 water garden

3 Bilbao Guggenheim
(Arch: Frank O. Gehry & Associates)

VISITOR CENTRES

A development of the site-related museum is the visitor centre, the major vehicle of the heritage business's demand for 'experiences'. The visitor centre is also a reflection of an age which is so culturally insecure that continual interpretation – of our heritage and contemporary culture – is now required.

The current Lottery-funded visitor centres must serve multiple functions in order to meet Millennium Commission funding criteria: learning, regeneration, sustainability, and, least of all, the display of objects. The role of the visitor centre as interpreter of a particular subject or theme is generally closely related to its location, and thus its relationship with the site is all-important.

The Grampian Archeaolink (1997) by Edward Cullinan, with a content of archaeology, regional history and folklore, blends into the hilly forested landscape with the aim of providing a window into the surroundings. The planning of the site with references to surrounding features is very important. The building is formed by making an incision in the ground, allowing the landscape to roll on over while using the undulations of the land to offer surprise panoramas from within. There was a need to provide distinct outdoor exhibition areas housing historically separate exhibitions; it was achieved by the use of embankments emanating from the central site to produce exhibition areas in quadrants with quite separate characteristics. The building is positioned to draw visitors' attention to various significant views and relationships, and there are strategic views out of perimeter rooms surrounding

a central auditorium. A long wholly glazed hallway gives fully revealed panoramic views of the open landscape circulation and orientation area, and is a foil to the dark spaces of the exhibition. (See **4**.)

The Slimbridge Visitor Centre (1998) by ECD Architects provides a home and administration centre for the Wildfowl and Wetlands Trust, the worldwide authority on wetlands habitat. A strong line of linked buildings houses the centre's functions plus the visitor centre, an observation tower, restaurant, wildlife garden, maintenance yard and replacement housing for onsite staff. (See **5**.)

The Heathrow Airport Visitor Centre (1995) by Bennetts Associates provides a distinct architectural focal point, pulling together and packaging the various activities of air travel. It houses a permanent exhibition for terminal 5 plans, and also plays a high-profile community role, with job centre, community information desk and noise complaint service. The centre's ideological links are with the locals rather than passengers, and it has no obvious link with the main body of the airport complex. It faces the NE runway for plane spotting

The Bracknell Visitor Centre, 'Weather Watch Discovery Centre' (1997) by David Marks and Julia Barfield explains how weather works and the evolution of weather measurement and forecasting. With a weather-responsive tower as a landmark, electronic information, audio-visual programmes supplying information, interactive displays and computer games, the discovery centre acts as a link between technology and the environment.

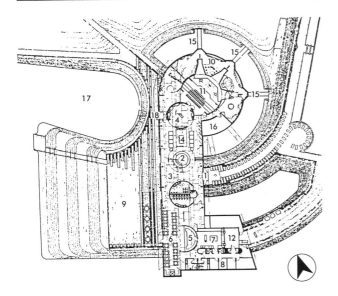

1 entrance; 2 reception; 3 concourse; 4 computer interpretation; 5 servery; 6 café; 7 kitchen; 8 offices; 9 arena; 10 ambulatory; 11 auditorium; 12 staff; 13 WCs; 14 shop; 15 light chutes; 16 plant; 17 base of ramp; 18 bridge over

4 Grampian Archeaolink Visitor Centre, layout plan: the building is aligned with Berry Hill Fort and the distant sacred mountain, Bennachie
(Arch: Edward Cullinan)

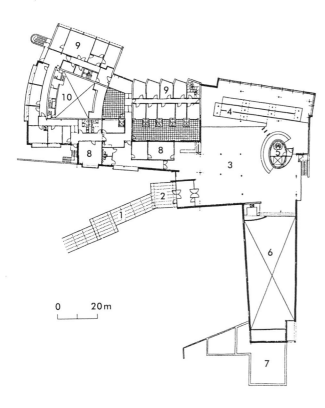

1 boardwalk; 2 main entrance; 3 entrance/exhibition space; 4 ramp down to exhibition space; 5 observation tower; 6 void over restaurant; 7 kitchens etc. below; 8 meeting rooms; 9 offices; 10 void above lecture theatre

5 Slimbridge Wetlands Conservation Centre: first floor, entrance level
(Arch: ECD Architects)

DESIGN OF THE MUSEUM *planning, space requirements*

Although new buildings are comparatively rare, there is much work in converting, refurbishing and upgrading existing museums and galleries.

Museums and galleries are often housed in historic buildings and are, as such, major exhibits in their own right. Birmingham's Gas Hall Gallery (1993) by Stanton Williams, for example, was originally an Edwardian municipal hall.

The client The client is likely to be the museum curators or conservators who have the objects to display and know all about them. Access to such specialist knowledge is important to the design process.

Design issues and criteria Space requirements are governed by the size of the collection, the method of display, the size of the artefacts and the projected rate of growth of the collection. Generally, larger artefacts require significantly more display space if their full impact is to be communicated.

High-capacity floor loading is an important consideration for locations of heavy items in exhibition and storage areas, and has to be provided for anticipated numbers and likely distribution of visitors.

Typical schedule of accommodation This includes exhibition rooms, auditorium, multiple-use event spaces, library, shop, workshops, conservation areas, offices, cafeteria etc.

- Shop: should be accessible without having to enter the museum/gallery. At the same time, it should not be too dominant; shoppers have to be reminded where the shop is.
- 'Resource centre': in main gallery space or store area, where researchers can handle and examine objects under controlled environmental conditions and approved supervision.
- High-quality lecture spaces and seminar rooms: extra income as conference suites.

Special temporary exhibitions These are important in attracting visitors to museums, which therefore need to provide good facilities for such events. Particular needs are for workshop access with clear wide access to the gallery, and also provision for deliveries, from the street, of construction materials and loaned objects in large crates.

Utilisation of floor space The average ratio of gallery to non-gallery space in the UK is 48:52, with permanent displays taking up 40% of the total area. Non-gallery space includes areas devoted to storage, curatorial activities, visitor facilities and education.

Display and storage requirements

museums type	display	storage
	(% ground floor area)	
national	35	29
local authority	57	25
independent	58	12
all museums	53	19

(from Manual of Museum Planning)

Storage Compact mobile shelving reduces storage space. Storage space required should be calculated on the basis of the volume of all objects in the collection with allowances for planned annual growth and unplanned donations (15% extra space).

EXTENDING THE MUSEUM WINGS

Space in finite buildings on prime sites has to be used effectively, so non-public facilities such as offices, reserve storage and conservation workshops can be in remote ancillary buildings. Extra display space can be created in various ways: e.g. mezzanine floors have been inserted at the London Transport Museum (1994) by Dry Butlin Bicknell, and in Vienna a new basement has been excavated at the Museum of Applied Art (1993) by Sepp Mueller Architekt.

Adding wings can transform existing buildings into mazes. Wings that read as separate structures are more successful, such as at the Stuttgart Staatsgalerie, Venturi, and Scott Brown and Associates' Sainsbury Wing in London; both use elements of the original. Stirling's Clore Gallery at the Tate Museum blends in with the Tate at one end while at the other declares itself contemporary and apart.

ACCESS AND CIRCULATION *planning, public space and orientation*

Access is, in its widest sense, a major preoccupation with museums. Most importantly it is about routes and progression, but also covers many other aspects.

The entrance This can be accessible and democratic or ceremonial and imposing. An entrance at ground level is welcoming, particularly if combined with an open, diaphanous (rather than a closed, bastion-like) appearance to the public; on the other hand, the ascent of a monumental staircase makes entering the building a ceremony.

Berlin's New National Gallery (1968) by Mies van der Rohe, where visitors leave the street and climb a staircase before arriving at an enormous empty concrete plinth which looks over the entire area, is contrasted by Stirling's Staatsgalerie which has no central, well-defined entrance, but a ramp which allows the visitor to enter, circle, or ascend the museum to the top.

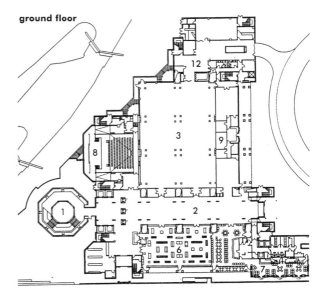

ground floor

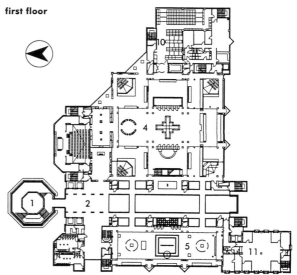

first floor

part E–W section

1 hall of steel; 2 the street; 3 temporary gallery; 4 war gallery; 5 tournament gallery; 6 museum shop; 7 bistro; 8 cinema; 9 photographic studio; 10 exhibition preparation/storage; 11 offices; 12 restaurant; 13 hunting gallery; 14 oriental gallery

6 Royal Armouries, Leeds: lower two floors given over to accessible and revenue-generating public areas such as bar, restaurant, shop and cinema, and also a library and education centre; museum proper is on the first and second floors and their respective mezzanines; at south end is the administration block and to the east a goods, storage and conservation block (Arch: Derek Walker Associates)

Visitor orientation A very important aspect of museum design; the visitors need a clear idea of the layout of the exhibition rooms. At the Tate Modern, Herzog & de Meuron have made the ground level an open public space from which the entire gallery can be seen, and with glass monitors indicating the exhibits and their location to provide orientation 'so people don't feel lost'.

The central orientation space is repeated in many notable examples: at the Stuttgart Staatsgalerie the vast, welcoming atrium hall or rotunda, from which the entire organisation of the building can be instantly perceived, is required not only by the increased number of visitors but also by the need to render complex options clearly visible.

A central atrium Interconnecting all the rooms with a central atrium enables visitors to orient themselves and choose the rooms they wish to visit.

A glazed roof over the central court cleared of its accretion of buildings at the National Maritime Museum Neptune Court, Greenwich by Rick Mather Architects & BDP has sorted out circulation problems while substantially increasing exhibition space. Legibility and orientation have been achieved by new bridges and internal streets to allow direct access to the galleries. Similarly, a glazed roof high above the courtyard of the Wallace Collection (2000), also by Rick Mather Architects, provides a new focus and helps to orientate visitors.

The 50 m tall atrium at the Bilbao Guggenheim forms the key circulation and orientation space of the museum.

Circulation and planning Frank Lloyd Wright's innovative New York Solomon R. Guggenheim Museum (1959) gave circulation a high priority, at the price of inherent inflexibility. Visitors ascend by elevator and walk down the spiral ramp encircling the central atrium, but have restricted space to look at the works.

Sources of design for the Getty Center, Los Angeles (1998) by Richard Meier & Partners include the 'Dulwich unit', a cubic naturally top-lit gallery coupled into a nine-bay or four-bay square plan. These squares then form the basis of the museum clusters organised around a major patio and are interspersed with atria and external terraces (see **7**). The galleries follow the successful layout of the top floor of the Uffizi in Florence (see **8**) where the main circulation route embraces a courtyard, providing a point of external orientation while linking a series of independent galleries. The sequence of viewing can be determined by the visitor, who can bypass specific areas without the loss of the general sense of position.

The ambition to both allow the viewing of a collection chronologically, while at the same time accessing individual components of the exhibition directly, formed the brief for the Museum of Scotland. Galleries are planned as a set sequence tracing the narrative of Scottish history. Earliest settlements are in the depths of the basement and the subsequent eras of Scottish history described as visitors move up through five progressively luminous floors. The journey culminates with the view from the roof, setting the museum and its contents in the

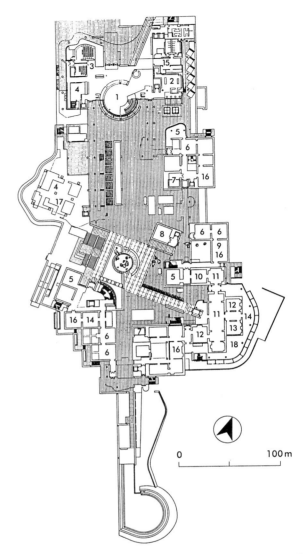

1 rotunda/information; 2 bookshop; 3 orientation theatres; 4 void; 5 information; 6 sculpture; 7 art lift; 8 family centre; 9 drawing; 10 tapestry; 11 great hall; 12 Regency; 13 Rococo; 14 transition; 15 offices above; 16 painting galleries above; 17 loan/special exhibits above; 18 decorative arts terrace above

7 Getty Center, Los Angeles: entry level plan (Arch: Richard Meier & Partners)

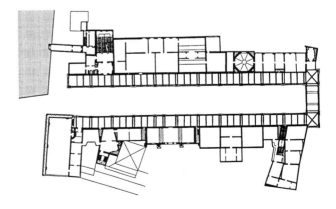

8 The Uffizi Gallery in Florence, Giorgio Vasari, 1570: top floor plan
(Present arrangement: Ignazio Gardella, Giovanni Michelucci, Carlo Scarpa and Guido Morozzi, 1956)

real context of the city. General circulation or orientation space is provided by a large triangular hall between the inner core and the outer spaces, which is flooded in daylight like an internal courtyard (see **9**).

The new layout for the New Earth Galleries at the Natural History Museum (1993) by Pawson Williams Architects takes visitors 12 m up to the top floor on a long central escalator from the atrium to upper gallery, passing through a 10 m diameter rotating steel globe, an allegorical representation of the earth. Then the visitor can explore the exhibits on the way down. The atrium is visible from one end of each of the gallery floors, and acts as a reference point for disorientated visitors (see **10**).

Norman Foster used the 4.2 m gap between the original house of the Royal Academy and the main galleries as a fulcrum, exposing and lighting two façades and linking all five floors with a new steel and glass staircase and lift, giving direct access to the Sackler Galleries (1991).

At the National Maritime Museum, Neptune Court, galleries are reached directly through an arcade onto the internal streets. Views to the outside orientate visitors while new bridges and internal streets run around the central podium making possible a circuit of galleries within the original building (see **11**).

Access for people with disabilities The building should accommodate the needs of people with any kind of disability.

- Entrance: Ideally the building should be accessible to all through the main entrance. Where there are conservation constraints with an historic building, changing the main point of entry for everyone can avoid the need for harmful alterations. Otherwise a separate route for wheelchair users and others may be necessary.

- Circulation: If possible all visitors, with or without disabilities, should use the same routes throughout. Where space permits, the preferred method of changing levels is a ramp. Otherwise provide a lift device, independently operable: – stairlift or, better still, a platform stairlift for wheelchair users – vertical hydraulic-type platform lift – stair climbers for wheelchair users (this is a last resort as it does not allow independent access.

- WCs for disabled users at all levels.

- Staff needs: Access is required for staff with disabilities to all offices and stores, with accessible toilet facilities on the office level. This would open up these areas to disabled students, researchers and colleagues from elsewhere wishing to study items in store.

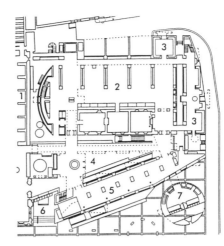

1 original museum
2 main gallery
3 study galleries
4 central orientation space and ticket hall
5 temporary exhibition space
6 restaurant and schools entrance
7 tower

0   10 m

9 Museum of Scotland, Edinburgh: ground floor plan
(Arch: Benson + Forsyth)

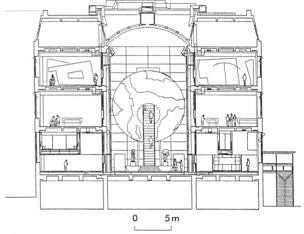

0   5 m

10 New Earth Galleries, Natural History Museum, London: main atrium, lateral section
(Arch: Keith Williams, while at Pawson Williams Architects)

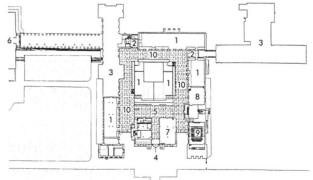

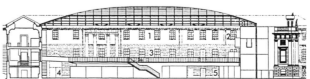

ground floor

1 galleries
2 reconfigured stair core
3 'back of house'
4 main entrance
5 foyer/tickets
6 Queen's House
7 shop
8 schools
9 lecture theatre
10 exhibition 'streets'

0   20 m

section

1 Neptune court
2 reconfigured North Block
3 exhibition podium
4 exhibition 'streets'
5 foyer/tickets

11 Neptune Court, National Maritime Museum, Greenwich
(Arch: Rick Mather Architects & BDP)

COMMUNICATION SIGNAGE

Even when the design of the building itself is the main influence on circulation patterns, signage plays an important part in the visitor's effective use of a museum or gallery. Museums without prescribed circulation routes, such as the Royal Armouries in Leeds, are dependent on signage. Effective signage does not necessarily rely on words: for foreign visitors and children colour-coding and pictograms can work well. In the children's area of the Science Museum, 'The Basement' (1995) by Ben Kelly, signage is fundamental: 2500 children move through the galleries per day, so colour-coding and pictograms featuring children address the needs of designing for the movement of people.

The building itself can fulfil the function of a sign. For instance, the Victoria and Albert 'Boilerhouse' extension is proposed as a 'museum without walls', which will act as a visual, physical and virtual gateway to the collection of 4.5 million objects. The interlocking spiral tangentially links space after space, inviting visitors to turn corners to the next glimpsed event.

IT increasingly plays its part in informing visitors about the contents of the building; the Tate Modern is an unprecedented public museum space with a new kind of civic programme – screening, performances and events. The galleries 'announce their contents' through the internal façade, like a series of big screens.

DESIGN FOR CURATORIAL NEEDS AND CONSERVATION WORK *research, store*

An important part of the function of a major museum or gallery is the work of its professional team, who require highly specialised accommodation. This can be in affordable space away from the central site, where storage can be provided in conditions that are right.

The V & A's research and conservation centre (1995) by Austin-Smith:Lord, re-houses all of the museums' conservation departments, curatorial, research and educational departments, plus administration offices. The centre provides accommodation to handle the museum's collection of nearly 1.5 million objects and one million books. State-of-the-art workshops have been inserted into the existing building, providing:

- paper conservation department (needing the supply of 14 different types of water), which has raised access floors to take IT networks
- records office
- curatorial office for the department of dress and textiles
- cellular offices for senior curators
- staff common room
- textile and carpet conservation, including space for washing and drying large carpets and tapestries.

The photography department has a lead-lined X-ray facility for exploring the condition of artefacts. It also has double-height space for the photography of larger objects (door heights along the ground-floor routes open to a maximum height of 4.5 m to allow these objects to be circulated).

Provision has been made for specialist spot extraction for the different processes involved, supplies of specialist gases, deionised and other water, detection facilities, black-out facilities etc.

The layout facilitates the movement of large objects, and in the north yard rolled carpets and heavy pieces of sculpture can be moved by fork lift. Sculpture conservation has 'dirty work areas' for stone cutting and grinding; these are fitted with specialised dust extraction equipment.

Oxford Museum service store and laboratory by W. S. Atkins (1994) needed a central repository and laboratory to store, conserve, study and catalogue its 600 000 preserved artefacts. The building has two distinct functions; tall storage for the bulkier items and domestic-scale laboratories and offices where conservation work and cataloguing can take place.

DETAILED DESIGN *display techniques, fittings, materials*

A museum or gallery display is composed of permanent and temporary exhibits in varying proportions. Temporary exhibitions can amplify and extend permanent exhibitions, and provide an opportunity to display material normally kept in storage.

Certain basic guidelines apply to the wide field of designing for exhibits:

- *Walls*: Uninterrupted surfaces are needed for displaying artefacts. Fabric-covered or plasterboard-clad hardboard are easily repaired and can be fixed directly to walls. These porous materials help to control relative humidity by absorbing and releasing moisture.
- *Floors, floor finishes*: Quiet, comfortable, attractive, hard-wearing, light-reflective and capable of taking heavy loads. Usually wood, stone or carpet are most suitable.

Basic floor loading for museums and galleries is 4 kN/m^2 (BS 6399: Part 1, 1984). Additional allowances may be required for particularly heavy exhibits, display partitioning, or loads from artefacts suspended from the underside of upper floors. For a display of large objects loading capacity of up to 10–15 kN/m^2 may be necessary. The use of compact storage units, which can increase storage capacity by 75%, requires a minimum loading capacity of 7.5 kN/m^2. (See below.)

Typical specified floor loadings	
function	*typical floor loading (kN/m^2)*
exhibition space	4–5
circulation	4–5
toilets	2
catering	3
retail	4 + (depending on storage)
storage	5–15
offices	2.5
workshops	5–7.5
plant	7.5–10
allowance for suspended exhibits	up to 2.5

(Lord, G.D. and Lord, B. (eds) (1991) *The Manual of Museum Planning*, HMSO, London)

Object display Most importantly, individual items must be placed at an appropriate viewing level, in suitable light. Each object must be given a visual context. Emphasis on particular objects is achieved through design, restricted viewing, positioning etc. The presentation of information about individual objects has to be made in the context of the overall strategy for information, which includes the look of the message, editing, graphics, signs and titles, information panels, labelling the objects, 'keying' of information etc.

Case design Display cases can be a very important part of museum furnishings. Visual and practical matters have to be considered (e.g. backgrounds, which are important in the context of the individual case and the total design of the exhibition, and have to be selected with reference to the compatibility of materials, both of the objects and with their surroundings within the case). Cases also have to be designed for various aspects of maintenance access, including the objects housed within, the services (such as lighting, humidification equipment etc.) and the case itself. (See **12**.)

A screen system Where insufficient wall area is available for display/hanging, screen systems are important. At the Gas Hall, Birmingham, a grid of stainless steel sockets is spread throughout the hall for fixing an innovative demountable screen system to increase hanging space. The main screen module of blockboard with hardwood lippings and aluminium edge fixings is 3.25 m high and 1.86 m wide. A stainless steel barrier can be fitted to maintain a protective distance between visitors and the display. The barriers can be linked in 'runs' to create walls of modules. Screens weigh up to 200 kg, so a handling system has been devised for operation by two trained staff, allowing repositioning of the screens and their movement to the gantry-hung storage room.

INFORMATION TECHNOLOGY *virtual reality, new technology*

The electronic revolution is having an impact on museums and the type of visitor is changing, becoming more diversified and more demanding. For the new generation viewing is not enough; interaction is expected. Virtual reality provides a strong context for art and a greater possibility for viewer interaction than any other means yet devised.

Now technology can extend an institution far beyond its physical confines, taking information and original computer art into homes worldwide. This means that the programme of the museum becomes more important than its shell or individual spaces. The museum can incorporate micro-galleries offering computerised images of art along with extensive information about it, including objects in other institutions. Video, computers, CD-ROMs and telecommunications have to be integral, supplementing our way of seeing art.

The use of CD-ROM stations throughout the National Museum of Photography, Film and TV (1984) by Austin-Smith:Lord enhances access to the

  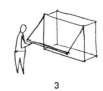

1 hinged-side access: provides good visibility; case dimensions should relate to arm's length for dressing; if cases are placed together, fitting lining panels is difficult unless divided into convenient sections

2 hinged-front access: permits easy dressing; large cases may require a transom for stability, which will limit sizes of lining panels and inserted display blocks

3 top-hinged: strong opening stays are required for safety

  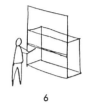

4 sliding front: provides good visibility, easy to dress; a single sliding panel may need support when fully opened; lining panels may need to be in sections to pass through the opening

5 two sliding panels: used where space is limited on both sides of the case; glass 'overlaps' when closed, and when sealed with dust-excluding strip, which may be distracting (some patent sliding systems provide a butt junction)

6 sliding upwards: weight of glass can present problems and be dangerous when in open position, strong 'stops' and supports are required

7 sliding downwards

8 lift-off front: provides maximum access for lining panels, display blocks and placing objects, but the weight of glass may require two people to open the case

9 demountable case system: useful for temporary and travelling exhibitions; even when construction is simple a team may be needed for erection

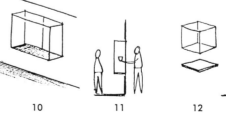 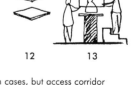

10/11 rear access: useful for large walk-in cases, but access corridor reduces gallery space; difficult to see the effect when dressing the case, and to make adjustment at front once dressed

12/13 lift-off 'shade' or 'hood' case: good visibility if constructed with edge-to-edge glass or perspex; covers too heavy to be manageable in larger sizes without risk to object displayed

12 Access to display cases
(Hall, M. (1987) *On Display: A Design Grammar*, Lund Humphries Publishers Ltd, London)

collections by providing an information interface between the visitor and the exhibit. This protects the collection from over-exposure, a lot of it being light-sensitive, delicate and easy to damage. The use of CD-ROM stations is also very popular, so a computer-based access system is being integrated into the fabric of the museum. CD-ROMs of exhibits enable a large amount of relevant data to be made available, while a research room allows examination when necessary.

The proposed UCL museum embodies the museum as art object. Switches in the floor will respond to pressure of user's feet to activate panels of liquid crystal glass, changing them from cloudy to clear. The façade will change constantly in response to number and position of visitors in the building. Visitors wanting to see actual paintings or drawings can summon them from a virtual-reality set-up. The appropriate paternoster will then deliver the object to the correct floor for the viewer to examine it.

Particularly important for a gallery showing cutting-edge exhibits, such as the Whitechapel Art Gallery by John Miller and Partners (1998), is the provision of servicing for audio-visual facilities anywhere in the gallery. This is essential for the increasing use of video as an art medium.

ENVIRONMENT

The design of servicing (i.e. climate, security, storage, handling and conservation) is as important as that of the galleries themselves.

Basic environmental requirements

The overriding objective is to achieve and maintain suitable stable indoor relative humidity and temperature conditions with minimum mechanical intervention. The balance of various aspects of the building's environmental performance is important: for example, in achieving a compromise on temperature to match the needs of objects with those of people. Also, the conservator needs to ensure the artefacts deteriorate as slowly as possible, while the exhibition designer needs to display the objects with maximum effect and for visitor satisfaction.

Most collections are vulnerable to damage caused by humidity, airborne pollutants, temperature fluctuations and the effects of light. The open display of objects in conditions that are comfortable for human occupation risks considerable damage to the artefacts themselves.

Museum conservation uses chemistry and physics to understand and treat the deterioration of the constituent materials of objects. Since deterioration is often caused by the interaction of materials with their environment, conservation has developed to include an understanding of the built environment and its effect on collections.

The conservators' specialist contribution can range from monitoring environmental threats to collections, to evaluating the suitability of display and construction materials in terms of their chemical stability. A conservator should be brought in at an early stage to participate in developing the project criteria, and to contribute during the feasibility stage, with information on health and safety matters, and the scope of environmental and engineering services.

Within the context of optimum services design, careful consideration should be given to minimising the risk to the collections when locating service installations and routeing service ducts.

Passive design; 'buffer' characteristics of building There is a growing preference among UK museums for a holistic approach to design, maximising the use of passive design features while minimising dependence on active systems to control the environment.

Passive design measures and simplified environmental control systems should always be investigated first. The running costs of maintaining a uniform environmental control throughout the building can be reduced by introducing a sustainable methodology at early stage of design (see **13**).

Less intensively used and visited collections can exploit the natural stability of building fabric and contents to 'buffer' rapid temperature and humidity

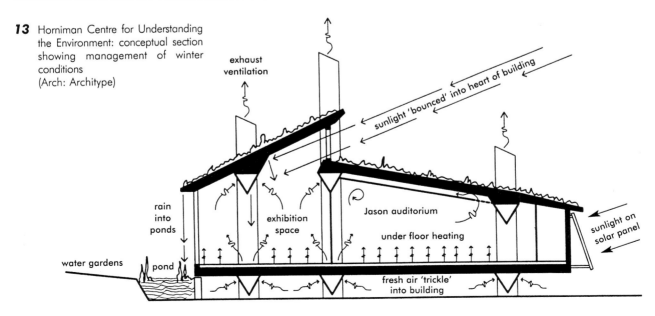

13 Horniman Centre for Understanding the Environment: conceptual section showing management of winter conditions (Arch: Architype)

exhaust ventilation

sunlight 'bounced' into heart of building

rain into ponds

exhibition space

Jason auditorium

under floor heating

sunlight on solar panel

water gardens

pond

fresh air 'trickle' into building

changes. This can be achieved by exploiting the 'thermal flywheel' and 'sponge' characteristics of a building. A high thermal mass of structure allied with porous finishes can be used to create an inherently stable environment. This can be enhanced by the use of external insulation, small windows or shaded shuttered ventilation openings where heat losses and gains can be dealt with at the window and not in the room. Furniture can also contribute to moisture buffering properties.

Heavy structure stabilises the Museum of Scotland, Edinburgh, from temperature and humidity swings. Galleries are mechanically ventilated, with controlled environments to display cabinets for sensitive exhibits.

The Grampian Visitor Centre, Archeaolink, utilises ground-locked surfaces creating a thermal flywheel effect, providing a heatstore in winter and cooling in summer. The passive annual heat storage principle is used to create a low-energy building.

Minimisation of energy use; sustainable methodology
Certain rules of thumb are applicable to new or refurbishment work regarding management priorities for environmental control and energy efficiency practice:

- be simple; specify low-energy features
- find out where energy is used
- identify where it can be saved.

Building services could then be lower powered designs used either as 'trickle chargers' to achieve desired average conditions or as 'trimmers' to stop conditions drifting too far off course.

Sensitive exhibits could be kept within buffered display cases or areas. Low control is acceptable in low-occupancy areas (e.g. store rooms and reserves). More input is needed in areas of high heat gains from lighting and/or large numbers of people introducing more moisture.

MGC standard rules for low-energy design:
- Avoid the 'uniform environment' approach to design.
- Use a zone strategy whereby 'sensitive' areas are grouped together.
- Set widest possible environmental control parameters.
- Use passive design features to create slow environmental change rates.
- Use low-energy features such as high-frequency lighting and condensing boilers.
- Adopt appropriate operation and control features.

Environmental management objectives:
- Avoid environmental change which causes stress to objects.
- Achieve balance between needs of objects and those of visitors: fresh air, comfortable temperatures for visitors; lighting sufficient to see collection but not enough to damage it.
- Well-designed showcases create environmental zoning, providing protection against high numbers of visitors and consequent fluctuations of temperature and humidity.
- Ensure that the energy saving does not override conservation; the collection needs stable conditions at all times.

Air conditioning and close control systems
Building services installations that can facilitate the close control of RH, particulate and gaseous pollutants, UV-light exposure and temperature fluctuations make a significant contribution to the preventive conservation of artefacts. However, air conditioning is only justified if most of the collection is sensitive to small environmental fluctuations, and a large throughput of visitors is common.

The installation of environmental control and lighting can present a dilemma on architectural conservation and environmental grounds. Art collectors demand full air-conditioning and onerous lighting controls before lending objects, but installation of air conditioning in existing buildings is very disruptive, and energy intensive once commissioned.

The failure of the system can make matters worse (e.g. humidifier system failure giving excessive moisture levels or over-ventilation in winter resulting in excessively low humidity levels).

A highly technical solution is appropriate in large, intensively used, highly managed national facilities such as the National Gallery, but it is important to explore the range of variations in conditions which are acceptable for a lower energy solution.

Air conditioning should only be viewed as the correct solution if the majority of a museum's collection requires tight control, and then only after careful consideration of capital and running costs.

'Environmental zoning' can be used to reduce the need for air conditioning in existing buildings. This can be achieved by the division of museum spaces into critical and uncritical areas, and grouping the most sensitive exhibits together in easily controlled zones or display cases.

Example: environmental zoning
At the London Transport Museum, air conditioned gallery pods are slotted in to house sensitive displays of old maps and documents, while vehicles are on display with minimum climate modification. (Arch: Dry Butlin Bicknell)

Air conditioning; temperature and humidity control
There is no absolute agreed level of heating and humidity control. The control bands of a particular collection depend on the state of preservation and previous conditions the objects have been kept in.

Temperature is the least critical environmental factor but important as a means of controlling humidity levels. Low temperatures help reduce chemical and biological decay, but a desirable temperature is often governed by human comfort requirements, which should not exceed 19°C.

Relative humidity (RH) is a more important factor in conservation than temperature, as high humidity poses the greatest potential risk. Dry conditions inhibit corrosion, chemical and biological attack, but organic material such as wood and textiles shrink and may become brittle. In damp conditions, corrosion occurs in some unstable materials, and most organic materials are at risk attack from moulds, insects and fungi. Some moulds can propagate at RHs as low as 60%, but the real danger starts at 75% RH. A generally acceptable level of control for sensitive or delicate objects is 55±5% RH.

Short-term fluctuations in moisture levels are particularly damaging to artefacts, and this can happen with an influx of large numbers of visitors. Such variations are considered to be as damaging as excessive, long-term dryness or moisture. Most artefacts can be safely exhibited and stored in environments with a RH range of 45–60%, provided that the buffering effect of the building's thermal mass and porous finishes can be used to control short-term fluctuations.

Air quality and ventilation

Air quality is not just about external pollution but also the reduction of internally generated pollutants, both gaseous and particulates. All fitting-out materials should be checked to conform to conservation quality standards. Plywood, composite boards, paints and carpet tiles generate pollutants. Composite boards are not suitable for housing museum objects. Samples of materials can be sent to the British Museum Testing Service for assessment of conservation acceptability.

The impact of gaseous pollution depends on location and the type of exhibit. Atmospheric pollutants such as sulphur dioxide and hydrogen sulphide are the commonest substances causing surface damage to objects. For particularly fragile exhibits a filtration system for removing both particulate and gaseous pollutants can be specified and be as high as 95% efficient. Where gaseous pollutants are present, activated charcoal filters fitted to the air-handling units should be considered as minimum provision.

Typical air-quality requirements for a fine-art gallery are maximum levels for sulphur dioxide and nitrous oxide pollution of $10\,\mu g/m^3$ and ozone pollution of $2\,\mu g/m^3$.

Ventilation is required primarily for people's health and comfort, but also where condensation and humidity pose the greatest risks. For example, at the American Air museum, Duxford (1998) by Foster and Partners, the basic function of the building is to protect the aircraft from further environmental damage. The exhibits are sensitive to humidity, not temperature change. The main space has to be kept at 50% RH, while the temperature is free-running. As people are moving around the site, it is acceptable to have summer temperatures 2°C below the outdoors level and in winter 2–3°C above. The design maximum is 28°C externally.

At the Techniquest Science museum, Cardiff Bay by Ahrends Burton & Koralek (1995), ventilation needs to be variable to deal with a wide-ranging occupant load – a maximum of 1200 at one time at peak periods, down to 150 a day. Natural ventilation is provided by clerestory windows and low-level 'hit and miss' dampers depending on the space temperature and CO_2 concentration, together with displacement ventilation.

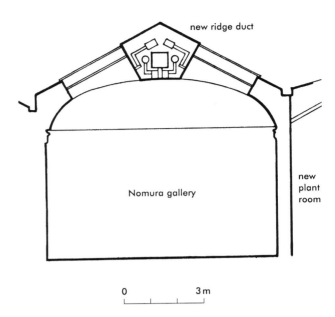

14 The Nomura Gallery at the Tate: low-profile approach has been adopted as the prototype for refurbishment of the entire grade 1 listed gallery; ridge duct incorporates the air-conditioning supply and return, fixed and adjustable light fittings, public address loudspeakers and various sensors; a new roof structure has been built over the existing one to support the new ridge duct, with double-glazed laylights fitted with automatic sun louvres and daylight controls, as well as air distribution ductwork and service catwalks
(Arch: John Miller & Partners Architects; services engineers: Steenson Varming Mulcahy)

The Spirit Building by HOK at the Natural History Museum houses a collection of creatures preserved in formaldehyde, a very unstable substance which would explode if allowed to get too hot. Here a solar chimney uses convection currents to draw heat from the building.

The specification of close control systems involves significantly increased capital and revenue expenditure, and their adoption may result in serious long-term cost penalties for the end user. However close control is a prerequisite for international artefact loan and a RH of 50–55±3% has become the established international standard. Sufficient equipment capacity is required to respond to rapid change in humidity.

These standards apply to all areas where the loaned item or its packing may be located, such as display, shipping, storage, conservation and circulation areas.

Capital costs of services installations can vary significantly, related to the degree of control over environmental conditions that is required and also the extent to which the building fabric itself can be used to control the internal environment. Many museums specify separate summer and winter environmental control schedules for energy efficiency reasons.

Example: low-cost solution

To overcome problems of high levels of humidity and carbon dioxide caused by visitors at the Courtauld Institute Galleries at Somerset House:

(1) Ventilation is increased by harnessing the stack effect, by which natural convection currents draw used warm air through opened-up chimney stacks. Stacks are lined with 175mm diameter metal ducting with mechanical fans at the chimney terminals. Carbon dioxide sensors are installed in the galleries which activate fans when necessary.

(2) Humidistat controlling a humidifier and a dehumidifier are installed in each room to ensure ambient RH stays within 10% of 55%.

(3) An electronic building management system synchronises equipment and keeps constant records of temperature and levels of RH and CO_2 in each gallery, so the system can be regularly appraised and adjusted.

For a table of recommended figures for temperature, relative humidity and particle filtration in the following situations, refer to the CIBSE *Lighting Guide: Lighting for Museums and Art Galleries* (1994) '*Museums in the Spotlight*':

(1) close environmental control design standards

(2) good quality control standards (art galleries)

(3) collections in display cases (broadband control standards for collections held in display cases).

BS 5454: 1989 *Recommendations for storage and exhibition of archival documents* is the basic source of information for environmental design and provides set criteria for temperature and humidity conditions. However it is increasingly recognised that conditions can be varied for different artefacts and different buildings.

Example: lenders' environmental requirements

The modern exhibition space created at the Gas Hall, Birmingham, (1994 National Portrait Gallery extension) by Stanton Williams has to meet the environmental requirements of art lenders', who insist on close control at touring exhibitions, with strict lighting levels and fire and security provisions.

(1) The gallery is maintained at around 22°C and 55% RH. Air is filtered to reduce potential damage by gaseous contaminants.

(2) Environmental and security data is recorded, as lenders increasingly require documentary evidence of conditions before agreeing to participate in exhibitions.

(3) The basement exhibition preparation area, delivery lift and loading area are all maintained at the same levels of temperature and humidity as the gallery hall.

(4) The raised steel access floor with maple flooring forms a pressurised floor void serving as the plenum for supply of conditioned air to the exhibition space.

(5) A glazed revolving door at the hall's entrance slows the entry of visitors, giving the environmental system the chance to adjust when 300 visitors, the maximum number, are trying to gain admission.

LIGHTING

The need for lighting

Usually display lighting should aim to present the exhibits accurately in terms of the whole object and its details, while making the display attractive. This generally requires a combination of ambient and accent lighting. Lamps achieving good colour rendering must be used.

The light level needs to be sufficient to provide a balance between the lighting of the object on display and the whole visual field. Exhibits should be brightest to ensure optimum visibility of the display.

Fundamental questions are:
- whether lighting should be natural or artificial or what balance.
- whether daylight is to be for display or only gallery space
- whether sunlight is to be excluded from the gallery and, if so, what sun-screening system is required.

At least three independent lighting systems will be required:

(1) working lights for use during installation, cleaning, maintenance, dismantling, and security patrols outside opening hours

(2) emergency lighting for visitor safety

(3) display lighting (see **15**).

Factors to be considered in designing the display lighting scheme are:
- Psychological: how exhibits are seen, perception of building, mood in public galleries, lighting of routes. The even, steady flow of artificial light allows viewing the contents of the museums as static objects; the moving, changing quality of natural light produces a more complex environment, where conditions change and affect the viewing of the contents.
- Physiological: illumination, contrast, reflectance, efficiency, uniformity, glare, colour, photo-degradation.

Too much contrast can lead to problems with vision. Many picture galleries work with a contrast ratio of 2:1 whereas in museum displays the contrast ratios are much higher.

Recommended lighting levels (lux)
- office: 300 ambient, 500 task
- demonstration theatre: seating area 300, demonstration area 600
- exhibition hall: 500/300/100

1 wall-washing
2 downlighting
3 uplighting
4 diffused
5 directional spot (accent)
6 lighting of pale objects
7 increased illumination for dark objects

note on fluorescent fittings: modern fluorescent lighting is nearly indistinguishable from natural daylight in colour rendering; walls can be washed with even light rather than cause distracting pools of light; the fittings can be concealed easily

15 Display-lighting techniques
(Hall, M. (1987) *On Display: A Design Grammar*, Lund Humphries Publishers Ltd, London)

- workshop: 200/500/750
- circulation areas 200, shop 600, toilets 150.

Use of daylight

In the cool, northern European climate, daylighting is the best passive solar option available, possibly with a daylight illuminance control system. Some advantages of windows and rooflights are:

- reduced energy consumption
- view of exterior and some sparkle enlivens space
- variable light pattern
- strong contrast through sunlight can add interest, defining form and texture.

The roof lanterns of the Dulwich Picture Gallery (John Soane, 1812), the first public gallery in Britain, have been repeated and developed ever since.

The key visual element of the conversion of Giles Gilbert Scott's power station into the Tate Modern is the 'light beam', which runs the length of the building as an additional floor, containing café, restaurant and member's room/bar. This is two floors within a glass rooftop structure running the building's entire 155 m length. It allows light to penetrate into the galleries below and gives views out.

The refurbishment of the first-floor galleries of the National Portrait Gallery by CZWG opened them up to natural light with half-open shutters to the windows. Paintings on the opposite wall are cantilevered at an angle from the wall to avoid glare, and also provide visitors with a greater sense of immediacy as they enter.

Lighting techniques

The CIBSE Lighting Guide: Lighting for Museums and Art Galleries (Museums in the Spotlight) includes a section suggesting lighting techniques for specific classes of exhibit:

- Lighting of galleries for temporary exhibitions and outdoor sculpture displays.
- Historic buildings: lighting of the building itself or use as a museum or gallery.
- Display of exhibits in some form of visual context: the 'experience' type of display, where objects are displayed in a representation of the real environment. Light pattern, colour and animation may be used in a manner similar to theatre lighting techniques. This can be automatically linked to an audio-visual presentation.

Types of artificial light

Types of light source include the following:

- Tungsten, low-voltage tungsten-halogen spotlights, fluorescent.
- Fluorescent strip lighting can be nearly indistinguishable from natural daylighting in colour rendering. Fittings can be concealed easily and wash walls with even light rather than causing pools of light.
- Velarium (ceiling diffusers; daylight or artificial light).
- Flexibility can be achieved with various combinations; close grid or continuous track, combination, tungsten, light spill from display cases, baffled sources.
- Lamp miniaturisation through the use of fibre optics has opened up new opportunities, giving sparkle and reducing heat build-up.

At the Henry Moore Institute, Sculpture Gallery and Study Centre, Leeds (1993) by Edward Jones and Jeremy Dixon Architects, by lowering the ceiling height a series of plug-in points enables space to be lit by one or many lamps. Small dichromatic tungsten-halogen lamps with a cool ultraviolet filter were used, with the option of changing wattage from 20 to 50. In the larger gallery 5° lights were used; the effect is like dappled sunlight. An electrosonic control system linked to a photocell alters artificial light as daylight fluctuates. The quality of lighting gives the character.

Colour appearance This relates to 'coolness' or 'warmth' of light which affects the mood of the spaces (see table below).

Characteristics of light: sources and character		
	focused	unfocused
natural:	south light	north light
	sunlight and daylight	overcast/daylight
	☐ warm and variable	☐ cool and uniform
	☐ contrast and shadows	☐ flat and soft shadows
	☐ bright and glaring	☐ lower contrasts
artificial:	incandescent and discharge	fluorescent and discharge
	sources (clear glass)	and incandescent (frosted)
	☐ warm (>cool)	☐ cool (>warm)
	☐ contrast and shadows	☐ low modelling
	☐ directional light	☐ diffused
(Mark Major © 1994)		

The colour rendering properties of different lamps varies greatly and the colour of lighting can also be affected by the reflection from a strongly coloured surface.

Tinted glass also changes colour rendering properties. Colour rendering of the exhibits must be the starting point of the lighting scheme. White light consisting of whole of the visible spectrum is needed for proper colour rendering of works of art. Tungsten filaments of incandescent lamps are biased towards the red end of the spectrum while fluorescent lamps are generally biased towards the green, blue and yellow. The designer should aim to keep an element of blue in the lighting as yellow makes things look dimmer.

Problems caused by light

Problems for visitors The geometry governing the eye lines of visitors and the light cast by luminaires, shadows, light levels and reflections have to be carefully designed (see **17**).

Glare causes discomfort or disability, and can be direct or reflected. It can be avoided in the design of the building envelope by orientation of windows, rooflights, provision of shading devices, diffusers, overhangs etc.

Glare from reflecting surfaces (e.g. the surface of exhibits or the glass of a display case) can also be a problem. To avoid direct glare all light sources must be screened from normal directions of view. Where there is free circulation of visitors around objects consider the comfort of lighting from all angles; where there is a controlled viewing angle, the design of lighting to avoid spillage and resultant glare is easier.

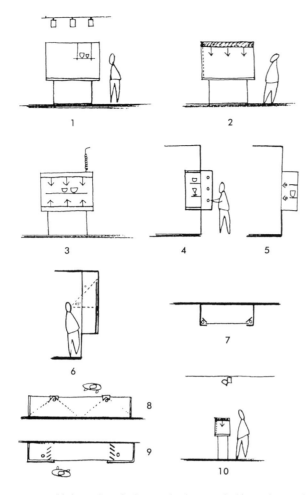

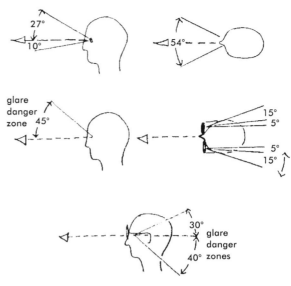

1,2 field of vision
3 potential distraction zone
4,5 greater limitations on lighting imposed by visitors wearing glasses

17 Sight and light angles
(Hall, M. (1987) *On Display: A Design Grammar*, Lund Humphries Publishers Ltd, London)

Contrast: keep general levels below 300 lux where there are mixed light-sensitive exhibits because of the problems of adaptation as visitors move around.

Reflectance: ambient spaces can be illuminated up to 300 lux, but higher levels can introduce glare and reflections. Glass frames and cabinets can act as total or partial mirrors obscuring the object within. To avoid reflected glare any bright source must be excluded from the area seen by reflection in the exhibit – this area is often described as the 'offending zone'. (See **18**.)

1 external lighting: through glass top, but heat may build up unless 'cool' light source is used; objects can cast shadows when lit by slanting light and possible problems of glare
2 integral lighting: light box separated from case interior by diffusing glass or louvres (with clear glass panel excluding dust); fluorescent for even, well-distributed light, or tungsten, for highlighting, can be accommodated
3 lighting from below as well as from upper light box to reduce effect of shadows and to light undersides of objects; light source must be masked, usually by louvres
4 backlighting: fluorescent tubes behind diffusing material, usually opal perspex; tubes must be evenly spaced, at some distance from diffuser; ideally fitted with dimmers to control brightness
5 strip lights (fluorescent or tungsten) attached to shelf ends inside the case, illuminating both above and below a shelf; can only be used for objects with no conservation risks
6 fluorescent lighting: behind case fascia panel (without diffusing panel separating light from case interior); angles of vision must be calculated to avoid glare from light source
7 vertical lighting (plan view): slim fluorescent tubes set in case corners, forming light columns; suitable for wall cases with solid sides
8 fluorescent column (plan view): set behind case uprights; a possible solution for lighting in old wall cases
9 side lighting (plan view): louvres essential to mask fluorescent tubes; accurate calculation of light spread is needed to ensure even illumination on case back panel
10 internal case lighting: slim lightbox for miniature fluorescent or incandescent lamps; brightness at eye level should be carefully controlled; wiring to the lightbox, housed in case corner, may be distracting

16 Lighting cases
(Hall, M. (1987) *On Display: A Design Grammar*, Lund Humphries Publishers Ltd, London)

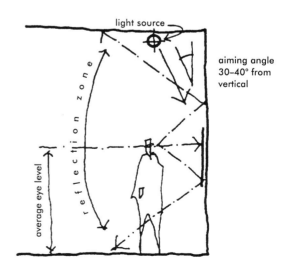

18 Reflections and aiming angle/location for artificial light source
(diagram: Mark Major © 1994)

Damage caused by light (Photodegradation) All spectral white light can damage artefacts, particularly daylight. Chemical changes can occur such that colours fade, papers discolour, and certain materials become more brittle. For example, pigment can fade in a water-colour or fibres be destroyed in a tapestry.

The harmful, ultra-violet component of light may be filtered to some degree, although this has some effect on colour. An assessment must always be made of the likely photochemical action of light on any object with reference to other factors such as RH and high temperatures.

Control of light damage In many cases the very fact that an object is on display means that damage will occur. The object of the lighting design is to minimise this problem without seriously affecting the ability of the gallery visitor to see clearly. Light exposure should be minimised outside gallery opening hours.

The degree of damage is affected by the spectral distribution of the light, as well as the illuminance level and the exposure time. Ultra-violet filters or secondary glazing is needed on all light sources shining directly onto objects to eliminate radiation damage. UV filter films or interlayers to laminated glass should be used on all external windows.

In the case of spectral distribution, galleries are recommended to reduce UV radiation to no more than 75 microwatts per lumen, but even this level may be too high a maximum exposure value to avoid pigment damage: current filters can reduce levels to below 10 microwatts per lumen, and ultra-violet light must be filtered out completely to show priceless old masters.

Levels for conservation activities need to be much higher, with levels of up to 1000 lux being acceptable when exposure is limited to short periods.

The CIBSE Lighting Guide: Lighting for Museums and Art Galleries (*Museums in the Spotlight*) includes a table giving recommended maximum illuminances and cumulative exposure values. This categorises three main exhibit types:
(1) objects insensitive to light (e.g. metal, stone and glass)
(2) objects moderately sensitive to light (e.g. oil paintings)
(3) objects highly sensitive to light (e.g. textiles, documents and most natural history exhibits).

SECURITY

Thefts are increasing during opening hours and methods of display and vigilance are important to reduce attempts to damage displays as well as steal exhibits. Methods of control include closed-circuit TV, warders, alarms, and fire detection systems.

Fire risk The risk is relatively low, but protection should be provided by fully addressable alarm systems. First-aid fire fighting is best by sprinkler system and water still represents the best fire-fighting agent for most applications. However, there is a problem of secondary damage in conventional sprinkler systems; water can rapidly destroy paintings, textiles and decorative finishes. Where there is an unacceptable risk of accidental water release because of sprinkler head failure, 'pre-action' systems should be used in preference to dry-pipe sprinklers.

Pulsing 'water mist' prevents fire from spreading and prevents a conflagration, cooling without wetting surfaces. This is a potential replacement for Halon and most powders, which reduce the combustion efficiency, but Halon is being phased out for environmental reasons.

Theft and damage These are major risks. A balance has to be achieved between the provision of direct fire escape routes and designing the layout to maximise security.

Security systems should include barriers and display cases, intruder detection to external openings, deadlocks and non-removable hinges to external doors, infra-red movement detectors and colour closed-circuit TV systems.

Warders The number of warders can dictate the method of display (e.g. whether objects can be on open display or in cases. The arrangement of cases, screens and solid divisions must be considered in relationship to the value and nature of the collection and the supervision of the warders. Blind areas and deep shadows should be avoided.

Barriers In open displays where there is no conservation problem unobtrusive 'psychological' barriers can be employed to indicate a 'no-go' or 'do not touch' area (e.g. guard ropes or placing the objects on a plinth). Another deterrent is to display security devices prominently.

Vandalism This always has to be taken into account. Shatterproof glass or perspex should be considered for casing valuable objects or those of a politically sensitive nature.

OFFICES

Santa Raymond

Notes
- Some important aspects of design relevant to offices are also found in other sections.
- Metric is generally used in this section, but agents and space planners normally use Imperial measurement.

INTRODUCTION

The design of office buildings is changing fast. Technology, globalisation and demographics are revolutionising the way workplaces are used. Office buildings, once seen primarily as a symbol of corporate power, must now be adaptable over time, flexible in use, easy to maintain, accessibly located and ecologically sound. They must also provide users with an effective and enjoyable environment, and financiers with a solid return.

Once it was considered sufficient to provide a shell into which individual modules were fitted in a standard format. Now the demand for 'long life, loose fit' has never been more pertinent. Thus, this section of the handbook works from the inside out. Having first considered influences in both the historical and modern-day contexts, and what space is used for and how this manifests itself in physical terms, information is provided on different types of space, technological and service aspects, and furniture, before considering the building as a whole.

Throughout, offices are considered in the global context. The local situation influences the way people work, and thus the way buildings are used. While the 'universal style' of glazed façades is found (and desired) world-wide, the interiors are laid out in many different ways. Office fit-outs reflect the cultural demands of the user, wherever their location. Differences between cultures can cast useful light on design parameters. Due to land costs, for instance, densities in British city offices are generally much higher than in most Europeans cities. The demands of differing climatic conditions become ever more central to the design agenda, with ecological considerations fuelling the tension between aesthetics and practicalities.

As with all projects, office legislation is increasingly onerous. Clients too are becoming more demanding. In the past, offices were perceived as an overhead; now they are seen as a positive ingredient of business success. The cost of space provision is a fraction of what many workers are paid, but with increasing sophistication of environments and expensive technology, the total cost per head in central city areas can almost equal the annual salary of lowest paid staff. However, the right office adds value in terms of how the business operates and how staff, suppliers and customers perceive the operation.

1 Reception Area at St Luke's Advertising Agency, London (Arch: Gareth Wright)

This reception space brings together many aspects of modern office design, with short-term work, meeting and refreshment areas right by the entrance, and the receptionist managing diaries and room bookings.

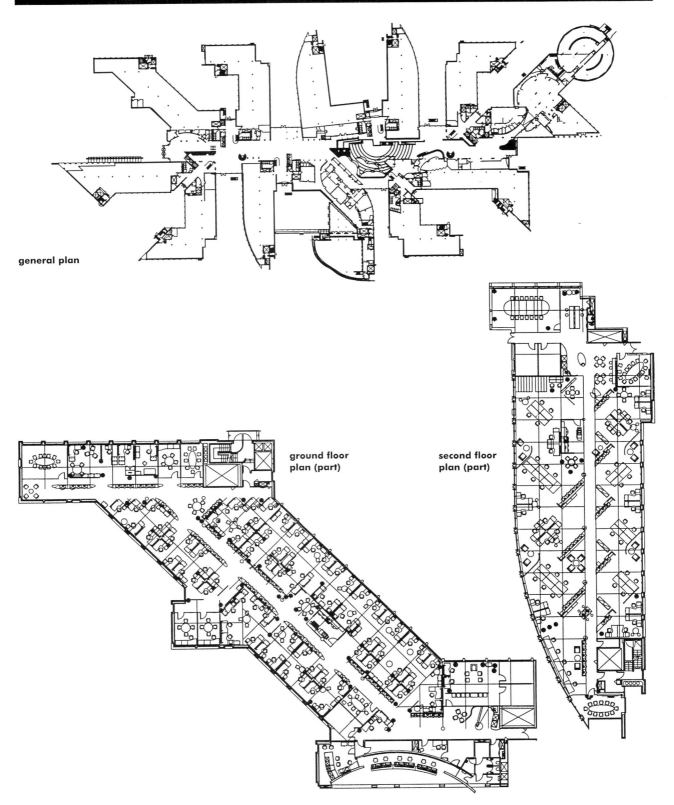

general plan

ground floor
plan (part)

second floor
plan (part)

2 British Airways Waterside, Harmondsworth, Middx
(Arch: Niels Torp & RMJM)

This 120 000 m² complex comprises six office 'houses' joined by a central 'street' 175 m long and about 12 m wide. The glazed street contains sculpture, trees, cafés and casual seating, with shops, meeting and support spaces along both its sides. Parking for 1850 cars is situated underground.

The four-storey houses provide 50 000 m² gross of workspace for 3000 people at 9 m² net/person. All workstations are open plan,

and many are shared, but there are numbers of meeting rooms and spaces, generally situated in the centre of the plan.

The triple glazed 'street' construction is conceptually a meniscus, with a simple tube and rod supporting frame. Generally, a concrete frame structure is used elsewhere.

The latest technology encourages flexibility, and an ongoing briefing process allowed maximum user participation.

HISTORY

The office, as defined in the dictionary as 'a place for transacting business', is coming into its own as never before. Communication is seen increasingly as the primary function of office space. Individual tasks requiring concentration or privacy may well take place at home, as they did when paperwork – the keeping of records – first started. Balancing the needs of concentration and confidentiality with those of communicating, is the central dilemma of office design.

Monks can be seen as the first office workers, concentrating for hours on writing and decorating manuscripts. The word 'bureau' describing the desk, which was for centuries an integral part of the furnishings of any dwelling of substance, came from the coarse cloth or 'bure' used by monks to protect delicate parchment from the work table on which it was placed. Today, some form of bureau, which contains and protects work tools and equipment, is used by many home workers.

By the 14th century, administrating large estates – whether royal, noble, common or ecclesiastical – required dedicated space. Later, the legal profession evolved, as did the use of written documentation, which required storage space. These activities were usually based within the domestic environment.

Business people started meetings outside the home in places such as coffee houses. These provide a useful model for the design of environments that encourage interaction in the modern context.

Banks and other major businesses developed during the 18th century, but it was not until railways provided transport that workers were easily able to congregate in central locations. The layout of early offices followed that of factories. This was further encouraged by the introduction in manufacture of 'scientific management' between the two world wars. Based on the sensible rationalisation of processes, the concept became mechanistic and inhumane, affecting not just factories but offices as well. The residue of this approach is only now being replaced.

In early offices, staff were generally housed in large open-plan spaces, with surveillance being an important aspect, and furniture and aesthetic echoing that of the school. Managers worked in home-like offices equipped mainly with domestic furniture. As with technology today – but much more slowly – electricity, typewriters and the telephone were instrumental in changing the way people worked.

Often striving for innovation, and intended to enhance the public image of the organisation, many early office buildings remain outstanding examples of the architecture of their time. From the magnificent brick structures, like those of Sullivan in Chicago, buildings became higher and then more transparent. Miessian structures, faced in steel and glass, took over – to an extent – from brick and concrete.

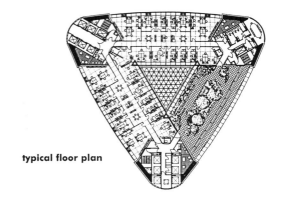

typical floor plan

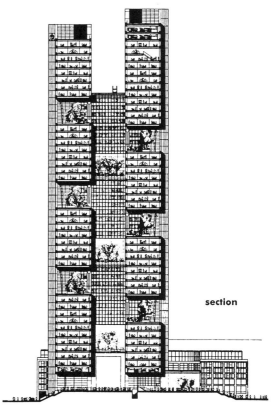

section

3 Commerzbank Headquarters, Frankfurt, Germany (Arch: Foster and Partners)

At 53 storeys and 260 m in height, the Commerzbank was the highest building in Europe when construction was completed in 1997.

The triangular plan provides narrow office floor plates around a central atrium. Four-storey gardens bring daylight and fresh air into the atrium. With openable windows, perimeter heating, interpane blinds and individual environmental control, energy consumption is much reduced. The gardens form useful space for refreshment and relaxation.

Providing space for 2400 workstations, the building has a net area of 52 700 m² (gross 120 736 m² (including 300 car and 200 bicycle spaces). Shops, a banking hall, apartments, a galleria with restaurants and spaces for cultural events forge a link at street level with the city fabric.

With a reinforced concrete rigid frame system at basement level, pairs of vertical masts enclose services and circulation cores in the corners of the plan, and support eight-storey Vierendeel beams that in turn support the clear-span office floors.

It was not until after the Second World War that the approach to the design of interior space started to change. In the USA, 'bull-pen' divisions were added to the usual open-plan and cellular space. It was Europe which led the way towards a more relaxed approach. During the 1960s 'office landscaping' in Germany stripped away both walls and hierarchy. Plants were introduced to provide focus and a sense of place, and desk layouts became less regimented and more humane in feel and scale. Generally, accommodated in deep-plan buildings, there were virtually no cellular spaces – neither personal offices nor meeting rooms. This lack of separation perhaps explains – alongside economic considerations – the short life of this movement. However, its long-term influence on workplace thinking has been critical. From this concept the 'combi-office' developed, with one- or two-person offices surrounding open space for group interaction. While this is still popular in Scandinavia and Germany, and does provide optimum conditions for many situations, it is an extravagant use of space.

During the early 1970s, Dutch architect Herman Hertzberger designed the Centraal Beheer Building to be once again human in scale. Comprising clusters of units for eight to ten people, the concept was that of a small village. Although the clustering is now seen to be inflexible, the 'street' concept which is central to many well-considered developments is a clear descendant. Niels Torp's SAS headquarters in Stockholm and BA Waterside (see **2**) are two examples of this.

The street is seen to foster communal activities. Acting as primary circulation space, radiating from this – in the out-of-city context – are blocks of low, narrow-plan office accommodation in one of several configurations. Advantages of this include flexibility in allowing multi-tenanting, a friendly atmosphere and the possibility of planning gain through the street not being deemed office space. In more confined situations the atrium may well perform the same function as the street, as may other types of generous circulation space.

Some users continue to demand deep-plan buildings. Some activities (e.g. share-dealing) are seen to function best in large open spaces. Additionally, the large floor plate provides maximum flexibility for the adaptable division of the space. However, not only do certain countries such as Germany require that workstations are set within a maximum distance of a window, but moves toward natural ventilation make deep plans less desirable.

Many organisations now experiment with 'new' or 'advanced' ways of working in order to encourage effective working or reduce costs. However, for such organisational change to succeed, the work environment must be designed to facilitate this. Thus the designer's role has never been more important.

TRENDS

The debate about open versus cellular space, privacy versus communality, shared desking versus dedicated desking continues but there are certain aspects of office design philosophy which are more generally accepted. Central to these is diversity. Theorists and practitioners describe advanced workspace in many ways: as caves and commons; cells, hives, clubs and dens; team, breakout and task spaces, and so on. Advanced workspace for advanced ways of working is about the individual: the individual person, task, process, group, sector or location.

Technology

Information and communications technology (ICT) powers the changing way that business and building processes are carried out. Equipment becomes smaller and more integrated. Flat screens allow narrow desks and thus reduced workstation footprints. Voice activation requires effective acoustic solutions. Wireless technology encourages mobile furniture and more relaxed layouts.

While the use of mobile equipment increases, the ergonomic and other dangers of overuse require sensible management, and a diversity of equipment becomes essential.

Integrated business and building management systems (BMSs) allow individuals to control their own environments – light, heat, air, sound – via the terminal, telephone or other gizmo. The building fabric reacts to integrate internal demands with external conditions, and in the most economic way. In their intelligence, simplicity becomes a key feature of building installations.

Occupancy

Technology is allowing people to work when and where it suits them best. This may well be out of the office, but even if they are in the office, workers tend to be away from their desks much of the time.

Encouraging sales and marketing staff to be out with the customer is a driver in advanced work-styles. If they are only in the office two days a week, or two hours a day, desk sharing appears to make sense (see **4**).

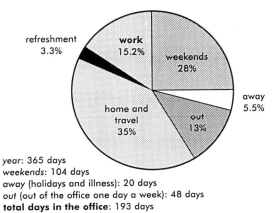

year: 365 days
weekends: 104 days
away (holidays and illness): 20 days
out (out of the office one day a week): 48 days
total days in the office: 193 days

home and travel (2/3 of each day): 128 days
refreshment (lunch coffee etc.) 12 days

work: 53 days (average time desk is fully occupied)

4 How workspace is used during the year

Demographics

Staff demand interesting work, to have control over what they do, and to be well remunerated in terms of cash, benefits and training. But they also demand a good working environment. A well-designed building can help to attract and retain staff, and enable them to work better.

Hierarchy is being reduced in many sectors. Knowledge, once the preserve of the mature, is now most available to the more computer-literate younger generation. Conversely, with people expected to live longer, and the wisdom of the over fifties in demand, the workplace must cater for older people.

Advanced workplaces for advanced work-styles

Attribute	Effect
Technology	Opens up the world
Interaction	Encourages innovation
Comfort	Attracts and retains key staff
Flexibility	Allows for different situations
Adaptability	Allows for major change
Diversity	Something for everyone

Flexibility

With many clients unable to forecast future requirements, adaptability in the long term and flexibility in the short term are fundamental aspects of office design. Organisations need buildings that allow change in the number of workers and in the tasks they carry out. Parts of the building may need to be used differently, even let or sold. This factor has implications for many aspects of the design, including the position of cores, and the building systems.

Accessibility

Buildings must now be equally useable for everyone: the needs of wheelchair users are a major issue, and so too are those of people with hearing or visual impairment. Beyond toilets, signage and refuges in case of fire, sensual climates are designed to help with way-finding and place-making. Sound, vision, smell and touch combine to inform and comfort all those who pass through the environment.

The other side of accessibility is security, and there is increasing emphasis on this in all its forms. Entry points which are friendly, but secure; data which is accessible from anywhere, but only by those with authorisation; open communication, but no risk of industrial espionage.

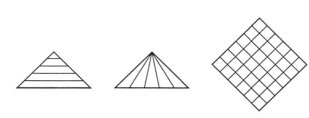

yesterday: *hierarchy*   today: *teams*   tomorrow: *networks*

5 Organisational scenarios

Fitness for purpose

Workstations used to be rolled out by the meter: everyone was supplied with exactly the same furniture and equipment, regardless of task, although position in the company might have some bearing, with more senior staff having larger workspaces or offices. Now the wise company considers need. Workstations are large or small depending on task. Offices are allocated to those who need space for concentration or for confidentiality. Meeting spaces and rooms are available as needed. Other spaces are provided that fit the company or department processes (see **5**). Furniture, furnishings and equipment are provided as appropriate.

Data management

To facilitate advanced work-styles, the provision of effective management and storage of paper and electronic information is essential. Only with information centrally filed, and handled by professionals, can workers operate with maximum efficiency and flexibility (see **6**).

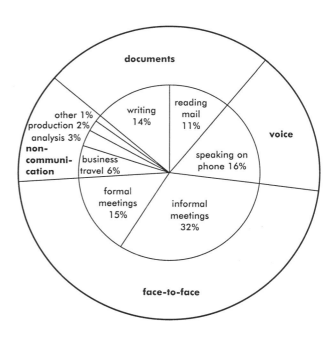

6 Different executive tasks to be accommodated

Ecology

Organisations are finding that 'acting green' is good for their business images and also for their bottom lines. Designers are thus expected to consider all aspects of environmental friendliness, from energy conservation to the embodied energy of materials.

Recycling – whether of packing materials, business waste or the use of recycled materials in the building's construction – is also part of this major trend.

Ambience

Good design has an accepted added value. An attractive office impresses possible new recruits, as well as customers, and staff work better if they feel the office raises spirits in the morning. The positive effects of colour are seen as useful; some firms enhance their air conditioning with carefully contrived smells; and Feng Shui is taken seriously by many organisations.

Paintings on the walls are described as 'a window into another world', and exhibitions by local artists can usefully foster relationships with local communities.

This all works best when the designer has considered these aspects early in the project, where art works form an integral part of the concept, and lighting is designed to enhance them.

Home-working

Home-working, at least part of the time, is now adopted by many workers. They benefit in terms of time with the family and reduced time and cost of travel. The business benefits from quality work carried out in the privacy of the home, and from the possibility of the resultant empty desk being shared. The community benefits from reduced congestion, pollution and energy use, and also the person's presence in the community. However, there must be suitable physical space in the home for working. Much of the design of this is covered by office legislation, but the relationship between the home worker and the employer requires careful consideration in terms of what is supplied and under what conditions.

Costs

Organisations scrutinise the cost of space using every possible technique to maximise space usage and minimise running costs. Conversely, the positive effect of attractive space is seen as useful in improving productivity.

Calculating life-in-use costs, as opposed to construction costs only, is changing the approach to the provision of space. This applies most importantly with user-occupiers, who are concerned with long-term issues. However, even developers and funders find that low service and maintenance costs make buildings more desirable.

Client

The voice of any one user client is not now heard above all the others; it is a question of listening, learning and integrating them all. Primarily, the client for an office building will be the financier, developer or user-occupier. However, people working in the building – executives, staff, and facilities team – will also be clients as will, to an extent, visitors or people passing-by. The office designer juggles the specific, and possibly conflicting, requirements of all these different users.

Building, design and construction teams

The building design, construction, management and maintenance teams are joining together to co-operate in making the life-in-use of the building as effective as possible. Increasingly, those responsible in the long term are an integral part of the concept design process (see **7,8,9**). As the complexities of office construction increase and demands become more stringent, so the combined knowledge and skills of all parties are required at the table from the earliest of stages.

The architect's role in the design of offices has changed, but has never been more critical. In a team of specialists, only the architect is aware of the big picture. Architects may no longer conduct the orchestra, nor indeed compose more than the outline of the music, but it is they who resolve the dilemmas of conflicting demands. And it is they who still can invent volumes that sing, and surfaces which take the breath away.

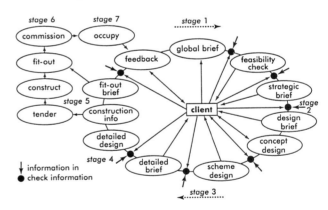

8 Effective briefing for office development

7 Players in the office game

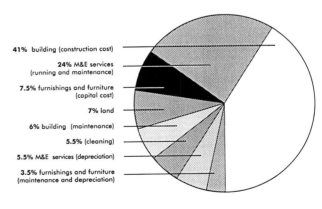

9 Total investment in an office building; discounted to present value, occupants' staff costs are excluded

SPACES

Space, and the way it is laid out, should reflect the needs of the user of that space. However, in office buildings there are many different users so the way space is used varies quite dramatically. The developer and tenant require maximum flexibility; the office workers, maximum comfort; the facilities managers, ease of maintenance. The chief executive wants space that impresses both shareholders and customers by looking good on the balance sheet as well as on the street.

Advanced work-styles are affecting the use of space, and thus its design. The functions of the main components of workspace – primary, support, ancillary and social – are increasingly overlapping (see **10**). Space may still underwrite hierarchy, but new ways of working and stringent budgets increasingly challenge this (see **11**).

Precise demands depend on business sector, task and individual characteristics. Traders and journalists often concentrate best with a high degree of background noise, call-centre operators with a medium level, while the writing of reports requires maximum peace. These tasks will probably take place in 'primary space', though many people write reports at home, and some people get the inspiration for this in a café setting.

Although spaces may be dedicated (personal offices or workstations), the practice of sharing facilities (hot-desking or officing) is on the increase, and is used for short- and long-term working.

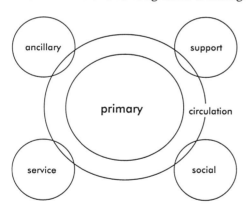

10 Types of space in the office

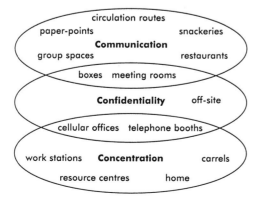

11 Work settings which serve the 3Cs

Primary space
Spaces for solitary work include:
- **Workstations:** basic configuration of work surface, chair, storage and equipment, possibly with some screening.
- **Carrel:** screened area, containing single or multiple workstations.
- **Personal offices:** fully enclosed spaces, usually with a door, for one or more people.
- **Cell:** non-dedicated, fully enclosed space for quiet or confidential working.

Spaces for collective work include:
- **Team rooms:** enclosed spaces for long-term team-working, which clients may also use.
- **Team spaces:** areas for teams; often changing configuration frequently.
- **Group spaces:** dedicated 'family' space for groups of people who may, or may not, work as teams.
- **Meeting points:** extended workstations to allow for informal meetings.
- **Meeting areas:** open spaces with formal or informal meetings furniture.
- **Meeting rooms:** enclosed spaces with formal or informal meetings furniture, plus special facilities such as electronic whiteboards, and audio-visual or video-conferencing equipment.

Support spaces
Support spaces serve the operation of the whole building, and may also present a public face. These include:
- **Reception areas:** balancing control and welcome, with a reception desk, visitor seating and display; provision for security and deliveries.
- **Restaurants:** including cafés and eating areas with formal or informal seating which may be used all day for group or individual working.
- **Resource centres:** balancing control with service, the resource centre may well house samples and videos as well as paper and electronic reference material.
- **Gardens, terraces and atriums:** potential use as workspaces, climate permitting.
- **Training suites:** a flexible layout of workstations allows for different learning configurations.
- **Presentation suites:** varying from a single room to an auditorium with supporting facilities, these will contain audio-visual and video-conferencing equipment.
- **Reprographic units:** for the production of in-house documentation.
- **Shops:** retail elements may include a delicatessen, newsagent, chemist, hairdresser, travel agent, cleaners and even a chain store/restaurant.
- **Clubrooms and bars:** these facilities are required in some cultures.
- **Health centres:** varying from workout equipment in a small room to a gym, swimming pool and dance areas with changing rooms attached.
- **Medical centres:** may be needed for periodic medical and dental consultations.
- **Day-care centres:** may cater for both the elderly and the young.

Ancillary space

Spaces which support departments or floors of an office – involving refreshment, paper handling and personal care – include:

- **Paper processing centres:** areas, often screened or enclosed, containing copiers, printers, faxes, binders, shredders and stationery storage.
- **Filing centres:** group, team or general filing and reference material, positioned in cabinets, cupboards or high-concentration systems.
- **Refreshment points:** tea kitchens or vending areas.
- **Toilets:** including showers, and enough flexibility to allow varying ratios of male to female staff, and also increased staff density.

Service space

Service space includes:

- **Mail room:** business processes will dictate layout and size.
- **Serveries, kitchens and ancillary areas:** dictated by functional needs, available space and service provision.
- **Staff rooms:** toilets, showers, changing rooms and sitting spaces for catering, maintenance and visiting staff.
- **Storage:** for furniture, office supplies, cleaning equipment, and maintenance supplies; and secure storage for office equipment.
- **Service storage:** for deliveries, and for waste that may be separated into clean, dirty, recycling, and compacted.
- **Plant rooms:** a main plant room and a patch or control room to each floor or area.
- **Security rooms:** housing CCTV monitors and workstations for security staff.

Circulation space

Circulation space – which covers both primary and secondary circulation routes – includes:

- **Corridors and passages:** enclosed or open routes through the building, providing clear direction and the opportunity to interact.
- **Lifts, lift lobbies and staircases:** position and design again encourages interaction.
- **Escalators:** their capacity provides an excellent means of moving people quickly and visibly between levels.
- **Refuges:** a well protected safe area for temporary use by those with special needs.
- **Delivery areas and goods lifts:** positioned for easy access to all parts of the building.

Off-site space

Consideration may need to be given to off-site space, including:

- **Satellite offices:** these will contain long- or short-term workspace, and meeting places, but usually only minimum support facilities.
- **Home space:** requires the same practical and legislative consideration as the space at central office.
- **Third-party space:** car parks, clients' offices, serviced or drop-in offices should all provide facilities to a reasonable standard.

LAYOUT

The way that interiors are laid out varies greatly between countries and companies, depending on land values, national cultures, company strategies and local legislation. Company strategies related to hierarchy – which may reflect national cultures – have a major bearing on the way space is allocated. The traditional solution provides offices and workstations sized and positioned to reflect status, whereas the advanced solution offers a variety of closed and open settings to reflect individual need and best practice functionalism (see **12**).

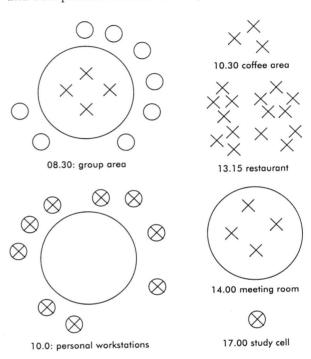

12 Different spaces which may be used in the course of a day

Space standards

Space standards are seen to relate to full-time equivalent employees (FTEs), which means that two people working half-time count as one FTE.

Space per person may refer to net space FTE in an office or workspace and it may include a proportion of secondary circulation. However, normally when referring to space per person it is assumed to include not just secondary circulation, but an aggregated proportion of support and ancillary space too – meeting and break-out areas, restaurant, resource centre, coffee and paper processing points, as well as back-of-house space. While taking a figure of $16\,m^2$ per person shows how many people will fit in a given space, the actual dedicated space per desk space could be as low as $6\,m^2$. 'Space per person' could be lower still where workstations are used by more than one person, or the space is really being 'squeezed'.

With rental levels in the City of London being nearly twice those of Frankfurt or Stockholm, there is increased pressure to optimise space usage. Thus the average gross space per employee may be $16.8\,m^2$ in London and $25.5\,m^2$ in Frankfurt.

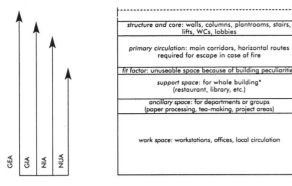

structure and core: walls, columns, plantrooms, stairs, lifts, WCs, lobbies

primary circulation: main corridors, horizontal routes required for escape in case of fire

fit factor: unuseable space because of building peculiarities

support space: for whole building* (restaurant, library, etc.)

ancillary space: for departments or groups (paper processing, tea-making, project areas)

work space: workstations, offices, local circulation

*note: this may be the whole building or the whole area which is occupied by tenant or owner

Space standards relate to the net usable area (NUA) of a building.

GEA: the gross external area is the whole building area around the outside of the outer walls.

GIA: the gross internal area is the area within the internal faces of external and atrium walls, including core area, but excluding roof plant and totally unlit spaces.

NIA: the net internal area excludes the core area. It is also known as NFA (net floor area) and NLA (net lettable area).

NUA: net usable area is the same as NIA but excludes primary circulation.

Core: area includes lifts, stairs, common lobbies, plant and service areas, ducts, toilets and the area of internal structure.

Primary circulation: links major routes within NIA with fire escapes.

Secondary circulation: connects workspaces and cellular spaces to primary circulation.

Fit factor: varies greatly between buildings, and relates to the amount of space that is wasted. The shape of the building, and the position of columns and mullions, can reduce the number workspaces that can be fitted in a space.

Efficiency: a ratio of 80% NIA to GIA is good, whereas 70% is not considered good enough. A ratio of 85% NUA to NIA is good; less than 75% is poor. Primary circulation may take up 15–20%, and internal partitions 5–15%, depending on cellularisation. A fit factor of 3% is good but over 10% is too much. Efficiency can be increased by adopting large buildings that are square rather than a linear on plan, optimising position and number of core elements and reducing envelope thickness.

13 Building area

Additive and subtractive approaches to using space

Additive At its simplest, this takes a gross figure of 15–20 m² per person and multiplies it by the projected working population, to arrive at a required NIA (net internal area).

A slightly more accurate approach is to take 12–14 m² per person and multiply by the working population. This provides the NUA (net usable area). Add 15–20% for primary circulation, 10% for partitions, and 10% for the building inefficiency factor. This provides the required NIA.

Subtractive Take GIA (gross internal area) as 100%. Subtract 20% for the core, which at 80% gives NIA (net internal area). Subtract 15% for primary circulation. This gives 65% NUA (net usable area). Divide this by 12–14 m² to discover the FTE (full-time equivalent) number of people that can be accommodated.

Circulation

The way people move around a building will affect how much they interact. Major focuses, such as café or library, can be positioned in such a way that encounters – and thus communication – are facilitated. Small seating areas along circulation routes, attractive lighting and colour, and views out, can all encourage casual interaction.

Fire escape routes must be easy to identify for all building users, including those with special needs.

Widths for horizontal circulation presuming a density of 1 person/7 m² of NIA:

Primary circulation	1.5–2.0 m²+
Secondary circulation	0.9–1.5 m²+
Tertiary circulation	0.55–0.75 m²+
Lift lobbies	3.0 m²+

Relationships (see *14,15*)

Appropriate adjacencies are critical to the well-ordered business, though these could change over time. Members of a department or business unit are most often co-located, but where this is less rigid there is more chance of potentially valuable cross-fertilisation. Managers may well work close to their teams, rather than in a specifically managerial area.

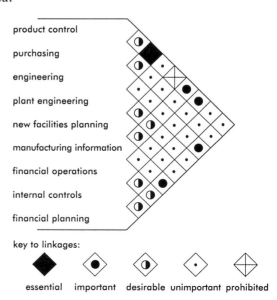

product control
purchasing
engineering
plant engineering
new facilities planning
manufacturing information
financial operations
internal controls
financial planning

key to linkages:

essential   important   desirable   unimportant   prohibited

14 Adjacency matrix, indicating the importance of being co-located

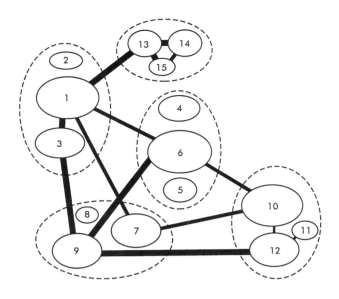

1 product control	9 financial planning
2 purchasing	10 procurement
3 engineering	11 plant
4 plant engineering	12 electrical and mechanical
5 new facility planning	13 invoice control
6 manufacturing information	14 staff
7 financial operations	15 order schedules
8 internal controls	

15 Relationships, indicating relationships between workgroups and their relative size

Meeting rooms and spaces (see **17**)

How space for meetings is designed and allocated is central to the advanced workplace. Meeting rooms that are shared, and can be booked, are taking the place of meeting spaces in personal offices. Meeting spaces take up less space than meeting rooms, and they are more often furnished with lounging furniture – sofas, occasional chairs and even beanbags – than enclosed space. Small meeting rooms, for up to four people, are in higher demand in most organisations than large rooms. Where presentations take place, more space will be needed for audio-visual or video-conferencing equipment.

Reception areas (see **18**)

Reception may still be a desk by the door or at the end of an echoey marble hall, but increasingly reception areas are the heart of the organisation. The receptionist may well be responsible for office co-ordination, diaries and the booking of space, as well as welcoming and directing visitors.

Where the café is positioned alongside reception, it provides the opportunity for visitor meetings outside any security girdle. With customer-focused businesses, there may be small meeting rooms adjacent to reception.

Considerations include the relationship between the street entrance and reception (with clear sight-lines and screening to reduce draughts), visitor seating, toilets and refreshments, and displays of corporate brochures, posters, awards or videos.

Levels of security range from the receptionists having a good memory for faces, through various types of electronically controlled barriers, to the inclusion of separate security desks with surfaces on which to check bags.

Workstations and offices (see **16**)

Offices cost more in space, construction and servicing than open-plan workstations, but offer individual privacy. Visual privacy may be achieved with screens, but oral privacy requires walls, or partitions providing reasonable acoustic attenuation.

Sizes of individual footprints vary greatly depending on culture, status and location. The net size of a minimum workstation may be as little as 2.8 m² (or even less in touch-down situations), with a general workstation at 3.5 m², and 6.5 m² for managerial positions. However, allowing for local circulation this will increase to the normal minimum of between 6 m² and 9 m² per person.

The smallest individual office is usually about 12 m² net, but cells for short-term work may be half that. Beyond this, the size of offices varies dramatically.

The size of group and team rooms will depend on workstation number, size and configuration, and the amount and type of meeting space and storage that are included.

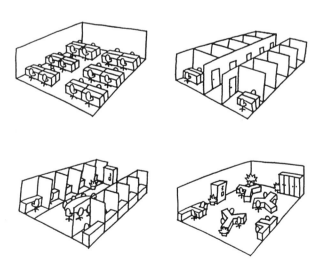

16 Office types: open-plan, cellular, combi-office, office landscape

Refreshment areas

As a central element of advanced workplace culture, corporate restaurants and cafés should be designed to accommodate not just eating, but meetings and solitary working as well. Refreshment areas provide invaluable workspace throughout the day. Tea kitchens and vending machine areas also provide useful space for both relaxing and discussions.

Excellent ventilation is essential to prevent the smell of food tainting both the immediate atmosphere and that of surrounding areas. Other considerations include visibility (attracting people to eat there), user and service access, the availability of services, suitable floor loadings, plus the provision of natural lighting wherever possible.

Although the design of restaurants, cafés and the ancillary accommodation is covered elsewhere in this handbook, there are certain aspects which are peculiar to the corporate environment. These relate to their specific functions of supporting comfortable eating in an attractive – and possibly different – atmosphere, ease of communication for those visiting the office for a short time, confidential meetings and work requiring deep concentration. This requires special attention to the provision of furniture, lighting and acoustics. Efficient but quiet handling of dirty crockery, ease of cleaning during use, and ready availability of power and data sockets are also critical considerations. Payment may well be cashless, and queuing should be avoided because it is probably time wasted at the employer's expense.

The restaurant location, and its relationship to the rest of the workspace, can strongly affect its success. No longer relegated to cheap basement space, it may offer rooftop views or take pride of place alongside the reception area.

In kitchenette and vending areas, safety legislation has reduced the permissible number of kettles and coffee makers: these kitchens may well contain a drinks vending machine and microwave instead. Careful lighting, durable but attractive surfaces and appropriate furniture, as well as cupboards, sink, refrigerator and dishwasher, will make these useful areas.

Criteria for corporate restaurants

Numbers: realistic take-up depending on location; sittings.

Proportion: of different types of staff.

Other facilities: executive dining rooms, sandwich bars, delicatessen, venderettes etc.

Food: type, range etc.

Opening hours: all day, lunchtime only, etc.

Use: outside meal times; cleaning.

Services: lighting; data and power outlets.

Furniture: for quick turn-around, or long-term working.

Ambience: workspace continued, or something quite different.

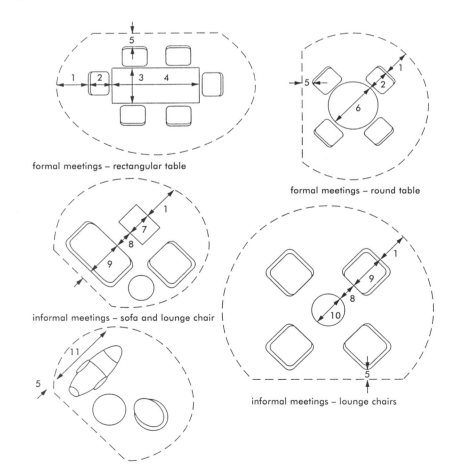

formal meetings – rectangular table

formal meetings – round table

informal meetings – sofa and lounge chair

informal meetings – lounge chairs

informal meetings – lounger and lounge chair

	(cm)
1 circulation space	65–75
2 conference chair	50–70
3 table width	90–120
4 table length	200–250
5 distance to wall	10–30
6 round table	120–140 diameter
7 low rectangular table	60–100
8 leg room	40–60
9 sofa and lounge chair	80–100
10 low round table	50–80 diameter
11 lounger	160–190

17 Meetings spaces

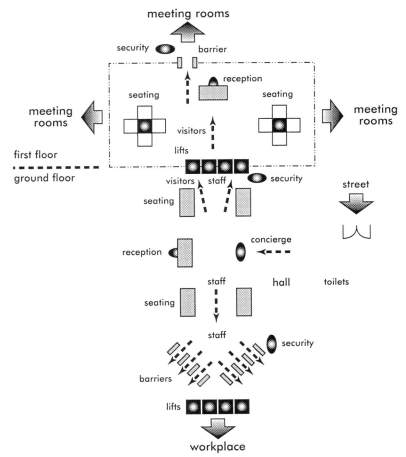

18 A reception complex at PricewaterhouseCoopers, Embankment Place, London (Arch: Terry Farrell & Partners Ltd)

Resource centres

The library for occasional research is transforming into the brain of the organisation. It is now the centre of electronic storage and information. Added to books, periodicals, catalogues, samples and microfiche are computer terminals that may well be used for accessing the Internet, intra- or extra-nets, as well as CD-ROMs. They may also be used for training. Skilled librarians provide technical assistance, and help with access to both paper and electronic information.

Shelving, racking, drawers and cupboards are needed for storage. Staff need workstations with horizontal surfaces for processing books and documents. They need easy views of access points, and as much of the rest of space as possible.

Users need formal desking, informal seating and possibly cells or booths for individual work or study.

Paper processing areas

Photocopiers, printers and faxes may be situated at the end of a block of workstations. However, they may need to be in a screened area to reduce disturbance, and also to encourage their function as gossip centres. Stationery stores, mail points, shredders, binders and work surfaces for correlation may also be included, as may space for hanging coats.

In flexible working situations, storage is required for personal belongings, which may be housed in trolleys, bags or other mobile containers.

Retreats

Smokers need space that is well ventilated, and situated in such a way that non-smokers are in no way affected. With the right furniture and lighting, it may also be used as workspace.

Muslims needs space for prayer, and all-night workers need a quiet place for a nap.

For at least some of the time, people are working at home more and more and the layout of their workspaces needs to be as efficient as that in the office. Conversely, how people choose to work at home can provide useful indicators as to what they find comfortable in the office. Home offices may be designed specifically for the person concerned, or as part of a general office initiative for home-working. The relationship between the main and home office can be quite complex. Office legislation applies, in principle, to home offices, but is difficult to supervise. Furniture, equipment and services may be supplied and maintained by the facilities department, or not, depending on a number of factors.

TECHNOLOGY AND POWER

Technological advances are changing the way people work, and as systems become ever more sophisticated their impact on buildings and the way they are used is increasingly powerful. Networked systems encourage freedom of location – off-site working, tele-working and home-working. Theoretically, using modern technology should result in a reduction in paper consumption, but this has proven to be less radical than would be expected. Both the requirement for paper contracts and records, and people's unease at relying on electronic storage, means that paper storage is still a major space issue in most offices.

The intelligent building is controlled by ecologically sensitive programmes. The personal environment is controlled via the PC, telephone, etc., and integration of interfaces between different technological systems and the people they serve becomes increasingly simple.

Integration of design is essential, but total integration of installation can prove too complicated in the long run. Elements have different life cycles, and difficulties with one part can affect the whole. Thus there is an argument for integration only where it is essential. Similarly, wire-free installations provide tremendous opportunities, but can have drawbacks such as cost and security. In addition, there may be health implications.

VDUs

At least 80% of the working population have access to a VDU and use them for three hours a day, or more. However, large monitors and keyboards are now giving way to laptops, docking stations, flat screens, palm pilots, voice or wand activation, and so on.

In some business sectors, such as merchant banking, staff require as many as six monitors to keep ahead of global trends in trading. As the use of paper decreases, more people will find two or split screens a necessity to avoid printing off documentation for reference.

Flat screens have major implications for the design of offices, as not only are they more elegant but, in requiring less depth, they also enable work surfaces to be shallower.

Telephony

Telephones and computers are coming together and taking over each other's tasks. Handsets may be free-range or corded, but either way systems can be programmed so that calls reach recipients wherever they are around the world.

Simple video-conferencing may take place at the workstation, but more complex meetings require rooms with special lighting, furniture and equipment carefully designed to facilitate the process. Although this type of communication does not replace meeting together in one place, those who know each other consider it a useful tool. Others find telephone conferencing equally good.

Some firms have protocols, which restrict the use of cellphones except at the desk, thus reducing the disturbance which ambulatory telephoning causes.

Information management

The full potential of flexible working only becomes effective where all information, whether paper or electronic, is kept centrally and managed by professionals. Information is then available from anywhere (with authorisation), and filing is arranged in a standard format. Likewise, reference material can be kept centrally, and made available by a librarian, who also provides a search and general help service.

Business management systems

While BMSs often only control lighting, the heating, ventilation and air conditioning (HVAC) systems and security, they can be designed to integrate many aspects of the building systems, including solar control by movable louvres and blinds, solar panels, wind stack direction and fire detection. Systems should be able to operate on a part-floor basis, and also relate to the possible future billing of tenants.

Access can be controlled by swipe cards or their equivalent, which can also include a cashless vending facility.

Power

Power consumption rarely exceeds $15\,W/m^2$, though risers/busbars should be rated to $25\,W/m^2$, plus 15–25% spare ways. Small power (240 V single phase) only is required, except in certain locations such as kitchen and workshops where 415 V three phase may be necessary. Floor outlets are provided at one per $5{-}10\,m^2$.

Standby power for emergency lighting is required, as are standby generators in some situations.

Cabling

Infra-red and other wireless systems have advantages, but cable management is still a critical element of any fit-out. Cabling may run in the floor with floor boxes or 'power standards', in the ceiling with 'power poles' or curly cabling, or around the perimeter of the building in conduit (at skirting or desk height). Cables may also run in furniture and screens. Data and power cabling must terminate in easily accessible positions for the users – preferably at work-surface level. Outlets need to be sufficient in number to serve all appliances without doubling up. Power and data cabling should be separated.

Cabling may be 'flood' or 'structured' and be in copper or fibre-optic. Large amounts of data require ISDN or similar lines for telephones and category 5 or 6 cabling for the computer systems, though all data may be carried by combined cabling. Main risers should be within 80 m horizontal run of any part of the serviced floor plate.

Cordless equipment may reduce the amount of data and power outlets to an extent, but cabling is still required for charging and high-speed transactions.

Equipment rooms

Each floor or large area requires a patch room where technology is handled locally. A controlled environment (dust-free, dry and secure) may be needed for the main equipment room or suite, serving the whole building or organisation. Off-site backup equipment or storage is also essential.

Control

While control may be local or central, users are more comfortable (and are prepared to accept lesser conditions) if they feel in personal control of their environment. Local controls may well be overridden by default systems which relate to external conditions or the time of day.

Local control may be via traditional switches or thermostats, computer or telephone, or help-desk personnel. Buildings may be divided into modules for heating and lighting, with perhaps a six workstation/two office area having its own control system which any occupant can access. Modules may be smaller on the perimeter of the building, where there is more volatility.

Remote systems include timers, infra-red movement detectors, light level monitors and centrally controlled thermostats.

ENVIRONMENT

Environmental conditions affect how people feel about the office more than any other design element. It is proven that inadequate fresh air and light reduces productivity. How badly an unsatisfactory sound climate affects output is less clear, but certainly people complain that noise in open-plan spaces makes concentration difficult.

Air, heat and cooling

People prefer natural ventilation and windows that open, but this is often not practicable. However, where climate, noise, pollution, security and plan form allow it, mixed mode ventilation can be adopted, with air conditioning, heating or comfort cooling as required. The fabric of the building may be used to assist air handling, such as displacement ventilation via atriums, stacks or double-skin façades. Structural mass, such as exposed concrete slabs, are used for climate control in retaining heat or cooling. Chilled ceilings and beams can also prove effective, as can heat exchangers and heat sinks.

Deep-plan buildings almost certainly require air conditioning, but in many other situations a degree of natural ventilation can still be introduced. Even in extreme climates, there are usually periods of the year when air conditioning can be dispensed with. Likewise, pollution may require filtration rather than full air conditioning, and systems can be devised to enable natural ventilation to be used even in high-security situations.

However, an air conditioning system requires less management, and though more expensive to run, is cheaper to install than a dual system. Air conditioning is seen – in the global context – as providing the optimum level of comfort for the user. Therefore, financiers and developers generally require office buildings to be fully air conditioned, even where this is not necessary.

In some European countries, such as Germany, opening windows provide natural ventilation for most offices, usually with perimeter heating. However, such buildings require careful design and management to ensure they are draught free, and that cross-ventilation is not blocked by partitions or screens.

The most appropriate system of ventilation, heating and cooling (low or high velocity, with or without terminal reheat and variable air volume etc.) will depend on the individual building and its situation. However, the percentage of fresh air introduced into the system (outside-air exchange rate), though reducing the efficiency of the system, also reduces levels of pollutants and thus of incidents of sick building syndrome (SBS).

Certain areas, such as toilets, food preparation areas, reprographic rooms and laboratories may require special extraction. Special care is needed to ensure that cooking smells do not escape into work areas.

Recommended temperatures are 21°C, with maximums of 24°C in summer and 22°C in winter, with fresh air provision of 8–12 litres per second per person.

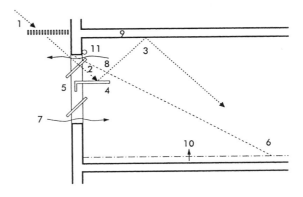

1 sunlight deflected by louvres, or	6 the window head limits how far light penetrates into the room
2 alternatively sunlight is deflected by 'light shelves' as part of the window	7 fresh air comes in at low level
3 and bounces up onto the ceiling and into the room	8 hot air goes out at high level
	9 the structure will cool the air
4 sunlight may also be reduced by 'light shelves'	10 the floor void may have room for auxiliary ventilation
5 and by special glazing	11 blinds reduce light and glare (and may provide privacy)

19 The naturally ventilated building – sunlight, daylight and air

Light (see 19)

Lighting is critical to how well people work, and how comfortable they feel. Legislation dictates lighting levels, and a lack of glare on computer screens, but much can be done with the control of natural light and the creative use of artificial light. Lighting affects what things look like, both in form and colour. The appearance of the interior or exterior of a building can be totally changed with imaginative lighting. The quantity of light needed for tasks is affected by age, with people of 60 needing four times the illuminance levels required by 20-year-olds.

Colour temperature, varying as it does from the warmth at 3000 K of a incandescent lamp to 5000 K of a cool fluorescent lamp or summer sunshine at midday, can also make an impact.

Daylight

The quality and quantity of light in an interior is dictated by the plan of the building and the way the skin of that building is designed. Narrow-plan buildings provide maximum daylight penetration, with the light from atriums in deep-plan buildings mimicking this to an extent.

Control is critical to satisfactory design, both in keeping too much light out and encouraging appropriate light penetration. Light is most effectively controlled outside the skin of the building, with overhangs, low head heights to windows or louvres. Such measures are normally not required on the north side of a building, unless there is reflected glare off adjacent structures. Louvres may be positioned in various ways, and be fixed or movable; however, they can prove hazardous in areas with high levels of wind. At skin level, shutters, solar glass or even plants are used for control. Internally, various types of blinds reduce or eliminate glare, but also cut out daylight and exterior views.

The optimum standards for visual comfort are >0.5% minimum daylight factor and >2–5% average daylight factor (with the daylight factor being lux inside/lux outside × 100%).

Artificial light

The type and position of luminaires can be used to enhance both the look and feel of a space. Uplighters, bouncing light off the ceiling, provide the most attractive and glare-free environment, but some accent lighting may be needed to avoid blandness. Lighting from downlighters, while more efficient, can be harsh and create reflective glare. Where there is sufficient ceiling height, suspended luminaires, which provide mainly uplighting but also some downlighting, can be most effective. Spotlights, whether recessed, surface mounted or hung from a track, provide sparkle and focused illumination, but can cause discomfort if wrongly positioned.

Task lights, either free-standing or built into the workstation, both augment ambient lighting for those who need higher lighting levels and also provide accent lighting. Accent lighting to art works, landscaping or other special features can provide useful interest. This can include emphasising special elements such as doorways or corridor junctions. Areas such as the café may well benefit from dramatic lighting, though it should be sufficient for meetings and other work situations.

Fluorescent lamps provide the most economic lighting, and with high-frequency ballast units they can be dimmed and do not have a visible flicker. Incandescent lamps – ordinary tungsten, tungsten halogen and low-voltage lamps – can all be used to good effect, but they have high energy consumption and low lamp life.

Ambient lighting for corridors, toilets, store rooms etc. can be 100–200 lux; general office space requires 300–500 (with light from an overcast sky being around 5000 lux). The desired uniformity ratio (minimum daylight factor/average daylight factor) is 0.8 over the designated task area.

1 ceiling void
2 ducts
3 gap at the top of partition
4 through partition construction
5 gaps/joints at ends/between panels
6 floor void (not usually a problem unless used as air plenum)
7 gaps under partitions (only with demountable systems)
8 structure-borne sound only likely for direct machine vibrations
9 for effective sound insulation, floor and ceilingvoids must be sealed along the partition line

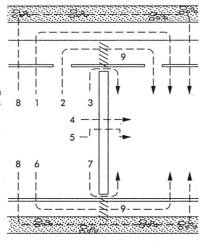

20 Noise paths, showing acoustic paths around partitions

	sound (liked)	noise (disliked)
audibility (loudness)	is it loud enough?	is it quiet enough?
intelligibility (clarity)	is it clear enough?	is it masked/diffused enough?

21 Sound and noise

Emergency lighting, to illuminate escape routes, can be incorporated in normal luminaires. These can be powered by batteries, or by a separate power source (which will also supply critical business activities). Statutory regulations not only control the amount and location of emergency lighting, but also its maintenance.

Sound (see **20,21**)

Noise is considered a major downside of open-plan officing. It interferes with people's ability to concentrate and may thus make them less productive. Conversely, in certain situations, such as trading floors, a degree of 'buzz' is considered essential.

Measures to lower the level of noise include reducing or eliminating noise sources, blocking noise sources, absorbing or diffusing noise, and masking it. Noise can be blocked with heavy or special acoustic walls and partitions. Careful detailing is required to junctions and openings, and partitions should run through floor and ceiling voids to the structure. Absorbent ceiling, floor, wall and screen finishes can help reduce the impact of noise. Air conditioning, music or artificial noise can make people less aware of noise, as can the discreet sound of voices.

Layout and protocol too can affect the transfer of sound, with the direction that people face, whether they are standing or sitting, and how loud they talk, all having an impact. Lower densities, with the resultant increased space between people, can improve the acoustic climate. Ceiling height, as well as finish, can be used to alter the acoustics.

Residual noise, after attenuation, should be no more than $45–50\,LA_{eq}$ for open-plan offices, $40–45\,LA_{eq}$ for cellular offices, and $30–40\,LA_{eq}$ for meeting rooms. Reverberation times should range from 0.4 seconds for a room of $50\,m^2$ to 0.7 seconds for a $500\,m^2$ room.

Plumbing

Hot and cold water services and drainage will be required for all sanitary installations, cleaners' cupboards, tea kitchens, vending, restaurant and café areas. Some facilities in specialist organisations, such as laboratories, may also require sanitary provision, as will any day-care, health or fitness facilities. Taller buildings require protected risers for fire fighting.

For both single sex and unisex toilets, provision can be calculated at 1 person per 14 m² NIA, based on 120% of the population (60%:60% male-to-female ratio). Where toilets are unisex, the calculation is based on 100% of the population. However, to provide for maximum adaptability over time, higher occupancy rates and differing gender balances are worth considering.

Water storage is calculated as 10–20 litres per person per day, to reduce the risk of Legionnaires' disease through keeping the turnover high.

Lifts and escalators

The positioning of lifts and their lobbies, and their number and speed can be critical to how staff and visitors perceive the building. Lifts should move a minimum of 15% of the building's population within 5 minutes, with a maximum wait of 30 seconds and an actual car capacity of 80%.

For any building over 10 000 m² a separate goods lift is essential(with ease of access at all levels for bulky objects). Fire fighter's lifts may well be needed for high buildings.

Escalators can carry large numbers of people quickly, but they are expensive in terms of both money and space. They are thus generally only used in high-profile situations, such as to enter a first-floor office area from the street or to move large groups through a higher space.

SETTINGS

Furniture, fittings and decorative items are all included in settings.

Furniture, the primary element, should function well, look good, and be durable and replaceable. It must be also be possible to procure the specified items within the given timeframe. Testing out alternative workstations and chairs can prove a useful exercise.

European legislation now makes clear demands concerning the provision of suitable workplace design where VDUs are involved. Since nearly all workers in Europe now use VDUs for at least part of their working day, the relevant Directive covers the majority of workstations.

VDU Directive

EEC Directive 90/270 covers most aspects of workplace design associated with VDUs. It calls for:
- clear and controllable screen images
- movable base to the screen
- adjustable keyboard height and angle
- document holders
- adequate sized work surfaces
- low-reflectance surfaces
- stable and adjustable chairs
- footrests
- avoidance of glare and other environmental discomfort factors
- eye tests
- training in the use of equipment.

Workstations (see **22**)

Workstations should be designed to provide maximum comfort. Adjustable height work surfaces are not obligatory, but common sense dictates that two people of quite different heights should not be forced to use the same height work surfaces. However, where desks are shared, heights are unlikely to be adjusted between occupancy by different users (though this does depend on the ease of adjustment). Adjustability to standing height is being adopted by many firms, particularly on the continent.

For general computer work, a boomerang shaped work surface can work well. The keyboard is positioned directly in front of the screen, with surfaces for reference material easily accessible on either side. Where alternative work settings are provided, minimum size workstations may prove adequate.

The classic 'systems furniture' workstation consists of one or more work surfaces, perhaps a movable table element for meetings, space for personal and business storage, screening which may be used as pin-up space, and a cable management system.

More mobile workstations may be made up of furniture which is configured to fit immediate needs. Alternatively, built-in workstations or standard elements put simply together may prove effective and economic.

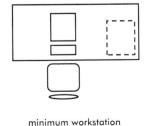

minimum workstation
(180 × 180 cm)

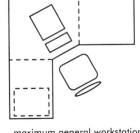

maximum general workstation
(180 × 180 cm)

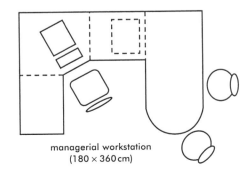

managerial workstation
(180 × 360 cm)

22 Typical workstations

Chairs (see 23)

A good chair is central to worker comfort. The VDU Directive requires that VDU operators be provided with fully adjustable chairs. The back and seat must be independently adjustable, as should seat(pan) and arm height. For those doing non-VDU centred tasks, seating is still important, though this will depend on length of use.

The occasional-visitor chair can be fairly basic, as can the seating in reception – though this should look good and not be too low. However, seating for meetings should be comfortable enough for several hours' use. This also applies to restaurant seating where it is also used for working, but it should be exceptionally durable and easily cleaned.

Storage (see 24)

Storage may be personal, group or general, and the amount and type will vary depending on business sector and department. It could be heavy, bulky or confidential, and may or may not require easy access. The more storage can be rationalised, the more flexible the organisation can become.

At the workstation, personal storage is needed for items including brief cases, handbags and other incidentals. Storage for stationery, small equipment, files and some reference material is also required within easy reach of the seating position. With shared desking, mobile pedestals, trolleys, bags or some other system should be provided, plus designated storage which is both neat and safe.

Groups require secure and tidy storage for coats and umbrellas. Space for reference material and files will also be needed, but in preference the majority of this is in a central resource centre.

Main storage areas include space for core business items, such as stationery and files (though dead files may well be stored off-site). Facilities management requires storage for housekeeping stores, cleaning equipment and materials.

Material may be accommodated on shelves, in cupboards or filing cabinets (vertical or horizontal). Bulk storage systems (sliding or revolving) can store large quantities of files and other information.

Paper storage

The average amount of paper storage per person varies from the academic at 12–15 linear meters to the mobile or space conscious groups at 0.5–2 linear meters. The average allowance in many businesses is 3–4 linear meters, though many staff use as much as 15 linear meters.

Capacities

The capacities of different storage systems in linear meters are:

Two-drawer filing cabinet	1
Cupboard/shelving four rows high	4
Revolving	11
Moving aisle	5.5
Revolving	50

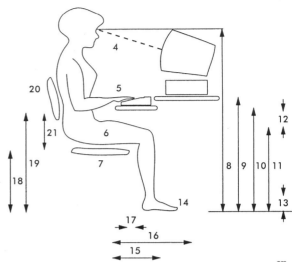

		cm
1	arm reach	40–60
2	distance to screen (more for large screens) plus document holder	50–75
3	elbow to keyboard reach	30–40
4	working angle from horizontal eye level to centre of screen	20–30°
5	neutral forearm and wrist angle	5–30°
6	open trunk to thigh angle	90–100°
7	adjustable seat (±5° from horizontal forwards and backwards)	40w × 36h × 40d
8	eye height to top of screen	100–140
9	general worktop height	65–76
10	keyboard height (rounded edges and wrist supports)	65–76
11	under desk knee clearance	50
12	clearance between thigh and work surface	20
13	under desk foot clearance	25
14	feet in firm contact with floor or footrest	
15	clearance for knees beneath desk	40–45
16	clearance for feet beneath desk	60
17	clearance between calf and front of seat	4–8
18	seat (pan) height	35–50
19	relaxed elbow height	55–75
20	seat back adjustable in height and angle (and position of lumbar support)	
21	armrest height above seat (adjustable and set back from seat edge 10cm)	20–25

23 Workstation ergonomics: average dimensions

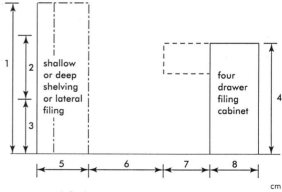

		cm
1	maximum reach (for the average woman)	195
2	optimum shelving zone (for storage of heavy items)	75–80
3	low zone, easy reach	70–75
4	maximum height for seeing into a drawer	140
5	depth of shelving	30–60
6	aisle width (allowing for door opening)	90–120
7	clearance for filing drawer to open	45–75
8	filing cabinet	50–80

note: lateral storage has twice the capacity of filing cabinets, so floor loadings need consideration

24 Dimensions for storage

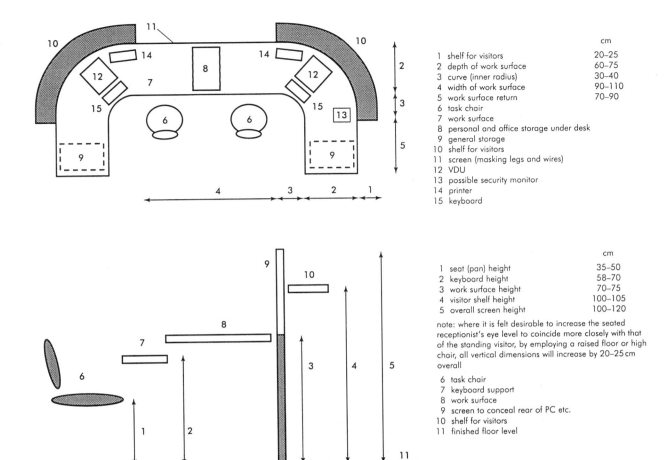

	cm
1 shelf for visitors	20–25
2 depth of work surface	60–75
3 curve (inner radius)	30–40
4 width of work surface	90–110
5 work surface return	70–90
6 task chair	
7 work surface	
8 personal and office storage under desk	
9 general storage	
10 shelf for visitors	
11 screen (masking legs and wires)	
12 VDU	
13 possible security monitor	
14 printer	
15 keyboard	

	cm
1 seat (pan) height	35–50
2 keyboard height	58–70
3 work surface height	70–75
4 visitor shelf height	100–105
5 overall screen height	100–120

note: where it is felt desirable to increase the seated receptionist's eye level to coincide more closely with that of the standing visitor, by employing a raised floor or high chair, all vertical dimensions will increase by 20–25 cm overall

6 task chair
7 keyboard support
8 work surface
9 screen to conceal rear of PC etc.
10 shelf for visitors
11 finished floor level

25 Reception desk

Screens

Screens are used to provide a degree of visual and acoustic privacy, but may also support shelving, cupboards and task lighting, house cable runs and can be used as pin-up boards by individuals or groups.

Where systems furniture is being used, screens may be an integral part of the workstation, supporting or being supported by the workstation, or they may be free-standing. Independent screens come in many different configurations, and may be so positioned to provide a feeling of intimacy to the individual or group.

Screen heights vary from 700 mm, to shield the under-desk area, to around 1800 mm, with heights in-between providing different degrees of privacy. Screens are also used to hide untidy cabling.

Fabric covered screens, containing absorbent material, usefully attenuate noise, but lightweight ones, constructed perhaps of perforated aluminium, have only a visual impact.

Meeting areas

With meeting areas varying from the space at the end of the desk or room to fully equipped video-conferencing and training rooms, furniture for meetings will depend on format and size of the space. Chairs and a table are the traditional basics of meeting rooms, but may be replaced for more informal sessions with sofas, lounge chairs, and even bean bags, with low tables for paperwork.

Reception area (see **25**)

With reception being the first – and often the only – introduction to an organisation, the quality of the furniture is especially important. Receptionists may work at standard workstations, or use an innovative meet and greet approach, but more frequently they sit behind specially designed desks. Flat screens are helping to make these more inviting, and reduce the amount of screening required. The purpose of these desks is to provide an efficient workstation while also allowing communication and surveillance. At the same time, they need to conceal untidy paperwork and cabling as well as sheltering the users from draughts coming in from the street.

Other furniture includes visitor seating, ranging from comfortable sofas and chairs to small areas with chairs and a table for short meetings, and touch-down desks for short periods of computer-based work. Stands may be provided to display promotional literature, framing for posters or art works, and shelving for products.

Restaurant

Serving counters are obtained from specialist suppliers, but their appearance should fit in with the overall design of the restaurant, as should other elements such as tills and dirty crockery collection points.

Seating may need to be sufficiently comfortable for long-term use, and tables positioned and of a height to support this.

Resource centre

Libraries are covered elsewhere in this handbook, but resource centres require not just furniture to support study, but also for meetings and training in adjacent spaces. Staff need generous workstations for processing material. Books, periodicals, files and electronic matter will require shelving and cupboards.

Signage

Flexible workers need to feel instantly at home when they arrive in the office for a few hours each week. Clear signage is essential for everybody, but especially for those with special needs. Raised and Braille lettering at critical points help those with visual impairment but specific help with way-finding for the hard of hearing is yet to be developed.

The design of the building can make it more easily navigable, with views out and changes of colour and texture. Technology too is helping, with touch-screens situated at critical points to illustrate the geography and help in locating personnel.

Window treatment

Windows may require blinds to control glare or ensure privacy. In some cases sheers or drapes may be appropriate to mask unattractive views, or reduce the 'black-hole' effect of glazing at night.

Art works

Where the inclusion of two- or three-dimensional art works is part of the scheme concept, both the decorative and place-making value is increased. Used to emphasise space, turn a corner or divide functions, art works – well lit – provide a useful and uplifting tool.

Plants

Plants and flowers make space more humane. Plants require good natural light or special lighting to a level of 600–700 lux, with a temperature of 21°C and relative humidity at 45–50%. Plants dislike draughts and radiant or hot ducted air. Watering systems, containers and positioning all require consideration.

Accessories

An integrated approach, including loose items such as waste-paper baskets and cutlery in the restaurant, should be a part of the overall design concept.

Procurement

The furniture may be procured from one or several different suppliers or manufacturers depending on the size and complexity of the contract. Devising a clear process for choice, with agreed criteria (design, quality, durability, delivery, ongoing availability, range and cost), showroom visits, trials and mock-ups can prove invaluable.

SHELL AND SCENERY

Buildings are comparatively permanent, while the organisations and activities within them are continuously changing. The building structure may well last 70 years or more; the skin 50 to 75 years. Environmental elements (services and cabling infrastructure) will last about 15 years. The scenery (fitting-out components such as ceilings, lighting and finishes) has a life-span of perhaps only 5 years. Settings (furniture and equipment) are moved as needs be to meet changing needs. (See **26**.)

'Shell and core' describes the building envelope, its structure and skin (walls and columns), and its servicing elements (stairs, lifts, lavatories, lobbies, ducts and plant rooms).

Factors that will affect the plan form and section include type of client, location, site conditions, planning restrictions, access, long- and short-term use of the building, organisational culture, required image, management, maintenance, budget and programme.

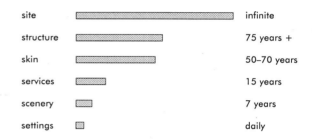

site	infinite
structure	75 years +
skin	50–70 years
services	15 years
scenery	7 years
settings	daily

26 Life expectancy: shell, building services, scenery and settings all last for different lengths of time

Levels of completion

The main contract for an office building may just cover the shell and core, or it may include the fit-out ready for the occupiers to move in. The six basic levels of completion are shell only, shell and core, developer standard, category A (background fitting-out), category B (bespoke fitting-out) and fully furnished.

Shell: building structure and envelope only.

Shell and core: includes building structure, cores and external envelope complete; all vertical services (water, drainage, gas, lifts, HVAC plant and risers, electrical and data risers); perimeter heating (if any) installed; toilets fully plumbed and finished.

Developer standard: as for shell and core, but plus entrance hall, cores, staircases, toilets, and other common parts all fully finished. Office space is left as shell and core, except that part which may be fitted for display purposes.

Category A fit-out: some fitting-out of office space, including raised floors and carpeting, suspended ceilings and luminaires.

Category B fit out: as for category A, but with partitions and doors; horizontal services including HVAC ducting, sprinklers, power and data cabling, service terminals; built-in furniture and equipment in special areas such as reception, restaurant and kitchen; all finishes and decorations.

Fully furnished: the above plus loose furniture, equipment and tools; blinds and drapes; accessories, art works and plants.

Site

The site, its location, access and planning and other legislation will all have a major impact on the development of the design.

Location will prescribe densities of development to provide the necessary return to the financiers. Planning requirements may well dictate the volume, form and style of any building, the number of parking spaces and also such matters as access and landscaping.

Orientation, view, noise, wind direction, overlooking and overshadowing and access (by foot, bicycle, car and public transport) will all affect how the site is used. Orientating buildings east–west makes shading more difficult than for north–south, where generally only the south face requires sun breaks.

A site density for business parks of 45% gross external area (GEA) to site area is considered the norm, with 25% of the site area for landscaping. Larger buildings provide a higher density and generally lower energy consumption and capital costs. However, they are less flexible and there is less room for landscaping than with several smaller buildings.

Parking

Mobile working implies parking for cars, and the balance between the cost in space, construction and maintenance of car parking, local authority restrictions on car numbers, and staff demands becomes ever more intense.

For business parks, one car per 25 m² of GEA is assumed, with 25 m² per space as optimum, and aisles serving parking bays on both sides.

Floor plates (see 27)

The optimum width of a building is dictated by the distance through which daylight penetrates into a building. This is generally accepted to be about 5–7.5 m (or floor-to-ceiling height × 2.0–2.5). A double zone building, with workspace on either side of central circulation, would be 15–18 m in depth. Depths of less than 15 m are preferred for natural ventilation, but very narrow floor plates (narrower than 13.5 m) are less able to accommodate a mixture of open-plan and cellular workspace.

Atriums are often incorporated in deep-plan buildings to bring daylight into the centre of the building, thus providing the equivalent of two medium depth plates. However, some businesses require the total depth of the building to be as open as possible.

Structure

A steel structure has the advantage that it is relatively light, good for longer spans and greater depths, and for holes and fixings. It is more efficient for rectangular plans, whereas concrete is efficient in both square and rectangular situations, and for relatively short spans.

Standard loading allowances are taken as 2.5 kN/m² over 95% of the lettable floor area, with 7.5 kN/m² for 5% high-loading areas (which may be in the centre of the building adjacent to the core).

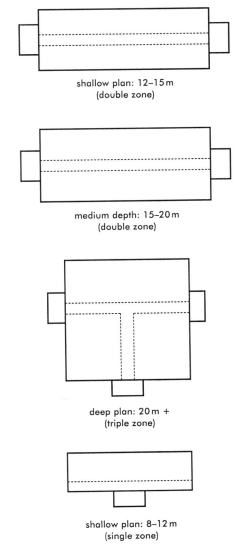

27 Building depths

Where longer spans and shallower floors are adopted, the extent of vibration from footfall etc. should be checked.

Skin

The envelope of the building must be watertight, airtight and meet thermal insulation requirements. The skin may be lightweight, and mainly glazed, or be faced with some apparently load-bearing material, such as stone or brick, with windows set within these panels. As its form varies dramatically, so does its function. The skin may let in the rain, or keep it out; it may be two part, with a maintenance walkway/ventilation stack between; there may be louvres that follow the sun, or blinds that adjust; the complex mechanics will almost certainly be controlled by a BMS.

The horizontal skin (the roof), though more traditional in construction, may well support solar collectors and stacks as well as the more usual air-handling plant.

Grids (see **28,29**)

With each element of the building having its own grid (from structure to ceiling tiles), integration of grids is essential.

The column grid should be as large as possible, and be a multiple of the space planning grid dimension. It may also relate to that of car parking, where this occurs within the building. Spans of 7.5 to 9.0 m are most economic.

The window mullion grid is most critical in cellular layouts where it dictates room size. A 3 m grid, which is not uncommon, works with a 1.5 m planning grid. Planning grids of 1.35 m and 1.2 m may also be adopted providing for rooms 2.7 m and 2.4 m in width.

Cores

Different elements of the core may be brought together in a single zone, or may be positioned separately with, for instance, staircases and toilets at the extremities, lifts in the centre, and ducts relating to the column grid.

The position of cores affects the way buildings can be used. Though fire regulations dictate the distances between staircases, the manner in which a building is subdivided depends on where cores are situated. A central core can prove economical, and allows for subdivision for different tenancies, but restricts the use of the floors as single open-plan entities. Cores at the perimeter can be effective, and if outside the envelope of the building may not count as office space for planning purposes.

Fire escape

The maximum travel distance in the UK to a means of escape in one direction only is 12 m, and 45 m in more than one direction (see **30**). The occupancy factor in open-plan offices exceeding 60 m² is 6 m² per person, or 7 m² per person for cellular offices.

Fire prevention also dictates the maximum volume of space that is acceptable without compartmentalisation to prevent the spread of fire. The volume of zones may be increased with the installation of automatic smoke vents, or by removing certain elements, such as staircases, outside the space.

Provision of escape for those with special needs, may require to include fireproof refuges and special secure escape routes.

Minimum widths for escape routes:

750 mm for 50 persons
850 mm for 110 persons
1050 mm for 220 persons
+5 mm per person above 220 persons

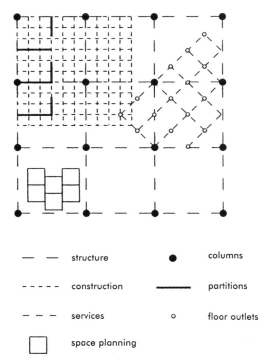

— — structure   ● columns

- - - - - construction   ▬▬ partitions

— – — services   ○ floor outlets

☐ space planning

28 Grids

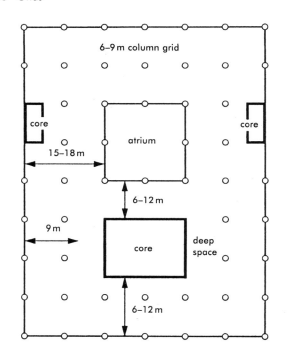

29 Plan form

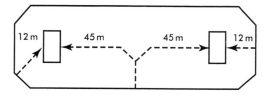

30 Fire escape routes: maximum distances for alternative exits or one only

Section (see *31*)

The height from the finished floor to the underside of the ceiling ranges from 2.6 m to 3.0 m. Suspended ceilings and raised floors provide space for ducting and cabling, but will increase the floor-to-floor height, and thus the overall height of the building. For column grids of up to 9 m centres, the services are usually run in a separate horizontal zone. With larger spans, the space between beams will often house service runs.

Raised floor zones are around 150 mm for cabling, or for special operations, such as trader dealing floors, 200–300 mm. Where air conditioning or ventilation is adopted the depth will increase to 300–450 mm. The lighting zone, which includes luminaires and suspended ceilings, is around 140 mm. The service zone in the ceiling will depend on what it contains.

Where structure is exposed, it can be used as a heat reservoir, and can also allow for increased floor-to-ceiling heights, at least in part, which is particularly desirable in open-plan areas.

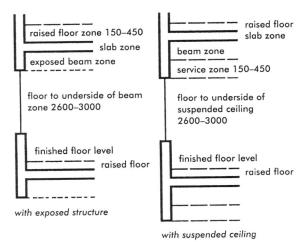

31 Vertical dimensions

Floors

In Europe and the USA, where raised floors are much less common, ducts in the floor slab provide limited cable provision. Cable-free equipment makes raised floors less important, and this helps with older or historic buildings, where the inclusion of a floor void is often not possible.

Design considerations for raised floors include:

- **Loading:** the system must be strong enough to take the required distributed and point loads without deflection or damage; and where it stands on legs, these must be able to transfer point loads to the structural slab without buckling or penetration.
- **Access:** access to the void is required for re-cabling and maintenance for electronic and power systems, and for maintenance and cleaning of ducting.
- **Terminals:** will be provided by floor boxes or standards for electronics and power, and by grilles for air handling.
- **Permeability:** vertical under-floor barriers may be required to prevent the spread of sound or fire.

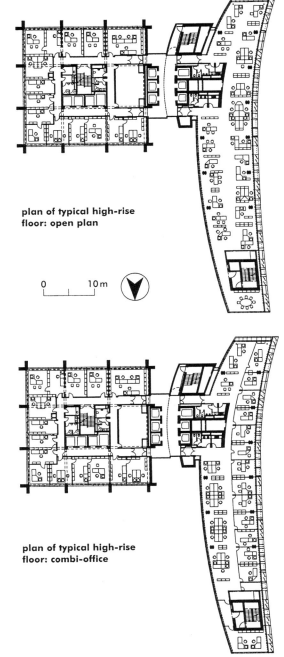

plan of typical high-rise floor: open plan

0   10 m

plan of typical high-rise floor: combi-office

32 GSW Headquarters, Berlin, Germany (Arch: Sauerbruch Hutton)

This development is made up of a number of parts. 47 900 m² in size, parking for 224 cars is mechanised as a result of a high water table. To an original square tower was added an 80 m high curved slab block, a three-storey street building with shops at ground level, and three other volumes containing a multipurpose entrance hall, conference facilities and offices. Each part has its own character. Most dramatic is the western façade of the high-rise block, where perforated metal shutters in bright colours form an ever-changing image as occupants exercise control.

Air movement is controlled externally with a 'wind roof' profile, and internally with a sophisticated façade design that pulls air in on the east façade from where it is then extracted via the solar flue of the multi-layered west façade. Air vents in internal partitions (designed to a high level of acoustic attenuation) allow air to pass between the openable windows. Only in winter months is mechanical ventilation required.

Walls and partitions

As well as dividing spaces, walls and partitions may be used to block vision, sound or fire. They may be fixed or demountable, but though theoretically a lightweight partition is easier to move, it may prove quicker and cheaper to move a 'dry-wall' partition.

Block or brick partitions will bear on the slab, and they may be load bearing. Lightweight ones (demountable or stud) stand on the raised floor. Plastered walls look good and wear well, but plasterwork is messy and slow.

Demountable partition systems can be quick to install, easy to relocate and provide adequate sound attenuation. However, they are expensive and have a limited life-span. With both sound and fire insulation it is essential to differentiate between the performance of a single panel (which may be high) and the wall (including door openings) as a whole. As with furniture, the design, quality, durability, delivery, ongoing availability, range and cost all require consideration.

The same issues need to be considered for mobile partitions to conference rooms and auditoria. In addition, means of support and storage require special consideration, as does acoustic performance, which may require the inclusion of pneumatic seals to the joints or an equivalent.

Ceilings

Acoustic panels fixed to a suspended aluminium or steel lightweight metal grid are found in the majority of offices. Panel size, appearance and performance vary greatly: large panels, curved panels, panels to withstand heavy impact, humidity and fire are available. Luminaires, sprinkler heads and air diffusers are all supported by the ceiling grid. Ducts and wiring are hidden above the ceiling, but are easily accessible for maintenance.

Panels in a suspended ceiling provide many advantages, but neat detailing around junctions can be difficult, and the grid lines can provide an excessive rhythm. A plasterboard ceiling, with either filled and taped joints, or a plaster skim, avoids this. Such ceilings may be essential in areas of complex configuration.

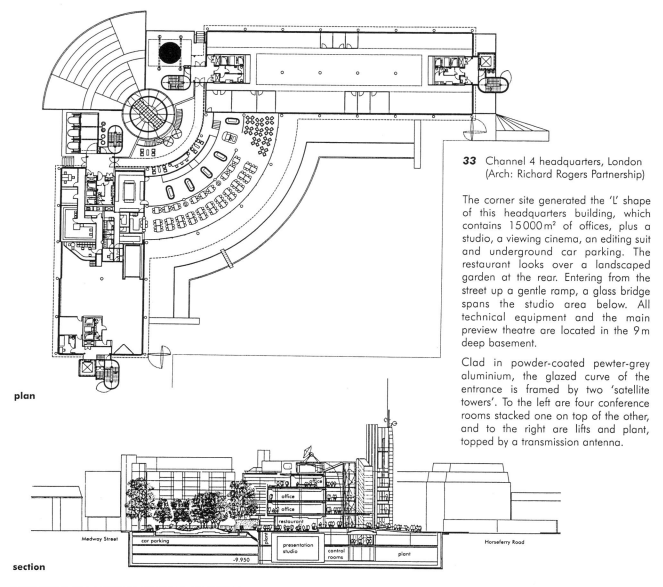

plan

33 Channel 4 headquarters, London (Arch: Richard Rogers Partnership)

The corner site generated the 'L' shape of this headquarters building, which contains 15 000 m² of offices, plus a studio, a viewing cinema, an editing suit and underground car parking. The restaurant looks over a landscaped garden at the rear. Entering from the street up a gentle ramp, a glass bridge spans the studio area below. All technical equipment and the main preview theatre are located in the 9 m deep basement.

Clad in powder-coated pewter-grey aluminium, the glazed curve of the entrance is framed by two 'satellite towers'. To the left are four conference rooms stacked one on top of the other, and to the right are lifts and plant, topped by a transmission antenna.

section

Floor finishes

Floors must wear well, be safe and communicate the desired image. Materials include timber, marble, vinyl, linoleum and steel. In British offices the most common floor covering is carpet, despite the consideration that hard materials are less likely to harbour pollutants.

The choice depends on appearance, cost and performance factors including safety, wear resistance, convenience, environment, ease of installation, and maintenance.

Careful consideration is required concerning reception flooring. Matting at the entrance removes dirt and moisture, but must be sufficient in quantity, be sensibly positioned and be flush with other floor finishes.

Wall finishes

Walls may be finished in plaster, marble, stone, tiles, timber, steel, aluminium, glass, mirror, various acrylic based materials and so on, but whatever the finish it must last well. Painted plaster or boarding remains a cheap option that can easily be refreshed, the colour scheme being easily adapted to the latest fashions. Special finishes (polished plaster or designer wallpaper) can look good, but they may not last well, and consideration of upkeep is an essential part of the design.

34 Menara Umno, Pulau Pinang, Malaysia (Arch: T. R. Hamzah & Yeang Sdn. Bhd)

section

25.353

roof (FFL)

21 81.900
20
19
18
17
16
15
14
13
12
11
10
9
8
7 28.000
6 23.000
5 18.000
4
3
2
1 3.300

This 21-storey building was designed to operate with natural ventilation or an air-conditioning system. With a narrow-plan construction, the maximum distance from an openable window is 6.5 m. It has a net area of 8200 m² (gross 10 900 m², including 94 car spaces), with a banking hall and auditorium situated at lower levels, and 14 floors of offices above.

Wing walls (in the end balcony zone) direct wind into pockets with adjustable 'air-locks' to bring air into the building. Cores and shading are positioned to provide maximum solar protection.

Designed to withstand earthquakes, a planar grid structure enhances the sway serviceability performance of the building.

By adopting a conventional reinforced concrete beam-and-slab system, local contractors were able to compete. A 22-month total construction programme was helped by using 'jump form' construction for the walls.

typical plan

0   10m

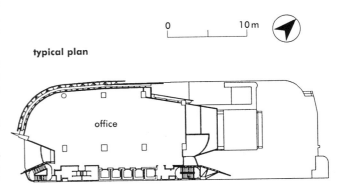

office

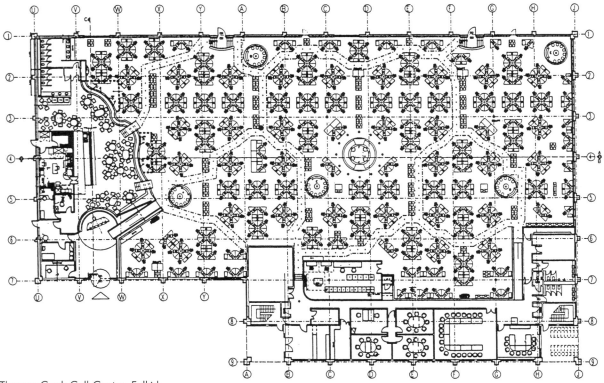

35 Thomas Cook Call Centre, Falkirk
(Arch: BDG McColl)

A 3700 m² warehouse building was converted to house 400 telesales staff set around a central control area, with a restaurant positioned by the entrance. Open except for meeting and training rooms, team meeting spaces are sunk into the 650 mm floor void.

A 'sensorama' walkway from reception uses light, smell and sound to provide a physical reminder of the holidays that are being sold. Murals of holiday scenes by local artists decorate the space throughout. Fairground-type masts display (with coloured lights) sales figures and team positions.

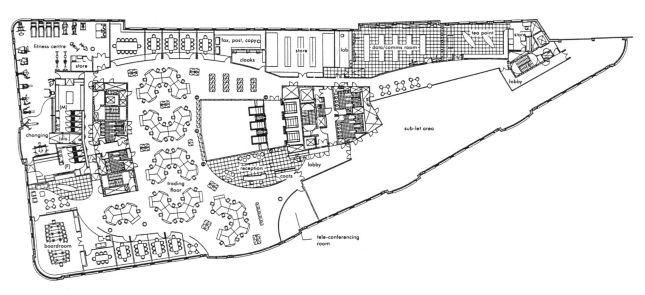

36 Trading space
(Arch: Pringle Brandon)

A foreign bank, operating in central London, asked for a quality office environment that would help attract and retain the highest calibre staff. With people working long hours, the office is intended to support their demanding lifestyles.

In a 1860 m² 'club' solution, 70 staff (traders and non-traders) sit at similar hi-tech, modular workstations arranged in clusters around the atrium. Surrounding them is a necklace of amenities

– glazed meeting rooms, video-conferencing, break-out spaces, cafés and a gym.

A new curved desk geometry delivers a variety of sinuous workstation layouts, such as honeycomb, rows and islands. Flat-panel displays allow for small, simple desks and provide a personalised and intimate environment that reflects the client's corporate culture.

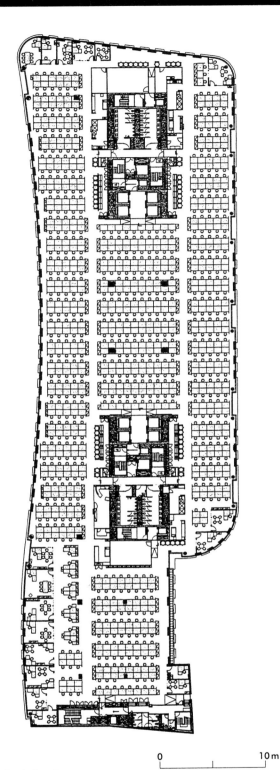

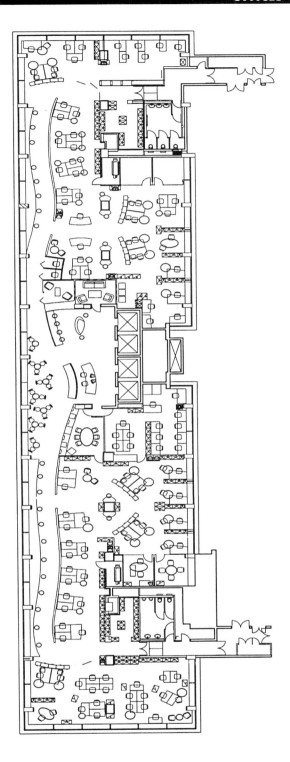

0   10m

37 Bank, London
(Arch: Pringle Brandon)

At an investment bank situated in Docklands, 650 traders are housed on a 5575 m² deep-plan dealing floor. The linear desking is amodular, allowing for individual desks to be any length. Desking has been designed for use with flat-panel displays, and allows for high-density occupation with ultra-flexibility for rapidly changing trading groups.

A further 1400 dealing positions are provided elsewhere, as is a 3715 m² data centre, offices, extensive client facilities and a staff restaurant.

38 Arthur Andersen, London: plan of consultancy floor
(Arch: BDG McColl)

This 820 m² narrow floor overlooking the Strand houses the consulting arm of accountancy firm Arthur Andersen. Acting as a base for 170 people, only support staff have PCs and dedicated desks; all others use laptops and fit into whatever space suits their needs and is available. This may be high touch-down desks along the window at the front of the building or communal tables in the central work area. Alternatively, they may choose the quiet 'Zen' zone (which features fish tanks and no telephones), a meeting room, or the collaborative zone (dubbed 'chaos') at the other end of the floor, where groups form and re-form using the mobile furniture.

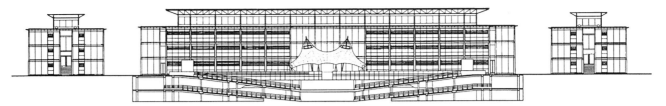

section and elevation

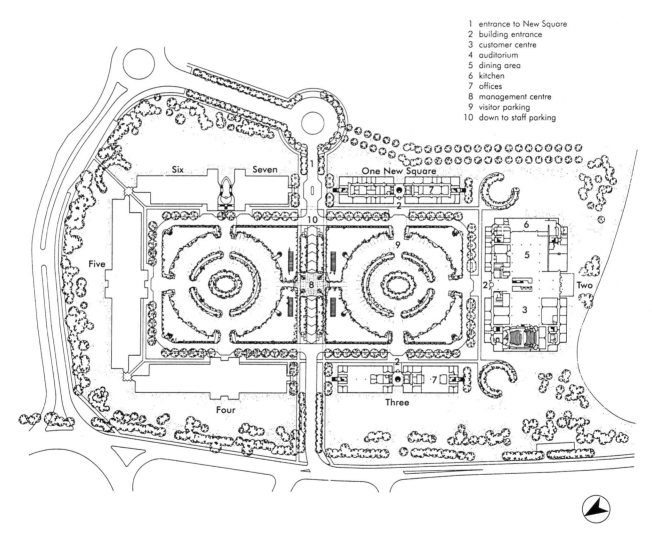

1 entrance to New Square
2 building entrance
3 customer centre
4 auditorium
5 dining area
6 kitchen
7 offices
8 management centre
9 visitor parking
10 down to staff parking

ground floor plan

39 IBM, Bedfont Lakes, W London
(Arch: Michael Hopkins & Partners)

The development of the business park at Bedfont Lakes, near Heathrow Airport, started in the late 1980s. IBM has three buildings, three stories in height, set around a landscaped courtyard. The 16 800 m² complex forms the base for at least 1500 sales and marketing staff, many of whom hot-desk when they come into the office. In each block, narrow-plan workspace surrounds two atria separated by a circulation core. The restaurant set in one of these is used all day for meetings and also sole working. Mainly open plan with some meeting rooms, there are also perimeter offices for certain staff members.

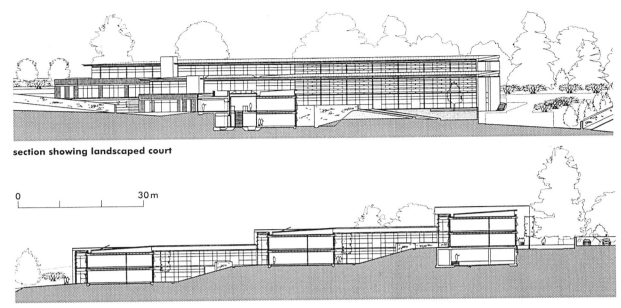

section showing landscaped court

0 ⊢———— 30 m

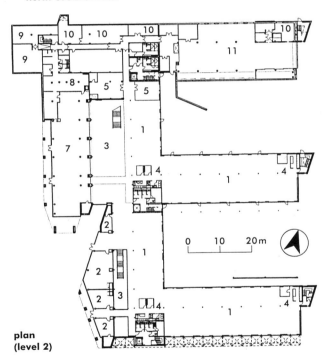

north–south section

1	open-plan office	6	communications room
2	meeting room	7	restaurant
3	street space	8	kitchen
4	business centre	9	store
5	post room/	10	plant
	reprographics	11	undercroft

plan (level 2)

0   10   20 m

This three-storey, 10 000 m² complex has three north/south facing wings which accommodate 580 workspaces. These are joined by a street, which is illuminated by north-facing roof lights.

A lightweight steel frame supports the pre-cast concrete shell units of the floor and roof slabs. The thermal mass of these, with effective solar control, provide for a maximum indoor temperature of 26°C with minimum mechanical systems.

Good daylighting, sophisticated building management control systems, solar panels for domestic hot water, rain and grey water management, and minimalisation of embodied energy, resource consumption and pollution, all make this an ecologically responsible building.

The 15 m deep plan allows for workstations either side of central circulation. Special lighting 'rafts' provide 400 lux with a mixture of direct and indirect lighting. Designed to assist the acoustic climate, the rafts also house the fire alarm system. Lighting is controlled by both daylight and presence detector sensors.

40 Wessex Water Operations Centre, Bath
(Arch: Bennetts Associates)

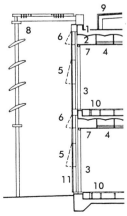

detail of office wing

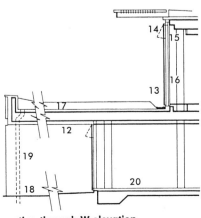

section through W elevation

1 exposed pre-cast concrete coffer units with in situ topping; 2 pre-cast unit visible through façade; 3 steel columns on 3 m grid (intermediate pre-cast concrete wall units provide thermal mass); 4 lighting raft with low-energy fittings and accoustic absorption in wings (each fitting controilled by daylight sensors and presence detectors); 5 manually operated windows; 6 BMS-controlled window with manual override button on façade; 7 anti-glare blinds; 8 fixed solar shading; 9 terne-coated stainless steel roof with rainwater collection to tank; 10 raised floor with perimeter trench heating; 11 full-height low-E double-glazed windows; 12 overhang shades restaurant windows; 13 full-height low-E and neutral solar control double-glazed units; 14 BMS-controlled windows interlinked with mechanical ventilation (to provide natural ventilation in mid-season or mechanical ventilation during high occupancy in summer); 15 blackout and glare blinds; 16 adjustable timber shutters; 17 grass landscaped roof; 18 Bath stone column cladding; 19 rainwater pipes discharge to natural swale drainage; 20 underfloor heating

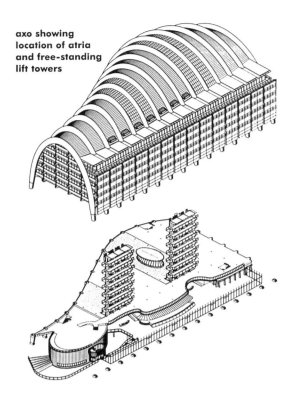

axo showing location of atria and free-standing lift towers

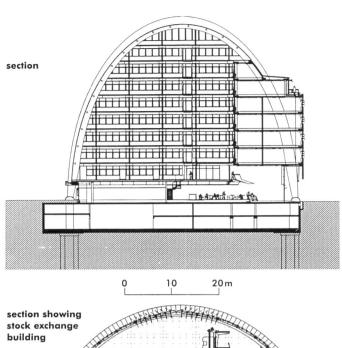

section

0   10   20 m

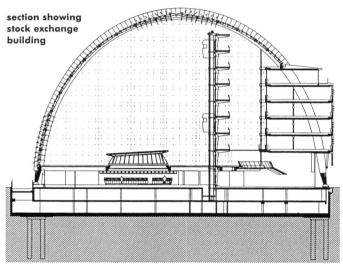

section showing stock exchange building

41 Ludwig Erhard Haus, Berlin
(Arch: Nicholas Grimshaw & Partners)

A tight site and a height restriction of 22 m at the eaves generated the design of this building, which accommodates at least 800 people in 18 000 m² of office space. A total area of 22 000 m² includes communications, exhibition, conference and lecture space, as well as parking for 250 cars and an entrance hall with an all-day restaurant with seating for 150 people.

Divided into three parts around two small atriums (which house the lifts), the complex construction comprises 15 steel arches spanning from between 33.7 to 61.2 m, set on a foundation slab. The nine column-free floors are suspended from the arches, which are reinforced with closed concrete shells set vertically between them.

Windows open in the glazed curtain wall façades. Internal finishes include glass partitions (unusual in Germany) and maple panelling in special areas, including the lifts, with stainless steel and aluminium fittings.

Although the home of the Berlin Stock Exchange, this is a multi-tenanted building with units of different sizes.

ground floor plan showing restaurant

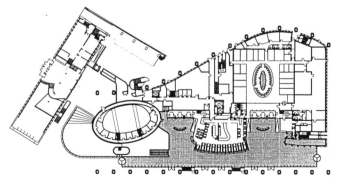

second floor plan

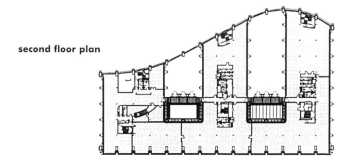

PUBS

See also Restaurants and Catering Facilities

THE PUB ATMOSPHERE

English pubs are famous as social institutions throughout the world: their atmosphere is very difficult to create afresh. Few modern designs have satisfactorily caught the right atmosphere; many originals have been insensitively altered, often first to so-called modern design, then back again to revival Victorian. A feature of successful pubs seems to be the breaking-up of space into small intimate areas which nevertheless retain a feeling of bustle all round. The traditional way to do this was with a central servery, with bars radiating around it. The good pub has something of theatre about it: good taste should be used sparingly; brashness and vulgarity have their place in interior fittings. Each pub has its own character, depending on its location, choice of beers, and even the time of year.

Some organisations have tried to keep the atmosphere of the traditional pub both in terms of physical atmosphere and the alcohol available (ideally, a choice of local beers) – for instance, CAMRA (the Campaign for Real Ale), and also some of the new, small companies in the brewery trade. They have tried to establish pubs in disused shop or commercial premises, challenging the traditional dominance of the large brewers. These designs tend to be traditional and revivalist, but nevertheless carefully created and often successful. In the 1960s and 1970s, many pubs lost the traditional beer pumps, which were replaced with pressurised keg beers.

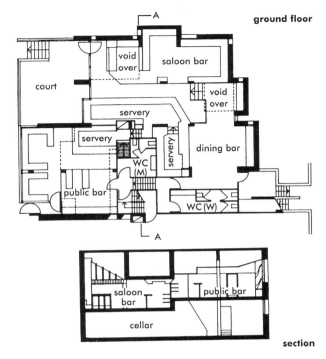

2 'Lord High Admiral', Westminster, London: a modern pub which successfully recreates the atmosphere of traditional English pub design, within a large-scale housing scheme; bars are separated, varying in design and comfort (Arch: Darbourne & Drake)

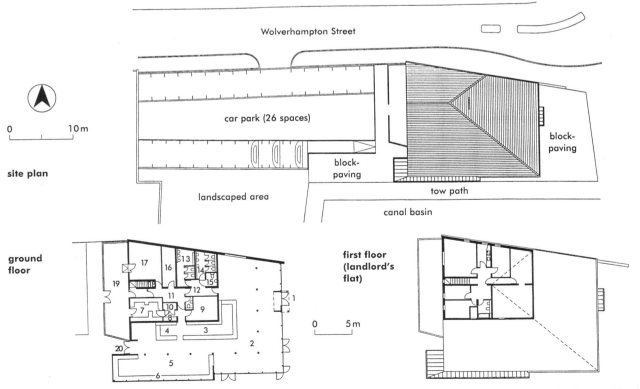

1 Pub at Town Wharf, Walsall, West Midlands (Arch: Sergison Bates & Caruso St John)

1 main entrance; 2 drinking area; 3 bar; 4 servery; 5 café area; 6 bench; 7 kitchen; 8 cutlery station; 9 bottle store; 10 dry store cupboard; 11 service corridor; 12 WC lobby; 13 toilets (M); 14 toilets (F); 15 WC (dis); 16 secure room; 17 cellar; 18 stairs to landlord's flat; 19 yard; 20 secondary entrance

PUB USAGE

This has traditionally been concentrated in the period after 9.00 PM, with lunchtime usage about one-third of this, although the relaxation of the licensing laws has allowed much more flexibility of opening hours, with many pubs now being open all day. Other recent changes include frequent provision of family rooms (to prevent under-18s coming into the bar).

There is now little distinction between pubs and licensed bars (see Restaurants); in theory the difference is that bars are intended for customers with less time, and often serve wine and more exotic drinks, snacks and light meals, whereas a pub traditionally serves beer and spirits, and is often intended for longer, evening drinking in more relaxing surroundings, with bar snacks often only available at lunchtime. It is now becoming common for there to be a restaurant in a separate room of the pub.

Bar servery The bar counter and back space are largely standardised, to suit drinks being served and storage of glasses etc.; at least one sink is also needed. A lockable shutter may be required if the area is used outside licensing hours.

Bars (drinking areas) There are usually at least two bars with different characteristics, and sometimes different prices (for instance, between the public bar and the lounge bar). There may be a separate games room (see **1**) and dining area. Public bar areas traditionally had a basic atmosphere, with simple seating and more high stools for drinking at the bar; the lounge bar had more comfortable seating. The designer needs to be clear if this traditional atmosphere is to be maintained, or whether a single bar area is more appropriate.

Delivery This is important consideration owing to the frequency and bulk of drink delivered. Delivery can be by large lorry or tanker, in kegs, barrels or crates. Suitable access to cellars is crucial (traditionally, but not necessarily, below ground). Storage for empties is also required. A delivery system from cellar to bar is required (it may be by hoist, electrical system, or pressure – hand pumps for draught beers or CO_2). More than one cellar may be necessary to suit the different temperatures required (e.g. for 'real ales' and the cooler beers gaining popularity in recent years).

Food Most pubs now also provide bar snacks. The growth of pre-cooked/chilled food and microwaves has led to a great increase in the variety of food provided: cooking equipment is therefore simpler than in the past, but must still be carefully integrated with the bar counter. A restaurant area is now common, requiring a separate kitchen and food preparation area.

Pub games Allow areas for pub games, generally darts, dominoes and pool, but there are some highly localised varieties. Video games, fruit machines and music are now considered essential by many brewers, but must be carefully placed to avoid annoying other users, who many want a quieter atmosphere.

Toilets The scale, siting and cleanliness of toilets are important: BS 6465 gives detailed information.

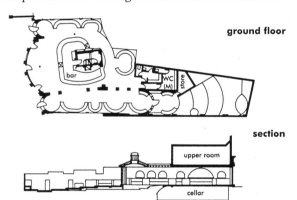

ground floor

section

5 'Markham Arms', Chelsea, London: a sympathetic conversion of a Victorian pub; original bow-front remains, with addition to rear, the geometry of the bow being repeated in the fixed seating arrangement
(Arch: Roderick Gradidge)

Licensing Act 1964

This covers premises where intoxicating liquor is sold. License applications are made to local licensing justices. Licenses are only granted if the premises are structurally suitable (the final decision resting with the justices), and further consent may be needed if other structural alterations are carried out at a later date. The licensing acts only control the sale of alcohol: the premises can be used for other purposes at any time, so the bar areas must be able to be closed and locked from the public when necessary. The fire officer will be consulted by the justices (and sometimes the police and the environmental health service), and the fire officer will probably also be consulted under separate applications for building regulations consent and under the Fire Precautions Act.

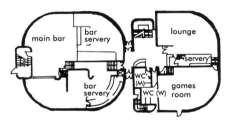

3 'The Fanciers', Northampton: a bright and breezy working men's club, with colourful use of materials, striped glass panels and curved corners; ground floor
(Arch: Roscoe Milne Partnership)

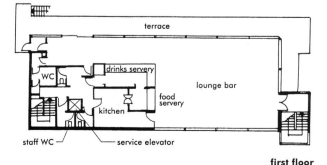

first floor

4 Foxhills Golf Club, Chertsey, Surrey
(Arch: Building Design Associates)

RELIGIOUS BUILDINGS

RELIGIOUS AFFILIATION

The approximate percentage of the adult UK population claiming active membership of a particular religion is as follows.

Trinitarian (Christian):

Anglican	3.1%
Protestant	4.1%
(Baptist, Methodist, United Reformed Church, Church of Scotland, other 'Free Church')	
Orthodox	0.5%
Roman Catholic	3.4%

Other religions:

Jewish	0.17%
Hindu	0.17%
Muslim	1.0%
Sikh	0.5%

CHRISTIAN CHURCHES

Anglicanism The Anglican communion exists in many countries. In England, it is the official state church, and in the UK it is therefore generally known as the Church of England; the monarch is the Supreme Governor, and the Archbishop of Canterbury is the primate. The Church of England was established as a result of Henry VIII's disagreement with the Papacy (the Act of Supremacy, 1534), and is often regarded as mid-way between Roman Catholicism and Protestantism; those closest to Catholic thinking are known as Anglo-Catholic.

Roman Catholicism is a world-wide religion, centred on the Pope in Rome, and claiming direct succession from St Peter, one of the 12 apostles of Jesus. Doctrine is summarised in the Nicene Creed. The Roman Catholic church is a large and complex organisation, with many religious orders. It could generally not be practised in the UK from the time of the Reformation until the Catholic Emancipation Act of 1829. In layout and services, great emphasis is usually placed on liturgy and tradition.

Eastern Orthodox A communion of self-governing churches developed from the Eastern Roman or Byzantine Empire, this now mainly describes the autonomous Greek Orthodox and Russian Orthodox Churches. The Trinity and the sacraments are considered of great importance.

Protestantism Sometimes known as 'Free Church' this has itself now split into many different groups, particularly with the growth of the evangelical and house-church movements over the last 30 years. High Church implies sympathy with Roman Catholicism; Low Church aligns with Methodism and the United Reformed Church. The traditional distinction of Low Church having chapels is now rare in the south of England.

The main Protestant denominations are as follows:

- *Methodism* was founded by John Wesley in the late 18th century, after gradual separation from the Church of England. Traditionally, Methodism has a strong emphasis on preaching, and the involvement of lay members. Similar to Low-Church Anglicanism.

- *Other Protestant denominations* include Baptists (who believe in baptism by total immersion), Presbyterians and Congregationalists, most of whom united in 1970 to form the United Reformed Church.

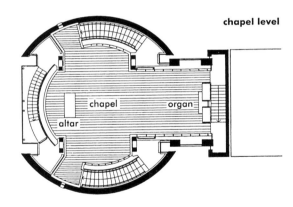

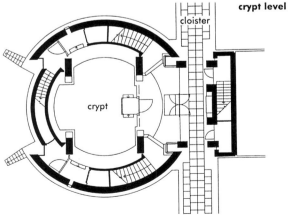

1 Traditional church layout, representing the cross on which Jesus died

2 Fitzwilliam College Chapel, Cambridge (Arch: MJP Architects)

- *The Salvation Army*, formed by William Booth in 1865 as a non-sectarian, evangelical Christian organisation, has a quasi-military structure, and its mission is to care for the poor and needy. Meetings are held in halls, and apart from a platform and seating there are virtually no liturgical requirements.
- *Quakers.* Generally known as the Quakers, the Society of Friends was established in the 18th century and they do not describe themselves as a church. They have no priesthood or formal liturgy. Their meeting halls are simple and usually rectangular; there is no altar, pulpit or font. Worship is often conducted largely in silence.

General arrangement

Declining congregations in the last 50 years have made many churches redundant. New forms of worship, and new uses for buildings, have had to be developed. Many denominations now share worship facilities although fundamental doctrinal differences remain: for instance, over the ordination of women, the interpretation of communion, and the role of the Papacy. Considerable co-operation often exists at a local level.

Some denominations have been re-established in the UK, coming from the USA (e.g. the Free Methodists). These denominations have no formal links with UK denominations of the same, or similar, names.

In Roman Catholic churches, the emphasis is now often placed on mass in the common tongue, rather than Latin. Protestants place more emphasis on preaching and communion carried out around 'Lord's Table'. Many newer religious sects have particular requirements related to special forms, singing, dancing and musical performances.

Most churches now have strong community concern; planning often relates to week-day uses – the key consideration is flexibility. Ancillary accommodation is usually required: for instance, meeting rooms (preferably for groups of different sizes), a coffee room, counselling room and office. Other factors include provision for people with mobility difficulties, good acoustic design (for both music and voice), security against crime, and adequate car parking space.

Traditional church services tend to emphasise importance of liturgy, mass (holy communion) and vestments etc., although the building layout may be informal. Less traditional services place more importance on preaching and individual participation.

A centralised plan is often popular with designers, but this is difficult to integrate with processional and ritualistic requirements. The importance of the priest, pastor or leader must not be lost.

Liturgical requirements

There are numerous items of equipment needed, depending on the religious attitude of the denomination or worshippers. Many will require individual design. Those generally encountered are noted below.

Altar or table This is the most important element in a church layout. Traditionally located at the east end (although there may also be subsidiary altars elsewhere). High Church uses the word altar, Low Church the word table. It is often located on a platform or raised area several steps above the nave. With a centralised plan, and in some experimental layouts, the altar is placed in the centre of the church. Size and ornamentation vary with each church; some altars are highly decorated, with elaborate cloths which need a suitable altar cloth chest.

Baptistry A receptacle for total immersion when initiates are baptised; used in Baptist and some evangelical denominations. It must be large enough to hold the minister and several initiates, and is usually covered when not in use. A heated water supply, steps on one side and drainage are required. Dressing and drying rooms (possibly both male and female) must be adjacent.

Communion rail The method of taking communion (or mass in High Church) varies between denominations and should be agreed at an early design stage. Communicants may have bread and wine passed around while seated, or may share a communal cup (and in both cases no communion rail will be necessary); or they may line up along a rail near the altar. The rail may need a rack for communion glasses, and must allow for elderly and infirm people kneeling adjacent (see **3**).

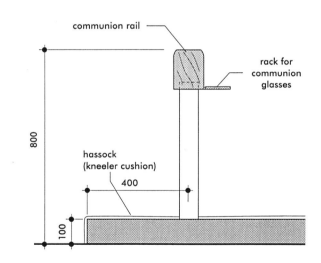

3 Communion rail

Confessional box Only found in High-Church buildings, this is an enclosure seating both priest and penitent, separated by a partition, in which the latter can talk in confidence to the priest.

Font Intended to hold water for baptisms, the font is traditionally at the entry to the church (i.e. at the west end), although it can now be located anywhere. Historically a large, carved object, with a cover, fonts are now often a simple bowl.

Lectern A book-rest, usually for the bible, located in the crossing or near the altar rail. Readings are made from a standing position, so the height of the lectern should be adjustable.

Pulpit Of major importance in Low-Church buildings, where preaching is given great prominence, the pulpit is usually elevated, with enclosed sides, and a book-rest and shelves.

Seating and pews Traditional layouts usually retain pews (often Victorian); other layouts often require a flexible space with individual upholstered chairs, with holders for order of service and hymn-books etc. (see **4**). Before adapting good-quality Victorian and pre-19th century pews, specialist advice should be sought. Choir stalls are sometimes required for choir seating. If worshippers are to kneel, a kneeler is required, sometimes hinged to the pew; otherwise a hassock (a decorated cushion) will be provided.

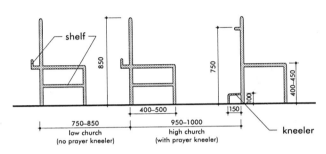

4 Seating/pews

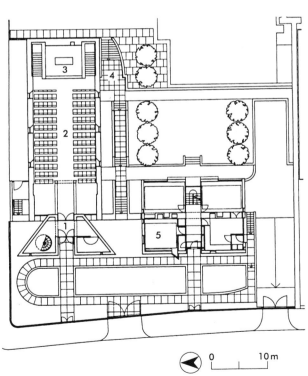

1 entrance 2 nave (seating for 140) 3 altar 4 vestry (below chancel) 5 vicarage

5 St Paul, Wightman Road, London (Anglican)
(Arch: Inskip & Jenkins)

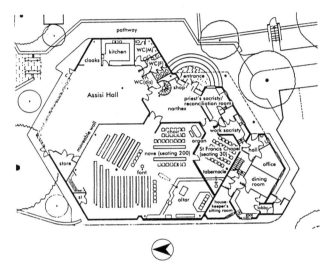

6 St Francis of Assisi, Crosspool, Sheffield (RC): the priest's accommodation is provided above the community facilites on the south side
(Arch: Vicente Stienlet)

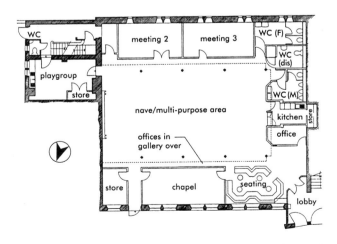

7 St Paul, Rossmore Road, London (Anglican): a re-ordering of a Victorian church to provide shared religious and community use
(Arch: Q. Pickard)

ground floor

first floor

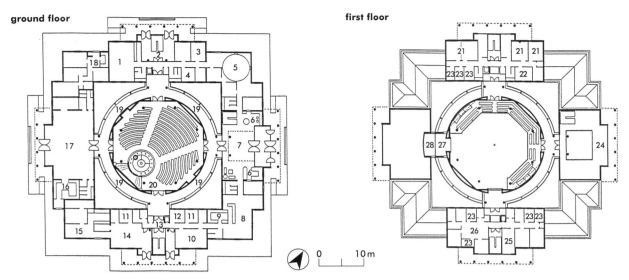

1 small hall; 2 lobby; 3 resource centre; 4 vestry; 5 chapel; 6 retail; 7 reception; 8 coffee shop; 9 kitchen; 10 meeting/activity room 11 couselling; 12 reception/admin; 13 lobby; 14 display area; 15 flat; 16 kitchen; 17 large hall; 18 warden's flat; 19 cloister; 20 worship area; 21 meeting room; 22 study; 23 counselling; 24 mezzanine; 25 common room; 26 reception; 27 organ; 28 projection

8 Church of Christ the Cornerstone, Milton Keynes: shared by five denominations (Anglican, Baptist, Methodist, Roman Catholic and URC)
(Arch: PDD Architects)

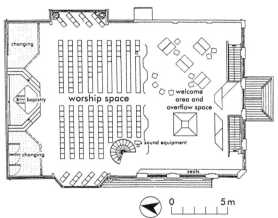

9 Emmanuel Christian Centre, Walthamstow: a Pentecostal church, with the worship hall on the first floor, and community facilities on the ground floor
(Arch: Praxis Architecture)

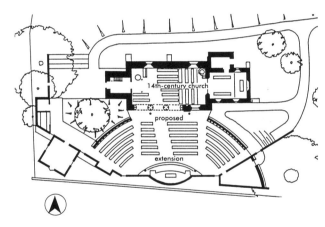

10 St Peter, Ditton, Kent (Anglican)
(Arch: Peter Melvin, Atelier MLM)

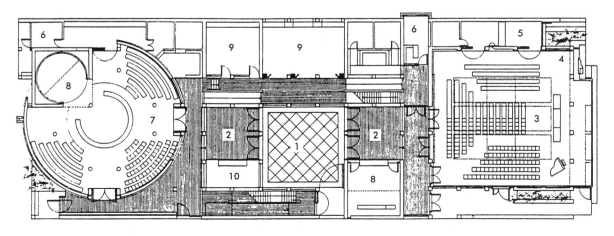

11 Bar Hill Ecumenical Church Centre
(Arch: Ivor Richards)

1 main entrance and courtyard; 2 entrance foyers and social spaces; 3 worship space (400 seats, shared Protestant/Roman Catholic); 4 sanctuary and bell tower; 5 prayer room; 6 vestry/office; 7 worship space (300 seats, shared Protestant/Roman Catholic); 8 chapels; 9 teaching and community rooms; 10 coffee bar

Organs

A specialist must be consulted at an early stage as organ requirements differ considerably depending not only on the volume and acoustics of the church, but also on musical style and type of accompaniment. The siting is critical: the organ should be free-standing (organ chambers are unacceptable); the location should not impede sound; the organ, organist and choir should be together and as near the congregation as possible; and the organ arrangement itself should be visually satisfying.

It should be noted that the primary purpose of a Roman Catholic and Anglican parish organ is liturgical accompaniment, while in a Low Church or evangelical group the organ is intended to provide musical accompaniment to singing.

The organ will often be very visible in the church: an unclad organ is unsightly, so it needs a well-designed case: a wooden structure enclosing the instrument, the front filled with decoratively arranged pipes. The purpose of the case is also protective and sometimes tonal, and should be finished to a high quality. The German term 'werk prinzip' is applied to what is considered to be the finest northern European organ arrangement, both musically and visually. Baroque and romantic organs of the 18th and 19th centuries are usually less satisfactory.

The internal atmospheric condition is very important: changes to heating, humidity or ventilation levels can drastically affect the performance of a traditional pipe organ.

Size of organ For a small church seating up to 150 people, a one-manual organ of three stops is adequate. In a medium church seating up to 300 people, a two-manual and pedal organ of 10 or 12 stops is needed, and possibly a third manual. For the largest churches and cathedrals, provide a three- or four-manual and pedal organ of about 35 stops.

Electronic organs These have recently improved dramatically in sound quality, and are now a serious alternative to pipe organs, particularly for smaller churches. Traditionally regarded as musically inferior, this is now much more doubtful. Their advantages are:
- much less space is required, and they can be easily repositioned to suit reordering or temporary rearrangements (e.g. at Christmas)
- little or no maintenance is required (a pipe organ requires regular, specialist maintenance)
- a great variety of sound can be produced
- they cost just a few thousand pounds.

However, they become obsolete quite quickly, and probably last no more than 20 to 30 years. Some models now available include pre-recorded hymn-book tunes, on computer disk, accessible simply by inputting the hymn number.

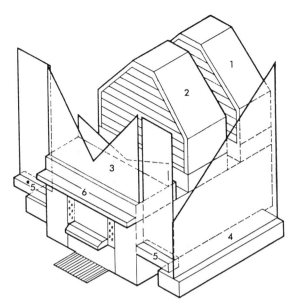

1 choir organ in box with louvred front; sound is masked by the swell organ standing in front of it; maintenance is by passage board between choir and swell organ

2 swell organ in box with louvred front; sound is masked by the great organ standing in front of it; maintenance is by passage board which also gives access to the great organ

3 great organ unenclosed and speaking from favourable position; large ranks on the front, small ranks on the rear

4 pedal organ divided and placed on both sides (or placed at rear behind choir organ) consisting of one or two ranks of large pipes which demand disproportionate amount of space

5 'off stand' block for display pipes, usually a mixture of dummies and pedal 4.9 m (16 ft) metal pipes

6 'off stand' block for display pipes, usually a mixture of dummies and great diapason 2.4 m (8 ft)

12 Diagrammatic layout of typical English organ (From Bradbeer)

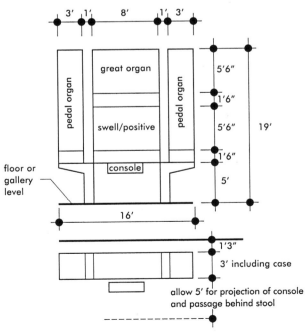

13 Space requirements for organ of two manuals and pedals (werk prinzip arrangement) (From Bradbeer)

MOSQUES

Note: spelling of words from languages which do not use the Roman alphabet is always open to more than one interpretation.

Introduction

Islam, together with Judaism and Christianity, are the three great monotheistic religions, and they share many holy texts.

The Arab prophet Muhammad was born in Mecca and about AD 610 he received revelations, which were subsequently recorded in the Qur'an (Koran), the Muslim holy book. In 622 Muhammad left Mecca for Medina, where he remained until his death in 632. In Medina, he became a both a religious and community leader. His legacy was sufficiently powerful that by 630 he had established control over all Arabia.

The five essential 'pillars of Islam' are:

(1) sincere reciting of the creed (the shahada)
(2) the formal prayer (the namaz) to be said five times a day
(3) the duty to share one's wealth through the giving of alms
(4) the requirement to fast during the month of Ramadan
(5) the pilgrimage to Mecca (the hajj), to be undertaken at least once.

There is no central authority or formal priesthood, but holy men and scholars (mullahs and ayatollahs) are accorded great respect. The main sectarian division is into Sunni and Shia believers, dating from 661.

Qur'an (Koran) The Muslim holy book, which sets out all that is necessary in order to lead a devout life. It is considered to be the direct word of God, as revealed to Muhammad by the angel Gabriel; the text is regarded as sacred and infallible, and is the main source of doctrine and law in Islam. It is poetry rather than prose, and is often chanted for liturgical purposes.

General arrangement

The word mosque is derived from the Arabic 'place of prostrations', (and it does not necessarily therefore have to be a building); it is both a house of worship and a symbol of Islam. Its built form is derived from that of the Prophet's house in Medina.

The mosque has a number of standard components, which will vary depending on whether it is local (masjid), congregational or principal (masid-i jami), or a Friday mosque (masid-i juma).

Traditionally, mosque design has followed climatic needs: for instance, shade and cooling has been obtained through use of arcades and courtyards incorporating areas of water. Open areas for prayer are, however, useless in wetter and cooler climates. In the West, there is an increasing practice to provide an Islamic Centre, comprising a mosque, library and lecture rooms, etc. Islam has also made an enormous contribution to architectural design in the areas of calligraphy, geometry and garden design.

Mosque design can be categorised into no more than five basic patterns:

- Arabia, Spain and Africa: the hypostyle hall and open courtyard
- Anatolia and SE Asia: a courtyard with a massive central dome or pyramidal pitched roofs
- Iran and central Asia: the bi-axial four-iwan type
- Indian subcontinent: an extensive courtyard and triple domes
- China: a walled garden enclosure with detached pavilions.

Detailed requirements

Planning generally For congregation, allow an area of 1 m² per person. When assembled in lines parallel to qibla wall, allow 1.2 m between lines when standing, and 0.8 m when sitting. Carpets and other floor coverings are required as the faithful remove footwear: storage space for shoes is required.

Congregational area A partly open courtyard (sahn) and partly roofed area for prayer, usually surrounded on three sides by colonnades. The open courtyard gives access to the roofed prayer hall (haram). All worshippers must face Mecca when at prayer, and should theoretically be equidistant from the qibla wall, thus forming parallel rows.

Decoration It is a generally accepted Islamic premise that the representation of living beings is unacceptable. This rigidly observed tradition does, however, allow free use of calligraphic devices from the Qur'an, which forms a valuable counterpart to otherwise plain surfaces and basic architectural forms.

Dikka A wooden platform, of single storey height with staircase access, positioned in line with the mihrab (sometimes located in the external courtyard). It is used for chanting and liturgical responses, particularly where there is a large congregation.

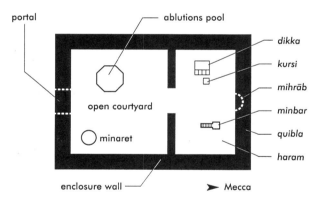

14 Main components of the mosque

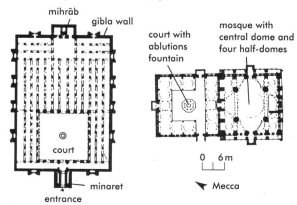

15 Simple mosque arrangement: Tlemcen Mosque of al-Mansur AD 1303–1306

16 16th-century mosque and court Sehzade Mehmet, Istanbul (Arch: Sinān)

Haram The sanctuary or covered prayer hall. Usually square or rectangular, with the roof either of a hypostyle pattern (i.e. a flat roof supported by a large number of evenly spaced columns) or covered by a large dome on pendentives, or a number of small domes.

Iwan Vaulted hall, one on each side of the courtyard.

Ka'bah The ancient shrine in Mecca; it is almost the only Islamic symbol.

Kulliye Associated buildings to a mosque (e.g. those used for medical or teaching purposes).

Kursi The lectern on which the Qur'an is rested; usually placed next to the dikka.

Maqsura Originally a raised platform with screens provided to protect the imman (the prayer leader); it is often offers an opportunity for special decoration.

Mihrāb The recess or niche, at the mid-point of the qibla wall, indicating the direction of Mecca. It is the most decorated feature of a mosque, although it is not in itself considered sacred. Its position is often emphasised by windows or a dome.

Minaret (mi'dinah) The original purpose was to ensure that the voice of the muezzin making the call to prayer five times a day (also the Friday sermon) could be heard over as large an area as possible. With the widespread use of loudspeakers, its function is now largely symbolic, and it can be omitted. The form of the minaret may be based on the lighthouse, but many other derivations are possible. Originally only one was provided, although two or four are sometimes found (and there are seven in Mecca).

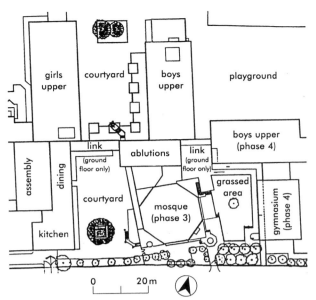

18 King Fahad Academy, London (Arch: Carnell Green)

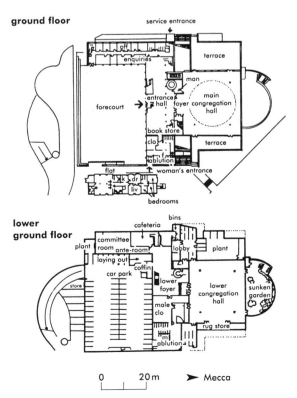

17 London central mosque (Arch: Gibberd & Partners)

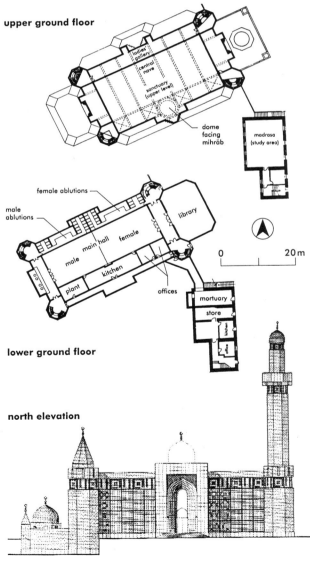

19 Great Mosque of Edinburgh (Arch: Basil Bayati Architecture & Urbanism Ltd)

Minbar The pulpit, always located to the right of the mihrāb. It is formed of a staircase, with a platform at the top, usually covered in a cupola-type roof. Sometimes absent from the smallest mosques, it varies from three steps to a highly decorated monumental staircase. The khutba (the oration or Friday sermon) is delivered from the minbar.

Portal This is intended to emphasise the change from the outside world to the enclosed, tranquil spaces of the mosque. The exterior of the mosque enclosure is usually plain, but the portal can be highly decorated.

Qibla The prayer-hall must have one wall (the qibla) facing Mecca

Segregation In most mosques, only male worshippers are permitted, although a gallery for women is often found. Some sects (e.g. Ishmailis) are fully integrated.

Washing facilities These must be provided as a requirement of the faith and are often a pool with running water (sometimes with a fountain) placed near the centre of the courtyard. It may, however, be purely decorative (particularly in European layouts), in which case the washing facilities will be next to the footwear storage area.

SYNAGOGUES

Introduction
Originally, worship centred around sacrifices made by the high priest in the temple, but sacrificial worship ended when the second temple was destroyed by the Romans in AD 70. By that time the synagogue was in common use.

As a result of the great age of Judaism, and the dispersion (diaspora) of the Jewish people (usually as a result of persecution), there are many different religious branches. It was not until the 1840s that most legal restrictions were removed from Jews in the UK, although informal toleration had existed for long before that. The United Synagogue was founded by Act of Parliament in 1870, and is still regarded as the largest grouping. Towards the end of the 19th century, great numbers of Jewish immigrants from Russia and eastern Europe introduced a very different Jewish tradition into the UK. Most were Orthodox Jews, speaking Yiddish, who formed new, small synagogues (called chevrot) outside the United Synagogue establishment. In 1887 the chevrot were formed into the Federation of Minor Synagogues.

There are many groupings in Anglo-Jewry, but the main divisions in the UK are generally considered to be as follows.

Orthodox (United Synagogue) Seeks to preserve traditional Judaism, and is considered to be the most influential group in the UK. Instrumental music is not used, and men and women are separated in the synagogue. The head is the Chief Rabbi, who is generally regarded as the spiritual leader of Anglo-Jewry.

Conservative (Federation of Minor Synagogues, formed 1887) Attempts to modify Orthodox Judaism, and is formed around smaller and more intimate congregations. Men and women are not segregated, and women can be accepted for ordination.

Reform Judaism Formed in the mid-19th century, it attempts a modern interpretation of Judaism; less emphasis is placed on ritual law and dietary requirements. Women take an active part in the service, part of which is in English. Both Conservative and Reform Judaism use a choir and organ. Reform Judaism has experienced considerable growth in the last 50 years.

Liberal and Progressive Synagogues Formed in the early 20th century to offer a radical departure from traditional Judaism. Its willingness to admit many who wish to convert to Judaism means the movement has experienced strong growth.

General arrangement
There is no formal architectural precedent for the synagogue (Greek for 'assembly', but gradually applied also to the building). Synagogues have three functions – as a place of worship, for study, and for social and community meetings – which tend to lead to a variety of built forms. Any place in which ten adult Jewish males congregate may be considered to be a synagogue.

The Talmud (the ancient collection of Jewish decisions and discussions about life and law) tends to set out the use of the synagogue, rather than the architectural form. This has often resulted in very basic, unassuming forms which have altered little over the centuries, often having a layout similar to an aisle-less chapel, or a mosque. The designs often tend to follow the architectural style of the country in which they are built. Increasingly they are multipurpose buildings incorporating community centres, sports and educational facilities, crèches and homes for the elderly.

The traditional alignment of the synagogue has been with the main prayer room on an east–west axis, with the ark at the east end, facing towards Jerusalem. Over the past two centuries, many European synagogues have tended to adopt a layout similar to a Christian church, with the bimah, ark and pulpit forming a uni-directional composition at the east end.

The Torah is the Jewish law, and comprises the first five books of the Bible (the Pentateuch). The Torah is hand-written on parchment scrolls and is kept in the ark in the synagogue. The rabbi is a teacher and spiritual guide, today having a role similar to clergy of other faiths. Ritual is very important.

Ritual requirements

Note that the spellings of Jewish terms can vary, often depending on whether translation is from Hebrew or Greek.

Ark The cabinet containing the Torah scrolls – the focal point of the synagogue, generally located at the east end. It may be free-standing, like a Christian altar, or it may be a niche in the east wall, where it can take the form of an apse. The original (portable) Ark of the Covenant had many uses; it was constructed during the time of Moses and is now lost.

Bimah The platform on which the reader's desk is placed for the reading of the Torah, usually with a surrounding railing. The bimah is the principal influence on the layout, and is often emphasised by more intense lighting. It has been located in various positions in the synagogue – sometimes at the W end, as a counterpart to the ark; sometimes in the centre. Over the past two centuries, the bimah tends to have moved to an eastern position adjacent to the ark.

Duchan The platform from which to recite the priestly benedictions.

Genizah The room (literally 'hiding space') in which to store unwanted manuscripts which may not be destroyed because of their sanctity.

Paroketh The curtain hanging in front of, or sometimes inside, the doors of the ark.

Mekvah Ritual bath of fresh-flowing water for the monthly cleansing by women. Usually placed near or below the synagogue.

Menorah The seven-branched candelabrum, positioned to the right of the paroketh (originally with seven branches, now with eight or nine).

Ner Tamid The lamp, which is continuously alight, located in front of the Ark.

Ornamentation Must be floral or geometric, in order not to contravene the second commandment, which proscribes the 'making of idols and graven images'.

Pulpit For the rabbi and cantor (one who chants the liturgy). Usually of modest design, it has no fixed location, but in Reform synagogues it is part of the bimah and ark composition.

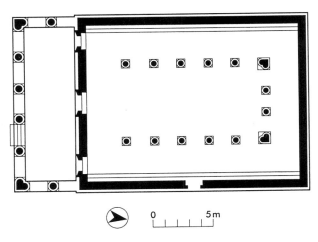

20 K'far Birim Synagogue, Israel (probably late Roman period) (From de Breffny)

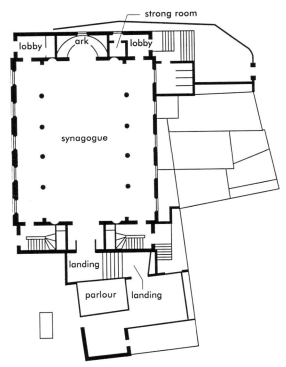

21 Great Synagogue, London (bombed 1941): built 1790–91, to seat 500 men on the main floor and 250 women upstairs; the bimah was a large platform in the centre (Arch: James Spiller; from Krinsky)

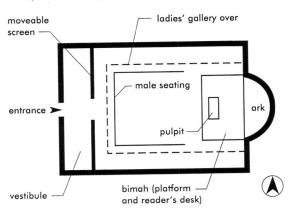

22 United Synagogue: standard layout

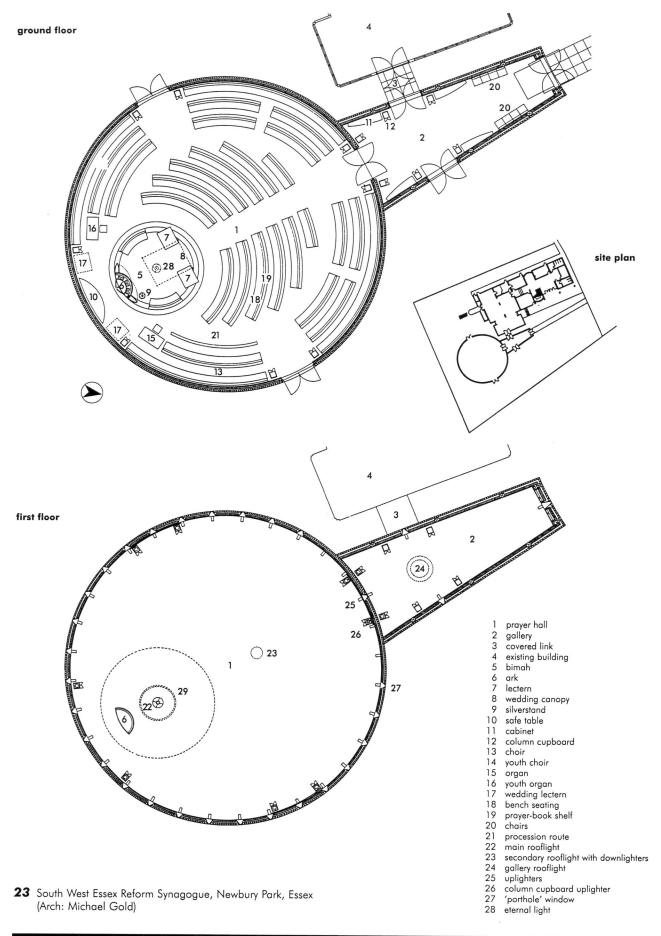

ground floor

site plan

first floor

1 prayer hall
2 gallery
3 covered link
4 existing building
5 bimah
6 ark
7 lectern
8 wedding canopy
9 silverstand
10 safe table
11 cabinet
12 column cupboard
13 choir
14 youth choir
15 organ
16 youth organ
17 wedding lectern
18 bench seating
19 prayer-book shelf
20 chairs
21 procession route
22 main rooflight
23 secondary rooflight with downlighters
24 gallery rooflight
25 uplighters
26 column cupboard uplighter
27 'porthole' window
28 eternal light

23 South West Essex Reform Synagogue, Newbury Park, Essex
(Arch: Michael Gold)

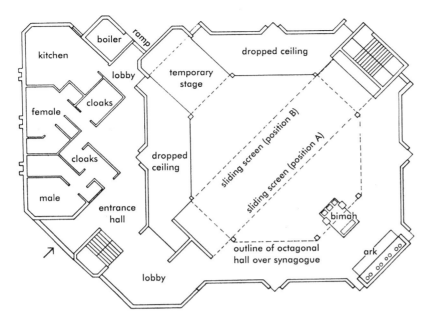

24 Pinner Synagogue, Middlesex
(Arch: Flinder Ashley Architects)

0   5   10m

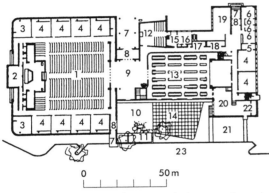

1 temple; 2 retiring room; 3 chair store; 4 classroom; 5 supply and mimeograph room; 6 office; 7 covered entrance; 8 vestibule; 9 lobby; 10 temple garden; 11 pool; 12 chapel; 13 social hall; 14 social garden; 15 ante-room; 16 rabbi office; 17 WC(F); 18 WC(M); 19 library; 20 stage; 21 kitchen; 22 dressing room; 23 driveway

25 Temple Beth El, USA: normal seating 1000 but can be extended to 1600; building includes provision for religious education, library and dramatic presentations
(Arch: Percival Goodman)

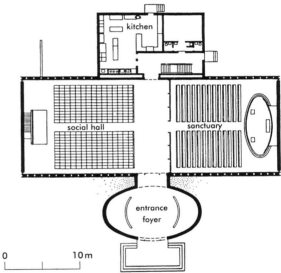

27 KTI Synagogue, New York, USA: accommodates up to 1000; flexible floor space for social and/or religious use
(Arch: Philip Johnson)

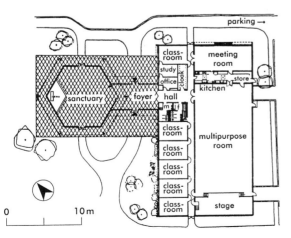

26 Jewish Center, West Orange, USA: all-week social, religious and educational use; chapel seats 250–350; multipurpose room up to 750 on high holy days
(Arch: David Brody Juster & Wisniewski)

HINDU TEMPLES

Hinduism

This is a western term for religious beliefs and practices intertwined with the history and social systems of India, and developed over some 4000 years. The practice of Hinduism varies enormously throughout India, and consequently abroad. There is no single organisational structure or creed, although Hinduism is generally characterised by the caste system. Hindus may believe in one God, no God, or many Gods, and there is a general belief in reincarnation, or rebirth in life after life. There is a great emphasis on ritual under the supervision of Brahman priests and teachers and there are numerous festivals. The liturgy is contained in the Veda. There are three categories of worship (temple, domestic and congregational) and pilgrimage to various sites is common. Shrines are found in most Hindu homes, where prayers are said daily and offerings are made to the gods. The decoration can be very ornate.

28 Venkateswara (Balaji) Temple of the United Kingdom, West Midlands: this Hindu temple complex comprises three buildings: temple, dining hall (used for multiple functions, e.g. dining, worship, weddings) and gopura (the ceremonial gateway, which also includes the priests' living accommodation)
(Arch: Associated Architects with Adam Hardy)

1 wall forming inner temple enclosure; 2 children's grassed play area; 3 paved terrace; 4 future shrine; 5 pergolas; 6 tank with island shrine pavilion; 7 steps down to pool; 8 pool with island shrine; 9 bridge over pool with central pavilion; 10 low brick wall marking outer temple enclosure; 11 gopura entrance; 12 shrines; 13 Mahamandapa seating space; 14 Shri Venkateswara shrine; 15 stairs; 16 battered retaining wall; 17 gateway to main temple; 18 priests' accommodation; 19 workshop; 20 balcony

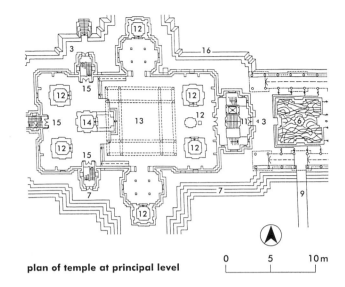

plan of temple at principal level

0   5   10m

gopura (gateway)

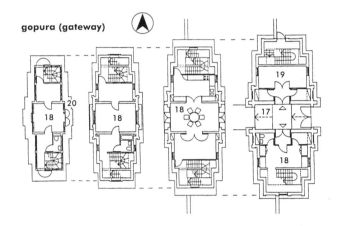

site plan

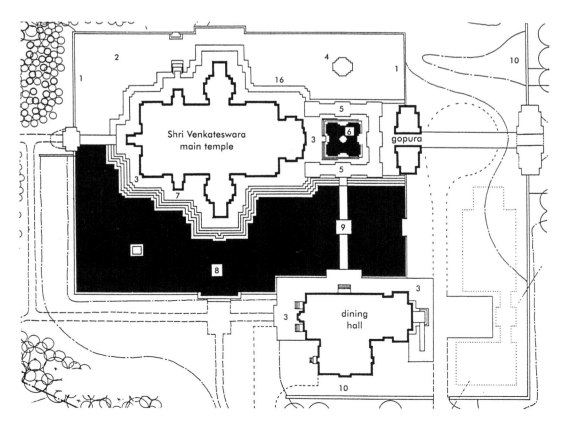

SIKH TEMPLES

Introduction

Sikhism is a religion founded by Guru Nanak in the early 16th century in the Punjab region of North India. It combines elements from both Hinduism and Islam, and aims for union with God through worship and service. The sacred scripture is the Guru Granth Sahib (also known as the Adi Granth) and salvation is considered to lie not only in faith but also in character. Sikhism is considered to be defined by Punjabi language and culture, but now that it is a world-wide religion, this can cause difficulties for those who have never been to the Punjab (the UK has the largest number of Sikhs outside India). The Golden Temple at Amritsar, Punjab (built 1577) is considered the central authority for Sikhism and there have been a number of modern reform movements which have attempted to reassert traditional Sikh beliefs.

There are no groupings or denominations, although some Sikhs name themselves after prominent Sikh leaders (e.g. Ramgashia or Rajput). There is no priesthood, and anyone can read the Guru Granth Sahib in the temple, although usually a paid Granathi (reader) is present to assist. The Granthi commands respect, but he has no particular social or religious status. Ceremonies and rites have in general been rejected as they are considered to encourage pride.

Gurdwara (temple) This is not only a place of worship but also 'the pivot of universal brotherhood' (G. S. Sidhu) where every aspect of spiritual and moral life is taught. Each temple has its own constitution, and is run by a management committee, elected annually from the Sangat (assembly or congregation). Women have equal rights.

The Sikh symbols Five articles must be worn on the body by a Sikh: Kesh (long, uncut hair), Kangha (comb, for cleaning and combing the hair), Karra (iron bangle, the symbol of perfection), Kachhehra (shorts or underwear, a symbol of continence and restraint of passion) and Kirpan (sword, a gift from the Guru; 'the mind made intense', not a weapon).

Festivals There are two main festivals that are celebrated (Baisakhi and Diwali), together with several lesser ones (Gurpurbs).

Detailed requirements

Temples: general design In India, temples are often built with onion domes surrounded by smaller ones, covered in gold leaf. Images are absent, being replaced by abstract patterns. In the UK, temples are usually housed in available buildings and are not purpose-designed. On entry to the temple, shoes should be removed and heads should be covered. Alcohol and tobacco are not permitted.

Guru Granth Sahib This is the Sikh Holy Book (also known as the Adi Granth)and it is brought out every morning at 5.00 AM and returned to a special room every evening. The original is in the Golden Temple at Amritsar, and was complied by Guru Arjan in 1604. It is the focal point of the temple, and is wrapped in cloth and located on a platform under a canopy. A whisk is usually waved over it as a sign of respect.

Langar (dining area) A feature of all temples, this is where visitors are invited to share a vegetarian meal (guru ka langar). Parshed (a sweet pudding) is served at the end of the service.

Nishan Sahib (flagpole) An external feature of every temple, it should be draped in yellow cloth and have a yellow flag decorated with the Sikh symbols (quoit and dagger in the centre, with two curved swords underneath).

Prayer hall The sangat (congregation) sit on the floor, women on one side, men on the other. They may come and go during the day as they wish, passing in front of the Guru Granth Sahib with hands folded, bowing, and offering gifts if they desire.

RESTAURANTS AND CATERING FACILITIES

F. Lawson

INTRODUCTION

The traditional divisions between formal restaurants, snack bars and pubs are now almost irrelevant as marketing trends dictate that many establishments are now given specific themes and cater for a particular sector of the market. In addition, following a general trend in the USA and as a result of time pressures in business life, many people wish to spend less time eating but this has not necessarily meant a deterioration in the quality of food offered. As well as moves towards themed restaurants and an expanded choice of cuisines from around the world, there has been huge growth in wine bars and coffee bars, generally also geared to specific markets.

Catering facilities are usually required in workplaces and other institutions (factories, offices, schools, hospitals) but there is also increasing provision for eating in the leisure and retail market (i.e. restaurants and bars linked to shopping, sports and entertainment centres).

PLANNING FACTORS

Location and type of provision must be related (e.g. for shoppers in a retail area, tourists in historical settings, business entertainment in commercial centres, casual passing trade in the high street).

Public access must look inviting and be separate from service access and waste disposal. Similarly, the exterior appearance should communicate clearly, with signs, lighting and menu displays, and convey an image of cleanliness. From outside, people should be able to view the interior seating, style and features (e.g. theme or ethnic origin). Each type of restaurant needs a different identity.

Branding now plays a key part in catering for specific types of customer (e.g. exclusive, family, vegetarian) although the image needs to be reinforced through known menu, quality of food and service, etc., to ensure repeat custom. Detailed analysis of consumer trends is essential.

The interior should create a good impression and a suitable atmosphere. Comfort should be related to the cost of the meal and length of stay, which will influence seating, furnishings, decorations, lighting, noise level and toilet facilities. Unconventional spaces can produce enjoyable surroundings (e.g. old cellars and warehouses). Note that period between refurbishment is usually quite short: about 7 years, or 4–5 years for fast-food and speciality restaurants.

Ambience is an important factor in restaurant design. Large regular spaces should be broken up into smaller more intimate areas, if necessary by screens or decorative features. Changes of level are not usually favoured by caterers but are acceptable providing they make a positive contribution to design, do not involve more than two or three steps, and the main part of the restaurant is on the same level as the kitchen. Raised seating areas should be

protected by balustrades. Many customers prefer a table at the side of a room, or in an alcove, rather than the central area; group bookings may require a more central position. The cash desk may be at the entrance, by service doors or within the kitchen area, depending on the management system.

For the highest quality restaurants, the initial impression is very important, requiring sufficient seating/table space and privacy. A bar is probably essential because customers often study the menu before being seated and the food preparation will probably take longer. Adaptability may be needed (e.g. partitioning to create a separate function area) and a change of atmosphere between lunch and evening may be important, which could require changes to the seating layout.

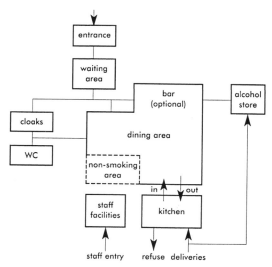

1 Diagrammatic layout

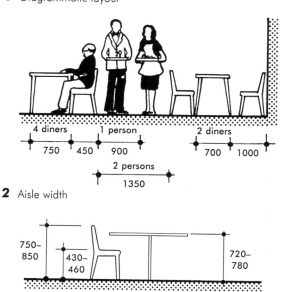

2 Aisle width

3 Chair and table heights

Lighting The choice of lighting is very important in creating an atmosphere that can be varied to suit different times of day or different customers and menus. During the day, it should be at a higher level and spread more generally, whereas at night there should be lower background lighting with individual table lights.

Guide to lighting levels:

restaurant	50–100 lux
lounge and bar	100 lux
reception	400 lux
corridors etc.	100–200 lux

Use classes Restaurants and takeaway premises in the UK are planning class A3 (food and drink for consumption on the premises, or hot food for consumption off the premises). Cafés and coffee bars etc. are usually planning class A1 (shops, including sales of sandwiches and cold (not hot) food for consumption off the premises). Therefore, cafés opening in shop premises do not require planning permission for change of use. Class A1 restrictions are poorly defined in law so they are usually negotiable: 80% takeaway service is often required, with only coffee and other non-alcoholic drinks on sale and food restricted to cakes and pre-prepared snacks etc., which must not be prepared on the premises. Class A3 permission is often much harder to obtain than class A1, and requires much greater provision (e.g. in WC and staff facilities), which necessitates larger premises but no greater sales potential.

Interior planning

Relationship of main elements The layout and relationship between different areas is dependent on the type of facility. Despite separate functional requirements, all elements (customer area, food preparation area, and counter or – in exclusive restaurants – interface with waiter) are interdependent and must be successfully integrated. Customer circulation should be planned so that there cannot be any confusion with service access and there should be an acoustic lobby between service doors connecting the restaurant and kitchen. The kitchen and preparation areas will equal about 50% of the dining space and ancillary and storage will be about 1.5–2 times the kitchen area. Any reduction in kitchen area tends to reduce efficiency and speed of service.

Customer requirements Include a menu display near entrance, sheltered entrance and an internal waiting area. There must be clarity in organisation between self-service, fast food, etc., and a separate smoking area.

Seating Restaurants should be planned so that a variety of seating arrangements is possible (e.g. tables for two and four, which can be placed together to give six, eight and ten places). Banquette or booth seating (**5**) can be considered but should be supplemented by normal tables to give flexibility. (**7**) shows typical table and counter layouts and local densities. Service aisles (**6, 7**) should be 900 mm (minimum) to 1350 mm wide if used both by trolleys and guests.

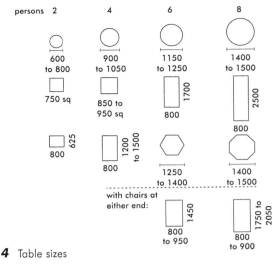

4 Table sizes

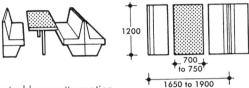

5 Typical banquette seating

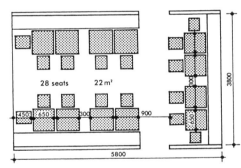

6 Minimum layout for part of restaurant: local density excluding main circulation and waiter stations and service areas

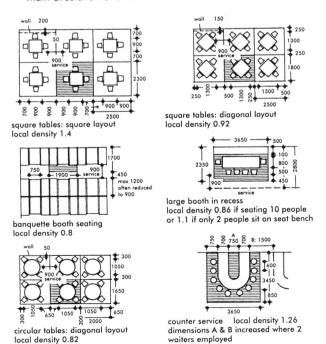

square tables: square layout
local density 1.4

square tables: diagonal layout
local density 0.92

banquette booth seating
local density 0.8

large booth in recess
local density 0.86 if seating 10 people
or 1.1 if only 2 people sit on seat bench

circular tables: diagonal layout
local density 0.82

counter service   local density 1.26
dimensions A & B increased where 2
waiters employed

7 Layout arrangement and densities

Waiter stations Located so as not to disturb the guests, the number will vary according to the standard of service. As a guide, use the following:

> restricted menu 1 waiter/waitress per 12–16 covers
> typical menu 1 waiter/waitress per 8–12 covers
> à la carte/de luxe 1 waiter/waitress per 4–8 covers

Provide head waiter stand in à la carte or de luxe restaurants.

Bars
Traditional and speciality restaurants frequently have aperitif bar for waiting customers and pre-meal drinks. These should be planned so as to allow the head waiter to take orders and call forward customers when tables are ready. Other types of bar include: roof top, pool side, beach, club areas. Bars need to comply with licensing laws.

Cocktail or aperitif bar If required, these should provide a comfortable intermediate waiting area between the entrance lobby and restaurant. Service may be by waiter so a long bar counter might not be required.

Main bar To encourage business from non-diners the main bar may have an external entrance. A fairly long bar counter supported by bar store with ice making machine and bottle cooler should be provided. The means to shut all bars securely during non-opening hours must be included, either by grill or shutter at the bar counter or by closing the room. The former has the advantage of allowing the room to be used as a lounge when the bar is closed. It should be possible to service bars without passing through public rooms. Space allowance for bars excluding counter:

> cocktail lounge
> (comfortable) 1.8–2.0 m²/person
>
> general bar
> (some standing and on stools) 1.3–1.7 m²/person

Cloakroom 0.04 m²/person. Probably unnecessary in a small restaurant or café, cloakrooms should be provided in higher quality restaurants, and are essential in function suites. Adequate security is essential: an attendant and ticket system may be necessary. Provision must allow customers to depart quickly after an event.

Furniture/equipment stores Allow 0.14 m²/person.

Other requirements Provision for dancing and live entertainment may need to be considered. A timber dance floor can be included either as a permanent area or one covered with carpet and used for other purposes. Timber floors require regular and careful maintenance. Allow 1.0–3.5 m²/couple. For live music, allow 1.5–2.0 m²/performer (more if a piano is needed), plus space for audio equipment and speakers etc.

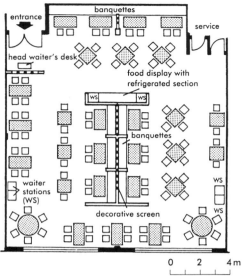

8 Traditional restaurant: 110 seats

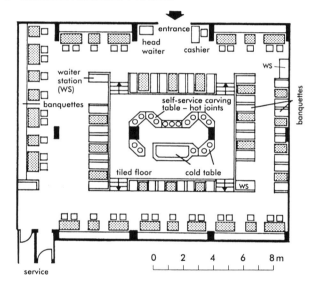

9 Restaurant seating 124 with self-service carving table

RESTAURANT TYPES AND SPACE ALLOWANCES
Traditional restaurant (8)
1.3–1.9 m²/person, according to type of business; formal atmosphere, with waiter service. There should be space for display table (e.g. flambé work) and the menu will include table d'hôte and à la carte. Tables will usually be for two persons with generous seating and spacing.

Carvery restaurant (9)
1.6 m²/person, including space for the carving table. The display table has hot and cold positions for self-service of joints, vegetables and sweets. Preparation, cooking and wash-up is done in the main kitchen.

Speciality/themed restaurant (10, 11)
2.0 m²/person, but space requirements can vary widely. Special decorative effects and furnishings are required to reflect dining theme; usually a specific menu. There may be display cooking, grill and dance floor, and probably a bar.

Snack bar service

1.5–2.2 m²/person, including counter and cooking. These are usually restricted to light meals, served at the counter or taken by customers to tables (there may be counter seating), and can be open 18 to 24 hours per day. Food is normally cooked within the counter area but back-up preparation, wash-up and storage is required. Optimum seating is 50 to 60; rapid turnover means that seating should not be too comfortable or spacious. The high occupancy rate means heavy wear, and surfaces must be robust.

Café service

0.83–1.5 m²/person. With a limited menu, cafés are usually family-run businesses and are designed on traditional lines with the kitchen separate from the dining room. Food may be collected by a waiter from a small service counter or hatch to kitchen.

Coffee bars

1.2–1.4 m²/person. Such speciality bars have become very popular. They are mainly self-service, varying from simple city-centre sites in converted buildings to larger purpose-built designs. The front counter may sell a variety of coffee beans, from green to full roast, with some free samples. The forward cooking area often has a counter, which may be decoratively screened, with preparation behind. Designs must have well-organised customer flow to make maximum use of often restricted sites.

Self-service

1.4–1.7 m²/person, with a long, continuous self-service counter, probably with a cash desk. Good circulation space is necessary and space for clearing trolleys (carts) is required. The counter must be planned to prevent long queues.

Motorway service stations prefer open service areas with separate counters serving hot and cold meals, snacks, sweets and drinks – a less formal arrangement, which also helps to reduce queuing.

Staff dining room

1.4 m²/person; with compact seating, this can be reduced to 0.9 m²/person. Usually self-service.

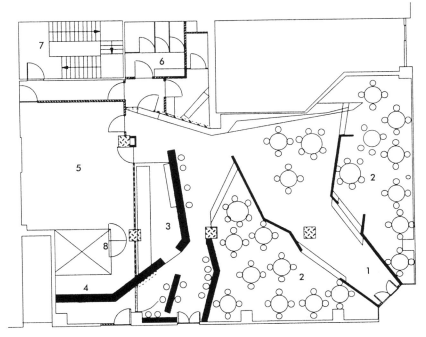

1 entrance; 2 eating areas; 3 bar; 4 takeaway counter; 5 kitchen; 6 WCs; 7 escape stair; 8 lift

10 Yeung's City Bar and Restaurant, Clerkenwell, London (Arch: Studio MG)

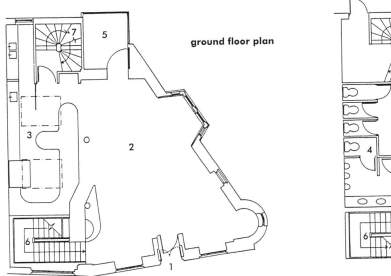

ground floor plan

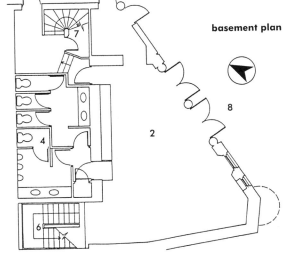

basement plan

1 main entrance; 2 dining areas; 3 preparation area; 4 WCs; 5 rear dining room; 6 public stair; 7 escape stair; 8 terrace
(n.b. staff area on first floor is not shown)

11 Pizza Express restaurant, Stockbridge, Edinburgh (Arch: Malcolm Fraser Architects)

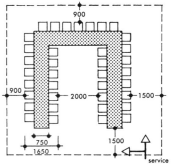

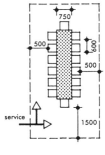

12 Space required for banqueting for 37 allowing for service

13 Space required for table seating 14 allowing for service: 2.0 m²/cover

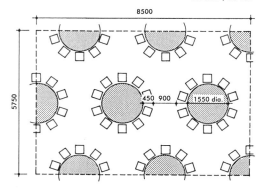

14 Banqueting seating at tables for ten (typical arrangement for large banquets): 1.2 m²/cover

Banquet/refectory layouts

0.8–1.6 m²/person. Banquets are traditionally laid out with a 'head table', sometimes on a dais, and side tables, the overall layout forming a T, U or E plan. The minimum distance between chair backs should be 1.5–2.0 m (see **12**). An alternative layout is for side tables to be circular, seating ten or more, for which the minimum distance between chair backs needs to be 900 mm (1.2 m is preferable) to allow adequate circulation of diners and staff (see **14**). With such large numbers, rapid waiter service is essential and access from the kitchen must not disrupt anyone making a speech from the head table. The area may need to be divisible: large, high quality, sound reducing partitions can be used. Note also that adjacent smaller rooms for meetings or seminars may be required.

Hotel restaurants (see also Hotels)

In medium and large hotels it is common to provide more than one restaurant, to give customers a choice of menu and price. Cheaper restaurants are usually coffee shops or cafeteria; the more expensive are (la carte. Large hotels may have additional specialist restaurants. Particularly in city centre hotels, restaurant may also be accessible from street to attract non-residential business.

In hotel restaurants, take-up of places can vary widely during the day (e.g. perhaps 80–90% for breakfast, 15–20% for lunch and 30–40% in the evening). This can result in considerable waste of resources so catering may therefore be franchised to a different organisation. Non-residential use can also be promoted to encourage greater take-up (e.g. business lunches). Seating capacities vary according to size of hotel, amount of potential outside business, location in relation to other restaurants, duration of guests' stay, and the amount of breakfast room service to be provided. In resorts and other suitable locations, provision should be made to serve meals in open air either by extension of one restaurant or by separate service.

15 Integrated refectory services, St Catherine's College, Cambridge (Arch: Arne Jacobsen)

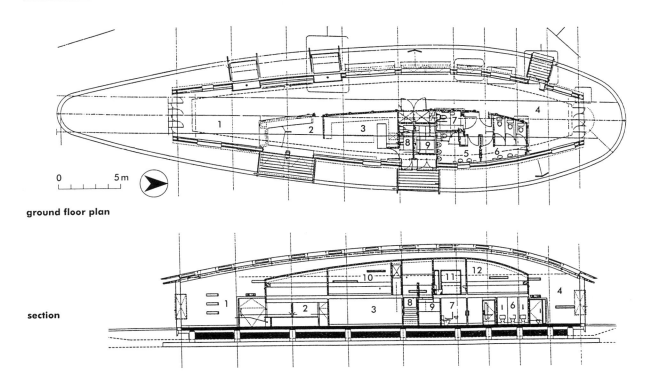

ground floor plan

section

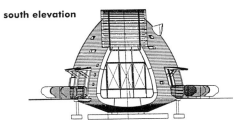

south elevation

1 café; 2 servery; 3 kitchen; 4 café/shop; 5 WC (M); 6 WC (F); 7 WC (dis); 8 staff
stair; 9 bin store; first floor: 10 office; 11 staff WC; 12 store

16 Café La Frégate, Jersey
(Arch: Alsop & Stormer in association with Mason Design Partnership)

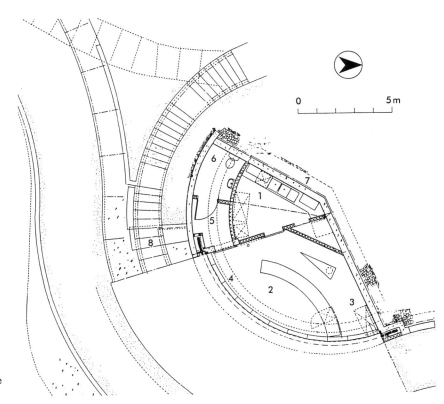

1 kitchen; 2 servery; 3 ice cream kiosk; 4 glass floor
panels; 5 store; 6 WC (dis); 7 reinforced concrete retaining
walls; 8 steps (leading to turf-covered roof over)

17 Headland Café, Bridlington, Yorkshire
(Arch: Bauman Lyons Architects)

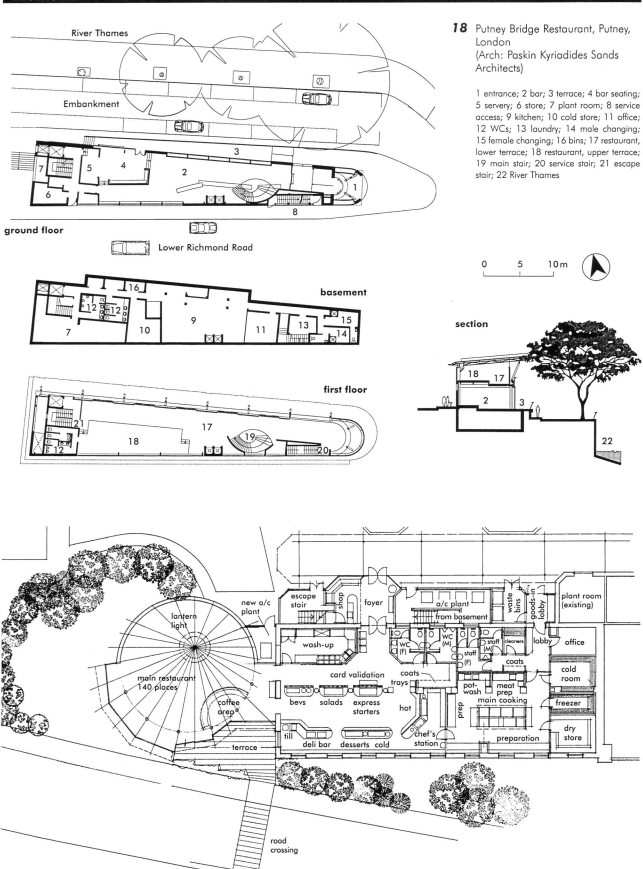

ground floor

River Thames

Embankment

Lower Richmond Road

basement

first floor

section

18 Putney Bridge Restaurant, Putney, London
(Arch: Paskin Kyriadides Sands Architects)

1 entrance; 2 bar; 3 terrace; 4 bar seating; 5 servery; 6 store; 7 plant room; 8 service access; 9 kitchen; 10 cold store; 11 office; 12 WCs; 13 laundry; 14 male changing; 15 female changing; 16 bins; 17 restaurant, lower terrace; 18 restaurant, upper terrace; 19 main stair; 20 service stair; 21 escape stair; 22 River Thames

0   5   10m

new a/c plant

escape stair

shop

foyer

a/c plant

from basement

waste bins

goods-in lobby

plant room (existing)

lantern light

wash-up

WC (F)

WC (M)

staff (F)

staff (M)

cleaners

lobby

office

main restaurant 140 places

card validation

coats

trays

coats

cold room

coffee area

bevs

salads

express starters

hot

pot-wash

meat prep

main cooking

freezer

prep

till

terrace

deli bar

desserts

cold

chef's station

preparation

dry store

road crossing

0   10m

19 Restaurant and catering facilities for a major pharmaceutical company: the kitchen is inside an existing listed building, the restaurant is a new building
(Arch: Williams Wren Partnership)

KITCHENS AND CATERING FACILITIES

General planning Kitchen requirements vary enormously depending on preparation methods used (see **21**, **22** for area calculations). An alternative method is to calculate areas as follows (including food store, cold room, wash-up, chef's office):

main restaurant kitchen area	$1.4\,m^2 \times$ no. of covers
banquet kitchen and service area	$0.2\,m^2 \times$ no. of covers
coffee shop kitchen	$0.3\,m^2 \times$ no. of covers
separate independent coffee shop	$0.45\,m^2 \times$ no. of covers

These allowances will need to be increased or reduced depending on whether the service is fully traditional or a convenience food operation. Allow approximately 50% extra for staff toilets ($0.4\,m^2$/person), locker and changing room ($0.6\,m^2$/person), canteen and other storage (see below).

Kitchen area generally The kitchen should be planned on one level to serve all catering outlets. If this is not possible, the main kitchen should be on the same level as the main restaurant, with preparation and stores on a different level. Banqueting and any other food service area not next to kitchen should be linked by service lifts (preferably not hoists) and stairs, and have their own forward service equipment. Kitchen, cold room and food store should be planned to be locked-off from staff when not in use. In large hotels food and drink stores should be under control of a storeman.

Plinths are required for some equipment. All wall corners should be protected. False ceilings should be of fire-resistant tiles with access panels to inspection covers, fire dampers etc. Doors should have vision panels and metal kick plates or automatic opening devices. Insect control devices will be needed (usually wall-hung electric units and fly screens over openings).

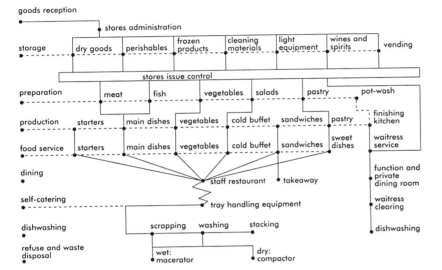

20 Kitchen flow diagram

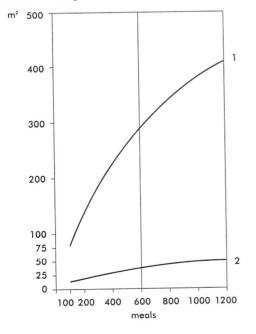

1 overall areas; 2 staff facilities

21 Area requirements: overall and staff facilities (note that areas are a guide only, and depend on exact facilities provided)

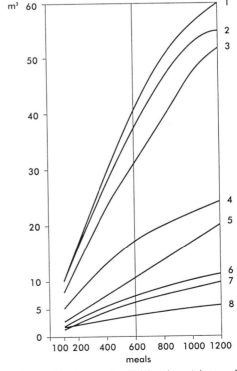

1 food production; 2 food preparation; 3 dishwashing; 4 dry store; 5 pot-wash; 6 refrigerated store; 7 frozen store; 8 cleaning materials

22 Area requirements: food production etc. (note that areas are a guide only, and depend on exact facilities provided)

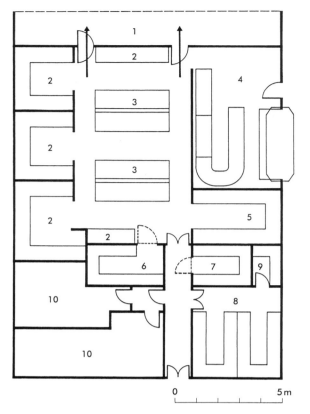

1 serving area; 2 preparation; 3 production; 4 dishwashing; 5 pot-wash; 6 cold room; 7 deep freeze; 8 dry store; 9 cleaning materials; 10 washroom/changing

23 Conventional/convenience kitchen (600 meals): typical layout (excluding administration and chef's offices)

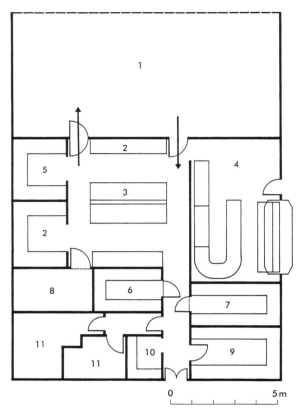

1 serving area; 2 preparation; 3 production/regeneration; 4 dishwashing; 5 pot-wash; 6 cold room; 7 deep freeze; 8 cold room; 9 dry store; 10 cleaning materials; 11 washroom/changing

24 Cook/chill kitchen (600 meals): typical layout (excluding administration offices)

Main types of kitchen

Conventional Raw materials are brought into the kitchen, cleaned, prepared and cooked using conventional cooking equipment. The cost of skilled labour and additional space requirements usually limit this type of kitchen to high quality restaurants.

Conventional/convenience (see **23**) A type commonly adopted for mid-range restaurants, and also most staff restaurants. Pre-prepared raw materials are used with various mixes. Output is maximised while limiting labour, equipment and space costs.

Cook/chill (see **24**) Items are prepared and cooked in a remote kitchen. The food is chilled after cooking, and is kept at 0 to 3°C for 1 to 5 days maximum before being re-heated in specially designed ovens immediately before service. Benefits include reduction of kitchen space (although servery and dishwashing areas remain the same), and lower labour costs, especially in the evenings and when overtime rates are greatest. The greatest benefit occurs where several sites can be serviced from one unit (e.g. in hospitals and large factories).

Cook/freeze Similar to cook/chill, but storage can be longer (up to 3 months) and frozen products are more robust (e.g. during transport). Note that temperature control (usually at -20°C) is very important and food can deteriorate dramatically when thawed.

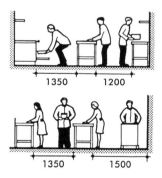

25 Minimum spaces between equipment to allow for circulation

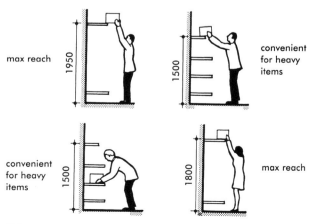

26 Limiting heights for store shelving

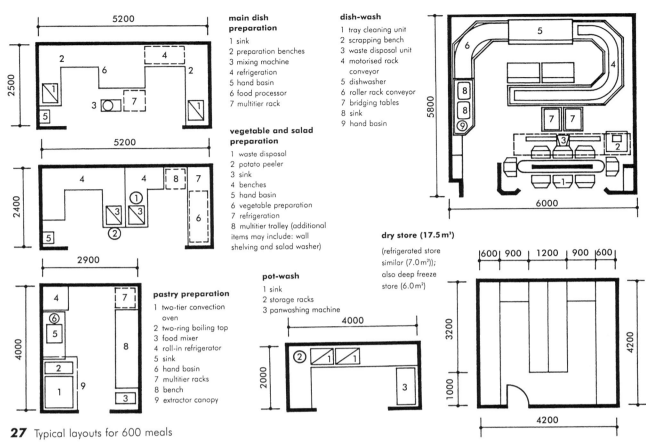

main dish preparation

1 sink
2 preparation benches
3 mixing machine
4 refrigeration
5 hand basin
6 food processor
7 multitier rack

vegetable and salad preparation

1 waste disposal
2 potato peeler
3 sink
4 benches
5 hand basin
6 vegetable preparation
7 refrigeration
8 multitier trolley (additional items may include: wall shelving and salad washer)

dish-wash

1 tray cleaning unit
2 scrapping bench
3 waste disposal unit
4 motorised rack conveyor
5 dishwasher
6 roller rack conveyor
7 bridging tables
8 sink
9 hand basin

pastry preparation

1 two-tier convection oven
2 two-ring boiling top
3 food mixer
4 roll-in refrigerator
5 sink
6 hand basin
7 multitier racks
8 bench
9 extractor canopy

pot-wash

1 sink
2 storage racks
3 panwashing machine

dry store (17.5 m²)

(refrigerated store similar (7.0 m²)); also deep freeze store (6.0 m²)

27 Typical layouts for 600 meals

Cooking area (see **27**) Open-plan area with a range of equipment to suit the type of food being prepared. Consultation with chefs, specialist designers or suppliers is essential. A continuous preparation/cooking process may be required. Main cooking equipment should either be in island units or against wall with extract canopies (see also ventilation, below).

Equipment Cooking equipment can include deep fat fryers, grills, steamers, boiling pans, pastry and roasting ovens, oven ranges, convection ovens, microwaves, infra-red heaters, boiling tables (hobs), bains-marie, and heated cabinets. It is generally stainless steel, free-standing and 750 mm deep. Ensure there is sufficient space around equipment for operation, movement of staff, food and containers, and cleaning and servicing.

Preparation areas (see **27**) Open-plan or bayed areas adjacent to cooking area. In smaller kitchens, these areas are usually not defined, but surround the production area. In larger kitchen, separate sections are usually adopted for vegetables, pastry, fish and meat, and general. Potato peelers and vegetable preparation machines may be required by the caterer, or can be bought pre-prepared. Benches are 600–750 mm deep and 900 mm high; they can have shelves above, at 1.5–1.8 m height.

Wash-up (see **27**) Most facilities include dish-washing machines; larger ones include an automatic conveyor system. Allow space for collecting dirty pans and dishes, washing, drying and stacking.

Food stores

Generally, these areas will depend on type of food (i.e. whether convenience food or fresh), location, and frequency of deliveries. Stores should all be separate areas.

Dry goods stores (see **27**) Have shelves (200 mm minimum above floor level to prevent damp) and storage units for flour, dried ingredients, cans and packets. The design should optimise linear storage.

For vegetable stores good air circulation is necessary.

Refrigerated stores are for perishable food (e.g. butter, cream, fresh meat, fish and drinks) and the temperature has to be kept between 0 and 3°C. They are normally modular, formed in 75 mm thick panels. In smaller kitchens, a refrigerated cabinet can be used instead.

Deep freezes are normally modular, formed in 75 mm thick panels, and with an insulated floor. The temperature must be kept between -18 and -21°C. In smaller kitchens, a cabinet freezer can be used instead.

Other stores

Crockery, cutlery, glass and silverware requires 0.14–0.2 m²/person.

For alcohol, allow 0.2 m²/person, divided into areas for beer and mineral bottles, kegs, white wine and spirits. Ease of delivery, access to servery and return of empties must also be considered.

Wine needs very careful storage (which can be for up to 20 years, or much longer for vintage port). Five main factors need to be considered:

- temperature: ideally between 10 and 12°C (white wine) and 14 and 16°C (red wine), although a gentle rise to moderate temperatures will cause little harm
- darkness: store away from daylight and definitely out of direct sunlight
- ventilation: a well-ventilated area is needed (to prevent contamination by odours and the growth of harmful bacteria)

- vibration: no vibration should be possible
- capital cost: storage quality will determine how long the wine can be kept, and hence its menu price.

Beers and spirits should ideally be stored at about 12°C; other points similar to wine storage.

Linen should be stored on slatted shelving. For each set of linen in use, five further sets are generally considered necessary, to allow for cleaning and reserve etc.

With refuse, the solution adopted will depend on method of storage and collection: i.e. bins or compactor (particularly useful for fast food packaging). Allow space for vehicles to back-up to receptacles and for washing down the storage area, bins etc.

Hygiene

Food hygiene regulations are rigorous and give considerable powers to local authorities to enforce hygiene requirements.

All surfaces in kitchen must be capable of being thoroughly cleaned. Floors usually should be of non-slip tiles, with wide radius coved skirtings, and the gradient of sloping floors should not be more than 1:20. Drainage channels in floor (with grease traps, located externally where possible) may be required in both kitchen and storage areas. There should be a recessed area at kitchen doors for ribbed rubber matting or other non-slip cleanable material. Walls in a kitchen are to be tiled up to 1.8 m; dwarf walls are to be tiled with an inclined top surface. A wash-hand basin must be provided in the kitchen area.

Staff facilities Washroom/toilet and changing facilities are a legal requirement and they should be of as high a standard as possible in order to retain good staff. For toilet provision see later.

Services

Generally, gas, water and plumbing supplies need to be run to within 1.0 m of appliances: final connection is made by specialists. Electricity demand can be considerable: ensure adequate provision, and emergency cut-outs. Gas is often preferred for cooking.

Light A good level of natural light is preferred: high-level windows above work tops, or rooflights can be considered. Openable windows must have fly screens. Where mechanical ventilation is provided, windows are to be non-openable, except for cleaning. Artificial lighting should be uniformly distributed: 400–500 lux in kitchen, 200 lux in stores and corridors.

Ventilation Food hygiene regulations require sufficient ventilation to remove steam, heat, oil and other fumes: condensation must be avoided. Mechanical extraction is required (extract velocity usually 7.7–10.2 m/s). Hoods are required over cooking equipment, preferably with vertical sides (extending to the ceiling, and 250 mm beyond the edge of equipment), automatic fire dampers, grease filters, air funnels over fryers, and enclosures to dishwashing equipment. Clear height to the underside of hoods: 2.15 m. Heat recovery systems are becoming common. Note that draughts likely to affect food or gas burners must be avoided.

temperature (°C):	heating	cooling (±1°C)
restaurants, bars	21	22
kitchens	15.6*–18	23
*legal minimum in work areas		

air changes/hour:	
cooking area	40
kitchen area	20–30 (or 20 l/m²)

Sound reduction Walling between kitchens and eating areas should be insulated, and a lobby may be needed. Sound absorbing surfaces can be useful to reduce background noise. Within the kitchen area, particularly noisy processes (e.g. dishwashing) can be screened and individual machines damped.

28 Example kitchen serving four restaurants: coffee shop 120 covers; main restaurant 100 covers; speciality restaurant 100 covers; staff dining room 80 covers; main food store in basement; also kitchen and service to function room

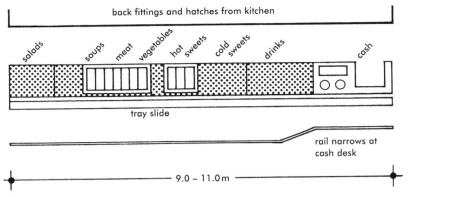

29 Self-service counter: single line arrangement

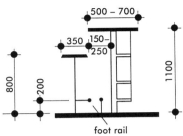

35 Bar counter: typical section

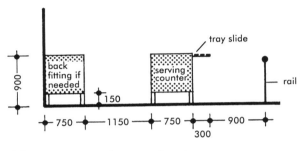

30 Self-service counter: typical section

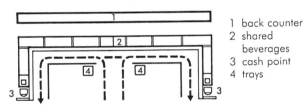

1 back counter
2 shared beverages
3 cash point
4 trays

31 Self-service counter: divergent flow arrangement

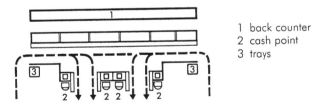

1 back counter
2 cash point
3 trays

32 Self-service counter: multiple outlet arrangement

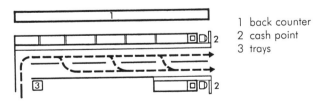

1 back counter
2 cash point
3 trays

33 Self-service counter: bypassing arrangement

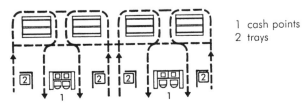

1 cash points
2 trays

34 Self-service counter: free-flow arrangement

COUNTERS/SERVING AREAS

Although not required in traditional restaurants with waiter service (except in bar area), in coffee bars and self-service restaurants the correct layout for counters or serving areas is a crucial part of the design. There is a fundamental difference between the counter in a snack/coffee bar (where customers are encouraged to remain at the counter) and the self-service counter (where customers must pass along the counter as quickly as possible). The layout of the menu, different foods, drinks and cash point at self-service counters follows established practice.

Self-service counters

Single-line arrangement is most common (**29, 30**); this has simplest flow, and requires only one cash desk, but can serve only 80 to 90 in 10 minutes. Parallel flow is similar but has two or more parallel counters.

Other layouts can be considered. Divergent flow (**31**) doubles the menu choice and customer flow. Multiple outlets (**32**) can increase customer flow by having several outlets and cash points; convergent flow is similar but has only one cash point. Bypassing (**33**) increases the flow by allowing customers to go to the cash point as soon as their choice has been made. Free-flow (linear) (**34**) has a separate counter for each menu; tray slides do not connect. Other free-flow patterns are also used (e.g. with counters not in line, or placed around perimeter).

Snack/coffee bar counters

Straight-run counters have the simplest layout, but greater service efficiency is obtained from U shapes (see **7**). For a typical cross-section see **35**.

WC PROVISION

General guidance for the UK is set out in BS 6465 (which collates information in Offices, Shops and Railway Premises Act, Factories Act, etc.). Recommended provision is complex: care is needed to establish the correct category. For cafés and coffee bars etc., if classed as shops (planning class A1 – see planning factors, above), a combined staff/customer WC may be acceptable, and a different calculation may apply, based on the area of the shop.

Staff provision (all categories) The minimum recommended provision for up to five staff is one WC and one hand-wash basin ('washing station'). For numbers above this, consult the relevant BS table. Note:
- more hand-wash basins (wbs) may be required if hands are soiled heavily
- an alternative chart gives numbers for male staff provision for WCs and urinals
- there is no requirement for separate male/female provision
- toilets must not be entered directly from food area, office or other working area
- where facilities are shared with customers, at least one additional WC should be provided.

Restaurants and coffee bars/cafés Recommended customer provision is set out in the BS, but see the note above about planning class. Note:
- provision is needed for cleaning facilities – at least one cleaner's sink.

Licensed bars and pubs Recommended customer provision is set out in the BS. Note:
- provision is needed for cleaning facilities – at least one cleaner's sink.

LEGISLATION

The legislation concerned with food hygiene, sales and consumption of alcohol, and public entertainment is extensive and complex; general health and safety legislation also applies, as do the requirements of the Offices Shops and Railway Premises Act where staff are concerned.

The Licensing Act, 1964 consolidated previous legislation and covers premises where intoxicating liquor is sold (including restaurants, canteens, clubs and pubs). Various licences are available, e.g.:
- on-licence: consumption on or off the premises (pubs, wine bars etc.)
- off-licence: consumption off the premises (shops and off-licences)
- restaurant: substantial meals on premises

- residential: residents and friends only (hotels)
- combined: restaurants and residential (hotels)
- members' clubs.

Licence applications are made to local licensing justices. Licences are only granted if the premises are structurally suitable (the final decision resting with the justices), and further consent may be needed if other structural alterations are carried out at a later date. In the case of a restaurant or guest house etc., the application can be refused if the premises are not 'suitable or convenient'. Note that the licensing acts only control the sale of alcohol: the premises can be used for other purposes at any time, so the bar areas must be able to be closed and locked from the public when necessary. The fire officer will be consulted by the justices (and sometimes the police and the environmental health service), and the fire officer will probably also be consulted under separate applications for building regulations consent and under the Fire Precautions Act.

The Private Places of Entertainment (Licensing) Act, 1967 covers licensing of private places of entertainment.

If public entertainment, music and dancing is to be provided, a licence is required from the local council (religious worship is excluded from these provisions). This is covered by the Local Government (Miscellaneous Provisions) Act, 1982. The requirements of an occasional licence are less onerous than a full licence.

The Food and Drugs Act, 1955 covers food factories, shops etc., and also farms. Food for human consumption must be fit, sound and wholesome. Ministers can make wide-ranging regulations relating to food hygiene. Premises are liable to inspection.

Under the Food Hygiene (General) Regulations 1970 there are numerous requirements relating to food hygiene, and its place and method of preparation. The enabling Act is the Food and Drugs Act. It is administered by the local authority. Relevant sections include:
- Part 3: handling of food to protect it from contamination, including wrapping, clothing and transport, and exclusion of people suffering from various infections
- Part 4: food premises, including drainage, water supply etc., and also ventilation and general cleanliness
- Part 5: administrative provisions.

The Food Safety (General Food Hygiene) Regulations 1995 have introduced further stringent provisions.

SHOPS AND RETAIL

INTRODUCTION

The traditional small shop, usually specialising in one or two products, has undergone fundamental changes in the last 50 years. The 'High Street', a feature of many villages and most towns, generally had numerous individual shops and a few larger department stores (the first department store is believed to be Bainbridge of Newcastle, *c*.1838). Many northern towns in the UK built shopping arcades in the late 19th century, to provide a better environment away from inclement weather and industrial smogs. Newcastle and Leeds, for instance, still have several very good arcades, often imitated on a smaller scale in local centres (e.g. Dewsbury, near Leeds). In London there are examples in Burlington Arcade (1819) and Leadenhall Market (1881).

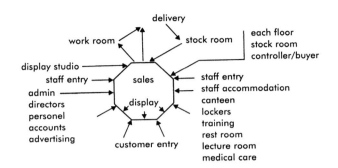

2 Plan analysis of room and routes of customers and goods

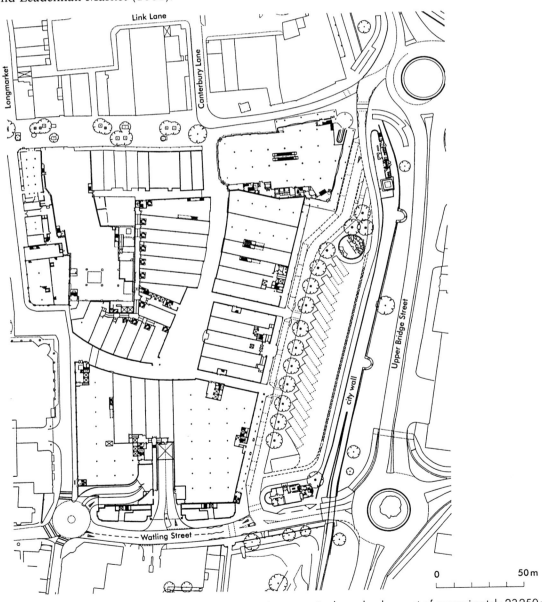

1 Whitefriars, Canterbury, Kent (Arch: Chapman Taylor)

an in-town, mixed-use development of approximately 23 250 m² (250 000 ft²) retail space, library/arts centre (375 m²; 4000 ft²), 16 residential units, 35 student accommodation units, 530 car parking spaces

3 White Rose Centre, Leeds
(Arch: BDP)

31 ha site, 60 000 m² retail floorspace (mostly on one floor), 4800 car parking spaces; two major department stores are used as 'anchors' at either end, with two others in the centre, and 85 smaller shops along the mall; the major stores have entrances directly from the parking areas; the internal mall is reduced visually by changes in direction and oval courts (which are colour-coded)

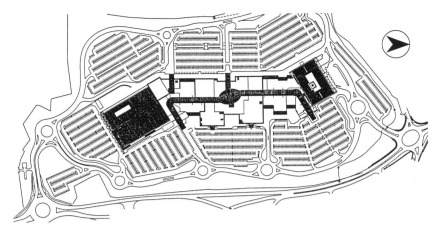

Supermarkets and superstores

The 'supermarket' was a real challenge to the traditional retail pattern. The first one may have been the Co-op in Manor Park, London (1948); self-service stores were also developed by Sainsbury and Tesco in the 1950s.

The coming of superstores – particularly in out-of-town, rural areas – fundamentally altered shopping patterns. In the 1980s, the Government encouraged these developments despite the misgivings of many planners and architects (over 50 regional shopping centres were proposed in 1986–88 alone). The result has generally been significant decline in the High Street, with many local shops unable to compete with the greater choice and lower prices offered by out-of-town centres. There has been a great increase in private car journeys (see also the note on PPG 13 below): car parking provision of several thousand spaces is generally required – nearly 5000 at the White Rose Centre, for instance, on the outskirts of Leeds (see **3**). The Government has now recognised the problems created by out-of-town centres and it is unlikely that many, if any, more will be built, despite the wishes of major retailers. Some commentators have suggested that the 'Bluewater' development in Kent may well be the last major greenfield centre to be built in the UK.

Over 200 towns have appointed a 'town centre manager' who (amongst many other activities) can generally provide guidance on local shopping policy, design of shop fronts, access and transport policy for the town, etc.

Planning Policy Guidance 6   PPG 6 (Town Centres and Retail Development suggests a 'sequential approach' to new retail development, with sites preferably in town centres, followed by edge-of-centre, district and local centres, and lastly out-of-centre sites – only acceptable where a range of transport is available. It is realised that this will require flexibility from all parties involved. Developers and retailers will need to accept a greater variety of scale, design and car-parking.

With retail developments over 2500 m² gross floor area (and sometimes smaller) regard must be paid to:
- whether the sequential approach has been adopted
- how local development plans will be affected
- the impact on existing town centres and the rural economy
- accessibility by both public and private transport
- overall effect on traffic patterns
- any significant environmental impact.

PPG 13 (Transport)   This attempts to contribute to the Government's sustainable development strategy by reducing the need to travel, particularly by private car. It also proposes better co-ordination of land uses, the sequential approach to retail development (see above), and better public transport. Structure plans should encourage the use of existing centres.

Current trends

These can be grouped into four categories:
- *Size:* stores are becoming larger.
- *Facilities:* some retail groups prefer to improve facilities within stores rather than enlarge – for instance, by providing more imaginative layouts including restaurant, demonstration and entertainment areas.
- *Traditional sites:* there is some movement back to town-centre sites (partly because of PPG 6) but this militates against standardisation and therefore increases costs (owing to difficult sites and planning restrictions). There is an encouraging trend for shared-use development, particularly for the incorporation of housing and community facilities. Parking facilities can also be shared (see **1**).

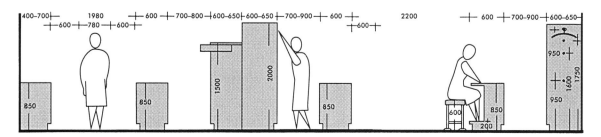

4 Typical section through sales floor

- *Internet developments:* (e-tailing), whereby shoppers order on-line and the store delivers to the home. The longer term potential of this is still uncertain, but if it becomes very popular, areas in many stores will become redundant.

New forms of retailing   Retail warehouse parks (which may have large showrooms), warehouse clubs and factory outlets are the major new forms of retailing currently emerging.

Shopping is now a leisure activity and a huge amount of marketing is aimed at identifying consumer trends and ensuring 'user satisfaction', attempting to give an emotional as opposed to a purely physical experience. Encouraging shoppers to spend, particularly in a very competitive environment, requires many subtle psychological techniques. Bookshops have coffee areas, with newspapers and magazines available, helping to increase 'dwell time'. Food supermarkets can display in the same area a different selection of food every day, sufficient for instance for a complete evening meal. The way that merchandise is arranged, the level and colour enhancement of artificial lighting, is very important.

While some stores have managed to reposition themselves to take advantage of changing trends, others – who a few years ago were household names, with apparently excellent management – have seemed unable to adapt and are suffering accordingly. Branding, rather than the product itself, is now seen to be increasingly important.

By the end of the 1990s, simple shed-like structures were no longer considered sufficiently inviting to customers, although there is an increasing need to standardise components in order to reduce costs and to allow the same components to be used on different sites.

Seventy per cent of the grocery trade is controlled by four retailers (and 96% by 12) and there is currently severe downward pressure on prices (partly due to governmental concerns; partly due to the entry of American stores).

Space planning of retail areas can be greatly influenced by the occupancy totals requirements of fire regulations (see Fire, below) and access for people with disabilities is also becoming increasingly important.

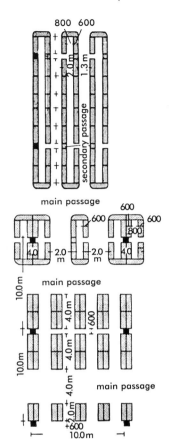

8 Typical arrangements of display units (solid squares represent structural columns)

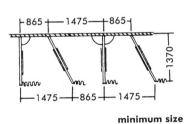

minimum size

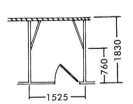

larger size

5 Fitting rooms

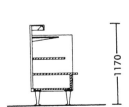

6 Free-standing hanging rack (length 1.525 m)

7 Self-selection unit (length varies); special merchandise needs special inserts

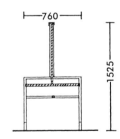

9 Millinery table

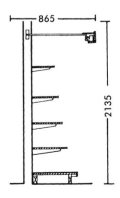

10 Back fixture with shelves only

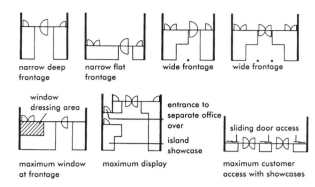

narrow deep frontage   narrow flat frontage   wide frontage   wide frontage

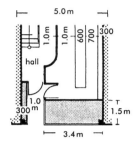

window dressing area

maximum window at frontage

entrance to separate office over

island showcase

maximum display

sliding door access

maximum customer access with showcases

11 Shopfront layout variations: deep window plans suitable for fashion furniture etc.; shallow for jewellery, books, stationery etc.

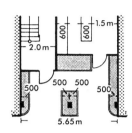

12 Display window extended by having shop entrance behind it and staircase to upper floors set back (minimum internal shop width 2.60 m)

13 Very deep shops often permit extensive display windows; impressive even if shop itself is small

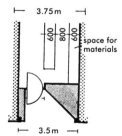

14 Deep shops may have wide vestibules with display windows at angles to entrance to attract customers from street traffic

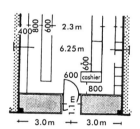

15 Central doors suitable for shops ≥ 6.0–6.2 m wide; counters may be installed on both sides; cash/wrap should be near door

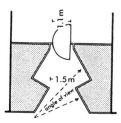

16 Narrow frontage: entrance can be recessed to provide larger display area with angled shopfront

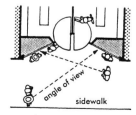

17 By slanting entire window area and having doors in same line, idea of **16** is developed to its logical conclusion

TERMINOLOGY

Retail premises are traditionally classified in several different ways:
- food stores
- comparison goods (from town-centre malls to retail warehouses)
- types of centre (e.g. local, district or regional)
- location.

'*Comparison shopping*' is a term often used to describe centres which have individual shop units, many of which may be selling comparable goods; they are an essential part of traditional town centres.

'*Convenience shopping*' covers supermarkets where an edge-of-centre location may be best, with car parking that allows shoppers to walk to the town centre for other business. The maximum walking distance is usually around 200–300 m.

DETAILED DESIGN

Planning: use classes   Three classes are used:
- A1: general retail
- A2: financial and professional services
- A3: food and drink.

These use classes are complex and care must be taken to ensure accurate definitions are applied. Changes within use class A usually require permission, although there are significant exceptions (e.g. change from class A3 to A1 no longer requires permission).

Space planning and structural grid:

	frontage width (m)	depth (m)
large units	7.30–9.00	9.15
small units	5.30–6.00	18.00–36.00

Aisles   Recommended minimum width, 1.98 m, with subsidiary aisles 990 mm. Counter height, generally, 920 mm. System modules vary according to type of shelving and bracketing used.

Lifts and escalators   These should be in groups, visible from entrance. Lifts in large stores are often placed in the centre of the building, not more than 50 m from any part of the sales floor, and are often combined with escalators, which is essential if 2000 people/hr or more must be transported. Escalators should run in successive series (return flights) to all sales floors, in both directions.

Food, alcohol, café, restaurant or medicines   Particular hygiene and security legislation applies and must be considered (see also Restaurants section).

Staff facilities   A rest room, locker room, drying arrangements for outdoor clothes, drinking water, WCs and washing facilities must be included. Separate entry to customers is desirable, depending on size of premises.

WCs   Recommended provision is complex and care is needed to establish the correct category. General guidance is set out in BS 6465 (which collates information in the Offices, Shops and Railway Premises Act, Factories Act, etc.). For small shops, a combined staff/customer WC may be acceptable (depending on the shop's area). If more than five staff are employed, or if in planning class A3 (food and drink), higher provision is required.

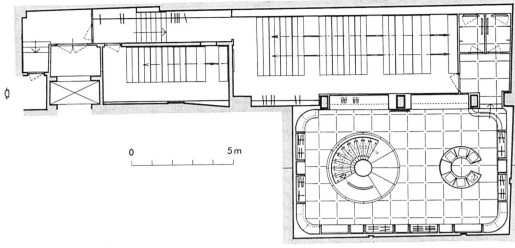

basement
plan

18 Specialist shop: 'Joan & David', New Bond Street, London W1 (Arch: Eva Jiricna Architects)

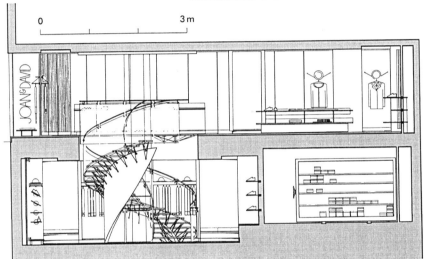

cross-section

Goods delivery In small shops, there may be only a single entrance for both customers and goods, but wherever possible, a separate goods entry should be provided. Goods delivery should be from a service yard with suitable unloading and turning space for large lorries (see also Vehicle Facilities section). Delivery may be via receiving room or stock room. Refuse and waste needs a separate circulation route (note that waste recycling may require several routes).

Fire Large shops and shopping centres are not adequately covered by the Building Regulations and require negotiation with local authorities and fire officers based on the size of sites and the number of people who could be caught in a fire (consult BS 5588). In the Building Regulations, shops come under different groupings depending on definitions: Part B (Fire) table D1 (purpose groups) classifies shops and commercial as group 4, although a shopping centre could also include groups 5 (assembly and recreation) and 7a (storage). B1 table 1 (occupancy totals – floor space factors) has different factors for concourses/ shopping malls (0.75 m²/person), and shop sales areas (2 m²/person or 7 m²/person, depending on merchandise and location). 'Small shops' (generally those with a maximum floor area of 280 m² per storey and in one occupancy) have some less onerous requirements.

SMALL SHOPS

The traditional corner shop and the small specialist shop (i.e. those selling primarily one product, such as greengrocers, bakers, fishmongers etc.) have generally been in decline since the 1970s. They are unable to complete on either price or variety with the local supermarket. Note, however, the advantage that the small shop is permitted to stay open for more than 6 hours on Sundays. In larger urban areas the small shop may be able to survive by offering a specialist service that the larger groups cannot offer.

There has recently (largely as a result of PPG 6) been some revival of interest in smaller shops on infill sites – often rebranded as 'convenience stores'. The main retailers claim that these sites are much less profitable, and it remains to be seen if they will survive on a long-term basis. There has also been considerable growth in shops at petrol stations, where it is often possible to expand provision to include food, snacks, newspapers, magazines etc.

Specialist shops (see *18,19,20*) The specialist small shop, particularly in the area of fashion, has become very popular, especially in the more affluent urban areas. Many of these shops are part of larger groups, appealing to a particular sector of the population, and with very large marketing budgets to promote their own image. Each shop must differentiate itself from what is in many ways a similar product being sold in numerous other outlets, and the brand name is the primary method; quality and price (the other traditional distinguishing criteria) are often of less importance. The theatrical atmosphere created in many of these specialist shops has to be cleverly designed to act as a backdrop to the merchandise, and has to be capable of rapid rearrangement or complete refitting.

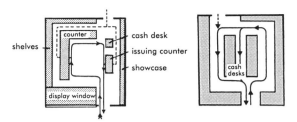

21 Properly placed fittings allow customers to move from entrance to sales counter, cash desk, issuing counter and exit without reverse circulation

22 No separation between customer and sales staff; whole room at disposal of customer (self-service)

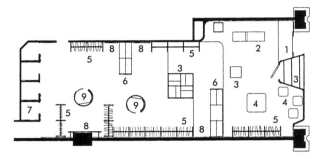

1 entrance; 2 cash desk; 3 showcase; 4 display cubes; 5 clothes racks; 6 display shelves; 7 changing room; 8 mirror; 9 store kiosks

19 Specialist shop: boutique in Champs Elysée, Paris (Arch: Isabelle Hebey)

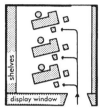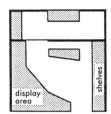

23 Shop for individual sales of a similar commodity (e.g. ticket sales)

24 Flower shop with large window and display area; rear of shop for arranging flowers

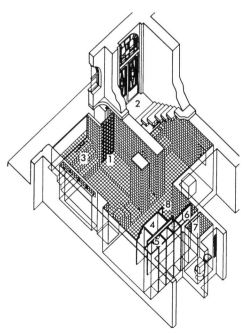

1 entrance to boutique; 2 entrance hall to appartments; 3 display platforms; 4 fitting room; 5 store cabins; 6 kitchen; 7 WC; 8 cash counter

20 Specialist shop: boutique where the sales message is more important than the product, Istanbul (Arch: Mehmet Konuralp)

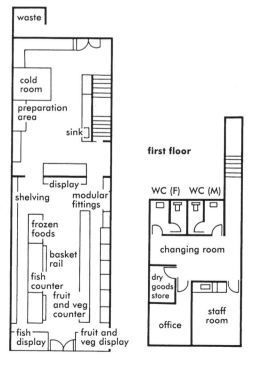

25 Typical example of small traditional food shop, with counter service: many such shops have now changed to self-service for pre-packaged goods, and counter service for fresh meat, pastries etc., with cash till(s) on exit route (see *15,21*)

MEDIUM-SIZE STORES AND SUPERMARKETS

These are normally considered to be self-service buildings on one level only. In general, 'superstores' have over 2500 m² trading floorspace and often stock non-food items.

A good example is the Sainsbury store at Tooting in south London (arch: Aukett Europe). It is a mid-size store of 2000 m² with 24 checkouts and 12 000 product lines. This is typical of a site envisaged by PPG 6 – an inner-city, mixed-use site with a two-storey technical college above the store, the car park (222 spaces) shared with the adjacent bingo hall, and excellent public transport links (e.g. adjacent underground station). The site area of 1.15 ha is only one-third the area of a pre-PPG 6 supermarket.

SHOPPING CENTRES/SUPERSTORES/HYPERMARKETS

A regional shopping centre (sometimes called a 'high street out of town') has over 50 000 m² gross floor space.

Out-of-town hypermarkets Basically these are single volume transfer sheds, with a gross area of 10 000 to 50 000 m², self-service, selling a maximum range of convenience and durable merchandise at low prices. Goods are delivered from manufacturers directly to on-site warehousing areas.

Location Usually out-of-town or urban perimeter, the road network is crucial to siting, as most customers come by car; the maximum driving time is 10 to 15 minutes from the centre of town for urban perimeter sites, or 25 minutes for out-of-town sites. Minimum catchment area is 80 000. Stores may be open 24 hours a day.

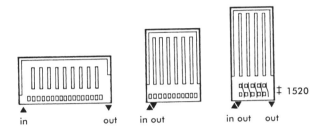

26 Supermarket layouts with checkout points related to width of frontage

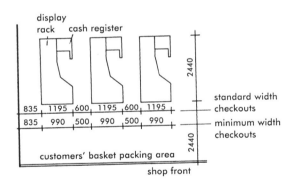

27 Layout of checkout points showing dimensions

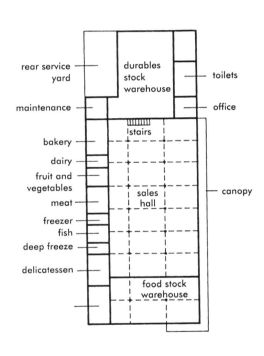

29 Diagrammatic layout of supermarket

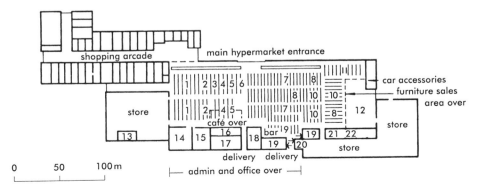

28 Layout of hypermarket with approximately 20 000 m² selling space; linked to shopping arcade of small shops

1 soft drinks and wine etc.; 2 groceries; 3 pharmacy and cosmetics; 4 dairy; 5 fruit and vegetables; 6 childrens clothing; 7 clothing; 8 household goods; 9 fancy goods; 10 shoes; 11 electrical; 12 furniture; 13 fire-fighting and sprinkler installation; 14 sub-station; 15 butchery preparation; 16 cooked meats; 17 fruit and vegetable preparation; 18 baker's and pastry shop; 19 changing room; 20 WCs; 21 boutique; 22 after-sales service

Car parking For food retail (above 1000 m²), one space/14 m²; non-food retail, one space/20 m² (maximum standards from PPG 13). There will often also be a petrol station and car maintenance facilities.

Ancillary accommodation Allow up to 50% gross area for warehousing, food preparation and staff facilities. Deliveries will probably be on a 24 hours a day basis. Parts of the structure may need to be designed for heavy warehouse loadings. Food preparation areas may be extensive and must comply with stringent food hygiene requirements (see Restaurants section).

Distribution warehouses (with internet delivery)

Some analysts are predicting that the growth of the internet will result in most shopping being carried out from the home, with delivery direct from warehouse to home. It is possible, therefore, that many larger shops could cease to exist, with most shopping being either from the local 'corner shop' or via the internet and home delivery; clearly this could have dramatic impact on many larger shopping centres. Other specialists dispute this scenario, and suggest that many people will always wish to see goods before buying, and enjoy 'the shopping experience', and that internet shopping, like mail order, will remain a small – albeit significant – part of the market. At the end of the 1990s, internet shopping was only 2% of the total (under £450 million). More probable is the provision of internet cafés in stores, although it has been suggested that such provision will have to be made much more inviting and relaxed than is currently the case if older and less computer literate people are to be encouraged.

Factory outlets

Essentially, single storey, simple boxes, usually arranged in a U-shape layout, they offer bargain shopping, convenience goods, and end-of-lines, with tenants on short leases (as product lines are often short). Well-established in the USA, they appeared in the UK in the late 1990s. As a result of their cost-conscious image, developers of factory outlets rarely consider it necessary to employ good design, and in some ways they are the antithesis of the large shopping centre where the developer deliberately concentrates on the customers' 'shopping experience'.

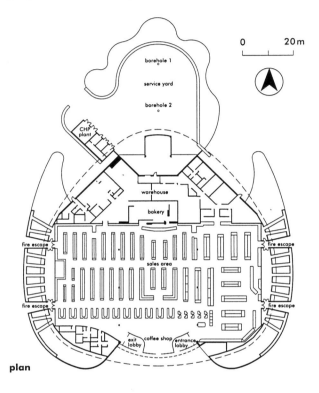

plan

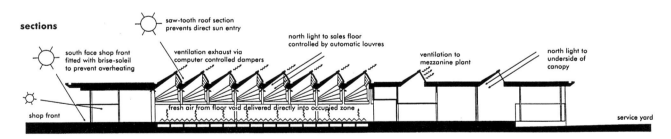

sections

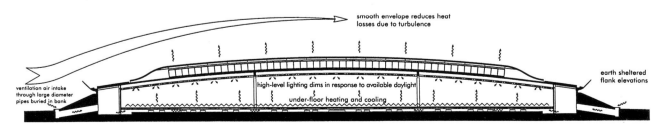

30 Sainsbury's at Greenwich Peninsula, London SE10: designed as a low-energy store, the building uses only 50% of the energy of an average store; natural daylight is used as much as possible and artificial lighting is carefully controlled (see section); a combined heat and power plant provides 85% of the electrical requirements (Arch: Chetwood Associates Ltd)

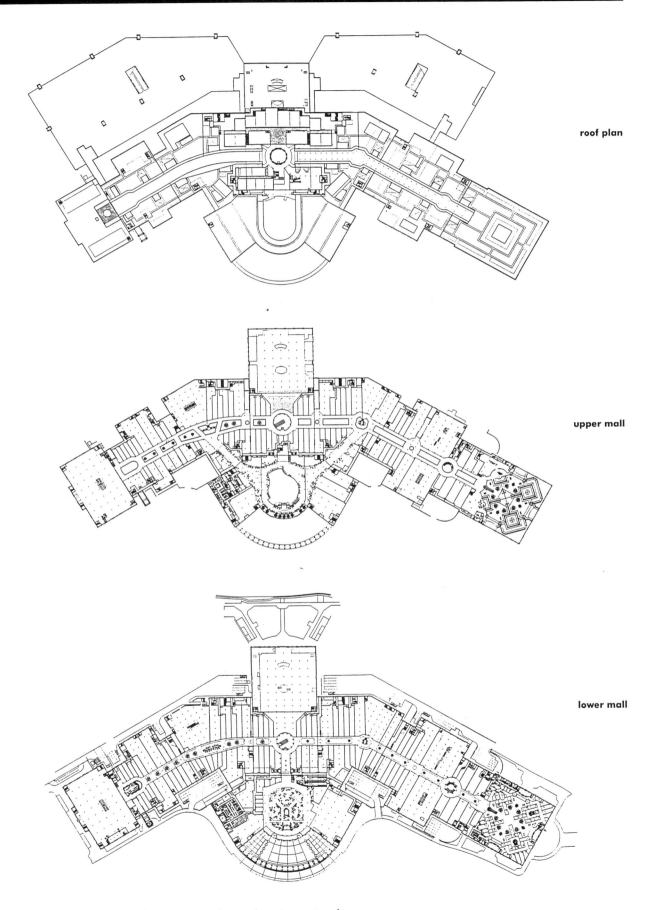

roof plan

upper mall

lower mall

31 The Trafford Centre, Manchester: an out of town shopping centre of
approximately 93 000 m² (1 million ft²)
(Design arch: Chapman Taylor; executive arch: Leach Rhodes Walker)

SPORTS FACILITIES

Sean Jones

INTRODUCTION

After covering the general design principles for these facilities, the requirements for individual sports are listed as follows:

- athletics (running tracks, shot, high jump, long jump, triple jump, discus and hammer, combined triple and long jump, javelin, pole vault)
- aikido, archery (clout, target), badminton, baseball, basketball, billiards and snooker, bowling (single and four rink), boxing, bowls (crown and lawn), cricket, croquet, curling, cycle racing, fencing pistes, football (American, association, Australian, five-a-side, Gaelic), rugby league, rugby union, gymnastics, handball, hockey, hurling, ice hockey, judo, karate, kendo, korfball, lacrosse, netball, polo, polo (bicycle), projectiles, real tennis, rackets, rounders, rugby fives, shinty, softball, squash, table tennis, trampoline, tug-of-war, volleyball, wrestling
- swimming
- tennis
- equestrian.

STADIUMS: GENERAL DESIGN

Directions in stadiums design and management: In a review of the trends and directions of arena and stadium developments around the world, the following three distinct generations of these types of facilities can be identified.

First generation

Following the establishment of codes in popular sports in the nineteenth century, the first generation of stadiums sought to give access to as many spectators as possible. Without mass media, the sport could only be experienced by attending in person. Major sporting encounters tended to be infrequent but attracted huge crowds. Very little emphasis was placed on comfort or ancillary facilities – capacity was the main criteria.

Second generation

Crowd numbers peaked during the 1950s in most developed countries, and have been in relative decline ever since. The advent of television increased access to popular sports to the extent that it is now possible to get a better view of the game in your own living room. Sports grounds became known as uncomfortable (sometimes dangerous) places where you were denied basic amenities and exposed to the rough and vulgar elements of society. The second generation of stadiums sought to win back the hearts and minds of the general public by offering a level of comfort, information and view of the game that could compete with what was available in their own living rooms. More comfortable seating, more seats under cover, adequate toilet facilities for men and women, access to a range of food and beverage outlets,

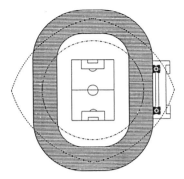

1 Wembley Stadium, London: built 1924, modernised for the 1948 Olympics and renovated again in 1985 (Arch: Simpson & Ayrton Architects)

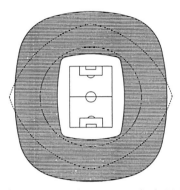

2 Azteca Stadium, Mexico City, Mexico: built 1966 exclusively for football

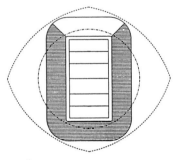

3 Welsh National Stadium, Cardiff: demolished in 1997 to make way for the Millennium Stadium (arch: HOK + Lobb Sports Architecture), the first stadium in the UK to have a closing roof (Arch: Osborne V. Webb)

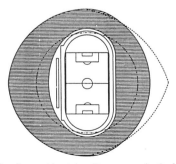

4 Olympic Stadium, Munich, Germany: built for the 1972 Olympic Games and designed primarily for athletic events (Arch: Gunther Behnisch; engr: Frier Otto)

large screen video displays and video monitors in concourse areas, advanced crowd management techniques to minimise queuing and delays both within the ground and in the car park, and so on. Venues that have successfully moved into the second generation have found their attendances stabilising. When this happens, the design and arrangement emphasis switches to the amount of money that each patron is invited to spend – spending per head is the key factor.

Third generation

The successful second-generation stadium is a sophisticated, capital intensive and profitable installation but it sits vacant for most of the year. Many attempts are made at inducing non-event day uses, such as receptions and functions, or alternatively at increasing the number of event days by housing a number of sports or teams. These strategies are vital to the success of major stadiums but they only hint at the emerging third generation of development – where stadiums become interlinked with other attractions in order to become self-sustaining venues in their own right. Integration with complementary facilities can generate year-round usage and return on capital investment. The rapid development in information technology and the advent of cable interactive television is creating more demand for sports programming. Broadcasting companies are investing in the latest generation of stadiums, and the needs of the entertainment industry are becoming increasingly predominant in the design and management of facilities. Good attendances are required less for their gate money and more for their value as a 'studio audience' when income from television becomes the major revenue source. To attract consistently large crowds, the venue must offer a wide range of activities so that, for example, five people attending on the same day can have five different experiences.

The range of facilities appearing at stadiums around the world is broad – indoor arenas for 10 000 to 15 000 spectators, hotel accommodation, themed retail arcades and stores, amusement arcades and attractions, cinemas and performance spaces, bowling alleys and swimming pools, health and fitness centres, child-care centres, offices for sports associations, parking stations and commuter interchanges, and so on. The objective is to reach a 'critical mass' where the facility draws people at times beyond the hosting of specific major events, so that the complex becomes a centre for community involvement for many interest groups, where sports is the main event but not the whole picture.

In the information age we are finding that cultural and ethnic differences are becoming strengthened; development considerations like market size, buying habits, cultural and regional attitudes and traditions cannot be transplanted from one place to another – what may work in a large market may not be viable in a smaller one, where it is often necessary to adopt more sensitive 'close-fit' solutions.

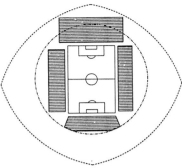

5 Highbury Stadium, Arsenal Football Club, London: an example of a typical British football ground with four separate stands – the east and west Art Deco styled stands were built in the 1930s, with more recent developments culminating in the North Bank Stand (arch: Lobb Sports Architecture) in 1993 (Arch: Ferrier & Binnie)

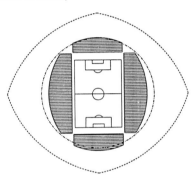

6 Sir Alfred McAlpine Stadium, Huddersfield: an RIBA 'Building of the Year', standing shaped like orange segments to provide optimum viewing for all spectators to watch football and rugby (see also **10,19,96**) (Arch: HOK + Lobb Sports Architecture)

7 Royals Stadium, Kansas City, USA: the Harry S. Truman complex was built in 1972 and designed specifically for baseball (Arch: HNTB Architects)

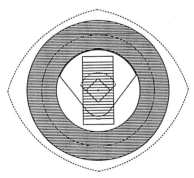

8 District of Columbia Stadium, USA: completely circular stadium used for both American football and baseball

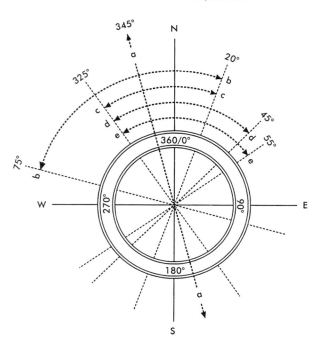

a best common axis for most sports: 345°

acceptable ranges for:

b association football and rugby: 285° to 20°
c most sports in multi-sports arenas: 325° to 20°
d hard court tennis, basketball, and netball: 325° to 45°
e cricket and baseball: 325° to 55°

9 Orientation

Location: town planning

As outlined in FIFA's *Technical Recommendations and Requirements for the Construction or Modernisation of Football Stadia*, published in 1995, it is of great importance that the location of the stadium and the angle of the pitch in relation to the sun, as well as prevailing weather conditions, are considered. It is recommended that when choosing a location there should be sufficient open space surrounding the stadium to allow for possible future development.

The location of the site should be accessible by motorway and rail from the city to make arrival and departure by spectators as simple as possible. The FIFA document and UEFA guidance also recommends that the environmental compatibility be a prime consideration in conjunction with community involvement when planning and constructing a new stadium facility.

Systems should allow easy access into, around and out of a major stadium complex, coupled with adequate monitoring and control systems to ensure any build-up of traffic congestion can be identified well in advance and dealt with by police and highways authorities.

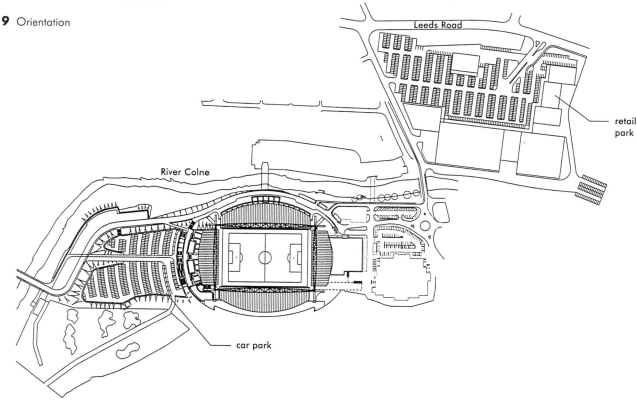

10 Sir Alfred McAlpine Stadium, Huddersfield: site layout showing hotel and other commercial facilities facing onto Leeds Road (see also **6,19,96**)
(Arch: HOK + Lobb Sports Architecture)

Sight-lines

One of the main parameters in the design of any grandstand or stadium is the desired standard of view for the spectator. More recently with the advent of all-seater stadiums the standard of view to be achieved has become much more important, in that the spectator should not feel the need to stand at key stages in the game to get a satisfactory view of the action. This is established by means of the sight-line calculation, which would generate a typical profile for the seating tier. As shown in the following diagrams a number of solutions can be studied by using alternative values in the calculation.

The factors affecting the calculation of the riser height (N) for the seating tier are:

N = riser height
R = height between eye and the 'point of focus' on the playing field
(the point of focus is often the near touchline)
D = horizontal distance from the eye to 'point of focus'
C = 'C' value (standard of view)
T = depth of seating row
(the *Guide to Safety at Sports Grounds*, published by The Stationery Office, outlines minimum requirements for seat widths and seating row depths).

A worked example to calculate the required riser height for a given 'C' value is given below, using the expression:

$$N = \frac{(R + C) \times (D + T)}{D} - R$$

The analysis of a proposed spectator position 20 m from the touchline (D), 5 m above the level of the point of focus on the pitch (R), using an 800 mm tread depth (T), with the requirement to achieve a 'C' value of 90 mm, would give a riser height as follows (all measurements in millimetres):

$$N = \frac{(5000 + 90) \times (20\,000 + 800)}{20\,000} - 5000$$

$$= \frac{5090 \times 20\,800}{20\,000} - 5000$$

$$= 5293.6 - 5000$$

$$= 293.6\,\text{mm riser height}$$

'C' value = 150 mm   excellent standard (may be used in the design of racecourse grandstands where many spectators wear hats)
= 120 mm   good viewing standard
= 90 mm   reasonable viewing standard, head tilted backwards
= 60 mm   between heads in row in front

Although the calculation method is simple, in reality the riser heights may have to be calculated many times over as the optimum solution for the section is investigated. For any change in the factors affecting the calculation of the riser height, the calculations for each row would have to be repeated.

Method of calculation The parameters that have an effect on the profile of the section resulting from the sight-line calculations are illustrated in the diagrams and set out below.

(1) The point of focus should first be established. This is often the near touchline or goal-line for end stands. However, with multipurpose stadiums accommodating a number of sports (e.g. an athletics track around the playing field), the point of focus may need to be adjusted to provide satisfactory viewing standards for both sports. As shown in the diagrams, moving the profile closer to the point of focus results in a steeper rake and an increase in height which may be unacceptable.

(2) The 'C' value then needs to be determined and again as can be seen in the diagrams alternative values can have a significant affect on the profile of the seating tier.

In a new design a 'C' value of 90 mm is an ideal starting point; however, in larger stadiums it is

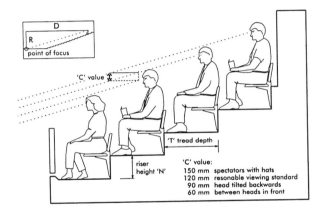

11 Stadiums: viewing standards

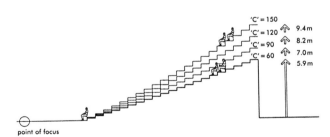

12 Stadiums: changing 'C' values (1)

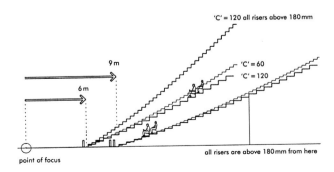

13 Stadiums: changing 'C' values (2), showing the effect of changing seating into standing

acknowledged that this is often difficult to achieve because the permitted angle of rake may be exceeded. A minimum 'C' value of 60 mm may be acceptable in certain cases.

(3) The distance from the point of focus and the first row of seats then needs to be determined. This is often fixed by requirements for service tracks around the playing area and the greater the distance the shallower the rake of the seating tier.

(4) The method of excluding spectators from the playing area (whether fences, moat or change in level) will influence the level of the front row relative to the pitch. Elevating the first row will increase the standard of view for the spectator; the angle of the seating tier will increase for a similar 'C' value.

The above factors in conjunction with site constraints, any limitations in height (of particular concern in urban locations) and cost constraints will enable the designer to develop the optimum profile for the stand.

Finally there are two further issues that should be checked to ensure a satisfactory solution is achieved. In the UK the *Guide to Safety at Sports Grounds* (also known as the *Green Guide*) stipulates that the gradient of the seating rows (angle of rake) should not exceed 34°. Elsewhere in Europe this figure varies so local legislation and appropriate codes of practice should be checked.

With the sight-line calculations the angle of the stand will approximate to a parabolic curve and so the risers will vary. This is acknowledged in the UK Building Regulations but again appropriate local legislation should be consulted. It should be noted that CEN, the European Committee for Standardisation, has carried out some initial draft studies into spectator facilities and criteria for spectator viewing.

Seating

Comfort, safety, durability and cost factors contribute to the decision on the type of seating to be used in stadium and grandstand developments. With an increased range and quality of facilities being included in stadium projects, the trend is to provide a greater range and increase in comfort rather than choose the cheapest solution.

To increase revenue potential, operators of stadium developments are providing various levels of club seating, private box balconies and VIP seating in addition to general spectator seating. These areas have increased comfort: the seats are more widely spaced, padded and may also have armrests.

There have been opposing views on the relative safety of various seating types but in the

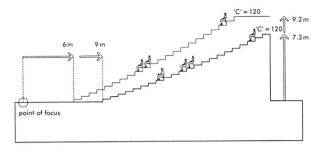

14 Stadiums: closer to focus

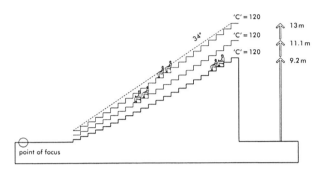

15 Stadiums: elevating first row

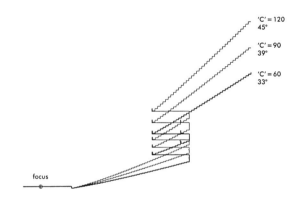

16 Stadiums: showing effect of changing viewing standards and effect on maximum angle of rake in a large stadium

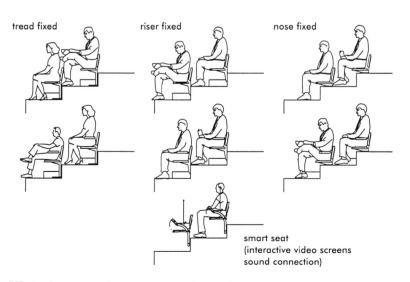

17 Stadiums: typical seating types (with or without arms)

recent *Technical Recommendations and Requirements for the Construction or Modernisation of Football Stadia*, produced by FIFA, it was stipulated that all seats should have backrests. While deemed as being more comfortable than the bench or 'tractor' style seats, the backrests provide an important safety function in preventing forward surges of spectators during exciting passages of play.

The FSADC (Football Stadia Advisory Design Council) *Guide to Seating* gives advice and guidance on the selection of materials and finishes for both the seats and supporting frames.

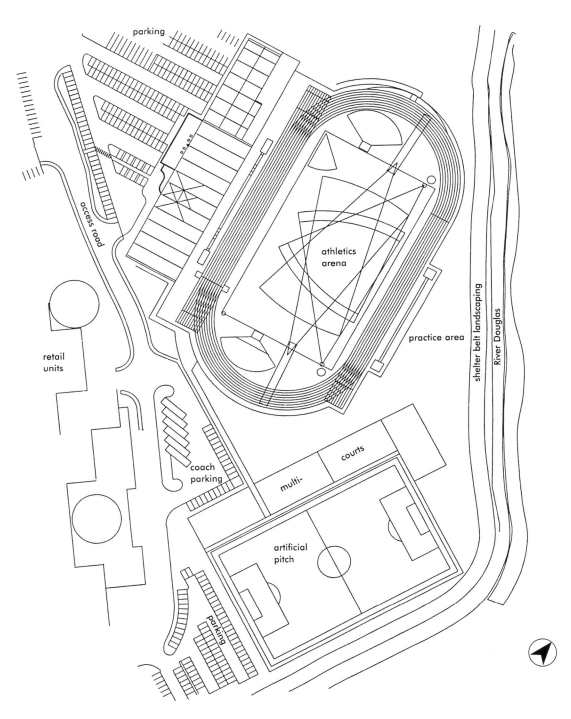

18 Robin Park Athletics Arena, Wigan
(Arch: HOK + Lobb Sports Architecture)

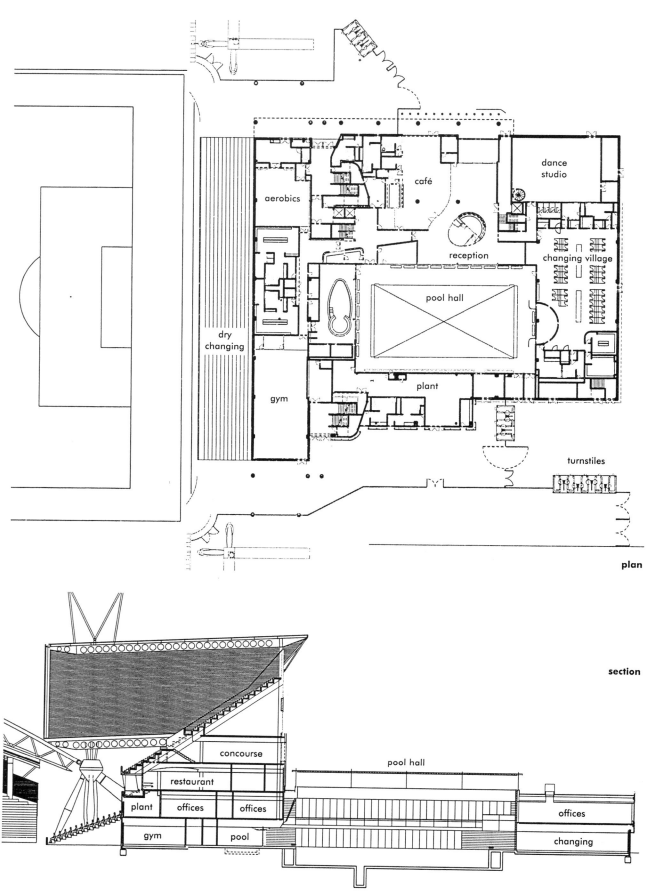

plan

section

19 Sir Alfred McAlpine Stadium, Huddersfield (see also
6,10,96): North Stand sports hall
(Arch: HOK + Lobb Sports Architecture)

ATHLETICS

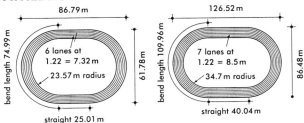

20 Outdoor running track: 200 m

21 Outdoor running track: 300 m

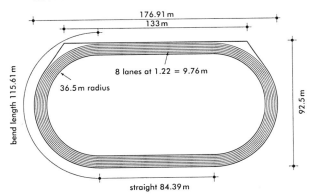

22 Outdoor running track: 400 m; based on standard 7-lane running track, for 6-lane all-weather surfaces reduce overall dimensions by 2.44 m (approximate overall size 179×106 m); major competitions and regional tracks require 8 all-weather lanes with 10-lane sprint straight, so increase overall dimensions by 2.44 m (approximate overall size 181×111 m)

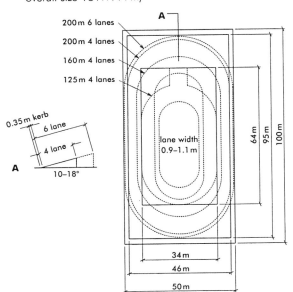

23 Indoor running track (dotted lines indicate space and clearance requirements)

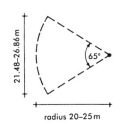

24 Shot

25 High jump

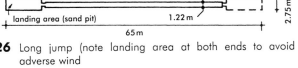

26 Long jump (note landing area at both ends to avoid adverse wind

27 Triple jump (senior and junior)

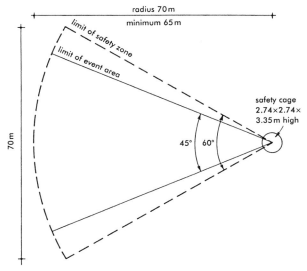

28 Discus and hammer (discus base 2.50 m; hammer base 2.135 m)

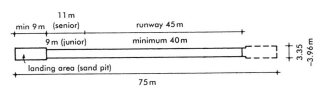

29 Combined triple and long jump

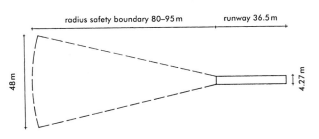

30 Javelin

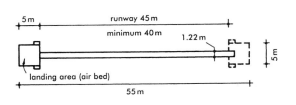

31 Pole vault

SPORTS PITCHES AND COURTS
Listed alphabetically

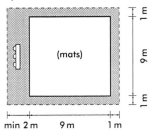

32 Aikido

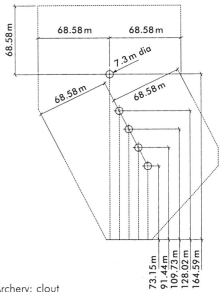

33 Archery: clout

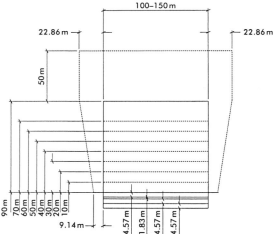

34 Archery: target

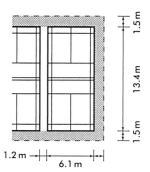

35 Badminton (minimum height 7.60 m)

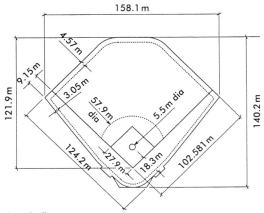

36 Baseball

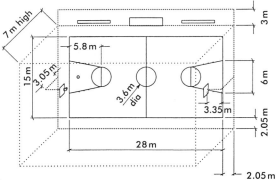

37 Basketball

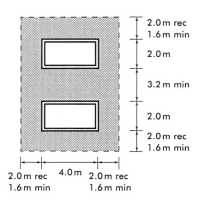

38 Billiards and snooker (agreed standards table: 3.50 × 1.75 m playing area)

39 Bowling: single rink in projectile hall

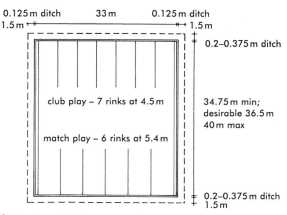

40 Bowling: 4 rinks minimum for recreation, 6 for tournaments

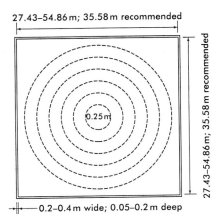

41 Bowls: crown

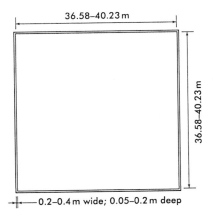

42 Bowls: lawn

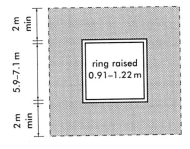

43 Boxing (for competition, in addition to accommodation for spectators the following are required: medical examination room, weighing room, gloving-up room, office, above-ring lighting and water supply to each corner)

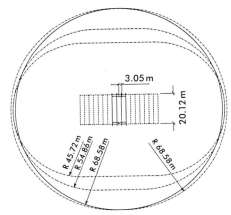

44 Cricket

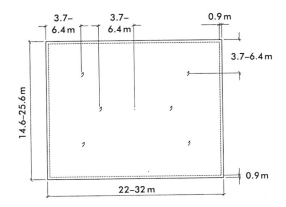

45 Croquet

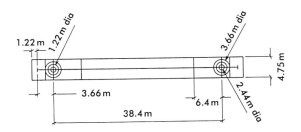

46 Curling

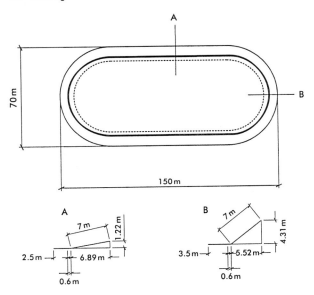

47 Cycle racing

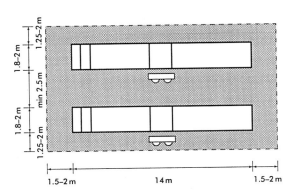

48 Fencing pistes

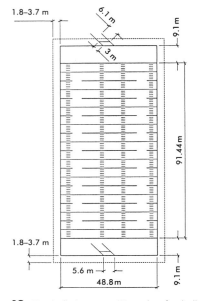

49 Football: American (Canadian football is a variant with slight differences in recommended pitch sizes)

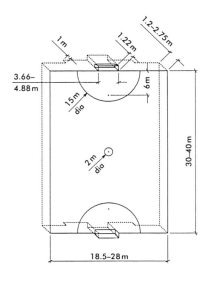

52 Football: five-a-side

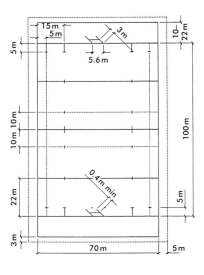

55 Football: rugby union

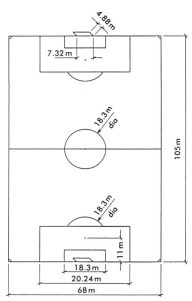

50 Football: association

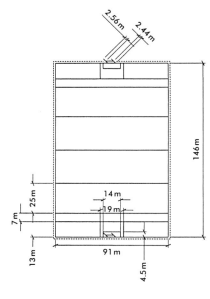

53 Football: Gaelic

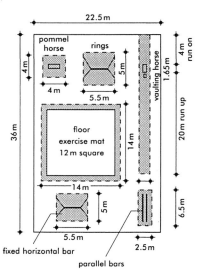

56 Gymnastics: men (minimum height 7.60 m)

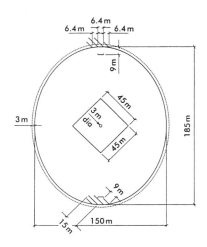

51 Football: Australian

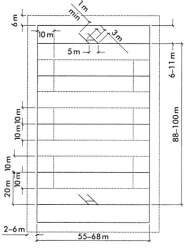

54 Football: rugby league

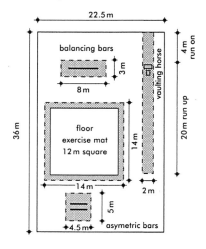

57 Gymnastics: women

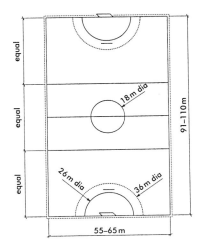

58 Handball (field handball of eleven-a-side on the pitch size shown here has largely given way to the Olympic indoor game)

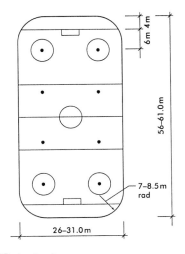

61 Ice hockey

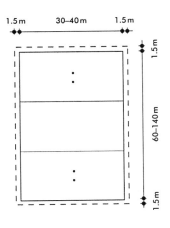

65 Korfball

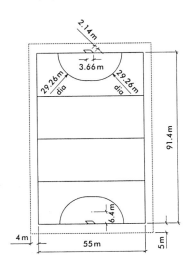

59 Hockey

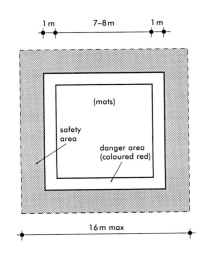

62 Judo

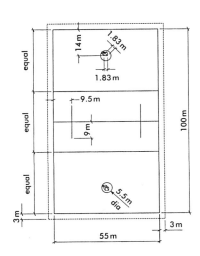

66 Lacrosse: men

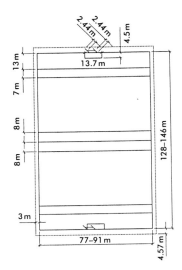

60 Hurling

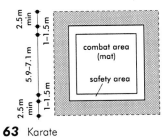

63 Karate

64 Kendo

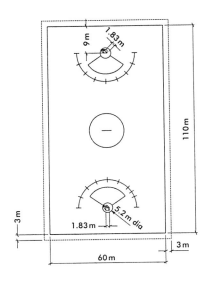

67 Lacrosse: women

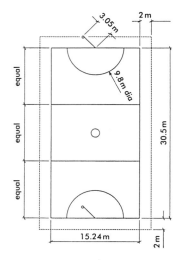

68 Netball

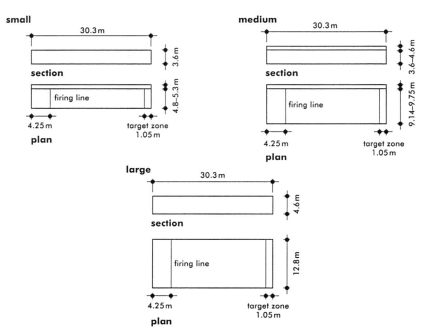

small

section

firing line

plan

4.25 m

target zone 1.05 m

30.3 m

3.6 m

4.8–5.3 m

medium

section

firing line

plan

4.25 m

target zone 1.05 m

30.3 m

3.6–4.6 m

9.14–9.75 m

large

section

firing line

plan

4.25 m

target zone 1.05 m

30.3 m

4.6 m

12.8 m

71 Projectile hall, section and plan

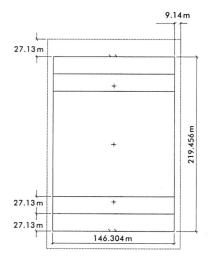

69 Polo

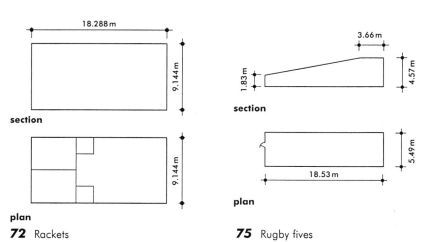

section

plan

18.288 m

9.144 m

9.144 m

72 Rackets

section

plan

3.66 m

1.83 m

4.57 m

5.49 m

18.53 m

75 Rugby fives

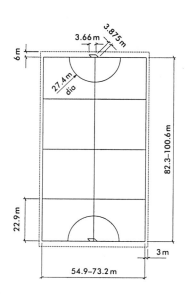

70 Polo (bicycle)

33.604 m

12.192 m

73 Real tennis (dimensions of court at Hampton Court)

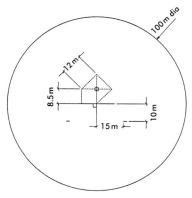

74 Rounders

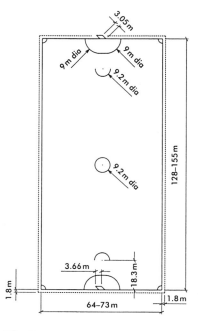

76 Shinty

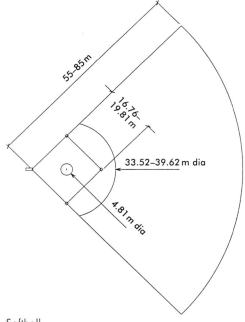

77 Softball

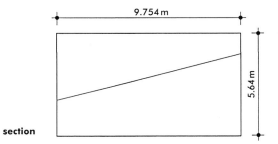

section

plan

78 Squash (note that dimensions and surface finishes are critical)

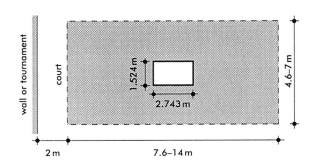

79 Table tennis (minimum height 4.20 m)

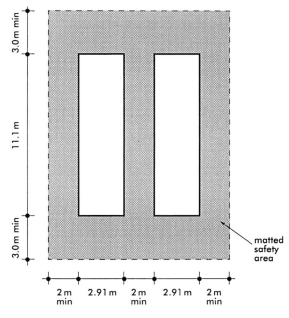

80 Trampoline

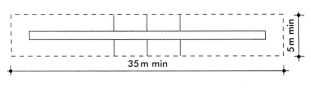

81 Tug-of-war

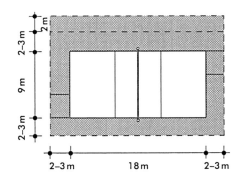

82 Volleyball

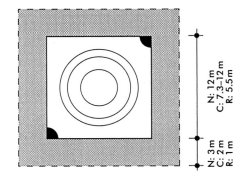

83 Wrestling (N national, C club, R recreation)

SWIMMING

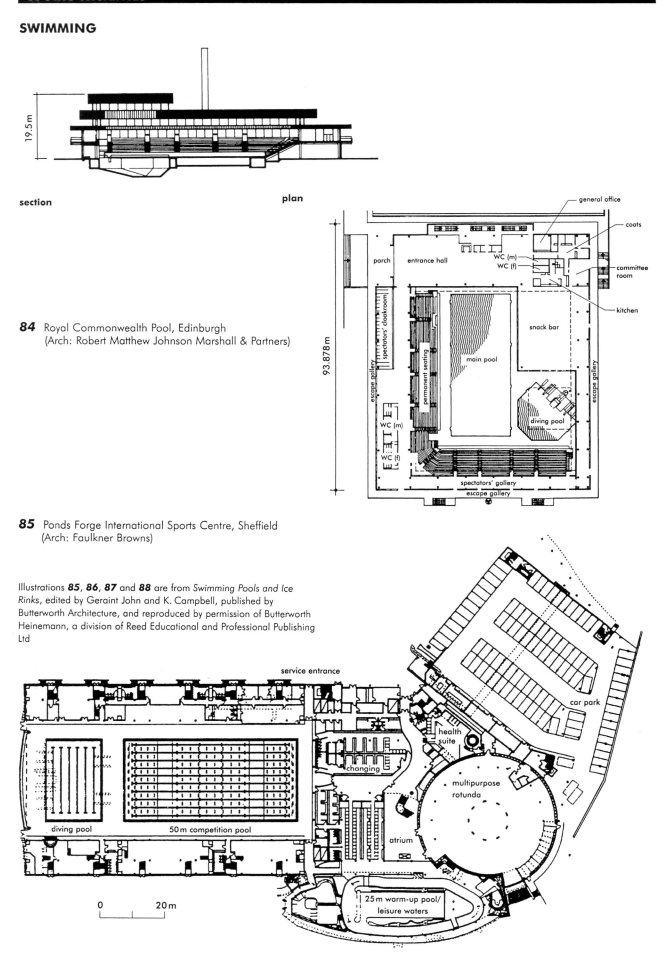

section   plan

84 Royal Commonwealth Pool, Edinburgh
(Arch: Robert Matthew Johnson Marshall & Partners)

85 Ponds Forge International Sports Centre, Sheffield
(Arch: Faulkner Browns)

Illustrations **85**, **86**, **87** and **88** are from *Swimming Pools and Ice Rinks*, edited by Geraint John and K. Campbell, published by Butterworth Architecture, and reproduced by permission of Butterworth Heinemann, a division of Reed Educational and Professional Publishing Ltd

SWIMMING

Introduction

The provision and design of public swimming pools has evolved during the 1990s and while originally it was normal for the competition type pool to be used by the public, the more specialist nature of the leisure pool has resulted in the development of specific pools to accommodate a wide range of other leisure uses.

In deciding the type of pool to be planned the likely main users should be established and the priority for different activities then determined. The accommodation required will vary with the size and type of pool but the maximum number of people able to use the pool will be determined by the water area and capacity of pool water treatment plant.

Further more detailed information can be obtained from the series of Guidance Notes prepared by the Sports Council on the design, planning, construction and services of swimming pools.

Swimming: pools for leisure

Some of the main features of pools specifically created for indoor leisure and recreational swimming are areas of shallow water with beach edges, infant pools, wave machines, water chutes, flumes and splash pools. These, together with the use of good quality materials, artificial sun bathing, planting, lagoons, islands, seating and refreshment areas for swimmers and spectators give a much greater range of experiences for the bather rather than the serious swimmer.

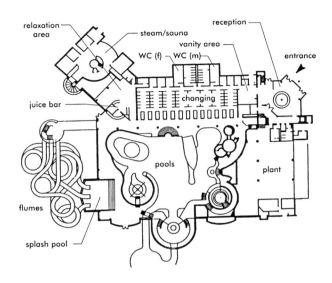

87 Coral Reef, Bracknell
(Arch: Sargent & Potiriadis)

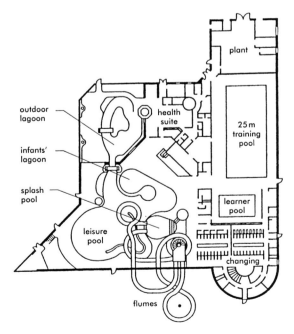

86 Perth Leisure Pool, Perth, Scotland
(Arch: Faulkner Browns)

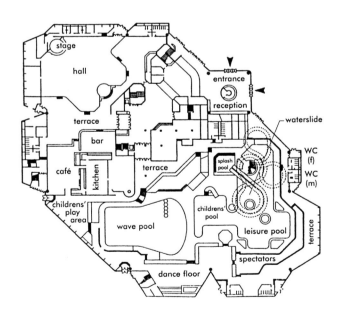

88 Sandcastle, Blackpool
(Arch: Charles Smith Architects)

Competition pools

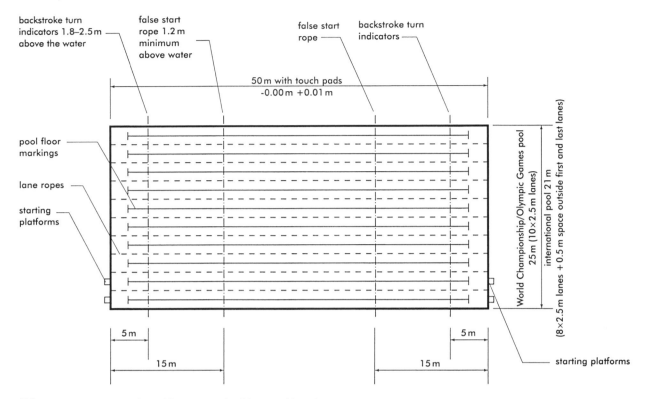

89 50 m swimming pool, to Olympic standard (nominal length 50 m, tolerance +0.03 m, –0.00 m at all points from 0.3 m above to 0.8 m below water level)

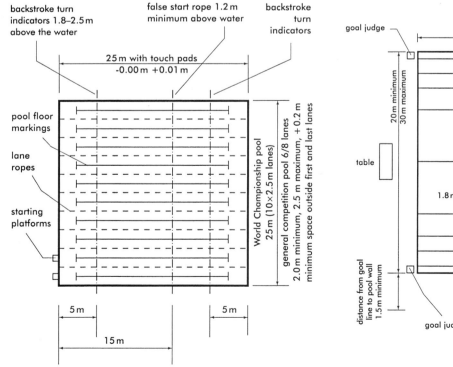

90 25 m swimming pool, to Olympic standard (nominal length 25 m, tolerance +0.02 m, –0.00 m at all points from 0.3 m above to 0.8 m below water level); note the 33¹/₃ m swimming pool is not now considered to be a standard type

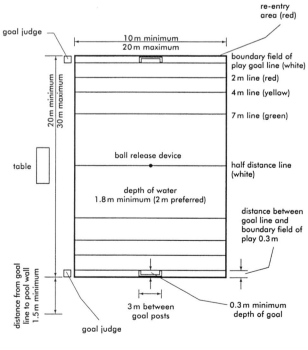

91 Water polo field of play dimensions, to Olympic standard; for other competitions, size is 20×8 m, minimum depth 1 m; allowance must be provided for referee to move freely from end to end of the field and for the goal judges at the goal line

Diving

Casual users of swimming pool facilities will use the 1 m and 3 m springboards but not the high fixed boards. As diving facilities are expensive to provide and supervise, fixed boards are therefore only planned on a regional basis. In order to fully utilise the diving pool, which is either in a separate pool or physically separated zone of a main pool, other leisure uses such as sub-aqua diving, water polo training, lane swimming or synchronised swimming should be considered.

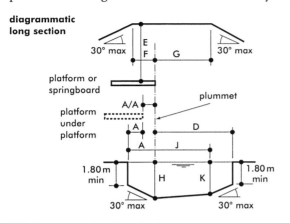

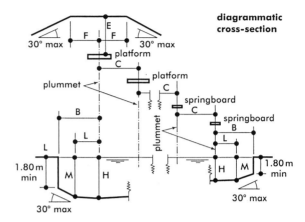

92 Dimensions for diving facilities

			springboard 1m horiz	springboard 1m vert	springboard 3m horiz	springboard 3m vert	platform 1m horiz	platform 1m vert	platform 3m horiz	platform 3m vert	platform 5m horiz	platform 5m vert	platform 7.5m horiz	platform 7.5m vert	platform 10m horiz	platform 10m vert
		length	4.80		4.80		5.00		5.00		6.00		6.00		6.00	
		width	0.50		0.50		0.60		0.60min, 1.50 pref		1.50		1.50		2.00	
		height	1.00		3.00		0.60–1.00		2.60–3.00		5.00		7.50		10.00	
A	from plummet back to pool wall	designation	A-1		A-3		A-1pl		A-3pl		A-5		A-7.5		A-10	
		minimum	1.50		1.50		0.75		1.25		1.25		1.50		1.50	
		preferred	1.80		1.80		0.75		1.25		1.25		1.50		1.50	
A/A	from plummet back to platform plummet directly below	designation									A/A5/1		A/A7.5/3,1		A/A10/5,3,1	
		minimum									0.75		0.75		0.75	
		preferred									1.25		1.25		1.25	
B	from plummet to pool wall at side	designation	B-1		B-3		B-1pl		B-3pl		B-5		B-7.5		B-10	
		minimum	2.50		3.50		2.30		2.80		3.25		4.25		5.25	
		preferred	2.50		3.50		2.30		2.90		3.75		4.50		5.25	
C	from plummet to adjacent plummet	designation	C1-1		C3-3,3-1		C1-1pl		C3-3,3-1pl		C5-3,5-1		C7.5-5,3,1		C10-7.5,5,3,1	
		minimum	2.00		2.20		1.65		2.00		2.25		2.50		2.75	
		preferred	2.40		2.60		1.95		2.10		2.50		2.50		2.75	
D	from plummet to pool wall ahead	designation	D-1		D-3		D-1pl		D-3pl		D-5		D-7.5		D-10	
		minimum	9.00		10.25		8.00		9.50		10.25		11.00		13.50	
		preferred	9.00		10.25		8.00		9.50		10.25		11.00		13.50	
E	from plummet, on board to ceiling	designation		E-1		E-3		E-1pl		E-3pl		E-5		E-7.5		E-3
		minimum		5.00		5.00		3.25		3.25		3.25		3.25		4.00
		preferred		5.00		5.00		3.50		3.50		3.50		3.50		5.00
F	clear overhead behind and each side of plummet	designation	F-1	E-1	F-3	E-3	F-1pl	E-1pl	F-3pl	E-3pl	F-5	E-5	F-7.5	E-7.5	F-10	E-10
		minimum	2.50	5.00	2.50	5.00	2.75	3.25	2.75	3.25	2.75	3.25	2.75	3.25	2.75	4.00
		preferred	2.50	5.00	2.50	5.00	2.75	3.50	2.75	3.50	2.75	3.50	2.75	3.50	2.75	5.00
G	clear overhead ahead of plummet	designation	G-1	E-1	G-3	E-3	G-1pl	E-1pl	G-3pl	E-3pl	G-5	E-5	G-7.5	E-7.5	G-10	E-10
		minimum	5.00	5.00	5.00	5.00	5.00	3.25	5.00	3.25	5.00	3.25	5.00	3.25	6.00	4.00
		preferred	5.00	5.00	5.00	5.00	5.00	3.50	5.00	3.50	5.00	3.50	5.00	3.50	6.00	5.00
H	depth of water at plummet	designation		H-1		H-3		H-1pl		H-3pl		H-5		H-7.5		H-10
		minimum		3.40		3.70		3.20		3.50		3.70		4.10		4.50
		preferred		3.50		3.80		3.30		3.60		3.80		4.50		5.00
J K	distance and depth ahead of plummet	designation	J-1	K-1	J-3	K-3	J-1pl	K-1pl	J-3pl	K-3pl	J-5	K-5	J-7.5	K-7.5	J-10	K-10
		minimum	5.00	3.30	6.00	3.60	4.50	3.10	5.50	3.40	6.00	3.60	8.00	4.00	11.00	4.25
		preferred	5.00	3.40	6.00	3.70	4.50	3.20	5.50	3.50	6.00	3.70	8.00	4.40	11.00	4.75
L M	distance and depth each side of plummet	designation	L-1	M-1	L-3	M-3	L-1pl	M-1pl	L-3pl	M-3pl	L-5	M-5	L-7.5	M-7.5	L-10	M-10
		minimum	1.50	3.30	2.00	3.60	1.40	3.10	1.80	3.40	3.00	3.60	3.75	4.00	4.50	4.25
		preferred	2.00	3.40	2.50	3.70	1.90	3.20	2.30	3.50	3.50	3.70	4.50	4.40	5.25	4.75
N	maximum slope to reduce dimensions beyond full requirements	pool depth	30°													
		ceiling	30°													

note: dimensions C (plummet to adjacent plummet) apply to platforms with widths as detailed; if platform widths are increased, then C is to be increased by half the additional width(s)

93 Dimensions for diving facilities: note that width of 10 m platform may be increased to 3 m

From Federation Internationale de Natation Amateur (FINA)/Amateur Swimming Association (ASA) handbook and information literature

Changing rooms

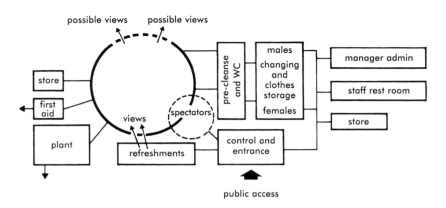

94 Circulation and grouping of elements

Over the past few years the majority of pool users have been from the adult population and this has meant that the expectation is for a much higher standard of changing and related areas. The fundamental decision in changing facilities is whether they are to be single or mixed sex. There is a clear trend towards mixed-sex changing areas. These areas are generally referred to as changing villages and can give much greater flexibility in accommodating differing proportions of males and females. For the majority of public pools, perhaps the ideal arrangement would be to have a main mixed-sex changing area supplemented by two group changing areas adjacent.

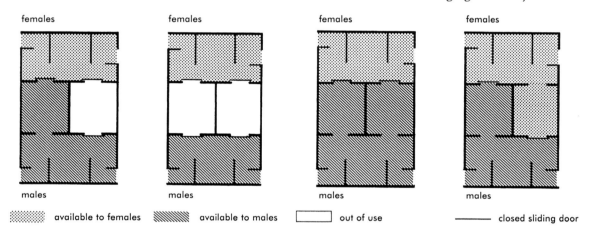

95 Changing area planned so that two central spaces can be used at different times by either sex

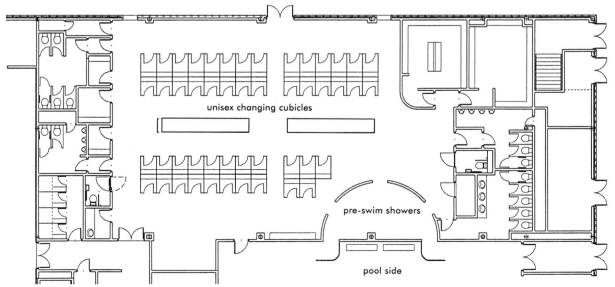

96 Changing Village, Sir Alfred McAlpine Stadium, Huddersfield (see also **6,10,19**)
(Arch: HOK + Lobb Sports Architecture)

Pool: typical details

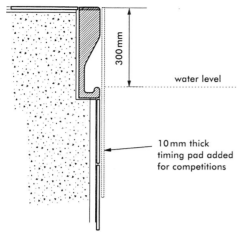

97 Raised edge detail: best applied at ends of main pools

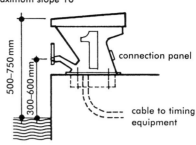

100 Diagram of starting platform (cable to timing equipment only built-in for major pool centres)

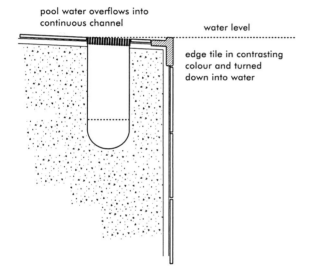

98 Deck edge detail suitable for sides of main pools (used in conjunction with **97**)

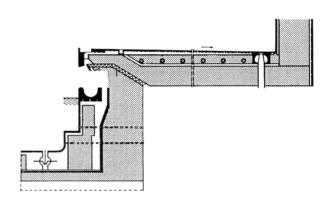

101 Pool edge with Wiesbaden type overflow: resting ledge and gangway in multipurpose pool

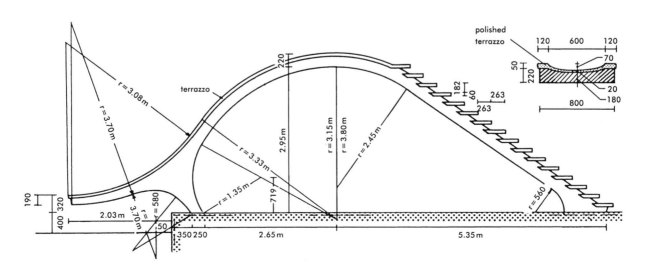

99 Water chute, Bad Kissingen, Germany

TENNIS

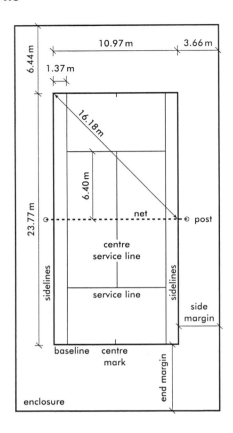

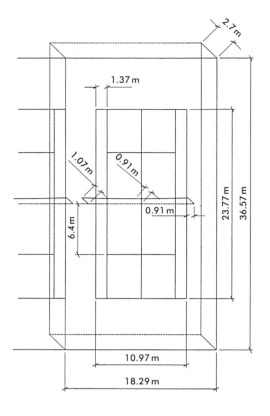

103 Lawn tennis court

enclosure dimensions relating to standards of play	international and national official championships (m)	county and club recommended (m)	recreational (m)
end margin	6.40	6.40	5.49
side margin	3.66	3.66	3.05
minimum enclosure size for one court	36.58×18.29	36.58×18.29	34.75×17.07
width for courts in one enclosure		33.53	31.70
width added for each iadditional court		15.24	14.63

102 Playing space required for courts of different standards according to requirements of the UK Lawn Tennis Association

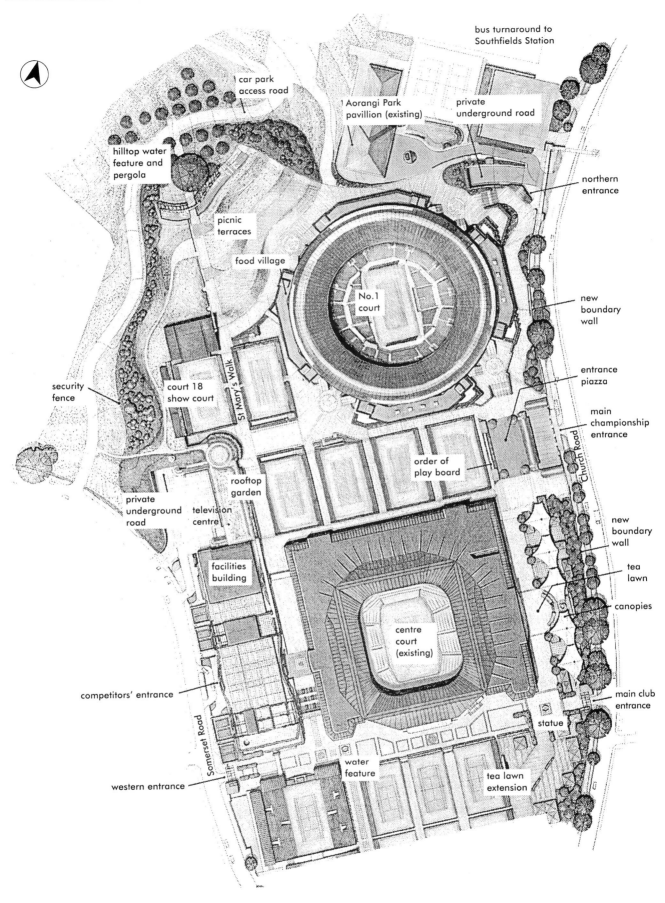

bus turnaround to
Southfields Station

car park
access road

Aorangi Park
pavillion (existing)

private
underground road

hilltop water
feature and
pergola

northern
entrance

picnic
terraces

food village

No.1
court

new
boundary
wall

security
fence

court 18
show court

entrance
piazza

main
championship
entrance

order of
play board

private
underground
road

rooftop
garden

television
centre

new
boundary
wall

facilities
building

tea
lawn

canopies

St Mary's Walk

Church Road

competitors' entrance

centre
court
(existing)

main club
entrance

Somerset Road

statue

western entrance

water
feature

tea lawn
extension

104 New No 1 Court development for the All-England Lawn
Tennis and Croquet Club at Wimbledon
(Arch: Building Design Partnership)

EQUESTRIAN

Indoor schools: location

In the past the location of riding schools was usually a result of the development of existing buildings. Additions were made to the stables of an old country house and portal framed structures built over an existing area provided an indoor facility for all-weather teaching.

Siting and access

Essential requirements for any site are as follows:

- good access for heavy vehicles in addition to cars
- access to open country and/or bridlepaths
- adequate services (possibly including fire hydrants)
- turning space for horsebox trailers, with space for lowering ramps to the side and rear
- access for fire appliances
- access for hay delivery vehicles (note: minimum gate width 3 m, minimum clearance height 4.5 m).

The stables should be sited an adequate distance away from adjacent houses and any loose boxes should be protected from prevailing winds.

Low lying sites which are prone to collecting water and are usually frosty in winter are to be avoided.

Planning and layout

The planning of installations breaks down into three main categories: instruction, horse management and administration.

Traditionally the plan usually arranges loose boxes looking inwards to a courtyard, with only a covered way in front of each box. Later developments totally enclosed the loose boxes, arranging them either side of a corridor. This enabled them to be serviced by a tractor and trailer circulating through the block. The main disadvantages were the extra cost, including the additional fire precautions required, and that horses can become bored with a limited view of the outside. However, the enclosed solution achieved much better working conditions for stable hands, and offered easier control of heating and ventilation, plus the ability to eliminate draughts. A calmer, quieter environment could also be achieved with enclosed boxes if the site was near roads or railways.

Other general principles that should be considered are that the indoor school should preferably be located away from the stable so that the instructor's commands cannot be heard by horses at rest. The risk of fire in stables necessitates special planning considerations. Straw stores require a minimum 1 hour fire resistance from other parts of the building or a fire break of at least 4.5 m is recommended.

Space requirements

There are many different standards of covered school. For example, the UK National Equestrian Centre has a riding area of 61 × 24.4 m, large enough to contain an international size arena and hold dressage and show jumping events, with seating for 300 along one long side. At the other end of the scale, it is possible to provide an area under a Dutch barn. The sides are only clad for 3 m from the eaves, and wattle hurdles enclose the floor.

Whatever the standard of building, the essential indoor riding space should be not less than 42×22 m, giving a clear floor space of 40×20 m, which is required for elementary dressage. Surrounding walls should incorporate tilted kickboards.

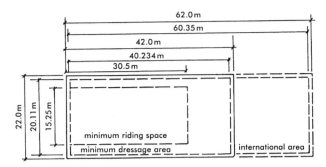

105 Riding school area: minimum height needed for jumping, 4 m (5 m preferred); spectator seating must be 20 m away; judges box and collection/mounting area also needed

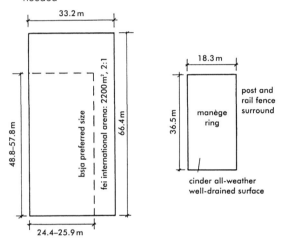

106 Indoor show jumping arena with collecting ring, warm-up and practice jump space; for mounting/collecting area allow for 20–30 horses at 3.5–5.0 m² each

107 Manège ring

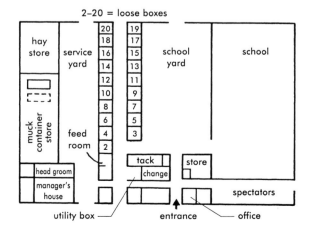

108 Lea Bridge Riding School, Lea Valley Regional Park, London
(Arch: J M V Bishop & M J Quinton)

Riding centre premises

The schedule of accommodation required is as follows.

(A) Instructional

- indoor school and areas
- outdoor manège
- grass paddocks (minimum 8000 m²)
- outdoor show jumping ring
- outdoor dressage area
- cross-country training area
- club room
- lecture room
- canteen
- storage for jumps, cavaletti etc. (approx 5% activity area).

(B) Horse management

- stables (loose boxes)
- utility box
- sick box (approximately 3.5 × 4.5 m).

The sick box should be away from other boxes, but within sight of other horses. A sling suspended from a beam with block and chain may also be needed. Larger establishments may need a completely isolated box for infectious diseases.

- feed store
- feed room
- tack room
- hay and straw store.

The hay and straw store is generally a Dutch barn type structure, the size depending largely on the number of horses and method of buying. One horse requires approximately 9 kg of hay and half a bale of straw per day. An additional 10%, approximately, extra volume should be allowed to accommodate new stock and for air circulation.

- smithy: possibly 10–15 m² (may be a mobile blacksmith)
- veterinary store
- muck store.

Muck stores are traditionally open bunkers with brick or block walls, but skip type containers have become more commonly used in recent times. The size depends on the number of horses and management, but generally allowance should be made for an average of 5.6 m³ per horse per week.

(C) Administration

Typically, areas are provided for reception, manager's office, staff room, first aid room, toilets, changing rooms, plant and residential accommodation as appropriate for managers, groom and stable hands.

Workshops and garaging for horseboxes, tractors etc. are also required.

a travelling room; b tack room; c drying room; d grinding room; e mash boilers; f feed area; g pharmacy; h office; i WC and shower; j reception; k main entrance; l boiler room; m female; n male; o night watch room; p staff room; q store; r washdown; s hay and straw; t yard; u WC; v kitchen

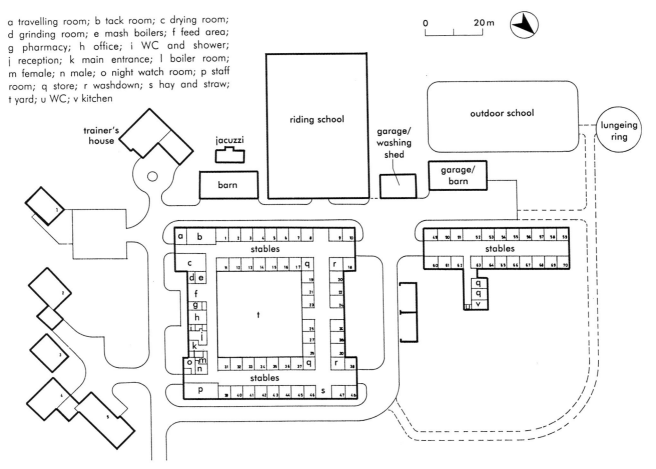

109 Oak Stables, Newmarket, Suffolk (Arch: David Cowan Associates)

THEATRES AND ARTS CENTRES

Kate Pickard

INTRODUCTION

The design of contemporary auditorium structures has developed to accommodate a range of functions and these new styles now accompany traditional historical theatre buildings. Considerable revival in the design of the theatre and auditorium has seen a move away from decorative architectural expression towards providing more multipurpose, flexible and functional structures. In addition, flexible seating and storage facilities, along with variable stage openings and mobile ceilings, allow adaptation of audience capacity and acoustic dynamics. These unified elements of contemporary design cater for all types of productions – from the staging of modest amateur dramas to large-scale orchestral concerts, opera and musicals.

Theatres and arts centres vary in their ranges of facilities, and their use of the structural space. This is evident in established buildings but even more so in recent contemporary designs, where art exhibition spaces, shops, restaurants and even tourist information services are included.

Traditionally, theatre buildings have been substantial and sometimes awe-inspiring structures, with elaborate interiors and grand carpeted stairways leading to the main auditorium. Traditional designs remain from the Victorian period when decorations and furnishings were lavish. These grand sophisticated theatres tend to accommodate large-scale touring productions, and will

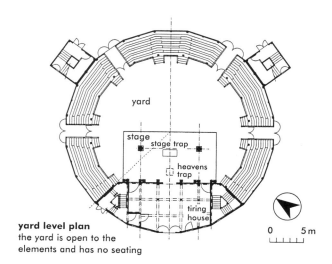

yard level plan
the yard is open to the elements and has no seating

1 Globe Theatre, Bankside, London SE1: an attempt by the American actor/director Sam Wanamaker to recreate the theatre of 1599 used by Shakespeare, with materials and layout resembling the original as closely as possible; new work includes a theatre design by Inigo Jones, exhibition and shop areas, a restaurant, and associated theatre facilities (Arch: Parameta Architects)

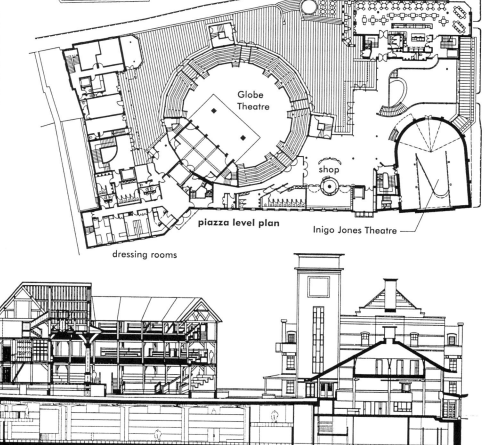

piazza level plan

section
galleries are roofed and have simple wooden benches

sometimes have a theatrical company in residence. 'Fringe' or amateur theatres often convert existing buildings, to accommodate workshops and studios designed for a specific company and their particular performance type. The auditoriums are smaller, often with steeply raked seating and intimate performance space. Some of these theatres may also have a café/bar/restaurant, close to the box office. Whether the main building accommodates rehearsal studios and production workshops varies according to the theatrical company in residence.

Arts centres are often designed to serve a more interactive purpose between production and arts education. These developments are often located within more of a community type setting. Extensive facilities can be incorporated into restricted sites. Sometimes existing buildings or community centres are used, and instead of large lobbies and foyers leading to a grand auditorium, there are more functional spaces for workshops, experimental/ studio theatre, and interactive performance areas. Administration offices and information centres are often located on site, as well as conference rooms and function suites. Arts centres may accommodate a variety of functions, such as public and private social events, exhibitions, weddings and meetings. In recent years, 'arts centres' and 'theatres' are more and more being merged together within contemporary buildings. Fully fitted with multimedia technology and facilities to serve a variety of functions, these modern structures can cater for most performances,

from large sale box office touring productions, to intimate dramas and workshops.

The main task of the architect is to maintain the balance between commercial, artistic and spectator requirements. Location of the building is very important, and although traditionally theatres tended to be situated in cultural centres in towns and cities, arts centres can also be located within smaller residential areas, and sometimes even villages, according to the project specifications. The theatre structure should not be insensitive to the geographical location and must maintain continuity with its surroundings, revitalising public areas and creating an inspirational and sculptural use of space. The geography and history of either existing or new sites is essential to the architectural form.

ORGANISATION

Theatres may be arranged in three main divisions (see **2**):

- **Reception/front of house:** entrance hall, foyers, box office, cloakroom, toilets, corridors and stairways. Optional: shop, exhibition space, restaurant and bar, tourist information office, administration office.
- **Auditorium:** main seating area. Optional: box/studio theatre.
- **Stage/backstage:** main stage, wings, back stage area, dressing rooms. Optional: scenery shop, wardrobe/costume shop, workshops and education rooms, and kitchen/staff room.

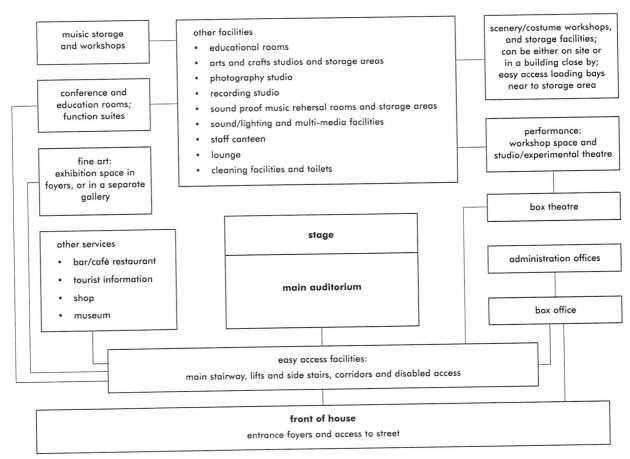

2 Multifunction theatres and arts centres: organisational diagram

Areas vary in content and size depending on type of theatre: drama and musical auditoriums, or an arts centre for amateur theatre and education. A 'bricks and mortar' theatre is one without an in-house performing company.

RECEPTION/FRONT OF HOUSE

The reception area of the building should have a sensitive relationship with the landscape. Some contemporary designs have used sophisticated glass façades and bright lighting in the entrance foyer, allowing the interior to spill out onto the street and creating a more inviting access for the public. Other structures are more sculptural, with large open plans and interesting uses of natural lighting. It is important that the organisation within the supporting spaces that lead to the auditorium is clear and welcoming. The main reception area may include a box office/information desk, cloakroom, and access to toilets. Sometimes, lobbies make available walls for art exhibition areas and multimedia displays, animating the public areas. A restaurant or bar/café is good for creating an atmosphere, and can overlap into open lobby areas, or can be accessed through corridors/doors leading from the reception areas. Access to the main auditorium should be prominent, and a choice of lifts, stairs or a grand stairway should be available. Other optional facilities include a shop, information services, conference rooms, function suits, and museum or gallery spaces. Access for people with disabilities, congestion and draughts are common problems with theatre foyers; clarity of circulation is paramount. A range of disabilities should be catered for, including lifts from the entrance hall to the auditorium. Some foyers occupy just the 'prow' of the building, whilst others are located around the front and sides. Doors should open outwards, against the exit flow in the corridor and should be self-closing. In many cases, especially in traditional theatre buildings, the main stairway leading to the auditorium is located prominently in the principal foyer.

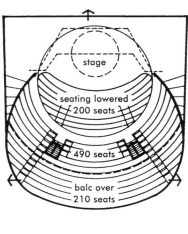

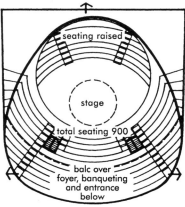

3 New London Theatre, Drury Lane, London: revolving stage and front stalls with adjustable height seating (can be either in the round or proscenium – 1106 seats in total); backstage facilities include nine dressing rooms (Arch: Tvrtkovic & Kenny Chew & Percival)

4 Circle level Olivier Auditorium, National Theatre, London: 1169 seats; two adjoining theatres (Lyttelton, 891 seats and Cottesloe, 400 seats); backstage areas (accessible to performers with disabilities) include dressing rooms, green room, quick change room and five rehearsal rooms (Arch: Denys Lasdun)

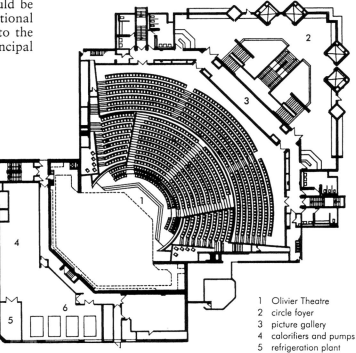

1 Olivier Theatre
2 circle foyer
3 picture gallery
4 calorifiers and pumps
5 refrigeration plant
6 boilers

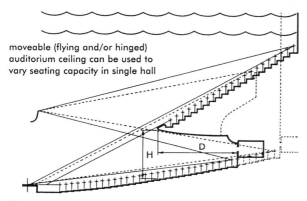

moveable (flying and/or hinged) auditorium ceiling can be used to vary seating capacity in single hall

5 Attached balcony (solid lines), flying balcony (dashed lines)

The auditorium longitudinal sections shown (**5—10**) have the same numbers of rows.

The maximum recommended D:H for balcony overhangs is 1:1 for concerts and 2:1 for opera and drama. Flying balconies may allow a greater D:H ratio by allowing reverberant energy to reach rear seats from behind. Balcony overhangs must be positioned clear of projection beams. The sight-line angle from the balcony to the stage should be no more than 30° and the last rows should have clear sight-lines to the central speaker cluster.

Convex and irregular surfaces aid sound diffusion. Domes, vaults and other large concave surfaces may cause acoustic problems.

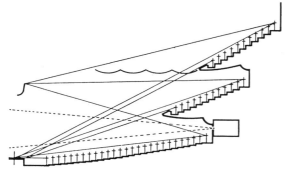

6 Two attached balconies

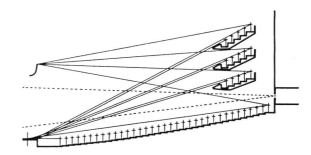

10 Three flying balconies

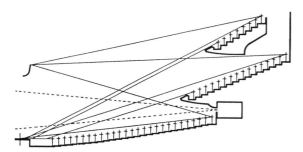

7 Attached lower balcony, flying upper balcony

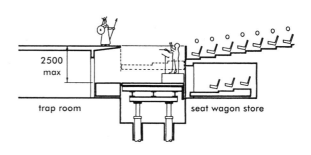

2500 max

trap room   seat wagon store

11 Typical orchestra pit lift detail

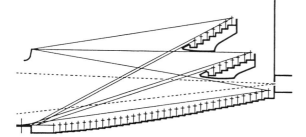

8 Two flying balconies

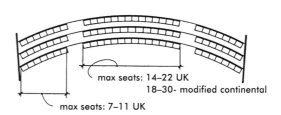

max seats: 14–22 UK
18–30- modified continental

max seats: 7–11 UK

12 Multiple aisle detail

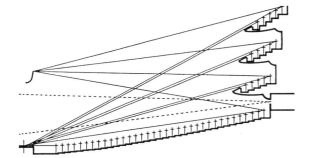

9 Three attached balconies

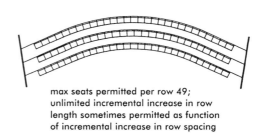

max seats permitted per row 49; unlimited incremental increase in row length sometimes permitted as function of incremental increase in row spacing

13 'Continental' seating

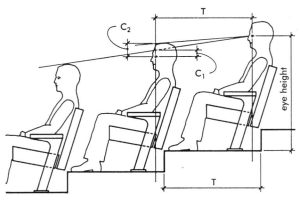

14 Typical seated spectator

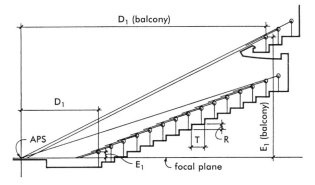

15 Constant rise floor slopes

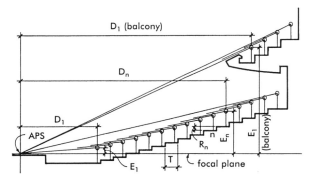

16 Iscidomal floor slopes

SIGHT-LINES

14 shows a typical seated spectator:
  eye height: 1120 ± 100 mm
  tread of seating tier (row spacing) T: 800–1150 mm
  head clearance C:
  C_1 = 60 mm minimum (view between heads in front)
  C_2 = 120 mm (reasonable viewing standards)
Rise R (see **15**): difference in height between adjacent seating platforms.

Floor slope (see **15**, **16**)

The arrival point of sight (APS) is the intersection of the highest sight-line at a focal plane positioned 50 mm above the stage platform. Distance D is the horizontal distance from the eye of a seated spectator to the APS.
  D_1 = distance from eye of front row to APS
  D_n = distance from eye of given row n to APS
Elevation E is the vertical height of the eye of a seated spectator above the focal plane.
  E_1 = vertical height of eye of first row above focal plane
  E_n = vertical height of eye of given row n above focal plane
  E_1 = 0 establishes maximum stage height allowable (i.e. 1060 mm)

With a constant rise floor slope (see **15**) the sight-lines from rows are parallel and the APS is determined by the intersection of the sight-line from the last or highest row at the focal plane.

$$R = \frac{T}{D_1}\left[E_1 + (N-1) + C\right] \qquad D_1 = \frac{T}{R-C}\left[E_1 + (N-1)\,C\right]$$

$$E_1 = \frac{D_1}{T}\,(R-C) - C\,(N-1)$$

N = number of rows in seat bank

With an iscidomal floor slope (see **16**) more efficient use is made of the given total rise. The exponential shape of the floor results from the generation of sight lines a single focal point or APS.

$$E_n = D_n\left[\frac{E_1}{D_1} + C\left(\frac{1}{D_1} + \frac{1}{D_2} + \frac{1}{D_3} + \ldots + \frac{1}{D_{n-1}}\right)\right] \quad R_n = E_n - E_{n-1}$$

The type and scale of performance will dictate the range of performing area sizes (see **17**). It may be desirable for performing space to accommodate a variety of performing area sizes. Containment of the audience within a 130° peripheral spread of vision from a performer at the point of command will help promote maximum visual and aural communication between the performer and the spectators.

The largest performing area should fall within a boundary defined by the 130° angle of peripheral of vision from seats at ends of the front rows (see **18**). The limit of the centre of action is defined by a 60° angle of normal, accurate, polychromatic vision from seats at ends of the front rows. The point of command should logically fall within the centre of action.

The boundary limit of the seating area in an auditorium might be defined by a given constant angle of peripheral spread of vision to the sides of given stage openings. Limits of both 30° and 60° angles of peripheral spread of vision related to various openings are illustrated in **19**.

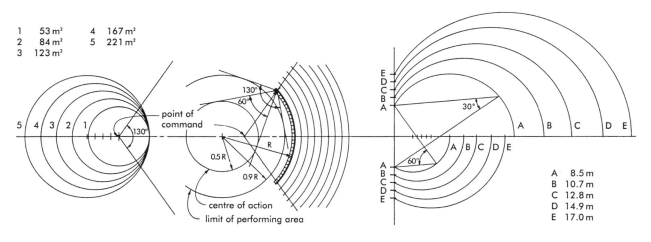

1	53 m²	4	167 m²
2	84 m²	5	221 m²
3	123 m²		

A	8.5 m
B	10.7 m
C	12.8 m
D	14.9 m
E	17.0 m

17 Range of performing area   **18** Relationship between performing area and seating   **19** Viewing angle fields from stage opening

AUDITORIUM

The audience can enter the auditorium, either from the foyer at the rear, from the sides of the seating rows, or from an opening within the seating ranks. In open stages, the stage area and auditorium are one space; traditional proscenium stages can have spectacular engaging forestage openings and elaborate comfortable interiors. Contemporary designs tend to be more simple and elegant in their approach, accommodating forestage grids, lighting bridges, acoustic devices and multipurpose panels, arranged around walls and ceilings. Acoustic and visual requirements must be considered at the outset. This will determine seating arrangements, layout and materials used for ceilings, walls, floors and chairs. The auditorium must be completely protected from any external sound, and internal sound from rehearsal rooms or the studio. In some cases, sound locks have been used on the doors. Concrete and brick in walls and ceilings is not only non-absorbent, and therefore internally acoustically dynamic, but is also good at excluding external sound.

Floors and ceilings

Floors are often carpeted, although timber boards are preferable acoustically. Floor layouts can be flexible for variable seating and acoustic requirements. High ceilings are required for concerts, musicals and opera, providing longer reverberation time: typical hall volume – $20.5 \, m^3$–$35 \, m^3$/audience seat. Lower ceilings should be used for drama and speech – $7.5 \, m^3$–$14 \, m^3$/audience seat. Acoustic requirements may dictate that reflective surfaces at the ceiling of the orchestra enclosure extend out above audience seating. In contemporary auditoriums, ceilings are movable with large panelling in segments that can be opened and closed on systems of winches and flying grids. These variables allow for the widely diverging acoustic requirements of electronic and live orchestral music as opposed to speech and drama.

1 auditorium (stalls, balcony, circle, upper circle)
2 stage
3 forestage (three double-level lifts) – stage front, orchestra pit, or seating
4 front of house
5 portico to Margaret Powell Square
6 art gallery (spaces arranged as cube, square and long) including workshop and education facilities
7 restaurant and tourist information
8 dressing rooms and offices
9 landscaped court
10 multi-storey car park

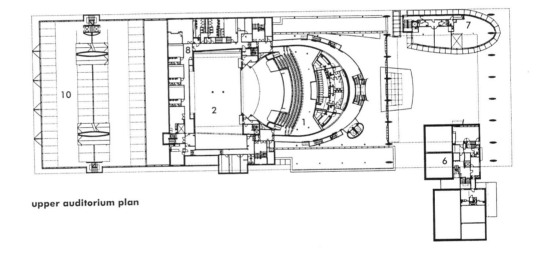

upper auditorium plan

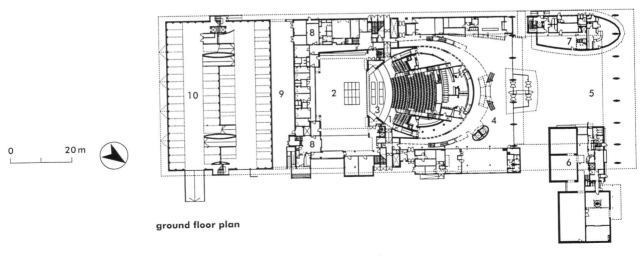

0   20 m

ground floor plan

20 Milton Keynes Theatre and Gallery: designed for drama, dance, opera and music; normal auditorium arrangement is 'lyric mode' (1250 or 1400 seats), but the ceiling can be raised for orchestral performances to provide 1600 seats, or lowered to close the upper circle for amateur drama etc. (950 seats)
(Arch: Blonski Heard Architects)

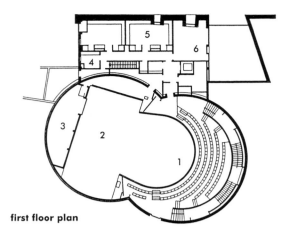

first floor plan

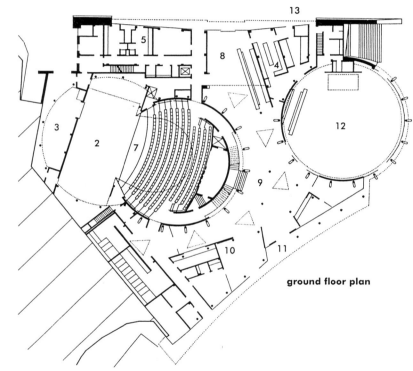

ground floor plan

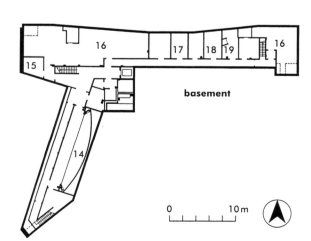

basement

0   10m

Seating

Flexible seating allows greater capacity and variation, and slide-away rows can be used to expose larger floor surface. In some cases, forestage seating can be moved into storage below the stage, and the front stalls seating can be moved back beneath the rear stalls, allocating standing room for large concerts. Circling screens can be used to reduce the size of the auditorium capacity while openings in the screen allow for seating slips, standing spaces and lighting slots. The minimum clearway between seats increases with the number of seats in a row. Rows can be designed in a variety of forms for various audience requirements; with a smaller audience, straight rows are possible. Adequate room must be allowed for wheelchair access and turning space.

The various seating row layouts are:
- straight
- straight with curved ends
- curved
- angled
- straight rows in blocks at different angles

For open stages and auditoriums with no balconies, seating can be steeply raked. When balconies are used, then the raking intensity can be reduced, allowing more height for balconies. Small box or studio auditoriums can use very steep raking to compact seating and allow a clear view of the open stage area. Every seat should allow viewing of the main central areas of the stage. Obviously it is ideal to try to achieve a clear line of sight of the whole stage area from every seat, but in compact theatres with a proscenium stage, some seats will have sight-lines into the back stage area from one angle, and seats in the upper level balconies will be looking down onto the stage and may not see the full back-drop sets on stage. The seating design must be considered in conjunction with the stage proportions and acoustics.

section

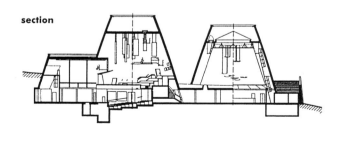

1 circle; 2 stage; 3 scene dock; 4 kitchen; 5 dressing rooms; 6 office; 7 auditorium (483 fixed seats); 8 bar; 9 foyer; 10 tourist information; 11 entrance; 12 café/performance space (150 chairs); 13 terrace; 14 orchestra pit; 15 band room; 16 plant; 17 staff room; 18 wardrobe; 19 store

21 Landmark Theatre and Arts Complex, Ilfracombe, Devon: the main auditorium has a proscenium; the performance space (12 on plan) is a café in the daytime, but this can be adapted in the evenings for cabaret, dances etc. (Arch: Tim Ronalds Architects)

Gangways

Aisles and gangways can be placed down the rows in any number. The minimum width is 1100 mm, and is determined by the number of seats. When the aisle is steeply raked, steps must extend to the full width of the gangway, and the step risers must be consistent. Railings should be provided especially when the raking is steep.

Balconies (see 5–10)

Steeply raked, multi-tiered auditoriums are common, with some theatres having up to three balconies. Balconies can be straight or curved; curved cascades create a sense of continuity and intimacy. Balconies can be used for upper and lower circles; front and back stalls and boxes by the side of the stage with loose seating or standing space. The steeper the rake, the greater the risk of sight-line cut-off caused by overhead balconies. However, a steeply raked auditorium does provide a dramatic arrangement for the gathering of a large audience, creating an exciting sense of the space within the structure's interior, as well as an ideal enclosure for the performance. The angles and sight-lines should be taken into consideration, especially with the design of the back stage area in accordance with the boxes to the side of the stage. In open staged theatres, there are no balconies, but steeply raked seating allows for considerable sound control for the seats furthest away from the stage. Often, manually controlled lighting devices are given space at the rear, or adjacent to the stage.

Exits

The requirements are that for each level, two separate exits are provided for the first 500 seats, and an additional one for each 250 thereafter. All doors should open in the direction of escape from the auditorium. Each exit must lead, via a fire-resistant enclosure, to a place of safety. Refer to the regulations for minimum exit widths per number of people.

STAGE/BACKSTAGE (see 22)

Not only is the performance space considerably different in each theatre or arts centre, but so also are the backstage areas and the extent of rehearsal and administration facilities that are catered for. The stage dimensions are largely dependent on the technical requirements of scenery dimensions and the type of performance being hosted.

Main stage

There are a variety of stage designs used in traditional and contemporary theatre designs.

Proscenium stage (see 3,21)   Traditionally used extensively, this form of stage is both versatile and flexible. The proscenium opening separates the performance area from the audience, and packs away the backstage areas. In some contemporary designs, the size is flexible for a more versatile performance area (see **24**). The proscenium height and width depend on technical and visual requirements: widths for drama are from 8 to 10 m, and 12 to 20 m for multipurpose venues.

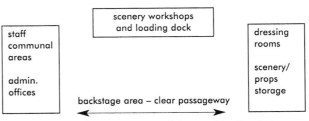

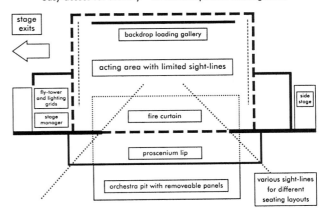

22 Stage and backstage: diagrammatic layout

A fire curtain drops from just inside the lip of the opening and should extend below the stage level, sometimes through the floor. An apron can extend from the proscenium opening and fire curtain. There may even be small side stages placed in the sides of the proscenium frame. These stages should relate to the main performance space, and sizes can vary. They may be used for extra scenery and possibly performance space, so good circulation and access backstage is essential.

There may also be stairs and step units, ramps, runways and an orchestra pit that may be closed or partially open (see **11**). The platforms in the orchestra pit can sometimes be altered according to acoustic or visual requirements.

Thrust stages These extend from the proscenium, bringing the performance into the audience area, and come in a variety of forms and sizes:

- oval or quarter circle
- square, or rectangular
- long and thin, with seats on either side.

Open stage (or arena stage) A form of Roman or early Renaissance theatre design which was also used in the Elizabethan period (see **1**). An open performance area is at floor level, or can be raised, and surrounded by the audience. Stage shapes and sizes are variable:

- part, half or fully open
- round or oval
- square, rectangular or polygonal.

In some theatres, the seating surrounds most, if not all, of the stage areas – theatre-in-the-round (see **3, 23,25**), where the actors may use the same entrances as the audience. A more intimate relationship with the audience is created. Lighting grids, sound technology and scenery devices are sometimes provided within the auditorium space or the upstage wall. For backdrops to the acting area, a back wall is required.

The box/studio theatre

For intimate and experimental plays, the box theatre is an enclosed room with simple lighting and sound equipment. There is minimal space for audience seating, which is either in front of a miniature proscenium or around an open stage or round stage. In most cases, seats are flexible and backstage areas are minimal or even non-existent. Sometimes the actors will use the same entrances as the audience, so it is important that there are different access points around the room to allow easy audience access. The stage may be raised using movable boxes, the space available for sets is minimal, and the seat raking may also be on boxes. In other cases, the tight theatre space will be fully equipped, with a slightly larger audience capacity. Drapes around the walls offer acoustic variables.

Stage floor

A resistant surface is desirable and a non-reflective and non-slippery finish is advisable: hardboard is often used. Ideally, a material that does not easily mark is recommended and removable panels are even better. The materials used for the floor must be fire resistant and must not warp or shrink.

Often the floor has a variety of trap doors (see **1**); a series of lifts can be incorporated for maximum flexibility, but these are expensive. The stage may be formed of modular sections which can be removed.

The basement should be easily accessed, with minimum headroom of 2.5 m.

Some stages can be raised, tilted or revolved, in part or in whole (e.g. see **3**). Some stages are slightly raked, which can give better sight-lines but may cause considerable problems with scenery.

The stage is often raised up to 1100 mm above the level of the auditorium, with a curved or angled front edge.

1 removable tier; 2 stage; 3 balcony; 4 director's office; 5 president's box; 6 cooling tower; 7 room; 8 foyer (light booth above); 9 shop; 10 mechanical equipment; 11 lounge; 12 lobby (rehersals) 13 vestibule

23 Arena Stage Theatre, Washington DC, USA: upper level plan (Arch: Harry Weese)

24 Chequer Mead Arts Centre, East Grinstead, West Sussex: an adaptable proscenium, allowing for an open stage (Arch: Tim Ronalds Architects)

first floor plan (auditorium)

0   10m

ground floor plan

1 stage; 2 auditorium (320 seats); 3 dressing room 1; 4 shower; 5 lift; 6 WC (dis); 7 control room; 8 workshop; 9 service yard; 10 kitchen; 11 café/foyer; 12 gallery; 13 entrance and box office; 14 office; 15 meeting room; 16 arts and crafts studio; 17 rehearsal room; 18 WCs; 19 gallery/circle; 20 dressing room 2

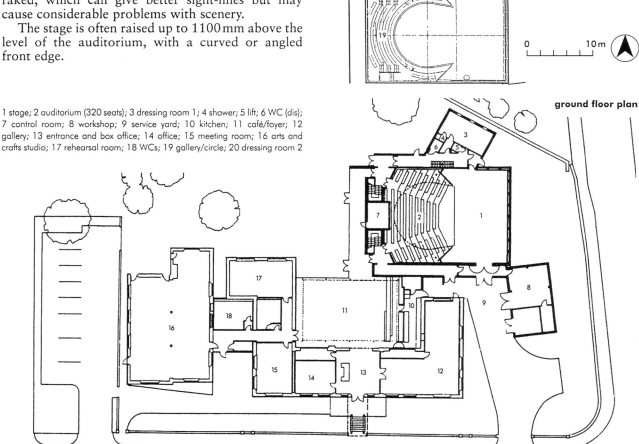

SUPPORTING AREAS

Orchestra pit

This is more common in traditional theatres. Although technology allows for more recorded music to be used, live music should be catered for in multipurpose performance spaces. The orchestra area is in front of the stage, and sometimes under the stage, depending on how important it is for the audience to see the orchestra (see **11**). Pit lifts can be used for flexible seating or staging requirements.

Considerations include:

- Both performers and the orchestra must be able to see the conductor.
- The conductor's eye level must not be lower than the stage.
- The pit should not extend further than 2 m under the stage.
- The maximum depth below the stage level should be 2.5 m.
- Space for 60–120 musicians should be provided (approximately 1 to 1.5 m²/musician, but much more for some instruments).

Wings

The extent of facilities that need to be considered in the supporting areas around the stage vary considerably according to the type of theatre and performance type. The kind of machinery involved could be:

- **Bridges:** long platforms that span the width of the proscenium, and will need space behind the top of the proscenium arch
- **Wagon stages:** large mobile platforms that support fully-built sets that will need room to enter and leave up-stage, and at both sides
- **Fly-tower:** a grid that suspends lighting and scenery above the stage. Adequate room is required for winches or rope ties to be operated off-stage at either side, or a motor room for motorised flying systems.
- **Additional stage lighting galleries:** either side off-stage.
- **Scenery loading docks.**

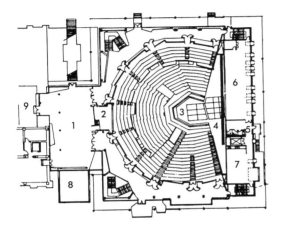

1 upper lobby; 2 control booth; 3 forestage; 4 space stage; 5 stage door; 6 costumes; 7 green room; 8 Walker Art Centre; 9 court

25 Tyrone Guthrie Theatre, Minneapolis, USA: a three-quarter arena stage; plan at balcony level (Arch: Ralph Rapson)

orchestra floor

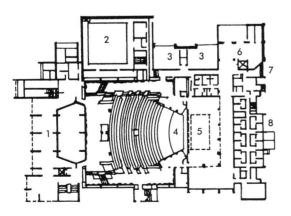

first balcony floor

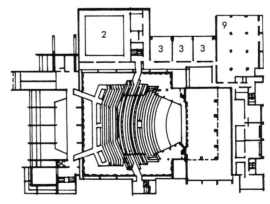

1 upper lobby; 2 upper part studio theatre; 3 meetings; 4 orchestra stage; 5 drama stage; 6 receiving; 7 office and entrance; 8 dressing rooms; 9 mechanical equipment

0   20m

26 Hamilton Place, Ontario, Canada (Arch: Garwood-Jones)

Backstage area (see 22)

This is the main circulation area around the stage and provides space for the movement of scenery, actors and any extra necessities. Sometimes in large theatres there is a need for a considerable open-plan area to overcome congestion problems. A lobby of some form is usually required to prevent light and sound from spilling onto the stage area. Normally there should be a passageway around the back of the stage to allow actors to transfer between stage entrances quickly. Facilities possibly needed in the immediate backstage area include:

- dressing rooms
- staff rooms
- kitchen and lounge area where staff and performers can gather
- scenery and properties storage area
- wardrobe storage area.

Other facilities in supporting areas

Some theatres may only have facilities for performances, the administration, rehearsals, and set/costume-making being maintained in another building close by. However, in many establishments, including arts centres, there is a need to consider a range of additional areas for administration and performance facilities. These include:

- Scenic shop: where sets and properties are made on site; in some cases conveniently near the stage area, especially where large-scale drops are hung. These areas must be large and adequate for complex technical purposes (e.g. carpentry benches and wood storage) and designed to the size of the largest scenery. In some cases the paint shop is separate to the workshop, and backdrops are either elevated on frames or laid out on the floor. In all types of workshop, there needs to be storage for cleaning and working material. Acoustic restrictions should protect the workshops from the rest of the theatre and large gates or roller shutters may be required for easy passage. There may need to be access for large goods vehicles and loading docks. In theatres where the workshops are separate to the auditorium theatre building, or where touring companies are accommodated, there needs to be a separate loading dock somewhere in the back stage area, close to storage facilities. There may also need to be an office for the head of design.

- **Props workshops:** similar to scenic workshop, for the making of furniture and smaller items.
- **Props store:** for the storage of stage furniture and extras.
- **Costume workshop:** where costumes are made. Dense storage and shelving may be required as well as working surfaces and large walk-in cupboards.
- **Wardrobe:** where costumes are stored in hung railings and storage compartments.
- **Wig storage and hair dressers.**
- **Rehearsal studios and workshop spaces:** large spacious areas for acting, dance and music. Wooden floors are the most common, with surrounding mirrors or plain interior. Sometimes room for simple lighting, sound and curtain devices may be required.
- **Control room (for sound and projection):** these are both usually placed at the rear of the auditorium or in the wings of the stage area. Projection is either used for scenic effects, or films (see also Cinemas). Often the soundboard is included inside the auditorium.
- **Piano store/music store.**
- **Recording studios:** possibly with tape storage cupboards.
- **Administration offices:** typical office layout.
- **Staff facilities:** including kitchen/laundry/canteen and staff communal areas, toilets, cleaners' stores and security control rooms.

REGULATIONS

The Theatres Act, 1968 states that every building for public performance of stage plays must be licensed by the local authority. Music and dancing premises are similarly controlled by the local authority, but under other legislation. Local authorities have the power to make regulations affecting the construction and equipment, and how the building is to be maintained in a safe condition, but apart from this the Building Regulations and Fire Officer's guidelines etc. apply in the normal way.

VEHICLE FACILITIES

Helen Dallas

Including car parks, petrol stations, bus and coach stations

There continues to be an increase in vehicle numbers, with a corresponding demand for facilities to serve the car and the owner: petrol garages, high-road service stations, car parks, car showrooms and repair garages. This section firstly examines vehicle sizes and their requirements for movement and road design, then studies the design of the different facilities in detail.

DETAILED DESIGN

Vehicle sizes

Car sizes vary, but a typical size (see **1**) is used for design of parking spaces, roadways and junctions. Similar standard information is used for other vehicle types (see **2,3**).

Roadways

Space for vehicles to travel and manoeuvre depends on the conditions under which they operate. For major roads national highway authorities lay down maximum permitted dimensions, axle loads and turning circles. They recommend road widths, sight-lines and other characteristics of major urban and rural roads. At bends, in particular, allowance must be made for the manoeuvring of different vehicles (see **4**).

On residential roads where traffic flows are light, some tolerance in dimensions is acceptable (e.g. to preserve existing features). Road widths narrower than 5.50 m can be acceptable (see **5,6,7,8**). Parking provision conditions the adequacy of road width. Where roads give direct access to dwellings and parking spaces, roadways are likely to be used for casual parking. Where this does not happen, widths are largely determined by the considerations of moving traffic. Narrowed sections may be used to discourage parking (e.g. where there may be danger at a pedestrian crossing).

The concept of traffic calming, incorporating measures to slow down or restrict certain forms of vehicle, has become a key to reducing vehicle associated problems within urban areas. The Highways (Traffic Calming) Regulations 1993 and the Highways (Road Humps) Regulations 1996 have been introduced to enable the implementation of schemes, incorporating rumble strips, humps, narrowings, chicanes, one-way throttles, mini-roundabouts, view blocking and surface treatments (see **9**).

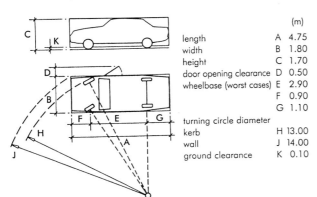

	(m)
length	A 4.75
width	B 1.80
height	C 1.70
door opening clearance	D 0.50
wheelbase (worst cases)	E 2.90
	F 0.90
	G 1.10
turning circle diameter	
kerb	H 13.00
wall	J 14.00
ground clearance	K 0.10

1 Typical car dimensions

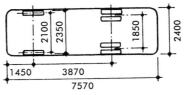

2 Typical dimensions: refuse vehicle

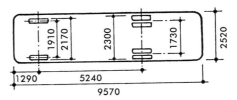

3 Typical dimensions: furniture removal van

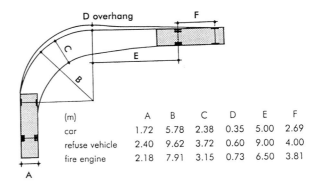

(m)	A	B	C	D	E	F
car	1.72	5.78	2.38	0.35	5.00	2.69
refuse vehicle	2.40	9.62	3.72	0.60	9.00	4.00
fire engine	2.18	7.91	3.15	0.73	6.50	3.81

4 Turning through 90°: dimensions for different vehicles

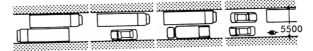

5 Normal maximum width for residential traffic 5.50 m: allows all vehicles to pass one another with overall tolerance of 500 mm for largest vehicle

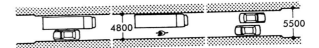

6 Carriageway of 4.80 m allows wide car and furniture removal van to pass each other with overall tolerance of 500 mm but is too narrow to allow free movement of large vehicles

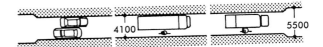

7 At 4.10 m carriageway is too narrow for large vans to pass vehicles other than cyclists; cars can pass each other with overall tolerance of 500 mm

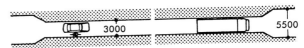

8 Width of 3.0 m minimum between passing bays in single track system

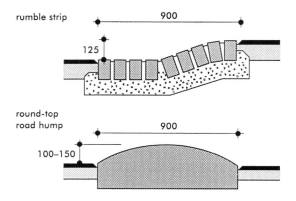

9 Details of typical traffic calming measures

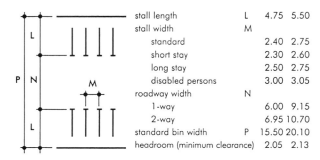

stall length	L	4.75	5.50
stall width	M		
standard		2.40	2.75
short stay		2.30	2.60
long stay		2.50	2.75
disabled persons		3.00	3.05
roadway width	N		
1-way		6.00	9.15
2-way		6.95	10.70
standard bin width	P	15.50	20.10
headroom (minimum clearance)		2.05	2.13

10 Recommended parking dimensions, 90° layout (m)

Parking configurations

Dimensions of vehicle parking spaces in parking bays range from 1.80×4.60 m to 2.50×6.00 m (see **10**), but slightly longer for parallel parking (see **11**). An increase in bay size is usually adopted for open-air parking or where a high proportion of larger cars and vans is likely. While 90° parking is more economical in space requirements (20–22 m² per car), 45° parking (23–26 m² per car) can be more convenient (see **12**). Vehicle parking spaces for people with disabilities should be wider: for semi-ambulant persons bay widths should be increased to 2.80 m; for wheelchair users to 3.00 m. Within larger and multi-storey car parks, both 90° and angled bays are used depending on overall widths available and lane patterns.

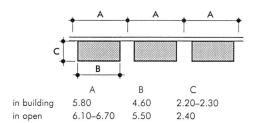

	A	B	C
in building	5.80	4.60	2.20–2.30
in open	6.10–6.70	5.50	2.40

11 Parallel parking (m)

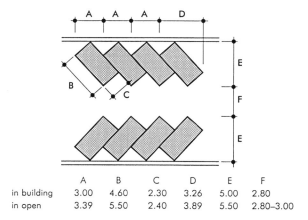

	A	B	C	D	E	F
in building	3.00	4.60	2.30	3.26	5.00	2.80
in open	3.39	5.50	2.40	3.89	5.50	2.80–3.00

12 Angled parking, 45° (m)

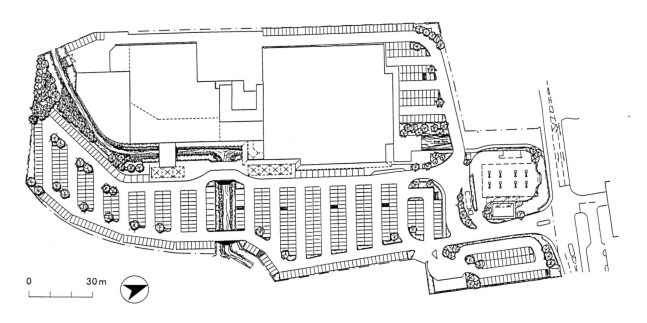

0   30 m

13 J Sainsbury/Homebase, Cardiff: commercial parking arrangement and petrol station

(Landscape arch: Munro & Whitten; arch: Jonathan Smith & Partners)

CAR PARK DESIGN

External or single-level parking

Single-storey open car parks can be required for both private and public use: for example, parking courts to residential flats developments, adjacent factories and offices, town-centre parking, tourist sites, supermarkets and multiplex cinemas.

Large open-plan parking areas often need to be broken down in scale by incorporating:

- variety in surfaces – coloured bricks, tarmacs, brushed concrete and grassblocks (note the need for resistance to attack by oil or petrol)
- screening or separation to delineate areas and help locate vehicles – level changes, signing, fencing and planting
- use of landscaping to soften hard expanses – individual trees between parking bays, low-level planting beds between back-to-back parking, at ends of run and adjacent pedestrian routes.

Location Parking arrangements should be clear and organised, using road markings and signs, preferably with one-way systems. Keep dead ends as short as possible so that the driver can view vacant spaces. Consider the passing of vehicles while waiting for another to reverse and depart. With larger car parks adopt a centralised route (may be two-way), with choice of one-way loops leading off. Long-stay car parks (e.g. for commuters) can have longer parking aisles and slightly narrower parking stalls (2.3 m), compared with short stay/rapid turnover (2.5 m). Plan large parking areas with

variable/peak usages, with both regular and overspill spaces.

Certain facilities may require a setting-down or taxi area immediately adjacent to an entrance (e.g. in case of poor weather, or for elderly or infirm visitors). Spaces may need to be allocated for people with disabilities, important personnel or shoppers with young children.

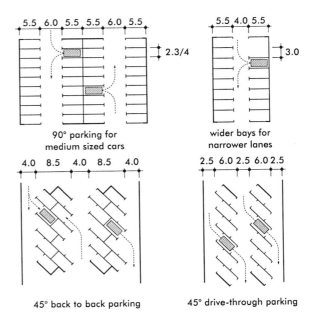

14 Typical layouts using 90°and angled parking (m)

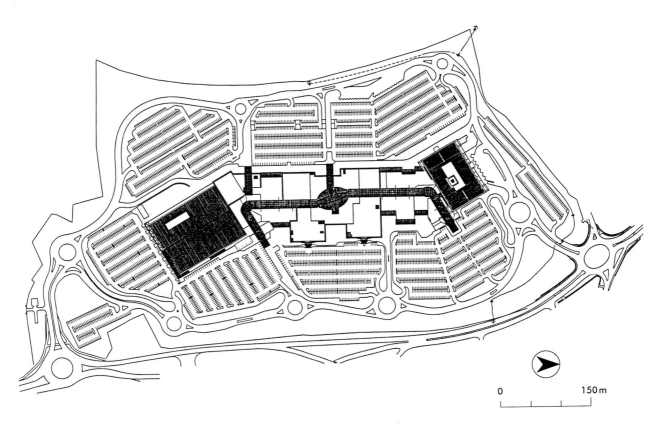

15 White Rose Shopping Centre, Leeds
(Arch: Building Design Partnership)

Multi-storey car parks

These are usually constructed to serve town centres, directly relating to shopping precincts or at various locations providing for visitors, shoppers and workers. Access should be clearly signed approaching the car park, preferably located off a main distributory road. Access design is subject to approval by Local Authority traffic engineers to ensure adequate space for entrance queueing and safe egress into traffic flows.

Arrangements The minimum acceptable plot size is 2.5 m² to allow for the structure and an economical aisled layout. A two parallel bin system is normally used to provide a sensible circulation arrangement, with one-way traffic flows having upward and downward routes separated (see **16**). This allows for maximum traffic capacity. Dynamic capacity is reduced if two-way traffic flows exist or mixed upwards and downwards circulation is used. Cul-de-sac driveways are undesirable. Economy is achieved by using the longest practicable aisle length. The downward routes should be short to expedite exit, with upwards routes devised to give the best possible search pattern for vacant stalls.

Typical floor arrangements include:

- Split level layout: arrangement widely adopted. Two bins so arranged that adjacent parking levels are separated by half-storey height. Short interconnecting ramps are used between levels (see **17**).
- Warped-slab layout: parking levels constructed with uninterrupted horizontal external edge; steady transition of gradients constructed to give internal interconnection of parking levels. Compared with split-level layout the need for ramps at either end of building is eliminated (see **18**).
- Parking ramp layout: parking level constructed as a long ramp, which has a significant effect on elevational appearance. To keep to acceptable gradients a long building is required. When necessary the exit can be speeded up by adopting an external helical ramp (see **19**).
- Flat-slab layout: external ramp used to interconnect level parking areas (see **20**).

Movement within car park For vehicles there should be an efficient path around the car park to locate a space, then to proceed quickly to the exit. Clear signing is required, usually combining ground route markings and mounted signs.

For pedestrians the location of exits, whether stairs or lifts, should be visible from any point within the car park. Standard green and white or illuminated signs must be provided. Space is required around exit positions and pay machines safe from vehicle flows.

Stairs The number and location of escape stairs is subject to minimum distances from any point within car park. They should be of generous width, open balustraded, well lit (preferably with natural light), ventilated and fitted with glazed doors top and bottom for user safety. Installation of lifts (average eight-person size) is required if there are two floors or more.

Security Both for vehicles and users, this is very important, and may be enhanced by ensuring:

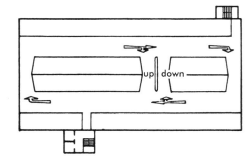

16 Typical multi-storey car-park arrangement

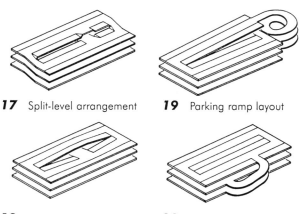

17 Split-level arrangement **19** Parking ramp layout

18 Warped-slab layout **20** Flat-slab layout

- there are no concealed or dead spaces not visible during general use
- that the division between two halves of a split-level layout is not blocked off visually
- all areas are well lit
- there is no further access to the car park other than through the designated vehicular and pedestrian entrances
- closed circuit TV monitoring systems and/or regular patrols are provided.

Control systems These are required to control entry into the car park and operate payment methods. Busy town-centre car parks should have indication of spaces available at or near the entry. Sophisticated electronic systems are now available to meet control requirements. The entrance should be obvious, with height restrictions and charges clearly displayed. Barriers can serve to slow down vehicles, and incorporate ticket machines. Subject to the flow of vehicles per hour, provision of two or more entrance/exit barrier positions may be required.

Alternative payment systems are available, such as a fixed charge paid on entry to a machine or cashier, which reduces need for a barrier at the exit. Graduated time charges, payable on exit, pay and display systems, or the purchase of tickets off-site can also be considered.

Construction Non-combustible materials are necessary to achieve the required structural fire resistance. Concrete column, beam and slab constructions are generally used as impact damage is negligible and limited surface treatment is needed. Columns should fit bay spacings, and be located to the rear to limit restriction of parking. Floors are often solid reinforced concrete slabs, pre-cast units or ribbed/coffered systems, which increase overall height but allow for services and lighting. External elevations should be partially open for fire protection and fume escape. Upstand is required at perimeters to restrain vehicle impact: typically, this is concrete, brick or steel.

The designer is often required to consider the external massing, using a range of materials and smaller elements to break down the scale or incorporate features sympathetic to the location. The problem can be alleviated if sunken parking systems are used (see **22**).

1 Avenue de Chartres
2 coach park
3 main access road
4 disabled parking
5 toilet block on ground floor below
6 footpath/cycleway
7 River Lavant
8 railway station

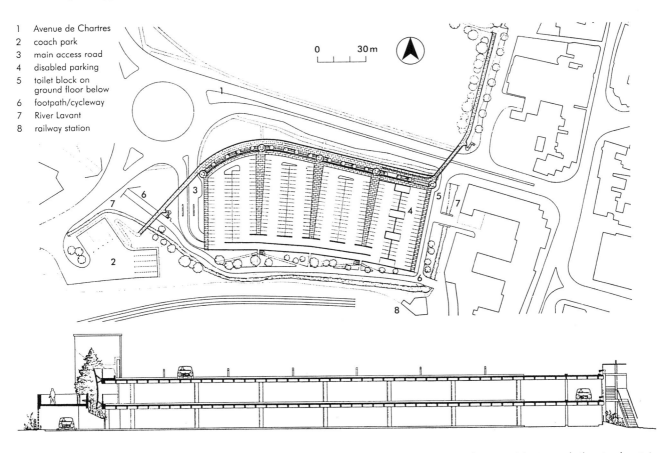

21 Avenue de Chartres car park, Chichester: first floor plan and section
(Arch: Birds Portchmouth Russum)

Car access is from the Avenue de Chartres roundabout. A distribution road parallel to the River Lavant gives access on each of the three levels to the four parking compartments, with a total capacity of 900 spaces. Having parked, the visitor can walk along generous pedestrian aisles towards the circular stair towers which give access to the elevated walkway. A system of pedestrian ramps at the north-east corner gives visitors with prams and trolleys direct access to all levels. Public toilet facilities are accessed at ground level through the base of the north-east stair tower. The disabled parking area is separated from the vehicular circulation and located at the closest point to the city centre

22 Mechanised car-parking system (by Double Parking Systems; drawings reproduced with consent)

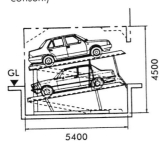

lift for two or four vehicles which can be independently removed

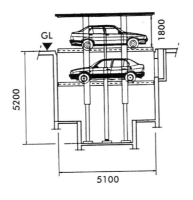

unit for one, two or four vehicles: unit designed to be completely below ground, and can therefore be located in courtyard etc.

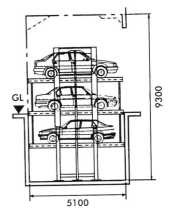

unit for three or six vehicles (top vehicle is above ground)

PETROL STATIONS

The majority of petrol stations are linked to the main oil companies, but there has been a significant increase in new outlets developed with supermarkets. Companies present a 'branded' image of high technology using sophisticated pumps, canopy structures, modern materials and bright lights. The range of facilities offered in association with the sale of petrol is growing, including car washing, car accessories and, in particular, the shop, offering confectionery, newspapers, convenience foods and snacks.

DETAILED DESIGN

Planning The size of facilities is determined by location, ease of access, typical traffic flows and competitors. Entrance and exits must allow easy steering onto the site and space is needed for cars to queue while waiting for a vacant pump; it should also be easy to steer away from the pump, with no obstruction of exits and good visibility when pulling out onto the road (see **23**). Provide good entry/exit sight-lines. Access may be by one-way flow onto the site or combined in-and-out routes, depending on the location (e.g. approaching a roundabout).

Planning, construction, installation, operation and maintenance of filling stations should be in accordance with Health & Safety document HS(G)41, with licensing required under The Petroleum (Regulation) Acts 1928 and 1936.

Pumps Consider the number of pumps required by the likely filling at peak times, usually mornings and evenings, noting that a car is on site before starting to fill for up to 4.5 minutes, filling for 1.5 minutes and then waiting for payment transaction for 2.5 minutes or more. A memory system at the control counter is imperative to allow for quick release of the pumps. Combinations of pumps are required, offering unleaded, 4 star, diesel etc. Pump positions are determined by the minimum safe separation from public thoroughfares and buildings.

Air and water This provision must be sited away from pumps, with adequate parking space. Likewise, car-wash systems should be set apart, and allow for queueing space and any necessary protection when adjoining other property.

Payment Customers generally make payments to a cashier controlling pump operations, unless the petrol station is not self-service. The cashier needs to be able to view all pump positions clearly. Payment can be made within a shop or through an external till window at night. Modern pumps can incorporate a credit card payment mechanism.

Petrol storage The potential hazards mean that storage is carefully controlled. Construction and operation of tanking is controlled under the Petroleum (Consolidation) Act 1928. New underground tanks are either glass fibre (to BS 4994) or twin-wall steel (to BS 2594), with size determined by the anticipated usage and frequency of deliveries. Pipes of medium-density polyethylene or nylon lead to capping/filling points. Petrol leakage detection systems are required and facilities for containment must be incorporated. Forecourt surfacing should be chosen so as to minimise

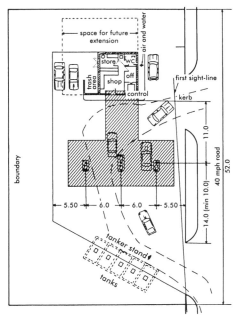

23 Typical layout allowing two cars to enter at same time (m)

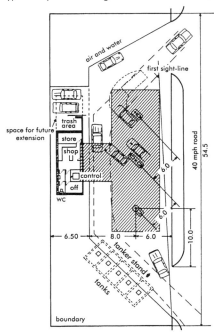

24 Typical echelon layout suits narrower sites (m)

staining from oil and petrol, to support the weight of tankers and must be non-slip for customer safety.

Canopy A canopy is required to cover all filling positions with approximately 3.50m projection on both sides beyond the pumps; the height needed above filling areas is 3.85m or more. The construction must be non-combustible, generally with steel posts supporting a cantilevered lightweight steel canopy, and designed to counteract wind lift, particularly in exposed areas. Covering can vary: metal or transparent sheeting, or occasionally flexible fabrics. The perimeter of the canopy is often required to support large fascia signs. Lighting, attached to or set within the canopy, must be of a good standard to enable the pump readout to be viewed easily and for security. These and other fittings need to be vapour resistant and flameproof.

Shop/facilities Increasingly large, shops have well-lit interiors and wide glazed frontages to encourage interest. There should be a direct route to the cashier, with space for queueing, and produce displayed in perimeter wall cabinets/shelving plus low-level central shelf units that do not impair the cashier's vision. Some incorporate fast-food service, either automated or under franchise. Other facilities might include public telephones and toilets.

Service stations
These are located to serve motorways or major trunk roads. The government regulates the number of service stations alongside motorways and also their parking provision for cars and lorries, toilets, shops and 24-hour opening. New stations are subject to strict planning controls and are often now sited at junctions for wider use and ease of servicing. In planning the station, there needs to be adequate approach runs for vehicle speed control, good signing for separation of lorries, cars and petrol and catering for long- and short-stay parking.

Facilities These include toilets, shops, fast-food outlets, cafeterias, telephones, ATMs, amusement arcades, petrol stations, vehicle recovery, with the larger service stations incorporating motels.

VEHICLE SHOWROOMS
Car retailers are becoming increasingly aware of the need for good design in showrooms to heighten product appeal. Showrooms serve specific makes of vehicle and operate independently, under franchise or as authorised groups. Dealerships are commonly linked for cost efficiency, flexibility of space and servicing facilities.

Siting The preference is for prominent positions (e.g. on main roads leading into town centres), with wide frontages and adequate space to the rear for servicing and storage of vehicles.

Showroom floor areas These should be the maximum possible size for the site. Allow approximately 10–25 m² (subject to size and status) per vehicle to give sufficient room for customers to move around them, see the cars from a distance and allow doors and bonnets to be left open. The space should be light and airy, which is often achieved by featuring plenty of glazing to the frontage together with good artificial lighting using appropriate accents. The decor is likely to be 'branded'. A stylish and comfortable reception area is important, with customer seating and space for discussing sales and financial arrangements. The showroom may incorporate a turntable for special displays. A sheltered position for clean vehicle entry is needed, using sliding door access.

External areas Space is often provided outside for displaying used vehicles and for a dedicated customer parking area. Consider the storage of new vehicles for peak sales periods, and the associated security problems. If linked with servicing facilities, the two areas should be separated, with servicing up to the rear; the customer service point is often combined.

VEHICLE SERVICES
Currently, vehicle service premises range from small independents operating from locally available space to large purpose-built facilities, using wide buildings incorporating a series of service bays, often as part of a group or specialist operation (e.g. exhaust or tyre replacement).

Service bays The overall recommended size is 9.0×4.0 m. Bays can incorporate either service pits or two-level hydraulic or mechanical lifts, the latter needing 4.8 m clear headroom. Pits are essential for commercial vehicles. The Road Traffic Act 1972 issues strict guidelines for premises and equipment involved in MOT testing. A registered garage needs to dedicate a bay for testing with an adjacent safe viewing area. Certain equipment can be transported between bays on high-/low-level rails or trolleys. Supplies of air, water, oil and grease are needed to serve all bays. Workbench areas should be located to the side or rear of bays, for working and tool points. Easy access should be available to storage of regular spares, such as bulbs, plugs, valves, etc. Each bay should have its own entry door for ease of vehicle turnover and reduction in heat loss. Floor surfacing must be non-slip and sealed to protect it from oil and petrol leaks.

Additional spaces These may include separate accommodation for body fitting and spraying of vehicles. A clean reception, customer waiting areas, employee toilets and office space should be provided in proportion to the size of operation.

Services Special provision may also include:
- extracts for fume removal and welding activity
- ducted heating systems or high-level radiant fittings
- portable lighting for viewing under vehicles
- security installations for MOT stations
- storage and disposal of batteries, oil contaminated components and tyres.

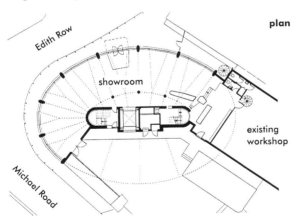

plan

showroom

existing workshop

Edith Row

Michael Road

elevation

25 Harley Davidson Showroom, London SW6 (Arch: Cullum & Nightingale)

BUS AND COACH STATIONS

Provision for buses and coaches plays an important role within vehicle facilities. Town centres must be planned to accommodate stopping areas for buses and adequate space for manoeuvring, with safe waiting and access for passengers (see **26**).

Large bus depots still exist in cities but de-regulation has led to smaller fleet numbers and greater variation in vehicle size (see **27**).

Parking configurations Multiple parking of buses and coaches must be considered within depots, stations and designated areas adjacent to tourist attractions, exhibition centres etc. Excepting garaging situations, where parking arrangements are organised around timetabling and maximum use of space, right-angle or 45° bays are used (see **28,29,30**), with sufficient allowance for ingress and egress, preferably one-way. Nearby movement of pedestrians should be carefully controlled and crossings marked.

Design requirements With the growth of long-distance coach travel, stations are required to operate in a similar manner to those for railways. At main stations a good standard of accommodation should be provided, comprising information, reservations and ticket offices, passenger waiting areas/rooms, left luggage, toilets, cafés and kiosks, together with staff offices and rest rooms. Subject to individual company arrangements, some provision may be required for bus/coach maintenance, re-fuelling and cleaning.

TRANSPORT INTERCHANGES

With demands to integrate further the different transport systems, interchanges are required, serving either to combine the location of bus and train services for the benefit of passengers and community (generally in town centres) or to encourage commuters to park their vehicles and continue their journeys by public transport.

Careful segregation is necessary for each sector (trains, buses, taxis, short- and long-stay parking and passengers), utilising separate levels, access points and effective signing. Accommodation requirements combine those for bus/coach stations, railway stations and car parks.

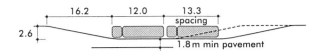

26 Typical lay-by dimensions for buses/coaches (m)

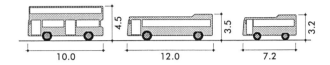

27 Typical bus/coach dimensions (m)

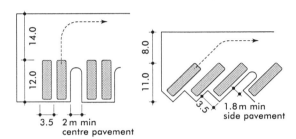

28 Bus/coach parking at 90° (m)   **29** Bus/coach parking at 45° (m)

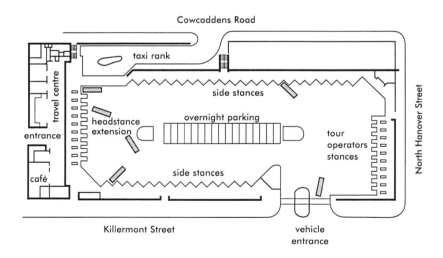

30 Buchanan Bus Station, Glasgow (Arch: The Jenkins Group)

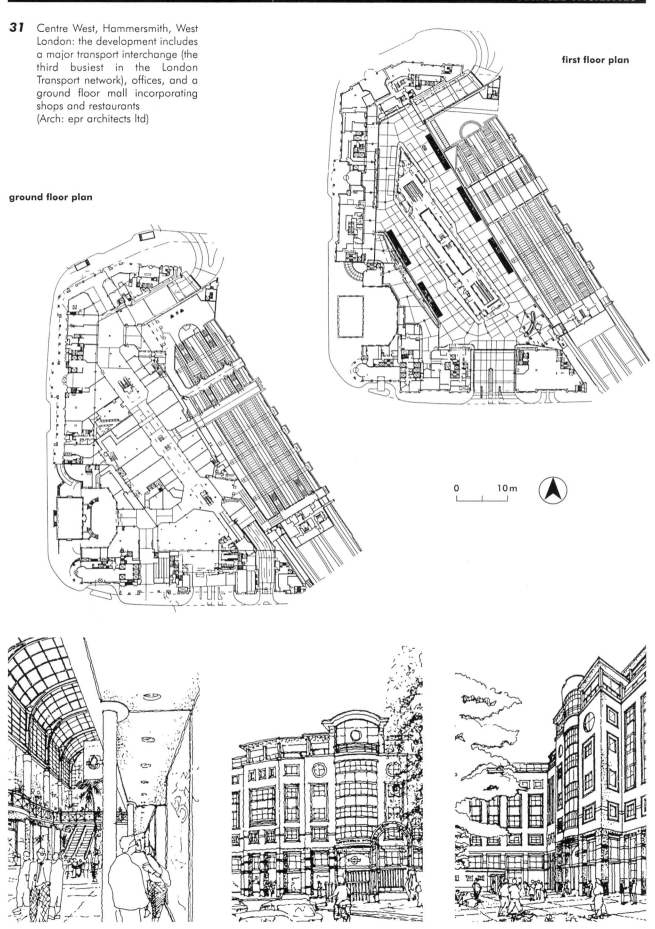

31 Centre West, Hammersmith, West London: the development includes a major transport interchange (the third busiest in the London Transport network), offices, and a ground floor mall incorporating shops and restaurants
(Arch: epr architects ltd)

first floor plan

ground floor plan

0   10m

sketch views

YOUTH HOSTELS

INTRODUCTION

The term 'youth hostel' in the UK may legally only be applied to accommodation run by the Youth Hostels Association (YHA), now a registered trade mark. There are many other types of 'hostel', which can be grouped into two main categories: 'backpacker hostels' for travellers, run by organisations other than the YHA, and residential hostels, run by local authorities or charities to cater for specific needs (see Housing and the section on Halls of Residence and Hostels). The aims of the YHA are 'to help all, especially young people of limited means, to a greater knowledge, love and care of the countryside, particularly by providing Hostels or other simple accommodation for them in their travels, and thus to promote their health, rest and education'.

The YHA was founded as a charity in 1930 and has around 240 hostels in England and Wales (around 80 in Scotland). Hostels vary from simple buildings in remote locations to city locations offering more facilities.

Traditionally, youth hostels provided a basic, if not spartan, level of accommodation for those wishing to walk or cycle in the countryside. Maximum length of stay in a hostel was three days, travel by car was not allowed until the early 1970s, and accommodation costs were kept low partly by giving each hosteller a task (e.g. sweeping floors, or cleaning the kitchen).

Since the 1970s, however, the YHA has developed a different policy of providing a much greater variety of accommodation which is intended to appeal to a wider cross-section of the population. Family rooms are often available and, sometimes, family annexes (with fully-equipped, self-contained facilities). Some hostels have special facilities for those with disabilities; all hostels should be designed to avoid access discrimination. Hostels are often in converted buildings, sometimes historic houses. Some city centre hostels are providing specific facilities for day visitors. Note that non-YHA hostels, such as those run, financed or grant-aided by local authorities or government agencies, may have different guidelines.

TYPES OF YOUTH HOSTEL

YHA hostels are divided into several groups:
(1) Hostels in popular cities and towns.
(2) Busy hostels with a wide range of facilities, which are especially suitable for groups and popular with families.
(3) Medium-sized hostels in country and coastal locations.
(4) Small hostels of a simple style, often in remote areas, which are particularly attractive to walkers and cyclists.
(5) 'Camping barns' – a network of farm buildings in some of the more remote areas with very basic accommodation (e.g. flush toilet, cold water and no heating).

DETAILED DESIGN

The following is based on information provided by the International Youth Hostel Federation (IYHF) and YHA (England & Wales), and John Bothamley who prepared the Hostel Design Manual.

General points

The following guidelines are intended as a general framework, and are subject to updating to reflect current attitudes; the guidelines may well not be suitable for simple hostels, but should be regarded as essential for all new hostels and for major works at existing ones. Standards are generally those adopted by tourist boards.

YHA hostels have traditionally been closed during the day, although this practice is now changing. Consequently, an external storage room with drying facilities has sometimes been provided for use when the hostel is closed. A changing room near the entrance may also be desirable to allow hostellers to remove wet or muddy clothing and boots.

Cycles A lit, lockable and weatherproof cycle store is required.

Dormitories All hostels must have separate dormitories for men and women, with separate access; areas should be 4 m² per single or double bunk, 5 m³ per person. Adequate ventilation must be provided (commonly taken to mean 1/20th of the floor area). Traditionally, dormitories are used by either sex as bookings demand. Four- and six-bed dormitories are generally considered to be the maximum size for new hostels. Consideration should also be given to: possible future sub-division; the top bunks folding against the wall; additional privacy provided by partitions at bed-ends; and improving sound insulation.

Dormitory equipment There must be adequate hanging, storage and seating facilities, plus at least one 13 amp socket outlet, one mirror, a metal or flame-resistant litter receptacle, and window curtains or blinds. Partitions can greatly improve privacy. Dimmable or individual lights are recommended.

Dormitory bedding Sheet sleeping bags must be available, together with duvets and blankets. Facilities (e.g. a linen store) must be provided to allow adequate storage and airing of bedding.

Eating areas These will be dependent on locality and style of hostel: a strong local identity is important. Large hostels might have a cafeteria, restaurant and bar (see also Kitchens).

Entrance porch and shelter This is essential, and consider also notices and if an envelope reservation system is needed. A toilet should be accessible during times when the hostel is closed.

Entrance area/reception Must allow for flow to other areas and may need to act as an assembly area for large groups. Prominent signage and information is desirable. Entrance doors must be suitable for rucksacks etc.

Family rooms   Areas are as for dormitories, with four or five beds generally provided. One bunk bed may also be convertible to a double bed. Disabled access may be particularly important. Layout generally is as *1*.

Leaders' accommodation   Areas are as for dormitories, but in single or twin rooms (see *3*). Location away from groups, and a separate common room, may be desirable.

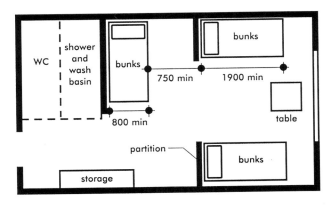

1   Dormitory/multi-bedded room: diagrammatic layout (not to scale)

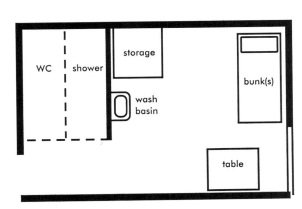

3   Leaders' accommodation: diagrammatic layout (not to scale)

Kitchen (self-catering)   Once very popular, self-catering is now less so; facilities should be provided in a separate room, with an adjacent eating area. Layout should be simple and robust (see *2*).

Kitchen (commercial)   Where meals are provided, local health regulations must be complied with. The area for a 100 bed hostel is approximately 40 m². Guests will generally collect meals from a counter.

Hostel shop   One must be provided, and be capable of supplying food for evening meals and breakfasts for hostellers.

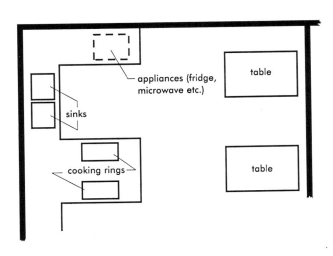

2   Self-catering kitchen: diagrammatic layout (not to scale)

Laundry   Adequate washing and drying facilities must be provided (but a local laundry may be an alternative).

Leisure areas   These will vary enormously depending on which groups the hostel is catering for. Games rooms, amusement machines, tables and bars may be provided, as well as a quiet area and a smoking-permitted area.

Maintenance   This must be considered at the design stage: hostel materials are subjected to very hard use. Designs should be stylish but tough, ease of cleaning is one of the most important considerations.

Meeting rooms   May be required (45 m² minimum), and should include facilities for slide and video viewing, blinds and adjustable light levels. Could also be used as relaxing area for guests or seasonal bedspace.

Multi-bedded rooms   See 'dormitories'.

Offices & Support areas   Includes front desk, for reception; storage for records; mail box; and notice board. Must have a direct view of entrance doors, and view of access routes to the rest of hostel (see also 'entrance area'). Other support areas may include a small workshop, storage for linen, cleaning materials etc., and room for extra staff when required for peak periods.

Parking (cars and coaches)   Hostellers are encouraged to travel by public transport, but some simple provision for car parking should be provided. Separate coach parking may also be required.

Seating areas   For relaxation, meeting up etc., these should be comfortable and adaptable seating is required. A separate area for TV and music should be provided.

Secure storage   This is essential.
- Luggage storage: must be suitable for large rucksacks etc, and some sports equipment. City centre hostels probably require individual cabinets (may be coin operated).

- Personal belongings: open storage may be acceptable, depending on location, with one shelf or cupboard per guest (approximately 500 × 600 × 700 mm).
- Valuables storage (e.g. for wallets and passports): must be lockable; possibly located in the office or secure area.

Services   Adequate heating and ventilation is essential, as are drying facilities. Adaptable ducting should be provided to allow for telephone, cable TV, computer and other communications cabling.

Security   Important, but it should be discreet. Zones could be as follows:
- entrance hall – all-comers
- day rooms – day visitors/guests/staff
- sleeping accommodation – guests/staff
- staff accommodation – staff only.

Entrance security should be kept to a minimum, but the main entrance should be visible from the reception desk. An electronic card entry system may be suitable in city centre hostels.

Signage   This should be in accordance with IYHF standards (detailed information on colours, symbols and lettering is available). Consider also multilingual signs and tactile signs for the partially-sighted. External signs should be included on public transport noticeboards and local road signs.

Toilet provision   Must be one WC per 12 persons, and there must be separate provision for men and women (see also 'entrance porch').

Washing provision   Must be one washbasin per six persons, and one shower per 15 persons. There should be a changing area adjacent to each shower, with adequate privacy and changing facilities. Washrooms must have adequate coat hooks, mirrors, shelves and shaver points etc.

Warden/staff   The warden or other responsible person must normally be present in the hostel at all times it is open. Wardens' accommodation should be self-contained, preferably away from busy hostel areas, and never under dormitories. Areas should be approximately 80 m² for the warden/manager, and 50 m² for an assistant (where required).

Environmental awareness

To comply with the IYHF Environmental Charter, all materials are required to be the most 'environmentally friendly' in their use category. Precise cost/benefit calculations should be made, and due allowance made for maintenance costs.

New buildings should: use standard material sizes where possible; use recycled products when available and economical; be adaptable; and allow for relevant waste storage.

A waste plan should be prepared, allowing for suitable storage and collection (which may be by individuals and companies, at varying times). Investigate if food waste can be recycled via a compost heap into landscaped areas adjacent to hostel.

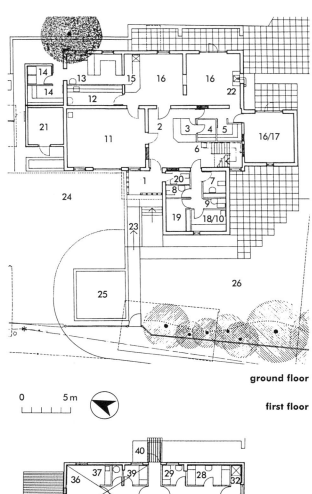

ground floor

first floor

0   5m

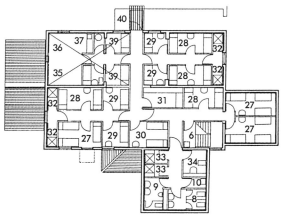

1 entrance lobby; 2 hall; 3 reception; 4 small office; 5 store; 6 stair lift (dis) 7 WC(dis); 8 WC(F); 9 WC(M); 10 cleaner's cupboard; 11 class/meeting room 1; 12 self-catering kitchen; 13 main kitchen; 14 kitchen store; 15 servery; 16 dining rooms; 16/17 dining overflow/meeting room 2; 18 laundry; 19 drying room; 20 WC; 21 plant room; 22 stove; 23 ramp; 24 vehicle turning area; 25 parking; 26 garden; 27 six-bed dormitory; 28 four-bed dormitory; 29 two-bed dormitory; 30 four-bed room (dis) 31 linen store; 32 shower; 33 shower (dis); 34 WC(dis)
hostel staff accn: 35 living room; 36 dining area; 37 kitchen; 38 bathroom; 39 bedroom
40 emergency escape

4   Rochester Youth Hostel, Gillingham, Kent: a former oast house (hop-drying kiln, once a common feature in Kent but now generally redundant), converted to provide hostel facilities
(Arch: Peter Beake Partnership)

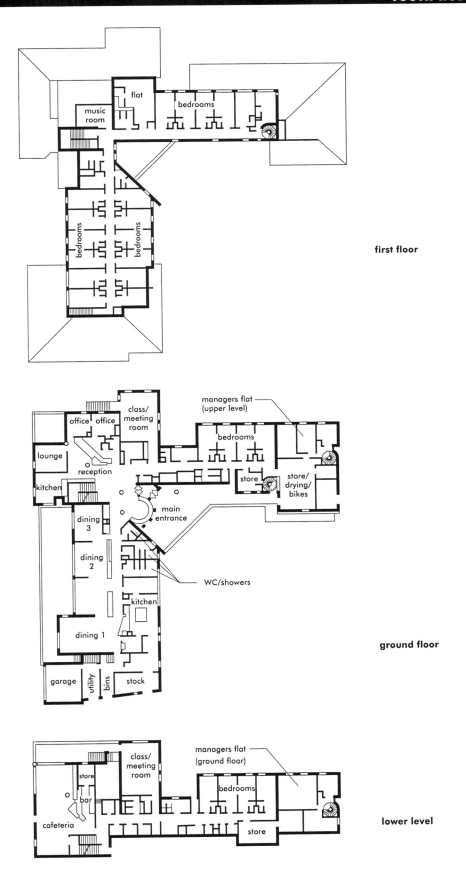

first floor

ground floor

lower level

4 Youth Hostel in Annecy, France:
(Arch: TRUELLE Architects (Paris))

contemporary hostel, considered typical example of good modern hostel design, incorporating many of the features in the IYHF design manual; the second floor contains more bedrooms

ZOOS AND AQUARIUMS

Patricia Beecham

INTRODUCTION: ZOOS

The good modern zoo is a cultural institution that manages and exhibits a collection of wild animals with the purpose of communicating ideas rather than merely displaying collections. It has to balance public education through entertainment with conservation, scientific research, technological development and fund raising.

Good zoo design and an ever-developing emphasis on animal welfare are inseparable. The modern zoo must provide acceptable conditions within which animals can breed, raise young, and behave as naturally as possible, which means the designer must be concerned about the animal's behavioural needs. The zoo must provide the visiting public with a positive image of both the animal and its captive environment in a way that promotes sympathy and respect. A generally more informed interest in wildlife due to television makes the public more critical of the environment in which the animals are displayed.

The dominance of landscape which emerged in the 1970s is not purely for sense of display, but part of the move towards a more naturalistic and stimulating environment, taking account of the psychological and physical needs of the animals.

The success of any zoo depends largely on the interest it generates. Visitors have to be in a comfortable environment while looking at attractive exhibits to heighten awareness of the conservation problems faced by the species and of strategies being used to overcome these problems.

London Zoo can be taken as a good example of a zoo which reflects the development of mainstream ideas about zoo design. Opened in 1826, it is the oldest surviving example of the proper zoological garden, rather than an exhibition of animals in a menagerie. Early innovations at London Zoo, which were subsequently adopted at other world zoos, include the first reptile house, opened in 1849, followed by the first public aquarium in 1853 and the first insect house in 1889. London Zoo includes within its grounds practically every type of exhibition building which has been developed within the past 170 years.

The changes in the design of the buildings during the zoo's history not only reflect progress in animal care but also changing attitudes of the public to the concept of wild animal display.

Architects have been responsible for much of the zoo's raised profile throughout the 20th century. Contemporary architectural thinking has been exemplified by the modernist functionalist penguin pool, 1934 (see **1**), the large tensile structure of the Snowdon Aviary, 1962–4, by Cedric Price, and the new brutalism of the elephant and rhino house, 1962–5 (see **2**).

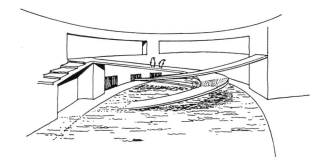

1 The penguin pool, London Zoo: listed building; modernist functionalist; slender curved reinforced-concrete ramps used to create simple planes and sweeping surfaces
(Arch: Lubetkin with Ove Arup, 1934)

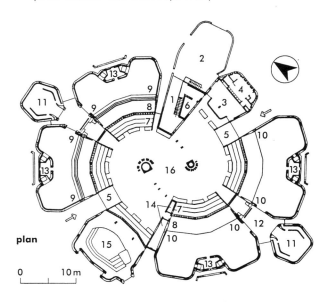

plan

0   10 m

1 ramp from service yard; 2 service yard; 3 mess room; 4 staff WCs; 5 public entrance; 6 store; 7 stepped viewing area; 8 animal ditches; 9 rhino dens; 10 elephant dens; 11 sick bays; 12 den lobbies; 13 drinking trough area; 14 main rising ducts; 15 elephant pool; 16 public space

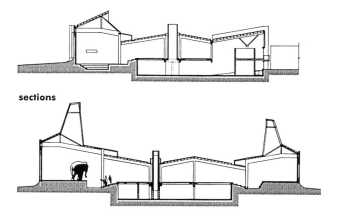

sections

2 Elephant and rhinoceros house, London Zoo: listed building; architecturally significant example of new brutalism
(Arch: Sir Hugh Casson, Neville Conder and Partners; illustration used with permission from Casson Condor Partnership)

Attitudes change, and around 1960 international orthodoxy in zoo architecture began to place a strong emphasis on landscape and the simulation of an animal's natural habitats. A quiet deferential tone was set by later buildings, praised for leaving visitors with a memory of plants and animals rather than architecture. One of the first new major exhibits since 1976 is the African Aviary (see **10**) and this is a hi-tech design also reticent about its presence, where the enclosures have been landscaped by filmset designers to imitate African habitats.

There are continuing attempts to resolve the conflict between animal needs and the desire of a broad section of the public to see animals naturalistically and entertainingly displayed. General approval of the more 'humane' environment of large enclosures outweighs the fact that the animals can at times disappear from public view. A benefit comes from the reward of having a 'discovery' factor.

DETAILED DESIGN

General zoo planning

In practice, most British zoos have an inheritance of cramped and inadequate buildings, and the commission, design and production as one complete

zoological enterprise is unusual, Marwell Zoo, Winchester, being one such exception.

The range of structures usually required at a large urban zoo include the following:
- animal houses
- aquarium
- reptile house
- aviaries
- ponds, pools and enclosures
- gates, tunnels and bridges
- visitor amenities and children's zoo
- auxiliary buildings, such as offices, library, prosectorium (pathology and post-mortem; animal hospital and pathology lab; research centre; education department; centre for life studies)
- service and staff buildings
- statues, memorials and markers.

Staff Categories of staff working on the site will include: curators, vets, head keepers, keepers, catering managers, security and transport staff, administrative staff and director.

In relation to both the range of structures and categories of staff, decisions have to be made about food delivery, preparation and storage, methods of catching animals, waste disposal and movement of on-site service vehicles.

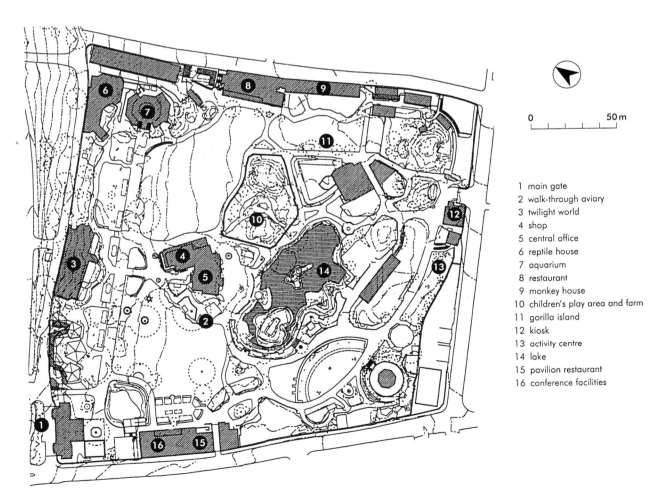

1 main gate
2 walk-through aviary
3 twilight world
4 shop
5 central office
6 reptile house
7 aquarium
8 restaurant
9 monkey house
10 children's play area and farm
11 gorilla island
12 kiosk
13 activity centre
14 lake
15 pavilion restaurant
16 conference facilities

3 Bristol Zoo: site plan
(Arch: LMP Architects)

Visitors Visitors' requirements to consider include: car parks, pedestrian entrance, (see **4**) and transport, as well as the location of sales kiosks, seats, rain shelters, food, and lavatories.

Zoo Licensing Act, 1981 This ensures that zoos meet minimum standards of animal welfare and visitor safety and has been drawn up in consultation with the Federation of Zoological Gardens of Great Britain and Ireland. Consideration should also be given to ensure the safety, effectiveness and comfort of the keepers.

Beyond the design factors of safety, public health and animal regulations, zoo buildings also need to provide security for the animals against malicious human behaviour. Zoos are a target for vandals, thieves, animal rights campaigners and sadists.

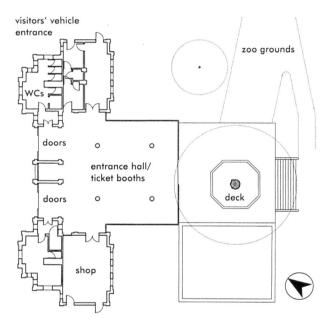

4 Bristol Zoo Entrance: ground floor
(Arch: LMP Architects)

Exhibit design

There are five basic patterns of zoological display arrangement, the oldest being the 'systematic' basis, where similar groups are kept in separate areas. A variation on this, allowing more diversification, is the Zoogeographic theme of display, in which animals are arranged in groups according to their continent of origin. Three further systems are based on habitat, popularity and behaviour. Of these, the last, the 'behavioural' zoo, is the most recent concept in zoo planning. These are built around the basic activities – sleeping/resting, foraging, movement and social interaction of the animals. Most zoos have been planned to include a selective combination of these five themes.

Elements of enclosure, physical boundaries, temperature, humidity and vegetation must be designed with particular reference to the needs of each species so that the animal can accept this artificial habitat as its territory. Animals in the wild are principally occupied by finding food. In captivity they need to be kept mentally alert and physically active; thus the quality of space is important. A habitat must be designed which will enable the animal to carry out its normal activities as far as possible, for example by allowing tree-dwelling animals the choice of not coming to ground level.

There are many aspects of designing to minimise stress. For instance, enclosures should provide 'escape' or 'avoidance' areas where individuals can retreat, and should avoid acutely angled corners where less dominant animals can be trapped. However, there should be no 'blind spots' in the enclosures where animals cannot be seen by the keepers. Elements should be included which will help to maximise behavioural opportunities. For example, water fulfils various functions, including swimming, wallowing, feeding and washing.

Thoughtful well-researched design can determine the behaviour of the exhibits in a manner which allows them to pursue their normal behaviour patterns in a contrived environment without detriment to the individuals. An example is in the exhibition of nocturnal animals, largely developed at Bristol Zoo. This exhibition was an important innovation in terms of lighting and illusionistic display. Successful experiments with lighting were made in reversing the animals' daily cycle, allowing their most active period to coincide with visiting hours.

Guidelines to creating an illusion of space include arranging the viewing distance to vary with the size and activity of the animal and the character of its environment, darkening viewing areas to avoid reflections on glass and providing a dark matt finish to exhibit backgrounds to complement the colour of animals.

Careful use of vegetation and observation areas can give the public the impression that they are 'entering' the realm of the animals rather than viewing them from outside. This helps to create receptivity towards educational materials.

Checklist of key design considerations for enclosure
   (1)   basic requirements
   (2)   indoor accommodation
   (3)   public space
   (4)   main exhibit area
   (5)   Off-view holding and service areas
   (6)   environmental control.

Construction

Easily cleaned impervious materials reduce the dangers of infection from bacteria and parasites; however, the risks of physical disease from non-sterile enclosures are often counteracted by improvement in the animals' psychological health.

It is particularly important to design within parameters dictated by conservation and environmental issues. Care must be taken in the use of materials, particularly timber, from an ecological perspective (e.g. recycled polypropylene was substituted for cedar shingles for the recent London Zoo reindeer den (Wharmby Kozdon Architects, 1994)). Environmentally progressive suppliers should be found when real wood is required.

Barriers against animal escape

To encourage a sense of involvement between people and animals the separation between them should be as natural as possible; the public now prefer not to be aware of caging.

Variations on water-filled moats or dry moats are very effective, combined with a vertical barrier where necessary, but then have the disadvantage of increasing distance. Carefully considered electric fencing can be effective in various situations, including the control of gorillas and chimpanzees.

Glass barriers can enable close proximity between viewer and subject, but also present problems such as the need for regular cleaning, and of reflection which has to be overcome by attention to lighting or the angle and profile of the glass.

Graphics

Signs, labels and graphics are integral to, and inseparable from, the exhibit as a whole. The animal, the enclosure and its furnishings, and all associated written and artwork become, in total, 'the exhibit', moving towards an 'interpretative zoo'. The public are used to professional advertising, and they can only be coaxed into reading information.

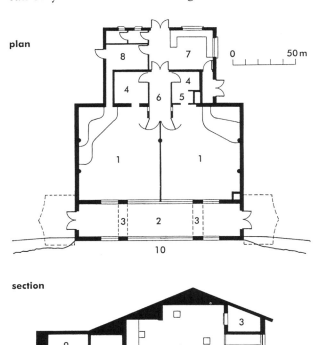

1 'gymnasium' type habitat with heated raised terraces; **2** public viewing area with 38 mm multi-laminated glass viewing screens to habitat; **3** overhead glass-sided orangutan transfer tunnel to landscaped water-moated island habitat; **4** holding area; **5** crush; **6** keepers' service corridor; **7** staff; **8** plant; **9** haystore; **10** moat

5 Indoor facilities for the Sumatran orangutan 'Home Habitat' at Durrell Wildlife Conservation Trust, Jersey, Channel Islands: designed to enable animals to move arboreally; capable of maintaining a family group of five to six individuals with separation facilities, and, if necessary, be capable of holding two social groups
(Arch: J. Douglas Smith, Architect)

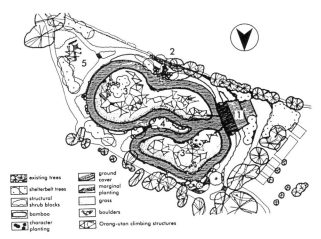

existing trees; shelterbelt trees; structural shrub blocks; bamboo; character planting; ground cover; marginal planting; grass; boulders; Orang-utan climbing structures

1 orangutan house; **2** conservation education 'long-house'; **3** island habitat with climbing structures; **4** viewing island; **5** children's play area

6 Outside habitat of the Sumatran orangutans at Durrell Wildlife Conservation Trust
(Landscape arch: Colvin and Moggeridge)

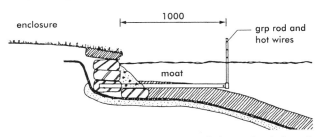

7 Barrier detail surrounding orangutan habitat island, Durrell Wildlife Conservation Trust

(illustrations 5,6,7 reproduced, with permission, from Mallinson, J.J.C. and Carroll, J.B. (1995) 'Integrating Needs in Great Ape Accommodation: Sumatran Orang-Utan *Pongo pygmaeus abelli* "Home Habitat" of JWPT', in: *Proceedings of the International Orangutan Conference: The Neglected Ape*, Nadler R.D., Galdikas B., Sheeran L., and Rosen N. (eds), Plenum Press, New York)

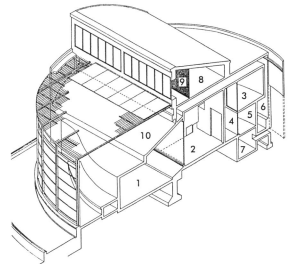

1 nocturnal viewing gallery; **2** nocturnal exhibit; **3** nocturnal holding area; **4** keeper safety porch; **5** keeper store; **6** keeper access; **7** heating; **8** holds for external exhibit; **9** keeper access; **10** external diurnal exhibit

8 Madagascar Centre, London Zoo: originally designed as Gorilla House, 1933, by Berthold Lubetkin in collaboration with Ove Arup; listed building conversion by Avanti Architects to house endangered species from Madagascar
(Arch: Avanti Architects Ltd)

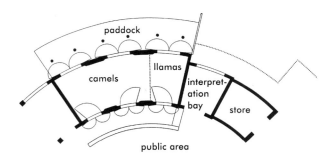

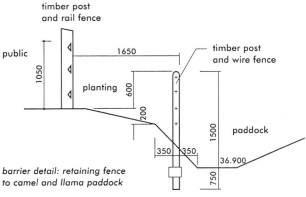

barrier detail: retaining fence
to camel and llama paddock

9 Camel house, Ambika Paul Children's Zoo, London Zoo
(Arch: Wharmby Kozdon Architects)

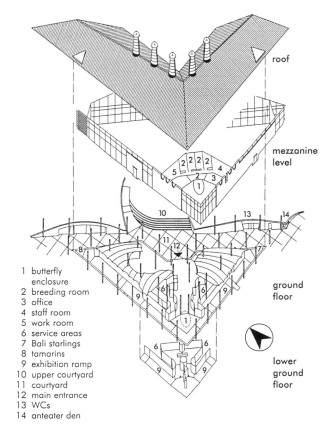

1 butterfly
 enclosure
2 breeding room
3 office
4 staff room
5 work room
6 service areas
7 Bali starlings
8 tamarins
9 exhibition ramp
10 upper courtyard
11 courtyard
12 main entrance
13 WCs
14 anteater den

11 Millennium Conservation Centre – The Web of Life,
London Zoo
(Arch: Wharmby Kozdon Architects)

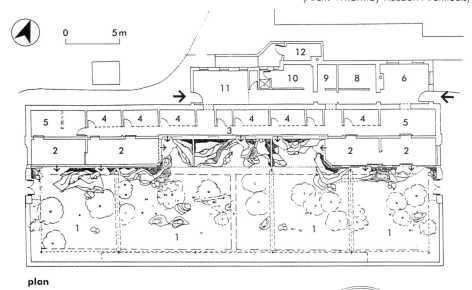

plan

1 aviary
2 shelter
3 service corridor
4 holding cage
5 cage room
6 food preparation
7 staff corridor
8 food store
9 office
10 changing room
11 mess room
12 boiler

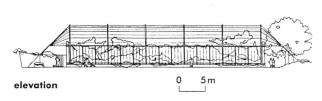

elevation

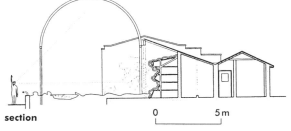

section

10 African (Eastern) Aviary, London Zoo: high hooped tubular
frames and fine piano wire
(Arch: John S Bonnington Partnership)

INTRODUCTION: AQUARIUMS

Experiments were first made with freshwater aquariums in the mid-19th century (R. Warington, 1849), followed shortly after by the first marine aquariums using manufactured substitute sea water (P. H. Gosse, 1854). After the opening of the first public aquarium at London Zoo in 1853 others began to appear all over the world, and by the end of the 19th century the attitude that aquariums should be principally scientific rather than decorative had become established.

With this background, and the policy of specialisation now adopted by many major aquariums, they are in many ways ahead of their zoological counterparts. Many recent aquariums have been designed to relate directly to their immediate coastline, and present their displays realistically in an ecological and geographical context. This diversification of the building type is expected to continue as new aquariums seek to differentiate themselves from existing more general exhibitions.

In the past two decades the number of aquariums as independent institutions and not necessarily part of zoological gardens has grown rapidly worldwide. As an aquarium has a definable space requirement it can be housed in a multi-storey building on an urban site. It can be a commercial component of a regeneration strategy instrumental in revitalising run-down areas, particularly those associated with a waterfront. A new aquarium can also be seen as a vehicle to increase visitor attendance and revenue as part of a zoo.

It is possible to accurately assess cost, attendance and operating expenses of a new aquarium, and there have been enough new facilities in the past decade to provide useful comparisons.

Exhibit design

Flexibility built into a new aquarium allows for periodic alterations and new exhibits, which is important to its continuing commercial success. Consequently it will be more responsive to new developments in exhibition techniques and will be able to respond to the increasingly sophisticated demands of its visitors.

In an aquarium complex with several display areas, the sequence of exhibits and information must be easily understood by visitors. The sequence may combine large tank displays housing a variety of animals, with small tanks showing aspects of aquatic life in detail. The trend is to encompass entire ecosystems and present living animals within the context of their habitat, in its widest sense, while also conveying information on animal behaviour, ecological and geographical aspects, water conservation and pollution, the fishing industry and tidal mechanics.

The exhibits can be reinforced by a variety of multi-sensory techniques and employ multi-media presentations. Each display addresses a particular theme where biological information can be provided by interactive devices.

Recent aquarium designs endeavour to recreate a complete aquatic ecosystem in which natural replenishment is possible. The specific environmental and behavioural needs of the exhibits have to be taken into account; from the provision of rock arrangements to accommodate rock dwellers and to allow fish to escape predators, to providing open space for sharks to follow their continuous swim-glide existence. The successful exhibit has to combine the design skills of the architect and set designer with the expertise of the biologist.

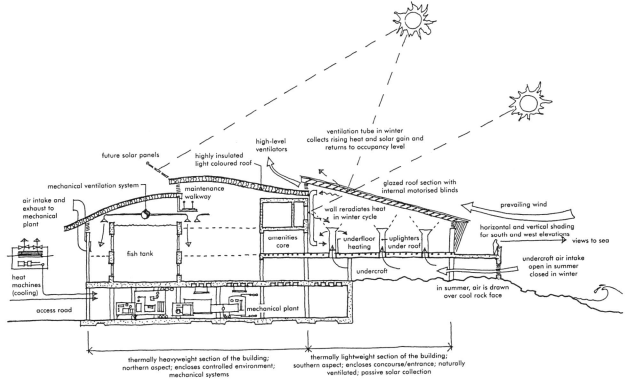

12 Environmental section from earlier scheme for National Marine Aquarium (Arch: Lacey Hickie Caley)

Water treatment

Water quality is of the utmost importance, as it provides the life-support medium for the animals. Water treatment must remove animal wastes, prevent the growth of harmful micro-organisms, remove toxic chemicals and maintain water clarity for viewing. It is necessary to control salinity, hardness and algal growth. It is also necessary to manage turbidity (resulting from suspension of fine air bubbles, silt etc.), colour and light levels.

An aquarium building needs a specific engineering system to service the tanks, requiring approximately 90% of the building's area. The equipment includes filters, sterilisers, pumping systems, heaters, reserve tanks, piping etc. Most aquariums have been located near the sea and have an unlimited supply of sea water. The water quality in the tanks is maintained by an 'open system', directly circulating fresh sea water. When fresh sea water is unavailable as a result of location or impurities, a closed system in which water is recirculated becomes necessary.

Water management filter systems include sand and gravel filters, diatomaceous earth filters, biological and ultra-violet filters. Treatment to eliminate micro-organisms and algae include chlorine, ozone, ultra-violet radiation, copper salts and protein skimmers. Each species requires a specialist designed system.

Exhibit construction

Improvements in glass and acrylic, from which are made the viewing panels used for enclosing aquarium tanks and marine animal pools, have enabled the visitor to have a close view of aquatic life.

Despite the advances in glass technology in recent years it cannot offer the versatility provided by acrylics. Not only can acrylic be manufactured in curved shapes but it is also possible to achieve virtually invisible full-strength joints between panels of very considerable thickness and strength. In addition, it can be shaped into dome and cylindrical sections. Dome windows that project into the tank and tunnels heighten the underwater experience, while cylindrical tanks are particularly effective when displaying shoaling fish.

Acrylic is a good insulator and can cope with temperature differentials such as with hot, humid or cold water exhibits) that could promote condensation. Acrylic panels can be assembled with mullions, sealant joints or with bonded joints. The latter joints can be almost invisible but if created without structural mullions they have to be designed to incorporate a high factor of safety.

The following sizes have been achieved with acrylic elements: window panel 7.3 m by 2.4 m high by 200 mm thick (Living Sea, Epcot, USA); seamless cylindrical tank 1.8 m in diameter (Monterey Bay, USA); tunnel 19.8 m long, 1.5 m in radius (Great Barrier Reef, Australia).

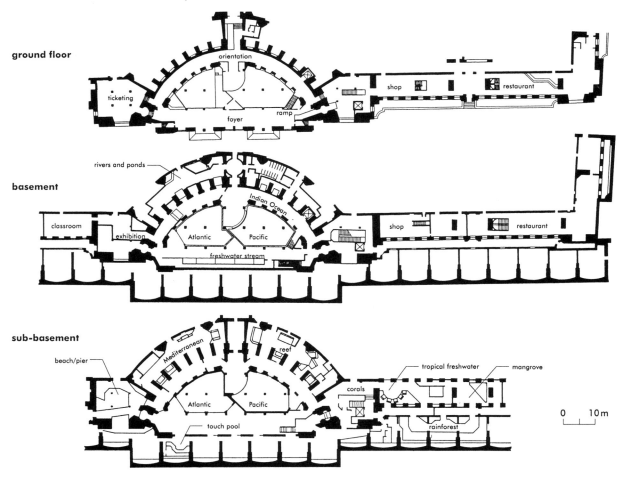

13 The London Aquarium, County Hall
(Arch: Renton Howard Wood Levin Partnership)

Various factors determine the decision to use acrylic or glass. Acrylic can be scratched by pinipeds (seals, walruses and sea-lions) and turtles; on the other hand, glazed exhibits require colour filtration to compensate for the greenish tinge. To reduce the likelihood of condensation, glass panels have to incorporate an intermediate space filled with inert gas, or the space can be ventilated to remove condensation. Fire presents a hazard to both glass and acrylic: the former will crack, and the latter is inflammable, so floodlights and heaters have to be located with care. However, the major limiting factor is more usually the available financial resources, particularly in the UK and Europe, and 25 mm glass has major cost advantages over annealed glass laminates and acrylic.

Lighting

Good lighting design is a fundamental component of a successful aquarium. 'Aquarium principle' lighting was introduced with the early aquariums, where the viewing area receives only indirect light from top-lit tanks. This method remains the logical basis for exhibition design, whereby light sources should be hidden and directed away from the visitors. For tanks combining underwater tunnel viewing with side panel viewing lighting is more complex. If it is the intention to suggest a natural underwater habitat, the appearance through the water of other visitors, or the reflection of signs and light sources will destroy the impression. Location of light sources can give an impression of greater space; by locating floodlights over a large tank at the opposite end

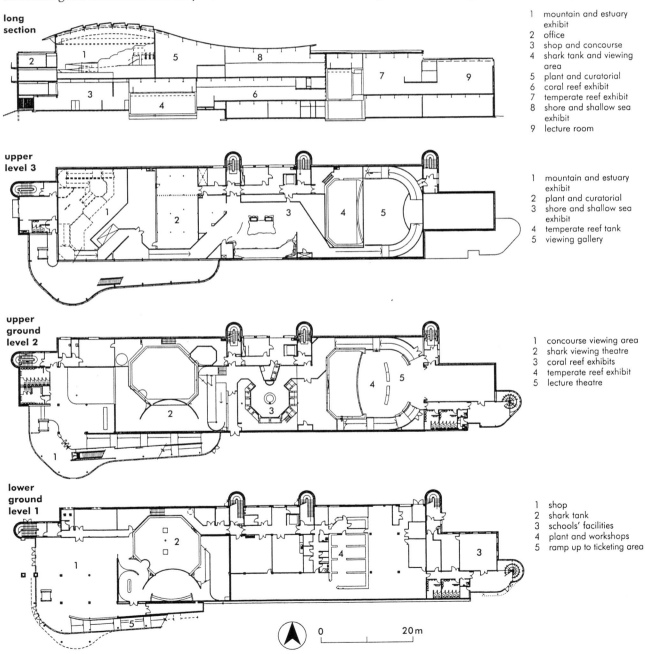

14 National Marine Aquarium, Plymouth
(Arch: Lacey Hickie Caley)

from the public access the impression of a great volume and depth of water with shafts of light penetrating to the sea bed is achieved.

Lighting can be designed to reflect the quality of the daylight found in the region forming the subject of the exhibition. This can be achieved by varying the angle, intensity and colour of the lights. Fluorescents, giving a predominantly cool, all-pervasive light source, represent the quality in temperate zones, while warmer incandescent and metal halide sources give the effect of tropical light. Within these general categories particular effects such as dappled light through overhead leaf canopies or shafts of sunlight penetrating deep ocean waters can be achieved.

Visitors Visitors' requirements include facilities in common with all visitor centres: car parking, entrance area, gift shop, food, lavatories etc. An increasingly important feature of a successful aquarium is a focus such as a significant display or a 'touch pool' with raked seating.

MARINE ANIMAL PARKS, OCEANARIUMS ETC.
Such centres have until recently been based on entertainment run on a commercial footing, often incorporating a stadium for shows, designed to exploit the intelligence and exuberant behaviour of dolphins, porpoises and killer whales. Now the general trend is away from pure entertainment and towards recreating an environment in which animals can carry out their natural patterns of behaviour, rather than 'perform'.

Species exhibited include cetaceans (whales, porpoises and dolphins), pinipeds (seals, walruses and sea-lions) and smaller water-dependent mammals such as the otter.

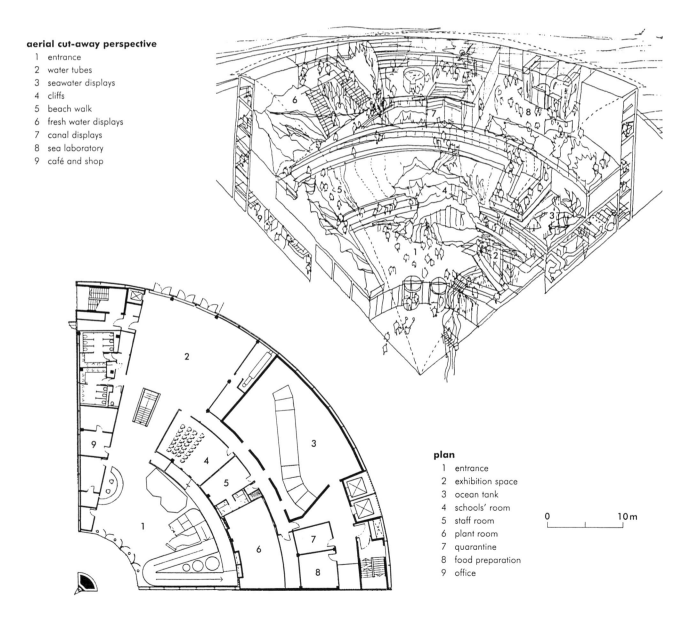

aerial cut-away perspective
1 entrance
2 water tubes
3 seawater displays
4 cliffs
5 beach walk
6 fresh water displays
7 canal displays
8 sea laboratory
9 café and shop

plan
1 entrance
2 exhibition space
3 ocean tank
4 schools' room
5 staff room
6 plant room
7 quarantine
8 food preparation
9 office

0   10m

15 National Sealife Centre, Birmingham
(Arch: Foster & Partners)

DESIGN FOR ACCESSIBILITY

Stephen J. Thorpe

INTRODUCTION

It is now recognised that those who use the built environment have a wide range of capabilities and that the needs of those who have specific physical or sensory impairments often coincide with the needs of many other users. The design solution to this is the integrated or inclusive approach. In summary, environmental design should be broad enough overall and in detail to suit the widest practicable range of users, including most disabled people. However, it is not universal design: some special provision will still be needed to suit either severe disability or social convention.

A positive outcome of an inclusive approach should be that design from the outset addresses this range of capability and need. This should eliminate the paradox of earlier special provision which tended both to disadvantage disabled people, for example by requiring them to travel further to an accessible entrance, and to deny their potential independence, for example by requiring them to seek assistance in using buildings.

Legislation and other official guidance tends to perpetuate the special approach but its scope is widening and, in particular, guidance is becoming more soundly based and better researched.

Inclusive design extends from the basic organisation of a building – its approach, levels, routes, spaces – through to the selection or detailing of fittings and finishes, such as door handles, railing systems, taps, electrical and manual controls.

Although careful selection is always necessary, an increasing number of products now respond to informed user demands – diminishing or impaired faculties are recognised and features such as good grip, contrast and simplicity of operation are incorporated.

An important factor in the design of properly accessible environments is a sound understanding of the principles involved. This avoids unthinking application of guidelines, supports design decisions in non-standard contexts and encourages imaginative solutions. The guidance in this section will concentrate on principles in relation to different building elements and contexts rather than on the more specific directions listed in the following pages or in references.

Earlier literature tended to concentrate on the wheelchair user as the most easily identifiable in terms of space and reach. However, the needs of those who walk but have limited mobility or who are sensorily impaired are also demanding and published guidance now reflects this.

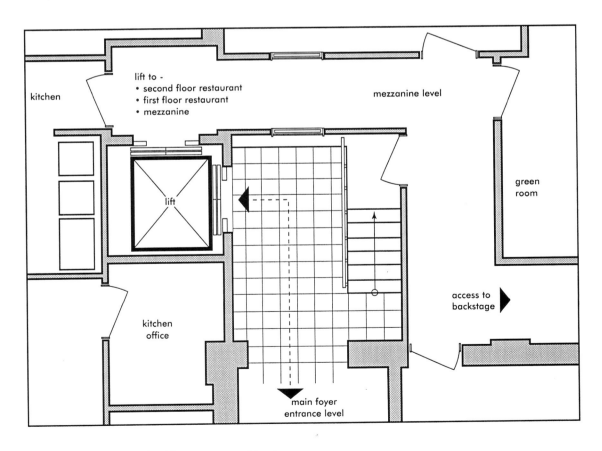

1 Snape Maltings Concert Hall: wheelchair access to all levels
(Arch: Penoyre & Prasad Architects)

GUIDANCE AND PRINCIPLES

Before presenting specific guidance, there follows a brief note on different impairments.

Wheelchair users

A wheelchair user may operate his or her manual or electric chair independently but other users may require the assistance of a companion to push and manoeuvre their chair and this requires additional space. Electric buggies or scooters can be significantly larger than the standard wheelchair range so openings and spaces based on conventional wheelchair dimensions may not be adequate.

Ambulant people

An ambulant person in this context is one who walks but with a degree of impairment, perhaps relying on sticks or a walking frame. In any case they will rely on support and resting points. They will value the spaces necessary for wheelchair passage and manoeuvring. The pressure needed to open or operate doors may be more critical for them than for a wheelchair user. They will usually prefer well detailed steps to a ramp for better stability and support. However some will not be able to manage more than a single shallow step and for them an easy going ramp may in fact be preferable.

Physical impairment

Physical impairment may also affect a person's ability to exert upper body pressure or to manipulate controls and this must be considered.

Sensory impairment

A person with sensory impairments may experience difficulty in approaching and using buildings unless the layout, finishes, detailing and equipment compensate for their specific impairments, usually of sight or hearing.

APPROACHES

Access to a building by car   This is important to many people with disabilities, whether they are drivers or passengers. From parking space or drop-off point the route to the entrance should be as short as possible and protected or covered if possible, with any ramps or steps carefully detailed.

Approach routes   Generally, these should avoid changes in level and should exploit ground and building levels to avoid specific ramps or steps as far as possible. Where they are unavoidable provide options: ramps (see **2**) suit wheelchair users and some ambulant people but steps are preferred by most of the latter.

On steps, handrails should be provided to each side. They should be continuous (i.e. across landings) and should extend beyond top and bottom steps to provide support at these critical points. On wider flights a double central handrail may be a better option, particularly in historic buildings where side or wall-fixed rails may be difficult to install or undesirable. On ramps, handrails will be needed by ambulant users for support and they may be required generally for protection.

Along routes   Slip-resistant surfaces should be used and the route must avoid potential hazards. Contrast should be provided to identify critical features such as stair nosings and support rails.

Tactile paving   This is recommended at critical points, such as crossings and other hazards, and detailed guidance is available. However, other ways of imparting tactile or auditory information may be more appropriate.

Signing   This should follow current guidance and be provided consistently and continuously along a route to remove any uncertainty about the destination.

ENTRANCES

The principal entrance   This should be usable by everyone. Where an alternative principal entrance is provided, for example to suit car users, it should lead directly to the main entrance foyer or reception. The entrance should always be identifiable within the building façade and allow views into the building for reassurance.

Thresholds   These should be as near level as practicable, with a maximum overall height of 15 mm and with a tapered section.

Good lighting   Entrances must be well lit and wherever possible weather protection should be provided.

Doors   Ease of operation is essential and opening pressure needs to be kept below 30 N. This will normally require easy-entry or low-energy operators or fully automated doors. In the latter case hinged or pivoted doors may be suitable in smaller buildings but should be single swing; elsewhere, sliding and/or folding doors are preferred.

Revolving doors   The smaller ones are unsuitable and the larger ones are not easily negotiated by anyone with impaired mobility so revolving doors should be avoided.

Door detailing (see **3**)   This is critical. Ensure adequate clear opening width (with buggies and

ramps no steeper than 1 in 12 (shallower preferred); alternative and adjacent steps where steeper than 1 in 20; slip-resistant surface

weather protection where possible; lighting to illuminate door and controls

1200   landing clear of door swing or face

2 Ramps

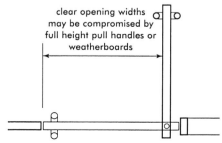

clear opening widths may be compromised by full height pull handles or weatherboards

3 Door detailing

scooters in mind), good contrast, ease of location and simple operating mechanisms. Avoid any visual ambiguity caused by inappropriate glazing (e.g. confusing reflections or misleading views of the interior) while ensuring that vision panels suit wheelchair users.

Lobbies (see **4**) Where these are necessary, they should allow manoeuvring clear of door swings and should where possible avoid the need to turn.

Lighting In lobbies, lighting should be at a transitional level between internal and external levels, and preferably use sensors to respond to changes in external lighting levels.

Reception spaces Reception areas should provide a clear introduction to the building, with straightforward unobstructed routes to the enquiry desk, lift, stairs and waiting area. A screened telephone point is helpful, especially in buildings where visitors will need to call taxis or waiting colleagues. Any cleaning matting should be firm and adequate in extent to clean wheelchair wheels.

Enquiry desk The detailing and equipment should enable anyone to approach and communicate easily.

Security People with disabilities must be able to negotiate screens and barriers without the need for special arrangements. Digital or card operated controls should be within reach and not require fine manipulation. Proximity devices are preferable.

Short-rise lifts These are a means of overcoming a change of level associated with an entrance. In existing buildings where the level change occurs externally it may be possible to lower the entrance and make the change inside where the lift will be protected from the elements and better supervised (see **5**).

INTERNAL CIRCULATION

Layout The organisation or pattern of any building should be readily understood using detailing appropriate to its nature and function. Large open spaces may need routes defined by floor contrast (e.g. pvc/carpet), reinforced by signing and lighting. Such routes should always lead to specific elements such as stairs, lifts, enquiry points. Initial design and subsequent management should ensure that these routes are unobstructed. More complex layouts will need logical patterns, good signing and memorable features (e.g. doors, stairs and daylighting).

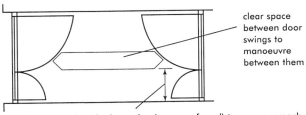

clear space between door swings to manoeuvre between them

at least 300 mm beside door edge (more preferred) to ease approach to operate and pull door; may be provided by fixed leaf

4 Lobbies

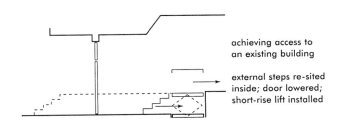

achieving access to an existing building

external steps re-sited inside; door lowered; short-rise lift installed

5 Short-rise lifts

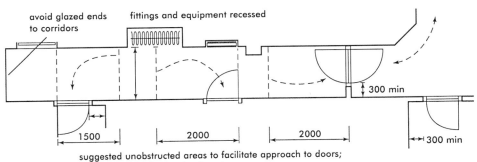

avoid glazed ends to corridors

fittings and equipment recessed

300 min

1500   2000   2000

300 min

suggested unobstructed areas to facilitate approach to doors; 1200 min width for turning into doorway; note 300 min beside door in corridor

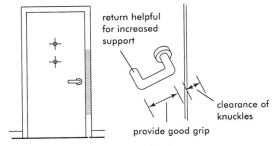

return helpful for increased support

clearance of knuckles

provide good grip

vision fittings: duplicate at lower level; distinguish: door frame/wall or screen door/fittings

6 Internal circulation and doors

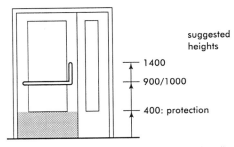

suggested heights

1400

900/1000

400: protection

distinguish regular leaf; where two-way, clarify pull/push; glazing wherever possible, especially in circulation routes

7 Double doors

Seating Where distances are substantial, such as in supermarkets or large stores, seating is desirable. There may be management objections but integrated seating, perhaps of the perching type, should be considered and placed at key points in the circulation routes, such as heads of stairs and lift waiting areas.

Doors

In normal use, doors must be positioned in rooms or circulation areas so as to allow sufficient space for them to be approached and operated simply. They should also be detailed for ease of use. (See **6**.) Alternative types of door may suit particular circumstances.

Self-closing doors These can present problems and excessive opening pressure, in excess of 30N, should be avoided by means of low energy operators, automation or magnetic hold-open devices, as appropriate.

Double doors (see **7**) These should always provide adequate clear opening to one leaf. Where this is not possible, such as in a listed building, ensure that the second leaf can be easily unfastened independently (e.g. by espagnolette or single lever multi-locking.

Sliding doors Such doors should have simple pull handles combined with locking devices and be very smooth running. Sufficient space must be allowed for the approach, operation and manoeuvring to pass through the opening. The clear opening width may need to be more than usual to allow for passage through at an angle.

Reduced swing doors These are easy to operate and may save space in confined areas, such as lavatories, and thus offset their relatively high cost.

Vertical circulation

Lifts and stairs should be integrated within the circulation pattern. This is particularly important where lifts are installed in existing buildings.

Lifts The location of the lifts should be clearly indicated by signs and access should be by direct routes across large spaces. Adequate waiting space off routes is desirable.

An eight-person lift provides adequate internal car size for a wheelchair user and companion but reversing out will be necessary. Larger lift sizes may be desirable if there is likely to be considerable foot and wheeled traffic. Other lift passengers may need support from grabrails or perching seats.

It may be acceptable for a passenger lift to be used for transporting goods but the converse is never acceptable.

Controls and information should be carefully considered and detailed both inside and outside lifts, including floor-level indicators and lift-coming signs. There may be a conflict between heights and legibility and duplication of controls may be necessary in multi-storey buildings.

Where possible avoid designing to minimum standards, particularly with door opening widths and internal car sizes, and especially where larger than normal wheelchairs or buggies might be circulating.

Escalators Some with impaired mobility find escalators difficult to manage so they should always be supplemented by lifts in close proximity.

Stairs (see **8**) For many users, stairs are potentially hazardous and must be carefully detailed with particular attention to nosings, handrails and support, contrast between surfaces, and lighting. Such considerations should not be overruled by the desire for spectacular effect, especially within entrance areas.

Short-rise lifts As an alternative to steps, and to avoid space-consuming ramps, short-rise lifts can be useful in negotiating differences in level. Rises of up to 4m are technically possible. These lifts are available as complete packages but they can be detailed to suit the building context or to incorporate an appropriate level of security.

Stairlifts Available with a seat and/or wheelchair platform, these lifts can suit a wide range of stair configurations. While they may resolve access problems in specific or small existing buildings, they may be incompatible with general use of stairs or unsuitable where the stairs are part of an escape route.

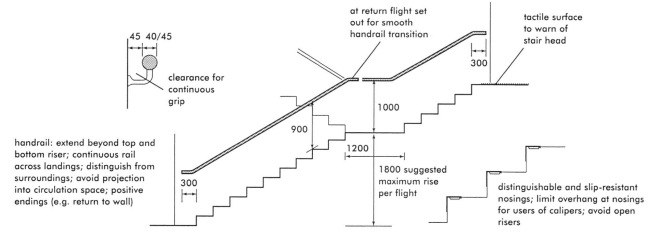

8 Stairs

Flooring considerations

Floor surfaces must be suitable for the areas concerned. For example, where there is a potential hazard, such as inside entrances and in lavatories, they should be effectively slip resistant. The same applies to stairs and ramps, including the approaches. Carpets should be reasonably firm to ease the passage of wheelchairs and cause no difficulties for ambulant users walking with a frame, for instance.

LAVATORIES

These are a serious concern for many people with disabilities and the one area where special provision seems justified. Nevertheless the principles of inclusive design should still be followed as far as possible.

Unisex WC A unisex lavatory allows the person to be assisted by a partner or companion of the opposite sex, although social convention usually requires such facilities to be entered separately from single-sex areas. The demand for unisex facilities is limited and in many buildings accessible lavatories can be incorporated within regular provision so they are also available for general use. To follow this principle it will be necessary to provide regular facilities which are easily accessible in their approaches as well as their internal layouts. Where existing buildings are converted this may not always be possible but disabled people should still not be required to travel further to a lavatory than other building users, and preferably not to another floor.

Wherever possible, accessible facilities should not be locked and they should be clearly signed as part of general signing to lavatories. Where unisex facilities are provided the locations should be clearly indicated at the building's entrance or reception area.

Detailed layout

The standard WC layout for a wheelchair user appears detailed and prescriptive but it is also designed to be suitable for as wide a range of users as possible. Illustration **9** shows the basic principles of space and relationship between fittings.

The peninsular layout (i.e. with full access either side of the WC) can offer more flexibility but it means the basin cannot be reached directly from the WC, which is crucial for some users. It should, therefore, be used only where specific building requirements justifies it, or as a supplement to the standard layout.

Regular lavatory layouts should suit people with mobility impairments, and this is achieved principally by providing more clear space between the WC and door swing. Handbasins are desirable and should be incorporated where possible. Such an upgrading of the often restricted compartment would obviously benefit many users and not just people with impaired mobility.

SHOWERS, BATHROOMS, CHANGING FACILITIES

The same inclusive principle should be followed in these related areas. There is usually no reason why facilities detailed to suit users with disabilities should not be generally available to all users, although the building's management may wish to ensure that accessible facilities are always vacant for those who specifically need them.

Particular care should be taken over critical aspects: these include slip-resistant flooring, flush detailing of drainage and junctions between surfaces or spaces, positioning controls and fittings so they can be easily reached, safe water temperatures, good supports, adequate space for assistance where necessary, and suitable storage. Signing of accessible facilities should be integrated with general signing.

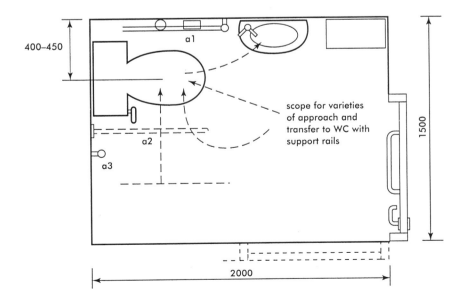

9 WCs

KITCHENS

If kitchens are incorporated in non-domestic buildings they should as far as possible follow the principles set out in the housing section, the key issues being flexibility of worktop height and related controls. To meet the demands of restricted reach, space standards may need to be higher than conventional tight planning allows.

COUNTERS AND WORK SURFACES

Detailing to provide flexibility will vary to suit visitors to a building and those who work within it. The design of reception counters and other visitor or customer transaction points should be inclusive rather than providing separate facilities for those with disabilities. This might entail adding a section at a lowered height. The full range of activities should be facilitated by detailing and/or equipment.

Security issues often conflict with such requirements and a balance must be struck with optimum access in mind.

WINDOWS AND EXTERNAL DOORS

Inclusive principles should be applied to all the functions of windows, including views out, ventilation, security and screening. Controls and handles should be within easy reach and simple to operate, preferably with one hand, as with some projecting or pivoted windows. Sliding windows may prove to be awkward unless fitted with very smooth running tracks.

All external doors should have adequate clear opening, particularly if they are sliding doors, with level or minimal thresholds. If they are hinged, doors should be fitted with restraints to prevent violent opening or closing. Emergency doors for evacuation purposes should also have simply operated fittings.

CONTROLS (see *10*)

Suitable controls should satisfy three inclusive criteria: they must be reachable, be easy to manipulate and give legible information.
- To be easily reached, controls need to be within a height range generally between 600 mm and 1200 mm. Whether the approach is sideways or head-on may determine the limits of this range.
- Ease of manipulation requires controls which are simple to locate and easy to grip and operate, such as large or full plate switches, large knobs or levers. Operation must not require excessive force.
- Legible information requires large numerals and raised surfaces to give a clear indication of such things as direction and extent of range.

Electronic control These criteria can be reasonably satisfied by electronically controlled doors and windows, curtains, taps, stopcocks etc., and can enable people with disabilities to successfully control their own environment, particularly in places of employment.

PROTECTION

Wheelchairs in particular, but also buggies, can potentially damage wall surfaces, angles, doors and

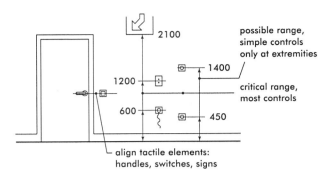

10 Controls

their linings. Integrated detailing such as splayed or rounded angles and general spaciousness with generous door opening widths should reduce the problem. Elsewhere, specific, discreet protection should be incorporated, again from the outset rather than after the event.

SUPPORT

People with impaired mobility frequently need support and this should be incorporated in the detailing of some of the elements such as staircases and specifically in accessible toilets. It may be possible to incorporate supports into counter fronts or similar fittings. Some fittings, such as basins and door handles, may also be used to provide support and they should be robust in design and detailing.

INFORMATION

A building should inform users as fully as possible and its layout, detailing and use of contrast – handrails, walls, doors, floor surfaces – should reduce the need for specific signing, which will thereby make it more easily negotiated by visually impaired people. Care should be taken to avoid features that might cause disorientation: for example, mirrors or other reflecting surfaces can confuse people, especially those with visual impairments. Mirrors are particularly unsuitable alongside stairs, where they may present a double image of the handrail, or when fixed to columns and causing dematerialisation of the building at critical points.

Signs

Signs should be clearly laid out, evenly lit, positioned to be seen from both wheelchair and standing level and should be consistently provided, especially along lengthy routes where constant reassurance is important. Whether fixed, suspended or free standing, in principle there should be a stark contrast between the signs and their immediate background which should in turn contrast with the building background.

Design and technology

Careful design and technology is necessary to communicate information to those with impaired hearing. Well-considered lighting, backgrounds and the positioning of windows can facilitate lip reading. Induction loop or infra-red systems can be used to amplify sounds both within rooms and at points of interaction such as counters or ticket offices. These two systems are simple in principle but they have specific advantages and disadvantages depending on the building context and should not be installed without expert advice.

SPECIFIC BUILDINGS

Much of the guidance given here is general and should be applicable in most building contexts. However individual building types do present specific problems, often of a basic nature, but if the inclusive design principle is applied from the outset it should be possible to resolve them, possibly by rethinking the usual solution from scratch rather than by resorting to special accessible alternatives.

EXISTING BUILDINGS

Improving accessibility within existing buildings may be a demanding process. A properly undertaken audit is a prerequisite to establishing the optimum level of accessibility to aim for.

Some reference has been made within this section to existing buildings but in summary the key considerations are as follows.

- Minimising compromises on basic requirements such as door widths and other space standards, support and contrast.
- The integration of new lifts within existing layout, particularly where a specific route is followed. This may be important in public and cultural buildings such as galleries and museums.
- The discreet use of technology. As set out earlier this may help to overcome specific barriers presented by existing building features such as changes in level or doors.

LEGISLATION

Key documents on accessibility are:

Building Regulations Part M
First published in 1987, these regulations currently apply to new or substantially reconstructed non-domestic buildings to which the public have access. From October 1999 its application extended to housing. Research into further widening its application to include work to existing buildings has been undertaken but no proposals have been made.

Disability Discrimination Act 1995
This concerns access by people with disabilities to education, employment, goods, services and facilities. From October 2004 suppliers of goods, services and facilities must remove the physical barriers which prevent access thereto by such people.

Buildings constructed since the introduction of Part M of the Building Regulations and which comply with its requirements and provisions will, to some extent, be deemed to satisfy this requirement of the Act. However, owners of other existing buildings with inbuilt inaccessibility must determine what is the optimum degree of accessibility which will indemnify them against any claims of discrimination. An access audit, as described below, will be helpful.

GUIDANCE

British Standards
Key standards in this context are:
- BS 5810:1979 Code of practice for access for the disabled to buildings. Much of the guidance here is incorporated into the current Part M of the Building Regulations.
- BS 5619: 1978 Code of practice for design of housing for the convenience of disabled people.

These two standards are in the process of being incorporated into a more comprehensive Standard based on input from people with disabilities, designers and specially commissioned research. The result is BS 8300, published in October 2001.

- BS 5588 Part 8: 1988 Fire precautions in the design, construction and use of buildings: Code of practice for means of escape for disabled people.

This established sound principles for evacuation by people with disabilities from buildings in the event of an emergency. It is currently under revision.

Key principles are the concept of refuges, use of evacuation lifts and effective management of evacuation, all of which remove any restrictions on access to multi-storey or complex buildings for people with disabilities.

- BS 4467: 1991 Guide to the dimensions in designing for elderly people.

Listed and historic buildings
PPG15 Planning Policy Guidance Note: Planning and the Historic Environment, published in 1994, established the principle that conservation of a building's special historic or architectural interest could, given careful design and management, be compatible with the provision of access around, into or within it. In support of and elaborating on this principle, English Heritage published its own illustrated guidance, Easy access to historic buildings, in 1995.

Audits
The audit concept, involving a rigorous and systematic assessment of a building in terms of its accessibility, has become firmly established. In its developed form (that is, supplemented by a programme to implement change), it is likely to be a strategic tool for building owners seeking to satisfy the requirements of the Disability Discrimination Act from 2004. It is also a requirement for applicants seeking Lottery funding that an access audit is carried out and its findings incorporated.

Other guidance and research
As would be expected much recent guidance now promotes inclusive design. Organisations producing guidance that is well researched and considered include:
- Centre for Accessible Environments
- Royal National Institute for the Blind
- The University of Reading (Research Group for Non-Handicapping Environments)

Access officers
Most UK local authorities have appointed access officers whose role is to monitor building proposals, provide informed advice on access provision, especially in problematic cases, and to prepare the authority's policy on accessibility.

DRAWING PRACTICE AND PRESENTATION

John Cavilla

INTRODUCTION AND GOOD PRACTICE

All practitioners should be able to produce drawings, and related information such as schedules, to a good standard. It is important for them to remember that drawings, particularly production/working drawings, have two purposes:

(1) to convey information to others with minimum confusion
(2) to enable them to clarify their own visions.

They must also be able to read the drawings of others so that the information can be integrated and translated into a real product.

It is worth quoting from a Building Economic Development Committee report entitled *Achieving quality on building sites*: 'Poor production drawings have too often been the cause of a low-quality finished product, poor cost control and failure to meet completion dates. Well-organised, complete and co-ordinated production drawings are a prerequisite for the management of construction.'

TRADITIONAL DRAWING SKILLS

Pencil drawing

Line drawing in pencil is the most difficult of the skills to master and requires dedicated practice. Such mastery is rewarding, however, giving the ability to produce design drawings which exhibit 'depth' and provoke the imagination, to produce complete working drawings, and also to construct the skeleton for detailed drawings completed in ink.

The grade, or 'softness', of lead determines the density of line and so the correct choice is an important contribution to the quality of drawing produced. For the normal range of drawing types 2H, H, HB and B are all that are needed (see *1*).

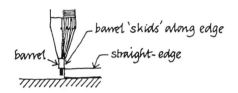

1 Pencil lead grades

Two types of pencil should be considered: the 'clutch' pencil, and the 'fine-line'.

Clutch pencil leads These are approximately 100 mm long with a diameter of 2 mm, and they require sharpening; however it is a simple process to maximise the life of the sharpened point by rotating the pencil from side to side as the line is drawn, using a relaxed grip. About 90% of the length of the leads can be used, they are extremely strong, and so are very cost effective (see *2*).

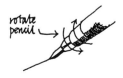

2 Preserving the sharpened point

Fine-line pencils With these, line drawing is simplified. Unlike the clutch pencil the leads vary in diameter to satisfy the type of line being drawn (0.3 mm, 0.5 mm, or 0.7 mm are the most popular). These pencils can present problems; for a comfortable drawing angle the lead is relatively thin and easily broken. In addition, wearing down of the lead can cause the pencil barrel to skid along the edge of a set-square or parallel-motion (see *3*).

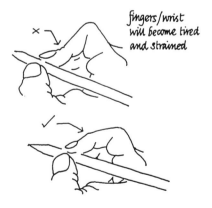

3 Simple problem with 'fine point' pencils

Whichever type of pencil is chosen a useful tip is to purchase separate ones for differing degrees of softness of lead. So buy pencils of varying colours or, if only one colour is available, wrap pieces of drafting tape around them to create a code. The result will be a dramatic increase in speed when interchanging.

When drawing with pencil (and with pen) ensure that the hand is relaxed and the grip is provided by the fingers; failure to follow this principle will result in the hand becoming tired and strained, and may even cause long-term injury to tendons (see *4*).

4 Using a relaxed grip

Regardless of the final purpose of the drawing it is good practice to employ pencil 'guidelines', which should be light, clear and accurate. A sharp point to the lead must be maintained (see also the following section on ink drawing). On completion of the guidelines the lining-in process can proceed to produce the completed drawing, using a softer lead to give the desired effect; employ a firm grip but avoid pressing. HB grade is ideal for secondary detail, such as suggestion on elevation of brick courses, roof tiles, and vegetation. B might be used for more emphasis in shadow, but there is a danger of smudging with softer leads and if an area has to be corrected it can be difficult to 'make good' that part of the drawing.

Ink drawing

This is the simplest form of line drawing to execute, and for reprographic purposes maximises the clarity provided by tracing paper and film.

Pencil guidelines should be drawn using, say, a 2H lead with minimum pressure; a lead softer than this will deposit more graphite on the paper and hence make it difficult to achieve a consistent, dense, ink line. Maintaining a good point on the lead is essential (avoid 'chisel' ends at all costs) so that the minimum width of pencil line is produced and maximum adhesion between ink and paper is achieved; if the ink simply sits on a broad pencil line it will easily be removed when cleaning-up the drawing with a soft eraser on completion.

Angle the nib across the straight-edge. This achieves two things: (1) it enables clear sight of the guideline and (2) it avoids the danger of ink being drawn under the straight-edge by capillarity (see **5**).

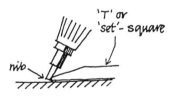

5 Angling the pen nib across the straight-edge

To avoid smudging of the ink, *lift* the straight-edge away from the line, do not drag it.

Errors on tracing paper or film can be erased by skimming the edge of a flexible razor blade, lightly held between thumb and fingers, across the ink line. This process leaves a rough surface which will make any new ink line across it go fuzzy. To restore the smooth finish to the paper, rub over the area with a hard *ink* eraser. This is one occasion when cheapest is often best, as good quality blades tend to be stiffer and increase the chances of damaging the surface of the paper.

Additional tips

To avoid back strain while line drawing, have the board tilted at a steep angle (45°–60°), but at a lower angle (say, 20°–30°) for any freehand detail or lettering, as support is then needed for hand, wrist and forearm (see **6**).

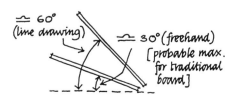

6 Comfortable working angles

Aim to draw all horizontal lines, working down the sheet, and then all vertical lines, working left to right (if right handed), to avoid smudging and the constant swapping of T-square and set-square. Resist the temptation to complete isolated parts of the drawing. There are generally two accepted ways of producing the junctions of straight lines (see **7**):

(1) crossing them very slightly (say, 1 mm) to give crispness at the junction – this needs practice and should not develop into indiscriminate crossing with no evidence of consistency and care

(2) drawing the lines so that they meet precisely at the junction – this is the traditional engineering technique and gives a neat, clean finish (if executed well), but it is marginally slower than crossing and introduces the danger that the lines may not quite meet, so giving a rounded effect.

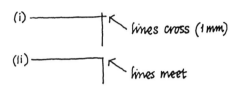

7 Junction of straight lines

Where curves and straight lines meet, draw the curved one first, then the straight line to meet it. It is difficult to get a curve to fit existing straight lines without producing a kink at the join (see **8**).

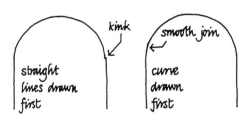

8 Intersection of curved and straight lines

Be aware that many templates for drawing circles and fittings have a right and a wrong way up: the right way takes advantage of a built-in lip to avoid problems of capillarity (see **9**).

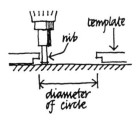

9 Using a template

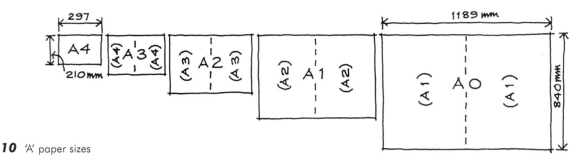

10 'A' paper sizes

ORGANISATION OF DRAWINGS

Paper
Drawing paper is available in standard 'A' sizes, convenient for folding, posting and handling. Each size is half the area of the next one in the sequence, but of the same proportions, A4 being the smallest, A0 the largest (see **10**).

Title panels
While a standard 'title panel' may at first seem to some to stifle an imaginative drawing layout, it is important to appreciate that for ease of reference in a set of project drawings a consistent arrangement, which is easily understood by others, is essential.

BS 1192:Part 1:1984 (*Construction Drawing Practice*) recommends contents for title panels, and some layout suggestions are offered here. The panel must be designed so that the recipient can immediately identify the project, the purpose of the drawing, the scale(s) used, details of any revisions, the date on which it was issued, and a contact name. Whatever style is adopted it should be remembered that the panel must be visible after folding for posting or archiving, and so should be placed in the bottom right-hand corner. (See **11**, **12**).

On many projects it has become common practice to photo-reduce drawings for record purposes or for general circulation. Where this process is anticipated a drawn scale may be incorporated next to the title panel so that where dimensions have not been shown an estimate can be made although this, of course, should never be used to override the need for accurate dimensioning. Any such drawn scale should be of adequate size and simplicity to remain clear at the reduced size: too often they are added with little thought as to whether they will actually serve their purpose, and so they become illegible.

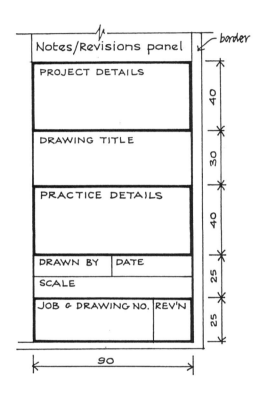

11 Typical title panel

Folding of drawings
The method of folding aims to reduce larger sheets to a standard A4 size (i.e. the smallest convenient unit) and present the title panel in the bottom right-hand corner. BS 1192 offers guidance on folding sequences, including techniques to allow for binding along the left-hand edge. (See **12**.)

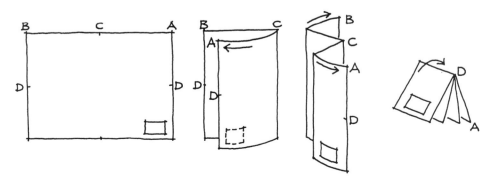

12 Folding drawings (example of A1 shown)

PROJECTIONS

In building drawing a 'projection' is a method of representing a solid object (i.e. something three-dimensional) in two dimensions. There are several projections in use, each of which has a particular function, but frequently a combination of them may express a difficult detail more clearly than just one.

Across the construction industry there is often confusion regarding the correct titles or arrangement; BS 1192 names and compares projections. The following is an outline of the principles of the more common projections and, where appropriate, references to variations in name that may be encountered. BS 1192 refers to them as 'parallel projectors', where all parallel faces on an object remain parallel when drawn: that is projections which do not display perspective relative to vanishing points.

Orthographic projection

This is the most popular projection used in the construction industry. It consists of an ordered arrangement of 'plans', 'sections', and 'elevations' (see **13**, and Sections below).

The arrangement is derived from the orthographic projection used in engineering drawing (i.e. the UK version known as 'first angle' and the American version known as 'third angle'). The construction industry uses a compromise between these two versions, but with flexibility: for example, the size of the drawing sheet frequently dictates the arrangement adopted. Therefore, in most building drawings it is not strictly correct to refer to them being specifically first or third angle (see **14**).

The plan is normally a horizontal section taken at about 1200 mm above floor level (typically just above window cill so that maximum information can be shown – e.g. window/radiator relationship). The plan may also be an elevation (e.g. that of a completed roof), see **14**.

The vertical section (see also Sections, below) is an essential part of an orthographic, and whenever possible it should be placed adjacent to the elevation to which it most closely relates; its position should be clearly indicated on the plan.

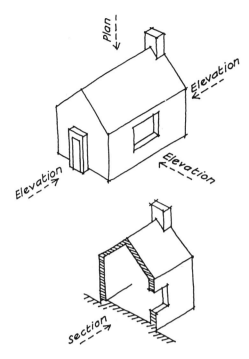

13 Definition of terms

Sometimes it may not be possible to contain the full set of elements on one drawing sheet, to a consistent scale. In such cases it would be appropriate to reduce the scale for the elevations, or to prepare a sheet of elevations alone; the elevations are normally the best choice for special treatment because they show less detail and relatively little annotation.

A disadvantage with the orthographic projection is that sometimes it may be difficult for the reader of the drawing to envisage junctions of faces of a building, or to understand complicated details, because each element of the drawing is two-dimensional and depth may not be easy to appreciate. Other parallel projections exist which give a three-dimensional effect; the examples which follow are described by their British Standard names but reference is also made to their more popular names.

14 Building in
        orthographic
        projection

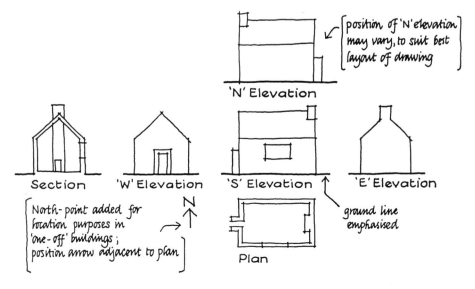

Isometric projection

BS 1192 gives this name but shows it as a sub-set within the 'axonometric' group. This may be confusing to some as axonometric is often understood to be a unique projection in itself (see also Planometric, below).

The isometric is a very useful projection which creates a view which is readily appreciated; the value of it in clarifying detail cannot be over-emphasised (see **15**).

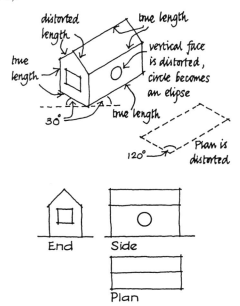

15 Isometric projection

Note that only lines which are drawn vertically or at 30° to the horizontal baseline remain their true length, all others become distorted; note also that the right-angle on plan is distorted to either 120° or 60°.

To simplify the process of drawing the elements whose lengths become distorted (e.g. the verge of a pitched roof), first draw the 'containing box', then locate known points by marking-off true lengths (see **16**).

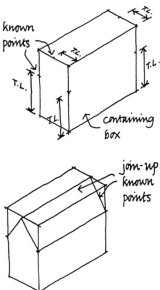

16 Constructing an isometric using true lengths

Curves also become distorted. They can be constructed by drawing the true curve and placing a grid of lines across it; the grid can then be reproduced on the face of the isometric (see **17**).

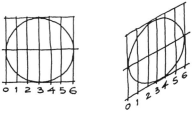

17 Drawing curves in isometric

Planometric

BS 1192 gives this name as a sub-set within the 'oblique' group; it is popularly called 'axonometric' and this name is supported by well-known standard texts on draughtsmanship (see notes in Isometric, above).

The planometric employs a similar principle to the isometric, but has a true plan and so is easier to prepare. However, it does not give as realistic a view. It is normally set at an angle of 45° to the baseline, but if preferred can be set at, say, 30°/60° (see **18**). Frequently it is used for pictorial views of kitchen designs.

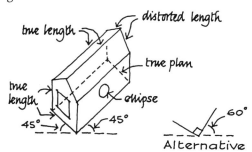

18 Planometric projection

Cavalier and cabinet projections

Classified as 'oblique' projections by BS 1192, these are seldom used in building drawing. They are designed to give a feeling of depth to the drawing while emphasising one elevation. The cavalier is simpler to draw but it has a rather unreal appearance (see **19**).

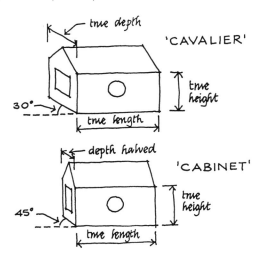

19 Oblique projections

SECTIONS (vertical sections and horizontal plans)

(Note: see also Orthographic projections, above.) A section is the drawing of an object as though it has been cut through. In building drawing it is usual to refer to the vertical projection as a 'section' and the horizontal as a 'plan' (see **20**).

(Note that the far window reveal is not cut through and so is in elevation. The normal convention is that the outline of the part in section is drawn with a thick line and the elevation with a thin line).

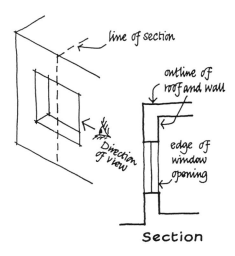

20 Principles of sections

The location of the vertical section is indicated on the plan and given a reference (e.g. A–A, C–C); the line and direction of the section may be shown in several ways (see **21**). These are normally the most significant element of a drawing, giving important information on construction and dimensions. However, the most informative sections are frequently avoided because they are also often the most difficult to draw (e.g. a staircase, or a hipped-end to a roof): this temptation should be resisted if possible.

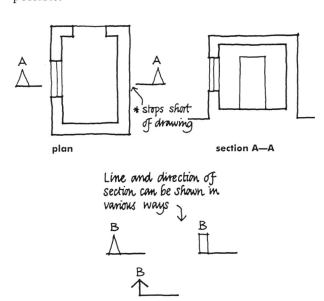

21 Locating sections

It is standard practice to 'hatch' sections to indicate the nature of the materials which are bisected. BS 1192 shows standard symbols for materials, but some are quite time-consuming to produce and so alternatives are frequently preferred. See **22** for a table of British Standard conventions, with popular alternatives where appropriate, and **24**.

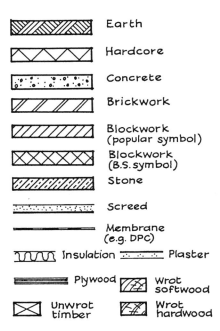

22 Representing materials in section

The amount of information shown on a section (plan or vertical) varies with the function of the drawing and the scale used (e.g. below 1:50 would not normally show detail beyond outline) – see **23**.

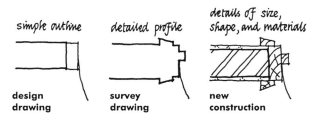

23 Relating information to function and scale of drawing

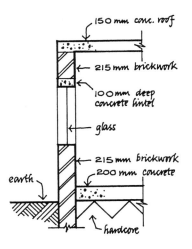

24 Typical hatching in sections

Points to remember:

(1) When the scale of the section drops below 1:50 hatching is normally abandoned (e.g. 1:100 is drawn as just an outline).

(2) Below 1:20 it is difficult to show detail such as the thickness of wall plaster, although descriptive notes may be added.

(3) Never attempt to hatch 100% of a drawing as this makes it congested and it is very time-consuming; limit hatching to junctions of differing materials and extremities of materials (e.g. the end of a wall) – see **25**.

(4) Hatching is seldom adequate on its own and so descriptive notes are added to support it.

(5) Secondary elements such as plaster, glass, ceiling tiles, etc., are normally shown with a *thin* outline (even though they are in section and would therefore logically have a thickened outline) – see **26**.

(6) While (3) above may be considered a time-saving device, always be aware that some forms of short-cut which are in common use may in fact cause problems for the reader of the drawing. A typical example is that of door swings shown on plan, which are sometimes indicated by simple 45° lines whereas it is more sensible to show the curve as a quadrant of a circle. This serves two purposes: it clarifies which side the door is hung and exposes potential clashes with walls and fittings (see **27**).

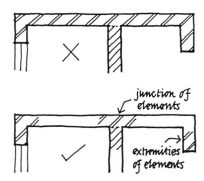

25 Economic hatching of materials

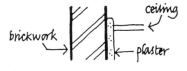

26 Indicating secondary elements

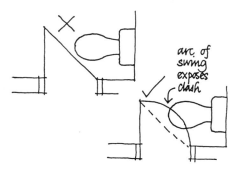

27 Drawing door swings

SCALES

Choosing the most appropriate scale for a drawing is a vital part of planning the process, and may set the pattern for subsequent drawings on a project. Select a scale which gives a drawing which is clear, accurate, and above all, achieves its objectives in terms of conveying information. It may also be appropriate to vary the scales of components of a drawing (see Orthographic projections, above), for example to highlight detail.

Examples of popular scales are:

- Block plans (site and surroundings): 1:2500, 1:1250.
- Site layout (building outline and position of fences, paths, roads, etc.): 1:500, 1:200.
- General (layout of rooms and principal construction features): 1:100, 1:50, 1:20.
- Details (doors, windows, eaves, fittings, etc.): 1:20, 1:10, 1:5, 1:1 (i.e. full-size).

(Note: it is generally agreed that 1:2 (i.e. half full-size) is not a good scale to choose as it is easily mistaken for full-size, and hence has frequently been the cause of confusion.)

Whatever scale is chosen, aim for consistency and accuracy in related drawings. For example if the ground floor plan is drawn at 1:50 then the other floor plans (first, second etc.) should also be drawn at 1:50, even if on different sheets.

traditional scales (expressed as ratio)		metric scales		remarks
		preferred	other	
full size	[1:1]	1:1		no change
half full size	[1:2]		1:2	no change
4″ = 1′0″	[1:3]			
3″ = 1′0″	[1:4]			
		1:5		
2″ = 1′0″	[1:6]			
1½″ = 1′0″	[1:8]			
		1:10		
1″ = 1′0″	[1:12]			
¾″ = 1′0″	[1:16]			
		1:20		
½″ = 1′0″	[1:24]			
			(1:25)	(limited use)
⅜″ = 1′0″	[1:32]			
¼″ = 1′0″	[1:48]			
		1:50		
1″ = 5′0″	[1:60]			
³⁄₁₆″ = 1′0″	[1:64]			
⅛″ = 1′0″	[1:96]			
		1:100		
1″ = 10′0″	[1:120]			
³⁄₃₂″ = 1′0″	[1:128]			
¹⁄₁₆″ = 1′0″	[1:192]			
		1:200		
1″ = 20′0″	[1:120]			
			(1:250)	(limited use)
¹⁄₃₂″ = 1′0″	[1:384]			
1″ = 40′0″	[1:480]			
		1:500		
1″ = 50′0″	[1:600]			
1″ = 60′0″	[1:720]			
1″ = 1 chain	[1:792]			
1″ = 80′0″	[1:960]			
		1:1000		
total:	24	9	1 (2)	

28 Metric and traditional scale ratios compared

Scale rules

Choose a good quality scale-rule (i.e. in the UK look for the 'BS 1347' stamp when purchasing). There are two formats available, two-sided oval, and triangular; they are available in 300 mm and 150 mm (oval only) lengths. It is ideal to have one of each length, the 150 mm size fitting easily into the pocket for site use.

The simple two-sided oval type is eminently satisfactory for general use, the shape enabling close reading of distances. However, it should always be remembered that scale-rules are for measuring and not for use as a straight-edge for drawing, or for cutting paper. The triangular type is very popular but generally more expensive than oval; it may also be argued that the additional scales provided are of limited value (e.g. 1:75) and those covered by the oval type satisfy all normal requirements.

LETTERING

All construction drawings require supporting titles and descriptive notes. Sometimes no more than a main title is needed, plus subtitles for the principal components of the drawing. However, more comprehensive descriptive notes may be required to support detailed construction. Each level must be capable of being easily read and should not degenerate into an attempt to impress with an 'architectural' style. It is therefore important, indeed vital, that a good standard of lettering is mastered; poor-quality lettering can ruin what may otherwise be a good drawing.

Two methods are generally used: (1) freehand, (2) stencilling. A corporate approach may dictate the choice, but above all it should be legible, quick to produce, and consistent.

Freehand

This is the quickest method, but frequently the most abused, due often to a lack of an understanding of the characteristics of the basic alphabet chosen, and a reluctance to practice. A good-quality freehand adds personality to the drawing. Three styles are considered below: modified roman, italic, and personal handwriting.

Modified roman This is probably the simplest solution, particularly in upper case; its style can be varied without loss of legibility (e.g. upright or sloping to the right) and if produced neatly is very easy to read. Many who use this style do struggle with the lower case, however, so emphasis should be placed upon this when mastering the alphabet. The main advantage with modified roman is clarity; its main disadvantage, compared with other freehand styles, is slowness.

See **29** for a guide to forming the letters. (Note that in upper case the central point of the 'M' and 'W' is taken the full height of the letter.)

Using guidelines, draft the letters lightly in pencil to establish proportion and spacing, then line in. A common problem is that of not achieving a balanced spacing between the letters. This is caused typically by maintaining a consistent *distance* between letters, as with a typewriter (e.g. see **30**). The aim should be to space by equalising the approximate *area* between letters (see **31**).

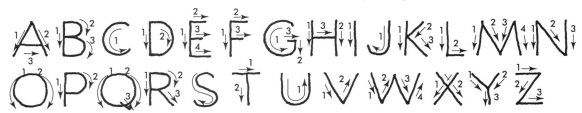

29 Lettering: modified roman

30 Spacing letters by distance

31 Spacing letters by area

Italic This is a popular style which is attractive, easy to read, and is the fastest form of freehand lettering. It would normally be used for detailed notes, in combination with modified roman titles and subtitles.

Unfortunately, italic is also the most abused, because of a failing to study and practice the basic shapes of the letters, so that it often becomes

unreadable. The only solution is to learn from a recognised work, examples are *Italic Handwriting*, by Tom Gourdie, and *The Art of Handwriting*, by John Le F. Dumpleton. These authors emphasise the repetitive shapes which occur across ranges of letters, highlighting that mastery of these shapes produces the simplicity, clarity and speed of true italic (see **32**).

32 Italic lettering

ABCDEFGHIJKLMN
OPQRSTUVWXYZ
abcdefghijklmnopqrstuvwxyz

Personal handwriting Everyday, untrained, personal handwriting should not be used, as normally the shape of letters will have evolved over many years and little attention paid to form in the early stages of development.

General comments

(1) Establish a hierarchy of lettering so that the eye is easily directed through the various components of the drawing (e.g. on a plan 'KITCHEN' might be considered more important than 'sink unit' or 'washing machine'). As well as upper and lower case, this can be done by varying the size and/or the style, and, when drawing in ink, using varying sizes of pen.

Examples for a typical A1 drawing:

- **Main titles** 6 mm roman, upper case, in size 0.8 pen.
- **Subtitles** (e.g. plan, elevation): 4 mm roman, upper case, 0.5/0.7 pen.
- **Other titles** (e.g. room names): 3 mm roman, upper case, 0.4/0.5 pen.
- **Detailed notes** 3 mm (overall) roman lower case, or 3 mm italic, 0.35 pen.

(2) Always use guidelines. These can be drawn in light pencil, or can be the lines on gridded paper (with varying square grid sizes) under the tracing paper. There is no doubt that using gridded paper (an A4 sheet for each of the sizes referred to in (1) above) speeds up the task, and gives greater control over shape and spacing of letters.

(3) Complete the line drawing before commencing lettering.

(4) Few people write naturally at the angle presented by a drawing fixed to a board so remove the drawing on completion and turn it to a comfortable angle (see **35**).

Stencilling

The principal advantage of stencilled lettering in ink is that it gives instant consistency and this may suit a practice where freehand may not be seen as giving the degree of control desired, for example where drawings may be revised by a second person, or where several are contributing to a set.

Always hold the stencil against a straight-edge (i.e. T-square or set-square), and ensure that the pen is the correct size for it (this information will be stamped on the face of the stencil). A pen that is too small will display kinks at changes in direction (e.g. the upper case 'N').

The main problem is speed when compared to freehand; stencilling is much slower and, in addition, individuality is destroyed. There is the opportunity to combine styles, perhaps using stencil for the title panel and main drawing title, but freehand for the remainder.

Organisation of drawing titles and notes

Positioning subtitles When adding subtitles (e.g. elevation, plan) it is sensible practice to start them from the extreme left-hand side of the element in question; this gives freedom to vary the length of the title, and also to continue an excessively long one on to a second line. Attempting to centre the title on the element is difficult and seldom works (see **33**).

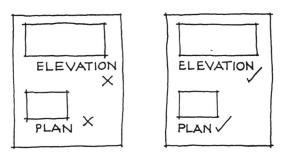

33 Positioning subtitles

Detail annotation It should be noted that the recommendations which follow are based on sound practice, but are not necessarily in agreement with the BS 1192 reference to 'leader lines'. The objective of any annotation should be to contribute to a drawing with simplicity and clarity, and in a format that will be readily understood by others. There should be a conscious effort made to ensure that whatever system is used it is consistent through all drawings on a project.

On a very detailed drawing, a large number of descriptive notes may be needed. These should be neatly and thoughtfully positioned so that they are easy to read and duplication of notes is kept to a minimum. They should be as near to the item as possible, without obliterating other elements. If several notes are needed they should be given a common left-alignment, and with an arrow from the note to the detail (see **34**).

Never use plain straight lines from a note to a detail as they can easily be confused with construction lines (see 'w' in **34**). Always make the direction arrow simple and consistent with a clear open arrowhead (see 'x' and 'y') and do not cover the drawing with 'snakes' (see 'z').

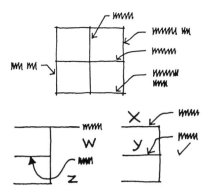

34 Correct use of arrows for annotation

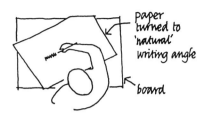

35 Lettering at a natural angle

Dimensioning

Dimensioning is one of the most important elements of a construction drawing. Dimensions should be clearly and correctly presented, leaving no doubts about size and position of the building and its components. Contractors, engineers, quantity surveyors etc. should not be expected to add up rows of intricate dimensions to ascertain, for example, an overall size of a building. This is the designer's responsibility: the excavation stage is too late to discover that a building will not fit on the site. A disciplined system of dimensioning should be adopted throughout a set of project drawings so that all parties recognise a consistent pattern of presentation.

Acquire a feel for the degree of accuracy that can be achieved in the construction processes. For example, bricklayers are frequently expected to build traditional walls specified to an accuracy of 1 mm on the drawings: in practice, this cannot be achieved with such a variable component as a brick, 5 mm being a more appropriate expectation. A pre-formed panel manufactured under factory conditions, however, presents a need for more accurate dimensioning of surrounding elements. Seek feedback from contractors to establish whether this aspect of the drawings on a project has been successful.

EXPRESSING SIZES

The construction industry generally recognises only millimetres (mm), metres (m) and kilometres (km), although centimetres (cm) are also used in some European countries. BS 1192 recommends that millimetres only are shown if the dimension is less than one kilometre. However, this convention is not wholly accepted; hence many variations are adopted. A commonly recommended format is as follows:
- 35 mm is shown as 35
- 350 mm as 350
- 3 m 500 mm as 3500
- 35 metres as 35 000.

Note that in dimensions exceeding one metre (e.g. 3 metres 500 millimetres) a space can be left between the thousands and hundreds (i.e. 3500). Many designers express this as 3.500 and this is acceptable although not strictly in accordance with the recommendations; if this style is adopted then 350 mm will become .350. Also note that the full three figures to the right of the decimal point are shown (i.e. not 3.5). Where the decimal point is used

it is usually entered on the base line (i.e 3.500) rather than raised. (Owing to space restrictions this book generally uses mm only up to 9999 and m beyond this (e.g. 10.0).)

PRESENTATION OF DIMENSION LINES AND SIZES

Dimension lines can take various forms (see **36**a–d).
(a) While this is popular for all classes it is particularly recognised as the normal method for showing co-ordinating dimensions (say, centre-lines of rows of columns). The head of the arrow should form a right angle (i.e. 90°).
(b) For speed and neatness this has become a popular technique for both overall and element dimensions; the oblique stroke should be kept a consistent length (say, 3 mm).
(c) This version is normally used for dimensions of elements. While acceptable it can present difficulties in achieving consistency, and slight variations in the size of the head tend to show up; it can also be time-consuming.
(d) This is recognised as an acceptable method for elements, but it is traditionally used on engineering drawings and is not popular in construction drawing as consistency is difficult to achieve and hence may cause the appearance to become rather untidy.

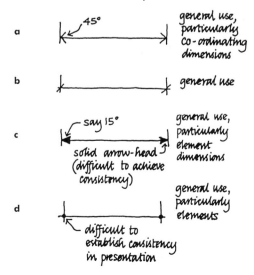

36 Dimension lines

Plans

Figures appear above the dimension line, and are read from bottom to top and right to left. Where a line of individual dimensions occurs, include an overall (or 'tying-in') dimension which shows the sum of the elements (see **37**).

On large buildings of frame construction it is good practice to create 'grid-lines' which coincide with centre-lines of key features such as columns; these give consistent and accurate reference points for other information such as cladding (see **38**).

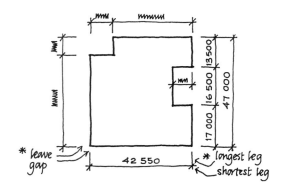

37 Principles of dimensioning elements and of tying-in

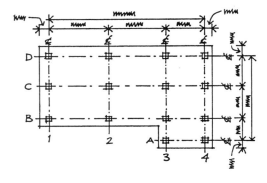

38 Dimensioning plans of framed buildings

Plans taken at ground level should also convey information regarding (1) the 'building-line', or adjacent fixed features, so that the structure can be accurately positioned, and (2) the position and value of the 'datum' for establishing heights (see Vertical sections, below).

Vertical sections

When marking dimensions on a section relate them to a 'datum' (i.e. a fixed point at a known height which can be clearly located, e.g. at DPC level or the top of the structural ground floor). Never relate them to external ground level as this may vary around the building. Assume the datum to be at a height of +100 m and in turn relate this to an existing known feature, for example an inspection chamber cover. By fixing the datum at 100 m this will ensure that, under normal circumstances, all levels will remain positive, even if there is a deep basement (see **39**).

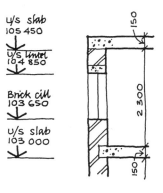

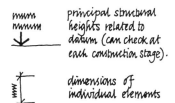

39 Dimensioning vertical sections

BIBLIOGRAPHY AND REFERENCES

AIRPORTS

Ashford N.J. Stanton H.P.M. and Moore C.A. (1991) *Airport Operations*, Pitman, London.

Ashford N.J. and Wright P. (1991) *Airport Engineering*, John Wiley & Sons, New York.

Blow C.J. (1996) *Airport Terminals*, 2nd edn, Butterworth Heinemann, Oxford.

Doganis, Rigas (1992) *The Airport Business*, Routledge, London and New York.

Edwards, Brian (1997) *The Modern Terminal: new approaches to airport architecture*, E & FN Spon, London.

Hart W. (1986) *The Airport Passenger Terminal*, John Wiley & Sons, New York.

Horonjeff, Robert (1992) *Planning and Design of Airports*, 4th edn, McGraw-Hill, New York.

Whitelaw, Jackie (ed.) (1995) *21st Century Airports*, Thomas Telford Publications, London.

Wickens A.H. and Yates L.R. (eds) (1995) *Passenger Transport after 2000AD*, Chapman & Hall, London.

Wright A.J. (1991) *World Airports*, Ian Allan, London.

BUSINESS PARKS

English Estates (and others) (1986) *Industrial and Commercial Estates, Planning and Site Development*, Thomas Telford, London.

Segal Quince & Wicksteed Ltd (1995) *Technology Parks in London*, London Planning Advisory Committee, London.

CINEMAS

Barron M. (1993) *Auditorium Acoustics and Architectural Design*, E & FN Spon, London.

British Industrial-Scientific Film Association (1979) *Film Guide for the Construction Industry*, Construction Press, Lancaster.

BS 5382: 1976, *Specification for Cinematograph Screens*.

BS 5550: Part 3: 1986, Specification for the position and dimensions of the maximum projectable image area on 35 mm motion picture film.

Part 7: 1990, *Specifications and measurements for the B chain electro-acoustic response of motion picture control rooms and indoor theatres.*

Part 8: 1989, *Glossary of terms used in the motion picture industry.*

BS 5588, *Fire Precautions in the design, construction and use of buildings*:

Part 6: 1991, *Code of practice for assembly buildings.*

Part 8: 1988, *Code of practice for means of escape for disabled people.*

BS CP 1007: 1955, *Maintained lighting for cinemas.*

Cinematograph Safety Regulations (1959), HMSO, London.

Knopp L. (1955) *The Cinematograph Regulations 1955*, Cinema Press, London.

COMMUNITY CENTRES

Hanson D. (1971) *The Development of Community Centres in County Durham (excluding County Boroughs) 1919–1968*, MEd Thesis, University of Newcastle.

Taylor M. (1983) *Resource Centres for Community Groups*, Community Projects Foundation, London.

CREMATORIA

Cremation Acts, 1902 and 1952.

Cremation Regulations, 1952, 1965, 1979.

Cremation (Amendment) Regulations, 1985.

Department of the Environment (1978) *The Siting and Planning of Crematoria* (LG1/232/36), HMSO, London.

DoE (1995) *Secretary of State's Guidance – Crematoria* (PG5/2(95)), HMSO, London.

Environmental Protection Act, 1990.

Local Government Act (Burial and Cremation), 1972.

Statutory Rules and Orders, 1930.

Cremation Society of Great Britain: Brecon House, Albion Place, Maidstone, Kent, ME14 5DZ.

EDUCATION: SCHOOLS

Dearing, R. (1993) *The National Curriculum and its Assessment: Final Report.*

Department for Education and Employment (1999) *Raising Standards: Opening Doors – Developing Links Between Schools and Their Communities*, DfEE, London.

Department for Education and Employment (1999) *BB91 Access for Disabled People to School Buildings*, The Stationery Office, London.

Department for Education and Employment (1999) *Designing for 3 to 4 Year Olds*, DfEE, London.

Department for Education and Employment (1999) *BB90 Lighting Design for Schools*, The Stationery Office, London.

Department for Education and Employment (1998) *BB89 Art Accommodation in Secondary Schools*, The Stationery Office, London.

Department for Education and Employment (1997) *BB87 Guidelines for Environmental Design in Schools* (Revision of Design Note 17), The Stationery Office, London.

Department for Education and Employment (1997) *BB86 Music Accommodation in Secondary Schools*, The Stationery Office, London.

Department for Education and Employment (1997) *BB85 School Grounds: A Guide to Good Practice*, The Stationery Office, London.

Department for Education and Employment (1997) *BB84 School Boarding Accommodation: A Design Guide*, The Stationery Office, London.

Department for Education and Employment (1996) *BB83 Schools' Environmental Assessment Method (SEAM)*, The Stationery Office, London.

Department for Education and Employment (1996) BB82 *Area Guidelines for Schools*, HMSO, London.

Department for Education and Employment (1996) *BB81 Design and Technology Accommodation in Secondary Schools: A Design Guide*, HMSO, London.

Department for Education and Employment (1996) *Managing School Facilities Guide 4: Improving Security in Schools*, HMSO, London.

Department for Education (1996) *Managing School Facilities Guide 3: Saving Energy*, HMSO, London.

Department for Education and Employment (1996) *BB80 Science Accommodation in Secondary Schools: A Design Guide*, HMSO, London.

Department for Education (1995) *BB79 Passive Solar Schools: A Design Guide*, HMSO, London.

Department for Education and Employment (1995) *Making IT Fit* (video and associated leaflet), DfEE, London.

Department for Education (1993) *BB78 Security Lighting*, HMSO, London.

Department for Education and Employment (1992) *BB77 Designing for Pupils With Special Educational Needs: Special Schools*, HMSO, London.

Department of Education and Science (1991) *BB72 Educational Initiatives in City Technology Colleges*, HMSO, London.

Department of Education and Science (1990) *BB71 The Outdoor Classroom*, HMSO, London.

Department of Education and Science (1987) *BB67 Crime Prevention in Schools: Practical Guidance*, HMSO, London.

Department of Education and Science (1984) *BB61 Designing for Children with Special Educational Needs: Ordinary Schools*, HMSO, London.

Department of Education and Science (1983) *DN32 Designing 8–12 Middle Schools*, DfEE Publications Centre, London.

The Education (School Premises) Regulations 1996, HMSO, London.

EDUCATION: UNIVERSITIES AND COLLEGES

Dearing, Sir Ron (1997) *Higher Education in the learning society, report of the National Committee*, The National Committee of Inquiry into Higher Education, UK.

DfEE/DES, *Design Notes 20,33,37,41,44,45,49,50*, Architects and Building Group, London.

Further Education Funding Council (1993) *Guidance on Estate Management*, FEFC, Coventry.

FEFC (1996) *Estate Management in Further Education Colleges: A Good Practice Guide*, FEFC, Coventry.

FEFC (1997) *Accommodation Strategies, Guidance for Colleges*, Supplement to Circular 97/19, FEFC, Coventry.

Higher Education Funding Council for England (1993) Strategic Estate Management, HEFCE, Bristol.

Kedney R. and Kelly J. (1992) 'FE: the built environment and incorporation', *Coombe Lodge Report*, vol. 23 no. 2, The Further Education Staff College, Blagdon, Bristol.

Kenny, Grace (1988) 'Section 4: Buildings', in Locke, M. (ed.) *College Administration, A Handbook*, 2nd edn, Longman in association with National Association of Teachers in Further and Higher Education, Harlow.

Kenny, Grace and Foster, Ken (1986) *Managing Space in Colleges*, 2nd edn, Management in Colleges Series, no. 1, Further Education Staff College, Blagdon, Bristol.

National Audit Office (1996) *Space Management in Higher Education: A Good Practice Guide*, NAO, London.

FARMS

Astley-Cooper P. (1991) *Farm and Rural Building Pocketbook*, Farm and Rural Buildings Centre, Kenilworth.

Barnes M. and Mander C. (1986) *The Farmer's Guide: Farm Building Construction*, (2nd edn, 1992), Farming Press, Ipswich.

Bell B. (1981) *The Farm Workshop* (2nd edn, 1992), Farming Press, Ipswich.

BS 5061, *Specification for cylindrical forage tower silos and recommendations for their use*.

BS 5502, *Buildings and structures for agriculture: General design*: Parts 20 to 23, 25, 30 to 33 *Livestock Buildings*: Parts 40 to 43, 49 to 52 *Crop Buildings*: Parts 60, 65, 66, 70 to 72, 74, 75 *Ancillary Buildings*: Parts 80, 81, 82.

BS 5545, *Milking machine installations*.

BS 6180, *Code of practice for protective barriers in and about buildings*.

Clarke P.O. (1985) *Buildings for Beef Production*, 3rd edn, Cement and Concrete Association.

Control of Pesticides Regulations 1986, HMSO, London.

Council for the Protection of Rural England (February 1991) *Building Responsibilities: the case for extending planning control over agricultural and forestry buildings*.

Council for the Protection of Rural England (May 1990) *A Place in the Country: Planning Control over Agricultural Workers' Dwellings*.

Countryside Commission (1996) *Countryside Design Summaries*, Countryside Commission, Cheltenham

Countryside Commission (1993) *Design in the Countryside*, CCP418, Countryside Commission, Cheltenham.

Department of the Environment Planning Research Programme (1995) *Planning for Rural Diversification, A Good Practice guide*, HMSO, London.

DoE Planning Research Programme (1995) *Planning Controls over Agricultural and Forestry Development and Rural Building Conversions*, HMSO, London.

DoE/MAFF, (1995) Rural England: White Paper – *A Nation Committed to a Living Countryside*, HMSO, London.

English P.R., Fowler V.R., Baxter S.H. and Smith W.(1988) *The Growing and Finishing Pig*, Farming Press Ltd, Ipswich.

Halley's Agricultural Notebook (Annual), Primrose McDonald.

Hardy R. and Meadowcroft S. (1986) *Indoor Beef Production*, (2nd edn, 1990) Farming Press, Ipswich.

Health and Safety Executive (1988) *Storage of approved pesticides: guidance for farmers and other professional users*, HSE Guidance Note CS19.

Land Use Consultants (1991) *Permitted Development Rights for Agriculture and Forestry*, HMSO, London.

Loynes I.J. (1992) *Planning Dairy Units*, Farm and Rural Buildings Centre, Kenilworth.

Ministry of Agriculture, Fisheries and Food (1991) *Code of Good Agricultural Practice for the Protection of Water*, (1992) *Air*, and (1993) *and Soil*, MAFF.

Nix J., *Farmer's Handbook* (Annual), Wye College.

Noton N.H. (1982) *Farm buildings*, College of Estate Management, Reading.

SI No. 1086 (1995) *The Dairy Products (Hygiene) Regulations*, HMSO, London.

SI No. 324 (1991) *The Control of Pollution (Silage, Slurry and Agricultural Fuel Oil) Regulations: Guidance Notes for Farmers*, HMSO, London.

Southorn N. (1996) *Farm Buildings – Planning and Construction*, Melbourne: Inkata (a division of Butterworth Heinemann, Oxford).

Thickett B., Mitchell D. and Hallows B. (1988) *Calf Rearing*, Farming Press.

Warth K. (1997) *Stables and Other Equestrian Buildings: a guide to Design and Construction*, Allen, London.

Woodforde J. (1983) *Farm Buildings in England and Wales*, Routledge & Kegan Paul, London.

FIRE STATIONS

Central Fire Brigades Advisory Council (1985) *Report of the Joint Committee on Standards of Fire Cover*, HMSO, London.

Greater London Council (1971) *Fire Stations*, Department of Architecture and Civic Design, GLC, London.

London Fire and Civil Defence Authority (1994) *London Fire Brigade Fire Station Brief*, commissioned by the LFCDA Property Client Group.

HALLS OF RESIDENCE AND HOSTELS

See Housing and Residential Accommodation

HEALTH SERVICE BUILDINGS

Building Design Partnership/Department of Health and Social Security (1979) *Interstitial Space in Hospitals outside North America*, BDP/DHSS, London.

Cox A. and Groves P. (1981) *Design for Health Care*, Butterworth, Kent.

James, Paul and Noakes, Tony (1994) *Hospital Architecture*, Longman, Harlow.

MARU with The Nuffield Trust (1999) *Healthcare Building for Tomorrow: Developing a 2020 Vision*, The Architectural Press, London.

Mathers & Haldenby (1979) *Interstitial Space in Health Facilities*, M&H, Canada.

MPA Health Strategy and Planning (1998) *The Millennium Hospital*, London, MPA, London.

Secretary of State for Health (2000) *The NHS Plan*, Stationery Office, London.

Stone P. (1980) *British Hospitals and Health-Care Buildings*, The Architectural Press, London.

NHS Estates, Design Guides (1991 and 1993) *Design of Community Hospitals, Options for the 90s: Accommodation for adults with acute mental illness*, Stationery Office, London.

NHS Estates, Estate Code (1992–1994) *Environments for quality care: Health Buildings in the Community*, Stationery Office, London.

NHS Estates, Health Building Notes (1988–1998) Nos 1, 2, 4, 6, 8, 10, 12, 13, 15, 20, 21, 22, 23, 26, 27, 29, 35, 36, 37, 42, 46, 47, 52, 53, 55, Stationery Office, London.

NHS Estates, Health Facilities Notes (1993–1998) Nos 01, 02, 07, 08, 09, 13, Stationery Office, London.

NHS Estates, Health Guidance Notes (1989–1998) *Magnetic Resonance Imaging, Telemedicine, Structure Cabling for IT systems*, Stationery Office, London.

NHS Estates, Health Technical Memorandum 81 (1996) *Firecode - Fire Precautions in New Hospitals*, Stationery Office, London.

HOSPICES

There are various statutory instruments and instructions issued under the following Acts: Medicines Act, 1968; Midwives Act, 1951; Misuse of Drugs Act, 1971 (and related regulations); National Health Services Act, 1977; Registered Homes Act, 1984. For example:

SI No. 798 (1973) *Misuse of Drugs (Safe Custody) Regulations*.

SI No. 1578 (1984) *Nursing Homes and Mental Nursing Homes Regulations*.

SI No. 1346 (1984) *Registered Homes Tribunal Rules*.

DHSS Circulars HC (84) and LAC (84) 15.

HOTELS

Baud-Bovy M. and Lawson F.R. (1999) *Tourism and Recreation Planning and Design*, The Architectural Press, Oxford.

Lawson F.R. (1995) *Hotels and Resorts Planning, Design and Refurbishment*, The Architectural Press, Oxford.

Lawson F.R. (1994) *Restaurants, Clubs and Bars: Planning, Design and Investment*, The Architectural Press, Oxford.

Lawson F.R. (2000) *Congress, Convention and Exhibition Facilities: Planning, Design and Management*, The Architectural Press, Oxford.

Rutes W. and Penner R. (1985) *Hotel Planning and Design*, Watson Guptill, New York.

HOUSING AND RESIDENTIAL ACCOMMODATION

NB: There are numerous publications relating to residential accommodation, and the following should be regarding as only a small selection. Numerous British Standards and other national and local government publications, as well as those in the voluntary and private sector, have an influence on housing. Some of the older government publications are difficult to obtain as they may no longer be in print.

Brewerton J. and Darton D. (eds) (1997) *Designing Lifetime Homes*, Joseph Rowntree Foundation, York.

BS 8220, *Guide for security of buildings against crime*.

BS EN 5103.

Building Research Establishment (1993) *Housing Design Handbook: Energy and Internal Layout*, BRE, Watford.

Cantle E.F. and Mackie J.S. (eds) (1983) *Homes for the Future*, Institute of Housing and RIBA, London.

Colquhoun I. (1999) *RIBA Book of 20th Century British Housing*, Butterworth Heinemann, Oxford.

Colquhoun I. and Fauset P.G. (1991) *Housing Design in Practice*, Longman, Harlow.

Department of the Environment (1995) *Our Future Homes*, HMSO, London.

Department of the Environment, Transport and the Regions/Housing Corporation (1999) *Housing Quality Indicators*, HMSO, Norwich.

Essex County Council, (new edn, 1997) *Essex Design Guide for Residential and Mixed Use Areas*, Essex County Council, Chelmsford.

Goodchild B. (1997) *Housing and the Urban Environment*, Blackwell Science, Oxford.

Hawkesworth R. (1993 – vol. 1; 1998 – vol. 2) *Housing Design in the Private Sector*, Serious Graphics, University of Portsmouth Enterprise Ltd, Portsmouth.

Housing Acts, 1985 and 1996.

Housing Corporation (periodically updated) *Procedure Guide and Good Practice Guide*, Housing Corporation, London.

Housing Corporation (1993, 1995) *Scheme Development Standards*, Housing Corporation, London.

Lincolnshire County Council (1996) *Lincolnshire Design Guide for Residential Areas*, Lincolnshire County Council, Lincoln.

Llewelyn-Davies (1994) *Providing More Homes in Urban Areas*, University of Bristol (SAUS Publications) and Joseph Rowntree Foundation.

Lund B. (1996) *Housing Problems and Housing Policy*, Longman, London.

National House-Building Council (NHBC) (updated regularly) *NHBC Standards*, National House-Building Council, Amersham.

Parker Morris Report (1961) *Homes for Today and Tomorrow*, HMSO.

Stationery Office (1998) *Housing for Varying Needs: A Design Guide*: Part 1, Houses and Flats, Stationery Office, Edinburgh.

PPG 3 Housing (currently being revised), HMSO.

Department of the Environment
Circular 36/67, *Housing Standards*.
Circular 1/68, *Metrication of Housebuilding*.
Circular 12/92, *Houses in Multiple Occupation*.

DoE Design Bulletins (all published by HMSO, now The Stationery Office). These bulletins give much useful technical information, mainly relating to housing issues, although much of the information could now be out of date and many of the bulletins are out of print. The most useful are: DB 6, 14, 24 (parts 1 and 2), 29, and 32.

DB1 *Some Aspects of Designing for Old People* (1968)
DB2 *Grouped Flatlets for Old People* (1968)
DB3 *Service Cores in High Flats* (in seven sections – 1962 to 1967)
DB4 *Swimming Pools* (1962)
DB5 *Landscaping for Flats* (1967)
DB6 *Space in the Home* (1968)
DB7 *Housing Cost Yardstick* (1963)
DB8 *Dimensions and Components for Housing* (imperial) (1963)
DB9 *Swimming Bath Costs* (1965)
DB10 *Cars in Housing 1: some medium density layouts* (1966)
DB11 *Old Peoples Flatlets at Stevenage* (1966)
DB12 *Cars in Housing 2: dimensions and multistorey parking garages* (1971)
DB13 *Safety in the Home* (metric edn) (1971)
DB14 *House Planning* (1968)
DB15 *Family Houses at West Ham* (1969)
DB16 *Co-ordination of components in housing* (metric edn) (1968)
DB17 *The Family at Home* (1970)
DB18 *Designing a Low-rise Housing System* (1970)
DB19 *Living in a Slum* (1970)
DB20 *Moving out of a Slum* (1970)
DB21 *Families Living at High Density* (1970)
DB22 *New Housing in a Cleared Area* (1971)
DB23 *Housing for Single People 1: how they live at present* (1971)
DB24 Part 1: *Spaces in the Home: bathrooms and WCs* (1972)
DB24 Part 2: *Spaces in the Home: kitchens and laundering spaces* (1972)
DB25 *The Estate outside the Dwelling* (1972)
DB29 *Housing for Single People 2: design guide* (1974)
DB30 *Services for Housing: Sanitary Plumbing and Drainage* (1974)
DB31 *Housing for the Elderly: size of grouped schemes* (1975)
DB32 *Residential Roads and Footpaths* (2nd edn, 1992)
DB33 *Housing Single People* (revised, 1978)

INDUSTRIAL BUILDINGS

Akerman K. (1991) *Building for Industry*, Watermark Publications (UK), London.

Bates W. (1978) *Introduction to the Design of Industrial Buildings*, Constrado, London.

Falconer P. and Drury J. (1975) *Building and Planning for Industrial Storage and Distribution*, The Architectural Press, London.

Institute of Logistics (1993) *Principles of Warehouse Design*, Institute of Logistics and Transport, Corby.

Mills E.D. (ed.) (1976) *Planning; Building for Habitation, Commerce and Industry*, Newnes-Butterworth, London.

Pemberton A.W. (1974) *Plant Layout and Materials Handling*, Macmillan, London.

Philips A. (1993) *The Best in Industrial Architecture*, BT Batsford, London.

Rider R. (ed.) (1998) *Designing for Deliveries*, Freight Transport Association, Tunbridge Wells.

Townroe P. (1976) *Planning Industrial Location*, Leonard Hill Books, London.

Webb J.D. (ed.)(1976) *Noise Control in Industry*, Sound Research Laboratories, Sudbury.

Wilkinson C. (1995) *Supersheds*, The Architectural Press, Oxford.

Legislation concerning industrial buildings includes: Clean Air Act, 1993; Control of Pollution Act; Control of Substances Hazardous to Health (CoSSH) Regulations; Factories Act, 1961; Fire Precautions Act 1971 (also SI 1989/76: Fire Precautions Order 1989); Health & Safety at Work etc. Act (including booklet 5, *Cloakroom Accommodation and Washing Facilities* and booklet 36, *First Aid in Factories*); Manual Handling Legislation; Offices Shops & Railway Premises Act, 1963; Petroleum (Consolidation) Act, 1928; Planning (Hazardous Substances) Act, 1990; Planning (Consequential Provisions) Act, 1990; Public Health (Recurring Nuisances) Act; Radioactive Substances Act; Town & Country Planning Act, 1990; Water Industry Act, 1991.

Statutory instruments:

Town & Country Planning (Use Classes) Order, 1987.

Statutory Regulations & Orders 1922:73 (as amended by SI 1961:2435) *Chemical Works Regulations*.

Statutory Regulations & Orders 1917:1067 (as amended by SR&O 1926:864 and SI 1961:2434) *Metal Works*.

Statutory Regulations & Orders 1964:966 *Sanitary Convenience Regulations*.

Statutory Regulations & Orders 1964:965 *Washing Facilities Regulations*.

BS 5588.

LABORATORIES

Advisory Committee on Dangerous Pathogens 1990: Categorisation of Pathogens According to Hazard and Categories of Containment (BS 5295).

Code of Practice for the Housing and Care of Animals used in Scientific Procedures (1989).

BS 3202:1991.

BS 7258:1990, *Fume Cupboards*.

Hain W. (1995) *Laboratories: A Briefing and Design Guide*, E & FN Spon, London.

Nuffield Foundation (1961) *The Design of Research Laboratories*, Oxford University Press, Oxford.

Radioactive Substances Act, 1993.

LANDSCAPE WORKS

Beazley E. (1990) *Design and Detail of Space Between Buildings*, E & FN Spon, London.

BS 340, *Specification for Precast Concrete Kerbs, Channels, Edgings and Quadrants*.

BS 368, *Precast Concrete Flags*.

BS 435, *Dressed Natural Stone Kerbs, Channels, Quadrants and Setts*.

BS 1722, *Specification for Fences*.

BS 3882, *Recommendations & Classifications for Topsoil*.

BS 3936, *Specification for Nursery Stock*, Parts 1–10 (*Trees and Plants*).

BS 4428, *Recommendations for General Landscape Operations*.

BS 4987, *Coated Macadam for Roads and Other Paved Areas*.

BS 5837, *Code of Practice for Trees in Relation to Construction*.

BS 6031, *Code of Practice for Earthworks*.

Colvin B. (1970) *Land and Landscape*, John Murray, London.

Department of the Environment (1980), *Design Bulletin 32, Residential Roads and Footpaths, Layout Considerations*, HMSO, London.

Fairbrother N. (1974) *The Nature of Landscape Design*, The Architectural Press, London.

Gibbons J. and Oberholzer B. (1991) *Urban Landscapes: A Workbook for Designers*, BSP, Oxford.

Hillier's Manual of Trees and Shrubs, Hillier & Sons.

Landscape: Guide to Sources of Information, (1978) HMSO, London.

Littlewood M. (1984) *Landscape Detail Handbook*, The Architectural Press, London.

Tandy C. (ed.) (1978) *Handbook of Urban Landscape*, The Architectural Press, London.

Weddle A.E. (1979) *Landscape Techniques*, Heinemann, London.

LAW COURTS

The Design Guide for Crown and County Courts, PSA Courts Group in association with the Lord Chancellor's Department.

Magistrates' Courts Design Guide (1991) HMSO, 1992.

Walker, Peter N. (1970) *The Courts of Law, A Guide to their History and Working*, David & Charles, Newton Abbott.

LIBRARIES AND LEARNING RESOURCE CENTRES

BS 5454: 1989, *Recommendations for storage and exhibition of archival documents*, BSI, London.

Higher Education Funding Council for England,

(1993) *Joint Funding Councils' Libraries Review Group: Report*, HEFCE, Bristol (known as the *Follett Report*).

International Federation of Library Associations and Institutions (1986) *Guidelines for Public Libraries*, ILFA, Paris, France.

Kelly T. (1973) *A History of Public Libraries in Great Britain*, Library Association, London.

Public Libraries and Museums Act, 1964

Thompson G. (1989) *Planning and Design of Library Buildings*, 3rd edn, Butterworth Architecture, Oxford.

MUSEUMS AND ART GALLERIES

Architectural Review (August 2000), 'Evolving Museums'.

Belcher M. (1991) *Exhibitions in Museums*, Leicester University Press.

Brawne M. (1982) *The Museum Interior: Temporary and Permanent Display Techniques*, Thames & Hudson, London.

Brawne M. (1998) *The Getty Centre*, 'Architecture in Detail' Series, Phaidon.

Boylan P. (ed.) (1992) *Museums 2000: Politics, People, Professionals and Profit*, Museums Association/Routledge, London.

Cassar M. (1994) *Environmental Management: guidelines for museums and galleries*, Routledge, London.

Darragh J. and Snyder J.S. (1993) *Museum Design: Planning and Building for Art*, Oxford University Press, Oxford.

Duncan C. (1995) *Civilizing Rituals: Inside Public Art Museums*, Routledge, London.

Henderson J. (1998) *Museum Architecture*, Mitchell Beazley, London.

Lord G.D. and Lord B. (eds) (1991) *The Manual of Museum Planning*, HMSO, London.

McKean C. (2001) *The Making of the Museum of Scotland*, NMS Publishing.

Matthews G. (1991) *Museums and Art Galleries: A Design and Development Guide*, Butterworth Architecture, Oxford.

Myerson J. (2000) *Making the Lowry*, Lowry Press.

Newhouse V. (1998) *Towards a New Museum*, The Monacelli Press.

Papadakis A.C. (ed.) (1991) *New Museums*, Architectural Design Academy Editions, London.

Pearce S.M. (1992) *Museums, Objects and Collections: A Cultural Study*, Leicester University Press.

Resource Publications (London): (Resource: the Council for Museums, Archives and Libraries, formerly the Museums and Galleries Commission):
> *Access to museums and galleries for people with disabilities.*
> *Guidelines on disability for museums and galleries in the UK.*
> *Improving museum security.*
> *Managing your museum environment.*
> *Museum collections in industrial buildings: a selection and adaptation guide.*
> *Perspectives on access to museums and galleries in historic buildings.*
> *Standards for touring exhibitions.*

Sixsmith M. (2000) *Designing Galleries*, Arts Council.

Steele J. (ed.) (1994) *Museum Builders*, Academy Editions, London.

Thompson J.M.A. (ed.) (1992) *Manual of Curatorship*, 2nd edn, Butterworth/Museums Association, London.

Thomson G. (1986) *The Museum Environment*, Butterworth, London.

Waterfield G. (ed.) (1991) *Palaces of Art, Art Galleries in Britain 1790–1990*, Dulwich Picture Gallery, Lund Humphries.

Walker D. and Wilson G. (1999) *The Making of a Museum*, Royal Armouries, London.

OFFICES

Arnoff S. and Kaplan A. (1995) *Total Workplace Performance: rethinking the office environment*, WDL Publications.

British Council for Offices (2000) *BCO Guide 2000: Best practice in the specification of offices*, BCO.

Becker F. (1990) *The Total Workplace: Facilities Management and the Elastic Organisation*, van Nostrand Reinhold, New York.

Becker F. and Steele F. (1994) *Workplace by Design - Mapping the High Performance Workscape*, Jossey-Bass Publishers.

Clements-Croome D. (2000) *Creating the Productive Workplace*, E & FN Spon, London.

Crane R. and Dixon M. (1991) *Architects' Data Sheets: Office Spaces*, Architecture Design & Technology Press, London.

Duffy F., Laing A. and Crisp V. (1993) *The Responsible Workplace*, Butterworth Architecture, Oxford.

Duffy F. (1997) *The New Office*, Conran, Octopus, London.

Laing A., Duffy F., Jaunzens D. and Willis S. (1998) *New Environment for Working*, Construction Research Communications Ltd.

Littlefair P. *et al.* (2001) *Office Lighting*, Building Research Establishment, Watford.

Marmot A. and Eley J. (1995) *Understanding Offices*, Penguin Books, Harmondsworth.

Marmot A. and Eley J. (2000) *Office Space Planning*, McGraw-Hill, London.

Myerson J. and Ross P. (1999) *The Creative Office*, Lawrence King Publishing.

O'Mara M. (1999) *Strategy and Place*, The Free Press.

Oseland N. and Bartlett P. (1999) *Improving Office Productivity: A Guide for Business and Facilities Managers*, Pearson Education Limited.

Pelegrin-Genel E. (1996) *The Office*, Flammarion.

Raymond S. and Cunliffe R. (1999) *eating@work*, Eclipse, London.

Raymond S. and Cunliffe R. (1999) *Sensible workplaces: a practical approach to intelligent buildings*, Eclipse, London.

Raymond S. and Cunliffe R. (1997) *Corporate reception areas: a design guide*, Eclipse, London.

Raymond S. and Cunliffe R. (1997) *Tomorrow's Office: creating effective and humane interiors*, E & FN Spon, London.

Sunstrom E. (1999) *Supporting Workteam Effectiveness*, Jossey-Bass Publishers.

Sunstrom E. (1986) *Workplaces: The Psychology of the Physical Environment in Offices and Factories*, Cambridge University Press, Cambridge.

Teunissen R. (1998) *High Performance Workplaces: Identifying Needs in Facilities Management European Practice*, Arko Publishers.

Van Meel J. (2000) *The European Office: office design in the national context*, 010 Publishers, Rotterdam.

Vischer J. (1996) *Workplace Strategies: Environment as a Tool for Work*, Chapman & Hall, London.

Worthington J. (1997) *Reinventing the Workplace*, The Architectural Press.

PUBS

See Restaurants

RELIGIOUS BUILDINGS

Allen W. (1981) *Acoustic Treatment for Places of Worship*, Ecclesiastical Architects & Surveyors Association, Newcastle upon Tyne.

Bradbeer F.H. (1967) 'Church Design: Principles of Organ Design', *Architects' Journal*, vol. 146, pp. 927–36.

de Breffny B. (1978) *The Synagogue*, Weidenfeld & Nicolson Ltd, London.

Brock P. (1985) *A Theology of Church Design*, Ecclesiastical Architects & Surveyors Association, Newcastle upon Tyne.

Council for the Care of Churches, (1985) *Church Organs*, CIO Publishing, London.

Frishman M. and Kahn H-U. (eds) (1994) *The Mosque*, Thames & Hudson Ltd, London.

Goring R. (ed.) (1992) *Chambers Dictionary of Beliefs and Religions*, W & R Chambers Ltd, Edinburgh.

Krinsky C.H. (1985) *Synagogues of Europe*, Architectural History Foundation/Massachusetts Institute of Technology Press, Cambridge, Massachusetts.

Lindsay P. (1993) *Synagogues of London*, Vallentine Mitchell, London.

du Quesnay H. (1991) *Faith Communities Handbook*, Hertfordshire County Council.

Sidhu G.S. (1988) *The Gurudwara* [*The Sikh Temple*], Sikh Missionary Society UK, Southall, Middlesex.

RESTAURANTS AND CATERING FACILITIES

Dartford J. (1990) *Dining Spaces*, Architecture Design & Technology Press, London.

Crane R. and Dixon M. (1990) *Food Preparation Spaces*, Architecture Design & Technology Press, London.

Lawson F.R. (1995) *Hotels and Resorts*, Architectural Press/Butterworth Architecture-Heinemann, Oxford.

Lawson F.R. (1994) *Restaurants, Clubs and Bars*, 2nd edn, Butterworth Heinemann, Oxford.

Smith D. (1978) *Hotel and Restaurant Design*, Design Council Publications, London.

Pertinent legislation includes: Model Water Bylaws (Department of the Environment); Workplace (Health, Safety & Welfare) Regulations, 1992; Environment Protection Act, 1990; Food & Drugs Act, 1955; Food Hygiene (General) Regulations, 1970; Food Safety Act, 1990; Food Safety (General Food Hygiene) Regulations, 1995; Local Government (Miscellaneous Provisions) Act, 1976 (Section 20); Local Government (Miscellaneous Provisions) Act, 1982; Licensing Acts, 1953 and 1964; Private Places of Entertainment (Licensing) Act, 1967.

SHOPS AND RETAIL

Beddington N. (1991) *Shopping Centres*, Butterworth Architecture, Oxford.

BS 5588: Part 2 (*Shops*) and Part 10 (*Shopping complexes*), BSI, London.

Building, 16 June 2000 (supplement), Builder Group, London.

Department of the Environment, Transport and the Regions, *The impact of large foodstores on market towns and district centres*, HMSO, London.

Department of the Environment (revised 1996) PPG 6, *Town Centres and Retail Development*, HMSO, London.

DoE (1994) PPG 13, *Transport*, HMSO, London.

DoE/BDP Planning/Oxford Institute of Retail Management (1992) *The Effects of Major Out-of-Town Retail Developments*, HMSO, London.

McGoldrick P.J. and Thompson M.G. (1992) *Regional Shopping Centres: out-of-town versus in-town*, Avebury Ashgate Publishing Ltd, Aldershot.

Prior J. (1999) *Sustainable Retail Premises: An Environmental Guide to Design and Management of Retail Premises*, Construction Research Communications, London.

Scott N.K. (1989) *Shopping Centre Design*, E & FN Spon, London.

SPORTS FACILITIES

John G. and Campbell K. (1993), *Outdoor Sports, Handbook of Sports and Recreational Building Design*, Vol. 1, Butterworth Architecture and the Sports Council, Oxford.

John G. and Campbell K. (1995), *Indoor Sports, Handbook of Sports and Recreational Building Design*, Vol. 2, Butterworth Architecture and the Sports Council, Oxford.

John G. and Sheard R. (1997) *Stadia: A Design and Development Guide*, The Architectural Press, Oxford.

Kit Campbell Associates (1993), *Changing Changing: A Report to the Sports Council*, Sports Council, London.

Sports Council, *Guidance Notes*, English Sports Council, London.

Individual sports

Athletics: International Amateur Athletic Federation, *Official Handbook 1996–7* (revised edition), IAAF. (See also IAAF *Track and Field Facilities Manual 1995*.)

Football, American: American National Football League, *Rules of American Football*, NFL.

Football, Association: Federation Internationale de Football Association (FIFA) (1995) *Technical Recommendations and Requirements for the Construction or Modernisation of Football Stadia*, FIFA.

Football, Australian: British Australian Rules Football League, *A Fundamental Guide to the Game*.

Football, Gaelic: Gaelic Athletic Association, *Playing Rules for Football and Hurling*, GAA.

Football, Rugby League: Rugby Football League, *International Laws of the Game*, RFL, Leeds.

Football, Rugby Union: Rugby Football Union, *Laws of the Game*, RFU, Twickenham.

Hockey: Hockey Rules Board (1990) *Rules of the Game of Hockey*, HRB.

Hurling: Gaelic Athletic Association, *Playing Rules for Football and Hurling*, GAA.

Swimming: Dawes, J. (1979) *Design and Planning of Swimming Pools*, Architectural Press, London.

Swimming: Federation Internationale de Natation Amateur (FINA)/Amateur Swimming Association (ASA), Information Literature.

Swimming and Skating: John G. and Campbell K. (eds) (1996) *Swimming Pools and Ice Rinks, Handbook of Sports and Recreational Building Design*, Vol. 3, Butterworth Architecture and the Sports Council, Oxford.

Tennis: UK Lawn Tennis Association.

THEATRES AND ARTS CENTRES

Appleton I. (1996) *Buildings for the Performing Arts: A Design and Development Guide*, Butterworth Architecture, Oxford.

Earl J. and Sell M. (eds) (2000) *Theatres Trust Guide to British Theatres 1750–1950*, A&C Black, London.

Forsyth M. (1987) *Auditoria: Designing for the Performing Arts*, Mitchell Publishing, London.

Ham R. (1987) *Theatres: Planning Guidance for Design and Adaptation*, The Architectural Press, London.

Head L. (ed.) *British Performing Arts Yearbook 2000/2001*, Rhinegold Publishing, London.

Home Office (1990) *Guide to Fire Precautions in Existing Places of Entertainment and Like Premises*, HMSO London. (Note: not for new designs; only existing buildings.)

Leacroft R. (1988) *Development of the English Playhouse*, Methuen, London.

Leacroft R. and Leacroft, H. (1984) *Theatre and Playhouse*, Methuen, London.

Strong J. (undated) *Encore: Strategies for Theatre Renewal*, Theatres Trust Charitable Fund, London.

Pertinent legislation includes: Theatres Act, 1968; Cinemas Act, 1985; Private Places of Entertainment Act, 1968; BS 5588: Part 6, *Places of Assembly*.

VEHICLE FACILITIES

Department of Transport, *Layout of Major/Minor Junctions*, DTp-TA 20/84, HMSO, London.

Freight Transport Association, (1983) *Designing for Deliveries*, FTA, Tunbridge Wells.

Institution of Highways and Transportation with Department of Transport (1987) *Roads and Traffic in Urban Areas*, HMSO, London.

McCluskey J. (1992) *Road Form and Townscape*, Butterworth Architecture, London.

Tandy C. (1972) *Handbook of Urban Landscape*, The Architectural Press, London.

Pertinent legislation and guidance includes: Health & Safety Document HS(G)41; Highways Act, 1980; Highways (Traffic Calming) Regulations, 1993; Highways (Road Humps) Regulations, 1996; Petroleum (Regulation) Acts, 1928 and 1936; Petroleum (Consolidation) Act, 1928; Planning Policy Guidance Note 13, Transport (PPG 13); Road Traffic Acts, 1972, 1991; Road Traffic Regulations Act, 1984; Road Traffic Regulation (Parking) Act, 1986; Road Traffic Reduction Act, 1997; Transport Act, 1982.

YOUTH HOSTELS

International Youth Hostel Federation and Bothamley J. (1997) *Hostel Design Manual*, International Youth Hostel Federation, Welwyn Garden City, Hertfordshire.

ZOOS AND AQUARIUMS

Bendiner R. (1981) *The Fall of the Wild, The Rise of the Zoo*, Elsevier Dutton Co Inc., New York.

Hancock D. (1971) *Animals and Architecture*, Hugh Evelyn Limited, London.

Hediger H. (1965) *Man and Animals in the Zoo*, Routledge & Kegan Paul, London.

Ironmonger J. (1992) *The Good Zoo Guide*, HarperCollins, London.

Mallinson J.J.C. and Carroll J.B. (1995) *Integrating Needs in Great Ape Accommodation*, Jersey Wildlife Preservation Trust, Channel Islands.

Markowitz H. (1982) *Behavioural Enrichment in the Zoo*, Van Nostrand Reinhold, New York.

Polakowski K.J. (1987) *Zoo design: the reality of wild illusions*, University of Michigan.

Reid G. McG. (1994) *Live Animals and Plants in Natural History Museums*, Manual of Natural History Curatorship, HMSO, London.

Stevenson, M.F.(1983) 'The captive environment: its effect on exploratory and related behavioural responses in wild animals', in *Exploration in Animals and Humans* (eds John Archer and Lynda Byrke), Van Nostrand, New York.

Taylor L. (1993) *Aquariums, Windows to Nature*, Prentice Hall, New York.

Tudge C. (1991) *Last Animals at the Zoo*, Hutchinson Radius, London.

Wylson A. and P. (1994) *Theme Parks, Leisure Centres, Zoos and Aquaria*, Longman Scientific and Technical, Longman Group UK Limited.

Zoo Licensing Act (1981) HMSO, London.

Zuckerman S. (ed.) (1979) *Great Zoos of the World: their origins and significance*, Weidenfeld & Nicolson, London.

DESIGN FOR ACCESSIBILITY

BS 4467: 1991, *Guide to the dimensions in designing for elderly people*, BSI, London.

BS 5619: 1978, *Code of practice for design of housing for the convenience of disabled people*, BSI, London.

BS 5588: Part 8: 1988, *Fire precautions in the design, construction and use of buildings: Code of practice for means of escape for disabled people*, BSI, London.

BS 5810: 1979, *Code of practice for access for the disabled to buildings*, BSI, London.

BS 8300: 2001, *Code of Practice for the design of buildings and their approaches to meet the needs of disabled people*, BSI, London.

Centre for Accessible Environments.

Department of the Environment (1994) PPG 15, *Planning and the Historic Environment*, HMSO, London.

Disability Discrimination Act, 1995.

English Heritage (1995) *Easy Access to Historic Buildings*.

Royal National Institute for the Blind.

The University of Reading (Research Group for Non-Handicapping Environments).

DRAWING PRACTICE AND PRESENTATION

BS 1192: 1984, *Construction Drawing Practice*, BSI, London.
Part 1, *Recommendations for general principles*.
Part 2, *Recommendations for architectural and engineering drawings*.
Part 3, *Recommendations for symbols and other graphic conventions*.

Building Economic Development Office (BEDC) (1987) *Achieving quality on building sites*, NEDO, London.

Dumpleton J. Le F. (1965) *The Art of Handwriting*, Pitman, London.

Gourdie T. (1955) *Italic Handwriting*, Studio Vista, London.

Porter T. and Goodman S. (1982) *Manual of Graphic Techniques*, Vol. 5, Butterworth, London.

Porter T. and Greenstreet B. (1980–85) *Manual of Graphic Techniques* (Vols 1 to 4), Butterworth, London.

Reekie R.F. (1989) *Draughtsmanship, Architectural and Building Graphics*, Edward Arnold, London.

CONVERSION OF UNITS

LIST OF CONVERSION TABLES

metric	imperial
length	
1.0 mm	0.039 in
25.4 mm (2.54 cm)	1 in
304.8 mm (30.48 cm)	1 ft
914.4 mm	1 yd
1 000.0 mm (1.0 m)	1 yd 3.4 in (1.093 yd)
20.117 m	1 chain
1 000.00 m (1 km)	0.621 mile
1 609.31 m	1 mile
area	
100 mm² (1.0 cm²)	0.155 in²
645.2 mm² (6.452 cm²)	1 in²
929.03 cm² (0.093 m²)	1 ft²'
0.836 m²	1 yd²
1.0 m²	1.196 yd² (10.764 ft²)
0.405 ha (4 046.9 m²)	1 acre
1.0 ha (10 000 m²)	2.471 acre
1.0 km²	0.386 mile²
2.59 km² (259 ha)	1 mile²
volume	
1 000 mm³ (1.0 cm³; 1.0 ml)	0.061 in³
16 387 mm³ (16.387 cm³; 0.0164 l; 16.387 ml)	1 in³
1.0 l (1.0 dm³; 1 000 cm³)	61.025 in³ (0.035 ft³)
0.028 m³ (28.32 l)	1 ft³
0.765 m³	1 yd³
1.0 m³	1.308 yd³ (35.314 ft³)
capacity	
1.0 ml	0.034 fl oz US
1.0 ml	0.035 fl oz imp
28.41 ml	1 fl oz imp
29.57 ml	1 fl oz US
0.473 litre	1 pint (liquid) US
0.568 litre	1 pint imp
1.0 litre	1.76 pint imp
1.0 litre	2.113 pint US
3.785 litre	1 gal US
4.546 litre	1 gal imp
100.0 litre	21.99 gal imp
100.0 litre	26.42 gal US
159.0 litre	1 barrel US
164.0 litre	1 barrel imp
mass	
1.0 g	0.035 oz (avoirdupois)
28.35 g	1 oz (avoirdupois)
454.0 g (0.454 kg)	1 lb
1 000.0 g (1 kg)	2.205 lb
45.36 kg	1 cwt US
50.8 kg	1 cwt imp
907.2 kg (0.907 t)	1 ton US
1 000.0 kg (1.0 t)	0.984 ton imp
1 000.0 kg (1.0 t)	1.102 ton US
1 016.0 kg (1.016 t)	1 ton imp
mass/unit length	
0.496 kg/m	1 lb/yd
0.564 kg/m (0.564 t/km)	1 ton US/mile
0.631 kg/m (0.631 t/km)	1 ton imp/mile
1.0 kg/m	0.056 lb/in (0.896 oz/in)
1.116 kg/m	1 oz/in
1.488 kg/m	1 lb/ft
17.86 kg/m	1 lb/in
length/unit mass	
1.0 m/kg	0.496 yd/lb
2.016 m/kg	1 yd/lb

metric	imperial
mass/unit area	
1.0 g/m²	0.003 oz/ft²
33.91 g/m²	1 oz/yd²
305.15 g/m²	1 oz/ft²
0.011 kg/m²	1 cwt US/acre
0.013 kg/m²	1 cwt imp/acre
0.224 kg/m²	1 ton US/acre
0.251 kg/m²	1 ton imp/acre
1.0 kg/m²	29.5 oz/yd²
4.882 kg/m²	1 lb/ft²
703.07 kg/m²	1 lb/in²
350.3 kg/km² (3.503 kg/ha; 0.35 g/m²)	1 ton US/mile²
392.3 kg/km² (3.923 kg/ha; 0.392 g/m²)	1 ton imp/mile²
density (mass/volume)	
0.593 kg/m³	1 lb/yd³
1.0 kg/m³	0.062 lb/ft³
16.02 kg/m³	1 lb/ft
1 186.7 kg/m³ (1.187 t/m³)	1 ton US/yd³
1 328.9 kg/m³ (1.329 t/m³)	1 ton imp/yd³
27 680.0 kg/m³ (27.68 t/m³; 27.68 g/cm³)	1 lb/in³
specific surface (area/unit mass)	
0.823 m²/t	1 yd²/ton
1.0 m²/kg	0.034 yd²/oz
29.493 m²/kg	1 yd²/oz
area/unit capacity	
0.184 m²/l	1 yd²/gal
1.0 m²/l	5.437 yd²/gal
concentration	
0.014 kg/m³	1 grain/gal imp
0.017 kg/m³	1 grain/gal US
1.0 kg/m³ (1.0 g/l)	58.42 grain/gal US
1.0 kg/m³ (1.0 g/l)	70.16 grain/gal imp
6.236 kg/m³	1 oz/gal imp
7.489 kg/m³	1 oz/gal US
mass rate of flow	
0.454 kg/s	1 lb/s
1.0 kg/s	2.204 lb/s
volume rate of flow	
0.063 l/s	1 gal US/minute
0.076 l/s	1 gal imp/minute
0.472 l/s	1 ft³/minute
1.0 l/s (86.4 m³/day)	13.2 gal imp/s
1.0 l/s	0.264 gal US/s
1.0 l/min	0.22 gal imp/min
1.0 l/min	0.264 gal US/min
3.785 l/s	1 gal US/s
4.546 l/s	1 gal imp/s
28.32 l/s	1 ft³/s
0.0038 m³/min	1 gal US/min
0.0045 m³/min	1 gal imp/min
1.0 m³/s	183.162 gal US/s
1.0 m³/s	219.969 gal imp/s
1.0 m³/h	35.31 ft³/h
0.0283 m³/s	1 ft³/s
velocity	
0.005 m/s	1 ft/minute
0.025 m/s	1 in/s
0.305 m/s	1 ft/s
1.0 m/s	3.28 ft/s
1 000.0 m/hr (1 km/hr)	0.621 mile/hr
1 609.0 m/hr (0.447 m/s)	1 mile/hr

metric	imperial
fuel consumption	
1.0 l/km	0.354 gal imp/mile
1.0 l/km	0.425 gal US/mile
2.352 l/km	1 gal US/mile
2.824 l/km	1 gal imp/mile
acceleration	
0.305 m/s²	1 ft/s²
1.0 m/s²	3.28 ft/s²
9.806 m/s² = g (standard acceleration due to gravity)	g = 32.172 ft/s²
temperature	
X°C	($^9/_5$ X + 32) °F
$^5/_9 \times$ (X − 32) °C	X°F
temperature interval	
0.5556 K	1°F
1 K = 1°C	1.8°F
energy	
1.0 J	0.239 calorie
1.356 J	1 ft lbf
4.187 J	1.0 calorie
9.807 J (1 kgf m)	7.233 ft lbf
1 055.06 J	1 Btu
3.6 MJ	1 kilowatt-hr
105.5 MJ	1 therm (100 000 Btu)
power (energy/time)	
0.293 W	1 Btu/hr
1.0 W	0.738 ft lbf/s
1.163 W	1.0 kilocalorie/hr
1.356 W	1 ft lbf/s
4.187 W	1 calorie/s
1 kgf m/s (9.807 W)	7.233 ft lbf/s)
745.7 W	1 horsepower
1 metric horsepower (75 kgf m/s)	0.986 horsepower
intensity of heat flow rate	
1 W/m²	0.317 Btu/(ft² hr)
3.155 W/m²	1.0 Btu/(ft² hr)
thermal conductivity[1]	
0.144 W/(m.K)	1 Btu in/(ft² hr °F)
1.0 W/(m.K)	6.933 Btu in/(ft² hr °F)
thermal conductance[2]	
1.0 W/(m².K)	0.176 Btu/(ft² hr °F)
5.678 W/(m².K)	1.0 Btu/(ft² hr °F)
thermal resistivity[3]	
1.0 m K/W	0.144 ft² hr °F/(Btu in)
6.933 m K/W	1.0 ft² hr °F/(Btu in)
specific heat capacity	
1.0 kJ/(kg.K)	0.239 Btu/(lb °F)
4.187 kJ/(kg.K)	1.0 Btu/(lb °F)
1.0 kJ/(m³ K)	0.015 Btu/(ft³ °F)
67.07 kJ/(m³ K)	1.0 Btu/(ft³ °F)
specific energy	
1.0 kJ/kg	0.43 Btu/lb
2.326 kJ/kg	1.0 Btu/lb
1.0 kJ/m³ (1 kJ/l)	0.027 Btu/ft³
1.0 J/l	0.004 Btu/gal
232.1 J/l	1.0 Btu/gal

metric	imperial
refrigeration	
3.517 kW	12 000 Btu/hr = 'ton of refrigeration'
illumination	
1 lx (1 lumen/m²)	0.093 ft-candle (0.093 lumen/ft²)
10.764 lx	1.0 ft-candle (1 lumen/ft²)
luminance	
0.3183 cd/m²	1 apostilb
1.0 cd/m²	0.000645 cd/ft²
10.764 cd/m²	1 cd/ft²
1550.0 cd/m²	1.0 cd/in²
force	
1.0 N	0.225 lbf
1.0 kgf (9.807 N; 1.0 kilopond)	2.205 lbf
4.448 kN	1.0 kipf (1 000 lbf)
8.897 kN	1.0 tonf US
9.964 kN	1.0 tonf imp
force/unit length	
1.0 N/m	0.067 lbf/ft
14.59 N/m	1.0 lbf/ft
32.69 kN/m	1.0 tonf/ft
175.1 kN/m (175.1 N/mm)	1.0 lbf/in
moment of force (torque)	
0.113 Nm (113.0 Nmm)	1.0 lbf in
1.0 Nm	0.738 lbf ft
1.356 Nm	1.0 lbf ft
113.0 Nm	1.0 kipf in
253.1 Nm	1.0 tonf in
1356.0 Nm	1.0 kipf ft
3037.0 Nm	1.0 tonf ft
pressure	
1.0 Pa (1.0 N/m²)	0.021 lbf/ft²
1.0 kPa	0.145 lbf/in²
100.0 Pa	1.0 millibar
2.99 kPa	1 ft water
3.39 kPa	1 in mercury
6.9 kPa	1.0 lbf/in²
100.0 kPa	1.0 bar
101.33 kPa	1.0 standard atmosphere
107.25 kPa	1.0 tonf/ft²
15.44 MPa	1.0 tonf/in²

[1] k-value

[2] also known as U-value or thermal transmittance

[3] 1/k-value

Length

1 millimetres to inches

mm	0	1	2	3	4	5	6	7	8	9
	in									
0		0.04	0.08	0.11	0.16	0.2	0.24	0.28	0.31	0.35
10	0.39	0.43	0.47	0.51	0.55	0.59	0.63	0.67	0.71	0.75
20	0.79	0.83	0.87	0.91	0.94	0.98	1.02	1.06	1.1	1.14
30	1.18	1.22	1.25	1.3	1.34	1.38	1.41	1.46	1.5	1.57
40	1.57	1.61	1.65	1.69	1.73	1.77	1.81	1.85	1.89	1.93
50	1.97	2.00	2.05	2.09	2.13	2.17	2.21	2.24	2.28	2.32
60	2.36	2.4	2.44	2.48	2.52	2.56	2.6	2.64	2.68	2.72
70	2.76	2.8	2.83	2.87	2.91	2.95	3.0	3.03	3.07	3.11
80	3.15	3.19	3.23	3.27	3.31	3.35	3.39	3.42	3.46	3.5
90	3.54	3.58	3.62	3.66	3.7	3.74	3.78	3.82	3.86	3.9
100	3.94	3.98	4.02	4.06	4.09	4.13	4.17	4.21	4.25	4.29
110	4.33	4.37	4.41	4.45	4.49	4.53	4.57	4.61	4.65	4.69
120	4.72	4.76	4.8	4.84	4.88	4.92	4.96	5.0	5.04	5.08
130	5.12	5.16	5.2	5.24	5.28	5.31	5.35	5.39	5.43	5.47
140	5.51	5.55	5.59	5.63	5.67	5.71	5.75	5.79	5.83	5.87
150	5.91	5.94	5.98	6.02	6.06	6.1	6.14	6.18	6.22	6.26
160	6.3	6.34	6.38	6.42	6.46	6.5	6.54	6.57	6.61	6.65
170	6.69	6.73	6.77	6.81	6.85	6.89	6.93	6.97	7.01	7.05
180	7.09	7.13	7.17	7.21	7.24	7.28	7.32	7.36	7.4	7.44
190	7.48	7.52	7.56	7.6	7.64	7.68	7.72	7.76	7.8	7.83
200	7.87	7.91	7.95	7.99	8.03	8.07	8.11	8.15	8.19	8.23
210	8.27	8.31	8.35	8.39	8.43	8.46	8.5	8.54	8.58	8.62
220	8.66	8.7	8.74	8.78	8.82	8.86	8.9	8.94	8.98	9.02
230	9.06	9.09	9.13	9.17	9.21	9.25	9.29	9.33	9.37	9.41
240	9.45	9.49	9.53	9.57	9.61	9.65	9.69	9.72	9.76	9.8
250	9.84									

2 decimals of inch to millimetres

in	0.000	0.001	0.002	0.003	0.004	0.005	0.006	0.007	0.008	0.009
	mm									
0.0		0.0254	0.0508	0.0762	0.1016	0.127	0.1524	0.1778	0.2032	0.2286
0.01	0.254	0.2794	0.3048	0.3302	0.3556	0.381	0.4064	0.4318	0.4572	0.4826
0.02	0.508	0.5334	0.5588	0.5842	0.6096	0.635	0.6604	0.6858	0.7112	0.7366
0.03	0.762	0.7874	0.8128	0.8382	0.8636	0.889	0.9144	0.9398	0.9652	0.9906
0.04	1.016	1.0414	1.0668	1.0922	1.1176	1.143	1.1684	1.1938	1.2192	1.2446
0.05	1.27	1.2954	1.3208	1.3462	1.3716	1.397	1.4224	1.4478	1.4732	1.4986
0.06	1.524	1.5494	1.5748	1.6002	1.6256	1.651	1.6764	1.7018	1.7272	1.7526
0.07	1.778	1.8034	1.8288	1.8542	1.8796	1.905	1.9304	1.9558	1.9812	2.0066
0.08	2.032	2.0574	2.0828	2.1082	2.1336	2.159	2.1844	2.2098	2.2352	2.2606
0.09	2.286	2.3114	2.3368	2.3622	2.3876	2.413	2.4384	2.4638	2.4892	2.5146
0.1	2.54									

3 inches and fractions of inch to millimetres

in	1/16	1/8	3/16	1/4	5/16	3/8	7/16	1/2	9/16	5/8	11/16	3/4	13/16	7/8	15/16
	mm														
	1.6	3.2	4.8	6.4	7.9	9.5	11.1	12.7	14.3	15.9	17.5	19.1	20.6	22.2	23.8
1	25.4	27.0	28.6	30.2	31.8	33.3	34.9	36.5	38.1	39.7	41.3	42.9	44.5	46.0	47.6	49.2
2	50.8	52.4	54.0	55.6	57.2	58.7	60.3	61.9	63.5	65.1	66.7	68.3	69.9	71.4	73.0	74.6
3	76.2	77.8	79.4	81.0	82.6	84.1	85.7	87.3	88.9	90.5	92.1	93.7	95.3	96.8	98.4	100.0
4	101.6	103.2	104.8	106.4	108.0	109.5	111.1	112.7	114.3	115.9	117.5	119.1	120.7	122.2	123.8	125.4
5	127.0	128.6	130.2	131.8	133.4	134.9	136.5	138.1	139.7	141.3	142.9	144.5	146.1	147.6	149.2	150.8
6	152.4	154.0	155.6	157.2	158.8	160.3	161.9	163.5	165.1	166.7	168.3	169.9	171.5	173.0	174.6	176.2
7	177.8	179.4	181.0	182.6	184.2	185.7	187.3	188.9	190.5	192.1	193.7	195.3	196.9	198.4	200.0	201.6
8	203.2	204.8	206.4	208.0	209.6	211.1	212.7	214.3	215.9	217.5	219.1	220.7	222.3	223.8	225.4	227.0
9	228.6	230.2	231.8	233.4	235.0	236.5	238.1	239.7	241.3	242.9	244.5	246.1	247.7	249.2	250.8	252.4
10	254.0	255.6	257.2	258.8	260.4	261.9	263.5	265.1	266.7	268.3	269.9	271.5	273.1	274.6	276.2	277.8

4 feet and inches to metres

in	0	1	2	3	4	5	6	7	8	9	10	11
	m											
ft												
0		0.0254	0.0508	0.0762	0.1016	0.127	0.1524	0.1778	0.2032	0.2286	0.254	0.2794
1	0.3048	0.3302	0.3556	0.381	0.4064	0.4318	0.4572	0.4826	0.508	0.5334	0.5588	0.5842
2	0.6096	0.635	0.6604	0.6858	0.7112	0.7366	0.762	0.7874	0.8128	0.8382	0.8636	0.889
3	0.9144	0.9398	0.9652	0.9906	1.016	1.0414	1.0668	1.0922	1.1176	1.143	1.1684	1.1938
4	1.2192	1.2446	1.27	1.2954	1.3208	1.3462	1.3716	1.397	1.4224	1.4478	1.4732	1.4986
5	1.524	1.5494	1.5748	1.6002	1.6256	1.651	1.6764	1.7018	1.7272	1.7526	1.778	1.8034
6	1.8288	1.8542	1.8796	1.905	1.9304	1.9558	1.9812	2.0066	2.032	2.0574	2.0828	2.1082
7	2.1336	2.159	2.1844	2.2098	2.2352	2.2606	2.286	2.3114	2.3368	2.3622	2.3876	2.413
8	2.4384	2.4638	2.4892	2.5146	2.54	2.5654	2.5908	2.6162	2.6416	2.667	2.6924	2.7178
9	2.7432	2.7686	2.794	2.8194	2.8448	2.8702	2.8956	2.921	2.9464	2.9718	2.9972	3.0226
10	3.048											

5 metres to feet

m	0	1	2	3	4	5	6	7	8	9
	ft									
0		3.28	6.56	9.84	13.12	16.40	19.69	22.97	26.25	29.53
10	32.8	36.09	39.37	42.65	45.93	49.21	52.49	55.77	59.06	62.34
20	65.62	68.9	72.17	75.45	78.74	82.02	85.3	88.58	91.86	95.14
30	98.43	101.7	104.99	108.27	111.55	114.82	118.11	121.39	124.67	127.95
40	131.23	134.51	137.8	141.08	144.36	147.63	150.91	154.2	157.48	160.76
50	164.04	167.32	170.6	173.89	177.17	180.45	183.73	187.01	190.29	193.57
60	196.85	200.13	203.41	206.69	209.97	213.25	216.54	219.82	223.1	226.38
70	229.66	232.94	236.22	239.5	242.78	246.06	249.34	252.63	255.91	259.19
80	262.46	265.75	269.03	272.31	275.59	278.87	282.15	285.43	288.71	292.0
90	295.28	298.56	301.84	305.12	308.4	311.68	314.96	318.24	321.52	324.8
100	328.08	331.37	334.65	337.93	341.21	344.49	347.77	351.05	354.33	357.61
110	360.89	364.17	367.45	370.74	374.02	377.3	380.58	383.86	387.14	390.42
120	393.7	396.98	400.26	403.54	406.82	410.1	413.39	416.67	419.95	423.23
130	426.51	429.79	433.07	436.35	439.63	442.91	446.19	449.48	452.76	456.04
140	459.32	462.6	465.88	469.16	472.44	475.72	479.0	482.28	485.56	488.85
150	492.13	495.41	498.69	502.0	505.25	508.53	511.81	515.09	518.37	521.65
160	524.93	528.22	531.5	534.78	538.06	541.34	544.62	547.9	551.18	554.46
170	557.74	561.02	564.3	567.59	570.87	574.15	577.43	580.71	583.99	587.27
180	590.55	593.83	597.11	600.39	603.68	606.96	610.24	613.52	616.8	620.08
190	623.36	626.64	629.92	633.2	636.48	639.76	643.05	646.33	649.6	652.89
200	656.17	659.45	662.73	666.01	669.29	672.57	675.85	679.13	682.42	685.7
210	688.98	692.26	695.54	698.82	702.1	705.38	708.66	711.94	715.22	718.5
220	721.79	725.07	728.35	731.63	734.91	738.19	741.47	744.75	748.03	751.31
230	754.59	757.87	761.16	764.44	767.72	771.0	774.28	777.56	780.84	784.12
240	787.4	790.68	793.96	797.24	800.53	803.81	807.09	810.37	813.65	816.93
250	820.21									

7 metres to yards

m	0	1	2	3	4	5	6	7	8	9
	yd									
0		1.09	2.19	3.28	4.37	5.47	6.56	7.66	8.75	9.84
10	10.94	12.03	13.12	14.22	15.31	16.4	17.5	18.59	19.69	20.78
20	21.87	22.97	24.06	25.15	26.25	27.34	28.43	29.53	30.62	31.71
30	32.8	33.9	35.0	36.09	37.18	38.28	39.37	40.46	41.56	42.65
40	43.74	44.84	45.93	47.03	48.12	49.21	50.31	51.4	52.49	53.59
50	54.68	55.77	56.87	57.96	59.06	60.15	61.24	62.34	63.43	64.52
60	65.62	66.71	67.8	68.9	69.99	71.08	72.18	73.27	74.37	75.46
70	76.55	77.65	78.74	79.83	80.93	82.02	83.11	84.21	85.3	86.4
80	87.49	88.58	89.68	90.77	91.86	92.96	94.05	95.14	96.24	97.33
90	98.43	99.52	100.61	101.71	102.8	103.89	104.99	106.08	107.17	108.27
100	109.36	110.46	111.55	112.64	113.74	114.83	115.92	117.02	118.11	119.2
110	120.3	121.39	122.49	123.58	124.67	125.74	126.86	127.95	129.05	130.14
120	131.23	132.33	133.42	134.51	135.61	136.7	137.8	138.89	139.99	141.08
130	142.17	143.26	144.36	145.45	146.54	147.64	148.73	149.83	150.92	152.01
140	153.1	154.2	155.29	156.39	157.48	158.57	159.67	160.76	161.86	162.95
150	164.04	165.14	166.23	167.32	168.42	169.51	170.6	171.7	172.79	173.89
160	174.98	176.07	177.17	178.26	179.35	180.45	181.54	182.63	183.73	184.82
170	185.91	187.0	188.1	189.2	190.29	191.38	192.48	193.57	194.66	195.76
180	196.85	197.94	199.04	200.13	201.23	202.32	203.41	204.51	205.6	206.69
190	207.79	208.88	209.97	211.07	212.16	213.26	214.35	215.44	216.53	217.63
200	218.72	219.82	220.91	222.0	223.1	224.19	225.28	226.38	227.47	228.57
210	229.66	230.75	231.85	232.94	234.03	235.13	236.22	237.31	238.41	239.5
220	240.56	241.69	242.78	243.88	244.97	246.06	247.16	248.25	249.34	250.44
230	251.53	252.63	253.72	254.81	255.91	257.0	258.09	259.19	260.28	261.37
240	262.47	263.56	264.65	265.75	266.84	267.94	269.03	270.12	271.22	272.31
250	273.4									

9 kilometres to miles

km	0	1	2	3	4	5	6	7	8	9
	mile									
0		0.62	1.24	1.86	2.49	3.11	3.73	4.35	4.98	5.59
10	6.21	6.84	7.46	8.08	8.7	9.32	9.94	10.56	11.18	11.81
20	12.43	13.05	13.67	14.29	14.91	15.53	16.16	16.78	17.4	18.02
30	18.64	19.29	19.88	20.5	21.13	21.75	22.37	22.99	23.61	24.23
40	24.85	25.47	26.1	26.72	27.34	27.96	28.58	29.2	29.83	30.45
50	31.07	31.69	32.31	32.93	33.55	34.18	34.8	35.42	36.04	36.66
60	37.28	37.9	38.53	39.15	39.77	40.39	41.01	41.63	42.25	42.87
70	43.5	44.12	44.74	45.36	45.98	46.6	47.22	47.85	48.47	49.09
80	49.7	50.33	50.95	51.57	52.2	52.82	53.44	54.06	54.68	55.3
90	55.92	56.54	57.17	57.79	58.41	59.03	59.65	60.27	60.89	61.52
100	62.14									

6 feet to metres

ft	0	1	2	3	4	5	6	7	8	9
	m									
0		0.31	0.6	0.91	1.22	1.52	1.83	2.13	2.44	2.74
10	3.05	3.35	3.66	3.96	4.27	4.57	4.88	5.18	5.49	5.79
20	6.1	6.4	6.71	7.01	7.31	7.62	7.92	8.23	8.53	8.84
30	9.14	9.45	9.75	10.06	10.36	10.67	10.97	11.28	11.58	11.89
40	12.19	12.5	12.80	13.1	13.41	13.72	14.02	14.36	14.63	14.94
50	15.24	15.54	15.85	16.15	16.46	16.76	17.07	17.37	17.68	17.98
60	18.29	18.59	18.9	19.2	19.58	19.81	20.12	20.42	20.73	21.03
70	21.33	21.64	21.95	22.25	22.56	22.86	23.16	23.47	23.77	24.08
80	24.38	24.69	24.99	25.3	25.6	25.91	26.21	26.52	26.82	27.13
90	27.43	27.74	28.04	28.35	28.65	28.96	29.26	29.57	29.87	30.18
100	30.48	30.78	31.09	31.39	31.7	32.0	32.31	32.61	32.92	33.22
110	33.53	33.83	34.14	34.44	34.75	35.05	35.37	35.67	36.0	36.3
120	36.58	36.88	37.19	37.49	37.8	38.1	38.41	38.7	39.01	39.32
130	39.62	39.93	40.23	40.54	40.84	41.15	41.45	41.76	42.06	42.37
140	42.67	42.98	43.28	43.59	43.89	44.2	44.5	44.81	45.11	45.46
150	45.72	46.02	46.33	46.63	46.94	47.24	47.55	47.85	48.16	48.46
160	48.77	49.07	49.38	49.68	49.99	50.29	50.6	50.9	51.21	51.51
170	51.82	52.12	52.43	52.73	53.04	53.34	53.64	53.95	54.25	54.56
180	54.86	55.17	55.47	55.78	56.08	56.39	56.69	57.0	57.3	57.61
190	57.91	58.22	58.52	58.83	59.13	59.44	59.74	60.05	60.35	60.66
200	60.96	61.26	61.57	61.87	62.18	62.48	62.79	63.09	63.4	63.7
210	64.01	64.31	64.62	64.92	65.23	65.53	65.84	66.14	66.45	66.75
220	67.06	67.36	67.67	67.97	68.28	68.58	68.89	69.19	69.49	69.79
230	70.1	70.41	70.71	71.02	71.32	71.63	71.93	72.24	72.54	72.85
240	73.15	73.46	73.76	74.07	74.37	74.68	74.98	75.29	75.59	75.9
250	76.2									

8 yards to metres

yd	0	1	2	3	4	5	6	7	8	9
	m									
0		0.91	1.83	2.74	3.65	4.57	5.49	6.4	7.32	8.23
10	9.14	10.06	10.97	11.89	12.8	13.71	14.63	15.54	16.46	17.37
20	18.29	19.2	20.12	21.03	21.95	22.86	23.77	24.69	25.6	26.52
30	27.43	28.35	29.26	30.18	31.09	32.0	32.92	33.83	34.75	35.66
40	36.58	37.49	38.4	39.32	40.23	41.15	42.06	42.98	43.89	44.81
50	45.72	46.63	47.55	48.46	49.38	50.29	51.21	52.12	53.04	53.95
60	54.86	55.78	56.69	57.61	58.52	59.44	60.35	61.27	62.18	63.09
70	64.0	64.92	65.84	66.75	67.67	68.58	69.49	70.41	71.32	72.24
80	73.15	74.07	74.98	75.9	76.81	77.72	78.64	79.55	80.47	81.38
90	82.3	83.21	84.12	85.04	85.95	86.87	87.78	88.7	89.61	90.53
100	91.44	92.35	93.27	94.18	95.1	96.01	96.93	97.84	98.76	99.67
110	100.58	101.5	102.41	103.33	104.24	105.16	106.07	106.99	107.9	108.81
120	109.73	110.64	111.56	112.47	113.39	114.3	115.21	116.13	117.04	117.96
130	118.87	119.79	120.7	121.61	122.53	123.44	124.36	125.27	126.19	127.1
140	128.02	128.93	129.85	130.76	131.67	132.59	133.5	134.42	135.33	136.25
150	137.16	138.07	138.99	139.9	140.82	141.73	142.65	143.56	144.48	145.39
160	146.3	147.22	148.13	149.05	149.96	150.88	151.79	152.71	153.62	154.53
170	155.45	156.36	157.28	158.19	159.11	160.02	160.93	161.85	162.76	163.68
180	164.59	165.51	166.42	167.34	168.25	169.16	170.08	170.99	171.9	172.82
190	173.74	174.65	175.57	176.48	177.39	178.31	179.22	180.14	181.05	181.97
200	182.88	183.79	184.71	185.62	186.54	187.45	188.37	189.28	190.2	191.11
210	192.02	192.94	193.85	194.77	195.68	196.6	197.51	198.43	199.34	200.25
220	201.17	202.08	203.0	203.91	204.83	205.74	206.65	207.57	208.48	209.4
230	210.31	211.23	212.14	213.06	213.97	214.88	215.8	216.71	217.63	218.54
240	219.46	220.37	221.29	222.0	223.11	224.03	224.94	225.86	226.77	227.69
250	228.6									

10 miles to kilometres

mile	0	1	2	3	4	5	6	7	8	9
	km									
0		1.61	3.22	4.83	6.44	8.05	9.66	11.27	12.87	14.48
10	16.09	17.7	19.31	20.92	22.53	24.14	25.75	27.36	28.97	30.58
20	32.19	33.8	35.41	37.01	38.62	40.23	41.84	43.45	45.06	46.67
30	48.28	49.89	51.5	53.11	54.72	56.33	57.94	59.55	61.16	62.76
40	64.37	65.98	67.59	69.2	70.81	72.42	74.03	75.64	77.25	78.86
50	80.47	82.08	83.69	85.3	86.9	88.51	90.12	91.73	93.34	94.95
60	96.56	98.17	99.78	101.39	103.0	104.61	106.22	107.83	109.44	111.05
70	112.65	114.26	115.87	117.48	119.09	120.7	122.31	123.92	125.53	127.14
80	128.75	130.36	131.97	133.58	135.19	136.79	138.4	140.01	141.62	143.23
90	144.84	146.45	148.06	149.67	151.28	152.89	154.5	156.11	157.72	159.33
100	160.93									

Area

11 square centimetres to square inches

cm²	0	1	2	3	4	5	6	7	8	9
	in²									
0		0.16	0.31	0.47	0.62	0.78	0.93	1.09	1.24	1.4
10	1.6	1.71	1.86	2.02	2.17	2.33	2.48	2.64	2.79	2.95
20	3.1	3.26	3.41	3.57	3.72	3.88	4.03	4.19	4.34	4.5
30	4.65	4.81	4.96	5.12	5.27	5.43	5.58	5.74	5.9	6.05
40	6.2	6.36	6.51	6.67	6.82	6.98	7.13	7.29	7.44	7.6
50	7.75	7.91	8.06	8.22	8.37	8.53	8.68	8.84	9.0	9.15
60	9.3	9.46	9.61	9.77	9.92	10.08	10.23	10.39	10.54	10.7
70	10.85	11.01	11.16	11.32	11.47	11.63	11.78	11.94	12.09	12.25
80	12.4	12.56	12.71	12.87	13.02	13.18	13.33	13.49	13.64	13.8
90	13.95	14.11	14.26	14.42	14.57	14.73	14.88	15.04	15.19	15.35
100	15.5	15.66	15.81	15.97	16.12	16.28	16.43	16.59	16.74	16.9
110	17.05	17.21	17.36	17.52	17.67	17.83	17.98	18.14	18.29	18.45
120	18.6	18.76	18.91	19.07	19.22	19.38	19.53	19.69	19.84	20.0
130	20.15	20.31	20.46	20.62	20.77	20.93	21.08	21.24	21.39	21.55
140	21.7	21.86	22.01	22.17	22.32	22.48	22.63	22.79	22.94	23.1
150	23.25	23.41	23.56	23.72	23.87	24.03	24.18	24.34	24.49	24.65
160	24.8	24.96	25.11	25.27	25.42	25.58	25.73	25.89	26.04	26.2
170	26.35	26.51	26.66	26.82	26.97	27.13	27.28	27.44	27.59	27.75
180	27.9	28.06	28.21	28.37	28.52	28.68	28.83	28.99	29.14	29.3
190	29.45	29.61	29.76	29.92	30.07	30.23	30.38	30.54	30.69	30.85
200	31.0	31.16	31.31	31.47	31.62	31.78	31.93	32.09	32.24	32.4
210	32.55	32.71	32.86	33.02	33.17	33.33	33.48	33.64	33.79	33.95
220	34.1	34.26	34.41	34.57	34.72	34.88	35.03	35.19	35.34	35.5
230	35.65	35.81	35.96	36.12	36.27	36.43	36.58	36.75	36.89	37.05
240	37.20	37.36	37.51	37.67	37.82	37.98	38.13	38.29	38.44	38.6
250	38.75									

13 square metres to square feet

m²	0	1	2	3	4	5	6	7	8	9
	ft²									
0		10.76	21.53	32.29	43.06	53.82	64.58	75.35	86.11	96.88
10	107.64	118.4	129.17	139.93	150.66	161.46	172.22	182.97	193.75	204.51
20	215.29	226.01	236.81	247.57	258.33	269.1	279.86	290.63	301.39	312.15
30	322.92	333.68	344.45	355.21	365.97	376.74	387.5	398.27	409.03	419.79
40	430.56	441.32	452.08	462.85	473.61	484.38	495.14	505.91	516.67	527.43
50	538.2	548.96	559.72	570.49	581.25	592.02	602.78	613.54	624.31	635.07
60	645.84	656.6	667.36	678.13	688.89	699.65	710.42	721.18	731.95	742.71
70	753.47	764.24	775.0	785.77	796.53	807.29	818.06	828.82	839.59	850.35
80	861.11	871.88	882.64	893.41	904.17	914.93	925.7	936.46	947.22	957.99
90	968.75	979.52	990.28	1 001.04	1 011.81	1 022.57	1 033.34	1 044.1	1 054.86	1 065.63
100	1 076.39	1 087.15	1 097.92	1 108.68	1 119.45	1 130.21	1 140.97	1 151.74	1 162.5	1 173.27
110	1 184.03	1 194.79	1 205.56	1 216.32	1 227.09	1 237.85	1 248.61	1 259.38	1 270.14	1 280.91
120	1 291.67	1 302.43	1 313.2	1 323.96	1 334.72	1 345.49	1 356.25	1 367.02	1 377.78	1 388.54
130	1 399.31	1 410.07	1 420.84	1 431.6	1 442.36	1 453.13	1 463.89	1 474.66	1 485.42	1 496.18
140	1 506.95	1 517.71	1 528.48	1 539.24	1 550.0	1 560.77	1 571.53	1 582.29	1 593.06	1 603.82
150	1 614.59	1 625.35	1 636.11	1 646.88	1 657.64	1 668.41	1 679.17	1 689.93	1 700.7	1 711.46
160	1 722.23	1 732.99	1 743.75	1 754.52	1 765.28	1 776.05	1 786.81	1 797.57	1 808.34	1 819.1
170	1 829.86	1 840.63	1 851.39	1 862.16	1 872.92	1 883.68	1 894.45	1 905.21	1 915.98	1 926.74
180	1 937.5	1 948.27	1 959.03	1 969.8	1 980.56	1 991.32	2 002.09	2 012.85	2 023.62	2 034.38
190	2 045.14	2 055.91	2 066.67	2 077.43	2 088.2	2 098.96	2 109.73	2 120.49	2 131.25	2 142.02
200	2 152.78	2 163.55	2 174.31	2 185.07	2 195.84	2 206.6	2 217.37	2 228.13	2 238.89	2 249.66
210	2 260.42	2 271.19	2 281.95	2 292.71	2 303.48	2 314.24	2 325.0	2 335.77	2 346.53	2 357.3
220	2 368.06	2 378.82	2 389.59	2 400.35	2 411.12	2 421.88	2 432.64	2 443.41	2 454.17	2 464.94
230	2 475.7	2 486.46	2 497.23	2 507.99	2 518.76	2 529.52	2 540.28	2 551.05	2 561.81	2 572.57
240	2 583.34	2 594.1	2 604.87	2 615.63	2 626.39	2 637.16	2 647.92	2 658.69	2 669.45	2 680.21
250	2 690.98	2 701.74	2 712.51	2 723.27	2 734.03	2 744.8	2 755.56	2 766.32	2 777.09	2 787.85
260	2 798.62	2 809.38	2 820.14	2 830.91	2 841.67	2 852.44	2 863.2	2 873.96	2 884.73	2 895.49
270	2 906.26	2 917.02	2 927.78	2 938.55	2 949.31	2 960.08	2 970.84	2 981.6	2 992.37	3 003.13
280	3 013.89	3 024.66	3 035.42	3 046.19	3 056.95	3 067.71	3 078.48	3 089.24	3 100.01	3 110.77
290	3 121.53	3 132.3	3 143.06	3 153.83	3 164.59	3 175.35	3 186.12	3 196.88	3 207.65	3 218.41
300	3 229.17	3 239.94	3 250.7	3 261.46	3 272.23	3 282.99	3 293.76	3 304.52	3 315.28	3 326.05
310	3 336.81	3 347.58	3 358.34	3 369.1	3 379.87	3 390.63	3 401.4	3 412.16	3 422.92	3 433.69
320	3 444.45	3 455.22	3 465.98	3 476.74	3 487.51	3 498.27	3 509.03	3 519.8	3 530.56	3 541.33
330	3 552.09	3 562.85	3 573.62	3 584.38	3 595.15	3 605.91	3 616.67	3 627.44	3 638.2	3 648.97
340	3 659.73	3 670.49	3 681.26	3 692.02	3 702.79	3 713.55	3 724.31	3 735.08	3 745.84	3 756.6
350	3 767.37	3 778.13	3 788.9	3 799.66	3 810.42	3 821.19	3 831.95	3 842.72	3 853.48	3 864.24
360	3 875.01	3 885.77	3 896.54	3 907.3	3 918.06	3 928.83	3 939.59	3 950.36	3 961.12	3 971.88
370	3 982.65	3 993.41	4 004.17	4 014.94	4 025.7	4 036.47	4 047.23	4 057.99	4 068.76	4 079.52
380	4 090.29	4 101.05	4 111.81	4 122.58	4 133.34	4 144.11	4 154.87	4 165.63	4 176.4	4 187.16
390	4 197.93	4 208.69	4 219.45	4 230.22	4 240.98	4 251.74	4 262.51	4 273.27	4 284.04	4 294.8
400	4 305.56	4 316.33	4 327.09	4 337.86	4 348.62	4 359.38	4 370.15	4 380.91	4 391.68	4 402.44
410	4 413.2	4 423.97	4 434.73	4 445.49	4 456.26	4 467.02	4 477.79	4 488.55	4 499.31	4 510.08
420	4 520.84	4 531.61	4 542.37	4 553.13	4 563.9	4 574.66	4 585.43	4 596.19	4 606.95	4 617.72
430	4 628.48	4 639.25	4 650.01	4 660.77	4 671.54	4 682.3	4 693.06	4 703.83	4 714.59	4 725.36
440	4 736.12	4 746.88	4 757.65	4 768.41	4 779.18	4 789.94	4 800.7	4 811.47	4 822.23	4 833.0
450	4 843.76	4 854.52	4 865.29	4 876.05	4 886.82	4 897.58	4 908.34	4 919.11	4 929.87	4 940.63
460	4 951.4	4 962.16	4 972.93	4 983.69	4 994.45	5 005.22	5 015.98	5 026.75	5 037.51	5 048.27
470	5 059.04	5 069.8	5 080.57	5 091.33	5 102.09	5 112.86	5 123.62	5 134.39	5 145.15	5 155.91
480	5 166.68	5 177.44	5 188.2	5 198.97	5 209.73	5 220.5	5 231.26	5 242.02	5 252.79	5 263.55
490	5 274.32	5 285.08	5 295.84	5 306.61	5 317.37	5 328.14	5 338.9	5 349.66	5 360.43	5 371.19
500	5 381.96									

in²	0	1	2	3	4	5	6	7	8	9
	cm²									
0		6.45	12.9	19.36	25.81	32.26	38.71	45.16	51.61	58.06
10	64.52	70.97	77.41	83.87	90.32	96.77	103.23	109.68	116.13	122.58
20	129.03	135.48	141.94	148.39	154.84	161.29	167.74	174.19	180.65	187.1
30	193.55	200.0	206.45	212.9	219.35	225.8	232.26	238.71	245.16	251.61
40	258.06	264.52	270.97	277.42	283.87	290.32	296.77	303.23	309.68	316.13
50	322.58	329.03	335.48	341.94	348.4	354.84	361.29	367.74	374.19	380.64
60	387.1	393.55	400.0	406.45	412.91	419.35	425.81	432.26	438.71	445.16
70	451.61	458.06	464.52	470.97	477.42	483.87	490.32	496.77	503.23	509.68
80	516.13	522.58	529.03	535.48	541.93	548.39	554.84	561.29	567.74	574.19
90	580.64	587.1	593.55	600.0	606.45	612.91	619.35	625.81	632.26	638.71
100	645.16	651.61	658.06	664.51	670.97	677.42	683.87	690.32	696.77	703.22
110	709.6	716.13	722.58	729.03	735.48	741.93	748.39	754.84	761.29	767.74
120	774.19	780.64	787.1	793.55	800.0	806.45	812.9	819.35	825.81	832.26
130	838.71	845.16	851.61	858.06	864.51	870.97	877.42	883.87	890.32	896.77
140	903.22	909.68	916.13	922.58	929.03	935.48	941.93	948.39	954.84	961.29
150	967.74	974.19	980.64	987.1	993.55	1 000.00	1 006.45	1 012.9	1 019.35	1 025.8
160	1 032.26	1 038.71	1 045.16	1 051.61	1 058.06	1 064.51	1 070.97	1 077.42	1 083.87	1 090.32
170	1 096.77	1 103.22	1 109.68	1 116.13	1 122.58	1 129.03	1 135.48	1 141.93	1 148.38	1 154.84
180	1 161.29	1 167.74	1 174.19	1 180.64	1 187.09	1 193.55	1 200.0	1 206.45	1 212.9	1 219.35
190	1 225.8	1 232.26	1 238.71	1 245.16	1 251.61	1 258.06	1 264.51	1 270.97	1 277.42	1 283.87
200	1 290.32	1 296.77	1 303.22	1 309.67	1 316.13	1 322.58	1 329.03	1 335.48	1 341.93	1 348.38
210	1 354.84	1 361.29	1 367.74	1 374.19	1 380.64	1 387.09	1 393.55	1 400.0	1 406.45	1 412.9
220	1 419.35	1 425.8	1 432.26	1 438.71	1 445.16	1 451.61	1 458.06	1 464.51	1 470.96	1 477.42
230	1 483.87	1 490.32	1 496.77	1 503.22	1 509.67	1 516.13	1 522.58	1 529.03	1 535.48	1 541.93
240	1 548.38	1 554.84	1 561.29	1 567.74	1 574.19	1 580.64	1 587.09	1 593.55	1 600.0	1 606.45
250	1 612.9									

12
square
inches
to square
centimetres

ft²	0	1	2	3	4	5	6	7	8	9
	m²									
0		0.09	0.19	0.28	0.37	0.46	0.56	0.65	0.74	0.84
10	0.93	1.02	1.11	1.21	1.3	1.39	1.49	1.58	1.67	1.77
20	1.86	1.95	2.04	2.14	2.23	2.32	2.42	2.51	2.6	2.69
30	2.79	2.88	2.97	3.07	3.16	3.25	3.34	3.44	3.53	3.62
40	3.72	3.81	3.9	3.99	4.09	4.18	4.27	4.37	4.46	4.55
50	4.65	4.74	4.83	4.92	5.02	5.11	5.2	5.3	5.39	5.48
60	5.57	5.67	5.76	5.85	5.95	6.04	6.13	6.22	6.32	6.41
70	6.5	6.6	6.69	6.78	6.87	6.97	7.06	7.15	7.25	7.34
80	7.43	7.53	7.62	7.71	7.8	7.9	7.99	8.08	8.18	8.27
90	8.36	8.45	8.55	8.64	8.73	8.83	8.92	9.01	9.1	9.2
100	9.29	9.38	9.48	9.57	9.66	9.75	9.85	9.94	10.03	10.13
110	10.22	10.31	10.41	10.5	10.59	10.68	10.78	10.87	10.96	11.06
120	11.15	11.24	11.33	11.43	11.52	11.61	11.71	11.8	11,89	11.98
130	12.08	12.17	12.26	12.36	12.45	12.54	12.63	12.73	12.82	12.91
140	13.01	13.1	13.19	13.29	13.38	13.47	13.56	13.66	13.75	13.84
150	13.94	14.03	14.12	14.21	14.31	14.4	14.49	14.59	14.68	14.77
160	14.86	14.96	15.05	15.14	15.24	15.33	15.42	15.51	15.61	15.7
170	15.79	15.89	15.98	16.07	16.17	16.26	16.35	16.44	16.54	16.63
180	16.72	16.82	16.91	17.0	17.09	17.19	17.28	17.37	17.47	17.56
190	17.65	17.74	17.84	17.93	18.02	18.12	18.21	18.3	18.39	18.49
200	18.58	18.67	18.77	18.86	18.95	19.05	19.14	19.23	19.32	19.42
210	19.51	19.6	19.7	19.79	19.88	19.97	20.07	20.16	20.25	20.35
220	20.44	20.53	20.62	20.72	20.81	20.9	21.0	21.09	21.18	21.27
230	21.37	21.46	21.55	21.65	21.74	21.83	21.93	22.02	22.11	22.2
240	22.3	22.39	22.48	22.58	22.67	22.76	22.85	22.95	23.04	23.13
250	23.23	23.32	23.41	23.5	23.6	23.69	23.78	23.88	23.97	24.06
260	24.15	24.25	24.34	24.43	24.53	24.62	24.71	24.81	24.9	24.99
270	25.08	25.18	25.27	25.36	25.46	25.55	25.64	25.73	25.83	25.92
280	26.01	26.11	26.2	26.29	26.38	26.48	26.57	26.66	26.76	26.85
290	26.94	27.03	27.13	27.22	27.31	27.41	27.5	27.59	27.69	27.78
300	27.87	27.96	28.06	28.15	28.24	28.34	28.43	28.52	28.61	28.71
310	28.8	28.89	28.99	29.08	29.17	29.26	29.36	29.45	29.54	29.64
320	29.73	29.82	29.91	30.01	30.1	30.19	30.29	30.38	30.47	30.57
330	30.66	30.75	30.84	30.94	31.03	31.12	31.22	31.31	31.4	31.49
340	31.59	31.68	31.77	31.87	31.96	32.05	32.14	32.24	32.33	32.42
350	32.52	32.61	32.7	32.79	32.89	32.98	33.07	33.17	33.26	33.35
360	33.45	33.54	33.63	33.72	33.82	33.91	34.0	34.1	34.19	34.28
370	34.37	34.47	34.56	34.65	34.75	34.84	34.93	35.02	35.12	35.21
380	35.3	35.4	35.49	35.58	35.67	35.77	35.86	35.95	36.05	36.14
390	36.23	36.33	36.42	36.51	36.6	36.7	36.79	36.88	36.98	37.07
400	37.16	37.25	37.35	37.44	37.53	37.63	37.72	37.81	37.9	38.0
410	38.09	38.18	38.28	38.37	38.46	38.55	38.65	38.74	38.83	38.93
420	39.02	39.11	39.21	39.3	39.39	39.48	39.58	39.67	39.76	39.86
430	39.95	40.04	40.13	40.23	40.32	40.41	40.51	40.6	40.69	40.78
440	40.88	40.97	41.06	41.16	41.25	41.34	41.43	41.53	41.62	41.71
450	41.81	41.9	41.99	42.09	42.18	42.27	42.36	42.46	42.55	42.64
460	42.74	42.83	42.92	43.01	43.11	43.2	43.29	43.39	43.48	43.57
470	43.66	43.76	43.85	43.94	44.04	44.13	44.22	44.31	44.41	44.5
480	44.59	44.69	44.78	44.87	44.97	45.06	45.15	45.24	45.34	45.43
490	45.52	45.62	45.71	45.8	45.89	45.99	46.08	46.17	46.27	46.36
500	46.45									

14
square feet
to square
metres

15
square
metres
to square
yards

m²	0	1	2	3	4	5	6	7	8	9
	yd²									
0		1.2	2.39	3.58	4.78	5.98	7.18	8.37	9.57	10.76
10	11.96	13.16	14.35	15.55	16.74	17.94	19.14	20.33	21.53	22.72
20	23.92	25.12	26.31	27.51	28.7	29.9	31.1	32.29	33.49	34.68
30	35.88	37.08	38.27	39.47	40.66	41.86	43.06	44.25	45.45	46.64
40	47.84	49.04	50.23	51.43	52.62	53.82	55.02	56.21	57.41	58.6
50	59.8	61.0	62.19	63.39	64.58	65.78	66.98	68.17	69.37	70.56
60	71.76	72.96	74.15	75.35	76.54	77.74	78.94	80.13	81.33	82.52
70	83.72	84.92	86.11	87.31	88.5	89.7	90.9	92.09	93.29	94.48
80	95.68	96.88	98.07	99.27	100.46	101.66	102.86	104.05	105.25	106.44
90	107.64	108.84	110.03	111.23	112.42	113.62	114.82	116.01	117.21	118.4
100	119.6	120.8	121.99	123.19	124.38	125.58	126.78	127.97	129.17	130.36
110	131.56	132.76	133.95	135.15	136.34	137.54	138.74	139.93	141.13	142.32
120	143.52	144.72	145.91	147.11	148.31	149.5	150.7	151.89	153.09	154.28
130	155.48	156.68	157.87	159.07	160.26	161.46	162.66	163.85	165.05	166.24
140	167.44	168.64	169.83	171.03	172.22	173.41	174.62	175.81	177.01	178.2
150	179.34	180.59	181.79	182.99	184.18	185.38	186.57	187.77	188.97	190.16
160	191.36	192.55	193.75	194.95	196.14	197.34	198.53	199.73	200.93	202.12
170	203.32	204.51	205.71	206.91	208.1	209.3	210.49	211.69	212.89	214.08
180	215.28	216.47	217.67	218.87	220.06	221.26	222.45	223.65	224.85	226.04
190	227.24	228.43	229.63	230.83	232.02	233.22	234.41	235.61	236.81	238.0
200	239.2	240.39·	241.59	242.79	243.98	245.18	246.37	247.57	248.77	249.96
210	251.16	252.35	253.55	254.75	255.94	257.14	258.33	259.53	260.73	261.92
220	263.12	264.31	265.51	266.71	267.9	269.1	270.29	271.49	272.69	273.88
230	275.08	276.27	277.47	278.67	279.86	281.06	282.25	283.45	284.65	285.84
240	287.04	288.23	289.43	290.63	291.82	293.02	294.21	295.41	296.61	297.8
250	299.0	300.19	301.39	302.59	303.78	304.98	306.17	307.37	308.57	309.76
260	310.96	312.15	313.35	314.55	315.74	316.94	318.13	319.33	320.53	321.72
270	322.92	324.11	325.31	326.51	327.7	328.9	330.09	331.29	332.49	333.68
280	334.88	336.07	337.27	338.47	339.66	340.86	342.05	343.25	344.45	345.64
290	346.84	348.03	349.23	350.43	351.62	352.82	354.02	355.21	356.41	357.6
300	358.78	359.99	361.19	362.39	363.58	364.78	365.97	367.17	368.37	369.56
310	370.76	371.95	373.15	374.35	375.54	376.74	377.94	379.13	380.33	381.52
320	382.72	383.91	385.11	386.31	387.5	388.7	389.89	391.09	392.29	393.48
330	394.68	395.87	397.07	398.27	399.46	400.66	401.85	403.05	404.25	405.44
340	406.64	407.83	409.03	410.23	411.42	412.62	413.81	415.01	416.21	417.4
350	418.6	419.79	420.99	422.18	423.38	424.58	425.77	426.97	428.16	429.36
360	430.56	431.75	432.95	434.14	435.34	436.54	437.73	438.93	440.12	441.32
370	442.52	443.71	444.91	446.11	447.3	448.5	449.69	450.89	452.08	453.28
380	454.48	455.67	456.87	458.06	459.26	460.46	461.65	462.84	464.04	465.24
390	466.44	467.63	468.83	470.02	471.22	472.42	473.61	474.81	476.0	477.2
400	478.4	479.59	480.79	481.98	483.18	484.38	485.57	486.77	487.96	489.16
410	490.36	491.55	492.75	493.94	495.14	496.34	497.53	498.73	499.92	501.12
420	502.32	503.51	504.71	505.9	507.1	508.3	509.49	510.69	511.88	513.08
430	514.28	515.47	516.67	517.86	519.06	520.26	521.45	522.65	523.84	525.04
440	526.24	527.43	528.63	529.82	531.02	532.22	533.41	534.61	535.8	537.0
450	538.2	539.39	540.59	541.78	542.98	544.18	545.37	546.57	547.76	548.96
460	550.16	551.35	552.55	553.74	554.94	556.14	557.33	558.53	559.72	560.92
470	562.12	563.31	564.5	565.71	566.9	568.1	569.29	570.49	571.68	572.88
480	574.08	575.27	576.47	577.66	578.86	580.06	581.25	582.45	583.64	584.84
490	586.04	587.23	588.43	589.62	590.82	592.02	593.21	594.41	595.6	596.8
500	598.0									

17
hectares
to acres

ha	0	1	2	3	4	5	6	7	8	9
	acre									
		2.47	4.94	7.41	9.88	12.36	14.83	17.3	19.77	22.24

ha	0	10	20	30	40	50	60	70	80	90
	acre									
0		24.71	49.42	74.13	98.84	123.55	148.26	172.97	197.68	222.4
100	247.11	271.82	296.53	321.24	345.95	370.66	395.37	420.08	444.8	469.5
200	494.21	518.92	543.63	568.34	593.05	617.76	642.47	667.19	691.9	716.61
300	741.32	766.03	790.74	815.45	840.16	864.87	889.58	914.29	939.0	963.71
400	988.42	1 013.13	1 037.84	1 062.55	1 087.26	1 111.97	1 136.68	1 161.4	1 186.11	1 210.82
500	1 235.53	1 260.24	1 284.95	1 309.66	1 334.37	1 359.08	1 383.79	1 408.5	1 433.21	1 457.92
600	1 482.63	1 507.34	1 532.05	1 556.76	1 581.47	1 606.18	1 630.9	1 655.61	1 680.32	1 705.03
700	1 729.74	1 754.45	1 779.16	1 803.87	1 828.58	1 853.29	1 878.0	1 902.71	1 927.42	1 952.13
800	1 976.84	2 001.55	2 026.26	2 050.97	2 075.69	2 100.4	2 125.11	2 149.82	2 174.53	2 199.24
900	2 223.95	2 248.66	2 273.37	2 298.08	2 322.79	2 347.5	2 372.21	2 396.92	2 421.63	2 446.34
1 000	2 471.05									

yd²	0	1	2	3	4	5	6	7	8	9
	m²									
0		0.84	1.67	2.51	3.34	4.18	5.02	5.85	6.69	7.53
10	8.36	9.2	10.03	10.87	11.71	12.54	13.38	14.21	15.05	15.89
20	16.72	17.56	18.39	19.23	20.07	20.9	21.74	22.58	23.41	24.25
30	25.08	25.92	26.76	27.59	28.43	29.26	30.1	30.94	31.77	32.61
40	33.45	34.28	35.12	35.95	36.79	37.63	38.46	39.3	40.13	40.97
50	41.81	42.64	43.48	44.31	45.15	45.99	46.82	47.66	48.5	49.33
60	50.17	51.0	51.84	52.68	53.51	54.35	55.18	56.02	56.86	57.69
70	58.53	59.37	60.2	61.04	61.87	62.71	63.55	64.38	65.22	66.05
80	66.89	67.7	68.56	69.3	70.23	71.07	71.9	72.74	73.5	74.4
90	75.25	76.09	76.92	77.76	78.6	79.43	80.27	81.10	81.94	82.78
100	83.61	84.45	85.29	86.12	86.96	87.79	88.62	89.47	90.3	91.14
110	91.97	92.81	93.65	94.48	95.32	96.15	96.99	97.83	98.66	99.5
120	100.34	101.17	102.0	102.84	103.68	104.52	105.35	106.19	107.02	107.86
130	108.7	109.53	110.37	111.21	112.04	112.88	113.71	114.55	115.39	116.22
140	117.06	117.89	118.73	119.57	120.41	121.24	122.08	122.91	123.75	124.58
150	125.42	126.26	127.09	127.93	128.76	129.6	130.44	131.27	132.11	132.94
160	133.78	134.62	135.45	136.29	137.13	137.96	138.8	139.63	140.47	141.31
170	142.14	142.98	143.81	144.65	145.49	146.32	147.16	148.0	148.83	149.67
180	150.5	151.34	152.18	153.01	153.85	154.68	155.52	156.36	157.19	158.03
190	158.86	159.7	160.54	161.37	162.21	163.05	163.88	164.72	165.55	166.39
200	167.23	168.06	168.9	169.73	170.57	171.41	172.24	173.08	173.91	174.75
210	175.59	176.42	177.26	178.1	178.93	179.77	180.61	181.44	182.28	183.11
220	183.95	184.78	185.62	186.46	187.29	188.13	188.97	189.80	190.64	191.47
230	192.31	193.15	193.98	194.82	195.65	196.49	197.33	198.16	199.0	199.83
240	200.67	201.51	202.34	203.18	204.02	204.85	205.69	206.52	207.36	208.2
250	209.03	209.87	210.7	211.54	212.38	213.21	214.1	214.89	215.72	216.56
260	217.39	218.3	219.07	219.9	220.74	221.57	222.41	223.25	224.08	224.92
270	225.75	226.59	227.43	228.26	229.1	229.94	230.77	231.61	232.44	233.28
280	234.12	234.95	235.79	236.62	237.46	238.3	239.13	239.97	240.81	241.64
290	242.48	243.31	244.15	244.99	245.82	246.66	247.49	248.33	249.17	250.0
300	250.84	251.67	252.51	253.35	254.18	255.02	255.86	256.69	257.53	258.36
310	259.2	260.04	260.87	261.71	262.54	263.38	264.22	265.05	265.89	266.73
320	267.56	268.4	269.23	270.07	270.91	271.74	272.58	273.41	274.25	275.09
330	275.92	276.76	277.59	278.43	279.27	280.11	280.94	281.78	282.61	283.45
340	284.28	285.12	285.96	286.79	287.63	288.46	289.3	290.14	290.97	291.81
350	292.65	293.48	294.32	295.15	295.99	296.83	297.66	298.5	299.33	300.17
360	301.0	301.84	302.68	303.51	304.35	305.19	306.02	306.86	307.7	308.53
370	309.37	310.2	311.04	311.88	312.71	313.55	314.38	315.22	316.06	316.89
380	317.73	318.57	319.4	320.24	321.07	321.91	322.75	323.58	324.42	325.25
390	326.09	326.93	327.76	328.6	329.43	330.27	331.11	331.94	332.78	333.62
400	334.45	335.29	336.12	336.96	337.8	338.63	339.47	340.31	341.14	341.98
410	342.81	343.65	344.48	345.32	346.16	346.99	347.83	348.67	349.51	350.34
420	351.17	352.01	352.85	353.68	354.52	355.35	356.19	357.03	357.86	358.7
430	359.54	360.37	361.21	362.04	362.88	363.72	364.55	365.39	366.22	367.06
440	367.9	368.73	369.57	370.41	371.24	372.08	372.91	373.75	374.59	375.42
450	376.26	377.09	377.93	378.77	379.6	380.44	381.27	382.11	382.95	383.78
460	384.62	385.46	386.29	387.13	387.96	388.8	389.64	390.47	391.31	392.14
470	392.98	393.82	394.65	395.49	396.32	397.16	398.0	398.83	399.67	400.51
480	401.34	402.18	403.01	403.85	404.69	405.52	406.36	407.19	408.03	408.87
490	409.7	410.54	411.38	412.21	413.05	413.88	414.72	415.56	416.39	417.23
500	418.0									

16
square yards
to square
metres

acre	0	1	2	3	4	5	6	7	8	9
	ha									
		0.4	0.81	1.21	1.62	2.02	2.42	2.83	3.23	3.64

acre	0	10	20	30	40	50	60	70	80	90
	ha									
0		4.05	8.09	12.14	16.19	20.23	24.28	28.33	32.37	36.42
100	40.47	44.52	48.56	52.6	56.66	60.71	64.75	68.8	72.84	76.89
200	80.94	84.98	89.03	93.08	97.12	101.17	105.22	109.26	113.31	117.36
300	121.41	125.46	129.5	133.55	137.59	141.64	145.69	149.73	153.78	157.83
400	161.87	165.92	169.97	174.02	178.06	182.11	186.16	190.20	194.25	198.3
500	202.34	206.39	210.44	214.48	218.53	222.58	226.62	230.67	234.71	238.77
600	242.81	246.86	250.91	254.95	259.0	263.05	267.09	271.14	275.19	279.23
700	283.28	287.33	291.37	295.42	299.47	303.51	307.56	311.61	315.66	319.7
800	323.75	327.8	331.84	335.84	339.94	343.98	348.03	352.07	356.12	360.17
900	364.22	368.26	372.31	376.36	380.41	384.45	388.5	392.55	396.59	400.64
1 000	404.69									

18
acres to
hectares

Volume

19
cubic
centimetres
to cubic
inches

cm³	0	1	2	3	4	5	6	7	8	9
in³										
		0.06	0.12	0.18	0.24	0.31	0.37	0.43	0.49	0.55

cm³	0	10	20	30	40	50	60	70	80	90
in³										
0		0.61	1.22	1.83	2.44	3.05	3.66	4.27	4.88	5.49
100	6.1	6.71	7.32	7.93	8.54	9.15	9.76	10.37	10.98	11.59
200	12.2	12.82	13.43	14.04	14.65	15.26	15.87	16.48	17.09	17.7
300	18.31	18.92	19.53	20.14	20.75	21.36	21.97	22.58	23.19	23.8
400	24.41	25.02	25.63	26.24	26.85	27.46	28.07	28.68	29.29	29.9
500	30.51	31.12	31.73	32.34	32.95	33.56	34.17	34.78	35.39	36.0
600	36.61	37.22	37.83	38.45	39.06	39.67	40.28	40.89	41.5	42.11
700	42.72	43.38	43.94	44.55	45.16	45.77	46.38	46.99	47.6	48.21
800	48.82	49.43	50.04	50.65	51.26	51.87	52.48	53.09	53.7	54.31
900	54.92	55.53	56.14	56.75	57.36	57.97	58.58	59.19	59.8	60.41
1 000	61.02									

21
cubic
metres to
cubic feet

m³	0	1	2	3	4	5	6	7	8	9
ft³										
0		35.31	70.63	105.94	141.26	176.57	211.89	247.2	282.52	317.83
10	353.15	388.46	423.78	459.09	494.41	592.72	565.04	600.35	635.67	670.98
20	706.29	741.61	776.92	812.24	847.55	882.87	918.18	953.5	988.81	1 024.13
30	1 059.44	1 094.75	1 130.07	1 165.38	1 200.7	1 236.01	1 271.33	1 306.64	1 341.96	1 377.27
40	1 412.59	1 447.9	1 483.22	1 518.53	1 553.85	1 589.16	1 624.47	1 659.79	1 695.1	1 730.42
50	1 765.73	1 801.05	1 836.36	1 871.68	1 906.99	1 942.31	1 977.62	2 012.94	2 048.25	2 083.57
60	2 118.88	2 154.19	2 189.51	2 224.82	2 260.14	2 295.45	2 330.77	2 366.08	2 401.4	2 436.71
70	2 472.03	2 507.34	2 542.66	2 577.97	2 613.29	2 648.6	2 683.91	2 719.23	2 754.54	2 789.86
80	2 825.17	2 860.49	2 895.8	2 931.12	2 966.43	3 001.75	3 037.06	3 072.38	3 107.69	3 143.01
90	3 178.32	3 213.63	3 248.95	3 284.26	3 319.58	3 354.89	3 390.21	3 425.52	3 460.84	3 496.15
100	3 531.47	3 566.78	3 602.1	3 637.41	3 672.73	3 708.04	3 743.35	3 778.67	3 813.98	3 849.3
110	3 884.61	3 919.93	3 955.24	3 990.56	4 025.87	4 061.19	4 096.5	4 131.82	4 167.13	4 202.45
120	4 237.76	4 273.07	4 308.39	4 343.7	4 379.02	4 414.33	4 449.65	4 484.96	4 520.28	4 555.59
130	4 590.91	4 626.22	4 661.54	4 696.85	4 732.17	4 767.48	4 802.79	4 838.11	4 873.42	4 908.74
140	4 944.05	4 979.37	5 014.68	5 050.0	5 085.31	5 120.63	5 155.94	5 191.26	5 226.57	5 261.89
150	5 297.2	5 332.51	5 367.83	5 403.14	5 438.46	5 473.77	5 509.09	5 544.4	5 579.72	5 615.03
160	5 650.35	5 685.66	5 720.98	5 756.29	5 791.61	5 826.92	5 862.23	5 897.55	5 932.86	5 968.18
170	6 003.49	6 038.81	6 074.12	6 109.44	6 144.75	6 180.07	6 215.38	6 250.7	6 286.01	6 321.33
180	6 356.64	6 391.95	6 427.27	6 462.58	6 497.9	6 533.21	6 568.53	6 603.84	6 639.16	6 674.47
190	6 709.79	6 745.1	6 780.42	6 815.73	6 851.05	6 886.36	6 921.67	6 956.99	6 992.3	7 027.62
200	7 062.93	7 098.25	7 133.56	7 168.88	7 204.19	7 239.51	7 274.82	7 310.14	7 345.45	7 380.77
210	7 416.08	7 451.39	7 486.71	7 522.02	7 557.34	7 592.65	7 627.97	7 663.28	7 698.6	7 733.91
220	7 769.23	7 804.54	7 839.86	7 875.17	7 910.49	7 945.8	7 981.11	8 016.43	8 051.74	8 087.06
230	8 122.37	8 157.69	8 193.0	8 228.32	8 263.63	8 298.95	8 334.26	8 369.58	8 404.89	8 440.21
240	8 475.52	8 510.83	8 546.15	8 581.46	8 616.78	8 652.09	8 687.41	8 722.72	8 758.04	8 793.35
250	8 828.67									

23
litres to
cubic feet

litre	0	1	2	3	4	5	6	7	8	9
ft³										
0		0.04	0.07	0.11	0.14	0.18	0.21	0.25	0.28	0.32
10	0.35	0.39	0.42	0.46	0.49	0.53	0.57	0.60	0.64	0.67
20	0.71	0.74	0.78	0.81	0.85	0.88	0.92	0.95	0.99	1.02
30	1.06	1.09	1.13	1.17	1.2	1.24	1.27	1.31	1.34	1.38
40	1.41	1.45	1.48	1.52	1.55	1.59	1.62	1.66	1.7	1.73
50	1.77	1.8	1.84	1.87	1.91	1.94	1.98	2.01	2.05	2.08
60	2.12	2.15	2.19	2.22	2.26	2.3	2.33	2.37	2.4	2.44
70	2.47	2.51	2.54	2.58	2.61	2.65	2.68	2.72	2.75	2.79
80	2.83	2.86	2.9	2.93	2.97	3.0	3.04	3.07	3.11	3.14
90	3.18	3.21	3.25	3.28	3.32	3.35	3.39	3.42	3.46	3.5
100	3.53									

in³	0	1	2	3	4	5	6	7	8	9
cm³										
		16.39	32.77	49.16	65.55	81.94	98.32	114.71	131.1	147.48

20
cubic inches
to cubic
centimetres

in³	0	10	20	30	40	50	60	70	80	90
cm³										
0		163.87	327.74	491.61	655.48	819.35	983.22	1 147.09	1 310.97	1 474.84
100	1 638.71	1 802.58	1 966.45	2 130.32	2 294.19	2 458.06	2 621.93	2 785.8	2 949.67	3 113.54
200	3 277.41	3 441.28	3 605.15	3 769.02	3 932.9	4 096.77	4 260.64	4 424.51	4 588.38	4 752.25
300	4 916.12	5 079.99	5 243.86	5 407.73	5 571.6	5 735.47	5 899.34	6 063.21	6 227.08	6 390.95
400	6 554.83	6 718.7	6 882.57	7 046.44	7 210.31	7 374.18	7 538.05	7 701.92	7 865.79	8 029.66
500	8 193.53	8 357.4	8 521.27	8 685.14	8 849.01	9 012.89	9 176.76	9 340.63	9 504.5	9 668.37
600	9 832.24	9 996.11	10 160.0	10 323.9	10 487.7	10 651.6	10 815.5	10 979.3	11 143.2	11 307.1
700	11 470.9	11 634.8	11 798.7	11 962.6	12 126.4	12 290.3	12 454.2	12 618.0	12 781.9	12 945.8
800	13 109.7	13 273.5	13 437.4	13 601.3	13 765.1	13 929.0	14 092.9	14 256.7	14 420.6	14 584.5
900	14 748.4	14 912.2	15 076.1	15 240.0	15 403.8	15 567.7	15 731.6	15 895.5	16 059.3	16 223.2
1 000	16 387.1									

ft³	0	1	2	3	4	5	6	7	8	9
m³										
0		0.03	0.06	0.08	0.11	0.14	0.17	0.2	0.23	0.25
10	0.28	0.31	0.34	0.37	0.4	0.42	0.45	0.48	0.51	0.54
20	0.57	0.59	0.62	0.65	0.68	0.71	0.74	0.77	0.79	0.82
30	0.85	0.88	0.91	0.93	0.96	0.99	1.02	1.05	1.08	1.1
40	1.13	1.16	1.19	1.22	1.25	1.27	1.3	1.33	1.36	1.39
50	1.42	1.44	1.47	1.5	1.53	1.56	1.59	1.61	1.64	1.67
60	1.7	1.73	1.76	1.78	1.81	1.84	1.87	1.9	1.93	1.95
70	1.98	2.01	2.04	2.07	2.1	2.12	2.15	2.18	2.21	2.24
80	2.27	2.29	2.32	2.35	2.38	2.41	2.44	2.46	2.49	2.52
90	2.55	2.58	2.61	2.63	2.66	2.69	2.71	2.75	2.78	2.8
100	2.83	2.86	2.89	2.92	2.94	2.97	3.01	3.03	3.06	3.09
110	3.11	3.14	3.17	3.2	3.23	3.26	3.28	3.31	3.34	3.37
120	3.4	3.43	3.46	3.48	3.51	3.54	3.57	3.6	3.62	3.65
130	3.68	3.71	3.74	3.77	3.79	3.82	3.85	3.88	3.91	3.94
140	3.96	4.0	4.02	4.05	4.08	4.11	4.13	4.16	4.19	4.22
150	4.26	4.28	4.3	4.33	4.36	4.39	4.42	4.45	4.47	4.51
160	4.53	4.56	4.59	4.62	4.64	4.67	4.7	4.73	4.76	4.79
170	4.81	4.84	4.87	4.9	4.93	4.96	4.99	5.01	5.04	5.07
180	5.1	5.13	5.15	5.18	5.21	5.24	5.27	5.3	5.32	5.35
190	5.38	5.41	5.44	5.47	5.49	5.52	5.55	5.58	5.61	5.64
200	5.66	5.69	5.72	5.75	5.78	5.8	5.83	5.86	5.89	5.92
210	5.95	5.98	6.0	6.03	6.06	6.09	6.12	6.14	6.17	6.2
220	6.23	6.26	6.29	6.31	6.34	6.37	6.4	6.43	6.46	6.48
230	6.51	6.54	6.57	6.6	6.63	6.65	6.69	6.71	6.74	6.77
240	6.8	6.82	6.85	6.88	6.91	6.94	6.97	6.99	7.02	7.05
250	7.08									

22
cubic feet
to cubic
metres

ft³	0	1	2	3	4	5	6	7	8	9
litre										
0		28.32	56.63	84.95	113.26	141.58	169.9	198.21	226.53	254.84
10	283.16	311.48	339.79	368.11	396.42	424.74	453.06	481.37	509.69	538.01
20	566.32	594.64	622.95	651.27	679.59	707.9	736.22	764.53	792.85	821.17
30	849.48	877.8	906.11	934.43	962.75	991.06	1 019.38	1 047.69	1 076.01	1 104.33
40	1 132.64	1 160.96	1 189.27	1 217.59	1 245.91	1 274.22	1 302.54	1 330.85	1 359.17	1 387.49
50	1 415.8	1 444.12	1 472.43	1 500.75	1 529.07	1 557.38	1 585.7	1 614.02	1 642.33	1 670.65
60	1 698.96	1 727.28	1 755.6	1 783.91	1 812.23	1 840.54	1 868.86	1 897.18	1 925.49	1 953.81
70	1 982.12	2 010.44	2 038.76	2 067.07	2 095.39	2 123.7	2 152.02	2 180.34	2 208.65	2 236.97
80	2 265.28	2 293.6	2 321.92	2 350.23	2 378.55	2 406.86	2 435.18	2 463.5	2 491.81	2 520.13
90	2 548.44	2 576.76	2 605.08	2 633.39	2 661.71	2 690.03	2 718.34	2 746.66	2 774.97	2 803.29
100	2 831.61									

24
cubic feet
to litres

25
litres to
imperial
gallons

litre	0	1	2	3	4	5	6	7	8	9
	gal imp									
0		0.22	0.44	0.66	0.88	1.1	1.32	1.54	1.76	1.98
10	2.2	2.42	2.64	2.86	3.08	3.3	3.52	3.74	3.96	4.18
20	4.4	4.62	4.84	5.06	5.28	5.5	5.72	5.94	6.16	6.38
30	6.6	6.82	7.04	7.26	7.48	7.7	7.92	8.14	8.36	8.58
40	8.8	9.02	9.24	9.46	9.68	9.9	10.12	10.34	10.56	10.78
50	11.0	11.22	11.44	11.66	11.88	12.1	12.32	12.54	12.76	12.98
60	13.2	13.42	13.64	13.86	14.08	14.3	14.52	14.74	14.96	15.18
70	15.4	15.62	15.84	16.06	16.28	16.5	16.72	16.94	17.16	17.38
80	17.6	17.82	18.04	18.26	18.48	18.7	18.92	19.14	19.36	19.58
90	19.8	20.02	20.24	20.46	20.68	20.9	21.12	21.34	21.56	21.78
100	22.0									

27
litres to
US gallons

litre	0	1	2	3	4	5	6	7	8	9
	gal US									
0		0.26	0.53	0.79	1.06	1.32	1.59	1.85	2.11	2.38
10	2.64	2.91	3.17	3.43	3.7	3.96	4.23	4.49	4.76	5.02
20	5.28	5.55	5.81	6.08	6.34	6.61	6.87	7.13	7.4	7.66
30	7.93	8.19	8.45	8.72	8.98	9.25	9.51	9.78	10.04	10.3
40	10.57	10.83	11.1	11.36	11.62	11.89	12.15	12.42	12.68	12.95
50	13.21	13.47	13.74	14.0	14.27	14.53	14.8	15.06	15.32	15.59
60	15.85	16.12	16.38	16.64	16.91	17.17	17.44	17.7	17.97	18.23
70	18.49	18.76	19.02	19.29	19.55	19.82	20.08	20.34	20.61	20.87
80	21.14	21.4	21.66	21.93	22.19	22.46	22.72	22.96	23.25	23.51
90	23.78	24.04	24.31	24.57	24.83	25.1	25.36	25.63	25.89	26.16
100	26.42									

Mass

29
kilograms
to pounds

kg	0	1	2	3	4	5	6	7	8	9
	lb									
0		2.21	4.41	6.61	8.82	11.02	13.23	15.43	17.64	19.84
10	22.05	24.25	26.46	28.66	30.86	33.07	35.27	37.47	39.68	41.89
20	44.09	46.3	48.5	50.71	52.91	55.12	57.32	59.52	61.73	63.93
30	66.14	68.34	70.55	72.75	74.96	77.16	79.37	81.57	83.78	85.98
40	88.18	90.39	92.59	94.8	97.0	99.2	101.41	103.61	105.82	108.03
50	110.23	112.44	114.64	116.85	119.05	121.25	123.46	125.66	127.87	130.07
60	132.28	134.48	136.69	138.89	141.1	143.3	145.51	147.71	149.91	152.12
70	154.32	156.53	158.73	160.94	163.14	165.35	167.55	169.76	171.96	174.17
80	176.37	178.57	180.78	182.98	185.19	187.39	189.6	191.8	194.01	196.21
90	198.42	200.62	202.83	205.03	207.24	209.44	211.64	213.85	216.05	218.26
100	220.46	222.67	224.87	227.08	229.28	231.49	233.69	235.9	238.1	240.3
110	242.51	244.71	246.92	249.12	251.33	253.53	255.74	257.94	260.15	262.35
120	264.56	266.76	268.96	271.17	273.37	275.58	277.78	279.99	282.19	284.4
130	286.6	288.81	291.01	293.22	295.42	297.62	299.83	302.03	304.24	306.44
140	308.65	310.85	313.06	315.26	317.47	319.67	321.88	324.08	326.28	328.49
150	330.69	332.9	335.1	337.31	339.51	341.72	343.92	346.13	348.33	350.54
160	352.74	354.94	357.15	359.35	361.56	363.76	365.97	368.17	370.38	372.58
170	374.79	377.0	379.2	381.4	383.6	385.81	388.01	390.22	392.42	394.68
180	396.83	399.04	401.24	403.45	405.65	407.86	410.06	412.26	414.47	416.67
190	418.88	421.08	423.29	425.49	427.68	429.9	432.11	434.31	436.52	438.72
200	440.93	443.13	445.33	447.54	449.74	451.95	454.15	456.36	458.56	460.77
210	462.97	465.18	467.38	469.59	471.79	473.99	476.2	478.4	480.61	482.81
220	485.02	487.22	489.43	491.63	493.84	496.04	498.25	500.45	502.65	504.86
230	507.06	509.2	511.47	513.6	515.88	518.0	520.29	522.4	524.7	526.9
240	529.1	531.31	533.5	535.72	537.9	540.13	542.3	544.54	546.7	548.9
250	551.16	553.36	555.57	557.77	559.97	562.18	564.38	566.59	568.79	571.0
260	573.2	575.41	577.61	579.82	582.02	584.23	586.43	588.63	590.84	593.04
270	595.25	597.45	599.66	601.86	604.07	606.27	608.48	610.68	612.89	615.09
280	617.29	619.5	621.7	623.91	626.11	628.32	630.52	632.73	634.93	637.14
290	639.34	641.55	643.75	645.95	648.16	650.36	652.57	654.77	656.98	659.18
300	661.39	663.59	665.8	668.0	670.21	672.41	674.62	676.82	679.02	681.23
310	683.43	685.64	687.84	690.05	692.25	694.46	696.66	698.87	701.07	703.28
320	705.48	707.68	709.89	712.09	714.3	716.5	718.71	720.91	723.12	725.32
330	727.53	729.73	731.93	734.14	736.34	738.55	740.75	742.96	745.16	747.37
340	749.57	751.78	753.98	756.19	758.39	760.6	762.8	765.0	767.21	769.41
350	771.62	773.82	776.03	778.23	780.44	782.64	784.85	787.05	789.26	791.46
360	793.66	795.87	798.07	800.28	802.48	804.69	806.89	809.1	811.31	813.51
370	815.71	817.92	820.12	822.32	824.53	826.73	828.94	831.14	833.35	835.55
380	837.76	839.96	842.17	844.37	846.58	848.78	850.98	853.19	855.39	857.6
390	859.8	862.0	864.21	866.41	868.62	870.8	873.03	875.2	877.44	879.64
400	881.85	884.05	886.26	888.46	890.67	892.87	895.08	897.28	899.49	901.69
410	903.9	906.1	908.31	910.51	912.71	914.92	917.12	919.33	921.53	923.74
420	925.94	928.15	930.35	932.56	934.76	936.97	939.17	941.37	943.58	945.78
430	947.99	950.19	952.4	954.6	956.81	959.01	961.22	963.42	965.63	967.83
440	970.03	972.24	974.44	976.65	978.85	981.06	983.26	985.47	987.67	989.88
450	992.08	994.29	996.49	998.69	1 000.9	1 003.1	1 005.31	1 007.51	1 009.72	1 011.92
460	1 014.13	1 016.33	1 018.54	1 020.74	1 022.94	1 025.15	1 027.35	1 029.56	1 031.76	1 033.97
470	1 036.17	1 038.38	1 040.58	1 042.79	1 044.99	1 047.2	1 049.4	1 051.6	1 053.81	1 056.01
480	1 058.22	1 060.42	1 062.63	1 064.83	1 067.04	1 069.24	1 071.45	1 073.65	1 075.86	1 078.06
490	1 080.27	1 082.47	1 084.67	1 086.88	1 089.08	1 091.29	1 093.49	1 095.7	1 097.9	1 100.11
500	1 102.31									

gal imp	0	1	2	3	4	5	6	7	8	9
	litre									
0		4.55	9.09	13.64	18.18	22.73	27.28	31.82	36.37	40.91
10	45.46	50.0	54.55	59.1	63.64	68.19	72.74	77.28	81.83	86.38
20	90.92	95.47	100.01	104.56	109.1	113.65	118.2	122.74	127.29	131.83
30	136.38	140.93	145.47	150.02	154.56	159.1	163.66	168.21	172.75	177.3
40	181.84	186.38	190.93	195.48	200.02	204.57	209.11	213.66	218.21	222.75
50	227.3	231.84	236.39	240.94	245.48	250.03	254.57	259.12	263.67	268.21
60	272.76	277.3	281.85	286.4	290.94	295.49	300.03	304.58	309.13	313.67
70	318.22	322.76	327.31	331.86	336.4	340.95	345.49	350.04	354.59	359.13
80	363.68	368.22	372.77	377.32	381.86	386.41	390.95	395.5	400.04	404.59
90	409.14	413.68	418.23	422.77	427.32	431.87	436.41	440.96	445.5	450.05
100	454.6									

26 imperial gallons to litres

gal US	0	1	2	3	4	5	6	7	8	9
	litre									
0		3.79	7.57	11.36	15.14	18.93	22.71	26.5	30.28	34.07
10	37.85	41.64	45.42	49.21	52.99	56.78	60.56	64.35	68.13	71.92
20	75.7	79.49	83.27	87.06	90.84	94.63	98.41	102.2	105.98	109.77
30	113.55	117.34	121.12	124.91	128.69	132.48	136.26	140.05	143.83	147.62
40	151.40	155.19	158.97	162.76	166.54	170.33	174.11	177.9	181.68	185.47
50	189.25	193.04	196.82	200.61	204.39	208.18	211.96	215.75	219.53	223.32
60	227.1	230.89	234.67	238.46	242.24	246.03	249.81	253.6	257.38	261.17
70	264.95	268.74	272.52	276.31	280.09	283.88	287.66	291.45	295.23	299.02
80	302.81	306.59	310.37	314.16	317.94	321.73	325.51	329.3	333.08	336.87
90	340.65	344.44	348.22	352.01	355.79	359.58	363.36	367.14	370.93	374.72
100	378.51									

28 US gallons to litres

lb	0	1	2	3	4	5	6	7	8	9
	kg									
0		0.45	0.91	1.36	1.81	2.27	2.72	3.18	3.63	4.08
10	4.54	4.99	5.44	5.9	6.35	6.8	7.26	7.71	8.16	8.62
20	9.07	9.53	9.98	10.43	10.89	11.34	11.79	12.25	12.7	13.15
30	13.61	14.06	14.52	14.97	15.42	15.88	16.33	16.78	17.24	17.69
40	18.14	18.6	19.05	19.5	19.96	20.41	20.87	21.32	21.77	22.23
50	22.68	23.13	23.59	24.04	24.49	24.95	25.4	25.85	26.31	26.76
60	27.22	27.67	28.12	28.58	29.03	29.48	29.94	30.39	30.84	31.3
70	31.75	32.21	32.66	33.11	33.57	34.02	34.47	34.93	35.38	35.83
80	36.29	36.74	37.19	37.65	38.1	38.56	39.01	39.46	39.92	40.37
90	40.82	41.28	41.73	42.18	42.64	43.09	43.54	44.0	44.45	44.91
100	45.36	45.81	46.27	46.72	47.17	47.63	48.08	48.53	48.99	49.44
110	49.9	50.35	50.8	51.26	51.71	52.16	52.62	53.07	53.52	53.98
120	54.43	54.88	55.34	55.79	56.25	56.7	57.15	57.61	58.06	58.51
130	58.97	59.42	59.87	60.33	60.78	61.24	61.69	62.14	62.6	63.05
140	63.5	63.96	64.41	64.86	65.32	65.77	66.22	66.68	67.13	67.59
150	68.04	68.49	68.95	69.4	69.85	70.31	70.76	71.21	71.67	72.12
160	72.57	73.03	73.48	73.94	74.39	74.84	75.3	75.75	76.2	76.66
170	77.11	77.56	78.02	78.47	78.93	79.38	79.83	80.29	80.74	81.19
180	81.65	82.1	82.55	83.01	83.46	83.91	84.37	84.82	85.28	85.73
190	86.18	86.64	87.09	87.54	88.0	88.45	88.9	89.36	89.81	90.26
200	90.72	91.17	91.63	92.08	92.53	92.99	93.44	93.89	94.35	94.8
210	95.25	95.71	96.16	96.62	97 07	97.52	97.98	98.43	98.88	99.34
220	99.79	100.24	100.7	101.15	101.61	102.06	102.51	102.97	103.42	103.87
230	104.33	104.78	105.23	105.69	106.14	106.59	107.05	107.5	107.96	108.41
240	108.86	109.32	109.77	110.22	110.68	111.13	111.58	112.04	112.49	112.95
250	113.4	113.85	114.31	114.76	115.21	115.67	116.12	116.57	117.03	117.48
260	117.93	118.39	118.84	119.3	119.75	120.2	120.66	121.11	121.56	122.02
270	122.47	122.92	123.38	123.83	124.28	124.74	125.19	125.65	126.1	126.55
280	127.01	127.46	127.91	128.37	128.82	129.27	129.73	130.18	130.64	131.09
290	131.54	132.0	132.45	132.9	133.36	133.81	134.26	134.72	135.17	135.62
300	136.08	136.53	136.99	137.44	137.89	138.35	138.8	139.25	139.71	140.16
310	140.61	141.07	141.52	141.97	142.43	142.88	143.34	143.79	144.24	144.7
320	145.15	145.6	146.06	146.51	146.96	147.42	147.87	148.33	148.78	149.23
330	149.69	150.14	150.59	151.05	151.5	151.95	152.41	152.86	153.31	153.77
340	154.22	154.68	155.13	155.58	156.04	156.49	156.94	157.4	157.85	158.3
350	158.76	159.21	159.67	160.12	160.57	161.03	161.48	161.93	162.39	162.84
360	163.29	163.75	164.2	164.65	165.11	165.56	166.02	166.47	166.92	167.38
370	167.83	168.28	168.74	169.1	169.64	170.1	170.55	171.0	171.46	171.91
380	172.37	172.82	173.27	173.73	174.18	174.63	175.09	175.54	175.99	176.45
390	176.9	177.36	177.81	178.26	178.72	179.17	179.62	180.08	180.53	180.98
400	181.44	181.89	182.34	182.8	183.25	183.71	184.16	184.61	185.07	185.52
410	185.97	186.43	186.88	187.33	187.79	188.24	188.69	189.15	189.6	190.06
420	190.51	190.96	191.42	191.87	192.32	192.78	193.23	193.68	194.14	194.59
430	195.05	195.5	195.95	196.41	196.86	197.31	197.77	198.22	198.67	199.13
440	199.58	200.03	200.49	200.94	201.4	201.85	202.3	202.76	203.21	203.66
450	204.12	204.57	205.02	205.48	205.93	206.39	206.84	207.29	207.75	208.2
460	208.65	209.11	209.56	210.01	210.47	210.92	211.37	211.83	212.28	212.74
470	213.19	213.64	214.1	214.55	215.0	215.46	215.91	216.36	216.82	217.27
480	217.72	218.18	218.63	219.09	219.54	219.99	220.45	220.9	221.35	221.81
490	222.26	222.71	223.17	223.62	224.08	224.53	224.98	225.44	225.89	226.34
500	226.8									

30 pounds to kilograms

Density (mass/volume)

31 kilograms per cubic metre to pounds per cubic foot

kg/m³	0	10	20	30	40	50	60	70	80	90
	lb/ft³									
0		0.62	1.25	1.87	2.5	3.12	3.75	4.37	5.0	5.62
100	6.24	6.87	7.49	8.12	8.74	9.36	9.99	10.61	11.24	11.86
200	12.49	13.11	13.73	14.36	14.98	15.61	16.23	16.86	17.48	18.11
300	18.73	19.35	19.98	20.61	21.23	21.85	22.47	23.1	23.72	24.35
400	24.97	25.6	26.22	26.84	27.47	28.09	28.72	29.34	29.97	30.59
500	31.21	31.84	32.46	33.09	33.71	34.33	34.96	35.58	36.21	36.83
600	37.46	38.08	38.71	39.33	39.95	40.58	41.2	41.83	42.45	43.08
700	43.7	44.32	44.95	45.57	46.2	46.82	47.45	48.07	48.7	49.32
800	49.94	50.57	51.19	51.82	52.44	53.06	53.69	54.31	54.94	55.56
900	56.19	56.81	57.43	58.06	58.68	59.31	59.93	60.56	61.18	61.81
1 000	62.43									

Velocity

33 metres per second to miles per hour

m/s	0	1	2	3	4	5	6	7	8	9
	mile/hr									
0		2.24	4.47	6.71	8.95	11.18	13.42	15.66	17.9	20.13
10	22.37	24.61	26.84	29.08	31.32	33.55	35.79	38.03	40.26	42.51
20	44.74	46.96	49.21	51.45	53.69	55.92	58.16	60.4	62.63	64.87
30	67.11	69.35	71.58	73.82	76.06	78.29	80.53	82.77	85.0	87.24
40	89.48	91.71	93.95	96.19	98.43	100.66	102.9	105.13	107.37	109.61
50	111.85	114.08	116.32	118.56	120.8	123.03	125.27	127.5	129.74	131.98
60	134.22	136.45	138.69	140.93	143.16	145.4	147.64	149.88	152.11	154.34
70	156.59	158.82	161.06	163.3	165.53	167.77	170.0	172.24	174.48	176.72
80	178.96	181.19	183.43	185.67	187.9	190.14	192.38	194.61	196.85	199.09
90	201.32	203.56	205.8	208.04	210.27	212.51	214.75	216.98	219.22	221.46
100	223.69									

Pressure, stress

35 kilograms force per square centimetre to pounds force per square inch

kgf/cm²	0.0	0.1	0.2	0.3	0.4	0.5	0.6	0.7	0.8	0.9
	lbf/in²									
0		1.42	2.84	4.27	5.6	7.11	8.53	9.96	11.38	12.8
1	14.22	15.65	17.07	18.49	19.91	21.34	22.76	24.18	25.6	27.02
2	28.45	29.87	31.29	32.71	34.13	35.56	36.98	38.4	39.83	41.25
3	42.67	44.09	45.51	46.94	48.36	49.78	51.2	52.63	54.05	55.47
4	56.9	58.32	59.73	61.16	62.58	64.0	65.43	66.85	68.27	69.69
5	71.12	72.54	73.96	75.38	76.81	78.23	79.65	81.07	82.5	83.92
6	85.34	86.76	88.18	89.61	91.03	92.45	93.87	95.3	96.72	98.14
7	99.56	100.99	102.41	103.83	105.25	106.68	108.1	109.52	110.94	112.36
8	113.79	115.21	116.63	118.05	119.48	120.9	122.32	123.74	125.17	126.59
9	128.01	129.43	130.86	132.28	133.7	135.12	136.54	137.97	139.39	140.81
10	142.23									

37 kilonewtons per square metre to pounds force per square inch

kN/m² (kPa)	0	10	20	30	40	50	60	70	80	90
	lbf/in²									
0		1.45	2.9	4.35	5.8	7.25	8.7	10.15	11.6	13.05
100	14.50	15.95	17.40	18.85	20.30	21.75	23.21	24.66	26.11	27.56
200	29.01	30.46	31.91	33.36	34.81	36.26	37.71	39.16	40.61	42.06
300	43.51	44.96	46.41	47.86	49.31	50.76	52.21	53.66	55.11	56.56
400	58.01	59.46	60.91	62.36	63.81	65.26	66.71	68.17	69.62	71.07
500	72.52	73.97	75.42	76.87	78.32	79.77	81.22	82.67	84.12	85.57
600	87.02	88.47	89.92	91.37	92.82	94.27	95.72	97.17	98.62	100.07
700	101.52	102.97	104.42	105.87	107.32	108.77	110.22	111.68	113.13	114.58
800	116.03	117.48	118.93	120.38	121.83	123.28	124.73	126.18	127.63	129.08
900	130.53	131.98	133.43	134.88	136.33	137.78	139.23	140.68	142.13	143.58
1 000	145.03									

lb/ft³	0	1	2	3	4	5	6	7	8	9
	kg/m³									
0		16.02	32.04	48.06	64.07	80.09	96.11	112.13	128.15	144.17
10	160.19	176.2	192.22	208.24	224.26	240.28	256.3	272.31	288.33	304.35
20	320.37	336.39	352.41	368.43	384.44	400.46	416.48	432.5	448.52	464.54
30	480.55	496.57	512.59	528.61	544.63	560.65	576.67	592.68	608.7	624.72
40	640.74	656.76	672.78	688.79	704.81	720.83	736.85	752.87	768.89	784.91
50	800.92	816.94	832.96	848.98	865.0	881.02	897.03	913.05	929.07	945.09
60	961.11	977.13	993.15	1 009.16	1 025.18	1 041.2	1 057.22	1 073.24	1 089.26	1 105.27
70	1 121.29	1 137.31	1 153.33	1 169.35	1 185.37	1 201.38	1 217.4	1 233.42	1 249.44	1 265.46
80	1 281.48	1 297.5	1 313.51	1 329.53	1 345.55	1 361.57	1 377.59	1 393.61	1 409.62	1 425.64
90	1 441.66	1 457.68	1 473.7	1 489.72	1 505.74	1 521.75	1 537.77	1 553.79	1 569.81	1 585.83
100	1 601.85									

32 pounds per cubic foot to kilograms per cubic metre

mile/hr	0	1	2	3	4	5	6	7	8	9
	m/s									
0		0.45	0.89	1.34	1.79	2.24	2.68	3.13	3.58	4.02
10	4.47	4.92	5.36	5.81	6.26	6.71	7.15	7.6	8.05	8.49
20	8.94	9.39	9.83	10.28	10.73	11.18	11.62	12.07	12.52	12.96
30	13.41	13.86	14.31	14.75	15.2	15.65	16.09	16.54	16.99	17.43
40	17.88	18.33	18.78	19.22	19.67	20.12	20.56	21.01	21.46	21.91
50	22.35	22.8	23.25	23.69	24.14	24.59	25.03	25.48	25.93	26.38
60	26.82	27.27	27.72	28.16	28.61	29.06	29.5	29.95	30.4	30.85
70	31.29	31.74	32.19	32.63	33.08	33.53	33.98	34.42	34.87	35.32
80	35.76	36.21	36.66	37.1	37.55	38.0	38.45	38.89	39.34	39.79
90	40.23	40.68	41.13	41.57	42.02	42.47	42.92	43.36	43.81	44.26
100	44.7									

34 miles per hour to metres per second

lbf/in²	0	1	2	3	4	5	6	7	8	9
	kgf/cm²									
0		0.07	0.14	0.21	0.28	0.35	0.42	0.49	0.56	0.63
10	0.7	0.77	0.84	0.91	0.98	1.05	1.12	1.2	1.27	1.34
20	1.41	1.48	1.55	1.62	1.69	1.76	1.83	1.9	1.97	2.04
30	2.11	2.18	2.25	2.32	2.39	2.46	2.53	2.6	2.67	2.74
40	2.81	2.88	2.95	3.02	3.09	3.16	3.23	3.3	3.37	3.45
50	3.52	3.59	3.66	3.73	3.8	3.87	3.94	4.01	4.08	4.15
60	4.22	4.29	4.36	4.43	4.5	4.57	4.64	4.71	4.78	4.85
70	4.92	4.99	5.06	5.13	5.2	5.27	5.34	5.41	5.48	5.55
80	5.62	5.69	5.77	5.84	5.91	5.98	6.05	6.12	6.19	6.26
90	6.33	6.4	6.47	6.54	6.61	6.68	6.75	6.82	6.89	6.96
100	7.03									

36 pounds force per square inch to kilograms force per square centimetre

lbf/in²	0	1	2	3	4	5	6	7	8	9
	kN/m² (k Pa)									
0		6.9	13.79	20.68	27.58	34.48	41.37	48.26	55.16	62.06
10	68.95	75.84	82.74	89.64	96.53	103.42	110.32	117.22	124.11	131.0
20	137.9	144.8	151.69	158.58	165.48	172.38	179.27	186.16	193.06	199.96
30	206.85	213.74	220.64	227.54	234.43	241.32	248.22	255.12	262.01	268.9
40	275.8	282.7	289.59	296.48	303.38	310.28	317.17	324.06	330.96	337.86
50	344.75	351.64	358.54	365.44	372.33	379.22	386.12	393.02	399.91	406.8
60	413.7	420.6	427.49	434.38	441.28	448.18	455.07	461.96	468.86	475.76
70	482.65	489.54	496.44	503.34	510.23	517.12	524.02	530.92	537.81	544.7
80	551.6	558.5	565.39	572.28	579.18	586.08	592.97	599.86	606.76	613.66
90	620.55	627.44	634.34	641.24	648.13	655.02	661.92	668.82	675.71	682.6
100	689.5									

38 pounds force per square inch to kilonewtons per square metre

Refrigeration

39
watts to
British thermal
units per hour

W	0	1	2	3	4	5	6	7	8	9
	Btu/hr									
0		3.41	6.82	10.24	13.65	17.06	20.47	23.89	27.3	30.71
10	34.12	37.53	40.95	44.36	47.77	51.18	54.59	58.01	61.42	64.83
20	68.24	71.66	75.07	78.5	81.89	85.3	88.72	92.13	95.54	98.95
30	102.36	105.78	109.12	112.6	116.01	119.43	122.76	126.25	129.66	133.07
40	136.49	139.91	143.31	146.72	150.13	153.55	156.96	160.37	163.78	167.2
50	170.61	174.02	177.43	180.84	184.26	187.67	191.08	194.49	197.9	201.31
60	204.73	208.14	211.55	214.97	218.38	221.79	225.2	228.61	232.03	235.44
70	238.85	242.26	245.68	249.09	252.5	255.91	259.32	262.74	266.15	269.56
80	272.97	276.38	279.8	283.21	286.62	290.03	293.45	296.86	300.27	303.68
90	307.09	310.51	313.92	317.33	320.74	324.15	327.57	330.98	334.39	337.8
100	341.22									

Thermal conductance (U-value)

41
watts per
square metre
kelvin to
British thermal
units per
square foot
hour degree F

W/(m²K)	0.0	0.1	0.2	0.3	0.4	0.5	0.6	0.7	0.8	0.9
	Btu/(ft²hr°F)									
0.0		0.018	0.035	0.053	0.074	0.088	0.106	0.123	0.141	0.158
1.0	0.176	0.194	0.211	0.229	0.247	0.264	0.282	0.299	0.317	0.335
2.0	0.352	0.370	0.387	0.405	0.423	0.440	0.458	0.476	0.493	0.511
3.0	0.528	0.546	0.564	0.581	0.599	0.616	0.634	0.652	0.669	0.687
4.0	0.704	0.722	0.740	0.757	0.775	0.793	0.810	0.828	0.845	0.863
5.0	0.881	0.898	0.916	0.933	0.951	0.969	0.986	1.004	1.021	1.039
6.0	1.057	1.074	1.092	1.110	1.127	1.145	1.162	1.180	1.198	1.215
7.0	1.233	1.250	1.268	1.286	1.303	1.321	1.34	1.356	1.374	1.391
8.0	1.409	1.427	1.444	1.462	1.479	1.497	1.515	1.532	1.550	1.567
9.0	1.585	1.603	1.620	1.638	1.656	1.673	1.691	1.708	1.726	1.744
10.0	1.761									

Btu/hr	0	1	2	3	4	5	6	7	8	9
	W									
0		0.29	0.59	0.88	1.17	1.47	1.76	2.05	2.34	2.64
10	2.93	3.22	3.52	3.81	4.1	4.4	4.69	4.98	5.28	5.57
20	5.86	6.16	6.45	6.74	7.03	7.33	7.62	7.91	8.21	8.5
30	8.79	9.09	9.38	9.67	9.97	10.26	10.55	10.84	11.14	11.43
40	11.72	12.02	12.31	12.6	12.9	13.19	13.48	13.78	14.07	14.36
50	14.66	14.95	15.24	15.53	15.83	16.12	16.41	16.71	17.0	17.29
60	17.59	17.88	18.17	18.47	18.76	19.05	19.34	19.64	19.93	20.22
70	20.52	20.81	21.1	21.4	21.69	21.98	22.28	22.57	22.86	23.15
80	23.45	23.74	24.03	24.33	24.62	24.91	25.21	25.5	25.79	26.09
90	26.38	26.67	26.97	27.26	27.55	27.84	28.14	28.43	28.72	29.02
100	29.31									

40
British thermal units per hour to watts

Btu/(ft². hr°F)	0.00	0.01	0.02	0.03	0.04	0.05	0.06	0.07	0.08	0.09
	W/(m²K)									
0.0		0.057	0.114	0.17	0.227	0.284	0.341	0.397	0.454	0.511
0.1	0.568	0.624	0.681	0.738	0.795	0.852	0.908	0.965	1.022	1.079
0.2	1.136	1.192	1.249	1.306	1.363	1.42	1.476	1.533	1.59	1.647
0.3	1.703	1.76	1.817	1.874	1.931	1.987	2.044	2.101	2.158	2.214
0.4	2.271	2.328	2.385	2.442	2.498	2.555	2.612	2.669	2.725	2.782
0.5	2.839	2.896	2.953	3.009	3.066	3.123	3.18	3.236	3.293	3.35
0.6	3.407	3.464	3.52	3.577	3.634	3.691	3.747	3.804	3.861	3.918
0.7	3.975	4.031	4.088	4.145	4.202	4.258	4.315	4.372	4.429	4.486
0.8	4.542	4.599	4.656	4.713	4.77	4.826	4.883	4.94	4.997	5.053
0.9	5.11	5.167	5.224	5.281	5.337	5.394	5.451	5.508	5.564	5.621
1.0	5.678									

42
British thermal units per square foot hour degree F to watts per square metre kelvin

INDEX